Photoshop Elements 5

THE MISSING MANUAL

*The book that
should have been
in the box*®

Photoshop
Elements 5
THE MISSING MANUAL

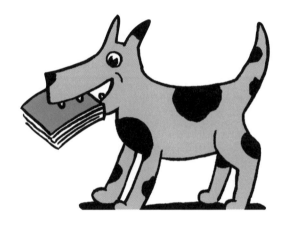

Barbara Brundage

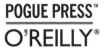
POGUE PRESS™
O'REILLY®

Beijing • Cambridge • Farnham • Köln • Paris • Sebastopol • Taipei • Tokyo

Photoshop Elements 5: The Missing Manual

by Barbara Brundage

Published by O'Reilly Media, Inc., 1005 Gravenstein Highway North, Sebastopol, CA 95472.

O'Reilly books may be purchased for educational, business, or sales promotional use. Online editions are also available for most titles (*safari.oreilly.com*). For more information, contact our corporate/institutional sales department: (800) 998-9938 or *corporate@oreilly.com*.

Printing History:

September 2006:   First Edition.

 This book uses RepKover,™ a durable and flexible lay-flat binding.

ISBN-10: 0-596-52728-4
ISBN-13: 978-0-596-52728-0

Table of Contents

Part Two: Elemental Elements

Part Three: Retouching

Foreword

The digital imaging landscape has changed dramatically since Adobe Photoshop Elements 4 was released. Because of the power, speed, flexibility, and incredible image quality of the most recent hardware, the adoption of digital cameras is at an all-time high. Never before have there been more applications to adjust and manipulate your images, and never before have there been more books to learn about these applications. It's a great time to be a digital photographer!

Both O'Reilly and Adobe recognize that you, as a user, have more choices than ever when it comes to your software and literature. Congratulations on choosing the best of both worlds—a fantastic book and an incredibly powerful piece of software. Between the most dynamic version of Elements yet, and a book that has followed each and every change along the way, you can rest assured that you have before you a winning team of knowledge and power.

I had the pleasure of working with Barbara Brundage the last time around, and I was extremely impressed with how thorough, detailed, accurate, and insightful her tutorials were. With *Photoshop Elements 5: The Missing Manual,* Barbara again brings clarity, creativity, and precision to even the most esoteric questions you might have.

This fifth release of Photoshop Elements introduces dozens of new features (there are even some that you can't find in its big brother, Photoshop!). Having spent the entirety of the development cycle using Elements 5, and having read this book end to end several times, I can tell you that you're holding one of the best tools to master both the old and new tricks in Elements 5.

I hope that you enjoy your time with this book, and the new release of Elements, as much I do.

—Bryan O'Neil Hughes
User Advocate, Adobe Systems, Inc.

The Missing Credits

About the Author

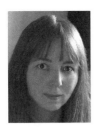

Barbara Brundage is the author of *Photoshop Elements 4: The Missing Manual*, and a member of Adobe's prerelease groups for Elements 3, 4, and 5. She's been teaching people how to use Photoshop Elements since it first came out in 2001. Barbara first started using Elements to create graphics for use in her day job as a harpist, music publisher, and arranger. Along the way, she joined the large group of people finding a renewed interest in photography, thanks to digital cameras. If she can learn to use Elements, you can, too!

About the Creative Team

Peter Meyers (editor) works as an editor at O'Reilly on the Missing Manual series. He lives with his wife and cat in New York City. Email: *peter.meyers@gmail.com*.

Nan Barber (copy editor) has worked with the Missing Manual series since its inception—long enough to remember booting up her computer from a floppy disk. Email: *nanbarber@oreilly.com*.

Michele Filshie (copy editor) is O'Reilly's assistant editor for Missing Manuals and editor of four Personal Trainers (another O'Reilly series). Before turning to the world of computer-related books, Michele spent many happy years at Black Sparrow Press. She lives in Sebastopol and loves to get involved in local politics. Email: *mfilshie@oreilly.com*.

Galen Fott (technical reviewer) is a writer, animator, puppeteer, and coauthor (with Deke McClelland) of several books on Photoshop Elements, including *Photoshop Elements 4 One-on-One* (Deke Press/O'Reilly). He is also a contributing editor to *PC Magazine*. Web: *www.grundoon.com*.

Bryan O'Neil Hughes (Foreword, technical reviewer) has been a member of Adobe's Photoshop Team since 1999. He has edited several books on both Photoshop and Photoshop Elements. Bryan's photographs have been published in a variety of magazines and Web sites, and even appear within Photoshop. Email: *bhughes@adobe.com*.

Rose Cassano (cover illustration) has worked as an independent designer and illustrator for 20 years. Assignments have ranged from the nonprofit sector to corporate clientele. She lives in beautiful Southern Oregon, grateful for the miracles of modern technology that make working there a reality. Email: *cassano@highstream. net*. Web: *www.rosecassano.com*.

Acknowledgements

Many thanks to Galen Fott and Bryan Hughes for reading this book and giving me the benefit of their advice and corrections, and additional thanks to Bryan for writing the Foreword. I'm also grateful for the help I received from everyone at Adobe, especially Rich Coencas, Barry Burris, Don Day, Mike Sobieski, Guy Nicholas, and Mark Dahm.

Special thanks also to graphic artist Jodi Frye (*www.frontiernet.net/~jlfrye/Jodi_ Frye*) for allowing me to reproduce one of her Elements drawings to show what can be done by those with more artistic ability than I have. My gratitude also to Florida's botanical gardens, especially McKee Botanical Garden (*www. mckeegarden.org*), Historic Bok Sanctuary (*www.boktower.org*), Heathcote Botanical Gardens (*www.heathcotebotanicalgardens.org*), and Harry P. Leu Gardens (*www.leugardens.org*), for creating oases of peace and beauty in our hectic world. Finally, I'd like to thank everyone in the gang over at the Adobe Photoshop Elements support forum for all their help and friendship.

The Missing Manual Series

Missing Manuals are witty, superbly written guides to computer products that don't come with printed manuals (which is just about all of them). Each book features a handcrafted index, cross-references to specific page numbers (not just "see Chapter 14"), and RepKover—a detached-spine binding that lets the book lie perfectly flat without the assistance of weights or cinder blocks.

Recent and upcoming titles include:

Access 2007: The Missing Manual by Matthew MacDonald

Access for Starters: The Missing Manual by Kate Chase and Scott Palmer

AppleScript: The Missing Manual by Adam Goldstein

AppleWorks 6: The Missing Manual by Jim Elferdink and David Reynolds

Creating Web Sites: The Missing Manual by Matthew MacDonald

CSS: The Missing Manual by David Sawyer McFarland

Digital Photography: The Missing Manual by Chris Grover and Barbara Brundage

Dreamweaver 8: The Missing Manual by David Sawyer McFarland

eBay: The Missing Manual by Nancy Conner

Excel: The Missing Manual by Matthew MacDonald

Excel 2007: The Missing Manual by Matthew MacDonald

Excel for Starters: The Missing Manual by Matthew MacDonald

FileMaker Pro 8: The Missing Manual by Geoff Coffey and Susan Prosser

Flash 8: The Missing Manual by Emily Moore

FrontPage 2003: The Missing Manual by Jessica Mantaro

GarageBand 2: The Missing Manual by David Pogue

Google: The Missing Manual, Second Edition by Sarah Milstein, J.D. Biersdorfer, and Matthew MacDonald

Home Networking: The Missing Manual by Scott Lowe

iLife '05: The Missing Manual by David Pogue

iMovie 6 & iDVD: The Missing Manual by David Pogue

iPhoto 6: The Missing Manual by David Pogue

iPod & iTunes: The Missing Manual, Fourth Edition by J.D. Biersdorfer

iWork '05: The Missing Manual by Jim Elferdink

Mac OS X Power Hound, Panther Edition by Rob Griffiths

Mac OS X: The Missing Manual, Tiger Edition by David Pogue

Office 2004 for Macintosh: The Missing Manual by Mark H. Walker and Franklin Tessler

PCs: The Missing Manual by Andy Rathbone

PowerPoint 2007: The Missing Manual by Emily Moore

QuickBooks 2006: The Missing Manual by Bonnie Biafore

Quicken for Starters: The Missing Manual by Bonnie Biafore

Switching to the Mac: The Missing Manual, Tiger Edition by David Pogue and Adam Goldstein

The Internet: The Missing Manual by David Pogue and J.D. Biersdorfer

Windows 2000 Pro: The Missing Manual by Sharon Crawford

Windows XP for Starters: The Missing Manual by David Pogue

Windows XP Home Edition: The Missing Manual, Second Edition by David Pogue

Windows XP Pro: The Missing Manual, Second Edition by David Pogue, Craig Zacker, and Linda Zacker

Windows Vista: The Missing Manual by David Pogue

Windows Vista for Starters: The Missing Manual by David Pogue

Word 2007: The Missing Manual by Chris Grover

Introduction

All of a sudden, everyone in the world seems to be getting a digital camera. And no wonder. When you go digital, you get instant gratification—you can preview your photos as soon as you take them, and there's no more wondering how many duds you're going to get back from the photo store.

You save a bundle on printing, too, since you can pick and choose which photos to print. Or maybe you're thinking that printing's pretty 20th century. Maybe you want to post your photos on a Web site, email them to friends, or create a really cool slideshow with fancy transitions and music.

If the digital camera bug has bitten you, you're probably aware of something else: The image-editing and picture-organizing software that comes with most cameras is pretty limited when it's time to spruce up your digital photos. Even if you're scanning in old prints and slides, you'll want a program that'll help you rejuvenate these gems and eliminate the wear and tear of all those years.

Enter Photoshop Elements 5: an all-in-one program that can help you improve your photos, keep them organized, and make top-notch prints and truly nifty creative projects.

Why Photoshop Elements?

Adobe's Photoshop is the granddaddy of all image-editing programs. It's the Big Cheese, the industry standard against which everything else is measured. Every photo you've seen in a book or magazine in the past 10 years or so has almost certainly passed through Photoshop on its way to being printed. You just can't buy anything that gives you more control over your pictures than Photoshop does.

But Photoshop has some big drawbacks—it's darned hard to learn, it's horribly expensive, and many of the features in it are just plain overkill if you don't plan to work on pictures for a living.

For several years, Adobe tried to find a way to cram many of Photoshop's marvelous powers into a package that normal people could use. Finding the right formula was a slow process. First there was PhotoDeluxe, a program that was lots of fun but came up short when you wanted to fine-tune *how* the program worked. Then Adobe tried again with Photoshop LE, which many people felt just gave you all the difficulty of full Photoshop but still too little of what you needed to do top-notch work.

Finally—sort of like "The Three Bears"—Adobe got it just right with Photoshop Elements. It took off like crazy because it offers so much of the power of Photoshop in a program that almost anyone can learn to use. With Elements, you too can work with the same wonderful tools that the pros use.

With the earliest versions of Elements, there was something of a learning curve. It was a super program but not one where you could just sit down and expect to get perfect results right off the bat.

In each new version, Adobe has added lots of push-button-easy ways to correct and improve your photos, and there are even more automated ways to do things in Elements 5. One-button fixes are a lot smarter, too. If you've used Elements before, you'll notice visibly better results with most of them in Elements 5. If you've been scared of Elements because you've heard about how tricky it is, you can stop worrying and jump right in.

What You Can Do with Elements 5

Elements not only allows you to make your photos look great, but it also helps you organize your photos and gives you some pretty neat projects to use them in. The program also comes loaded with lots of new ways to share your photos. The list of what Elements can do is pretty impressive. You can:

- Enhance your photos by editing, cropping, and color correcting them, including fixing exposure and color problems.

- Add all kinds of special effects to your photos, like turning a garden-variety photo into a drawing, painting, or even a tile mosaic.

- Combine photos into a panorama or a montage.

- Move someone from one photo to another, and even remove people (your ex?) from last year's holiday photos.

- Repair and restore old and damaged photos.

- Organize your photos and assign keywords to them so you can search by subject or name.

- Add type to your images and turn them into things like greeting cards and flyers.

- Create slideshows to share with your friends, regardless of whether they use Windows, Mac, or even just a cellphone.

- Automatically resize photos so that they're ready for email. Elements even lets you send your photos inside specially designed emails.

- Create digital artwork from scratch, even without a photo to work from.

- Create and share incredible Web photo galleries, and email-ready slideshows that will make your friends actually ask to see the pictures from your latest trip.

- Create and edit graphics for Web sites, including making animated GIFs (pictures that move animation-style).

- Create wonderful collages and photo layout pages that you can print or share with your friends digitally. Scrapbookers—get ready to be wowed.

It's worth noting, though, that there are still a few things Elements *can't* do. While Elements 5 handles text quite competently, at least as photo-editing programs go, it's still no substitute for PageMaker, InDesign, or any other desktop publishing program. And Elements can do an amazing job of fixing problems in your photos, but only if you give it something to work with. If your photo is totally overexposed, blurry, and the top of everyone's head is cut off, there may be a limit to what even Elements can do to help you out. (C'mon, be fair.) The fact is, though, you're more likely to be surprised by how much Elements *can* fix than by what it can't.

What's New in Elements 5

This book is about Photoshop Elements 5. Elements 5 is a huge upgrade from earlier versions, and it's really packed with exciting new features. If you have an earlier version of Elements, you'll find a number of similarities in the basic editing functions, but Elements 5 gives you a lot of new ways to tackle old projects. It's definitely a must-have update, no matter which version of Elements you might have used before. Along with a snazzy new look, some of the main changes in Elements 5 are:

- **True black-and-white conversion.** Elements has always let you remove color, but Elements 5 creates truly stunning black-and-white shots from your color photos (page 265).

- **Curves.** Not a drawing tool, but one of the most sophisticated color adjustment tools from Photoshop. It's come to Elements in a simpler, easy-to-use form (page 248).

- **Dozens of new graphics, frames, and special effects** to jazz up your photos (Chapter 13), and new alignment tools to help you position them just so.

- **Professional-looking new photo layouts** (page 397). Other great new projects include DVD cover inserts and CD/DVD labels.

- **Multi-page documents.** For the first time, you can create Elements files that are more than a single page long (page 403).

- **Web-based photo galleries.** Beautiful, interactive photo galleries that let viewers do things like scroll through pictures (as though on a gallery wall), or turn the pages like a book (page 447).

- **Mapping tools.** You can now view your photos like pins stuck in a Yahoo map. You can even share your maps with your friends so that they can click a spot on a map to see the photos you took of a particular location (page 441).

- **Multi-session burning for backup.** If you use the Organizer (page 43) to store your photos, no longer must you waste an entire CD to back up a couple of photos. You can tell Elements to leave the disc open so that you can come back and use it again and again till it's full.

- **Burst mode storage.** If you use your camera's burst mode (multiple shots in quick succession), you can tell the Organizer to automatically suggest stacks of the photos from each burst.

You'll also find new ways to sharpen your photos, more control of Layer styles—the list goes on and on. There's never been an Elements update with so many new features.

> **NOTE** The official system requirements for Elements 5 specify Windows XP with Service Pack 2. But, if you're a Service Pack 1 holdout, Elements should run just fine. However, remember that you're not as secure when using the online components of Elements as you would be with Service Pack 2.

If you've used Elements before and you're not sure which version you've got, a quick way to tell is to look for the version number on the CD. If the program is already installed, see page 13 for help figuring out which version you have.

Incidentally, all five versions of Elements are totally separate programs, so you can run all of them on the same computer if you like, as long as your operating system is compatible. (Adobe doesn't recommend trying to have more than one version open at a time, though.) So if you prefer the older version of a particular tool, you can still use it. As a matter of fact, if you're experienced in Elements and addicted to the many add-on tools and actions for Elements 3 and earlier versions, you definitely want to keep your old Elements around. (Adobe has taken steps to make sure that most of those tools *can't* work in Elements 4 and 5; more details on page 479.) If you've been using one of the earlier versions, you'll still feel right at home in Elements 5. You'll just find that it's easier than ever to get stuff done with the program.

If You Have a Mac

This book covers Elements 5 for Windows (the only version available at the time of writing). However, when Adobe releases Elements 5 for Mac, you can use this book with the Mac version as well. Just substitute Command (⌘) for Ctrl, and Option for Alt whenever you see keyboard shortcuts. About 98 percent of the Editor's functions work the same on both platforms. However, this book's sections on the Organizer apply only to Windows. (See page 14 for more on the difference between the Editor and the Organizer.)

Elements vs. Photoshop

It's very easy to get confused about the differences between Elements and the full version of Adobe Photoshop. Because Elements is so much less expensive, and because many of the program's more advanced controls are tucked away, a lot of Photoshop aficionados tend to view Elements as some kind of toy version of their program.

They couldn't be more wrong. Elements *is* Photoshop, but it's Photoshop adapted for use with a home printer and for the Web. The most important difference between Elements and Photoshop is that Elements doesn't let you work or save in CMYK mode, which is the format used for commercial color printing. (CMYK stands for Cyan, Magenta, Yellow, and blacK. Your inkjet printer also uses those ink colors to print, but it expects you to give it an RGB file, which is what Elements creates. This is all explained in Chapter 7.)

Elements also lacks several tools that are basic staples in any commercial art department, like Actions or scripting (to help automate repetitive tasks), the extra color control you can get from Selective Color, and the Pen tool's special talent for creating vector paths. Also, for some special effects, like creating drop shadows or bevels, the tool you'd use—Layer styles—doesn't have as many settings in Elements as it does in Photoshop (although Elements 5 gives you have many more settings options for Layer styles than previous versions). The same holds true for a handful of other Elements tools.

And although Elements is all most people will need to create graphics for the Web, it doesn't come with the ImageReady component of Photoshop, which lets you do things like automatically slice images for faster Web display. If you use Elements, you'll have to do those tasks manually or look for another program to help out.

The Key to Learning Elements

Elements may not be quite as powerful as Photoshop, but it's still a complex program, filled with more features than most people will ever end up using. The good news is that the Quick Fix window lets you get started right away, even if you don't understand every last option that Quick Fix presents you with.

As for the program's more complex features, the key to learning how to use Elements—or any other program, for that matter—is to focus only on what you need to know for the task you're currently trying to accomplish.

For example, if you're trying to use Quick Fix to adjust the color of your photo and crop it, don't worry that you don't get the concept of "layers" yet. You won't learn to do everything in Elements in a day or even a week. The rest will wait until you need it. So take your time and don't worry about what's not important to you right now. You'll find it much easier to master Elements if you go slowly and concentrate on one thing at a time.

If you're totally new to the program, you'll find only three or four big concepts in this book that you really have to understand if you want to get the most out of Elements. It may take a little time for some concepts to sink in—resolution and layers, for instance, aren't the most intuitive concepts in the world—but once they click, they'll seem so obvious that you'll wonder why things seemed confusing at first. That's perfectly normal, so persevere. You *can* do this, and there's nothing in this book that you won't be able to understand with a little bit of careful reading.

The very best way to learn Elements is just to dive right in and play with it. Try all the different filters to see what they do. Add a filter on top of another filter. Click around on all the different tools and try them. You don't even need to have a photo to do this. See page 39 for how to make an image from scratch in Elements and read on to learn about the many downloadable practice images you'll find at this book's companion Web site, *www.missingmanuals.com*. Get crazy—you can stack up as many filters, effects, and Layer styles as you want without crashing the program.

About This Book

Elements is such a cool program and so much fun to use, but figuring out how to make it do what you want is another matter. The manual that comes with Elements 5 is more like a quick reference guide and doesn't go into as much depth as you might want. The Elements Help files are very good, but of course you need to know what you're looking for to use them to your best advantage.

You'll find a slew of Elements titles at your local bookstore, but most of them assume that you know quite a bit about the basics of photography and/or digital imaging. It's much easier to find good intermediate books about Elements than books designed to get you going with the program.

Which is where the Missing Manual comes in. This book is intended to make learning Elements easier by avoiding technical jargon as much as possible, and explaining *why* and *when* you'll want to use (or avoid) certain features in the program. That approach is as useful to people who are advanced photographers as it is to those who are just getting started with their first digital camera.

NOTE This book periodically recommends *other* books, covering topics that are too specialized or tangential for a manual about Elements. Careful readers may notice that not every one of these titles is published by Missing Manual parent, O'Reilly Media. While we're happy to mention other Missing Manuals and books in the O'Reilly family, if there's a great book out there that doesn't happen to be published by O'Reilly, we'll still let you know about it.

You'll also find tutorials throughout the book that refer to files you can download from the Missing Manual Web site (*www.missingmanuals.com*) so you can practice the techniques you're reading about. And throughout the book, you'll find several different kinds of sidebar articles. The ones labeled "Up to Speed" help newcomers to Elements do things or explain concepts that veterans are probably already familiar with. "Power Users' Clinic" covers more advanced topics that won't be of much interest to casual photographers.

NOTE You'll see illustrations of Windows XP in this book. By the time you're reading this, you may be using Windows Vista, the next version of the Windows operating system. Elements 5 will most likely work just fine in Vista, but it's worth taking a quick look at one of the many Internet forums devoted to Elements (page 478) before you buy the program, just to be on the safe side.

About the Outline

This book is divided into six different parts, each of which focuses on a certain kind of task you may want to do in Elements.

Introduction to Elements

The first part of this book helps you get started with Elements. Chapter 1 shows you how to navigate Elements' slightly confusing layout and mishmash of programs within programs. You learn how to decide which window to start from, as well as how to set up Elements so it best suits your own personal working style. You'll also learn about some important basic keyboard shortcuts and where to look for help when you get stuck. Chapter 2 covers how to get photos into Elements, the basics of organizing them, and how to open files and create new images from scratch, as well as how to save and back up your images. Chapter 3 explains how to rotate and crop your photos, and includes a primer on that most important digital imaging concept—resolution.

Elemental elements

Chapter 4 tells you how to use the Quick Fix window to dramatically improve your photos. Chapters 5 and 6 cover two key concepts—making selections and layers—that you'll use throughout the book.

Retouching

Having Elements is like having a darkroom on your computer. In Chapter 7, you'll learn how to make basic corrections, such as exposure, color adjustments, sharpening, and removing dust and scratches. Chapter 8 covers topics unique to people who use digital cameras, like RAW conversion and batch processing your photos. In Chapter 9, you'll move on to some more sophisticated fixes, like changing the light, using the clone stamp to make repairs, making your photos more lively with hue/saturation, and changing the colors in an image. Chapter 10 covers converting your photos to black and white, and tinting and recoloring black and white photos. Chapter 11 helps you to use Elements' Photomerge feature to create multi-photo panoramas and to make perspective corrections to your images.

Artistic elements

This part covers the fun stuff—painting on your photos and drawing shapes (Chapter 12), using filters and effects to create a more artistic look (Chapter 13), and adding type to your images (Chapter 14).

Sharing your images

Once you've created a great image in Elements, you'll want to share it, so this part is about how to get the most out of your printer (Chapter 15), how to create images for the Web and email (Chapter 17), how to make slideshows and Web Galleries with your photos (Chapter 18), and all the fun projects you can create with Elements 5 (Chapter 16).

Additional elements

There are literally hundreds of plug-ins and additional styles, brushes, and other fun stuff you can get to customize your copy of Elements and increase its abilities; the Internet and your local bookstore are chock full of additional information. Chapter 19 offers a look at some of these, as well as information about using a graphics tablet in Elements and some resources for after you've finished this book.

The Very Basics

This book assumes that you know how to perform basic activities on your computer like clicking and double-clicking your mouse and dragging objects onscreen. Here's a quick refresher: to *click* means to move the point of your mouse or trackpad cursor over an object on your screen and press the mouse or trackpad button once. To *double-click* means to press the button twice, quickly, without moving the mouse between clicks. To *drag* means to click an object and use the mouse to move it, while holding down the button so you don't let go of it. If you're comfortable with basic concepts like these, you're ready to get started with this book.

In Elements, you'll often want to use keyboard shortcuts to save time, and this book gives keyboard shortcuts when they exist (and there are a lot of them in Elements). So if you see "Press Ctrl+S to save your file," that means to hold down the Control key while pressing the S key.

About → These → Arrows

Throughout *Photoshop Elements 5: The Missing Manual* (and in any Missing Manual, for that matter) you'll see arrows that look like this: "Go to Editor → Filter → Artistic → Paint Daubs."

This is a shorthand way of helping you find files, folders, and menu choices without having to read through excruciatingly long, bureaucratic-style instructions. So, for example, the sentence in the previous paragraph is a short way of saying: "Go to the Editor component of Elements. Click the Filter choice in the menu bar. In that menu, choose the Artistic section, and then go to Paint Daubs in the pop-out menu." Figure I-1 shows you an example in action.

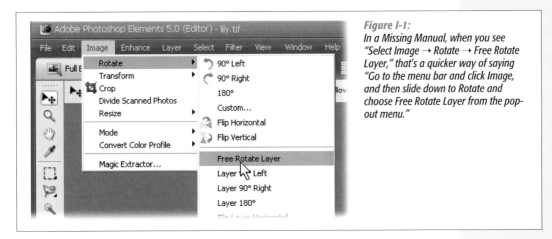

Figure I-1:
In a Missing Manual, when you see "Select Image → Rotate → Free Rotate Layer," that's a quicker way of saying "Go to the menu bar and click Image, and then slide down to Rotate and choose Free Rotate Layer from the pop-out menu."

File paths are shown in the conventional Windows style, so if you see "Go to *C:\ Documents and Settings\<your user name>\My Documents\My Pictures*," that means to go to your C drive, open the Documents and Settings folder, and look for your user account folder. In that folder, open the My Pictures folder that's inside it.

About MissingManuals.com

If you head on over to the Missing Manual Web site (*www.missingmanuals.com*), you can find links to downloadable images for the tutorials mentioned in this book, if you want to practice without using your own photos. (Or maybe you never take pictures that need correcting?)

A word about the image files for the tutorials: to make life easier for folks with dial-up Internet connections, the file sizes have been kept pretty small. This means you probably won't want to print the results of what you create (since you'll end up with a print about the size of a match book). But that doesn't really matter because the files are really meant for onscreen use. You'll see notes throughout the book about which images are available for any given chapter.

At the Web site, you can also find articles, tips, and updates to the book. If you click the Errata link, you'll see any corrections to the book's content, too. If you find something, feel free to report it by using this link. Each time the book is printed, we'll update it with any confirmed corrections. If you want to be certain that your own copy is up to the minute, this is where to check for any changes. And thanks for reporting any errors or corrections.

Safari® Enabled

When you see a Safari® Enabled icon on the cover of your favorite technology book, that means the book is available online through the O'Reilly Network Safari Bookshelf.

Safari offers a solution that's better than e-books. It's a virtual library that lets you easily search thousands of top tech books, cut and paste code samples, download chapters, and find quick answers when you need the most accurate, current information. Try it for free at *http://safari.oreilly.com*.

Part One:
Introductory Elements

1

Finding Your Way Around Elements

Photoshop Elements lets you do practically anything you want to your digital images. You can colorize black-and-white photos, remove demonic red-eye stares, or distort the facial features of people who've been mean to you. The downside is that all those options can make it tough to find your way around Elements, especially when you're new to the program.

This chapter helps get you oriented in Elements. You'll learn about what to expect when you start up the program and how to use Elements to fix your photos with just a couple of keystrokes. Along the way, you'll find out about some of Elements' basic controls and how to get hold of the program's Help files if you need them.

UP TO SPEED

Which Version of Elements Do You Have?

This book covers Photoshop Elements 5. If you're not sure which version of Elements you have, the easiest way to find out is to look at the program's icon (the file you click to launch Elements).

You can use this book if you have an earlier version of Elements because a lot of the basic editing procedures are the same. But Elements 5 is a pretty big update, so you'll find many new features, like Color Curves (page 248) and Black-and-White conversion (page 265), that won't be in your version of the program. There are *Missing Manuals* for Elements 3 and 4, too, and you may prefer to track down the right book for your version of Elements.

The Welcome Screen

When you launch Elements for the first time, you get a veritable smorgasbord of options, all neatly laid out for you in the Welcome screen (Figure 1-1).

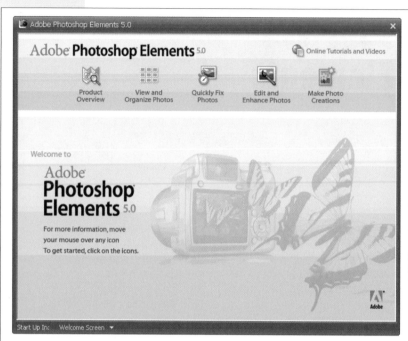

Figure 1-1:
The Elements Welcome screen gives you five main activities to choose from (there's also a Tutorials link in the upper-right corner). Hold your cursor over any of these options for more details about each choice. You can't bypass the Welcome screen just by clicking the Close button. When you do, the screen goes away—but so does Elements. Fortunately, you've got options: The box on page 15 tells you how to permanently get rid of the Welcome screen.

Interestingly, the Welcome screen isn't actually Elements. It's a launching pad that, depending on the button you click, starts up one of two different programs:

- **The Organizer,** which lets you store and organize your image files.

- **The Editor,** which lets you edit your images.

It's quite easy to get back and forth between the Editor and the Organizer—which you might call the two different faces of Elements—and you probably won't do much in one without eventually needing to get into the other. But in some ways, they still function as two separate programs. In any case, the Welcome screen offers you no less than five choices for how to get into Elements:

- **Product Overview** offers a round-up of all the features inside Elements.

- **View and Organize Photos** takes you to the Organizer, where you can store and sort all your images.

- **Quickly Fix Photos** brings you to the wonderful Quick Fix window (which is actually part of the Editor) where you can perform amazing color corrections with just a click.

• **Edit and Enhance Photos** takes you to the Editor, which is the digital darkroom/art studio where you can perform your most extensive edits.

• **Make Photo Creations** starts you up in the Editor with a new Photo Layout page to work on (see page 397), a great shortcut if you're into scrapbooking.

If you start in the Organizer, once you've located a photo to edit, you have to wait while the Editor loads. And when you have both the Editor and the Organizer running, quitting the Editor doesn't close the Organizer. You have to close both programs independently.

Adobe has built Elements around the assumption that most people work on their photos in the following way: First, you bring your photos into the Organizer to sort and keep track of them. Then, you open your photos in the Editor to work on them, and save them back to the Organizer when you're finished making changes. You can work differently, of course, like opening photos directly in the Editor and bypassing the Organizer altogether, but you may feel like you're always swimming against the current if you choose a different way of working. The next chapter has a few hints for disabling some Elements features if you really find they're getting in your way.

FREQUENTLY ASKED QUESTION

Say Goodbye to the Welcome Screen

How do I get rid of the Welcome screen?

If you get to feeling like you've been welcomed enough, you can turn off the Welcome screen. Then you don't have to click through it every time you start the program.

In the Welcome screen's lower-left corner, you can choose where you want Elements to start when you launch

the program: Editor, Organizer, or Welcome screen. Pick the one you want, and from now on, that's what opens first in Elements.

To get the Welcome screen back, from either the Editor or the Organizer, choose Window → Welcome.

Organizing Your Photos

The Organizer is where your photos come into Elements and go out again (when it's time to print or email them). The Organizer stores and catalogs your photos, and you automatically come back to it for any activities that involve sharing your photos, like printing a photo package or making a slideshow. The Organizer's main window (Figure 1-2) is sometimes called the *Photo Browser*. It lets you view your photos, sort them into collections, and assign keyword labels to them.

The Organizer has lots of really cool features you'll learn about throughout this book when they're relevant to the image-editing task at hand. The next chapter shows you how to use the Organizer to import and organize your photos, and Appendix A covers all the Organizer's different menu options.

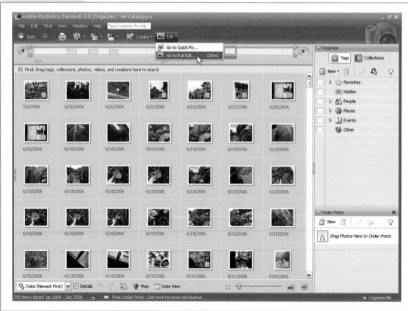

Figure 1-2:
The Photo Browser is your main Organizer workspace. Click the Edit button, as shown in the illustration, to go to either the Quick Fix or Full Edit. Click the Create button to the left of the Edit button, and you can choose to start all kinds of new projects with your photos. The Organizer also gives you another way to look at your photos, Date View, which is explained in Figure 1-3.

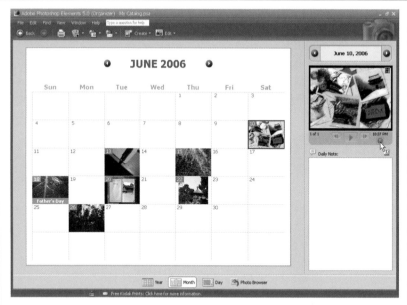

Figure 1-3:
Date View is a fun feature that lets you see your photos organized by the date you brought them into the Organizer. It's even laid out like a calendar. In the upper-right corner of the window you can play a little slideshow of all the pictures you took on a particular day. If you find a photo you want to edit or use in a project, then click the little binoculars (where the cursor is in the photo) to see that photo's location in the Photo Browser window. When you want to go back to the Browser without selecting any photos, just click the Photo Browser button at the bottom of the window.

Photo Downloader

Actually, Elements has one other component, which you may have seen already if you've plugged your camera into your computer after you installed Elements: the Photo Downloader (Figure 1-4).

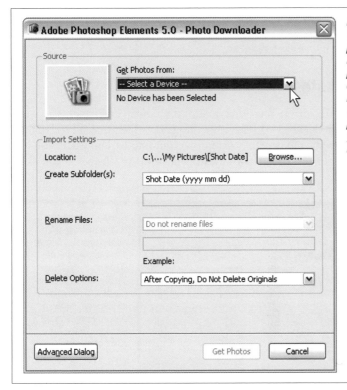

Figure 1-4:
The Adobe Photo Downloader is yet another program that you get when you install Elements. Its role in life is to pull your photos from your camera (or other storage device) into the Organizer. The Downloader runs even if Elements isn't currently open (although, as you'll learn in the box on page 36, you can disable the Downloader if you don't like it). After the Downloader does its thing, you end up in the Organizer.

This bumptious little program is meant to help you get your photos into the Organizer, and it's more zealous than a personal-injury lawyer on the scene of an accident. It sniffs out any device you attach to your computer that may possibly contain photos. and it races to the scene, elbowing the Windows Explorer dialog box out of the way. Depending on the speed of your computer, it may show up before the Explorer dialog box or slightly after it. You have to dismiss the Downloader first if you want to use another program to import your photos.

You can read more about the Downloader in the next chapter (page 32), including how to easily tame it so that you control when it appears. If you plan to use the Organizer to catalog your photos and assign keywords to them, then reading the section on the Downloader in Chapter 2 can help you avoid forehead-smacking moments.

Where the Heck Did Elements Go?

If you know that you've installed Elements but you can't seem to figure out how to launch it, no problem.

There should be a shortcut to Elements on your desktop once you've installed the program. You can also go to the

Start menu and click the Adobe Photoshop Elements 5.0 icon. If you don't see Elements in the Start menu, click the arrow next to "All Programs," and you should find it in the pop-up menu.

Editing Your Photos

In addition to the Organizer, the other main component of Elements is what Adobe calls the Editor (Figure 1-5). This is the fun part of Elements, where you get to edit, adjust, transform, and generally glamorize your photos, and where you can create original artwork from scratch with the drawing tools and shapes, if you like.

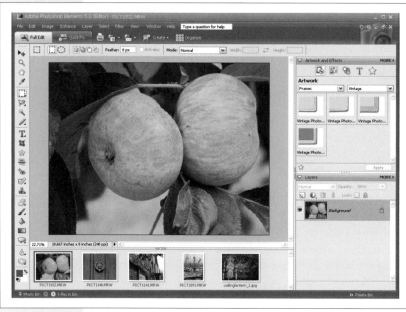

Figure 1-5:
The main Elements editing window, which Adobe calls Full Edit. In previous versions of Elements it was known as the Standard Editor, something you might want to remember in case you ever try any tutorials written for Elements 3 or 4.

You can operate the Editor in either of two different modes:

- **Quick Fix.** For many beginners, the Quick Fix (Figure 1-6) ends up as your main workspace. Adobe has gathered together the basic tools you need to improve most photos, and it's the one place in Elements where you can have a before-and-after view while you work. Chapter 4 discusses using Quick Fix in detail.

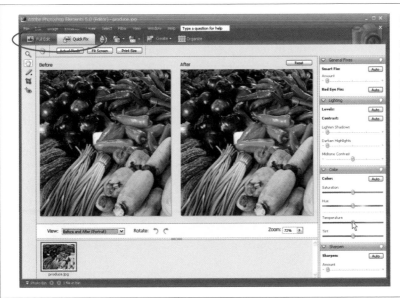

Figure 1-6:
The Quick Fix window is the only place in Elements where you can see a before-and-after view of your photo as you work. Use the navigation buttons at the top of the screen (circled) to navigate from Full Edit to the Quick Fix window and back again.

- **Full Edit.** The Full Edit window gives you access to Elements' most sophisticated tools. You have far more ways to work on your photo in Full Edit than in Quick Fix, and if you're fussy, it's where you'll do most of your retouching work. Most of the Quick Fix commands are also available via menus in the Full Edit window.

The rest of this chapter covers some of the basic concepts and key tools you'll come across in the Editor.

NOTE   If you leave a photo open in the Editor, when you switch back to the Organizer, you see a red band with a padlock across the photo's Organizer thumbnail as a reminder. To get rid of the lock and free up your image for Organizer projects, go back to the Editor and close the photo there.

POWER USERS' CLINIC

Doubling Up

Old Elements hands: If you prefer the double-columned Toolbox from Elements 1 and 2, good news—you can tear the Toolbox loose from its moorings and collapse it into a double row by grabbing its top edge and pulling it off the Options bar. But keep in mind that a double-columned Toolbox is a bit of a quirky creature. When you put it too close to the left edge of the screen, it springs back to its original form.

Another advantage to having a floating Toolbox is that you can use the Tab key to hide it along with your other loose palettes. Tab again to bring them all back. (Like the anchored Toolbox, the bins and top bars of Elements don't go away when you press the Tab key.)

Your Elements Tools

Elements gives you an amazing array of tools to use when working on your photo. You get almost two dozen primary tools to help you select, paint on, and otherwise manipulate your photos, and many of the tools have as many as four subtools hiding beneath them (see Figure 1-7). Bob Vila's workshop probably isn't any better stocked than Elements' virtual toolbox.

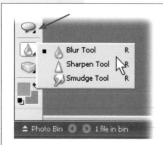

Figure 1-7:
Like any good toolbox, the Elements Toolbox has lots of hidden drawers tucked away in it. Many Elements tools are actually groups of tools, which are represented by tiny black triangles on the lower-right side of the tool icon (where the arrow is pointing in the illustration). Holding the mouse button down as you click the icon brings out the hidden subtools. The little black square next to the Blur tool means it's the active tool right now.

TIP When you want to explore every cranny of Elements, you need to open a photo (in the Editor, choose File → Open). Lots of the menus are grayed out if you have no file opened.

The long, skinny strip on the left side of the Full Edit window is the main Elements Toolbox, as you can see in Figure 1-5. It stays perfectly organized so that you can always find what you want without ever having to lift a finger to straighten it up. And what's more, if you forget what a particular tool does, then hold your mouse over the tool's icon and a label appears. To activate a tool, click it. Any tool that you select comes with its own collection of options, as shown in Figure 1-8.

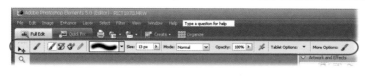

Figure 1-8:
When a tool is active, the Options bar changes to show its available settings (circled). Elements tools are highly customizable, letting you do things like adjust a brush's size and shape.

Other windows in Elements, like Quick Fix and the RAW converter (see page 211), also have toolboxes, but none is as complete as the one in Full Edit.

Don't worry about learning the names of every tool right now. It's easier to remember what a tool is once you've used it. And don't be concerned about how many tools you have available. You probably have a bunch of Allen wrenches in your garage toolbox that you don't use more than a couple of times a year. Likewise, you'll find that you tend to use certain Elements tools more than others.

TIP You can activate any tool with a keyboard shortcut, thereby saving a *ton* of time, since you don't have to interrupt what you're doing to trek over to the Toolbox. To see a tool's shortcut key, hover your mouse over the icon. It's the letter in parentheses in the tooltips text that pops up.

FREQUENTLY ASKED QUESTION

The Always-On Toolbox

Do I always have to have a tool selected?

Yes. When looking at the Toolbox, you may notice that the Marquee tool icon (the little dotted rectangle) is highlighted, indicating that the tool is active. You can deactivate it by clicking a different tool. But what happens when you don't want any tool to be active? How do you fix things so that you don't have a tool selected?

You don't. In the Editor, one tool must always be selected, so you'll probably want to get in the habit of choosing a tool that won't do anything damaging to your image if you click it accidentally. For instance, the Pencil tool, which leaves a spot or line where you click, is probably not a good choice. The Marquee selection tool, the Zoom tool, and the Hand tool are the safest choices.

Bins and Palettes

In the Editor, the two big space-consuming objects hogging the bottom and right side of your screen are called *bins*. The Photo bin, as shown in Figure 1-9, helps you keep track of which images are currently open.

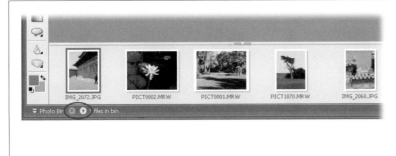

Figure 1-9:
The Photo bin runs across the bottom of your screen. It holds a thumbnail of every photo you have open. If you happen to have 73 photos open at once, you can scroll the bin to the left or right by clicking on either of the two triangle arrow buttons (circled). To change the active photo, click the thumbnail of the one you want and it moves to the front and becomes the active image.

The Photo bin is a useful feature, but unless you have a gigantic monitor, you may prefer to have the space for your editing work. To close the bin, click the Minimize button, just to the left of "Photo Bin." One very cool thing about the Photo bin is that even when it's closed, you can use the left and right arrows (the ones to the right of the Minimize button) to rotate through the open photos until you find the one you want.

The long wide strip down the right side of your screen is the Palette bin. Elements stores *palettes* in this bin, letting you do things like keep track of what you've done to your photo (Undo History) and apply special effects to your images (Artwork and Effects).

Taming the Palette bin

It's possible that you'll like the Palette bin, but many people don't. If you don't have a large monitor, you may find it wastes too much desktop acreage, and in Elements, you need all the working room you can get. Fortunately, you don't have to keep your palettes in the bin; you can close the bin and just keep your palettes floating around on your desktop, or you can minimize them.

You open and close the bin by clicking the Palette Bin button at the bottom of your screen (below the bin), or you can click the Palette bin's left edge (anywhere along the thin vertical bar). You can also pull palettes out of the bin by dragging the name bar of any palette. Figure 1-10 shows how to make your palettes even smaller once they're out of the bin. Freestanding palettes can also be combined with each other, as shown in Figure 1-11.

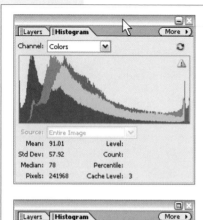

Figure 1-10:
You can free up even more space by collapsing your palettes, accordion-style, once they're out of the bin.

Top: To do so, double-click the palette's top bar. You can also toggle back and forth between expanded and contracted views by clicking the palette's Minimize button.

Bottom: A shrunken palette.

Only two palettes are in the Palette bin to start with (Layers, and Artwork and Effects). To see how many more palettes you actually have, check out the Window menu. When you select a new palette, by choosing it in the Window menu, it may appear in the bin first. If you've hidden the bin, it jumps back out at you with the new palette on display, and you'll have to haul the palette out if you don't want to use the bin. Some palettes, like Undo History, show up already floating, and you have to drag them into the bin if you want to corral them there.

> **NOTE** If you've been going crazy because you're trying to get rid of one of the bin's original palettes, but every time you close it, it just hops back into the bin, click the More button in the upper-right corner of the palette and turn off "Place in Palette bin when closed." Next time you close the palette, it goes away and won't return till you choose it again from the Window menu.

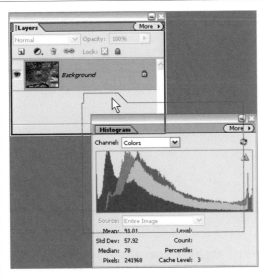

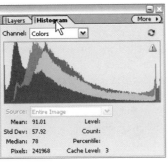

Figure 1-11:
You can combine two or more palettes together once you've dragged them out of the bin.

Top: The Histogram palette is being pulled into, and combined with, the Layers palette. To combine palettes, drag one of them (by clicking on the palette's name tab) and drop it onto the other palette (notice the dark black border that appears on the Layers palette, signaling it's "ready" to accept the Histogram palette).

Bottom: To switch from one palette to another after they're grouped, just click the tab of the one you want to use. To remove a palette from a group, just drag it off the palette window. If you want to return everything to how it looked when you first launched Elements, go to Window → Reset Palette Locations.

The Artwork and Effects palette

The Artwork and Effects palette is a special new feature in Elements 5. Adobe has simply crammed the program with all sorts of goodies like easily addable frames, graphics, and backgrounds. You have so many that creating a separate palette for each one would mean you'd need some kind of Palette Manager just to keep track of everything.

Adobe's solution to this surplus is a new palette, the Artwork and Effects palette, which is organized a little differently from your other palettes. When you want to use something from Artwork and Effects, first click the button at the top of the palette to enter the main category you want, as explained in Figure 1-12. Then use the pull-down menus to find the exact frame, filter, or whatever. You can learn more about working with this palette on page 344.

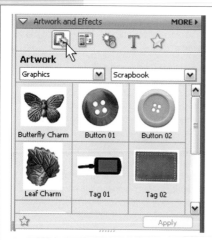

Figure 1-12:
From left to right, the buttons across the top of the Artwork and Effects palette take you to: Artwork (frames, backgrounds, clip art), Themes (for Photo Creations; see page 399), Special Effects (filters, effects, Layer styles), Text effects (see page 386), and your Favorites.

Elements Shortcuts

One thing that makes Elements kind of bewildering is the number of ways you have to perform almost any action. You can navigate from menus, use the Shortcuts bar, or, as most people find easiest, use keyboard shortcuts. In this book, when there's a keystroke that you can use to do something, it's usually the method you'll see. But often you have other ways to do the same thing that are equally good. It's your choice.

For instance, on the top of your screen, just below the menu bar, is the Shortcuts bar. If you're the kind of person who likes to click a button to make things happen, this is your part of Elements. When you pass your mouse over the Shortcut bar icons, you can see tooltips that tell you what each button does. Some people love the Shortcuts bar—others ignore it completely.

NOTE Elements has one palette-related quirk. In the Window menu, visible palettes should have a check next to their names. But if you collapse a palette, then even though the palette's name stays on your desktop, it remains unchecked in the Window menu. If you lose a collapsed palette (they occasionally get hidden behind the Options bar when you switch back and forth from Full Edit to Quick Fix or the Organizer), just select the palette's name again in the list to bring the palette back to the front where you can reach it. If all else fails, choosing Reset Palette Locations in the Window menu puts everything back to its original position.

Getting Help and the How To Palette

Wherever Adobe found a stray corner in Elements, they stuck some help into it. You can't move anywhere in this program without being offered some kind of guidance. Here are some of the ways you can summon assistance if you need it:

- **Options bar.** Enter a search term in the Help box, or use the Help menu (as shown in Figure 1-13), or just press F1.

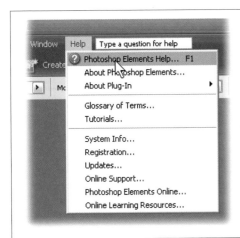

Figure 1-13:
Type a search term into the box marked "Type a question for help,"
or choose Help → Photoshop Elements Help, or simply press F1 to
see the Elements Help files. In the Help window, you can also browse
a topic list and a glossary.

- **Tooltips.** The text that pops up under your mouse as you move around Elements is linked to the appropriate section in Elements Help. Click a tooltip for more information about whatever your mouse is hovering over.

- **Dialog box links.** Most dialog boxes have links to Elements Help. If you get confused about what the settings for a filter do, for instance, then click the blue link text for a reminder.

If you call up the Help Center without typing a search term first, it's a bit confusing to find answers to your questions. Adobe now uses a sort of generic help center that corrals the help files for all its current program versions. This means, somewhat irritatingly, that when you first open the Adobe Help Center, it's set up to answer questions about the Adobe Help Center, not about Elements. To get to the Elements Help files, use the pull-down menu on the left side of the Help Window (Product Help for) to select Elements, and then type your search question.

The How To palette

If you need help figuring out where to begin a project, the Editor's How To palette gives instructions for lots of things you're likely to want to do in Elements (Figure 1-14). You can get directions for everything from making a photo look old-fashioned to creating fancy warped text effects. To see the How To palette, go to Window → How To.

Escape Routes

Photoshop Elements has a couple of really wonderful features to help you keep from making irrevocable screw-ups: the Undo command and the Undo History palette. After you've gotten used to them, you'll probably wish it were possible to use these tools in all aspects of your life, not just Elements.

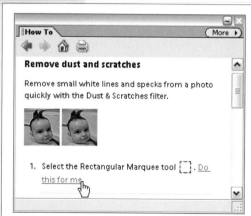

Figure 1-14:
The How To palette offers help with everything from basics, like opening a file, to more advanced projects, like changing an object's color. When you click "Do this for me," Elements runs the show while you just sit there and watch. It's always helpful to be able to watch an expert at work. (Sometimes, instead of doing the work for you, Elements just gives you very explicit directions for something you have to do yourself.)

Undo

No matter where you are in Elements, you can almost always change your mind about what you just did. Press Ctrl+Z and the last change you made goes away. Pressing Ctrl+Z works even if you've just saved your photo, but only while it's still open. (If you close your picture, your changes are permanent.) Keep pressing Ctrl+Z and you keep undoing your work, step by step.

If you want to redo what you just undid, just press Ctrl+Y. These keystroke commands are great for toggling changes on and off while you decide whether you really want to keep them.

> **NOTE** You do have some control over the keys you use for Undo/Redo, if you go to Edit → Preferences → General. Elements gives you two other choices, both of which involve the Z key in combination with the Control, Alt, and Shift keys.

Undo History palette

In the Full Edit window, you get even more control over the actions you can undo, thanks to the Undo History palette (Figure 1-15), which you open by choosing Window → Undo History.

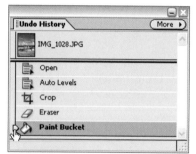

Figure 1-15:
For a little time travel, just slide the pointer up and watch your changes disappear one by one. You can only go back sequentially. Here, for instance, you can't go back to Crop without first undoing the Paint Bucket and the Eraser. Slide the pointer down to redo your work. You can also move to a different point in your work by just clicking the place in the list where you want to go, instead of using the slider.

This palette holds a list of the changes you've made since the last time you saved your image. Just push the slider up and watch your changes disappear one by one as you go. Undo History even works if you've saved your file: As long as you haven't closed your file, the palette tracks every action you take.

Be careful, though. You can back up only as many steps as you've set Elements to remember. Elements lets you keep track of as many as 1,000 actions. You can regulate this number in Preferences, as explained in Figure 1-16.

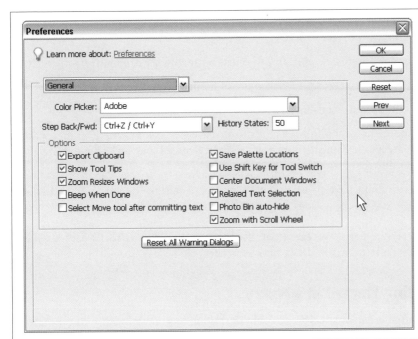

Figure 1-16:
You can set the number of steps the Undo History palette remembers in Edit → Preferences → General. Elements initially sets it to 50, but you can set it as high as 1,000. Beware, though—remembering even 100 steps may slow your system to a crawl if you don't have a super-powered processor, plenty of memory, and loads of disk space. If Elements runs slowly on your machine, then reducing the number of history states it remembers (try 20) may speed things up a bit.

The one rule of Elements

As you're probably beginning to see, Elements lets you work in lots of different ways. What's more, most people who use Elements approach projects in different ways. What works for your neighbor with his pictures may be quite different from how you would choose to work on the very same shots.

However, you'll hear one suggestion from almost every Elements veteran, and it's an important one: *Never ever work on your original. Always, always, always make a copy of your image and work on that.*

The good news is that if you store your photos in the Organizer, you don't need to worry about accidentally trashing your original. Elements automatically creates a copy when you edit a photo that's cataloged in the Organizer, so that you can always revert to your original.

NOTE The Organizer's *version sets* provide another great safety net. They let you make as many different editions of your photo as you like without compromising your original. Page 54 has full details.

If you're determined not to use the Organizer, follow these steps to make a copy of your image:

1. **Right-click the title bar of the Image window and choose Duplicate, or go to File → Duplicate.**

   The Image window is the small window within the Editor where your photo appears.

2. **Name the duplicate, and click the close button on the original.**

   Now the original is safely tucked out of harm's way.

3. **Save the duplicate using Ctrl+S.**

   Choose Photoshop (.psd) as the file format when you save it. (You may want to choose another format after you've read Chapter 3 and understand more about your different format options.)

Now you don't have to worry about making a mistake or changing your mind, because you can always start over if you want to.

NOTE Elements doesn't have an autosave feature, so you should get into the habit of saving frequently as you work. Read more about saving on page 52.

Getting Started in a Hurry

If you're the impatient type, and you're starting to squirm because you want to be up and doing something to your photos, here's the quickest way to get started in Elements: adjust the brightness and color balance all in one step.

1. **While you're in the Editor, open a photo.**

   Press Ctrl+O and navigate to the image you want, and then click Open.

2. **Press Alt+Ctrl+M.**

   You've just applied Elements' Auto Smart Fix tool (Figure 1-17).

Voilà! You should see quite a difference in your photo, unless the exposure, lighting, and contrast were almost perfect before. The Auto Smart Fix tool is one of the many easy-to-use features in Elements. (Of course, you may not like what just happened to your photo, but that's why you bought this book.)

If you're the really impatient type, you can jump right to Chapter 4 to learn about using the Quick Fix commands. But it's worth taking the time to read the next two chapters so you understand which file formats to choose and how to make some basic adjustments to your images, like rotating and cropping them.

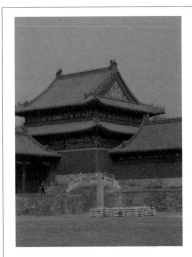
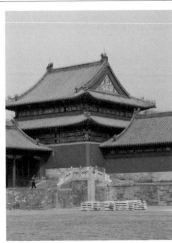
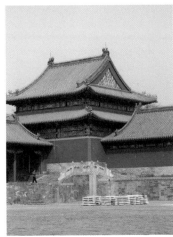

Figure 1-17:
Auto Smart Fix is the easiest, quickest way to improve the quality of your photos.

Top left: The original, unedited picture.

Top right: Auto Smart Fix makes quite a difference, but the colors are still slightly off.

Bottom: By using some of the other tools you'll learn about in this book (like Auto Contrast and Adjust Sharpness), you can make things look even better.

Importing, Managing, and Saving Your Photos

Now that you've had a look around Elements, it's time to start learning how to get photos *into* the program, and also how to keep track of where these photos are stored. As a digital photographer, you may no longer be facing shoeboxes stuffed with prints, but you've still got to face the menace of photos piling up on your hard drive. Fortunately, Elements gives you some great tools for organizing your collection and quickly finding individual pictures.

In this chapter, you'll learn how to import your photos from cameras, digital card readers, and scanners. You'll also find out how to import individual frames from videos, how to open files that are already on your computer, and how to create a new file from scratch. After that, you'll learn how to use the Organizer to sort and find your pictures once they're in Elements. Finally, you'll learn how to save the work you create in Elements and how to make backups.

Importing from Cameras

Elements gives you lots of different ways to get photos from camera to computer, but the simplest tool is the Adobe Photo Downloader. If you don't like the Downloader, read on. Later in this section, you'll learn about other ways to import your photos.

> **NOTE**   Take a moment to carefully read the instructions from your camera manufacturer. These directions should always take precedence over anything you read here that suggests doing something differently.

The Photo Downloader

You may have already made the acquaintance of the Photo Downloader, since it automatically appears (Figure 2-1) whenever you connect a camera or card reader to your PC—even if Elements isn't running. The Downloader's job is pretty straightforward: to shepherd your photos as they make the trip to your PC and to make sure Elements knows where your new images are stored. Your job is to help it along by adjusting the following settings.

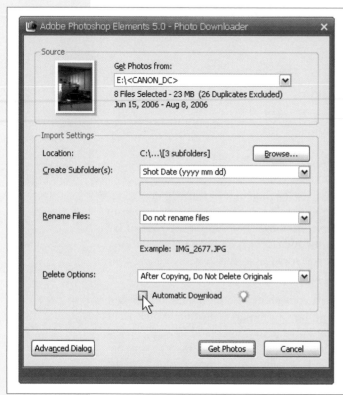

Figure 2-1:
When the Elements 5 Downloader first launches, you see this dialog box, which lets you choose where your photos go and what names they're given (say goodbye to names like IMG_0327.JPG). To start, choose your camera or card reader from the list of devices. If you want to browse through your photos to decide which ones to import, click Advanced Dialog, where you can pick and choose which photos to grab and fine-tune other settings.

- **Get Photos From.** Choose your camera or card reader from the list of available devices, as your first step to downloading.

- **Location.** Your photos usually get stored in a folder named after the date you imported them. (This folder is located inside the directory *C:\<your user name>\My Documents\My Pictures\Adobe\Digital Camera Photos*. If you download more photos the same day, you get a second folder, with the same name with "-1" added to it.) If you want to change where your photos are headed, then click the Browse button and choose another location. You can permanently change the standard location by going to Organizer → Edit → Preferences → Camera or Card Reader. Set a new location, and from now on, the Downloader always puts your photos in the folder you chose.

- **Create Subfolder.** If you want to have more organization, you can choose to put your files into a subfolder, inside the folder you chose in Location, with a name you pick (instead of a date-stamped one). You can also choose to have a subfolder named after the date and time of your import, or the date when the photo was shot. You can also choose not to create a subfolder at all (choose None from the pull-down menu), if you want all your photos to be imported into the same folder level that you chose in Location.

   TIP   When you give the folder a descriptive name, you can apply that name as a descriptive tag (label) to all the photos in the folder with just one click (once you're in the Photo Browser window). Read more about tags—and how they can help quickly find photos—later in this chapter.

- **Rename Files.** You can choose to give all the files a custom name, if you like. So if you type *obedience_school_graduation*, then you get photos named obedience_school_graduation001, obedience_school_graduation002, and so on, or you can choose to use a combination of a custom name and the shot date, if you prefer. You can also choose to use just the shot date or today's date, or the name of the subfolder. In each case, you'll get the three-digit number to distinguish the files. You can also choose to leave this setting at "Do not rename files," in which case you keep the camera's file names and numbers.

- **Delete Options.** You can choose to let the Downloader delete your files when done. Figure 2-2 explains more about this option.

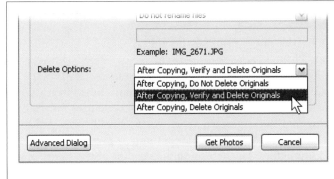

Figure 2-2:
The Downloader offers to delete the files from your camera or memory card reader once they've been imported. This feature seems handy, but prudent people may want to think twice about whether to actually delete the files. The Downloader's pretty reliable, but it's always a good idea to wait until you've been through all your photos before deleting the originals. If you must use this option, at least choose "After Copying, Verify and Delete Originals," which forces Elements to check that it's copied over your files correctly before deleting the originals.

- **Automatic Download.** If you like to live dangerously, you can turn on this checkbox and Elements will download any new photos it detects without showing you the dialog box. In almost all circumstances, it's best to leave Automatic Download off so that you have some control over what's going on. (This checkbox appears only after you've selected a device in the "Get Photos from" menu.)

The Elements 5 Downloader is smart enough to recognize any photos that it's already imported, and it doesn't reimport those. If you want to see your duplicates and maybe download them again, or if you want to pick and choose which photos to import, then click the Advanced Dialog button at the bottom of the window to bring up the larger dialog box shown in Figure 2-3.

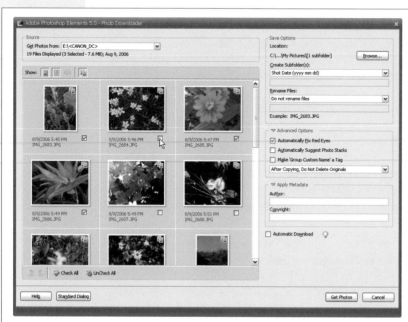

Figure 2-3:
When you want to pick and choose which photos to import, summon the Photo Downloader's Advanced Dialog.

This window gives you all the options you see in the regular Photo Downloader, plus a few more. The Advanced window is divided into two main parts. On the left side are the thumbnails of your photos. The little checkmarks next to each image indicate which photos will be imported; just turn off the checkboxes for the ones you don't want to bring into the Organizer. When you've already imported some of the images, the Organizer tells you so and doesn't import them again. You can also import video and sound files. The four buttons above the preview area let you choose which kind of files to see:

• **Hide Images.** If you want to temporarily hide your images (so you can look at just your video files, for instance), click this button or press Ctrl+M.

• **Video files.** This button is grayed out unless Elements finds any movie or video files on your memory card. If it does, you can hide them by clicking this button. You might do that if you're only interested in importing still photos right now. To see the video files again, click the button once more.

• **Audio files.** This button works just like the video button, but it becomes active when Elements finds audio files you may want to import.

- **Show Duplicates.** If Elements has already imported some of the photos on your memory card, but you want to see those files again, click this button and you can reimport them (or just see them for comparison's sake). In the preview area, the thumbnails of the files you've already imported will show an icon to indicate that they're duplicates. (You can see the icon on the upper-right corner of the thumbnails in Figure 2-3; it looks just like the Show Duplicates button.)

> **NOTE** Although much of this chapter talks about importing your pictures from a camera, most memory card readers work the same way. Use a card reader if you have one, since you'll spare your camera's batteries and you'll subject your camera to less wear and tear.

The right side of the window is where you can adjust the settings for where your pictures are stored and how their folders are named. Most of these choices are the same ones you get in the basic Photo Downloader, but you also get a few extras:

- **Automatically Fix Red Eyes.** When you leave the Automatically Fix Red Eyes checkbox turned on, Elements searches through all your newly imported photos looking for pictures of people with red eyes (caused by camera flash) and then fixes them automatically. It sounds great, but it's not 100-percent reliable and tends to "fix" things like bright white teeth as well. It's not destructive, because Elements makes a Version set (see page 54) with your original, so you can ditch the new version if you don't like what Elements did. But the extra time it takes and the time you waste looking for mistakes mean you're better off leaving this option turned off and using another method to fix red eyes later. See page 95 for more about Elements' Red Eye tool.

- **Automatically Suggest Photo Stacks.** The Organizer lets you group related photos together into stacks (see page 490). Turn this box on to use the new auto-stack feature, where Elements automatically finds photos that should be grouped together. This feature works only for photos taken in your camera's burst mode. In other words, photos of the same subject, taken very close together in time.

- **Make "Group Custom Name" as a Tag.** If you chose a custom name for your images, you can assign the name as a tag here. (Tags are explained on page 46.)

- **Apply Metadata.** If you want to write your name or copyright information right into the file's metadata (see page 51) so that anyone who views your file will know it's yours, you can do that here.

Once you're done adjusting the Downloader's settings, click Get Photos. The Downloader gets your photos and launches the Organizer so you can review your pictures.

> **NOTE** You can tell the Organizer to "watch" folders that you often bring graphics (or even sound files or video) into. When you set a watched folder, Elements keeps an eye on it and lets you know when you have new photos there. Elements either imports the new files or tells you they're waiting for you, depending on which option you choose. See page 486 for more about watched folders.

Disabling the Photo Downloader

If it annoys you to have the Downloader popping up whenever you hook up your camera or pop a Photo CD into your drive, Adobe has made it very easy for you to turn the Downloader off.

If you look down at your system tray (the row of icons in the bottom-right corner of your screen), you see an icon for the Photo Downloader along with whatever other icons are sitting there. Click the Downloader icon and choose Disable to shut it down; then just turn it on (by clicking again and choosing Launch) when you want to import photos, as shown in Figure 2-4. When you choose Exit, the icon disappears until the next time you restart your computer.

If you don't want to use the Photo Downloader at all, you can disable the Downloader by going to Organizer → Edit → Preferences → Camera or Card Reader, and turning it off. If you do choose this option, you can still use the Get Photos command when you're in the Organizer, even though you've turned off the Downloader.

If you disable the Downloader, you can still use any of the standard Windows photo-opening options like Windows Imaging Assistant, or just copy the files to a folder via the Windows dialog box that pops up when Windows detects your camera or card reader.

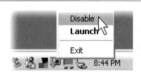

Figure 2-4:
If you prefer not to use the Downloader all the time, it's quite simple to turn it off here in your system tray. Just right-click the Downloader icon and choose Disable; choose Launch to start it up again. If, on the other hand, you always have trouble getting the Downloader to launch, in the Organizer, go to File → Get Photos → From Camera or Scanner, and the Downloader should start for you.

Opening Stored Images

If you've got photos already stored on your computer, you have several options for opening them with Elements. If the file format is set to open in Elements, then double-click the file's icon to launch Elements and open the image. (If you want to change which files open automatically in Elements, see the box on page 37.) You've also got a few ways to open files from within Elements:

- **From the Organizer, for files not yet in the Organizer.** Go to File → Get Photos → From Files and Folders, or press Ctrl+Shift+G, and then select your file. The other options in the Get Photos menu (like opening files stored on a mobile phone) are covered on page 483.

  You can also select an image that's stored in the Organizer and open it directly in the Editor. To do so, in the Organizer, click the file's thumbnail, and then press Ctrl+I, or go to Edit → Go to Full Edit. If you'd rather go to Quick Fix (see page 91), choose Edit → Go to Quick Fix instead.

- **From the Editor.** Go to File → Open or press Ctrl+O and select your file.

Picking the File Types That Elements Opens

How do I stop Elements from opening all my files?

Many people are dismayed to discover that once they install Elements, it opens every time they double-click any kind of graphics file—whether they want the file to open in Elements or not.

You can control the file types associated with Elements by going to Edit → File Association in the Editor. Alternatively, the Windows operating system also lets you adjust which program opens when you double-click a file. First, find a file of the type you want to change. Then:

1. Right-click the icon of the closed file.

2. From the pop-up menu, choose Open With → Choose Program....

3. Select the program you want to use to open the file. Turn on "Always use the selected program to open this kind of file" to change the program for all files of this type.

Working with PDF Files

If you open a PDF file in Elements, you'll see the Import PDF dialog box (Figure 2-5), which gives you lots of options for how you want Elements to treat your file. You can choose to import whole pages or just the images on the pages, you can import multiple pages (if the PDF is more than one page), and you can choose the color mode (see page 40) and the resolution, as well as whether or not you want anti-aliasing (see page 117).

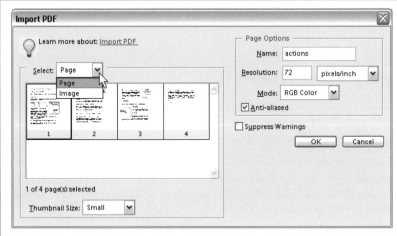

Figure 2-5:
You can open multi-page PDF files in Elements. Just click the thumbnail of the page you want (Shift+click to select multiple pages), and Elements opens it right up. You can catalog PDF files in the Organizer, too.

Scanning Photos

Elements comes bundled with many scanners because it's the perfect software for making your scans look their best. You have two main ways of getting scans into Elements. Some scanners come with a *driver plug-in*, a small utility program that lets you scan directly into Elements. Look on your scanner's installation software for information about Elements compatibility or check the manufacturer's Web site for a Photoshop plug-in to download. (If you can scan into Photoshop, you should be able to scan into Elements.) You may also be able to scan into Elements if your scanner uses the *TWAIN interface*, which is an industry standard used by many scanner manufacturers.

If you don't have any of these programs, you'll need to use the scanning program that came with your scanner. Then, once you've saved your scanned image in a format that Elements understands, like TIFF (.tiff, .tif) or Photoshop (.psd), open the file in Elements like any other photo.

To control your scanner from within Elements, you can choose to scan from either the Editor or the Organizer. In the Editor, go to File → Import, and you'll find your scanner's name on the list that appears. In the Organizer, go to File → Get Photos → From Scanner, or press Ctrl+U. You should check out your available options for both locations because they're probably different. For instance, you may find that you have different file formats available to you in the Editor than you do in the Organizer.

> **TIP** If you do a lot of scanning, check out the Divide Scanned Photos command (page 63) for helpful tips on how to quickly scan in lots of photos at the same time. Also, you can save yourself a lot of drudgery in Elements if you make sure your scanner glass and the prints you're scanning are both as dust-free as possible before you start.

Capturing Video Frames

Elements lets you capture a single frame from a video and use it the way you would any still photo. This feature works best if you choose a movie that's already on your computer (versus one that's streaming to your PC from across the Web).

Elements can read many popular video file formats, including .avi, .wmv, and .mpeg. You do need to have a program on your computer (besides Elements) that's capable of viewing the video file. For example, to view a QuickTime movie, you need to have QuickTime installed on your PC.

> **NOTE** The video capture tool in Elements isn't really designed for use with long movies. You'll get the best results with clips that aren't more than a minute or two long.

To import a video frame, in the Editor, go to File → Import → Frame From Video, and then in the Video import dialog box:

---

1. **Find the video that contains the frame you want to copy.**

   Click the Browse button and navigate to the movie you want. After you choose the movie, the first frame should appear in the window in the Frame From Video dialog box.

2. **Navigate to the frame you want.**

   Either click the Play button or use the slider below the window to move through the movie until you see what you want.

3. **Copy the frame you want by clicking Grab Frame.**

   You can grab as many frames as you want. Each frame shows up in the Elements Editor as a separate file.

4. **When you have everything you need, click Done.**

   While grabbing video frames is a very fun thing to be able to do, it does have certain limitations. Most importantly, your video is going to appear at a fairly low resolution, so don't expect to get a great print from a video frame.

Creating a New File

You can also create a new blank Elements document. You may want to create a new blank document when you're using Elements as a drawing program or when you're combining parts of other images together, for example.

To create a new file, go to the Editor, and choose File → New → Blank File (or press Ctrl+N) to bring up the New File dialog box. You have lots of choices to make each time you start a new file; they're all covered in the following sections.

> **NOTE**   You can't create a new blank file in the Organizer, but Elements gives you a quick short-cut from the Organizer to the Editor so you can open up a new, fresh file there. To open a new file, choose File → New → Blank File, and the Organizer creates a virgin file for you and automatically hops you over to the Editor. If you want to create a new file based on a photo that's in the Organizer, select the thumbnail, press Ctrl+C to copy it, and then choose File → New → Image from Clipboard in the Editor. Elements switches you to the Editor where you'll see your copied photo awaiting you, all ready to work on.

Picking a Document Size

The first thing you need to decide, logically enough, is how big you want your document to be. You can choose inches, pixels, centimeters, millimeters, points, picas, or columns as your unit of measurement. Just pick the one you want in the Width and Height pull-down menus and then enter a number. Or you can choose one of the many preset sizes shown in Figure 2-6.

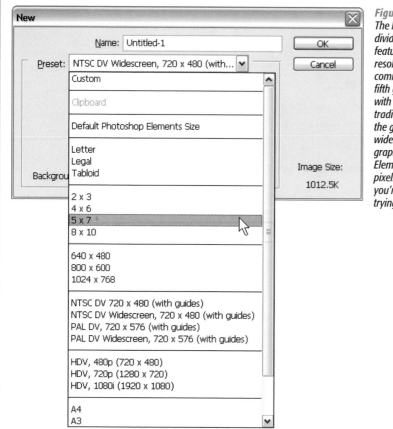

Figure 2-6:
The list of preset document sizes is divided into groups, each of which features popular file sizes and resolution settings for a variety of common uses. For example, the fifth group from the top (the one with the highlighted bar) includes traditional photo print sizes, and the group after that includes widely used choices for onscreen graphics. The default Photoshop Elements size is 4"×6" at 300 pixels per inch, which works well if you're just playing around and trying things out.

Choosing Resolution

If you decide not to use one of the presets, you need to choose a resolution for your file. You'll learn a lot about resolution in the next chapter (see page 82), but a good rough guide is to choose 72 pixels per inch (ppi) for files that you'll look at only on a monitor, and 300 ppi for files you plan to print.

Choosing Color Mode

Elements gives you lots of color choices throughout the program, but Color Mode is probably your most important one because it determines which tools and filters you can use in your document. There are three choices available in the Color Mode menu:

- **RGB Color Mode.** Choosing RGB (red, green, and blue) means that you're creating a color document, as opposed to black and white. You'll probably choose RGB Color Mode most of the time, even if you don't plan on having color in your image, because RGB gives you access to all of Elements' tools. Page 195 has lots more about picking colors. You can use RGB Color mode for black-and-white photos if you like, and many people do, since it gives you the most options for editing your photo.

- **Grayscale Mode.** Black-and-white photos are called *grayscale* because they're really made up of many shades of gray. In Elements, you can't do as much editing on a grayscale photo as you can in RGB (for example, you can't use some of the filters on a grayscale photo).

- **Bitmap Mode.** Every pixel in a bitmap mode image is either black or white. Use Bitmap mode for true black and white images—shades of gray need not apply here.

NOTE Sometimes you may need to change the color mode of an existing file to use all of Elements' tools and filters. For example, there are quite a few things you can do only if your file is in the RGB color mode. So if you need to use a filter (see page 342) on a black-and-white photo and your choice is grayed out, go to Image → Mode and select RGB Color. Choosing RGB Color won't suddenly colorize your photo; it just changes the way Elements handles the file. You can always change back to the original color mode when you're done. If you use the "Convert to Black and White" feature in Elements (see page 265), you still have an RGB mode photo afterwards, not a grayscale mode.

If you have a 16-bit file (see page 221), you need to convert it to 8-bit color, or you won't have access to many of the commands and filters in Elements. Make the change by choosing Image → Mode → 8 Bits/Channel. You're most likely to have 16-bit files if you import your images in RAW format (page 211); some scanners also offer you an option of creating 16-bit files. JPEG photos are always 8-bit.

Choosing Your File's Contents

The last choice you have to make when you start a new file is the *contents* of the file. Choosing your file's contents is where you tell Elements the color to use for the empty areas of the file, like the background. You can be a traditionalist and choose white (almost always a good choice), or else choose a particular color or transparency. More about transparency in a minute.

If you want to choose a color other than white, use the Foreground/Background color squares to do so, as shown in Figure 2-7.

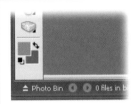

Figure 2-7:
To choose a new Background color, just click the Background color square (the green one shown here) to bring up the Color Picker. Then choose the color you want. Your new color appears in the square, and the next time you do something that involves using a Background color, that's the shade you get. The whole process of picking colors is explained in much more detail on page 195.

The third option is the most interesting: transparent. To understand transparency and why it's such a wonderful invention, you need to know that every digital image, every single one, is either rectangular or square. A digital image *can't* be any other shape.

But digital images can *appear* to be a different shape—sunflowers, sailboats, or German Shepherds, for example. How? By placing your object on a transparent background so that your object looks like it was cut out, so that only its shape appears, as shown in Figure 2-8. The actual photo is still a rectangle, but if you placed it into another image, you'd see only the shell and not the surrounding area, because the rest of the photo is transparent.

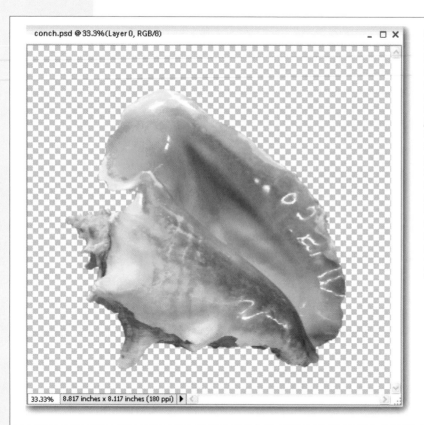

Figure 2-8:
The checkered background is Elements' way of indicating that an area is transparent. (It doesn't mean you've somehow selected a patterned background.) If you place this photo into another image, all you'll see is the shell itself, not the checkerboard or the rectangular outline of the photo. When you don't like the size and color of the grid, you can adjust them in Edit → Preferences → Transparency.

To keep the clear areas transparent when you close your image, you need to save the image in a file format that allows transparency. JPEGs, for instance, automatically fill transparent areas with solid white, so they're not a good choice. TIFFs, PDFs, or Photoshop files (.psd), on the other hand, let the transparent areas stay clear. Page 431 has more about which formats allow transparency.

Using the Organizer

The Organizer is where you keep track of your photos and start most of your projects for sharing your photos. You can see thumbnails of all your photos in the Organizer, assign keywords (called *tags*) to make it easier to find the pictures you want, and search for your photos in lots of different ways.

The Photo Browser is the main Organizer window. Date View is an alternate way to look at and search for your photos, as explained in Figure 2-9. But the Photo Browser is more versatile: It's your main Organizer workspace, which is what the rest of this section is about.

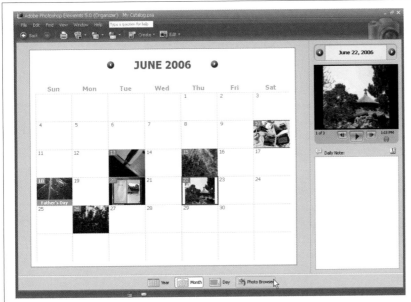

Figure 2-9:
Date View offers you the same menu options as the main Photo Browser window, but instead of a contact sheet-like view of your photos, you see your images laid out on a calendar. Click a date (in this example, June 22 is chosen), and in the upper-right corner of the screen, you can step through a slideshow view of that day's pictures. (You can choose which holidays appear on the calendar by going to Edit → Preferences → Calendar.) Date View is fun, and sometimes handy for searching, but it doesn't offer many useful functions that aren't also in the Photo Browser.

NOTE   If you want to explore the Organizer in depth, check out Michael Slater's books, *Organize Your Photos with Adobe Photoshop Elements* (Adobe Press), and his Web site, *www.photofanatic.com*. Michael is the developer of the program that became Photoshop Album and then the Elements Organizer. While his book hasn't been updated since Elements 3, his Web site may have an update for Elements 5.

The Organizer stores the information about your photos in a special database called a *catalog*. You don't have to do anything special to create this container— Elements creates your catalog (named *My Catalog*) automatically the first time you import photos. It's possible to have more than one catalog, but most people don't because you can't search more than one catalog at a time.

Your catalog can include photos stored anywhere on your computer, and even photos that you've moved to external hard drives and CDs. There aren't any limits on where you can keep your originals. But once your photos appear in the Organizer, you must move them from within the Organizer as opposed to using another method (like Windows Explorer), if you want the Organizer to know where you put them. You aren't limited to photos, either—you can store videos and audio files in the Organizer as well.

TIP   The Organizer lets you choose to edit in programs other than Elements by going to Organizer → Edit → Preferences → Editing → Use a Supplementary Editing Application. So if you want to supplement Elements with a program like Paint Shop Pro, or even Photoshop, it's easy to do.

WORKAROUND WORKSHOP

Avoiding the Organizer

Nobody's neutral about Adobe's decision to include the Organizer with Elements. People either love the Organizer or they hate it. If you're in the latter group, try to see if you can come to terms with the Organizer because it has some very useful features. You'll lose a lot if you give up the Organizer because it's the only place in Elements where you get a visual preview of your images before opening them.

However, if you find you just can't abide the Organizer, or if you prefer to use a different program to organize your photos—or you just like to be disorganized—then you can easily avoid the Organizer altogether.

In the lower-left corner of the Welcome screen, choose to always start up in the Editor.

Remember to keep "Include in Organizer" and version sets turned off in the Save dialog box whenever you're saving a picture.

You can also go to Control Panel → Administrative Tools → Services and find *Adobe Active File Monitor V5*. This is a *service*, a small program that always runs in the background when your computer is on, even when Elements is closed. Highlight Active File Monitor, and then go to Action → Properties and set the Startup to Manual.

The Photo Browser

The Photo Browser (Figure 2-10) may look a little intimidating the first time you see it, but it's really very logical.

At the top of your screen, just below the Organizer's menus, is the Shortcuts bar, your main navigational tool in the Organizer. By clicking the relevant icons, you can choose to import photos, print them, share them, create projects, edit your photos, or switch over to Date View.

The Timeline is just below the Shortcuts. Each little bump on the Timeline represents a group of photos (based on the sorting method you chose in View → Arrangement). The higher a bar is, the more photos in that batch. Click a bar to see thumbnails of all the photos from that date in the main window, which Adobe calls the *Image Well*. Directly below the Timeline is the Search bar, one of many ways to look for your photos.

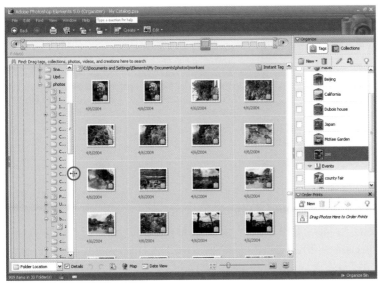

Figure 2-10:
The Photo Browser is your main Organizer workspace. You can customize it by dragging the dividers to make any area larger or smaller. Notice how the cursor changes shape (circled) when you're in the correct spot to drag a divider. When you go to View → Arrangement, or use the pop-up menu in the lower-left corner of the Photo Browser window, you can change the way your photos are sorted in the Photo Browser.

On the right side of the Photo Browser is the *Organize bin*. That's where you *tag*, or label, your photos with keywords for easy searching. (Tagging is probably the first thing you'll want to do to your photos in the Organizer; you'll find directions on how to tag on page 46.) At the bottom of the Organize bin is a shortcut staging area to make it easy to order prints. You can read about how to use it on page 410.

If you'd like to get a simultaneous look at your pictures and the folders on your PC where they're stored, go to View → Arrangement → Folder Location. A new pane on the left side of the Photo Brower's window appears, showing the folder structure, including the exact location of the current batch of photos. Click a folder's icon to see the photos it contains displayed in the Image Well.

You can also move your photos directly within this Folder view pane by dragging them between folders. Moving your photos via the Folder view pane is better than moving them by, say, using Windows Explorer, because doing so lets Elements keep track of where your photos are (Figure 2-11).

> **NOTE** Once you get your photos into the Organizer, you can use "View Photos in Full Screen" and "Compare Photos Side by Side" to see a larger, slideshow-like view of your photos and choose the ones you want to print or edit (see page 494). You can even choose music to accompany them. You can also click the Full Screen View button at the bottom of the Photo Browser window (to the right of the thumbnail size slider).

Elements 5 introduces another new way to view your images: arranged on a Yahoo map. When you first import your photos, Elements gives you the option of assigning them to a location on a map of your choice. Page 441 explains more about using Yahoo maps in the Organizer, and also about sharing your maps with your friends.

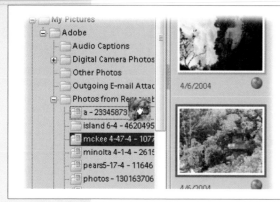

Figure 2-11:
If you want to move photos around on your PC after you've brought them into the Organizer, go to File → Move, or drag them within this pane of the Photo Browser. If you move photos around when you're not in the Organizer, Elements can't easily find them again. If Elements loses track of a photo, you can use the Reconnect command (File → Reconnect) to help Elements find it again.

Creating Categories and Tags

The Organizer's got a great system for quickly finding photos, but it works only if you use special keywords, called *tags*, which the Organizer uses to track down your pictures.

A tag can be a word, a date, or even a rating (as explained in the box on page 48). When you import photos to the Organizer, the photos are automatically tagged with the date of import (and with any other tag choices you may have made in the Downloader), but you may want to add more tags to make it easier to search for the subject of the photo later on. You can give a photo as many tags as you like.

Elements lets you group tags into *categories*. You get a certain number of preset categories, like People, Places, and Events, and you can create your own categories, too. You can also create as many subcategories within categories as you like. You may have a category of "Vacations," with "China trip" and "Cozumel" as subcategories, for instance. Your photos in those categories may have the tags "Jim and Helen," "silk factory," or "snorkeling."

Working with tags and categories

Elements gives you a few generic tags to help you get started, but you'll want to learn how to create your own tags, too. After all, by the time you've got 5,000 or so photos in the Organizer, searching for "Family" probably isn't going to help narrow things down.

When you're ready to create a new tag:

1. **Call up the Create Tag dialog box.**

   Press Ctrl+N, or from the Tags pane in the Organizer bin, click the New dropdown menu and choose New Tag. The Create Tag dialog box appears. (You also create new categories and subcategories from this dialog box.)

2. **Name the new tag and assign it to a category.**

Enter the name you want to use in the text box where it says Name. Then, assign the tag to a category by picking from the Category pull-down menu. (You can change the category later if you want.) You can also edit the icon for your tag, as explained in Figure 2-12.

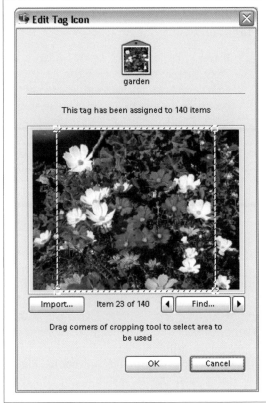

Figure 2-12:
Many people like to edit the icons Elements uses to represent different tags. Editing the icons makes it easy to search for a tag visually as well as by its name. To change the picture associated with a tag, click the tag in the Organize bin. Then, at the top of the bin, click the Edit Tag button (the pencil) → Edit Icon. In the Edit Tag Icon dialog box (shown here), the arrows on either side of the Find button let you step through all the photos that use that tag. (The Find button shows you those photos all at once.) Or, you can click the Import button to use a different image stored on your computer. Once you've chosen the picture you want, drag the dotted square to use only a certain part of your photo.

To assign the tag to a photo, just drag the tag's icon from the Organize bin onto the photo's thumbnail. It's as easy as that.

You can also delete tags, rearrange their order by dragging them, and even change the size of your tag icons by right-clicking a photo or tag and choosing what you want to do from the pop-up menu. You can also drag tags from one category to another in the Organize bin.

If you decide you want to remove a tag from a photo after you've assigned it:

- **From a single photo.** Right-click the photo's thumbnail, select Remove Tag, and then choose the tag you want to get rid of.

- **From a group of photos.** Select the photos, right-click one of them, select "Remove Tag from Selected Items," and then choose the tag you want to remove.

NOTE When an image first gets imported into the Organizer, the Image Well shows only the photos in the batch of photos you've just imported. You'll see an icon in the upper-right corner of the Image Well called Instant Tag (when in Folder view). Clicking it assigns the photo's folder name as a tag to all the photos in the group.

ORGANIZATION STATION

Special Tags

Elements starts you off with two special kinds of tags:

- **Favorites.** Favorites lets you assign a one- to five-star rating to your photos. It's a good way to mark the ones you want to print or edit. Ratings are a great search tool because you can tell Elements to find, say, all your pictures that have ratings of four or more stars. (See page 49 for details on how to perform a search.)

- **Hidden.** When you apply the Hidden tag to a photo, the photo isn't displayed in the Photo Browser until you click the search square next to the Hidden tag icon. The Hidden tag is useful for archiving those photos that didn't come out quite right but that you're not ready to trash. You can save these pictures (just in case) without having them cluttering up your screen while you're working with your good photos.

Creating Collections

You can also group your photos into *collections*, which are great for gathering together pictures taken at a particular event. They can also be used to prepare groups of photos that you plan on using in one of the Create projects, like slideshows or Photo Galleries (covered on page 447). When you create a collection, you're not actually making a copy of all the photos you're including; instead, you're simply creating a group of virtual "pointers" to each image. That means collections can hold as many pictures as you want without taking up much space and, even better, you can include individual pictures in multiple collections. Photos inside a collection can appear in any order you choose, which is important, for instance, if you want to control the order of photos in a slideshow.

NOTE Collections are also good for gathering together groups of photos you want to export for use with another program.

You work with collections very much the way you do with tags, but you start by clicking the Collections tab in the Organize bin. From there, the procedure works pretty much the same way as creating or editing a tag or a category.

NOTE For the most part, use collections for creating temporary groups of pictures that you plan on using in specific projects. When you want to create permanent groupings of your photos, it's usually better to do that by assigning the same tag to all the photos in the group.

Face Tagging

Elements includes an interesting way to sort through your photos so that you can easily tag them: Face Tagging. Go to Find → Find Faces for Tagging, or click the "Find Faces for Tagging" button at the top of the Organize bin. (It's the outline of a woman's head with a tag next to it.) Elements then searches through your catalog for photos with people in them, and opens a new window showing the results.

Face Tagging doesn't work quite the way you may have hoped: you can't somehow tell Elements to find all the photos with Aunt Hildegarde. Elements just looks for what it thinks are human faces, and then shows you every photo that includes what it takes to be a person.

If you think about it, this is a pretty tough thing for a program to do, so the results may include a number of things, like leaves or parts of buildings, that look like faces to Elements, but not to you.

So what's the point if Elements can't tell one person from another? Face Tagging is designed on the theory that you're most likely to want to tag pictures of your family and friends. By using Face Tagging, you can easily visually locate all the untagged photos of your grandfather in a group of faces, for instance, and quickly tag them all at once. The Face Tagging dialog box gives you access to all your tags, and it also includes a handy Recent Tags section that rounds up the last few tags you used so that you can quickly find them without having to navigate through the category structure to get to those tags.

Searching for Photos

Anyone who's been diligent enough to assign tags to all (or most) of their photos will be pleased to learn how easy Elements makes finding tagged photos. And as for the untagged masses? The good news is that Elements still gives you a few helpful ways to find your pictures. The next few sections take you through all your options.

Browsing through photos

When you don't know exactly which photo you're looking for, Elements gives you a few ways to search through groups of pictures. These methods are also great if you don't want to look through your entire collection.

- **Folders.** You can navigate through the folders stored on your computer, just as you would when using a program like Windows Explorer. First, turn on Folder view if you haven't already done so (View → Arrangement → Folder Location or use the pop-up menu in the lower-left corner of the Photo Browser window).

  Navigate by expanding the folders you want and working your way down to the ones that contain the photos you want. When you reach a folder that contains photos, the photos appear in the Image Well.

- **Timeline.** Each bar in the Timeline represents a group of photos. Click a bar, and you see the photos that were in that batch. The way the photos are grouped changes to match what you've chosen in View → Arrangement (Date (Newest First), Date (Oldest First), Import Batch, and so on).

- **Date View.** You see your photos, listed by date, on a calendar page. Just click the date of the group you want to see.

- **Map.** If you chose to situate your photos on a Yahoo map, you can click the Map button below the Image Well and then click the various pins you've stuck in the map to see your photos. (Page 441 has more on how to work with Yahoo maps.)

> **TIP** The Find menu, covered on page 491 also lets you search for photos with similar colors. Choose Find → By Visual Similarity with Selected Photo(s). This option is great when you're looking for similarly toned graphics to use in a project.

Using tags and categories to find photos

Of course, when you're looking for a particular picture, you can use all the previously listed ways to find photos and just keep clicking through groups of photos until you find the one you want. But searching by tags and categories is the easiest way to find a particular photo.

- **Organize bin.** Click the empty square next to a tag or category, and Elements finds all the photos associated with those tags and categories. (A pair of binoculars appears inside the square to indicate it's being used to search for photos.) Click as many tags and categories as you want, and Elements searches for them all.

  You can exclude a tag from a search by right-clicking the tag's name and, in the menu, choosing to exclude it. So you could search for photos with the tags "sports" and "rock-climbing," but not "broken leg," for instance.

- **Search bar.** The Organizer's Search bar gives you another way to perform a tag search. Figure 2-13 shows how to use it.

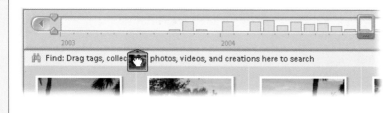

Figure 2-13:
To use the Search bar to find individual pictures, just drag any tag (or category) onto the bar with the binoculars. Your tag can hit the bar anywhere, not just on the binoculars icon itself.

Searching by Metadata

As explained in the box "Viewing Data About Your Images" on page 51, your camera stores a great deal of information about your images in the form of *metadata*. In the Organizer, you can search your photos by their metadata, looking for, say, all the photos you took with a particular camera model at a certain aperture and exposure. Figure 2-14 explains how.

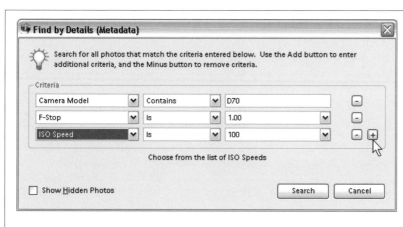

Figure 2-14:
To perform a search using your photos' metadata, go to Find → Find by Details (Metadata) to bring up this window. Choose the category of metadata from the drop-down menu on the left and enter your term or choose the exact setting in the box on the right. Click the + button to add additional search terms, up to a total of 10. To remove a criterion, click the search term's – button.

TIP If you want to share your tag information with people using Photoshop or with Photoshop Elements for Mac, go to File → Write Tag and Properties Info to Files. This transforms your tags into IPTC metadata keywords, which can then be read by programs like Photoshop, as well as the old File Browser in Elements 3, if you have friends still using that version.

INFORMATION STATION

Viewing Data About Your Images

The Organizer is just packed with information about your images. From captions you've written to statistics captured by your camera, the Properties window is chock full of interesting tidbits. To launch it, select any photo in the Organizer and press Alt+Enter, or right-click any photo and choose Show Properties from the pop-up menu. You get four different kinds of information to choose from, each of which you get to by clicking the icon on the top of the Properties window:

- **General.** This is information that includes the file's name, location (on your PC), size, date you took the picture, caption (just put your cursor in the box and start typing to add one), and a link to any audio files associated with it (see Chapter 18). You can also change the photo's file name here by highlighting the name and typing in a new one.

- **Tags.** If you've assigned any tags to your photo, they're listed here.

- **History.** History tells you when the file was created, imported, and edited, and also where you imported it from (your hard drive, for instance).

- **Metadata.** *Metadata* is information about the photo that's stored in the photo file itself. Most notably, this is where you view your *EXIF* (short for Exchangeable Image Format) data. EXIF data is information that your camera stores about your photos, including the camera you used, when you took the picture, the exposure, the file size, the ISO speed, aperture setting, and much more.

By paying attention to your EXIF data, you can learn lots about what works for making good shots...and what doesn't.

The Metadata screen includes many other kinds of information besides the EXIF data. Click the Complete button at the bottom of the window to see the full listing (clicking the Brief button shows you highlights only).

Saving Your Work

After all your organizing, editing, and resizing effort, you want to be sure you don't lose any of those files you struggled so hard to create. Saving your work is easy in Elements. (You don't need to do anything special to save information in the Organizer like tags or collections; you need to save only images you've created or changed, and you do that in the Editor.) When you're ready to save your file, press Ctrl+Shift+S to bring up the Save As dialog box, shown in Figure 2-15.

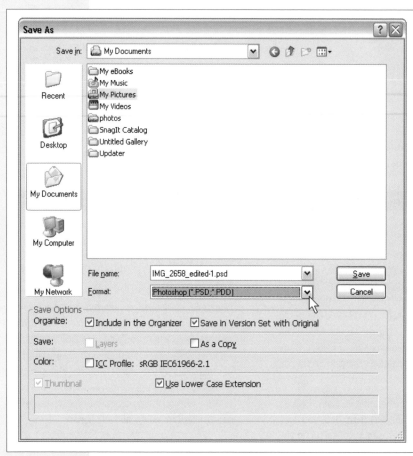

Figure 2-15:
The Elements Save As dialog box actually varies a little depending on what you're saving, but this example is pretty typical. When you click the Format pull-down menu (indicated by the cursor), you'll see a long list of file formats to choose from.

The top part of the Save As window is pretty much the same as it is for any program—you choose where you want to save your file, what you want to name it, and the file format you want. (More about file formats in a moment.) You also get some important choices that are unique to Elements:

- **Include in the Organizer.** This checkbox always appears turned on. Leave it on and your photo gets saved in the Organizer. Turn it off if you don't want the new file to go to the Organizer.

GEM IN THE ROUGH

Options for Saving Your Work

Elements gives you several options for saving a file. Before choosing, you need to consider whether you want to create version sets (page 54) of your photos.

To tell Elements how to react to the Save command, go to Editor → Edit → Preferences → Saving Files. You see a pull-down menu labeled On First Save. Here's what the three options do:

- **Always Ask.** Choose Always Ask and, when you press Ctrl+S, Elements brings up the Save As dialog box the first time you save—if it's the first time you've opened the file in this session of Elements. Close the file and reopen it while Elements is still running, and you won't see the Save As dialog box the next time you save. But once you exit Elements and start it again, you get the Save As dialog box the first time you press Ctrl+S.

- **Ask If Original.** If you're editing your original file and you don't have any version sets (page 54), you get the Save As dialog box the first time you save the file. On subsequent saves, or if you already have a version set, Elements just saves right over the existing version (unless you do a Save As to create a new one). This option is meant to make it easier to avoid inadvertently creating dozens of Organizer versions for each file as you edit it.

- **Save Over Current File.** When you select this option, Elements overwrites your existing file when you press Ctrl+S, without offering you the Save As

dialog box at all. This is the way Elements 2 and Photoshop behave when saving. If you choose this option and then decide you want to Save As instead of Save, press Ctrl+Shift+S (or just make your selection using the File menu).

You'll have certain situations where Elements presents you with the Save As dialog box no matter *what* you choose here. For instance, when you add layers (explained in Chapter 6) to a JPEG file, you can't save a JPEG with layers, so Elements brings up the Save As dialog box to let you choose a different file format for saving your work.

Leave the other two menus in the File Saving Options section set where Adobe put them (Image Previews → Always Save, and File Extensions → Use Lower Case), unless you have a specific reason to change them.

You can also control how well your image file works with other programs. Leave the Maximize PSD File Compatibility pull-down menu set to Always, unless you have a reason to change it. When Always is selected, a flattened image gets embedded in your file for the benefit of programs that don't understand Elements Layers. Doing so makes for a substantially larger file, but with disk space so cheap these days, it's usually best to let Elements maximize compatibility. If you choose Ask, you'll encounter the dialog box in Figure 2-16 when you save a layered .psd file.

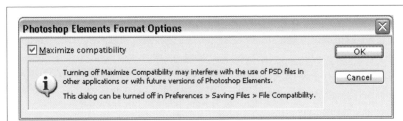

Figure 2-16:
Turn on the "Maximum compatibility" checkbox if you want people who don't have Elements to be able to open your image. The downside: bigger file size.

- **Save in Version Set with Original.** This option tells the Organizer to save your image (including any edits you've made) as a new version, separate from your original. Your photo gets the name of the original plus an ending to indicate it's an edited version.

  You can create as many versions as you want. Then you can go directly to any state that you've saved your image in. It's a very handy feature. When you choose to start a version set, from now on, you'll get the Save As dialog box every time you save (instead of being able to just save your changes). Elements does that to give you the chance to create a new version each time.

- **As a Copy.** When you save an image as a copy, Elements makes the copy, names it "[OriginalFileName] copy," and puts the copy away. The original version remains open. If you want to work on the copy, you must open it. Sometimes Elements forces you to save as a copy—for instance, if you want to save a layered image and you turn off the layers option. (See Chapter 6 for more about layers.)

- **Layers.** If your image has layers, then turn on this checkbox to keep them. When you turn off this setting, Elements usually forces you to save as a copy. To avoid having to save as a copy, flatten your image (page 164) before saving it.

- **ICC Profile.** You can choose to embed a color profile in your image. Page 183 explains color profiles.

- **Use Lower Case Extension.** Using Lower Case Extension causes Elements to save your file as yourfile.jpg rather than yourfile.JPG, for example. Leave this setting on unless you have a reason to turn it off.

The File Formats Elements Understands

Elements gives you loads of file format options. Your best choice depends on how you plan to use your image.

UP TO SPEED

File Formats

After you've spent hours creating a perfect image, you want other people to be able to see your picture, too. If everyone who wanted to view your images needed a copy of Elements, you probably wouldn't have a very large audience for your creations. So, Elements lets you save in lots of different *file formats*.

What does that mean? It's pretty simple, really. A file format is a way in which your computer saves information so that a program or another computer can read and use the file.

Because there are many different kinds of programs, and several different computing platforms, the kind of file that's best for one use may be a really poor choice for doing something else. That's why many programs, like Elements, can save your work in a variety of different formats, depending on what you want to do with your image. There are many formats, like TIFF and JPEG, that many different programs can read. Then there are other formats, like the .pub files that Microsoft Publisher creates, that are easily read only by the program that created the file.

- **Photoshop (.psd, .pdd).** The native file format for Elements or Photoshop. It's a good idea to save your files as .psd files before you work on them. A .psd file can hold lots of information, and you don't lose any data by saving in this format. Also, it allows you to keep layers, which is very important, even if you haven't used them for much yet.

- **Photo Creation Project (.pse).** This is a new format, only for multi-page Elements photo creations (see Figure 2-17).

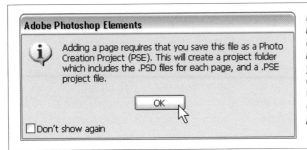

Figure 2-17:
If you add pages to one of the new Photo Creations (page 397) in Elements 5, you see this warning message box. Elements is telling you it needs to save your multi-page project in a format that almost no other programs can open. To learn more about working with this format, and how to get your project out of Elements for online printing or use by other programs, see the box on page 404.

- **TIFF (.tif, .tiff).** This is another format that preserves virtually all of your photo's information and allows you to save layers. TIFF files are used extensively in print production, and some cameras allow you to choose TIFF as a shooting option. Like Photoshop files, TIFFs can be very large.

- **JPEG (.jpg, jpeg, .jpe).** Almost everyone who uses a computer has run into JPEGs at one time or another. Most digital cameras offer the JPEG format as an option. Generally, when you bring a JPEG into Elements, you want to use another format when you save it, to avoid data loss. Keep reading for more about why.

- **JPEG 2000 (.jpf, .jpx, .jp2).** JPEG 2000 is a newer variation of the JPEG format that makes small files without losing any data and also supports transparency. There aren't many Web browsers that can display these files, though, so it's not a good choice for the Web.

- **PDF (.pdf, .pdp).** Adobe invented PDF, or Portable Document Format, which lets you send files to people with Adobe Reader (formerly, Acrobat Reader) so they can easily open and view the files. Elements uses PDF files to create presentations like slideshows.

- **CompuServe GIF (.gif).** These are used primarily for Web graphics and work well mainly for files without a lot of subtle shadings of color. See Chapter 17 for more on when to choose GIFs. They're also used for Web animations, called animated GIFs, which Elements can help you create (see page 434).

- **PICT (.pct).** PICT is an older Mac format that's still used by some applications. AppleWorks, for example, handles PICTs better than any other graphics format. Also, sometimes larger file formats like TIFFs generate their thumbnail previews as PICT resource files.

- **BMP (.bmp).** An old Windows standby. The small size of .bmp files makes them fast to display, so they're used for many graphics tasks by the Windows operating system.

- **PNG.** Another Web graphic format. See Chapter 17 for more information about these files.

- **Photoshop EPS (.eps).** Encapsulated PostScript format. Used to share documents among different programs, but generally you get best results with these if they're going to a PostScript Printer (laser printers are usually PostScript printers; inkjets usually aren't).

- **Digital Negative (.dng).** Elements can't save files in this format, but it can open DNG files. DNG is a new format developed by Adobe to create a more universal way to store all the different camera RAW file formats. You can download a special DNG converter from the downloads area of Adobe's support Web site (*www.adobe.com/downloads*) that lets you convert your camera's own RAW formatted photos into DNG files. DNG files aren't ready to use the way JPEG or TIFF files are; you still need to run your DNG files through the RAW converter before you can use them in projects. See page 223 for more about DNG.

The not-so-common file formats

Besides the garden-variety formats in the previous list, Elements lets you save in some formats you may never have heard of. Here's a list, and then you can forget all about them, probably.

COMPATIBILITY

Opening Obscure File Formats

Once in a while, you may run into a file that was created in a format that Elements doesn't understand. Sometimes you can fake Elements out and con it into opening the document by changing the file extension to a more common one.

For the few file formats that make Elements throw up its hands in despair, try IrfanView (*www.irfanview.com*), a wonderful free software program that can open almost any Windows-compatible format. You can even use Irfan-View to salvage damaged files sometimes, especially if you get an "invalid JPEG marker" error. If Elements balks at one of your files, first try opening and resaving the photo in IrfanView. If you're lucky, that may be all you need to do to make Elements recognize your file again.

Very rarely, you'll run across a file that makes even Irfan-View give up. If that happens, try a Google search. (Use the file's three- or four-letter extension as your search term.) It's unlikely to help you open it, but if you can figure out what it is, you can probably figure out where it came from and ask whoever sent it to you to try again with a more standard format.

- **Filmstrip.** This format is for use with Premiere, Adobe's video-editing program. You won't even see this option if Premiere isn't installed on your computer.

- **PIXAR.** Yup, *that* Pixar. This is the special format for the movie studio's high-end workstations, although if you're working on one of those, it's extremely unlikely that you're reading this page.

- **Scitex CT.** A format used for prepress work in the printing industry.

- **Photoshop Raw.** This format isn't the same as your camera RAW file, but rather an older Photoshop format that consists of uncompressed data.

- **Targa TGA,** or Targa, is a format developed for systems using the Truevision video board, but it has become a popular graphics format.

- **PCX.** A bitmap format used on different platforms.

About JPEGs

In the next chapter, you'll read about how throwing away pixels can lead to shoddy-looking pictures (page 88). Well, certain file formats were designed to make your file size as small as possible. They make the file smaller by throwing out information by the bucketful. These formats are known as *lossy* because they throw out, or lose, some of the file's data every time you save it, to make the file as small as possible.

Sometimes you want that to happen, like when you want a small-sized picture for a Web site. Therefore, many of the file formats that were developed for the Web, most notably JPEG, are designed to favor smallness over any other quality. They compress the file sizes by allowing some data to escape.

> **NOTE** Formats that preserve all your data intact are called *lossless*. (You may also run across the regrettable term *non-lossy*, which means the same thing.) The most popular file formats for people who are looking to preserve all their photos' data are Photoshop and TIFF.

If you save a file using the JPEG format, every time you hit the Save button and close the file your computer is squishing some of the data out of the photo. What kind of data? It's the information needed for displaying and printing the fine details. You don't want to keep saving as a JPEG over and over again. Every time you do, you lose a little more potential detail from your image. You can usually get away with saving as a JPEG once or twice, but if you keep it up, sooner or later you start to wonder what happened to your beautiful picture.

It's OK that your camera takes photos and saves them as JPEGs. Those are pretty enormous JPEGs, usually. Just importing a JPEG won't hurt your picture. But once you get your files into Elements, save your pictures as Photoshop or TIFF files while you work on them. When you want another JPEG as the final result, change the format back to JPEG *after* you're done editing it.

> **NOTE** Your camera may give you several different JPEG compression options to help you fit more pictures on your memory card. Always choose the *least* compression possible. Your photo file sizes are slightly larger, but the quality is much, much better. It's worth sacrificing the space.

Changing the File Format

It's very easy to change the format of a file in Elements. Just press Ctrl+Shift+S or go to File → Save As and, from the Format pull-down menu, select the format you want. Elements makes a copy of your file in the new format and asks you to name it.

Backing Up Your Files

With computers, you just never know what's going to happen, so "be prepared" is a good motto. If your computer crashes, it won't be nearly so painful if all your photos are safely backed up someplace else.

Saving to CDs and DVDs

Elements makes it very easy to save your files to any add-on storage device like a Zip drive or an external hard-drive. Of course, you can just do a Save As and choose your storage device as the destination, but it's also easy to back up to CDs (and DVDs, if you have a DVD burner).

Windows XP also has a CD-burning utility built right into the system. The box on page 62 explains how to use it. But when it comes to easy backups, you're in for a treat with the Elements Organizer. You can burn CDs or DVDs right from the Organizer, and it gives you many different options for backing up your photos and catalogs. All these options are covered in the next section.

> **NOTE** Elements 5 has a much-requested new feature for making backups: you can create *multi-session* discs. That means you can tell Elements to leave your CD or DVD open, so that you can come back later and use the disc again to add more files to it, instead of wasting an entire CD or DVD to burn a handful of pictures. To use this feature, go to Organizer → Edit → Preferences → Files and turn on "Enable multisession burning to CD/DVD."

Organizer Backups

The Organizer offers a really helpful way to back up your photos. It's one of the best parts of Elements, and it's certainly very thorough, even going so far as to remind you to label the disc you create. You can backup your catalog, or just copy specific photos. In Elements 5, the process is a little different, depending on which you choose. Just follow these steps:

1. **Call up the Backup dialog box, and let Elements make sure your catalog is in shape for backing up.**

   Go to File → Backup Catalog, or press Ctrl+Shift+B. Elements reviews your catalog and offers to reconnect any missing files, or you can reconnect them manually if you prefer. Page 486 has more on how to do that.

2. **Decide what kind of backup to make.**

In the window that opens, you have to decide whether to back up your whole catalog or make an incremental backup. *Full Backup* backs up *everything* in your catalog. Pick that one the first time you make a backup, or if you're backing up everything to move to a new computer. *Incremental Backup* finds only the stuff that's new since the last time you made a backup, and that's all it copies—a major time and space saver. (You must make a full backup at least once before Elements will let you do an incremental backup.)

Your backup will have the same name as your catalog. You can see the name in the dialog box, but you won't be allowed to change it. Click Next to continue.

NOTE   If you have multiple catalogs, you can back up only one catalog at a time.

3. **Choose a destination for your files.**

   Your choices include a CD, a DVD, or any hard drive connected to your computer (either built-in or external). Choose by selecting from the list in the Select Destination Drive box.

   If you're backing up to a hard drive, click the Backup Path Browse button to select the location where you want Elements to create your backup. Navigate through the folder structure in the window that appears, and create a new folder if you'd like to keep your backups tidy (a good idea). Once you're done, the path appears in the Backup window.

   If you're making an incremental backup, you have to show Elements where to find your previous backup. Either insert the CD or DVD with the original full backup, or click the letter name of the drive where you made your previous backup and use the "Previous Backup file" Browse button to show Elements the existing backup file.

4. **If you're backing up to a CD or DVD, insert your disc in the drive when Elements asks you to. (If you're backing up to any other kind of media, including internal or external hard drives, skip ahead to step 5.)**

   Elements needs to calculate how many discs you need to create your backup. As Elements burns each disc, it asks if you want Elements to verify the disc to be sure it's OK. You do. Elements prompts you to feed it more discs if your backup doesn't all fit on one disc.

   You can also change the write speed for your disc, if you wish. Just choose one of the other options from the pull-down menu. (A slower speed takes longer but may be more reliable.)

   NOTE   Always check your backup discs once you've burned them. Take a moment to put the disc in your computer and make sure that all your files are there. If there's an error, you want to know about it now, not six months later.

5. **Create your backup.**

Click Done, and Elements generates your backup. If you decide you don't want to make a backup, click Cancel instead.

If you chose to burn CDs or DVDs, don't forget to label the discs as Elements finishes burning them (see Figure 2-18).

NOTE These directions cover how to back up your images. It's not a bad idea to also back up your catalog database (the data file where the Organizer keeps track of where your photos are) every once in a while. To back up just the catalog information, use Windows Explorer to search for files with the extension .psa, and burn those files to CD or copy them to an external hard drive.

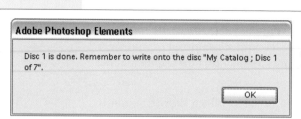

Figure 2-18:
The Organizer walks you through every step of backing up your photos. It doesn't forget a thing, even reminding you to write the disc's name on it when you're done.

Individual photo backup

You can back up your whole catalog, but you may occasionally want to back up just a few individual photos—those you just imported, for instance. Elements 5 makes this easy to do. It's very similar to making a catalog backup, but the first steps are a bit different:

1. **In the Organizer, select the files you want to back up.**

Ctrl+click the thumbnails to select only the ones you want. You can also press Ctrl+A to select all your photos and then Ctrl+click to deselect the ones you don't want.

2. **Tell Elements you want to copy your photos.**

Go to File → Copy/Move Offline, or press Ctrl+Shift+O. The Copy/Move Offline window appears.

3. **Decide whether you want to move your original file.**

If you turn on the Move Files checkbox, Elements moves your original file to your backup location, whether it's a CD or DVD, or just another location on your computer, leaving only a thumbnail in the Organizer. When you want to use that photo again, you'll be prompted for the CD or reminded that you need to reattach your external drive, if that's the destination you chose.

Leave the Move Files checkbox turned off if you just want to make a backup copy without moving your photo from its current location.

NOTE   If you choose to back up any files that are in stacks or version sets (page 490), then the checkboxes ("Include all files…") in the "Stacks and Version Sets" section become active. Turn these boxes on or off based on whether you want to include the related files.

Whatever options you choose in this window, when you're done here, click Next.

4. **Enter a name for your backup.**

   Pick a descriptive name (*April in Paris,* for example). If you don't enter a name, then your backup gets named after the current Elements catalog, even if you're copying only one photo.

5. **Follow the same procedure you'd use for backing up your catalog, beginning with step 3, above.**

   From this point on, the process and your options are identical, whether you're backing up an entire catalog or a single photo, except that Elements won't ask you for any existing backup files.

When you make copies of just a few photos (rather than the whole catalog), you're copying only the photos, not the catalog information about the photos. If you want to include your tag info along with the photos, before you start, go to File → Write Tag and Properties Info to Files. This makes your tags part of the files' EXIF data (see the box on page 51), so that if you send the photos to someone using Photoshop or another program that can read metadata, the tags appear as keywords.

NOTE   One drawback to including your tag and property info is that you can't use Elements to remove tags from the metadata later. So, for instance, if you attach a "stupid boss" tag to a photo, and then have second thoughts, you can remove that tag from your catalog, but it will still exist in any files you've emailed.

Online backups

Elements 5 also gives you quick access to making online backups of your photos. When you back up photos online, you're storing a copy of your photo on a computer server someplace else. Online backups provide an extra layer of security since your house can go up in smoke and you'll still have safe copies of your photos. The downside is that you have to pay to use this service, and it's pretty pricey for the amount of storage space you receive.

To check it out, in the Organizer, go to File → Online Backup. Elements launches your Web browser (if you're already connected to the Internet), or asks you to open an Internet connection. Then it takes you to Digital Iron Mountain, a commercial storage site that Adobe has chosen. Click Register to see the various plans they offer and to set up an account. In the future, just select the photos you want to back up and go to File → Online Backup to go straight to your Iron Mountain account.

Keep in mind that many other companies offer similar backup services at widely varying prices. Your Internet service provider may even offer some backup space as part of your monthly fee. Or search on Google for "online storage" and you'll find a slew of other options. Finally, a much more inexpensive way to create an off-site backup is to simply burn a full catalog backup, and give the discs to a friend or relative who doesn't live with you.

OUTSIDE ELEMENTS

Other Ways to Back Up

You can also easily burn your files to a CD right in Windows XP if you don't want to use the Organizer's backup feature. You may want to do so after downloading images from your camera, if you don't use the Adobe Downloader.

To back up to a CD, first be sure that burning is enabled for your CD burner. Go to My Computer → E Drive → Properties and turn on "Enable CD burning for this device." Oh, and no, you can't burn a CD without a CD burner. You'd be surprised how many people get confused by that. Then:

1. Put a blank CD in your CD tray.

2. Attach your camera or memory card reader.

3. Choose either to create a folder (if you're going to back up all your photos), or Shift+click the photos you want, and then click "Burn these files to a CD" in the preview window.

4. After your files have been copied, click the pop-up window in the System Tray to see them and select the Burn option.

Rotating and Resizing Your Photos

In the last chapter, you learned how to get your photos *into* Elements. Now it's time to look at how to trim off unwanted areas and straighten out crooked photos. You'll also learn how to change the overall size of your images and how to zoom in and out to get a better look at things while you're editing.

> **NOTE** From here through Chapter 14, you need to be in the Elements Editor. If you're still in the Organizer, press Ctrl+I to go to the Full Edit window.

Straightening Scanned Photos

Anyone who's scanned old photos can testify about the hair-pulling frustration when your carefully placed pictures come out crooked onscreen. Whether you're feeding in your precious memories one at a time or scanning batches of photos to save time, Elements can help straighten things out.

Straightening Two or More Photos at a Time

If you've got a pile of photos to scan, save yourself some time and lay as many of them as you can fit on your scanner. Thanks to Elements' wonderful Divide Scanned Photos command, you'll have individual images in no time.

Start by scanning in the photos (Figure 3-1). The only limit is how many can fit on your scanner at once. It doesn't matter whether you scan directly into Elements or use your scanner's own software. (See page 38 for more about scanning images into Elements.)

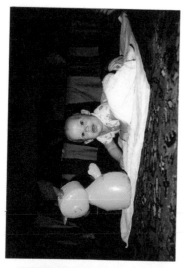

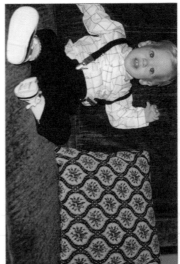

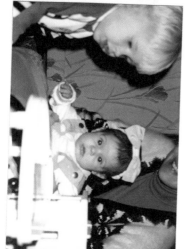

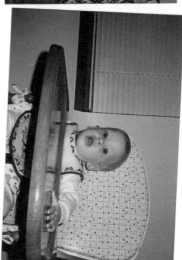

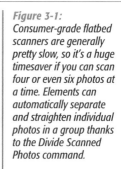

Figure 3-1:
Consumer-grade flatbed scanners are generally pretty slow, so it's a huge timesaver if you can scan four or even six photos at a time. Elements can automatically separate and straighten individual photos in a group thanks to the Divide Scanned Photos command.

TIP Sometimes it pays to be crooked. Divide Scanned Photos does its best work if your photos are fairly crooked, so don't waste time trying to be precise when placing your pictures on the scanner.

When you're done scanning, follow these steps:

1. **Open your scanned image file in the Editor.**

   It doesn't matter what file format you use when saving your scanned group of photos: TIFF, JPEG, PDF, whatever. Elements can read 'em all.

2. **Divide, straighten, and crop the individual photos.**

   Go to Image → Divide Scanned Photos. Sit back and enjoy the view as Elements carefully calculates, splits, straightens out, and trims each image. You'll see the individual photos appear and disappear as Elements works through the group.

3. **Name and save each separated image.**

   When Elements is done, you'll have the original group scan as one image and a separate image file for each photo Elements has carved out. Once you're done, import the cut-apart photos into the Organizer. To do that, just make sure that "Include in Organizer" is turned on in the Save As dialog box (page 52).

Elements usually does a crackerjack job splitting your photos, but once in a while it chokes, leaving you with an image file that contains more than one photo. Figure 3-2 shows you what to do when Elements doesn't succeed in splitting things up.

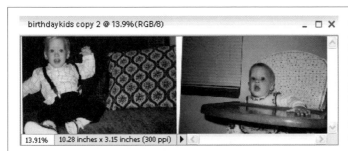

birthdaykids copy 2 @ 13.9%(RGB/8)

13.91%   10.28 inches x 3.15 inches (300 ppi)

Figure 3-2:
Sometimes Elements just can't figure out how to split up your photos, and you wind up with something like these two not-quite-split-apart images. Rescan the photos that confused Elements, but this time, make sure they're more crooked on the scanner and leave more space between them. Elements should then be able to split them correctly.

NOTE   Occasionally you may find that Elements can't accurately separate a group scan, no matter what you do. In that case, use the Marquee tool (page 113) to select each individual image, paste it into its own document (File → New → Image from Clipboard), and then save it.

Straightening Individual Photos

Elements can also straighten out and crop (trim) a single scanned image. Simply choose Image → Rotate → Straighten and Crop Image, and Elements tidies things up for you. You can also choose just Straighten Image if you'd rather crop the edges yourself. Better still, you can use Divide Scanned Photos on a single image, as explained in the previous section. (Cropping is explained on page 71.)

Rotating Your Images

Owners of print photographs aren't the only ones who sometimes need a little help straightening their pictures. Digital photos sometimes need to be rotated. For example, not all cameras output photos so that Elements (or any other image-editing program, for that matter) knows the correct orientation. Some cameras, for example, send portrait-orientated photos out on their side, and it's up to you to straighten things out.

Fortunately, Elements has rotation commands just about everywhere you go. If all you need to do is get Dad off his back and stand him upright, here's a list of where you can perform a quick 90-degree rotation on any open photo:

- **Quick Fix** (page 91). Click either of the Rotation buttons at the bottom of the preview area.

- **Full Edit.** Select Image → Rotate → 90° Left (or Right).

- **RAW Converter** (page 211). Click the left or right arrow at the bottom of the Preview window.

- **Organizer** (page 43). You can rotate a photo almost any time in the Organizer by pressing Ctrl plus the left or right arrow key. You can also choose Edit → Rotate 90° Left (or Right). Finally, there's a pair of Rotate buttons to click at the bottom of the Photo Browser window.

Those commands all get you one-click, 90-degree changes. But Elements has all sorts of other rotational tricks up its sleeve, as explained in the next section.

Rotating and Flipping Options

Elements gives you several ways to change the orientation of your photo. To see what's available, in the Editor, go to Image → Rotate. You'll notice two groups of Rotate commands in this menu. For now, it's the top group you want to focus on. (The second group does the same things, only those commands work on layers, which are explained in Chapter 6.)

In the first group of commands, you'll see:

- **Rotate 90° Left or Right.** This command produces the same rotation as the rotate buttons explained earlier. Use these commands for digital photos that come in on their sides.

- **Rotate 180°.** This turns your photo upside down and backward.

- **Flip Horizontal.** Flipping a photo horizontally means that if your subject was gazing soulfully off to the left, now she's gazing soulfully off to the right.

- **Flip Vertical.** This command turns your photo upside down without changing the left/right orientation (which is what Rotate 180° does).

    NOTE   When you're flipping photos around, remember you're making a mirror image of everything in the photo. So someone's who's writing right-handed becomes a lefty, any text you can see in the photo is backward, and so on.

- **Custom Rotate.** Selecting this command brings up a dialog box where, if you're mathematically inclined, you can type in the precise number of degrees to rotate your photo.

Figure 3-3 shows these commands in action.

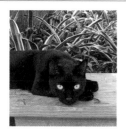
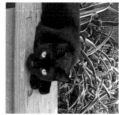
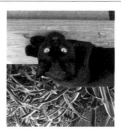
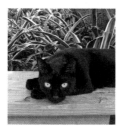
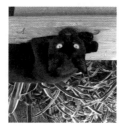
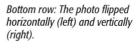

*Figure 3-3:
Even the most uncooperative cat
will turn somersaults for you if
you use the rotate commands.*

*Top row: From left to right, you
see the original, the photo
rotated 90 degrees to the right,
and the photo rotated 180
degrees.*

*Bottom row: The photo flipped
horizontally (left) and vertically
(right).*

If you want to position your photo at an angle on a page (as you would in a scrap-book), use Free Rotate Layer, described on page 70.

Straightening the Contents of Your Image

What about all those photos you've taken where the content isn't quite straight? You can flip those pictures around forever, but if your camera was off-kilter when you snapped the shot, your subjects will lean like a certain tower in Pisa. Elements has planned for this problem, too, by including a nifty Straighten tool that makes adjusting the horizon as easy as drawing a line.

> **TIP**   About 95 percent of the time, the Straighten tool will do the trick. But for the few cases where you can't get things looking perfect, you can still use the old school Elements method—the Free Rotate command, described on page 69.

Straighten Tool

If you can never seem to hold a camera perfectly level, you'll love the Elements Straighten tool. It lives just below the Cookie Cutter tool in the Full Editor's tool-box. To straighten a crooked photo:

1. **Open the photo, and then activate the Straighten tool.**

   Its icon is two little photos, one crooked and one not. Or, on the keyboard, just press P.

2. **Make any changes to the Options bar settings for the Straighten tool before you use the tool.**

   Your choices are described below.

3. **Tell Elements where the horizon is.**

Drag a line in your photo to show Elements where horizontal *should* be. Figure 3-4 shows how. Your line appears at an angle when you draw it. That's fine, because Elements is going to level out your photo, making your line the true horizontal plane in the image.

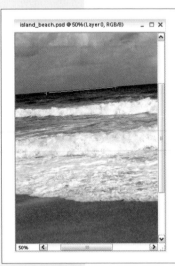 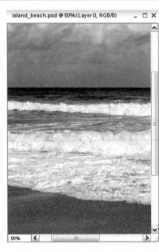

Figure 3-4:
Left: To correct the crooked horizon in this photo, just draw a line along the part that should be level. It's easiest to do this by choosing a clearly marked area like the horizon in this photo, but Elements doesn't need any visual help. You could draw a line across the middle of a lawn, for instance, and Elements would straighten the photo to that line.

Right: Elements automatically rotates the photo to straighten its contents. In this case, you see the results of selecting "Crop to Remove Background" (in the Options bar), which trims off all the ragged edges for you.

4. **Elements responds by automatically straightening your photo. It also crops the photo if you chose that setting in the Options bar.**

If you don't like what Elements did, press Ctrl+Z to undo it and draw another line. If you're happy, you're all done, except for saving your work (Ctrl+S).

TIP   If you have a photo of trees, sailing ships, skyscrapers, or any other subject where you'd rather straighten vertically than horizontally, just hold down Ctrl while you drag. The line you draw determines the vertical axis of your photo.

The Options bar gives you some choices about how to handle the edges of your newly straightened photo. Once your picture's straightened, the edges are going to be a bit ragged, so you can choose what you want Elements to do about that:

- **Grow or Shrink Canvas to Fit.** Elements adds extra space around the edges of your photo to make sure that every bit of the original edges is still there. It's up to you to crop your photo afterward (page 71).

- **Crop to Remove Background.** Elements chops off the ragged edges to give you a nice rectangular image.

- **Crop to Original Size.** Elements makes sure the dimensions of your photo stay exactly the same—even if that means including some blank spaces along the perimeter.

If your photo has layers (see Chapter 6), you can use the Straighten tool to straighten only the active layer (page 143) by going to the Options bar and turning off Rotate All Layers. If you want Elements to straighten your whole photo, leave this checkbox turned on.

> **NOTE** The Straighten tool is best for photos where you were holding the camera crooked. If you try it and it makes things look very odd in your photo, perhaps straightening isn't really what you need. Architectural photos, for instance, may look a bit crooked before you use this tool but a lot worse afterward. For example, now that house is *really* leaning, even though you're sure the ground line has been leveled correctly. If that happens, most likely your real problem is *perspective distortion* (a visual warping effect). To fix that, use Correct Camera Distortion (page 292).

Free Rotate

You can also use the Rotate commands to straighten your photos, or to turn them at angles for use in scrapbook pages or album layouts you create. The rotate command that's best for this use is Free Rotate Layer, which lets you grab your photo and spin it to your heart's desire. And if you aren't sure where straight is, Elements gives you some help figuring it out, as shown in Figure 3-5.

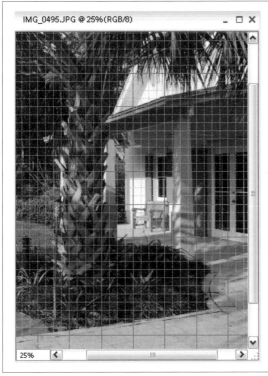

IMG_0495.JPG @ 25%(RGB/8)

25%

Figure 3-5:
If you need some help figuring out where straight is, in the Editor, go to View → Grid to toggle these handy guidelines on and off. You can adjust the grid spacing in Edit → Preferences → Grid. For a photo like this one, you could also change the color of the grid to make it show up better. To do that, click the color square in the grid preferences window and choose a color from the color picker (page 196).

All the rotate commands are also available for use on individual layers, incidentally. (Chapter 6 tells you all about layers, but you don't have to understand layers to use the Free Rotate Layer command.)

To use Free Rotate Layer:

1. **Go to Image → Rotate → Free Rotate Layer.**

   Elements asks you if it should "make this background a layer." Say yes. (Again, Chapter 6 tells you everything you need to know about layers.)

2. **Name the layer if you want to.**

   A dialog box appears, giving you a chance to name the layer. Do so if you want, then click OK.

3. **Use the handle or the curved arrows to adjust your photo (Figure 3-6).**

   Your picture may look kind of jagged while you're rotating. Don't worry about that—Elements smoothes things out once you're done.

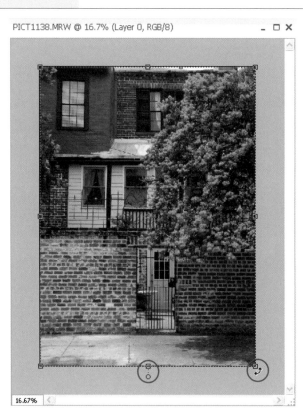

Figure 3-6:
Elements 5 gives you a new way to straighten the contents of your photo—or even spin it around in a circle. Just grab either the handle at the center bottom of your photo or a corner (both circled). If you grab a corner, your cursor turns into a two-headed arrow. Then drag to adjust your photo the way you'd straighten a crooked picture on the wall. Click the green OK checkmark when you're happy with what you've done, or the red "no" symbol to cancel.

4. When you've got your image positioned where you want it, click the green OK checkmark or press Enter. (If you don't like what you did, press the red "no" symbol to cancel the rotation.)

Now you've got a nice straight picture, but the edges are probably pretty ragged since the original had slanted, unrotated sides. You can take care of that by cropping your photo, which is covered in the next section.

Cropping Pictures

Whether or not you straightened your digital photo, sooner or later you'll probably need to *crop* it—trim it to a certain size. Most people crop their photos for one of two reasons: If you want to print on standard size photo paper, you usually need to cut away part of your image to make it fit on the paper. Then there's the "I don't want *that* in my picture" reason. Fortunately, Elements makes it easy to crop away distracting background objects or people you'd rather not see.

A few cameras produce photos that are proportioned exactly right for printing to a standard size like 4"×6". But most cameras give you photos that aren't the same proportions as any of the standard paper sizes like 4"×6" or 8"×10". (The width-to-height ratio is also known as the *aspect ratio*.)

The extra area most cameras provide gives you room to crop wherever you like. You can also crop out different areas for different size prints (assuming you save your original photo). Figure 3-7 shows an example of a photo that had to be cropped to fit on a 4"×6" piece of paper. If you'd like to experiment with cropping or changing resolution (explained on page 82), download the image in the figure (waterfall.jpg) from the "Missing CD" page at *www.missingmanuals.com*.

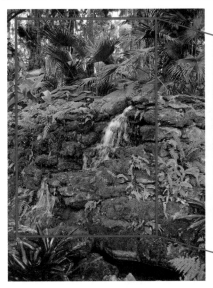
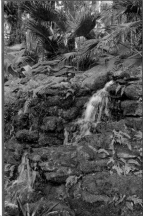

Figure 3-7:
When you print onto standard sized paper, you may have to choose the part of your digital photo you want to keep.

Left: The photo as it came from the camera.

Right: The results of cropping the image down to make it the correct shape for a 4"×6" print.

If your photo isn't in the Organizer, it's best to perform your crops on a copy, since trimming is going to throw away the pixels outside the area you choose to keep. And you never know—you may want those pixels back someday.

Using the Crop Tool

You can use the Crop tool in either the Full Edit or Quick Fix window. The Crop tool includes a helpful list of preset sizes to make cropping easier. If you don't need to crop to an exact size, here's how to perform basic freehand cropping:

1. **Activate the Crop tool.**

   Click the Crop icon in the Toolbox or press C.

2. **Drag anywhere in your image to select the area you want to keep.**

   The area outside the boundaries of your selection is covered with a dark shield. The dark area is what you're discarding. To move the area you've chosen, just drag the bounding box to wherever you want it.

   You may find the Crop tool a little crotchety sometimes. See the box on page 74 for help making it behave.

3. **To resize your selection, drag one of the little handles on the sides and corners.**

   They look like little squares, as shown in Figure 3-8. You can drag in any direction, so you can also change the proportions of your crop if you want to.

4. **If you change your mind, press Cancel (the "no" symbol) on the photo, or press the Escape key.**

   That undoes the selection so you can start over or switch to another tool if you decide you don't want to crop after all.

5. **When you're sure you've got the crop you want, press Enter, or press OK (the checkmark) on the photo, or double-click inside the cropping mask, and you're done.**

Cropping Your Image to an Exact Size

You don't have to eyeball things when cropping a photo. You can enter any dimensions you want in the width and height boxes in the Options bar, or, from the Aspect Ratio menu, you can choose one of the Presets, which automatically enters a set of numbers for you. The Aspect Ratio menu offers you several standard photo sizes, like 4"×6" or 8"×10", to choose from. The Use Photo Ratio choice in the Presets list lets you crop your image using the same width/height proportions (*aspect ratio*) as in the original. Figure 3-9 shows you a timesaver: how to quickly switch the width and height numbers.

> **NOTE** Although Custom is one of the Aspect Ratio menu choices, there's no reason to select it, since it's there to let you know you've entered a custom size. It selects itself when it's the right choice.

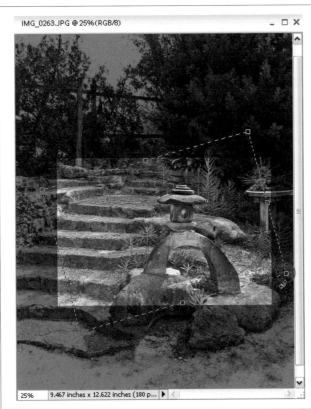

IMG_0263.JPG @ 25%(RGB/8)

25%   9.467 inches x 12.622 inches (180 p...

Figure 3-8:
If you want to change your selection from horizontal to vertical or vice versa, just move your cursor outside the cropped area and you'll see the rotation arrows (circled). Grab and rotate them, the same way you would an entire photo. Changing your selection doesn't rotate your photo—just the boundaries of the crop. When you're done, press Enter or the green checkmark (for OK) to tell Elements you're satisfied. The red "no" symbol cancels your crop. (The OK and Cancel symbols appear when you let go of the mouse.)

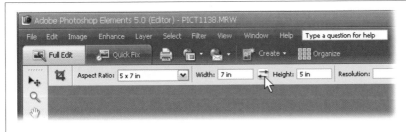

Figure 3-9:
If you want to change which number is the width setting and which is the height, just click these little arrows to swap them. So if you chose 5"×7" from the presets but want to switch to a landscape orientation, click the arrows below the cursor to get 7"×5" instead.

WARNING   If you enter a number in the Resolution box that's different from your image's current resolution, the Crop tool resamples your image to match the new resolution. (Resolution is explained in the section on resizing your image that starts on page 82.) See the section on Resampling (page 88) to understand what resampling is and why it isn't always a good thing.

Cropping with the Marquee Tool

The Crop tool is very handy, but it wants to make the decisions for you about several things you may want to control yourself. For instance, the Crop tool may decide to resample the image (see page 88) whether you want it to or not. The Crop tool gives you no warning that it's resampling. It just does it.

For better control, and also for making elliptical crop effects (great for oval vignettes), you may prefer to use the Marquee tool. It's no harder than using the Crop tool, but you get to make all the choices yourself.

There's one other big difference between using the Marquee tool and the Crop tool: with the Crop tool, all you can do with the area you selected is crop it. The Marquee tool, in contrast, lets you do anything else you want to your selected area, like adjust the color, which you may want to do before you crop.

TROUBLESHOOTING MOMENT

Crop Tool Idiosyncrasies

The Crop tool is crotchety sometimes. People have called it "bossy," and that's a good word for it. Here are some settings that may help you control it better.

- **Snap to Grid.** You may find that you just cannot get the crop exactly where you want it. Does the edge keep jumping slightly away from where you put it? Like most graphics programs, Elements uses a grid of invisible lines—called the *autogrid*—to help position things exactly. Sometimes a grid is a big help, but in situations like this, it's a nuisance.

If you hold down Ctrl, you can temporarily disable the autogrid. To get rid of it permanently, or to adjust the spacing on it, go to the View menu and turn off "Snap to Grid." You can adjust the grid settings in Edit → Preferences → Grid.

- **Clear the Crop Tool.** Occasionally you may find that the Crop tool won't release a setting you entered, even after you clear the Options bar boxes. If the Crop tool won't let you drag where you want and keeps insisting on creating a particular sized crop, you need to reset the Crop tool. Simply right-click it and choose Reset Tool from the shortcut menu, as shown in Figure 3-10.

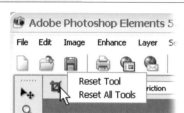

Figure 3-10:
If the Crop tool stops cooperating, there's an easy way to make it behave again. Click its icon in the Options bar, and then choose Reset Tool from the menu that appears. If you want to make sure that all your tools go back to their original settings, choose Reset All Tools.

To make a basic crop with the Marquee tool follow these steps:

1. **Activate the Marquee tool.**

   Click it in the Toolbox (the little dotted square) or press M. Figure 3-11 shows you the shape choices you get within the Marquee tool. For cropping, choose the Rectangular Marquee tool.

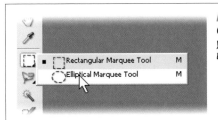

Figure 3-11:
Click the Marquee tool, and you can choose the shape from this menu, or you can choose the shape by clicking your choice in the Options bar when the tool is active. Both actions do the same thing.

2. **Drag the selection marquee across the part of your photo you want to keep.**

   When you let go, your selected area is surrounded by the dotted lines shown in Figure 3-12. These are sometimes called "marching ants." (Get it? The dashes look like ants marching around your picture.) The area inside the marching ants is the part of your photo you're keeping. (There's a lot more about making selections in Chapter 5.) If you make a mistake, press Ctrl+D to get rid of the selection and start over.

3. **Crop your photo.**

   Go to Image → Crop. The area outside your selection disappears, and your photo is cropped to the area you selected in step 2.

If you want to crop your photo to a particular aspect ratio, you can do that easily. Once the Marquee tool is active, but before you drag, go to the Options bar. In the Mode menu, choose Fixed Aspect Ratio. Then enter the proportions you want in the Width and Height boxes. Drag and crop as described earlier. Your photo will end up with exactly the proportions you entered in the Options bar.

You can also crop to an exact size with the Marquee tool:

1. **Check the resolution of your photo.**

   Take a look at the bottom of the image window and make sure the ppi number is somewhere between 150 and 300. 300 is best, for reasons explained on page 86. If the ppi is OK, go to step 2.

   If the ppi is too low, go to Image → Resize → Image Size. Change the number in the Resolution box to what you want. Make sure that the checkbox in the Resize dialog box that says Resample Image is turned off, and then click OK.

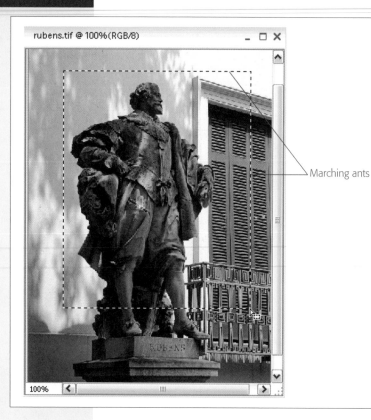

rubens.tif @ 100%(RGB/8)

100%

Marching ants

Figure 3-12:
When you let go after making your Marquee selection, you see the "marching ants" around the edge of your selection. You can reposition the marquee by dragging it. To do so, just put your cursor anywhere inside the selection marquee and then drag it.

2. **Activate the Marquee tool.**

   Click the Marquee tool in the Toolbox (the little dotted square) or press M. Choose the Rectangular Marquee tool.

3. **Enter your settings in the Options bar.**

   First go to the Mode menu and choose Fixed Size. Next, enter the dimensions you want in the Width and Height boxes.

4. **Drag anywhere in your image.**

   You get a selection the exact size you chose in the Options bar.

5. **Crop your Image.**

   Go to Image → Crop.

The Cookie Cutter tool also gives you a way to create really interesting crops, as shown in Figure 3-13.

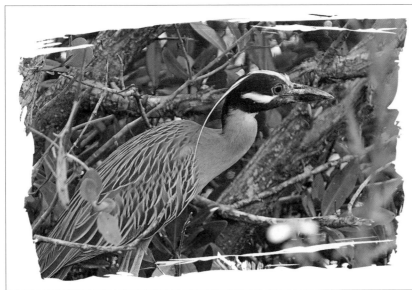

Figure 3-13:
With the Elements Cookie Cutter tool, you don't have to be square anymore. The Cookie Cutter tool lets you crop your images to a variety of different shapes, from the kind of abstract border you see here, to heart- or star-shaped outlines. You can read more about how to use the Cookie Cutter tool in Chapter 12.

TIP   If you're doing your own printing, there's really no reason to tie yourself down to standard photo sizes like 4" × 6"—unless, of course, you need the image to fit a frame of that size. But most of the time, your images could just as well be square, or long and skinny, or whatever proportions you want. You can be especially inventive when sizing images for the Web. So don't feel that every photo you take has to be straitjacketed into a standard size.

Zooming and Repositioning Your View

Sometimes, rather than changing the size of your photo, all you want to do is change its appearance in Elements so you can get a better look at it. For example, you may want to zoom in on a particular area, or zoom out, so you can see how edits you've made have affected your photo's overall composition.

This section is about how to adjust the view of your image inside Elements. Nothing you do with the tools and commands in this section changes anything about your actual photo. You're just changing the way you see it. Elements gives you lots of tools and keystroke combinations to help with these new views; soon you'll probably find yourself making these changes without even thinking about them.

Image Views

Before you start resizing your view of your photos, Elements gives you several different ways to position your image windows. When you first use Elements, if you have more than one photo open at a time, your photos tile themselves so that you can see them all simultaneously. If you have two photos open, for instance, each photo window spreads itself out to take half the available space on your desktop. You're not stuck with this layout, though.

When you go to Window → Images, you get several choices for how your image windows should display:

- **Maximize Mode.** Each photo window takes up the entire Elements desktop. You can also click the large square at the right of the Editor shortcuts bar to switch to this view.

    NOTE   In Maximize mode, you can only have one photo open at a time. Switch to Cascade or Tile if you want to work on two or more photos simultaneously.

- **Tile.** Your image windows appear edge to edge so that they fill the available desktop space. With two photos open, each gets half the window; with four photos, each gets one quarter of it, and so on. If you click the four squares in the Shortcuts bar, you get this view.

- **Cascade.** Your image windows appear in overlapping stacks. Most people find Cascade the most practical view when you want to compare or work with two images.

- **Match Zoom.** All your windows get the same magnification level as the active image window (the photo you're currently working on).

- **Match Location.** You see the same part of each image window, like the upper-right corner or the bottom left. Elements matches the other windows to the active window.

You also get four handy commands for adjusting the view of your active image window. Go to the View menu, and you see:

- **New Window for.** Choose this command and you get a separate, duplicate window for your image. This view is a terrific help when you're working on very fine detail. You can zoom way in on one view while keeping the other window in a regular view to help you keep your bearings for where you are in the photo. Don't worry about version control or keeping track of which window you're working in, since both windows just represent different glimpses of the same image.

- **Fit Screen.** This command makes your photo as large as it can be while still keeping the entire photo visible. You can also press Ctrl+0 for this view.

- **Actual Pixels.** Actual Pixels is the most accurate look at the onscreen size of your photo. If you're creating graphics for the Web, this view shows the size your image will be in your Web browser. The keystroke shortcut is Alt+Ctrl+0.

- **Print Size.** This view is really just a guess by Elements because it doesn't know exactly how big a pixel is on your monitor. But it's a rough approximation of the size your image would be if you printed it at the current resolution. (Resolution is explained in the section on resizing your photo, on page 82.)

TIP   You can also zoom in or out from this menu, but it's much faster to learn the keystroke shortcuts. The next section explains the Zoom tool in detail.

To adjust the view of a particular image, Elements gives you three useful tools: The Zoom tool, the Hand tool, and the Navigator palette, all of which are explained in the following sections.

The Zoom Tool

Some of Elements' tools require you to get a very close look at your image to see what's going on. Sometimes you may need to see the actual pixels as you work, as shown in Figure 3-14. The Zoom tool makes it easy to zoom your view in and out.

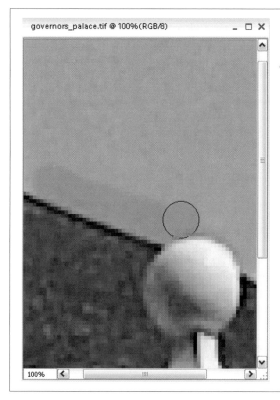

Figure 3-14:
There are times when you want to zoom way, way in when working in Elements. You may even need to go pixel by pixel in tricky spots, as shown here.

The Zoom tool's Toolbox icon is the little magnifying glass. Click it or press Z to activate the tool. Once the tool is active, you see two magnifying glasses in the Options bar. If you want to zoom in (to make the view larger), click the one with the + sign on it. To use the Zoom tool, you just click the place in your photo where you want the zoom to focus. The point where you clicked becomes the center of your view, and the view size increases again each time you click.

You can also select the Zoom Out tool in the Options bar, by clicking the magnifying glass with the – sign on it.

> **TIP** If you hold Alt as you click, the selected Zoom tool zooms in the opposite direction; for instance, the regular Zoom tool zooms out rather than in.

The Zoom tool has several Options bar settings you can use as well:

- **Zoom percent.** Enter a number here and the view immediately jumps to that percentage. 1600 percent is the maximum, and 1 percent is the minimum.
- **Resize Windows to fit.** Turn this option on, and your image windows get larger and smaller along with the image size as you zoom. The image always fills the entire window with no gray space around it.
- **Ignore Palettes.** This setting lets windows resize so that they don't stop getting larger when they reach the edge of a palette. Instead, they continue resizing *underneath* the palette. This choice isn't available until you turn on "Resize Windows to fit."
- **Zoom all windows.** If you have more than one image window, turn this option on, and the view changes in all the windows in sync when you zoom one window.

> **TIP** If you hold down the Shift key while you zoom, all your windows zoom together. You don't need to go to the Options bar to activate this feature.

The buttons for Fit on Screen, Actual Pixels, and Print Size are the same as the menu commands described in the preceding section.

> **TIP** You don't need to bother with the actual Zoom tool at all. You can zoom without letting go of the keyboard by pressing Ctrl+= to zoom in and Ctrl+– (that's the Ctrl key plus the minus sign) to zoom out. Just hold down Ctrl and keep tapping the equal or minus sign until the view is what you want. You can also zoom to 100 percent by double-clicking the Zoom tool's icon.
>
> It doesn't matter which tool you're using at the time—you can always zoom in or out this way. Because you'll do a lot of zooming in Elements, this keyboard shortcut is one to remember.

The Hand Tool

With all that zooming, sometimes you're not going to be able to see your entire image at once. Elements includes the Hand tool to help you adjust which part of your image appears onscreen. It's very easy to use. Just click the little hand in the Toolbox or press H to activate it.

When the Hand tool is active, your cursor turns to the little hand shown in Figure 3-15. Drag with the hand to move your photo around in the window. The hand tool is very helpful when you're zoomed in or working on a large image.

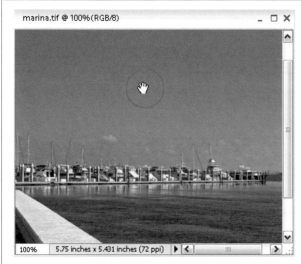

Figure 3-15:
The easiest way to activate the Hand tool is to press the Space bar on your keyboard. You can tell the Hand tool is active by this little white-gloved cursor (circled in red here). No matter what you're doing in Elements, pressing the Space bar calls up the Hand tool and it remains on until you release the Space bar. Then the tool you were previously using returns.

The Hand tool gives you the same Scroll All Windows option you have for the Zoom tool, but you don't have to use the Options bar to activate it. Just hold down Shift while using the Hand tool, and all your windows scroll in synch. The Hand tool also gives you the same three buttons (Fit Screen, Actual Pixels, and Print Size) that the Zoom tool does. Once again, they're the same as the menu commands described at the beginning of this section.

Figure 3-16 shows the Hand tool's somewhat more sophisticated assistant, the Navigator palette, which is very useful for working in really big photos or when you want to have a slider handy for micro-managing the zoom level. Go to Window → Navigator to call it up.

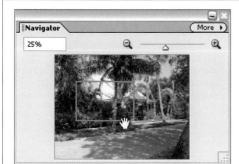

Figure 3-16:
Meet the Navigator. You can travel around your image by dragging the little red rectangle—it marks the area of your photo that you can see onscreen. You can also enter a percent number for the size you want your photo to display at, or move the slider or click the zoom in/out magnifying glasses on either side of the slider to change the view. The Navigator is just great for keeping track of where you are in a large image.

Changing the Size of Your Image

The previous section explained how to resize the view of your image as it appears on your monitor. But sometimes you need to change the size of your actual image, and that's what this section is about.

Resizing your photo brings you up against a pretty tough concept in digital imaging: *resolution*, which measures, in pixels, the amount of detail your image can show. Where it gets confusing is that resolution for printing and for onscreen use (like email and the Web) are quite different.

For example, you need many more pixels to create a good-looking print than you do for a photo that's going to be viewed only onscreen. A photo that's going to print well almost always has too many pixels in it for onscreen display, and as a result, its file size is usually pretty hefty for emailing. So you often need two different copies of your photo for the two different uses. If you want to know more about resolution, a good place to start is *www.scantips.com*.

This section gives you a brief introduction to both screen and print resolution, especially in terms of what decisions you'll need to make when using the Resize Image dialog box. You'll also learn how to add more canvas (more blank space) around your photos. You'd add canvas to make room for captions below your image, for instance, or when you want to combine two photos.

To get started, open a photo you want to resize and go to Image → Resize → Image Size (Figure 3-17).

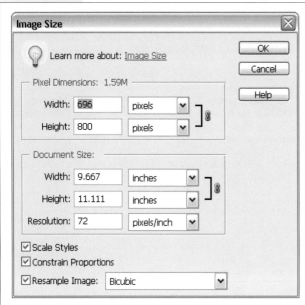

Figure 3-17:
The Image Size dialog box gives you two different ways to change the size of your photo. Use the Pixel Dimensions section when preparing a photo for onscreen viewing. (The number immediately to the right of Pixel Dimensions—here, 1.59 M— indicates the current size of your file in megabytes or kilobytes.) Before you can make any changes here, you must turn on Resample Image in the bottom part of the dialog box, since changing pixel dimensions always involves Resampling (see page 88). Use the Document Size section to prepare photos for printing.

Resizing Images for Email and the Web

It's important to learn how to size your photos so that they show up clear and easy to view onscreen. Have you ever gotten an emailed photo that was so huge you could see only a tiny bit of it on your monitor at once? That happens when someone sends an image that isn't optimized for viewing on a monitor. It's very easy to avoid that problem—once you know how to correctly size your photos for onscreen viewing.

If you look at the Image Size dialog box, you see two main sections. The top one says Pixel Dimensions and below that is Document Size. You'll use the Pixel Dimensions settings when you know your image is only going to be viewed onscreen. (Document Size is for printing.)

A monitor is concerned only with the size of a photo as measured in pixels, known as the *pixel dimensions*. On a monitor, a pixel is always the same size (unlike a printer, which can change the size of the pixels it prints out). Your monitor doesn't know anything about pixels per inch (ppi), and it can't change the way it displays a photo even if you change the photo's ppi settings, as shown in Figure 3-18. (It's true that graphics programs like Elements can change the size of your onscreen view by, say, zooming in, but most programs, like your Web browser, can't.)

All you have to decide is how many pixels long and how many pixels wide you want your photo to be. You control those measurements in the Pixel Dimensions section of the Image Size dialog box.

What dimensions should you use? That depends a little on who's going to be seeing your photos, but as a general rule, small monitors today are usually 1024 × 768 pixels. Some monitors, like the largest Dell and Apple models, have many more pixels than that, of course. Still, if you want to be sure that people who see your photo won't have to scroll, a good rule of thumb is to choose no more than 650 pixels for the longer side of your photo, whether that's the width or the height. If you want people to be able to see more than one image at a time, you may want to make your photos even smaller. Also, some people set their monitors to display only 600 × 800 pixels, so you may want to make even smaller images to send to them.

> **TIP**   To get the most accurate look at how large your photo truly displays on a monitor, go to View → Actual Pixels.

Also, although a photo is always the same pixel dimensions, you really can't control the exact inch dimensions at which those pixels display on other people's monitors. A pixel is always the same size on any given monitor (as long as you don't change the monitor's screen resolution), but different monitors have different sized pixels these days. Figure 3-19 may help you grasp this concept.

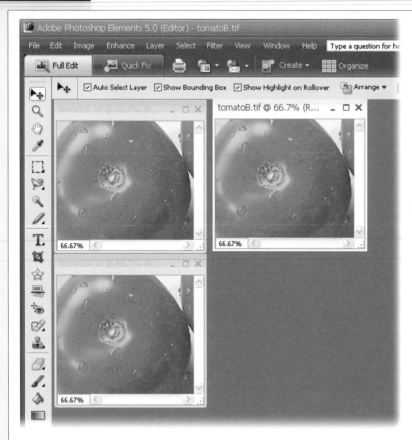

Figure 3-18:
This screenshot demonstrates that your monitor doesn't care about the ppi settings you enter. One of these photos was saved at 100 ppi, the second at 300 ppi, and the last at 1000 ppi. Can you tell which? No. They all display at exactly the same size on your monitor, because they all have exactly the same pixel dimensions, which is the only resolution setting your monitor understands.

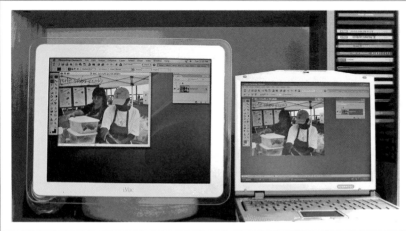

Figure 3-19:
Both these computers have a screen resolution of 1024 × 768 pixels, and the photo they're displaying takes up exactly the same percentage of each screen. But the picture on the left is larger because the monitor is physically larger—in other words, the pixels are bigger.

NOTE   In the following sections, you'll be learning what to do when you want to *reduce* the size of an image. It's much easier to get good results making a photo smaller than larger. Elements does let you *increase* the size of your image, using a technique called upsampling (explained on page 88), but you may get mediocre results. The section on resampling (page 88) explains why.

To resize your photos, start by making very sure you're not resizing your original. You're going to be shedding pixels that you can't get back again, so resize your photos using a copy (File → Duplicate) if your photo's not already in the Organizer.

1. **Call up the Image Size dialog box.**

   Go to Image → Resize → Image Size.

2. **In the Pixel Dimensions area, enter the dimension you want for the longer side of your photo.**

   Usually you'd want 650 pixels or less. Be sure that pixels show as the unit of measurement. You just need to enter the number for one side. Elements automatically figures the dimension for the other side as long as Constrain Proportions is turned on down near the bottom of the dialog box. (You need to turn on Resample Image before you can change the pixel dimensions.)

3. **Check the settings at the bottom of the dialog box.**

   Constrain Proportions should be turned on. (Scale Styles doesn't matter. Leave it on.) Resample Image should be turned on. (*Resampling* means changing the number of pixels in your image.) The Resample Image menu lists the different resampling methods. Adobe recommends Bicubic Sharper when you're making an image smaller, but you may want to experiment with the other menu options if you don't like the results you get when using Bicubic Sharper.

4. **Click OK.**

   Your photo is resized, although you may not immediately see a difference onscreen. Go to View → Actual Pixels, before and after you resize, and you can see the difference. Save your resized photo to make your size change permanent.

Sometimes Elements resizes an image automatically—for example, when you use the Organizer's E-Mail command (see page 436). But the method described here gives you more control than letting Elements make your decisions for you.

NOTE   If you're concerned about file size, use "Save for Web" (see page 429), which helps you create smaller files.

Resizing for Printing

If you want great prints, you need to think about your photo's resolution quite differently than you do for images that you're emailing. For printing, as a general rule, the more pixels your photo has, the better. That's the reason camera manufacturers keep packing more megapixels into their new models—the more pixels you have, the larger you can print your photo and still have it look terrific.

> **NOTE** Even before you take your photos, you can do a lot toward making them print well if you always choose the largest size and the highest quality setting on your camera (typically Extra Fine, Superfine, or Fine).

When you print your photo, you need to think about two things: the size of your photo in inches (or whatever your preferred unit of measurement is) and the resolution in pixels per inch (ppi). Those settings work together to control the quality of your print.

Your printer is a virtuoso that plays your pixels like an accordion. Your printer can squeeze the pixels together and make them smaller, or spread the pixels out and make them larger. Generally speaking, the denser the pixels (the higher the ppi), the higher the resolution of your photo, and the better it looks.

If you don't have enough pixels in your photo, the print will appear pixellated—very jagged and blurry looking. The goal is to have enough pixels in your photo so that they'll be packed fairly densely—ideally at about 300 ppi.

You usually don't get a visibly better result if you go over 300 ppi, though, just a larger file size. And depending on your tastes, you may be content with your results at a lower ppi. For instance, some Canon camera photos come into Elements at 180 ppi, and you may be happy with how they print. But 200 ppi is usually considered about the lowest density for an acceptable print. Figure 3-20 demonstrates why it's so important to have a high ppi setting.

To set the size of an image for printing:

1. **Call up the Image Size dialog box.**

   Go to Image → Resize → Image Size.

2. **Check the resolution of your image.**

   You want to look at the Document Size section of the dialog box (see Figure 3-17). Start by checking the ppi setting. If it's too low, like 72 ppi, go to the bottom of the dialog box and turn off Resample Image. Then enter the ppi you want in the Document Size area. The dimensions should become smaller to reflect the greater density of the pixels. If they don't, click OK, and open the dialog box again.

3. **Check the physical size of your photo.**

   Look at the numbers in the Document Size area. Are they what you want? If so, you're all done. Click OK.

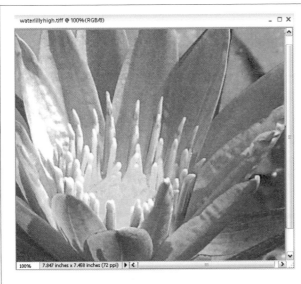

waterlillyhigh.tiff @ 100%(RGB/8)

100% | 7.847 inches x 7.458 inches (72 ppi)

Figure 3-20:
*Different resolution settings can dramatically alter
the quality of a printout.*

Top: A photo with a resolution of 300 ppi.

*Bottom: The same photo with resolution set to 72
ppi. Too few pixels stretched too far causes this
kind of blocky, blurry printing. When you can see
the individual pixels, a photo is said to be
pixellated.*

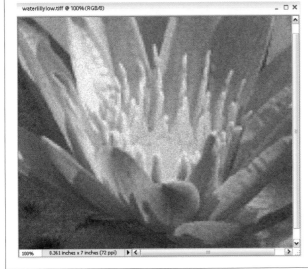

waterlillylow.tiff @ 100%(RGB/8)

100% | 8.361 inches x 7 inches (72 ppi)

4. **If your size numbers aren't right, resize your photo.**

   If the proportions of your image aren't what you want, crop the photo using
   one of the methods described earlier, and then come back to the Image Size dialog box. Don't try to reshape an image using the Image Size dialog box.

   Once you've returned to the Image Size dialog box, go to the bottom of the
   window and turn on Resample Image. Choose Bicubic Smoother in the menu.
   (This menu choice is Adobe's recommendation, but you may find that you prefer one of the other resampling choices.)

Now enter the size you want for the width or height. Make sure that Constrain Proportions is turned on. If it is, Elements will calculate the other dimension for you. (Scale Styles doesn't matter. Leave it on.)

5. **Click OK.**

Your photo is resized and ready for printing.

Resampling

Resampling is an image editing term for changing the number of pixels in an image. When you resample, your results are permanent, so you want to avoid resampling an original photo if you can help it. As a rule, it's easier to get good results when you *downsample*—that is, make your photo smaller—than when you *upsample*, which you do when you want to make your photo larger.

When you upsample, you're *adding* pixels to your image. Elements has to get them from somewhere, so it makes them up. Elements is pretty good at this, but these pixels are never as good as the pixels that were in your photo to begin with, as you can see from Figure 3-21. You can download the figure (russian_box.jpg) from the "Missing CD" page at *www.missingmanuals.com* if you'd like to try this out for yourself. Zoom in very closely so you can see the pixels.

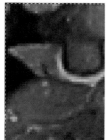 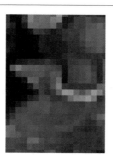 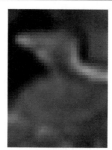

Figure 3-21:
Here's a close-up look at what you're doing to your photo when you resample it.

The photo as it came from the camera.

Downsampled to 72 ppi.

Upsampled back to the original resolution. See how soft the pixels look compared to the original?

When you enlarge an image to more than 100 percent of its original size, you'll definitely lose some of the original quality. So, for example, if you try to stretch a photo that's 3" wide at 180 ppi to an 8" × 10" print, don't be surprised if you don't like the results.

Elements offers you several resampling methods, and they do a very good job when you find the right one for your situation. You select them in the Resample Image menu in the Image Size dialog box. Adobe recommends choosing Bicubic Smoother when you're upsampling (enlarging) your images and Bicubic Sharper when you're downsampling (reducing) your photos, but you may prefer one of the others. It's worth experimenting with them all to see which you like.

Adding Canvas

Just like the works of Monet and Matisse, your photos appear in Elements on a digital "canvas." Sometimes you may want to add more canvas to make room for text or if you're combining photos into a collage.

To make your canvas larger, go to Image → Resize → Canvas Size. You can change the size of your canvas using a variety of measurements. If you don't know exactly how much more canvas you want, choose Percent. Then you can guesstimate that you want, say, 2 percent more canvas or 50 percent more. Figure 3-22 shows how to get your photo into the right place on the new canvas.

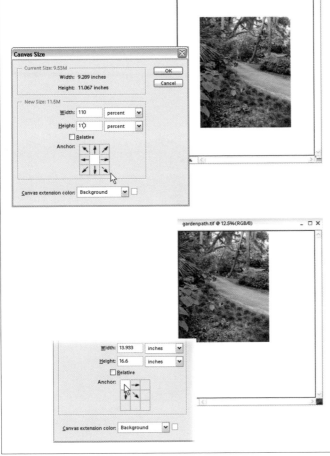

Figure 3-22:
The Canvas Size dialog box isn't as complicated as it looks. The strange little Anchor grid with arrows pointing everywhere lets you decide exactly where to add new canvas to your image. The white Anchor box represents your photo's current position, and the arrows surrounding it show where Elements will add the new canvas. By clicking in any of the surrounding boxes, you tell Elements where to position your photo on the newly sized canvas. In the top pair of images, the new canvas has been added equally around all sides of the existing image. In the bottom pair, the new canvas has been added below and to the right of the existing image.

NOTE   Changing the size of your canvas doesn't change the size of your picture any more than pasting a postcard onto a full-size sheet of paper changes the size of the postcard. In both cases, all you get is more empty space around your picture.

The Quick Fix

With Elements' Quick Fix tools, you can dramatically improve the appearance of a photo with just a click or two. The Quick Fix window gathers easy-to-use tools that help adjust the brightness and color of your photos and make them look sharper. You don't even need to understand much about what you're doing. You just need to click a button or slide a pointer, and then decide whether you like how it looks.

If, on the other hand, you *do* know what you're doing, you may still find yourself using the Quick Fix window for things like shadows and highlights because it's the only place in Elements that gives you a before-and-after view as you work. Also, the Temperature and Tint sliders can come in very handy for advanced color tweaking, like finessing the overall color of your otherwise finished photo. You even get two tools—the Selection brush and the Magic Selection brush—to help make changes to only a certain area of your photo.

In this chapter, you'll learn how to use all of the Quick Fix tools. You'll also learn about what order to apply the fixes so you get the most out of these tools. If you have a newish digital camera, you may find that the Quick Fix gives you all the tools you need to take your photos from pretty darn good (the way they came out of the camera) to dazzling.

> **NOTE** If an entire chapter on Quick Fix is frustratingly slow, you can start off by trying out the ultra-fast Auto Smart Fix—a quick-fix tool for the truly impatient. Page 28 tells you everything you need to know.

The Quick Fix Window

Getting to the Quick Fix window is easy. If you're in the Editor, go to the Shortcuts bar and click the Quick Fix button. If you're in the Organizer, go to the Shortcuts bar and click the Edit button's drop-down triangle, and then choose Go to Quick Fix. The Quick Fix window looks like a stripped-down version of the Full Edit window (see Figure 4-1).

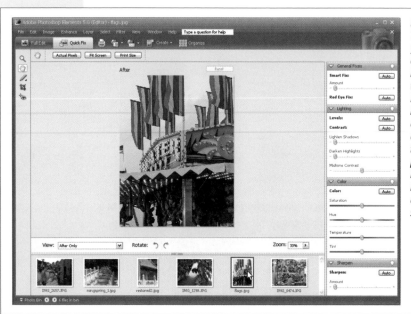

Figure 4-1:
The Quick Fix window. If you have several photos open when you come into the Quick Fix window, you can use the Photo bin (page 21) at bottom to choose the one you want to edit. Just click any of the image thumbnails and that photo becomes the active image—the one you see in the Quick Fix preview area in the center of your screen.

Your tools are neatly arranged on both sides of your image: On the left side, there's a five-item Toolbox; on the right side, there's a collection of quick-edit palettes stored inside the Control Panel. First, you'll take a quick look at the tools Quick Fix provides you with. Then, later in the chapter, you'll learn how to actually use them.

The Quick Fix Toolbox

The Toolbox holds an easy-to-navigate subset of the Standard Edit window's larger tool collection. All the tools work the same way in both modes, and you can also use the same keystrokes to switch tools here. From top to bottom, the Quick Fix Toolbox holds:

- **The Zoom tool** lets you telescope in and out on your image so that you can get a good close look at details or pull back to see the whole photo. (See page 79 for more on how the Zoom tool works.) You can also zoom by using the Zoom pull-down menu in the lower-right corner of the image preview area.

- **The Hand tool** helps move your photo around in the image window—just like grabbing it and moving it with your own hand. You can read more about the Hand tool on page 80.

- **The Magic Selection brush tool** lets you apply Quick Fix commands to select portions of your image. The regular Elements Selection brush is also available in Quick Fix. To get to the Selection brush, in the Toolbox, just click and hold on the Magic Selection brush icon, or click its icon in the Options bar when the Magic Selection brush is active. The difference between the two tools is that the Selection brush lets you paint a selection exactly where you want it (or mask out part of your photo to keep it from getting changed), while the Magic Selection brush makes Elements figure out the boundaries of your selection based on your much less precise marks on the image. The Magic Selection brush is much more automatic than the regular Selection brush.

To get the most out of both these tools, you need to understand the concept of selections. Chapter 5 tells you everything you need to know, including the details of using these brushes.

- **The Crop tool** lets you change the size and shape of your photo, by cutting off the areas you *don't* want (page 72).

- **The Red Eye tool** makes it a snap to fix those horrible red eyes in flash photos (page 95).

> **NOTE** If your photo needs straightening (page 67), you need to do that in Full Edit before bringing it into the Quick Fix window, since the Quick Fix Toolbox doesn't include the Straighten tool.

The Quick Fix Control Panel

The Control Panel, on the right side of the Quick Fix window, is where you make most of your adjustments. Elements helpfully arranges everything into four palettes—General Fixes, Lighting, Color, and Sharpen—listed in the order you'll typically use them. In most cases, it makes sense to start at the top and work your way down until you get the results you want. (See page 105 for more suggestions on what order to work in.)

The Control Panel always fills the right side of the Quick Fix screen. There's no way to hide it, and you can't drag the palettes out of the Control Panel as you can in Standard Edit mode. But you can expand and collapse them, as explained in Figure 4-2.

> **NOTE** If you go into Quick Fix mode *before* you open a photo, you won't see the pointers in the sliders, just empty tracks. Don't worry—they'll automatically appear as soon as you open a photo and give them something to work on.

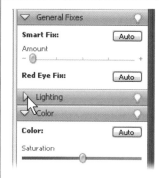

Figure 4-2:
Clicking any of these flippy triangles collapses or expands that section of the Control Panel. If you hardly ever use the tools in the Lighting section, for instance, you can collapse it so it scoots out of the way.

Different Views: After vs. Before and After

When you open an image in Quick Fix, your picture first appears by itself in the main window with the word "After" above it. Elements keeps the Before version—your original photo—tucked away, out of sight. But you can pick from three other different layouts, which you can choose at any time: Before Only, Before and After (Portrait), and Before and After (Landscape). The Before and After views are especially helpful when you're trying to figure out if you're improving your picture—or not—as shown in Figure 4-3. Switch between views by picking the one you want from the pop-up menu just below your image.

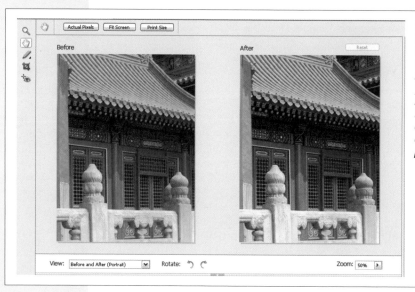

Figure 4-3:
The Before and After view in the Quick Fix window makes it easy to see how you're changing your photo. If you want a more detailed view, use the Zoom tool (the eyeglass icon) to focus on just a portion of your picture.

TIP   Quick Fix limits the amount of screen space available for your image. If you want a larger view while you work, click over to Standard Edit.

Editing Your Photos

The tools in the Quick Fix window are pretty simple to use. You can try one or all of them—it's up to you. And whenever you're happy with how your photo looks, you can leave Quick Fix and go back to the Full Edit window or the Organizer.

If you want to rotate your photo, you can do so here by clicking the appropriate Rotate button, below the image preview area. (See page 65 for more about rotating photos.)

> **NOTE**   If you click the Quick Fix Reset button, just above your image, you'll return your photo to the way it looked *before* you started working in Quick Fix. This button undoes *all* Quick Fix edits, so don't use it if you want to undo a single action only. For that, just use the regular undo command: Edit → Undo or Ctrl+Z.

Fixing Red Eye

Everyone who's ever taken a flash photo has run into the dreaded problem of *red eye*—those glowing, demonic pupils that make your little cherub look like someone out of an Anne Rice novel. Red eye is even more of a problem with digital cameras than with film, but luckily, Elements has a simple and terrific Red Eye tool for fixing it. All you need to do is click the red spots with the Red Eye tool, and your problems are solved.

To use the Quick Fix Red Eye tool:

1. **Open a photo.**

   The Red Eye tool works the same whether you get to it from the Quick Fix Toolbox or the main Toolbox in Full Edit.

2. **Zoom in so you can see where you're clicking.**

   Use the Zoom tool to magnify the eyes. You can also switch to the Hand tool if you need to drag the photo so that the eyes are front and center.

3. **Activate the Red Eye tool.**

   Click the Red Eye icon in the Toolbox or press Y.

4. **Click in the red part of the pupil with the Red Eye tool (see Figure 4-4).**

   That's it. Just one click should fix it. If a single click doesn't fix the problem, you can also try dragging over the pupil with the Red Eye tool. Sometimes one method works better than the other. You can also adjust two settings on the Red Eye tool: Darken Amount and Pupil Size, as explained later.

5. **Click in the other eye.**

   Repeat the process on the other eye, and you're done.

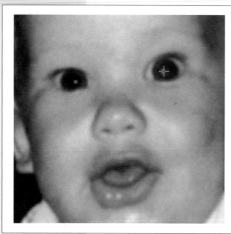

Figure 4-4:
Zoom in when using the Red Eye tool so you get a good look at the pupils. The eye on the left side of the picture has already been fixed. Don't worry if your photo looks so magnified that it loses definition— just make the red area large enough for a bulls-eye. Notice what a good job the Red Eye tool does of keeping the highlights (called catchlights) in the eye that's been treated.

POWER USERS' CLINIC

Another Red Eye Fix

The Red Eye tool does a great job most of the time, but it doesn't always work, and it doesn't work on animals' eyes. Elements gives you a couple of other ways to fix red eye that work in almost any situation. Here's one:

1. Zoom way, way in on the eye. You want to be able to see the individual pixels.

2. Use the Eyedropper tool (page 197) to sample the color from a good area of the eye, or from another photo. Confirm that you've got the color you want by checking the Foreground color picker (page 196).

3. Get out the Pencil tool (page 317) and set its size to 1 pixel.

4. Now click the bad or empty pixels of the eye to replace the color with the correct shade. Remember to leave a couple of white pixels for a catchlight.

This solution works even if the eye is *blown out* (that is, all white with no color information left).

If you're a layers fan, you can also fix Red Eye by selecting the bad area, creating a Hue/Saturation adjustment layer (page 166), and desaturating the red area, but this method doesn't work so well if the eye is blown out.

TIP You can also apply the Organizer's Auto Red Eye Fix in either the Quick Fix or Full Edit window. In the Quick Fix window, look for the Auto button in the Red Eye area of the Control Panel. In either Quick Fix or Full Edit, you can also activate the Red Eye tool and click the Auto button in the Options bar. The only tradeoff to using the Auto Red Eye Fix in the Full Edit window is you don't automatically get a version set (as you do when using the tool from within the Organizer). But you can create a version set when you save your changes, as explained on page 54.

If you need to adjust how the Red Eye tool works, the Options bar gives you two controls, although 99 percent of the time you can ignore them:

- **Darken Amount.** If the result is too light, increase the percentage in this box.

- **Pupil Size.** Increase or decrease the number here to tell Elements how much area to consider part of a pupil.

Smart Fix

The secret weapon in the Quick Fix window is the Smart Fix command, which automatically adjusts a picture's lighting, color, and contrast, all with one click. You don't have to figure anything out. Elements does it all for you.

You'll find the Smart Fix in the General Fixes palette, and it's about as easy to use as hitting the speed dial button on your phone: Click the Auto Smart Fix button, and if the stars are aligned, your picture will immediately look better. (Figure 4-5 gives you a glimpse of its capabilities. If you want to see for yourself how this fix works, download this photo—finch.jpg—from the "Missing CD" page at *www. missingmanuals.com.*)

> **TIP**   You'll find Auto buttons scattered throughout Elements. Elements uses them to make a best-guess attempt to implement whatever change the Auto button is next to (Smart Fix, Levels, Contrast, and so on). It never hurts to at least try clicking these Auto buttons; if you don't like what you see, you can always perform the magical undo: Edit → Undo or Ctrl+Z.

If you're happy with the Auto Smart Fix button's changes, you can move onto a new photo, or try sharpening your photo a little (see page 201) if the focus appears a little fuzzy. You don't need to do anything to accept the Smart Fix changes. But if you're not ecstatic with your results, take a good look at your picture. If you like what Auto Smart Fix has done, but the effect is too strong or too weak, press Ctrl+Z to undo it, and try playing with the Smart Fix Amount slider instead.

The Amount slider does the same thing the Auto Smart Fix does, only you control the degree of change. Watch the image as you move the slider to the right. If your computer is slow, there's a certain amount of lag time, so go slowly to give it a chance to catch up. If you happen to overdo it, sometimes it's easier to press the Reset button above your image and start again. Use the checkmark and the cancel button (which appear next to the General Fixes label, as shown in Figure 4-6) to accept or reject your changes.

> **TIP**   Usually you get better results with a lot of little nudges to the Smart Fix slider than with one big sweeping movement.

Incidentally, these are the same Smart Fix commands you see in two places in the Editor's Enhance Menu: Enhance → Auto Smart Fix (Ctrl+M), and Enhance → Adjust Smart Fix (Ctrl+Shift+M).

Sometimes Smart Fix just isn't smart enough to do everything you want, and sometimes it does things you *don't* want. The Smart Fix is better with photos that are underexposed than overexposed, for one thing. Fortunately, you still have several other editing choices, covered in the following sections. If you don't like the effect Smart Fix has had, undo it before going on to make other changes.

TIP   You can also apply the Smart Fix command from within the Organizer, so there's no need to launch the Editor at all if you just want this tool. Just click your photo and press Ctrl+Alt+M, or right-click your picture and choose Auto Smart Fix from the pop-up menu. You can also get to the Auto Smart Fix command via the Organizer's Edit menu.

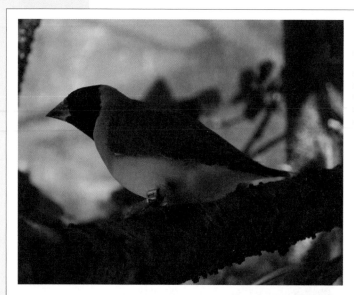

Figure 4-5:
Top: This photo is so dark you may think it's beyond help.

Bottom: The Auto Smart Fix button improved it significantly with just one click. (A click of the Auto Sharpening button, explained on page 104, was added to make it look really spiffy.)

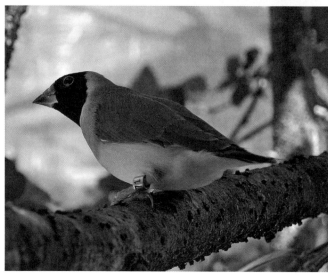

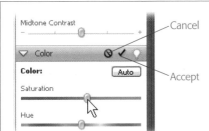

Figure 4-6:
When you move a slider in any of the Quick Fix palettes, the Cancel and Accept buttons appear in the palette you're using. Clicking the cancel symbol undoes the last change you made, while clicking the accept symbol applies the change to your image. If you make multiple slider adjustments, the cancel symbol undoes everything you've done since you clicked Accept.

Cancel

Accept

Adjusting Lighting and Contrast

The Lighting palette lets you make very sophisticated adjustments to the brightness and contrast of your photo. Sometimes problems that you thought stemmed from exposure or even focus may right themselves with these commands.

Levels

If you want to understand how Levels really works, you're in for a long technical ride. On the other hand, if you just want to know what it can do for your photos, the short answer is that it adjusts the brightness of your photo by redistributing the color information; Levels changes (and hopefully fixes!) both brightness and color at the same time.

If you've never used any photo-editing software before, this may sound rather mysterious, but photo-editing pros will tell you that Levels is one of the most powerful commands for fixing and polishing your pictures. To find out if its magic works for you, click the Auto Levels button. Figure 4-7 shows what a big difference it can make. Download this photo (squirrel.jpg) from the "Missing CD" page at *www.missingmanuals.com*, if you'd like to try this out yourself.

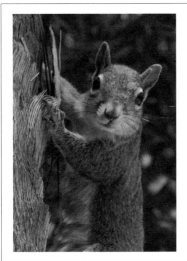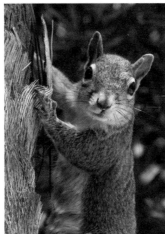

Figure 4-7:
A quick click of the Auto Levels button can make a very dramatic difference.

Left: The original photo of the squirrel isn't bad, and you may not realize how much better the colors could be.

Right: This image shows how much more effective your photo is once Auto Levels has balanced the colors.

What Levels does is very complex. Chapter 7 contains loads more details about what's going on behind the scenes and how you can apply this command much more precisely.

Calibrating Your Monitor

Why do my photos look awful when I open them in Elements?

Do you find that when you open your photos in Elements they look really terrible, even though they look decent in other programs? Maybe your photos are all washed-out looking, or reddish or greenish, or even black and white?

If that's the case, you need to calibrate your monitor, as explained on page 180. It's easy to do and it makes a big difference.

Elements is what's known as a *color-managed* application. You can read all about color management on page 178.

For now, you just need to understand that color-managed programs pay much more attention to the settings for your monitor than regular programs like word processors.

Color-managed programs like Elements are a little more trouble to set up initially, but the advantage is that you can get truly wonderful results if you invest a little time and effort when you're getting started. Also, if you don't calibrate your monitor, Elements can show its displeasure in odd ways that don't seem to have anything to do directly with color.

Contrast

The main alternative to Auto Levels in Quick Fix is Auto Contrast. Most people find that their images tend to benefit from one or the other of these options. Contrast adjusts the relative darkness and lightness of your image without changing the color, so if Levels made your colors go all goofy, try adjusting the contrast instead. You activate Contrast the same way you do the Levels tool: just click the Auto button next to its name.

> **NOTE** After you use Auto Contrast, look closely at the edges of the objects in your photo. If your camera's contrast was already high, you may see a halo or a sharp line around the photo's subject. If you see that line or halo, the contrast is too high and you need to undo Auto Contrast (Ctrl+Z) and try another fix instead.

Shadows and Highlights

The Shadows and Highlights tools do an amazing job of bringing out the details that are lost in the shadows or bright areas of your photo. Figure 4-8 shows what a difference these tools can make.

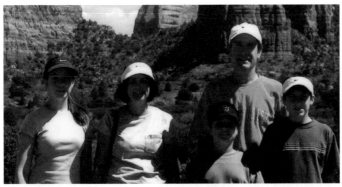

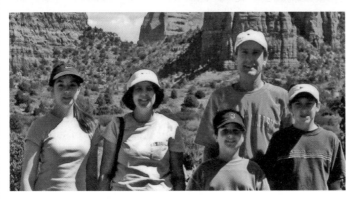

Figure 4-8:

Top: This photo shows a classic vacation picture problem: the day is bright, the scenery's beautiful, but everyone's faces are hidden in the dark shadows cast by their hats.

Bottom: The Shadows and Highlights tools brought back everyone's faces, but now they look a bit jaundiced. Use the color sliders to make them look healthy again.

The Shadows and Highlights tools are a collection of three sliders, each of which controls a different aspect of your image:

- **Lighten Shadows.** Nudge the slider to the right and you'll see details emerge from murky black shadows.

- **Darken Highlights.** Use this slider to dim the brightness of overexposed areas.

- **Midtone Contrast.** After you've adjusted your photo's shadows and highlights, your photo may look very flat and not have enough contrast between the dark and light areas. This slider helps you bring a more realistic look back to your photo.

> **TIP** You may think you only need to lighten shadows in a photo, but sometimes just a smidgen of Darken Highlights may help, too. Don't be afraid to experiment by using this slider even if you've got a relatively dark photo.

Go easy. Getting overenthusiastic with these sliders can give your photos a very washed-out, flat look.

Color

The Color palette lets you—surprise, surprise—play around with the colors in your image. In many cases, if you've been successful with Auto Levels or Auto Contrast, you won't need to do anything here.

Auto Color

Once again, there's another one-click fix available: Auto Color. Actually, in some ways Auto Color should be up in the Lighting section. Like Levels, it simultaneously adjusts color and brightness, but it looks at different information in your photos to decide what to do with them.

When you're first learning to use Quick Fix, you may want to try all three—Levels, Contrast, and Auto Color—to see which generally works best for your photos. Undo between each change and compare your results. Most people find they like one of the three most of the time.

Auto Color may be just the ticket for your photos, but you may also find that it shifts your colors in strange ways. Give it a click and see what you think. Does your photo look better or worse? If it's worse, just click Reset or Ctrl+Z to undo it, and go back to Auto Levels or Auto Contrast. If they all make your colors look a little wrong, or if you want to tweak the colors in your photo, move on to the Color sliders, explained in the next section.

Using the Color sliders

If you want to adjust the colors in your photo without changing the brightness, check out the Color sliders. For example, your digital camera may produce colors that don't quite match what you saw when you took the picture; or you may have scanned an old print that's faded or discolored; or you may just want to change the colors in a photo for the heck of it. If so, the sliders below the Auto Color button are for you.

You get four ways to adjust your colors here:

- **Saturation** controls the intensity of your photo's color. For example, you can turn a color photo to black and white by moving the slider all the way to the left. Move it too far to the right and everything glows with so much color that it looks radioactive.

- **Hue** changes the color from, say, red to blue or green. If you aren't looking for realism, you can have some fun with your photos by really pushing this slider to create funky color changes.

- **Temperature** lets you adjust color from cool (bluish) on the left to warm (orange-ish) on the right. Use Temperature for things like toning down the warm glow you see in photos taken in tungsten lighting, or just for fine-tuning your color balance.

• **Tint** adjusts the green/magenta balance of your photo, as shown in Figure 4-9.

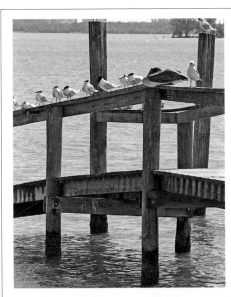

Figure 4-9:
Top: The greenish tint in this photo is a drastic example of a very common problem caused by many digital cameras.

Bottom: A little adjustment of the Tint slider clears it up in a jiffy. It's not always as obvious as it is here that you need a tint adjustment. If you aren't sure, the sky is often a dead giveaway. Is it robin's egg blue? If the photo's sky is that color and the real sky was just plain blue, tint is what you need.

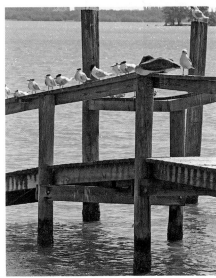

You probably won't use all these sliders on a single photo, but you can use as many of them as you like. Remember to click the checkmark that appears in the Color palette if you want to accept your changes. Chapter 7 has much more information about how to use the full-blown Editor to really fine-tune your image's color.

Sharpening

Now that you've finished your other corrections, it's time to *sharpen*, or improve the focus, of your photo. Most digital camera photos need some sharpening because the sharpening your camera applies is usually deliberately conservative. Once again, a Quick Fix Auto button is at your service. Give the Auto Sharpen button a try to get things started (see Figure 4-10).

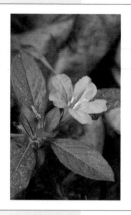 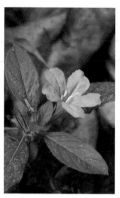 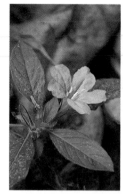

Figure 4-10:
Left: The original image. Like most digital photos, it could stand a little sharpening.

Middle: What you get with Auto Sharpen.

Right: The results of using the Sharpen slider to achieve stronger sharpening than Auto was initially willing to perform.

You should understand, though, that the sad truth is that there really isn't any way to actually improve the focus of a photo once it's taken. Software sharpening just increases the contrast where the program perceives edges, so using it first can have strange effects on other editing tools and their ability to understand your photo.

If you don't like what Auto Sharpening does (you very well may not), you can undo it (click the Cancel button on the Sharpen palette) and try the slider. If you thought the Auto button overdid things, go very gently with the slider. Changes vary from photo to photo, but usually Auto's results fall at around the 30 to 40 percent mark on the slider.

NOTE If you see funny halos around the outlines of objects in your photos, or strange flaky spots (making your photo look like it has eczema), those are artifacts from too much sharpening.

Always try to view Actual Pixels (View → Actual Pixels) when sharpening because that gives you the clearest idea of what you're actually doing to your picture. If you don't like what the button does, undo it, and then try the slider. Zero sharpening is all the way to the left. Moving to the right increases the amount of sharpening applied to your photo.

As a general rule, you want to sharpen more for photos you plan to print than for images for Web use. You can read lots more about sharpening on page 201.

> **NOTE** If you've used photo-editing programs before, you may be interested to know that the Auto Sharpen button applies the Unsharp Mask filter to your photo. The difference is, you don't have any control over the settings, as you would if you applied the mask from the Filters menu. But the good news is that if you want it, you can get this control—even from within Quick Fix. Just go to the Enhance Menu and choose Unsharp Mask, or, for even more control, check out the new Adjust Sharpness command just below it.

At this point, all that's left is cropping your photo, if you'd like to reduce its size. Page 71 tells you everything you need to know about cropping.

Quick Fix Suggested Workflow

There are no hard and fast rules for what order you need to work in when using the Quick Fix tools. As mentioned earlier, Elements lays out the tools in the Control Panel, from top to bottom, in the order that usually makes sense. But you can pick and choose which tools you want, depending on what you think your photo needs. But if you're the type of person who likes a set plan for fixing photos, here's one order in which to apply the commands:

1. **Rotate your photo (if needed).**

   Use the buttons below the image preview.

2. **Fix red eye (if needed).**

   See page 95.

3. **Crop.**

   If you know you want to crop your photo, now's the time. That way, you get rid of any problem areas before they affect other adjustments. For example, say your photo has a lot of overexposed sky that you want to crop out. If you leave it in, that area will skew the effects of the Lighting and Color tools on your image. So if you already know where you want to crop, do it before making other adjustments for more accurate results.

4. **Try Auto Smart Fix and/or the Smart Fix slider. Undo if necessary.**

   Pretty soon you'll get a good idea of how likely it is that this fix will do a good job on your photos. Some people love it; others think it makes their pictures too grainy.

5. **If Smart Fix wasn't smart enough, work your way down through the other Lighting and Color commands until you like the way your photo looks.**

   Read the sections earlier in this chapter to understand what each command does to your photo.

6. **Sharpen.**

Try to perform sharpening as your last adjustment because other commands can give you funky results on photos that have already been sharpened.

TIP When you're in Quick Fix mode, you can switch back to Full Edit at any point if you want tools or filters not available in Quick Fix.

Adjusting Skin Tones

If you're like most amateur photographers, your most important photos are pictures of people: your family, your friends, or even just fascinating strangers. Elements gives you yet another tool for making fast fixes—one that's designed especially for correcting photos that have people in them. This is the "Adjust Color for Skin Tone" command, available in both the Quick Fix and Full Edit windows.

The name "Adjust Color for Skin Tone" may be a bit confusing. What this command actually does is adjust your *entire* image based on the skin tone of someone in the photo. The idea behind "Adjust Color for Skin Tone" is that you may well be much more interested in the way the people in your photos look than in how the background looks. This command gives the highest priority to creating good skin color. It's an automatic fix, but there's a dialog box where you can tweak the results once you've previewed Elements' suggested adjustments. To use the "Adjust Color for Skin Tone" command:

1. **Call up the "Adjust Color for Skin Tone" dialog box.**

In either the Quick Fix or Full Edit, go to Enhance → Adjust Color → Adjust Color for Skin Tone. The dialog box shown in Figure 4-11 appears. You may need to move it out of the way of your photo so you can see what's happening.

2. **Show Elements an area of skin to sample for calculating the color adjustments.**

Once the dialog box appears, your cursor turns to an eyedropper. Just find a portion of your photo where your subject's skin has relatively good color, and click it.

3. **Tweak the results.**

Most of the time, Elements is a bit overenthusiastic in its adjustments. Use the sliders in the dialog box to get a more pleasing, realistic color. The Ambient Light slider works just like the Temperature slider in the Quick Fix control panel (page 102). Blush increases the rosiness of the skin as you move the slider to the right and decreases it to the left. Tan increases or decreases the browns and oranges in the skin tones. You may get swell results with your first click, or you may have to use all the sliders to get a truly realistic result. It all depends on the photo.

NOTE The "Adjust Color for Skin Tone" sliders are like the Quick Fix sliders in that you can get an idea of which way to move them by looking at the colors in the slider tracks in the dialog box.

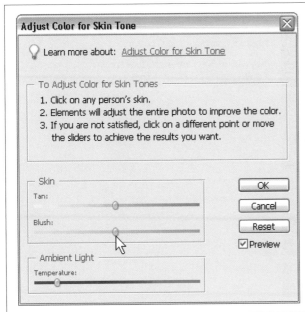

Adjust Color for Skin Tone

Learn more about: Adjust Color for Skin Tone

To Adjust Color for Skin Tones

1. Click on any person's skin.
2. Elements will adjust the entire photo to improve the color.
3. If you are not satisfied, click on a different point or move the sliders to achieve the results you want.

Skin

Tan:

Blush:

Ambient Light

Temperature:

OK

Cancel

Reset

☑ Preview

Figure 4-11:
When this dialog box appears, your cursor turns to a little eyedropper when you move it over your photo. Just click the best-looking area of skin you can find. After Elements adjusts the photo based on your click, you can use the sliders to fine-tune the results. Clicking different spots gives different results, so you may want to experiment by clicking different places.

You can preview the changes right in your photo as you work. If you mess up and want to start again, click Reset. If you decide you'd rather be using another tool instead, click Cancel.

4. **When you like what you see, click OK.**

Elements applies your changes. If you want to undo them, press Ctrl+Z.

"Adjust Color for Skin Tone" seems to work best on fair skin, and not so well on darker skin tones. And it's most suited for making fairly subtle adjustments, so you may have to reduce the amount of change from what Elements first did.

Also, notice that not only the skin tones are changing. Elements is adjusting *all* the colors in the photo in sync with the skin tones (Figure 4-12). Sometimes you may find you've acquired quite a color cast (see page 191) by the time you've got the skin just right. If this bothers you, try a different tool. On the other hand, you can create some very nice late afternoon light effects with this command. (In Elements 5, this tool is much more likely to give you a pleasing result on the first try than in Elements 4.)

While "Adjust Color for Skin Tone" is really meant as a kind of alternative fast fix, you may find it's most useful for making small final adjustments to photos you've already edited using other tools.

> **NOTE**   If you understand layers (explained in Chapter 6), you may want to make a duplicate layer and apply this command to your duplicate. Then you can adjust the intensity of the result by adjusting the layer's opacity (see page 151).

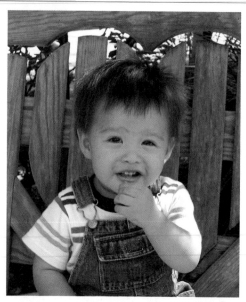

Figure 4-12:

Left: This photo shows a slight greenish cast, giving the little boy a somewhat unappealing skin tone.

Right: Adjust Skin Tone is able to warm up his skin tones, and it even removes the greenish tinge to the wood of the bench he's sitting on.

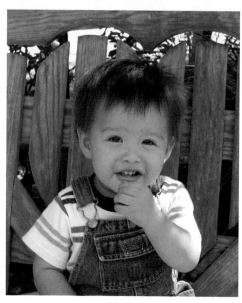

Part Two: Elemental Elements

2

Making Selections

One of Elements' most impressive talents is its ability to let you *select* part of your image and make changes only to that area. Selecting something tells Elements, "Hey, *this* is what I want to work on. Just let me work on this part of my picture and don't touch the rest of it." You can select your entire image or any part of it.

By using selections, you can fine-tune your images in very sophisticated ways. You could change the color of just one rose in a whole bouquet, for instance, or change your nephew's festive purple hair color back to something his grandparents would appreciate. Graphics pros will tell you that good selections make the difference between shoddy amateurish work and a slick professional job.

> **NOTE** The big secret to selecting is to take your time and be accurate. It's tempting to make your selections too quickly when you're first trying your hand at this, but you'll get better results if you don't rush. On the other hand, if you don't need your selections to be particularly precise, try out the Magic Selection brush (page 123).

Elements offers you a whole bunch of different selection tools to work with. You can draw a rectangular or a circular selection with the Marquee tools, for instance, or paint a selection on your photo with the Selection brush. When you're looking to pluck a particular object (a beautiful flower, for instance) from a photo, the Magic Extractor works wonders. For most jobs, there's no right or wrong tool; with experience you may find you tend to prefer working with certain tools more than others. Often you'll use more than one tool to create a perfect selection. Once you've read this chapter you'll understand all the different selection tools and how to use each one.

TIP   It's much easier to select an object that's been photographed against a plain background. So, if you know you're going to want to select a bicycle, for example, shoot it in front of a blank wall rather than, say, a hedge.

Making Quick Selections

Sometimes the only thing you want to do is select your entire photo. For instance, if you want to copy and paste your whole photo, you need to select all of it. Elements gives you some useful commands to help you make basic selections in a snap:

- **Select All** (Select → All or Ctrl+A) tells Elements to select your entire image. You'll see the "marching ants" (shown around the outline of the bell in Figure 5-1) around the outer edge of your entire picture.

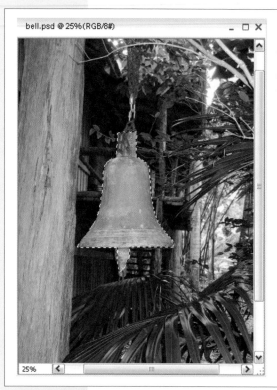

bell.psd @ 25%(RGB/8#)

25%

Figure 5-1:
The popular name for these dotted lines is "marching ants" because they march around your selections to show you where the edges lie. When you see the ants, your selection is active, meaning what you do next happens only to the selected area.

If you want to copy your image into another picture or program, performing a Select All is the fastest way to select the entire image. If your photo contains layers, which you'll learn about in Chapter 6, you may not be able to get everything you want with the Select All shortcut. In that case, the section about merging layers on page 162 explains what to do.

NOTE   If you're planning on copying an image to another program, like Microsoft Word or PowerPoint, make sure you've got Export Clipboard turned on in Edit → Preferences → General.

- **Deselect Everything** (Select → Deselect, Escape, or Ctrl+D) removes any current selection. Remember the keystroke combination because it's one you'll probably use over and over again in Elements.

- **Reselect** (Select → Reselect or Shift+Ctrl+D) tells Elements to reactivate the selection you just canceled. Use Reselect if you realize you still need a selection you just got rid of. Or you can just press Ctrl+Z to back up a step.

- **Hide a Selection** (Ctrl+H) keeps your selection active while hiding its outline. Sometimes the marching ants around a selection make it hard to see what you're doing, or they can be distracting. To see the ants again, press Ctrl+H a second time.

TIP   It's easy to forget you have a selection sometimes. When a tool acts goofy or won't do anything, start your troubleshooting by pressing Ctrl+H to be sure you don't have a hidden selection you forgot about.

Selecting Rectangular and Elliptical Areas

Selecting your whole picture is all well and good, but many times your reason for making a selection is precisely because you *don't* want to make changes to the whole image. How do you select just part of the picture?

Well, the easiest way is to use the Marquee tools. You already met the Rectangular Marquee tool back in Chapter 3, in the section on cropping (page 71). If you want to select a block of your image or a circle or an oval from it, the Marquee tools are the way to go. As the winners of "Most frequently used Selection tools," they get top spot in the Selection area of the Editor's Toolbox. You can modify how they work, like telling them to create a square instead of a rectangle, as explained in Figure 5-2.

To use the Marquee tools to make a selection:

1. **Press M or click the Marquee tool's icon in the Toolbox to activate it.**

   The Marquee tool is the little dotted square right below the Eyedropper icon. (Or it may appear as a little dotted oval, if you used the Elliptical Marquee tool last.)

2. **Choose the Shape you want to draw: rectangle or ellipse.**

   In the Options bar or in the Toolbox pop-out menu for the Marquee tools, choose the rectangle or the ellipse to set the shape.

3. **Choose a feather value if you want one.**

Feathering makes the edges of your selection softer or fuzzier for better blending. See the box on page 117 for a look at how feathering (and anti-aliasing) work.

4. **Drag in your image to make your selection.**

Wherever you initially place your mouse becomes one of the corners of your rectangular selection or a point just beyond the outer edge of your ellipse (unless you're using the "draw from center" option explained in Figure 5-2). The selection outline expands as you drag your mouse.

If you make a mistake, just press the Escape key. You can also press either Ctrl+D to get rid of all current selections, or Ctrl+Z to remove the most recent selection.

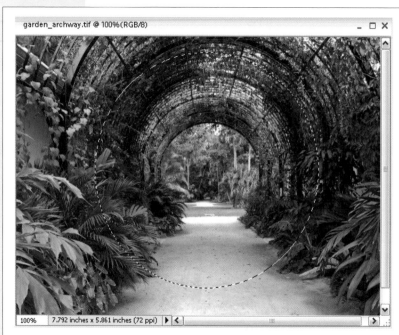

Figure 5-2:
The Marquee tools usually make oval or rectangular selections. To make a perfectly circular or square selection, hold down the Shift key while you drag. (If you're in the Elliptical marquee, it's a perfect circle; in the Rectangular marquee, it's a perfect square.) To draw your selection from the center, hold down Alt. It's easier to do it that way when you know the central point you want to include but aren't sure how much of the surrounding area you want.

The mode choices in the Options bar give you three ways to control the size of your selection: Normal lets you manually control the size of your selection; Fixed Aspect Ratio lets you enter proportions in the Width and Height boxes; and Fixed Size lets you enter specific dimensions in these boxes. The Anti-alias checkbox is explained in the box on page 117. Once you've made your selection, you can move the selected area around in the photo by dragging it (see page 76), or you can use the arrow keys to nudge your selection in the direction you want to move it. Changing the size of a Marquee selection once you've made it is pretty tricky, and it's far easier to just start over again, but you can add to or subtract from any selection you make in Elements. Page 116 tells you how.

Paste vs. Paste Into

Newcomers to Elements are often confused by the fact that there are two Paste commands in Elements: Paste and Paste Into Selection. Knowing what each one does will help you avoid problems.

- **Paste.** 99 percent of the time, Paste is the one you want. This command simply places your copied object wherever you paste it. Once you've pasted your object, you can move whatever you've pasted by moving the selected area.

- **Paste Into Selection.** This is a special command for pasting a selection into *another* selection. Your pasted object appears only *within* the bounds of the selection you're pasting into.

When you use Paste Into Selection, what you paste can still be moved around, but it won't be visible anywhere outside the edges of the selection you're pasting into. The Paste Into Selection is very handy if you want to do something like putting a beautiful mountain view outside your window. Select the window, copy the mountain (Ctrl+C), and then use Paste Into Selection to add the view. You can maneuver the mountain photo around till it's properly centered. And if you move it outside the boundary of your window selection, it just disappears.

Selecting Irregularly Sized Areas

It would be nice if you could always get away with making simple rectangular or elliptical selections, but is life really ever that neat? You aren't always going to want to select a block-shaped chunk of your image. If you want to change the color of one fish in your aquarium picture, selecting a rectangle or square isn't going to cut it.

Thankfully, Elements gives you other tools that make it easy for you to make very precise selections—no matter their size or shape. In this section, you'll learn how to use the rest of the Selection tools. But first you need to understand the basic controls that they (almost) all share.

Controlling the Selection Tools

If you're the kind of person who never makes a mistake and you also never change your mind, you can skip this section. If, on the other hand, you're human, you need to know about the mysterious little squares you see in the Options bar when the Selection tools are active (Figure 5-3).

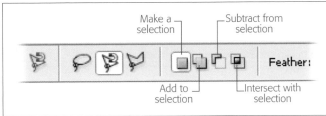

Make a selection
Subtract from selection
Add to selection
Intersect with selection
Feather:

Figure 5-3:
These cryptic squares can save you hours of time once you understand how to use them to tell the Selection tools how to behave.

These selection squares don't look like much, but they tell the Selection tools how to do their job: whether to start a new selection with each click, to add to what you've already got, or to remove things from your selection. They're available for all the Selection tools except the Selection brush and the Magic Selection brush, which have their own sets of options. From left to right, here's what they do:

- **Select** is the standard selection mode that you'll probably use most of the time. When you click this button to start a new selection, your previous selection disappears.

- **Add to Selection** tells Elements to add what you select next to what you've already selected. Unless you have an incredibly steady mouse hand, this option is a godsend because it's not easy to get a perfect selection on the first try. (Holding down the Shift key while you use any Selection tool also lets you add to a selection.)

- **Subtract from Selection** removes what you select next from any existing selection. (By holding down Alt while selecting the area you want to remove, you can accomplish the same thing.)

- **Intersect with Selection** is a bit confusing. It lets you take a selected area, make a new selection, and wind up with only the areas where both overlap selected, as shown in Figure 5-4. (The keyboard equivalent is Alt+Shift.)

Figure 5-4:
"Intersect with Selection" lets you take two separate selections and select only the area where they intersect. If you have an existing selection, when you select again your new selection includes only the overlapping area. Here, the top blue rectangle is the first selection, and the bottom purple square is the second. The light area shows the final selection after you let go of the mouse button.

The Magic Wand

The Magic Wand is a slightly temperamental—and occasionally highly effective—tool for selecting an irregularly shaped, but similarly colored, area of an image. If you have a big area of a particular color, the Magic Wand can find its edges in one click. It's not actually all that magical: all it does is search for pixels with similar color values. But if it works for you, you may decide it should keep the "magic" in its name because it's a great timesaver when it cooperates, as Figure 5-6 shows.

UP TO SPEED

Feathering and Anti-Aliasing

If you're old enough to remember what supermarket tabloid covers looked like before there was Photoshop, you probably had many a laugh at the obviously faked photos. Anyone could see where the art department had physically glued a piece cut from one photo onto another picture.

Nowadays, of course, the pictures of Elvis's and Cher's vampire baby from Mars are *much* more believable looking. That's because with Photoshop (and Elements) you can add *anti-aliasing* and *feathering* whenever you're making selections.

Anti-aliasing is a way of smoothing the edges of a digital image so that it's not jagged-looking. When you make selections, the Lasso tools and the Magic Wand let you decide whether to use anti-aliasing. It's best to leave anti-aliasing on unless you have a reason to want a really hard-looking edge on your selection.

Feathering blurs the edges of a selection. When you make a selection that you plan to move to a different photo, a tiny feather can do a lot to make it look like it's always been part of the new photo. The selection tools let you set a feather value before you use them, except for the Selection brush. Generally a 1- or 2-pixel feather gives your selection a more natural-looking edge without visible blurring.

If you apply a feather value that's too high for the size of your selection, you see a warning that reads "No pixels are more than 50% selected." Reduce the feather number to placate it.

A larger feather gives a soft edge to your photos, as you can see in Figure 5-5.

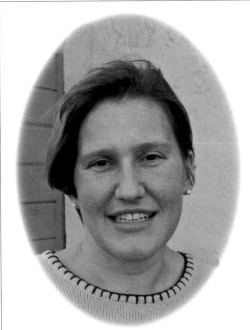

Figure 5-5:
Old-fashioned vignettes like this one are a classic example of where you'd want a fairly large feather. In this figure, the feather is 15 pixels wide. The higher the feather value, the softer the edge effect is.

Using the Magic Wand is pretty straightforward. You just click anywhere in the area you want to select. Depending on your *tolerance* setting (explained in the following bullet list), you may nail the selection at once, or it may take several clicks to get everything. If you need to click more than once, remember to hold down Shift so that each click adds to your selection.

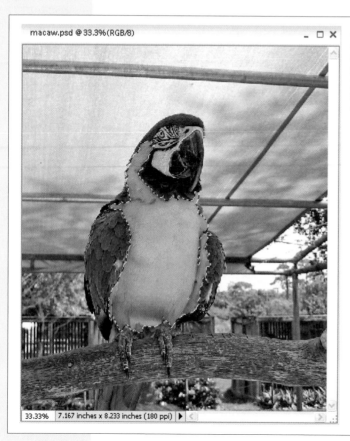

macaw.psd @ 33.3% (RGB/8)

33.33%   7.167 inches x 8.233 inches (180 ppi)

Figure 5-6:
Just one click with the Magic Wand created this selection. If there isn't a big difference between the color of the area you want to select and the colors of neighboring areas, the Wand isn't as effective as it is here.

The Magic Wand does its best job when you offer it a good solid block of color that's clearly defined and doesn't have a lot of different shades in it. But it's frustrating when you try to select colors that have any shading or tonal gradations. You have to click and click and click. Elements gives you two special Options bar settings that you can adjust to help the Wand do a better job:

- **Tolerance** adjusts the number of different shades that the tool selects at once. A higher tolerance includes more shades (resulting in a larger selection area), while a lower tolerance gets you fewer shades (and a more precise selection area). If you set the tolerance too high, you'll probably select a lot more of your picture than you want.

- **Contiguous** makes the Magic Wand select only color areas that actually touch each other (see Figure 5-7). It's on by default, but sometimes you can save a lot of time by turning it off.

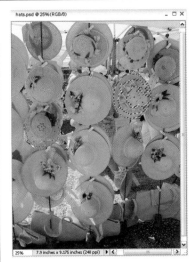 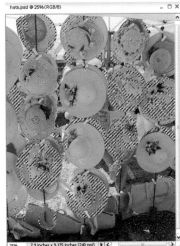

Figure 5-7:
In the left photo, the Contiguous checkbox has been turned on. By turning it off, as in the photo at right, you can select all the orange hats with just one click. If you want to quickly clean up the selection afterward, use the Selection brush (which is covered on page 125).

The big disadvantage to the Magic Wand is that it tends to leave you with unselected contrasting areas around the edge of your selection that are a bit of a pain to clean up. You may want to try out the Magic Selection brush (page 123) before trying the Magic Wand, especially if you want to select a range of colors. If you put a Magic Wand selection on its own layer (see Chapter 6 to understand how layers work), you can use the Defringe command (page 132) to help clean up the edges.

The Lasso Tools

The Magic Wand is great, but it works well only when your image has clearly defined areas of color. A lot of the time, you'll want to select something from a cluttered background that the Magic Wand just can't cope with. Sometimes you may think the easiest way would be if you could just draw around the object you want to select.

Enter the Lasso tool. There are actually three Lasso tools: the Lasso tool, the Polygonal Lasso tool, and the Magnetic Lasso tool. Each tool lets you select an object by tracing around it.

You activate the Lasso tools by clicking their icon in the Toolbox (it's just below the Marquee tool) or by pressing L, and then selecting the particular variation you want in the Options bar or the Toolbox pop-out menu. You then drag around the outline of your object to make your selection. The following sections cover each Lasso tool.

The basic Lasso tool

The theory behind the basic Lasso tool is very simple. Click the tool, and your cursor changes to the lasso shape shown in Figure 5-8. Just click in your photo, and then drag around the outline of what you want to select. When the end of your selection gets back around to join up with the beginning, you've got a selection.

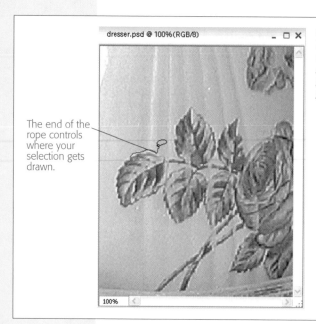

The end of the rope controls where your selection gets drawn.

Figure 5-8:
The end of the rope, and not the lasso loop, is the working part of the basic Lasso tool. If the cursor's shape bothers you, you can change it to crosshairs by pressing the Caps Lock key anytime as you select.

In practice, it's not always so easy to make an accurate selection with the Lasso, especially if you're using a mouse. A graphics tablet is a big advantage when using this tool, since tablets let you draw with a pen-shaped pointer. (There's more about graphics tablets on page 473.) But even if you don't happen to have a graphics tablet lying around, you can make all the tools work just fine with your mouse once you get used to their quirks.

It helps to zoom the view way in and to go very slowly when using the Lasso. (See page 77 for more information on changing your view.) Many people use the regular Lasso tool to quickly select an area that roughly surrounds their object, and then go back with the other selection tools, like the Selection brush or the Magnetic Lasso, to clean things up.

> **TIP** If you want to draw a straight line for part of your border, hold down Alt and click the points where you want your straight line to start and end.

If you want to get out of the Lasso tool before finishing your selection, press Escape. Once you have a selection, press Escape or Ctrl+D to get rid of it.

The Magnetic Lasso

The Magnetic Lasso is a very handy tool, especially if you were the kind of kid who never could color inside the lines or cut paper chains out neatly. The Magnetic Lasso snaps to the outline of any clearly defined object you're trying to select, so you don't have to follow the edge exactly.

As you might guess, the Magnetic Lasso does its best work on objects with clearly defined edges. You won't get much out of it if your subject is a furry animal, for instance. The Magnetic Lasso also likes a good strong contrast between the object and the background. (You can change the cursor shape with the Caps Lock key, just as with the regular Lasso.)

Click to start a selection. Then move your cursor around the perimeter of what you want to select; click again back where you began to finish your selection. You can also Ctrl+click at any point, and the Magnetic Lasso will immediately close up whatever area you've surrounded. You can also adjust how many points the Magnetic Lasso puts down and how sensitive it is to the edge you're tracing, as shown in Figure 5-9.

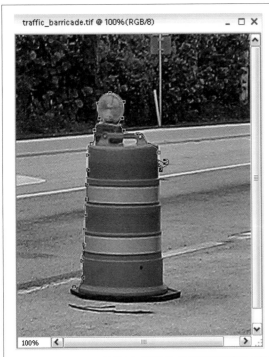

traffic_barricade.tif @ 100%(RGB/8)

100%

Figure 5-9:
One nice thing about the Magnetic Lasso is that it's easy to back up as you're creating your selection. As you go, it lays down the tiny boxes shown in this figure, which are called anchor or fastening points. If you make a mistake with the Magnetic Lasso, pressing Backspace takes you back one point each time you press the key. (If you want to completely get rid of a Magnetic Lasso selection you've begun but not completed, just press Escape.) If the Magnetic Lasso skips a spot or won't grab on to a spot where you want it to, you can force it to put down an anchor point by clicking once where you want the anchor to appear.

The Magnetic Lasso comes with four additional settings in the Options bar:

- **Width** tells the Magnetic Lasso how far away to look when it's trying to find the edge. The value is always in pixels, and you can set it as high as 256.

- **Edge Contrast** controls how sharp a difference the Magnetic Lasso should look for between the outline and the background. A higher number looks for sharper contrasts, and a lower number looks for softer ones.

- **Frequency** controls how fast Elements puts down the fastener points you see in Figure 5-9.

- **Use Tablet Pressure to Change Pen Width**—the little button with a pen at the right of the Options bar—only works if you have a graphics tablet. When you turn this setting on, how hard you press controls how Elements searches for the edge of objects you're trying to select. When you bear down harder, it's more precise. When you press more lightly, you can be a bit sloppier and Elements will still find the edge.

Many people live full and satisfying lives paying no attention whatsoever to these settings, so don't feel like you need to be fussing with them all the time. You can usually ignore them unless the Magnetic Lasso misbehaves.

> **TIP** You get better results with the Magnetic Lasso if you go more slowly than if you speed around the object. Like most people, the Magnetic Lasso does better work if you give it time to be sure of where it's going.

The Polygonal Lasso

At first, this may seem like a totally stupid tool. It works like the Magnetic Lasso, but it creates only perfectly straight segments. So you may think, "Well that's great if I want to select a Stop sign, but otherwise, what's the point?"

Actually, if you're one of those people who just plain *can't* draw, and you even have a hard time following the edge of an object that's already on the screen, this is the tool for you. The trick is to use very short distances between clicks. Figure 5-10 shows the Polygonal Lasso in action.

The big advantage of using the Polygonal Lasso over the Magnetic Lasso is that it's much easier to keep it from getting into a snarl. Your only options for this tool are Feather and Anti-alias, which are explained in the box on page 117.

Selecting with a Brush

Elements also gives you two very special brushes to help you make selections. The Selection brush has been part of Elements since Elements 2, so if you've used Elements before, you probably know how useful it is. You also get a very handy variation on the Selection brush: the Magic Selection brush. With this brush, Elements does most of the selecting work for you. You just make a quick scribble on the object you want to select, and Elements figures out the actual selection. It doesn't always work, but it's quite an amazing tool when it does.

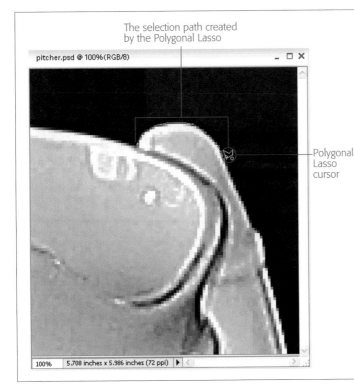

The selection path created
by the Polygonal Lasso

pitcher.psd @ 100% (RGB/8)

100%   5.708 inches x 5.986 inches (72 ppi)

Polygonal
Lasso
cursor

Figure 5-10:
If you have limited dexterity, the Polygonal Lasso tool and a lot of clicks eventually get you a nice accurate selection. You need to zoom way, way in to use this tool to select an object that doesn't have totally straight sides. Here, the Polygonal Lasso easily made it around the curve of the handle by clicking to make extremely short segments.

The Magic Selection brush and the Selection brush are grouped together in the Toolbox, and they appear in both Full Edit and Quick Fix because they're so useful. You may well find that with these two tools you rarely need the other selection tools anymore.

The Magic Selection Brush

You probably won't wonder why Adobe calls *this* tool "magic." The Magic Selection brush can make even the most complex selections as easy as doodling. It automates the whole process of selecting to an amazing degree. With this brush, you just make a few marks on the subject you want to select, as shown in Figure 5-11. Elements does all the calculating and creates the selection for you. If you want to practice the following steps on an actual picture, download the photo shown in Figure 5-11 (rose.jpg) from the "Missing CD" page at *www.missingmanuals.com*. Here's how to use the brush:

1. **Open a photo and activate the Magic Selection brush.**

    Click the brush in the Toolbox or press F. It's just below the Magic Wand in the Full Edit Toolbox (when you've got a single-row Toolbox), and just below the Hand tool in the Quick Fix Toolbox. (Make sure you've got the correct selection brush. The regular Selection brush shares the same Toolbox slot. You can quickly tell the icons apart by the dotted lines extending from the regular Selection brush icon. The Magic Selection brush looks more like a wand or a marker. If the wrong one is active, click the correct icon in the Options bar to switch.)

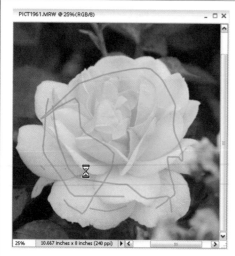

Figure 5-11:

Top: You may not even need to make this many marks on the object you want to select to tell Elements what to choose, depending on what your photo looks like. (The hourglass indicates that Elements is calculating where to make the selection.)

Bottom: Elements is able to use your scribbles as the basis for an almost perfect selection. Here, you'd need only to add the tiny shadowed area near the Magic Selection brush cursor (circled) for a flawless selection. Often it's easiest to switch to the regular Selection brush for this kind of cleanup.

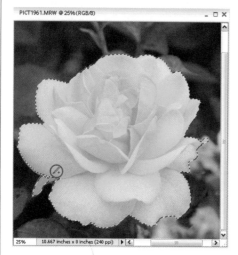

2. **Tell Elements what you want to select.**

   This is the amazing part of this tool. You don't need to outline the object at all. Just paint some marks on it with the Magic Selection brush, as shown in Figure 5-11, top. When you draw, try to cross the full range of tones and brightness you want, but the actual shape of your marks doesn't matter at all. You can draw a circle, a zigzag, lines—whatever suits the image. You may be able to select your object with just a dot or two if you're trying to select a particularly uniformly colored area.

When you let go of the mouse, Elements does some fast thinking and creates a selection based on what you marked. It's a bit like a more complex version of the Magic Wand, but you're not limited to a restricted color range the way you are with the wand.

3. **Adjust the result.**

The Magic Selection brush comes astonishingly close to a perfect selection if the conditions in your photo are good, but most of the time, you'll need to tweak your selection at least a bit. To add to your selection, in the Options bar, click the Foreground brush icon (with the + sign next to it) and make a mark or two someplace in the area you want to add. If Elements got too much the first time, click the Background brush icon (with the – sign next to it) and then make a mark in the area you want to remove.

The Magic Selection brush does its best work if the background of your photo isn't too busy, and if there's a good contrast between the object you want to select and the area around it. If what you're asking is too tough for Elements to figure out, you may see the progress bar flicker indecisively and then stop altogether. If that happens, try adding some additional marks to guide Elements or switch to another tool. Also, if you go back and forth too many times, adding to and subtracting from your selection, the Magic Selection brush can get confused and start to sulk, refusing to make a selection at all. If that happens, try switching to another tool and then go back to the Magic Selection brush to get a clean start.

In many cases, you'll find that the Magic Selection brush can only get you about 90 percent of the way to a perfect selection. It may be faster in the long run to switch to the Selection brush (explained in the next section) to clean up any small problem areas, as opposed to going over and over a selection with the Magic Selection brush.

> **NOTE**   If you plan to remove your selection from the surrounding area, you may want to try the Magic Extractor (page 128), rather than the Magic Selection brush.

The Selection Brush

The Selection brush is one of the greatest tools in Elements. It makes it really, really easy to make complex selections and to clean up the selections you've got. You can use it on its own or as a complement to the Magic Selection brush, described in the previous section.

With the Selection brush, you just paint over what you want to select. To do that, you drag over the area you want. You can let go, and each time you drag again, you automatically add to your selection. There's no need to change modes in the Options bar or hold down the Shift key the way you do with the other Selection tools.

Not only that, but the Selection brush also has a Mask mode, in which Elements highlights what *isn't* part of your selection. The Mask mode is great for finding tiny spots you may have missed and for checking the accuracy of your selection outline. In Mask mode, anything you paint over gets *masked* out. In other words, it's protected from being selected.

Masking is a little confusing at first, but you'll soon see what a useful tool it is. Figure 5-12 shows the same selection made with and without Mask mode.

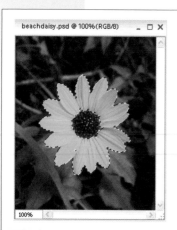 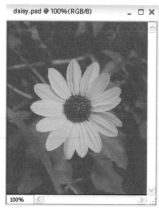

Figure 5-12:
Left: A selection made with the brush in Selection mode. It looks like a completed selection that you can make using any of the selection tools.

Right: The same selection in Mask mode. The red covers everything that is not part of your selection.

The Selection brush is pretty simple to use:

1. **Click the Selection brush in the Toolbox or press A.**

   The Selection brush is located in the Toolbox with the Magic Selection brush. You can easily tell which brush is active because the icon for the Selection brush shows the dotted lines (the "marching ants") that define the edges of a selection.

   In the Options bar, choose either Selection mode or Mask mode and the brush size you want.

2. **Drag over the area you want.**

   If you're in Selection mode, the area you drag over becomes part of your selection. If you're in Mask mode, the area you drag over is excluded from becoming part of your selection.

The Selection brush gives you several choices in the Options bar:

- **Brush.** You can use many different brushes depending on whether you want a hard- or soft-edged selection. If you want a different brush, just choose it from the menu here. (For more about brushes, see page 306.)

- **Size.** To change the brush size, type a size in the box, click the arrow, and use the slider. Or just press the close bracket key (]) to increase the size (keep tapping it until you get the size you want). The open bracket key ([) decreases the size of your brush. You can also just put your cursor on the word Size and scrub to the left or right to make the brush smaller or larger. (Don't know how to scrub? For more on this Elements feature, see page 308.)

TIP   The bracket key shortcut works with any brush, not just the Selection brush.

• **Mode.** This option is where you tell Elements whether you're creating a selection (Selection) or excluding an area from being part of a selection (Mask).

• **Hardness.** This option controls two things: the sharpness of the edge of your selection and its opacity. See Figure 5-13.

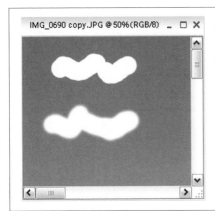

IMG_0690 copy.JPG @ 50% (RGB/8)   _ □ ✕

Figure 5-13:
The top selection was made at 100-percent hardness, and the bottom one is at 50 percent. (The selected area was then deleted to show you the outline more clearly.)

Switching between Selection and Mask mode is a good way to see how well you've done when you finish making your selection. In Mask mode, the parts of your image that are *not* part of your selection have a red film over them, so that you can clearly see the selected area only.

TIP   You don't have to live with the red mask color if you don't want to. To change the color of the mask, click the Overlay Color box in the Options bar while the Selection brush is active and in Mask mode. Use the Color Picker (page 196) to choose the color you prefer.

You can temporarily make the Selection brush do the opposite of what it's been doing by holding down Alt while you drag. For example, if you're in Selection mode and you've selected too large an area, Alt+drag over the excess to remove it. If you're masking out an area, Alt+drag to add an area to the selection. This may sound confusing, but some things are easier to learn just by doing them.

NOTE   The Selection brush is great for fine-tuning selections made with the other selection tools. Quickly switching to the Selection brush in Mask mode is a great way to check for spots you may have missed—the red makes it really easy to spot them.

Selecting Objects from an Image's Background

Ever feel the urge to pluck an object out of your photo's background? For example, maybe you want to take an amazing moon shot and stick it in another photo. The traditional procedure is to make your selection, invert it, and then delete the rest of the image. But Elements streamlines this process with yet another "Magic" tool—the Magic Extractor. It works much like the Magic Selection brush in that you just give Elements a few hints and let the program do the rest. When the Magic Extractor's done, your selection is isolated in all its lonely glory, surrounded by transparency and ready for use on its own. Like the Magic Selection brush, this tool does a surprisingly good job—most of the time. To conduct your own experiments, download the practice photo (coralbean.jpg) from the "Missing CD" page at *www.missingmanuals.com*.

The Magic Extractor has an elaborate dialog box with tools not found elsewhere in Elements. To see it, go to Image → Magic Extractor (see Figure 5-14). You see a full-screen dialog box, including a Toolbox on the left side, instructions across the top, a preview of your image, and a set of controls at right. It looks complicated, but it's really just a bunch of easy-to-use options for tweaking what you've got before Elements extracts your object for you. Here's how to use this timesaving new tool:

1. **Go to Image → Magic Extractor.**

   Your image appears in the preview area of the Magic Extractor window (Figure 5-14).

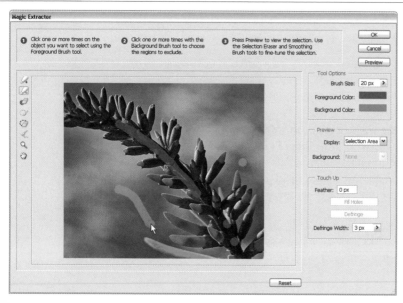

Figure 5-14:
Manually removing this spray of coral bean from its background would be a mighty long process. With the Magic Extractor, these few marks are all the help Elements needs to make the selection for you. (Because the blossom is red, this picture shows blue as the Foreground brush color and red as the Background brush color. That's reversed from the usual marker colors.)

TIP   The Magic Extractor sometimes has problems with very large files. If you need to extract an object from a hefty image, you may get better results if you crop away any large, unnecessary areas first. See page 71 for more about cropping.

2. **If necessary, change the marker colors.**

    On the right side of the window, you see two color squares. Usually, you'll see red for the Foreground brush (the one you use to mark what to keep) and blue for the Background brush (the one that tells Elements what to discard from your image). To make the brush tools easier to see, you can click the squares for the Color Picker (page 196), and choose new colors.

3. **Use the Foreground brush to tell Elements what you want to extract.**

    Make some marks on the object you want to remove from the image's background. You can draw lines, as shown in Figure 5-14, but making dots on your object may work just as well. With a little practice, you'll soon get the hang of knowing what kind of marks you need for each object.

4. **Click the Background brush and tell Elements what to exclude.**

    Similarly, make some marks in the areas you *don't* want Elements to include in your selection.

5. **Click the Preview button.**

    The Preview area shows what Elements thinks you want to do.

6. **If necessary, use the various tools to help Elements adjust the boundaries of your selection.**

    For example, if Elements left off an area you want, usually just one click with the Foreground brush is enough to tell Elements what you want to add. If there are spots missing within the selection, click the Fill Holes button. If you need to get a better view of your work, use the Zoom and Hand tools. (Both of these tools are explained in more detail on page 79.)

7. **Fine-tune the edges of your selection, if you wish.**

    Add a feather (page 117), defringe (page 132), or smooth the edges of the selection with the Smoothing brush.

8. **When you like what you see, click OK.**

    If you want to give up and try another method, click Cancel (in the Options bar) instead. Figure 5-15 shows what the Magic Extractor can do.

NOTE   If you understand layers (see Chapter 6), the Magic Extractor works only on the active layer of your photo. If you want to extract an object without wrecking the rest of your photo, make a duplicate layer (page 147) and work on that new layer.

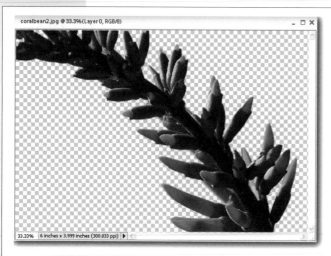

coralbean2.jpg @ 33.3%(Layer 0, RGB/8)

33.33%   6 inches x 3.999 inches (300.833 ppi)

Figure 5-15:
Just the few marks you saw in Figure 5-14
and a click of the Defringe button produce
this perfectly extracted selection, all ready to
move to another image.

The Magic Extractor gives you lots of ways to make sure that Elements gives you a perfect selection. The Toolbox contains a whole set of special tools just for the Extractor, as you can see in Figure 5-16. Each has its own keystroke to make it easy to switch tools while you work (given in parentheses after the tool's name in the list below). From top to bottom, you get:

- **Foreground brush** *(Keyboard shortcut: B)*. Use this brush to mark what you want to include in your extracted object. You can change the brush color using the square on the right side of the window.

- **Background brush** *(P)*. This brush tells Elements what you want to cut away from your selection. Like the Foreground brush, this brush has a color square on the right side of the window where you can choose a different marker color.

- **Point Eraser tool** *(E)*. If you mark something by mistake, use this tool to erase marks made with the Foreground and Background brushes.

- **Add to Selection tool** *(A)*. Use this tool to add to the selection you already have.

- **Remove from Selection tool** *(D)*. Whatever you paint over gets removed from your selection.

- **Smoothing brush** *(J)*. Once you've previewed your selection, you can use this brush to even out any ragged edges. Try the Touch Up commands from the right side of the window first because you may not need this brush.

- **Zoom tool** *(Z)* **and Hand tool** *(H)*. These are the same trusty standbys you use to adjust your view elsewhere in Elements. See page 79 for more about using the Zoom tool and page 80 for the Hand tool.

> **TIP**   Some of the fine-tuning tools, like the Smoothing brush, work much better if you zoom in pretty far before using them.

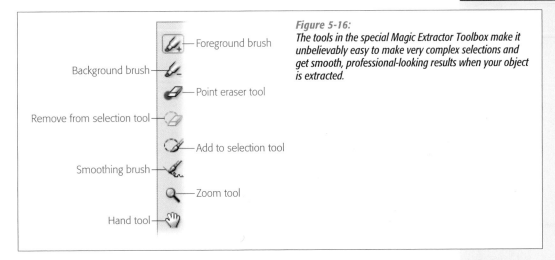

Figure 5-16:
The tools in the special Magic Extractor Toolbox make it
unbelievably easy to make very complex selections and
get smooth, professional-looking results when your object
is extracted.

So you can see exactly what you're doing, Elements gives you several ways to adjust the tools and also your view of the image. These are found on the right side of the window:

- **Tool Options.** You can use the color squares to choose different colors for the Foreground and Background brushes by clicking these squares and using the Color Picker (page 196). You can also adjust the brush size, but that's hardly ever necessary, unless the brush is too big for the area you want to select.

- **Preview.** Choose whether to see just the selected area or your entire image. You can also choose what kind of background you want to see your selection against to get a clearer view. For example, you can choose None (the standard transparency grid), or a black, gray, or white matte, which puts a temporary solid background to make it easier to check the edges of your selection. Mask is just like working with the Selection brush in Mask mode (page 125). You can paint more of a mask or remove the mask to reveal a larger selection. (Remember that what's masked *isn't* selected.)

Once you've previewed your selection, you also get some very helpful options for making sure your selection is absolutely perfect. Most of these options are on the right side of the dialog box, under Touch Up.

- **Feather.** Enter the amount, in pixels, to feather the edge of your selection. (Page 117 explains feathering.)

- **Fill Holes.** If Elements left some gaps in your selection, you may be able to fill them by clicking this button. This tool works only for holes that are completely surrounded by selected material, though. If the edges of your selection have bites out of them, use the Smoothing brush instead, or give the area an extra click with the Foreground brush.

• **Defringe.** If your selection has a rim of contrasting pixels around it, this command can usually eliminate them. Figure 5-17 shows what a difference defringing can make. You can choose a different number of pixels from the edge for Elements to consider when defringing, but the standard setting is usually fine.

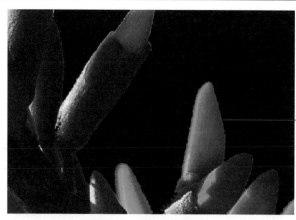

Raggedy, messy edges

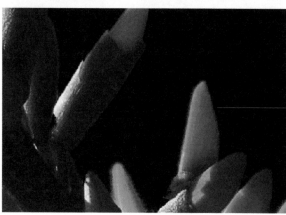

Smooth, neat edges

Figure 5-17:
Defringing is a huge help for cleaning up the edges of your selections.

Top: Here's a closeup of the extracted coral bean blossom. The black matte background makes the ragged edges stand out. If you look closely, you can see the ragged edges of the flower. If you place this image into another graphic, it will look like you cut it out with very dull nail scissors.

Bottom: The edges will blend into another image much more believably after you apply defringing. Here you can see how much softer the edges are after defringing. Now you can place the flower into another file without getting the cut-out effect.

TIP   If the edges of your selection are ragged but not contrasting, or if defringing alone doesn't clean things up enough, try the Smoothing brush (explained above). Just run it along the edge of your selection to polish it until it's smooth.

Extracting objects used to be a very time-consuming process, often involving expensive third-party plug-ins to make the job easier. But now the Magic Extractor is all you need in most situations.

Changing and Moving Selections

Now that you know all about how to make selections, it's time to learn about some of the finer points of using and manipulating them. Elements gives you several handy options for changing the areas you've selected and for actually moving images around once they're selected. You can even save a tough selection so you don't have to do *that* again.

Inverting a Selection

One thing you often want to do with a selection is *invert* it. That means telling Elements, "Hey, you know the area I've selected? Well, I want you to select everything *except* that area."

Why would you want to do that? Well, sometimes it's easier to select what you *don't* want. For example, suppose you have an object with a complicated outline, like the group of buildings shown in Figure 5-18. Say you want to put this building on your letterhead. It may be difficult to select. But the sky is just one big block of color. It's a lot faster to select the sky with the Magic Wand than to try to get an accurate selection of the building itself.

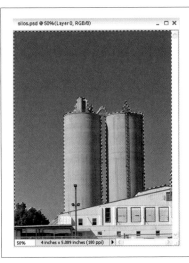 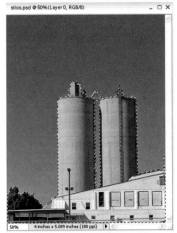

Figure 5-18:
Left: Say you want to make some adjustments to just the building in this photo. You could spend half an hour meticulously selecting it, or instead just select the sky with a click of the Magic Wand and invert your selection to get the silos. Here, the sky has the marching ants around it to show that it's the active selection—but that's not what you want.

Right: Inverting the selection (Select → Inverse) gives you the ants around the buildings without the trouble of tracing out all the ladders and pipes on the silos.

To invert a selection:

1. **Make a selection.**

   Usually, you first select what you *don't* want if you're planning to invert your selection. You can select with any tool that suits your fancy.

2. **Go to Select → Inverse.**

   Now the part of your image that you *didn't* select is selected.

Making a Selection Larger or Smaller

What if you want to tweak the size of your selection? Sometimes you may want to move the outline of a selection outward a few pixels to expand it. Figuring out how to do so confuses people because Elements offers two similar-sounding ways to do it: Grow and Expand. They sound like they should do the same thing, but there's a slight but important difference between them.

- **Grow** (Select → Grow) moves your selection outward to include more similar contiguous colors, no matter what shape your original selection was. Grow doesn't care about shape; it just finds more matching contiguous pixels.

- **Expand** (Select → Modify → Expand) preserves the shape of your selection and just increases the size of it by the number of pixels you specify.

- **Similar** (Select → Similar) does the same thing as Grow but looks at all pixels, not just the adjacent ones.

- **Contract** (Select → Modify → Contract) shrinks the size of a selection.

So what's the big difference between Expand and Grow? Look at Figure 5-19 to see how differently they behave.

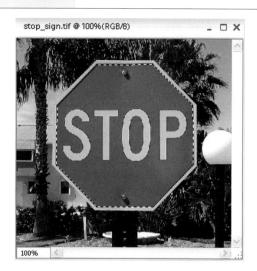

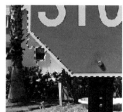

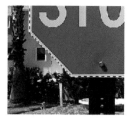

Figure 5-19:
Top: In the original selection, everything in the Stop sign has been selected except the small white border on the outside of the sign.

Bottom left: If you use Grow to enlarge the selection, you also get parts of the building that are similar in tone. As a result, your selection isn't shaped like a Stop sign anymore.

Bottom right: But if you use Expand instead, the selection still has the exact shape of the sign, only now the edges of the selection move outward to include the sign's white border area.

Smoothing and Bordering

Elements includes a couple of specialized commands for tweaking the edges of your selections.

- **Smoothing** (Select → Modify → Smooth) is a sometimes-dependable way to clean up ragged spots in a color-based selection (like you'd make with the Magic Wand, for instance). You enter a pixel value, and Elements evens out your selection based on the number you entered, by searching for similarly colored pixels.

  For example, if you enter 5 pixels, Elements looks at a 5-pixel radius around each pixel in your selection. In areas where most of the pixels are already selected, it adds in the others. Where most pixels aren't selected, it deselects the ones that are selected to get rid of the jagged edges and holes in the selection.

This is handy, but smoothing is sometimes hard to control, and it doesn't only affect the edge of your selection. Usually it's easier to clean up your selection by hand with the Selection brush than to use Smoothing.

- **Bordering** (Select → Modify → Border) adds an anti-aliased, invisible border to your image. You might say it selects the selection's outline. You would use it when your selection's edges are too hard and you want to soften them. Choose a border size and click OK. Only the border is selected, so you can also apply a slight Gaussian blur (see page 353) to soften it more if you like.

Moving Selections

Often you make selections because you want to move objects around—like putting that dreamboat who wouldn't give you the time of day next to you in your senior year class photo. You can move a selection in several ways.

Here's the simplest, tool-free way to move something from one image to another:

1. **Select it.**

   Make sure you've selected everything you want. It's really annoying when you paste a selection from one image to another and find you missed a spot.

2. **Press Ctrl+C to copy it.**

   Or you could use Ctrl+X if you want to cut it out of your original. Just remember that Elements leaves a hole if you do it that way.

   TIP   If you copy and paste a selection, and you see it's got partially transparent areas in it, back up and go over your selection again with the Selection brush using a hard brush, and then copy and paste again.

3. **Go to File → New → Image from Clipboard.**

   This creates a new document with just your selection in it. Or you can use Ctrl+V to paste it into another image or a document in another program. (Be sure you've turned on Export Clipboard in Edit → Preferences → General.)

The Move tool

You can also move things around *within* your photo by using the Move tool, which lets you cut or copy selected areas. Figure 5-20 shows how to use the Move tool to conceal distracting details in photos.

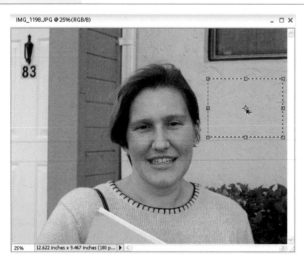

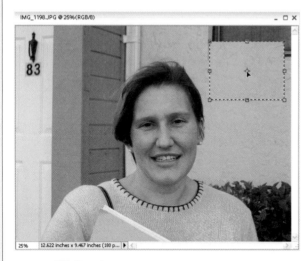

Figure 5-20:
Top: Here's the original version of the photo used for the feathered vignette on page 117. Let's say you wanted to get rid of the window in the upper-right corner of the top photo. By copying and moving a piece of the wall, you can cover up the window and create a simpler background to put the focus on the woman rather than the building. Here the area is selected prior to moving it.

Bottom: Hold down the Alt key while using the Move tool to copy a selected area. The piece of wall slides into its new position as a window hider. (If you use the Move tool without this keystroke modifier, Elements cuts away the selection, leaving a hole in your photo.)

The Move tool lives at the very top of the Standard Edit Toolbox. To use it:

1. **Make a selection.**

   Make sure your selection doesn't have anything in it that you don't want to copy.

2. **Switch to the Move tool.**

Click the Move tool or press V. Your selection stays active but is now surrounded by a rectangle with box-shaped handles on the corners.

3. **Move the selection and press Enter when you're satisfied with its position.**

As long as your selection is active, you can work on your photo in other ways and then come back and reactivate the Move tool. If you're worried about losing a complex selection, save it as described in the next section. If you're not happy with what you've done, just press Ctrl+D to deselect everything, and you can start over again.

You can move a selection in several different ways:

- **Move it.** If you just move a selection by dragging it, you leave a hole in the background where the selection was. The Move tool *truly* moves your selection. So unless you have something under it that you want to show through, that's probably not what you want to do.

- **Copy it and move the copy.** If you press the Alt key as you're moving, you'll copy your selection, so your original remains where it was. But now you'll have a duplicate to move around and play with.

- **Resize it.** You can drag the Move tool's handles to resize or distort your copy, which is great when you need to change the size of your selection. The Move tool lets you do the same things you can do with Free Transform (see page 297).

- **Rotate it.** The Move tool lets you rotate your selection the same way you can rotate a picture using Free Rotate (see page 69). Just grab a corner and turn it.

TIP   You can save a trip to the Toolbox and move selections without activating the Move tool. To move a selection without copying it, just place your cursor in the selection, hold down Ctrl, and move the selection. To move a copy of a selection, follow the same procedure but hold down the Alt key as well. You can drag the copy without damaging the original. To move multiple copies, just let go, then press Ctrl+Alt again and drag once more.

Adobe has added lots of new features to the Elements 5 Move tool, making it a great way to manage and move objects that you've put on their own layers (Chapter 6). Page 156 explains how to use the Move tool to arrange layered objects.

Saving Selections

You can tell Elements to remember the outline of your selection so that you can reuse it again later on. This is a wonderful timesaver and easy to do, too.

NOTE   Elements' saved selections are the equivalent of Photoshop's *alpha channels*. Keep that in mind if you decide to try tutorials written for Photoshop. Incidentally, alpha channels saved in files in Photoshop show up in Elements as saved selections, and vice versa.

To save a selection:

1. **Make your selection. Then choose Select → Save Selection, name your selection, and save it.**

   When you want to use the selection again, go to Select → Load Selection, and there it is, waiting for you.

   NOTE   When you save a feathered (page 117) selection, it's almost impossible to change the feather later on if you change your mind about how much feather you want. It's easier to save the hard-edged selection, load it, and then go to Select → Feather to add a feather if you need one. That way you can change the amount each time you use the selection, as long as you remember not to save the change to the selection.

Making changes to a saved selection

It's probably just as easy to start your selection over if you need to tweak a saved selection, but it is possible to make changes if you want. This can save you some time if your original selection was really tricky to create.

Say you've got a full-length photo of somebody, and you've created and saved a selection of the person's face (called, naturally enough, "Face"). Now, imagine that after applying a filter to the selection, you decide it would look silly to change only the face and not the person's hands, too.

So you want to add the hands to your saved selection. There are a couple of ways to do this.

The simplest is just to load up "Face," activate your selection tool of choice, put the tool in Add to Selection mode, and then save the selection again with the same name.

But how about if you've already selected the hands and you want to add *that* new selected area to the existing facial selection? Here's what you'd do:

1. **Go to Select → Save Selection.**

   Choose your saved "Face" selection. All the radio buttons in the dialog box become active.

2. **Choose "Add to Selection."**

   What you just selected is added to the original selection and saved, so now your "Face" selection also includes the hands.

Layers: The Heart of Elements

If you've been working mostly in the Quick Fix window so far, you've probably noticed that once you close your file, the changes you've made are permanent. You can undo actions while the file's still open, but once you close it, you're stuck with what you've done.

Well, in Elements, you can keep your changes and still revert to the original image if you use *layers*, a nifty system of transparent sheets that keep each element of your image on a separately editable sliver. Layers are one of the greatest image editing inventions ever. By putting each change you make on its own layer, you can constantly rearrange the composition of your image and add or subtract changes whenever you want.

If you use layers, you can save your file and quit Elements, and then come back days or weeks later and still undo what you did or change things around some more. There's no statute of limitations for the changes you make when using layers.

Some people resist learning about layers because they fear they're too complicated. But they're actually very easy to use once you understand how they work. And once you get started with layers, you'll realize that using Elements without them is like driving a Ferrari in first gear. This chapter gives you the information you need to get comfortable working with layers.

Understanding Layers

Imagine you've got a drawing of a room you're thinking about redecorating. Say the drawing features a few items in the room: the walls, the windows, and a piece of furniture or two. To get an idea of your different decorating possibilities, imagine that you've also got a bunch of transparent plastic sheets, each of which has some image on it that changes the room's look: a couch, a few different colors for the carpet, a standing lamp, and so on. Your decorating work is now pretty easy, since you can add and remove, and mix and match the transparencies with ease.

Layers in Elements work pretty much the same way. With layers, you can add and remove objects and also make changes to the way your image looks. And with any of these changes, you can modify or discard them later on.

If you look at Figure 6-1, you can see an Elements file that includes layers. Each object in that flyer is on a different layer, so you can easily remove or rearrange things. (If you want to follow along with a layers-heavy file, you can download a small version of this file from the "Missing CD" page at *www.missingmanuals.com*. Look for harvestfestsmall.psd.)

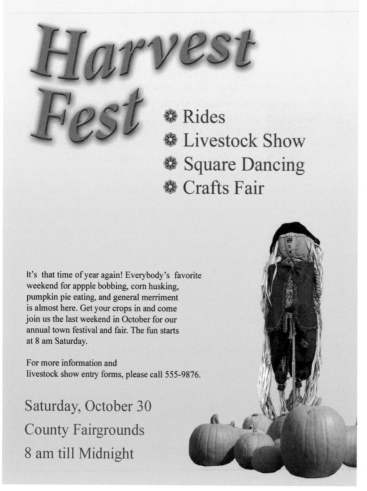

Figure 6-1:
Every object on this flyer—the background, the scarecrow, the pumpkins, each block of text—is on its own layer, which makes changing things a snap. Want to change the background, get rid of the pumpkins, or change the phone number? With layers, it's easy to do any of these things.

You can also use layers for many adjustments to your photos, giving yourself the chance to tweak or eliminate those changes later on. For instance, say you used Quick Fix's Hue slider but then decided the next day you didn't like what you did—you're stuck (unless you can dig out a copy of your original). But if you'd used a Hue/Saturation Adjustment *layer* to make the change, you could just throw out that layer and keep all your other changes intact (you'll learn about Adjustment layers later in this chapter). You can also use layers to combine parts of different photos together, as shown in Figure 6-2.

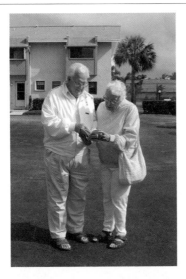

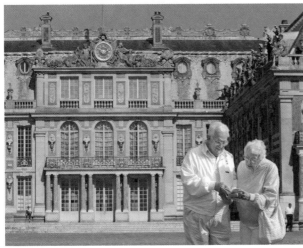

Figure 6-2:
Layers make it easy to combine elements from different photos. You may not be able to afford to send your grandparents on a real trip to Europe, but once you understand layers, you can give them a virtual vacation.

Once you understand how to use layers, you'll feel much more comfortable making radical changes to an image because mistakes are much easier to fix. Not only that, but by using layers, you can easily make lots of very sophisticated changes that are otherwise very difficult and time-consuming. But the main reason to use layers is for creative freedom. Layers make it easy to create lots of special effects that would be very difficult otherwise.

> **NOTE** Along with goodies like graphics and frames, the Artwork and Effects Palette contains a number of *smart objects*. These objects take on special powers when you add them to a layered file. For example, if you choose a new background from the palette, it automatically zips down to the bottom of the stack to replace your existing background, no matter which layer was active when you applied the new background. Page 402 explains how smart objects work.

The Layers Palette

The Layers palette is your control center for any kind of layer-related action you want to perform, like adding, deleting, or duplicating layers. Figure 6-3 shows you the Layers palette for an image that already has lots of layers.

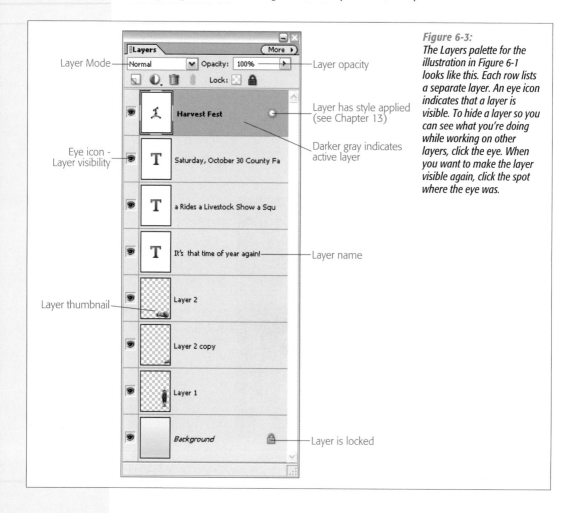

Figure 6-3:
The Layers palette for the illustration in Figure 6-1 looks like this. Each row lists a separate layer. An eye icon indicates that a layer is visible. To hide a layer so you can see what you're doing while working on other layers, click the eye. When you want to make the layer visible again, click the spot where the eye was.

It's important to have access to the Layers palette whenever you work with layers, not only for the information it gives you, but because you can do most layer manipulating more easily from the palette than directly in your image.

Each layer displays its name and a little thumbnail icon in the palette showing the layer's contents. You can adjust the size of the icon or turn it off altogether if you prefer, as shown in Figure 6-4.

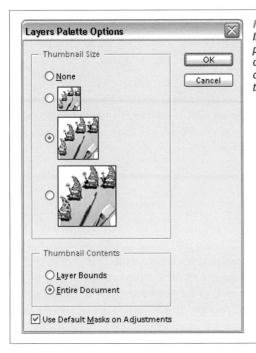

Figure 6-4:
If you want to change the size of the thumbnail icons in the Layers palette, click the More button in the palette's upper-right corner to open the Layers Palette Options box. At the bottom of the menu, choose Palette Options, and the dialog box shown here appears. In this case, the medium-size icon is selected.

The Layers palette usually contains one layer that's *active*, meaning that any action you take, like painting, is going to happen on that layer (and that layer only). The active layer is a darker gray so that you can see which one it is.

> NOTE   If you use the layer selection options described on page 158, you can wind up with multiple active layers or none, but for general working purposes, you usually want to have only one active layer.

When you look at an image that contains layers, you're looking down on the stack of layers from the top, just the way you would with overlays on a drawing. The layers appear in the same order in the Layers palette—the top layer of your image is the top layer in the stack in the Layers palette. (Layer order is important because whatever is on top can obscure what's beneath it.)

Elements lets you perform lots of different maneuvers right in the Layers palette. You can turn the visibility of layers off and on, change the order in which layers are stacked, link layers together, change the opacity of layers, add and delete layers—the list goes on and on. The rest of this chapter covers all these options and more.

A TIDY WORKSPACE

Managing the Layers Palette

The Layers palette sometimes gets into a fairly inconvenient location at the bottom of the Palette bin. The flippy triangle to the left of its name lets you open (or close) the palette; sometimes on small monitors, the palette contents are hidden below the bottom edge of the bin.

The Layers palette is important, so you probably want to get it out where you can see it all the time, at least while you're working with layered files. To do so, just grab the top bar of the palette near the name and pull it out of the bin onto your desktop. (For tips on keeping track of the Layers palette once it's out of the bin, look at page 22.)

You can collapse the Layers palette once it's on the desktop, but Elements gurus usually like to keep it easily accessible.

If you have a big monitor and have room to keep the Palette bin open while you work, it's fine to leave the Layers palette in the bin if you prefer. The idea is to get that palette where you can see it all the time and easily get to it with your mouse.

The Background

The bottom layer of any image is a special kind of layer called the *background*. If you bring any image or photo into Elements, the first time you open it, you'll see its one existing layer is called Background. (That's assuming that nobody else has already edited the file in Elements and changed things.) The name Background is only logical because whatever else you do will be on top of this layer.

> NOTE   There are two exceptions to the first-layer-is-always-the-background rule. First, if you create a new image by copying something from another picture, you'll just have a layer called "Layer 0." Background layers can't be transparent, so if you choose the Transparency option when creating a file from scratch, you'll have a Layer 0 instead of a Background layer.

Content-wise, the background can be totally plain or busy, busy, busy. A Background layer doesn't mean that it literally contains the background of your photograph—your entire photo can be a Background layer. It's entirely up to you what's on your Background layer and what you place on other, newly added layers. A common strategy for photographs is to keep your photo's image on the Background layer, and then perform adjustments and other embellishments (like adding type) on other layers.

Whatever you choose, there are a few things you *can't* do to backgrounds: If you want to change its blending mode (see page 153), opacity (page 151), or position in the layer stack, you need to convert the background into a regular layer.

TIP   The Background and Magic Erasers automatically turn a Background layer into a regular layer when you click a background with them. If you have a single object on a solid background and you want transparency around the object, one click with the Magic Eraser turns your background into a layer, eliminates a solid-colored background, and replaces it with transparency. (There's more on the Eraser tools on page 325.)

You can change a background to a regular layer by double-clicking the background in the Layers palette. Or, if you try to make certain kinds of changes to the background (like moving its position), Elements will prompt you to change the background to a regular layer.

You can also transform a regular layer into a Background layer if you want. The main reason to do this would be to send a layer zipping down to the bottom of the stack in a many-layered file. To do so:

1. **In the Layers palette, click the layer you want to convert to a background.**

2. **Select Layer → New → Background from Layer.**

   It may take a few seconds for Elements to finish calculating and respond after you tell it what to do. The layer you've changed moves down to the bottom of the layer stack in the Layers palette and automatically gets renamed "Background."

NOTE   You can't have more than one Background layer in an image. So what do you do if you want to change a regular layer to a Background layer and you've already got a Background layer? Well, you need to change the existing background into a regular layer first. Otherwise, the command is unavailable. (If you add a background from the "Artwork and Effects" palette, it automatically replaces the contents of your current background layer.)

COMPATIBILITY

Which File Types Can Use Layers?

You can add layers to any file you can open in Elements, but not every file format lets you *save* those layers for future use.

For instance, if your camera shoots JPEGs, you can open the JPEG in Elements and create lots of layers, but when you try to save the file, you'll see a warning reminding you that you can't have layers in a JPEG file.

Usually you'll want to choose either Photoshop (.psd) or TIFF as your format when saving an image with layers, because they both let you keep your layers for future use. PDF files can also have layers.

If someone using Photoshop sends you an image that has layers, you'll see them in the Layers palette when you open the file in Elements. Likewise, Photoshop can see layers you create in Elements.

If someone sends you a Photoshop file with *layer sets* (a way to group layers into what are essentially folders in the layers palette), Elements doesn't understand those, so ask the sender to expand the layer sets or convert the set to regular layers before sending you the file.

Creating Layers

Your image doesn't automatically have multiple layers. Lots of newcomers to Elements expect the program to be smart enough to put each object in a photo onto its own layer. It's a lovely dream, but even Elements isn't that brainy. To experience the joy of layers, you first need to add at least one layer to your image, which is what you'll learn how to do in the next few sections.

> **TIP** It may help you to follow along through the next few sections if you get out a photo of your own or create a new file to use for practice. Or, you can download either the harvestfestsmall.psd or leaves.jpg file from the "Missing CD" page at *www.missingmanuals.com*. (See page 39 for details on how to create a new file; if you do so, choose a white background.)

Adding a Layer

Elements gives you several different ways to add new layers. You can use any of the following methods:

- Select Layer → New → Layer.

- Press Ctrl+Shift+N.

- In the Layers palette, click the New Layer icon (the little square shown in Figure 6-5).

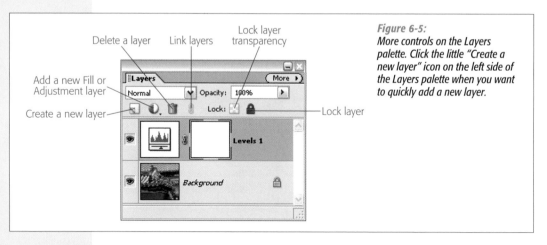

Figure 6-5:
More controls on the Layers palette. Click the little "Create a new layer" icon on the left side of the Layers palette when you want to quickly add a new layer.

When you create a new layer using any of these commands, the layer starts out empty. You won't see a change in your image until you use the layer for something (pasting something into the empty layer or painting on it, for example). If you look at the Layers palette, you'll see that any new layer you add appears just above the layer that was active when you created the new layer.

NOTE   The only practical limit to the number of layers your image can have is your computer's processing power. But if you find yourself regularly creating projects with upwards of 100 layers, you may want to upgrade to Photoshop, which has tools that make it easier to manage large numbers of layers.

Some actions create new layers automatically. For instance, if you drag an object in from another photo (see page 168 for instructions) or add artwork from the Artwork and Effects palette, the object automatically comes in on its own layer. And that's very handy for arranging the new item just where you want it, without disturbing the rest of your composition.

Deleting Layers

It's very easy to delete layers. Figure 6-6 shows the simplest way.

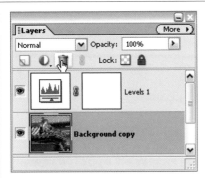

Figure 6-6:
To make a layer go away, you can either drag the layer to the Trash can icon on the Layers palette or, after selecting the layer, just click the "Delete layer" icon. Elements responds by asking if you want to delete the active layer. Say yes, and it's history. Once you delete a layer, it's gone forever.

Elements also gives you a few other ways to delete a layer. You can:

• Select Layer → Delete Layer.

• Right-click the layer in the Layers palette and choose Delete Layer from the pop-up menu.

• Click the More button on the Layers palette and choose Delete Layer from the pop-up menu.

Duplicating a Layer

Duplicating a layer can be very useful. Many Elements commands, like filters or color modification tools, won't work on a brand-new *empty* layer. This poses a dilemma because if you apply those changes to the layer containing your main image, you'll alter it in ways you can't undo later. The workaround is to create a *duplicate layer* and make your changes on that new layer. Then you can ditch the duplicate later if you change your mind, and your original layer is safely tucked away unchanged.

If all this seems annoyingly theoretical, try going to Enhance → Adjust Color → Adjust Hue/Saturation, for example, when you're working on a new blank layer, and see what happens. You'll see the dialog box shown in Figure 6-7 if you try to work on a blank layer.

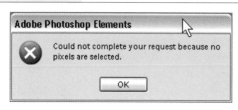

Figure 6-7:
The dreaded "no pixels are selected" warning means you're trying to make a selection or adjustment to empty space. There are several possible causes, but a very common one is trying to work on an empty layer. Other causes include too large a feather value on a selection (see the box on page 117), or trying to work in the empty part of a layer that contains only objects surrounded by transparency.

Elements gives you a few ways to duplicate an existing layer and its content. Select the layer you want to duplicate to make it the active layer, and then do one of the following:

• Press Ctrl+J.

• Choose Layer → Duplicate Layer.

• Right-click the Layer in the Layers palette and choose Duplicate Layer from the pop-up menu.

• Click the More button on the Layers palette and choose Duplicate Layer.

Creating a new layer using any of these methods copies the entire contents of the active layer into the new layer. You can then mess with the duplicate as much as you want without damaging the original layer.

GEM IN THE ROUGH

Naming Layers

You might have noticed that Elements isn't terribly creative when it comes to naming your layers. You get Layer 1, Layer 2, and so on. Fortunately, you don't have to live with those. It's quite easy to rename your layers in Elements.

Maybe renaming layers sounds like a job for people with too much time on their hands, but if you get started on a project that winds up with many layers, you may find that you can pick out the layers you want more quickly if you give them descriptive names.

Incidentally, you can't rename a Background layer. You have to change it to a regular layer first. Also, Elements

helps you out with Text layers (see page 379) by naming them using the first few words of the text they contain. To rename a layer:

1. **Double-click its name in the Layers palette.**

   The name turns to an active text box.

2. **Type in the new name.**

   You don't even need to highlight the text—Elements does that for you automatically.

As with any other change, you have to save your image afterward if you want to keep the name.

Copying and Cutting from Layers

You can also make a new layer that consists only of a *piece* of an existing layer. But first you need to decide whether you want to *copy* your selection or *cut it out* and place it on the new layer.

What's the difference? It's pretty much the same as copying versus cutting in your word-processing program. When you make a "New Layer via Copy," the area you select appears in the new layer while remaining in place in the old layer, too. On the other hand, "New Layer via Cut" removes the selection from the old layer and places it on a new layer, leaving a corresponding hole in the old layer. Figure 6-8 shows the difference.

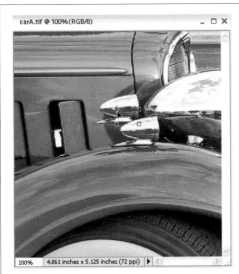

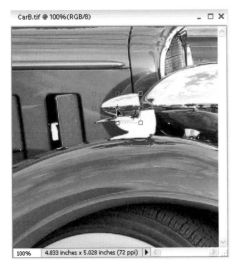

Figure 6-8:
The difference between "New Layer via Copy" and "New Layer via Cut" becomes obvious when you move the new layer so you can see what's beneath it.

Top: With "New Layer via Copy," the original light is still in place in the underlying layer.

Bottom: When you use "New Layer via Cut," the light leaves a hole behind.

Once you've selected what you want to move or copy, your new layer is only a couple of keystrokes away.

- **New Layer via Copy.** The easiest way to copy your selection to a new layer is to press Ctrl+J. You can also go to Layer → New → Layer via Copy. Whichever you use, if you didn't select anything before you use these keystrokes, your whole layer gets copied, so it's also a good shortcut for making a duplicate layer.

- **New Layer via Cut.** To cut your selection out of your old layer and put it on a layer by itself, press Ctrl+Shift+J, or go to Layer → New → Layer via Cut. Just remember that you'll leave a hole in your original layer when you do this.

If for some reason you want to cut and move the entire contents of a layer, you can press Ctrl+A first, although usually it's easier just to move your layer instead.

> **TIP** If you want to use a layer as the basis for a new document, Elements gives you a quick way to do so. Instead of copying and pasting, you can create a new document by going to Layer → Duplicate Layer. You get a dialog box containing a pull-down menu that gives you the option of placing the duplicate layer into your existing image, into any image currently open in the Editor, or into a new document of its own. (This maneuver only works from the menu. Ctrl+J doesn't bring up the dialog box.)

Managing Layers

The Layers palette lets you manipulate your layers in all kinds of ways, but first you need to understand a few more of the palette's cryptic little icons. Some of the things you can do with layers may seem tiresomely obscure when you first read about them, but once you're actually using layers, you'll quickly see why many of these options exist. The next few sections explain how to manipulate your layers in several different ways: how to hide them, how to group them together, how to change the way you see them, and how to combine layers together.

Making Layers Invisible

You can turn the visibility of layers off and on at will. This feature is tremendously useful, if you think about it. If the image you're working on has a busy background, for example, it's often hard to see what you're doing when you're working on a particular layer. Making the background invisible can really help you focus on the layer you're interested in. To turn off visibility, in the Layers palette, first select the layer you want to hide by clicking it, and then click the eye icon to hide the layer. Click the eye once more to make the layer visible again.

> **TIP** If you have a bunch of hidden layers and you decide you don't want them anymore, go to Layers Palette → More → Delete Hidden Layers to get rid of them all at once.

Adjusting Transparency

Your choices for layer visibility aren't limited to on and off. You can create immensely cool effects in Elements by adjusting the *opacity* of layers. In other words, you can make a layer partially transparent so that what's underneath it shows through.

To adjust the opacity of a layer, click the layer in the Layers palette and then either:

- Click in the Opacity box and type in the percentage of opacity you want.

- If you'd rather make the adjustment visually (as opposed to entering numbers), click the triangle to the right of the Opacity percentage and adjust the pop-out slider, or just put your cursor on the word Opacity and scrub left for less opacity and right for more. (Figure 6-9 explains the advantage of scrubbing.) (You can download leaves.jpg from the "Missing CD" at *www.missingmanuals.com*, if you'd like to experiment with creating Fill and Adjustment layers and changing their modes and opacity.)

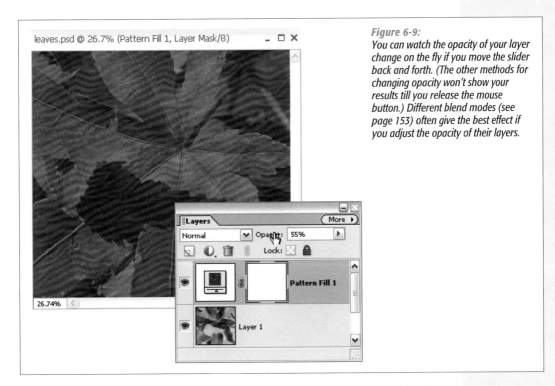

Figure 6-9:
You can watch the opacity of your layer change on the fly if you move the slider back and forth. (The other methods for changing opacity won't show your results till you release the mouse button.) Different blend modes (see page 153) often give the best effect if you adjust the opacity of their layers.

When you create a new layer using either the keyboard shortcut (Ctrl+Shift+N) or the menu (Layer → New → Layer), you can set the opacity right away in the New Layer dialog box. If you create a new layer by clicking the New Layer icon in the Layers palette, you need to Alt+click the New Layer icon—the New Layer dialog box appears and you can change the opacity.

NOTE You can't change the opacity of a Background layer. You have to convert it to a regular layer first.

Fading in Elements

One great thing you get in the full-featured Photoshop that Elements lacks is the ability to *fade* special effects and filters. Fading gives you great control over how much these tools change an image. (Often, filters generate harsh-looking results, and Photoshop's fade command helps adjust a filter's effect until it's what you intended.)

In Elements, you can approximate the Fade tool by applying filters, effects, or layer styles to a duplicate layer. Then, reduce the layer's opacity till it blends in with what's below (and change the blend mode if necessary) to get exactly the result you're looking for.

Locking Layers

You can protect your image from yourself by *locking* any of the layers. Locking keeps you from changing a layer's contents. You can also lock just the transparent parts of a layer if you want. When you do that, the transparent parts of your layer stay transparent no matter what you do to the rest of it (see Figure 6-10). (You're actually locking the pixels' current transparency level, so if you have pixels that are only partly transparent, they'll stay at their current opacity level, too.)

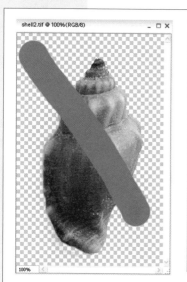
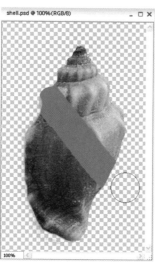

Figure 6-10:
After you've isolated an object on its own layer, sometimes you want to paint only on the object—and not on the transparent portion of the layer. Elements lets you lock the transparent part of a layer, making it easy to paint only the object itself.

Left: On a regular layer, paint goes wherever the brush does.

Right: With the layer's transparency locked, the stroke stops at the edge of the shell, even though the brush is now on the transparent portion of the layer.

To lock the transparent parts of a layer, select the layer and then click the little checkerboard in the Layers palette. It works like a button—when it's active, it shows an outline around it that makes it look pushed in. To unlock, just click the checkerboard again.

To lock the contents of a whole layer so that no changes can be made to it, click the little Lock icon in the Layers palette next to the checkerboard. Now if you try to paint on that layer or use any other tools, your cursor turns into the shape of the universal "no" symbol as a reminder that you can't edit that layer. You'll also see a Lock icon next to the layer name in the Layers palette. To unlock the layer, just click the Lock icon once more.

> **NOTE** Locking only preserves the layer from edits. It doesn't keep the layer from being merged into another layer or flattened, and it won't keep your image from being cropped.

Blend Mode

You also see another little menu in the Layers palette that says "Normal" or, in the New Layer dialog box, "Mode: Normal." This is the setting for your *blend mode*. When used with layers, blend modes control how the objects in a layer *blend* with the objects in the layer beneath it. By using different blend modes, you can make your image lighter, darker, or even make it look like a poster, with just a few bold colors in it. Blend modes can also control how some tools—those that have Blend Mode settings—change your image. Changing a tool's blend mode can sometimes dramatically change its results.

Blend modes are an awful lot of fun once you understand how to use them. You can use them to fix under-or overexposed photos, or to create all kinds of special visual effects. You can also use some of the tools, like the Brush tool, in different blend modes to achieve different effects. The most common blend mode is Normal, in which everything you do behaves just the way you would expect: an object shows its regular colors, and paint acts just like, well, paint.

Page 322 has lots more about how to use blend modes. For now, take a look at Figure 6-11, which shows how you can totally change the way a layer looks just by changing the layer's blend mode.

The blend modes are grouped together in the menu in categories according to the way they affect your image, but not every mode makes a visible change in every circumstance. Some of them may seem to do nothing—that's normal. It just means that you don't have a condition in your current image that's responding to that particular mode change. See the "Sharpening Your Images" section on page 201 for one example of a situation where a mode change makes an enormous difference.

Rearranging Layers

One of the truly amazing things you can do with Elements is move your layers around. You can change the order in which layers are stacked so that different objects appear in front of or behind each other. For example, you can position one object behind another if they're both on their own layers. Just grab the layer in the Layers palette and drag it to where you want it to be.

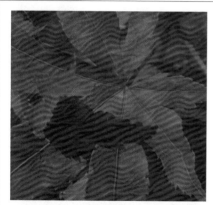

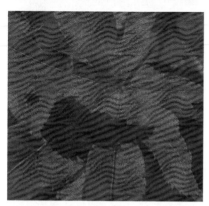

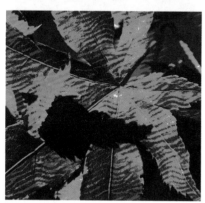

Figure 6-11:
This photo of some leaves has a Pattern Fill layer over it, showing three different modes. In normal mode, at 100-percent opacity, the pattern would completely hide the leaves, but by changing the blend mode of the pattern layer, you can create very different looks. (There's more about Pattern layers in the section "Fill and Adjustment Layers" on page 165.)

From top to bottom, the modes are: normal, dissolve, and hard mix. Notice how dissolve gives a grainy effect and hard mix gives a vivid, posterized look.

NOTE Remember, you're always looking down onto the layer stack when you look at your image, so moving something up in the list moves it toward the front of the picture.

Figure 6-12 shows the early stages of the flyer for a Fall Harvest Festival (originally shown in Figure 6-1). The pumpkins are already in place, and the scarecrow was dragged in from another image. The scarecrow comes in at the top of the stack, in front of the pumpkins. You can put the scarecrow behind the pumpkins by simply dragging the scarecrow layer beneath the pumpkin layer in the Layers palette.

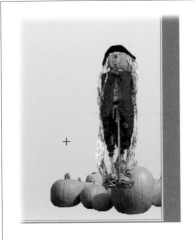 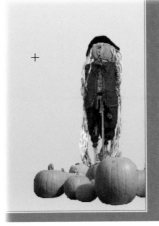

Figure 6-12:
Left: When you bring a new element into an image, it comes in at the top of the layer stack, making it the front object, like the scarecrow here.

Right: Move the new layer down in the stack, and the new object appears behind the existing content, just as the scarecrow moves behind the pumpkins here.

NOTE   The only kind of layer you can't move is a Background layer. If you want to bring a Background layer to another spot in the layer stack, first convert the Background layer to a regular layer (page 145), and then you can move it.

You can also move layers by going to Layer → Arrange and choosing the command of your choice:

- **Bring to Front** (Shift+Ctrl+]) sends the selected layer to the top of the stack so the layer's contents appear in the foreground of your image.

- **Bring Forward** (Ctrl+]) moves the layer up one level in the Layers palette, so it appears one step closer to the front of your image.

- **Send Backward** (Ctrl+[) moves the layer down one level so it's sent back one step in the image.

- **Send to Back** (Shift+Ctrl+[) puts the layer directly above the Background layer so it appears as far back as you can move anything.

- **Reverse** (no keystroke shortcut) switches two layers' locations in the stack, but you must select two layers in the palette (by Ctrl+clicking, for example) before this command becomes available.

TIP These commands (except Reverse) are now also available from the Move tool's Options bar or by right clicking in your photo when the Move tool is active. As a matter of fact, the Move tool is now a great way to rearrange layers in your image, as the next section explains.

Arranging layers with the Move tool

Adobe has given the Move tool a major makeover in Elements 5, making it more helpful when you're creating layered projects. Now you can locate and arrange layers right in your image window, without trekking all the way over to the Layers palette. (If you need a refresher on Move tool basics, check out page 136.)

To arrange layers with the Move tool:

1. **Activate the Move tool.**

   Click its icon in the Toolbox or press V.

2. **Select the layer(s) you want to move.**

   As soon as you activate the Move tool, you see the bounding box (the dotted lines) around the active layer in the Layers palette. As you move your cursor over your image, you see a blue outline around the layer that the cursor is over, no matter how far down the layer stack the object is, as shown in Figure 6-13. When you click to select the layer you want to move, the bounding box then appears around that layer. Shift+click to select multiple layers, and the bounding box expands to include all that you've selected.

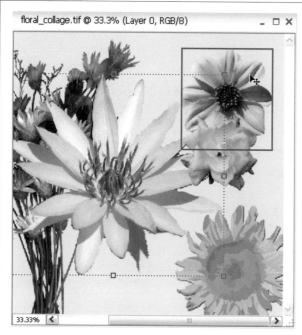

floral_collage.tif @ 33.3% (Layer 0, RGB/8)

33.33%

Figure 6-13:
The Elements 5 Move tool lets you select objects from any layer, not just the active one. When you move the cursor over any object, you see the blue outline around its layer. Here the water lily is the active layer (you can see the bounding box around it), but the Move tool is ready to select the pink flower, even though it's not on the active layer. If all these outlines annoy you, you can turn them off in the Options bar (via the Show Bounding Box or Show Highlight on Rollover checkbox). If you want to force the Move tool to concentrate only on the active layer, turn off Auto Select Layer.

3. **Move the Layer.**

For example, choose Layer → Arrange, or click the Arrange Menu in the Options bar, or right-click inside the bounding box in the image. You see the same choices (Bring to Front, Bring Forward, and so on) described in the previous section, except for Reverse, which is only available from the Layer menu. You can also use keystroke shortcuts (again, except for Reverse).

TIP   If you selected multiple layers, you may find that some of the commands are grayed out. If that's a problem, just click elsewhere in the image to deselect the layers and then send them one at a time instead of as a group.

Aligning and Distributing Layers

In Elements 5, it's now very easy to align objects in your image, thanks to the Move tool. *Aligning* arranges the objects on each layer so that they line up straight along their top, bottom, left, or right edges, or through their centers. So, for example, if you align the top edges of your objects, Elements makes sure that the top of each object is exactly in line with the others.

Evenly distributing the space between multiple objects is also a breeze. *Distributing* spaces out the distance between the objects, also letting you choose edges or centers as a guide. If you distribute the top edges, for example, Elements makes sure that there's an even amount of space from the top edge of one object to another. Use aligning for placing objects and distributing for allocating space.

TIP   Distributing objects in this way is especially handy when you're creating projects like those described in Chapter 15.

Aligning and distributing layers with the Move tool works much like rearranging layers:

1. **Activate the Move tool.**

Click its icon in the Toolbox or press V.

2. **Select the objects you want to align.**

This maneuver only works if each object is on its own layer. If you have multiple objects on one layer, move them to their own layers, one at a time, by selecting each object and then pressing Ctrl+Shift+J.

Shift+click inside the blue outline to select each layer you want to work with, or select the layers in the Layers palette.

3. **Choose how you want to align or distribute the objects by selecting from the Options bar menus.**

As shown in Figure 6-14, the Align and Distribute menus both give you the same choices: Top Edges, Vertical Centers, Bottom Edges, Left Edges, Horizontal Centers, and Right Edges.

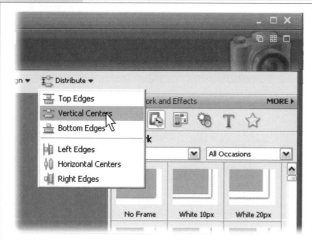

Figure 6-14:
You may get a little confused by the various ways you can arrange objects with the Move tool. The best way to find the choice you want is to look at the little thumbnails next to each label—they show you exactly how your objects will line up.

TIP   If you're confused about what the Align and Distribute menus do, just look at the thumbnails next to each menu item. You can apply as many different commands as you like, as long as the layers are still inside the bounding box. Figure 6-15 also gives you an example of how these commands work.

STAYING ORGANIZED

Selecting Layers

You can quickly target multiple layers when you want to manage them, like linking, moving, or deleting your layers. For your quick-selection pleasure, Elements gives you a whole group of layer selection commands, which you'll find in the Select menu. Here's what they do:

- **All Layers.** Choose this command and every layer except the Background layer gets selected. Even if you've turned off visibility (page 150) on a particular layer, that layer still gets selected.

- **Deselect Layers.** When you're done working with your layers as a group, you can choose this option and you won't have any layers selected until you click one.

- **Similar Layers.** This command is the most useful. Choose this option, and every layer of the same type gets selected, no matter where it is in the stack. So, for example, if you have a Text layer as your active layer when you choose Similar Layers, all your Text layers get selected. If, on the other hand, you had an Adjustment layer active, all your Adjustment layers get selected. You may use this command to quickly select a stack of Adjustment layers you want to drag to another image, for instance, using the technique on page 168.

You can also Shift+click to select multiple layers that are next to each other in the palette, or Ctrl+click to select layers that are separated. That way you can avoid the menu altogether. Once you're done, you can either use the Deselect Layers command from the menu, or just click another layer to make it the active layer.

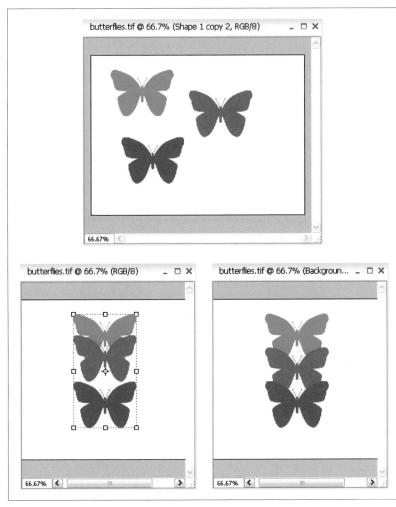

Figure 6-15:
Top: Each of these butterflies is on its own layer, but they need to be tidied up.

Bottom left: The result, after selecting the butterflies with the Move tool, and then picking Align → Center. As you see, the centers of the butterflies are now aligned, but they're not distributed evenly.

Bottom right: The butterflies after adding a trip to Distribute → Horizontal Centers. Note that they're evenly spaced but still pretty close together. That's because Distribute doesn't add any additional space between the outermost objects. If you want wider spacing between the shapes, make sure they're farther apart before you distribute them.

Grouping and Linking Layers

What if you want to move several layers at once? For instance, in the Harvest Festival image there are two layers with pumpkins on them. It's kind of a pain to drag each one individually if you need to move them in front of the scarecrow, for instance. Fortunately, you don't have to; Elements gives you a way to keep your layers united.

Linking layers

You can *link* layers together, and then they'll travel as a group, as shown in Figure 6-16.

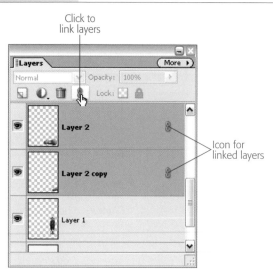

Click to
link layers

Figure 6-16:
Ctrl+click to select the layers you want to link, and then click the little chain (where the hand appears in the figure) to link two layers together. The chain icon appears to the right of each layer name to indicate that the chosen layers will now move as a group.

Icon for
linked layers

If you want to remove a link between layers, select the linked layers by Ctrl+click-ing each one and then click the same chain icon to turn it off again. You can always merge the layers (covered in the next section) into one layer if you want. Some-times, though, you'll want to keep layers separate, while still being able to move the layers as a group. Linking is the way to do that. You can also use the layer selection choices, described in the box on page 158, and skip the linking. As long as your layers all stay selected, they'll travel as a group. The advantage to linking is that your layers stay associated until you unlink them. There's no need to worry about accidentally clicking somewhere else in the palette and losing your selection group.

> NOTE The chain icon at the top of the Layers palette doesn't behave quite the same way as the transparency buttons do. You click the chain icon to link your layers, but it doesn't look any differ-ent once you've got some layers linked together (contrast that with the way the transparency but-tons look pushed in when active). The Linked layer chain next to the layer name is the only hint you get that a layer is linked.

Grouping layers

An even more powerful way to combine separate layers is to *group* them. Group-ing allows you to let one layer influence the other layers it's grouped with. Grouping layers isn't at all the same as linking them. It's probably easiest to under-stand grouping by looking at the example shown in Figure 6-17, which shows how you can crop an image on one layer using the shape of an object on another layer.

> NOTE If you group two layers together, the bottom layer determines the opacity of both layers.

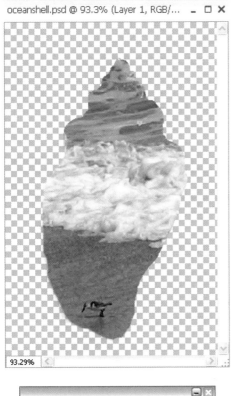

oceanshell.psd @ 93.3% (Layer 1, RGB/... _ □ ✕

93.29%

Figure 6-17:
This image began with a picture of a shell on one layer and a beach scene on the layer above it. At first, the beach image totally hid the shell, but interesting things happen when you group the layers. The beach layer gets cropped to the shape of the bottom layer, the shell. The little downward-bent arrow in the Layers palette indicates the beach layer is grouped.

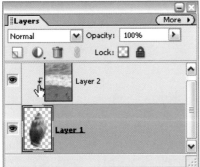

Once the layers are grouped, you can still slide the top layer around with the Move tool to reposition it so that you see exactly the part of it that you want. So in Figure 6-17, the beach layer was maneuvered around till the sandpiper showed in the bottom of the shell shape.

To group two layers together, make the top layer (of the two you want to group) the active layer. Then choose Layer → Group with Previous. You can also group layers using the keyboard. First, make sure the top layer is the active layer, and then press Ctrl+G. Another way to group is to do it right in the Layers palette.

Hold Alt, and in the Layers palette, move your cursor over the dividing line between the layers. Click when you see two linked circles appear by your cursor. Now your layers are grouped.

If you get tired of the layer grouping or you want to delete or change one of the layers, select Layer → Ungroup or press Ctrl+Shift+G to remove the grouping.

TIP   There's an even easier way to group layers. In the New Layer dialog box, there's a check-box for "Group with Previous Layer." Turn it on, and your new layer is pre-grouped with the layer below it.

POWER USERS' CLINIC

Stamp Visible

There are times when you want to perform an action on all the visible layers of your image without permanently merging them together. You can easily do this—and quickly, too, even if you have dozens of layers in your file—by using what Adobe calls the Stamp Visible command. The Stamp Visible command combines the contents of all your layers into a new layer at the top of the stack.

Stamp Visible lets you work away on the new combined layer while still preserving your existing layers untouched, in case you want them back later on. To use Stamp Visible, first create a new blank layer and make it the top layer of your image.

Next, either press Ctrl+Shift+Alt+E or hold down Alt while selecting the Merge Visible command from the Layers menu (or from the More menu in the Layers palette). You'll see the top layer fill itself with the combined contents of all your other layers.

If you want to keep a layer or two from being included in this new layer, just turn off the visibility of those layers you don't wish to include before using the Stamp Visible command.

If you have enough dexterity, you can even skip the layer creation step and press Ctrl+Shift+Alt+N+E to make the new layer and fill it at the same time.

Merging and Flattening Layers

By now, you've probably got at least an inkling of how useful layers are. But there is a downside to having layers in your image: they take up a lot of storage space, especially if you have lots of duplicate layers. Layers make files bigger. Fortunately, you aren't committed to keeping layers in your file forever. You can reduce your file size quite a bit—and sometimes also make things easier to manage—by merging layers or flattening your image.

Merging layers

Sometimes you may have two or more separate layers that really could be treated as one layer, like the pumpkins shown in Figure 6-18. You aren't limited to linking those layers together; once you've got everything arranged to your satisfaction, you can merge them together into one layer. Also, if you want to copy and paste your image, many times the standard copy and paste commands (page 115) will copy only the top layer. So it helps to get everything into one layer, at least temporarily.

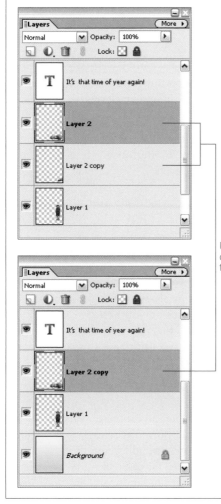

Use the Merge Down command to combine these two layers into one.

Figure 6-18:
Those pumpkins again. If you no longer need two separate pumpkin layers, you can merge the layers together.

Top: The Layers palette with the two separate pumpkin layers.

Bottom: The pumpkin layers merged into one layer.

You'll probably merge layers quite often when you're working with multi-layered files (for example, when you've got multiple objects that you want to edit simultaneously).

To merge layers, you have a few different options, depending on what's active in your image at the time. You can get to any of the following commands from the Layers menu, or from the More button on the Layers palette.

- **Merge Down.** This combines the active layer and the layer immediately beneath it. If the layer just below the active layer is hidden, you won't see this option in the list of choices.

- **Merge Visible.** This combines all the visible layers into one layer. If you want to combine layers that are far apart, just temporarily turn off visibility (by clicking the Eye icon) for the ones in between and for any other layers that you don't want to merge.

- **Merge Linked.** Click any of your linked layers and you see this command, which joins the linked layers into one layer.

- **Merge Clipping Mask.** You need to select the bottom layer of a group to see this command. Choose it, and the grouped layers join into one layer.

It's important to understand that once you merge layers and save and close your file, you can't just un-merge them again. While your file is still open, of course, you can use any of the undo commands (page 26), but once you've gotten past your undo limit, you're stuck with your merged layers.

> **NOTE** The box on page 162 shows you another way to combine all your layers, while still keeping a separate copy of the individual layers.

Sometimes if your layer contains type or shapes drawn with the Shape tool, you won't be able to merge the layer right away. Elements asks you to *simplify* the layer first. Simplifying a layer means that you have converted its contents to a raster object. In other words, now it's just a bunch of pixels, subject to the same resizing limitations as any photo would be. So, for example, if you have a type layer, you can still apply filters to the type or paint on it, but you can no longer edit the words. (See page 333 for more about simplifying and working with shapes, and see Chapter 14 for working with type.)

Flattening an image

While layers are simply swell when you're working on an image, they're a headache when you want to share your image, especially if you're sending it to a photo-printing service (their machines usually don't understand layered files). And even if you're printing at home, the large size of a layered file can make it take forever to print. Also, if you plan to use your image in other programs, very few non-Adobe programs are totally comfortable with layered files, so you may get some odd results if you feed them a layered file.

In these cases, you may want to squash everything in your picture into a single layer. It's very easy to do this in Elements. You simply flatten your image. Do so by going to Layer → Flatten Image, or on the Layers palette, choose More → Flatten Image.

> **NOTE** Saving your image as a JPEG file automatically gets rid of layers, too.

There's no keystroke shortcut for flattening, because it's something you don't want to do by accident. Like merging, flattening is a permanent change. Many cautious Elements veterans always do a Save As, instead of a plain Save, before flattening. That way you have a flattened copy and still have your working copy with the layers intact, just in case. Organizer version sets (page 54) can help you here, too, because they allow you to save different states of your image. So, you could have a version with layers and a flattened version, too.

> **NOTE** Flattening creates a background layer out of the existing layers in your image, which means that you lose transparency, just as with a regular background layer. If you want to create a single layer with transparency, use Merge Visible instead of Flatten Image.

Fill and Adjustment Layers

Fill layers and *Adjustment layers* are special types of layers. Adjustment layers let you manipulate the lighting, color, or exposure of the layers beneath them. If you're mainly interested in Elements to spruce up your photos, you'll probably use Adjustment layers more than any other kind. Adjustment layers are great because they give you the ability to undo or change your edits later on if you want to.

You can also use Adjustment layers to take the changes you've made on one photo and reapply those changes to another photo (see the box below). And after you've created an Adjustment layer, you can limit future edits so they affect only the area of your photo covered by the Adjustment layer.

You'll find out much more about all the things you can do with Adjustment layers in the next few chapters. For now, you just need to learn how to create and manipulate them.

Fill layers are just what they sound like: layers filled with a color, a pattern, or a gradient (a rainbow-like range of colors). There's more about gradients on page 362.

> **TIP** Digital photographers should check out the Photo Filter Adjustment layers. They let you digitally make the sort of adjustments that you used to do by attaching a colored piece of glass to the front of your camera's lens. You can read more about what you can do with photo filters on page 224.

GEM IN THE ROUGH

Adjustment Layers for Batch Processing

Page 227 shows you how to perform *batch* commands: simultaneously applying adjustments to groups of photos, using the Process Multiple Files tool. The drawback with Process Multiple Files is that you have access only to some of the auto commands there. So what do you do if you're a fussy photographer who's got 17 shots that are all pretty much the same and you'd like to apply the same fixes to all of them? Do you have to edit each one from scratch?

Not in Elements. You can open the photos you want to fix and then drag an Adjustment layer from the first photo onto each of the other photos (page 168 shows you how to drag layers between images). The new photo gets the same adjustments at the same settings. It's not as fast as true batch processing, but it saves a lot of time compared to editing each photo from scratch.

Adding Fill and Adjustment Layers

Creating an Adjustment or Fill layer is easy. In the Layers palette, just click the black-and-white circle, as shown in Figure 6-19. The button displays a menu of all the Adjustment and Fill layer choices in one list (the first three choices are Fill layers; the rest are Adjustment layers).

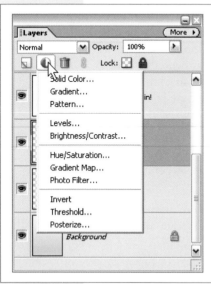

Figure 6-19:
To create a new Adjustment or Fill layer, click the black-and-white circle to get a drop-down menu that lets you choose the type of Adjustment or Fill layer you want. If you'd rather work from the menu bar, go to Layer → New Adjustment Layer (or Layer → New Fill Layer) and choose the layer type you want.

Whichever type of layer you choose, you get a dialog box that lets you tweak the layer's settings (the exception is Invert, which doesn't give you any choices). After you make your choices, click OK, and the new layer appears.

Elements gives you three Fill layer choices: Solid Color, Gradient (a rainbow-like range of colors), and Pattern. There's more about patterns on page 245 and about gradients on page 362.

The kinds of Adjustment layers you can select from are:

- **Levels.** This is a much more sophisticated way to apply Levels than using the Auto Levels button in Quick Fix or the Auto Level command from the Enhance menu. Page 184 has more information about using Levels. For most people, Levels is the most important Adjustment layer.

- **Brightness/Contrast.** This does pretty much the same things as the Quick Fix adjustment (covered on page 100).

- **Hue/Saturation.** Again, it's very much like the Quick Fix command (page 102), only with slightly different controls.

- **Gradient Map.** Gradient Map is very tricky to understand and is explained in detail on page 371. It applies a gradient based on a map of the luminosity values in your image. That means you can apply a gradient so that the colors aren't just distributed in a straight line across your image.

- **Photo Filter.** Use Photo Filter to adjust the color balance of your photos by adding warming, cooling, or special effects filters, just like you might attach to the lens of a film camera. See page 224.

- **Invert.** Invert reverses the colors of your image to their opposite values, for an effect similar to a film negative. See page 262.

- **Threshold.** Use this to make everything in your photo pure black and pure white. See page 262.

- **Posterize.** Reduces the numbers of colors in your image to give a poster-like effect. See page 262.

You can change the settings for a Fill or Adjustment layer by highlighting the layer in the Layers palette, and then going to Layer → Content Options, or by double-clicking the left icon for the layer in the Layers palette. The layer's dialog box reappears, and you can adjust its settings. Deleting Fill and Adjustment layers is a tad different from deleting a regular layer, as explained in Figure 6-20.

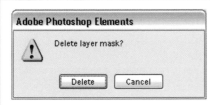

Figure 6-20:
When you click the Layers palette Delete icon, Elements asks you if you want to "Delete layer mask?" Click Delete. Then you have to click the Trash icon again to fully delete the layer. If you want to get rid of the layer in one go, you've got a few choices: use the Layer menu, right-click the layer in the Layers palette, or use the More button to delete it. In each case, you should see a Delete Layer choice. There's more about layer masks in the next section.

Layer Masks

Adjustment and Fill layers use something called a *layer mask*, which dictates which parts of the layer are affected when you make your changes (see Figure 6-21). By changing the area covered by the layer mask you can control which part of your image the layer adjustments affect.

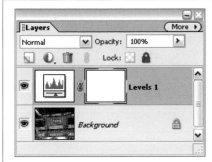

Figure 6-21:
Adjustment and Fill layers, like the Levels 1 layer shown here, always have two icons in the Layers palette: the left side shows what kind of adjustment the layer is making (Levels, in this case). You can double-click that icon to bring up the dialog box to make changes to your settings after the layer is in place. The right icon is for the Layer Mask, and you can use it to control the area that is covered by the adjustment.

Full Photoshop uses layer masks for many other purposes, but in Elements, these layers are the only place you encounter a layer mask. The great thing about layer masks is that you can edit them by painting on them, as explained on page 274. In other words, you can go back later and change the part of your image that the Adjustment layer affects.

Incidentally, the term layer *mask* may be a bit confusing if you're thinking about masking with the Selection brush. With the Selection brush, masking prevents something from being changed. A layer mask really works the same way, but by definition, it starts out empty; in other words, the mask can be used to prevent your adjustment from affecting parts of the layer, but not until you mask out parts of your image by painting on the layer mask. So to begin with, your entire layer is affected by your change. You can learn how to edit layer masks on page 224.

Moving Layers Between Images

If you use layers, it's extremely easy to combine parts of different photos together. Just put what you want from photo A into its own layer and then drag it onto photo B. The trick is that you have to drag the layer *from the Layers palette*. If you try to drop one photo directly onto another photo's window, you'll just wind up with a lot of windows stacked up on top of each other (unless you activate the Move tool, described on page 136). Figure 6-22 shows you the correct way to move a layer between photos.

TIP You can also drag a photo directly from the Photo bin into another image.

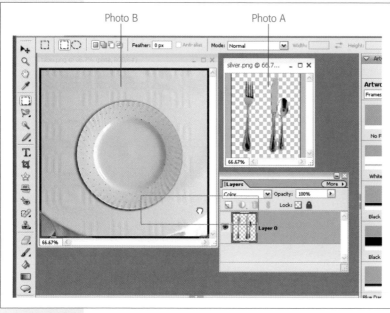

Figure 6-22:
This figure shows how to move objects from one photo to another, working from the Layers palette. Here, the goal is to get the silverware from photo A (whose Layers palette is visible) onto the tablecloth in photo B (whose image is visible). You always drag from the Layers palette onto a photo window when you combine parts of different images into a composite. (If you try to drag from a photo to a photo, it won't work unless you click the Move tool first.) Use the Move tool to adjust your object's placement once you've dropped it into the image.

NOTE You can't work with multiple images when you have your Elements screen view set to Maximize mode. Instead, go to Window → Images and choose Tile or Cascade. Cascade gives you the most flexibility for positioning your photos.

Here are a few points to keep in mind when you're copying a layer from one image to another:

- **Watch out for conflicting resolution settings** (see page 82). The bottom image (that is, the one receiving the moved layer) controls the resolution. So if you bring in a layer that's set to 300 pixels per inch (ppi), and place it on an image that's set to 72 ppi, the object you're moving will now be set to 72 ppi.

- **Lighting matters.** Objects that are lit differently will stand out if you try to combine them. If possible, plan ahead and choose similar lighting for photos you're thinking about combining.

- **Feather with care.** A little feathering (page 117) goes a long way toward creating a realistic result.

TIP If you'd like more practice using layers, visit the "Missing CD" page at *www.missingmanuals.com* and download the Table Tutorial. It walks you through most of the basic layer functions.

3

Part Three: Retouching

Basic Image Retouching

You may be perfectly happy using Elements only in Quick Fix mode. And that's fine, as long as you understand that you've hardly scratched the surface of what the program can do for you. Sooner or later, though, you're probably going to run across a photo where your best Quick Fix efforts just aren't good enough. Or you may just be curious to see what else Elements has under its hood. That's when you finally get to put all your image-selecting and layering skills to good use.

Elements gives you loads of ways to fix your photos beyond the limited options in Quick Fix. This chapter guides you through fixing basic exposure problems, shows you new ways of sharpening your photos, and most importantly, helps you understand how to improve the colors in your photos.

If you want to get the most out of Elements, you need to understand a little about how your camera, computer, and printer think about color. Next to resolution, color is the most important concept in Elements. After all, almost all the adjustments image editing programs make consist of changing the color of pixels. So quite a bit of this chapter is about understanding how Elements—and by extension, you—can manipulate your image's color.

> **TIP** Most of Elements' advanced-fixes dialog boxes have a "preview" checkbox, which lets you watch what's happening as your adjust the settings. It's a good idea to keep these checkboxes turned on so you can decide if you're improving things. And for a handy "before" and "after" comparison, toggle the checkbox on and off.

Fixing Exposure Problems

Incorrectly exposed photos are *the* number one problem all photographers face. No matter how carefully you set up your shot and how many different settings you try on your camera, it always seems like the picture you really, really want to keep is the one that's over- or underexposed.

The Smart Fix commands (page 97) can really help your photo, but if you've tried to bring back a picture that's badly over- or underexposed, you've probably run into the limitations of what Quick Fix can do. Similarly, the Shadows/Highlights command (page 176) can do a lot, but it's not intended to fix a photo whose exposure is totally botched—just ones where the contrast between light and dark areas needs a bit of help. And if you push Smart Fix to its limits, your results may be a little strange. In those situations, you need to move on to some of Elements' more powerful tools to help improve your exposure.

UP TO SPEED

Understanding Exposure

What exactly *is* exposure, anyway? You almost certainly know a poorly exposed photo when you see it: either it's too light or too dark. But what exactly has gone wrong?

Exposure refers to the amount of light your film (or the sensor in your digital camera) received when you released the shutter.

A well-exposed photo shows the largest amount of detail in *all* parts of your image—light and dark. In a properly exposed photo, shadows aren't just pits of blackness, and bright areas show more than washed-out splotches of white.

Deciding Which Exposure Fix to Use

When you open a poorly exposed photo in Elements, the first thing you need to do is figure out what's wrong with it, just like a doctor diagnosing a patient. If the exposure's not perfect, what exactly is wrong? Here's a list of common symptoms to help you figure out where to go next:

- **Everything is too dark.** If your photo is really dark, try adding a Screen layer, as explained on page 175. If it's just a bit too dark, try using Levels (see page 184).

- **Everything is too light.** If the whole photo looks washed out, try adding a Multiply layer (explained on page 175). If it's just a bit too light, try Levels (page 184).

- **The photo is mostly OK, but your subject is too dark or the light parts of the photo are too light.** Try the Shadows/Highlights adjustment (page 176).

Of course, if you're lucky (or a really skilled photographer), you may not see any of these problems, in which case, skip to page 184 if you want to do something to make your colors pop.

NOTE   You may have noticed that you didn't see Brightness/Contrast mentioned anywhere in the previous list. A lot of people tend to jump for the Brightness/Contrast controls when facing a poorly exposed photo. That's logical—after all, these dials usually help improve the picture on your TV. But in Elements, about 99 percent of the time, you've got a whole slew of powerful tools—like Levels and the Shadows/Highlights command—that can do much more than Brightness/Contrast can.

Fixing Major Exposure Problems

If your photo is completely over- or underexposed, you need to add special layers to correct the problems. You follow the same steps to fix either problem. The only difference is the layer blend mode (page 153) you choose: *Multiply layers* darken your image's exposure while *Screen layers* lighten it. Figure 7-1 shows Multiply layers in action (and also gives you an idea of the limitations of this technique if your exposure is really far gone). You can download the file window.jpg from the "Missing CD" page at *www.missingmanuals.com* if you'd like to try the different exposure fixes for yourself.

Be careful, though. If your entire photo isn't out of whack, using Multiply or Screen layers can ruin the exposure of the parts that were OK to start with, because they'll increase or decrease the exposure on the entire photo. Your properly exposed areas may blow out (see page 179) and lose the details if you apply a Screen layer, for example. So, if your exposure problem is spotty (rather than image-wide), try Shadows/Highlights (page 176) first. If your whole photo needs an exposure correction, here's how to use layers to fix it:

1. **Create a duplicate layer.**

   Open your photo and press Ctrl+J or go to Layer → Duplicate Layer. Check to be sure the duplicate layer is the active layer.

2. **In the Layers palette, change the mode for the new layer in the pop-up menu.**

   Choose Multiply, if your photo is overexposed, or Screen, if it's underexposed. Make sure you change the mode of the duplicate layer, not the original layer.

3. **Adjust the opacity of the layer if needed.**

   If the effect of the new layer is too strong, in the Layers palette, move the Opacity slider to the left to reduce the new layer's opacity.

4. **Repeat as necessary.**

   You may need to use as many as five or six layers if your photo is in really bad shape. If you need extra layers, you'll probably want them at 100 percent opacity, so you can just keep pressing Ctrl+J, which will duplicate the current top layer.

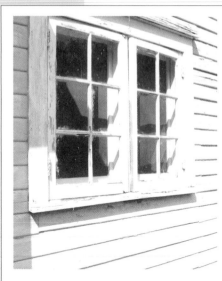

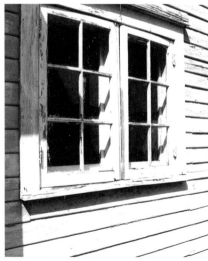

Figure 7-1:
For those who think photographically, each Multiply layer you add is roughly equivalent to stopping your camera down one f-stop.

Top: This photo is totally overexposed, and it looks like there's no detail there at all. Multiply layers darken things down enough to bring back a lot of the washed-out areas. This technique can bring up the detail quite a bit.

Bottom: As you can see in the corrected photo, even Elements can't do much in areas where there's no detail at all.

You're more likely to need several layers to fix overexposure than you are for underexposure. And, of course, there are limits to what even Elements can do for a blindingly overexposed image. Overexposure is usually tougher to fix than underexposure, especially if the area is blown out, as explained in the box "Avoiding Blowouts" on page 179.

The Shadows/Highlights Command

The Shadows/Highlights command is one of the best features in Elements. It's an incredibly powerful tool for adjusting only the dark or light areas of your photo without messing up the rest of it. Figure 7-2 shows what a great help it can be.

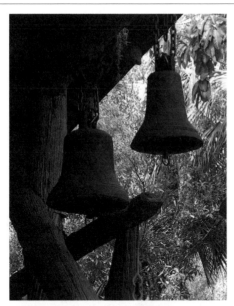

Figure 7-2:
Shadows/Highlights can bring back details from photos where you were sure there was no information at all.

Top: The original photo suffers from a severe case of extreme backlighting.

Bottom: The Shadows/Highlights tool brings out the hidden detail and reduces the background glare. If you look closely at the mouths of the bells and the wooden supports just below them, you can see the kind of noise that often lurks in underexposed areas. Those problems mean you may need to apply noise reduction (page 350) and tweak the saturation.

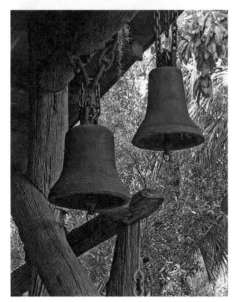

The Shadows/Highlights command in the Full Editor works pretty much the same way it does in Quick Fix (page 100). The single flaw in this great tool is that you can't apply it as an Adjustment layer (page 165), so you may want to apply Shadows/Highlights to a duplicate layer. Then, later on, you can discard the changes if you want to take another whack at adjusting the photo. In any case, it's not difficult at all to make amazing changes to your photos with Shadows/Highlights. Here's how:

1. **Open your photo and duplicate the layer (Ctrl+J) if you want to.**

   Duplicating your layer makes it easier to undo Shadows/Highlights later if you change your mind.

2. **Go to Enhance → Adjust Lighting → Shadows/Highlights.**

   Your photo immediately becomes about 30 shades lighter. Don't panic. As soon as you select the command, the Lighten Shadows setting automatically jumps to 25 percent, which is way too much for about 80 percent of your photos. Just shove the slider back to 0 to undo this change before you start making your corrections.

3. **Move the sliders around until you like what you see.**

   The sliders do exactly what they say: Lighten Shadows makes the dark areas of your photo lighter, and Darken Highlights makes the light areas darker. Pushing the slider to the right increases the effect for either one.

4. **Click OK when you're happy.**

The Shadows/Highlights tool is a cinch to use because you just go by what you're seeing. Keep these tips in mind:

- You may to want to add a smidgen of the opposite tool to balance things out a little. In other words, if you're lightening shadows, you may get better results by giving the Darken Highlights slider a teeny nudge, too.

- Midtone Contrast is there because your photo may look kind of flat after you're done with Shadows/Highlights, especially if you've made big adjustments. Move the Midtone Contrast slider to the right to increase the contrast in your photo. It usually adds a bit of a darkening effect, so you may need to go back to one of the other sliders to tweak your photo after you use it.

- You can overdo this tool. When you see halos around the objects in your photo, you've pushed the settings too far.

> **TIP**   If the Shadows/Highlights tool looks like it washed out your photo's colors—making every-one look like they've been through the laundry too many times—you can adjust the color intensity with one of the Saturation commands, either in Quick Fix or in the Full Editor (as described on page 251). Watch people's skin tones when increasing the saturation—if the subjects in your photo start looking like sunless-tanning lotion disaster victims, you've gone too far. You can also try adjusting colors with Elements' new Color Curves feature (page 248).

Controlling the Colors You See

You want your photos to look as good as possible and to have beautiful, breath-taking color, right? That's probably why you bought Elements. But now that you've got the program, you're having a little trouble getting things to look the way you want. Does this sound familiar?

Avoiding Blowouts

An area of a photo is *blown out* when it's so overexposed that it appears as just plain white—in other words, your camera didn't record any data at all for that area. (Elements isn't all that great with total black, either, but that doesn't happen quite so often. Most underexposed photos have some tonal gradations in them, even if you can't see them very well.)

A blowout is as disastrous in photography as it is when you're driving. Even Elements can't fix blowouts because there's no data for it to work from. So, you're stuck with the fixes discussed in this chapter, which are never as good as a good original.

When you're taking pictures, remember that it's generally easier to correct underexposure than overexposure. Keep that in mind when choosing your camera settings. If you live where there's extremely bright sunlight most of the time, you may want to make a habit of backing your exposure compensation down a hair. Depending on your camera, your subject, and the average ambient glare, you should try starting at −.3 and adjusting from there.

You can also try *bracketing* your shots—taking multiple shots of exactly the same subject with different exposure settings. Then you can combine the two exposures for maximum effect (the box on page 224 explains how to combine images).

- Your photos look great onscreen but your prints are washed out, too dark, or the colors are all a little wrong.

- Your photos look just fine in other programs like Word or Windows Explorer, but they look just awful in Elements.

What's going on? The answer has to do with the fact that Elements is a *color-managed* program. That means that Elements uses your monitor for guidance when deciding how to display images. Color management is the science of making sure that the color in your images is always exactly the same, no matter who opens your file or what kind of hardware they're viewing it on or printing it from. If you think of all the different monitor and printer models out there, you get an idea of what a big job this is.

Graphics pros spend their whole lives grappling with color management, and you can find plenty of books about the finer points of color management. On the most sophisticated level, color management is complicated enough to make you curl up, whimpering, into the fetal position and swear never to create another picture.

Luckily for you, Elements makes color management a whole lot easier. Most of the time, you have only two things to deal with: your monitor calibration and your color space. The following pages cover both.

> **NOTE** There are a couple of other color-related settings for printing, too, but you can deal with those when you get ready to print. Chapter 15 explains them.

Calibrating Your Monitor

Most of your programs pay no attention to what your monitor thinks, but a color-managed application like Elements relies on the *profile*—the information your computer stores about your monitor's settings—when it decides how to print or display a photo onscreen. If that profile isn't accurate, neither is the color in Elements.

So, you may need to *calibrate* your monitor, which is a way of adjusting its settings. A properly calibrated monitor makes all the difference in the world for getting great-looking results. If your photos look bad only in Elements, or if your pictures in print don't look anything like they look onscreen, the place to start is by calibrating your monitor.

Getting started with calibrating

Calibrating a monitor sounds horribly complicated, but it's actually not that difficult—some people think it's even kind of fun. You get an extra added benefit in that your monitor may look about a thousand times better than you thought it could. Calibrating may even make it easier to read text in Word, for instance, because the contrast is better.

Adobe gives you the Adobe Gamma Utility to calibrate your monitor. It installs right along with Elements. To get to it, go to Start → Control Panel → Appearance and Themes → Adobe Gamma. (If you can't find Adobe Gamma there, switch to Classic View.) Click the utility (in Classic View, double-click), and then follow the onscreen directions. Figure 7-3 shows you the Adobe Gamma window.

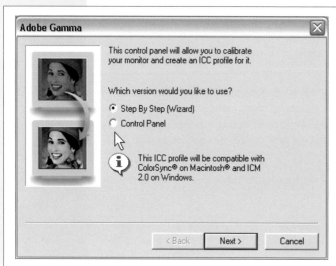

Figure 7-3:
Despite its intimidating name, the Adobe Gamma Utility is actually fairly easy to use, as you can see from this straightforward first screen. Choose the wizard if you've never calibrated your monitor before. If you want a step-by-step guide to using the Adobe Gamma Utility, Photoshop guru Ian Lyons has an excellent tutorial on his Web site at www.computer-darkroom.com/ps8_colour/ps8_2.htm. (It was written for Photoshop, but Adobe Gamma works the same no matter which program you use.)

If you have an LCD (flat panel) monitor, the bad news is that Adobe Gamma isn't really designed to work with LCDs. The good news is that sometimes it does help (despite Adobe's claims that it won't work with LCDs). It's certainly worth a try, and the odds are that you can improve your view at least a little, even if you can't make it perfect. If that doesn't help, you may want to try a third-party monitor-calibrating solution. Most of the good ones for LCDs use special hardware, so expect to spend some money if you need to go that route. Luckily, prices for calibration systems have dropped dramatically in the past year or two. (For example, if you shop around, you can find the Pantone Huey or the Colorvision Spyder2express for about $70.)

If your photos still look a little odd even after you've calibrated your monitor, you may need to turn on the Ignore EXIF setting in the Editor's preferences; see Figure 7-4.

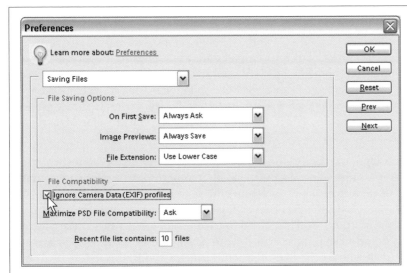

Figure 7-4:
If you still see a funny color cast (usually red or yellow) on all your digital camera photos, go to Edit → Preferences → Saving Files and turn on "Ignore Camera Data (EXIF) profiles." Some cameras embed nonstandard color information in their files, and Elements' Ignore EXIF utility just tells Elements to pay no attention to it, allowing your photos to display and print properly.

Choosing a Color Space

The other thing you may need to do to get good color from Elements is to check the *color space* Elements is using. Color space refers to which standard (out of several possibilities) Elements uses to define your colors. Color space can seem pretty abstruse the first time you hear about it, but it's simply a way of defining what colors mean. For example, when someone says "green," what do you envision: a lush emerald color, a deep forest green, a bright lime?

Choosing a color space is a way to make sure that everything—Elements, your monitor, your printer—that handles a digital file sees the same colors the same way. Over the years, the graphics industry has agreed on standards so that everyone has the same understanding of what you mean when you say red or green—as long as you specify which set of standards you're using.

Elements only gives you two color spaces to pick from: *sRGB* (also called *sRGB IEC61966-2.1* if you want to impress your geek friends) and *Adobe RGB*. When you choose a color space, you tell Elements which set of standards you want it to apply to your photos.

If you're happy with the color you see on your monitor in Elements and you like the prints you're getting, you don't need to make any changes. If, on the other hand, you aren't perfectly satisfied with what Elements is giving you, you'll probably want to modify your color space, which you can do in the Color Settings dialog box. Go to Edit → Color Settings or press Ctrl+Shift+K. Here are your choices:

- **No Color Management.** Elements ignores any information that your file already contains, like color space information from your camera, and doesn't attempt to add any color info to the file data. (When you do a Save As, there's a checkbox that offers you the option of embedding your monitor profile. Don't turn on this checkbox, since your monitor profile is best left for the monitor's own use, and putting the profile into your file can make trouble if you ever send the file someplace else for printing.)

- **Always Optimize Colors for Computer Screens.** Choose this option and you're looking at your photo in the sRGB color space, which is what most Web browsers use, so this is a good choice for when you're preparing graphics for the Web. Many online printing services also prefer sRGB files. (If you've used a previous version of Elements, this is the same as the old Limited Color Management option.)

- **Always Optimize for Printing.** This option uses the Adobe RGB color space, which is a wider color space than sRGB. In other words, it allows more gradations of color than sRGB. Sometimes this is your best choice for printing—but not always. So despite the note you'll see in the Color Settings dialog box about "best for printing," don't be afraid to try one of the other two settings instead. Many home inkjet printers actually cope better with sRGB or no color management than with Adobe RGB. (For old Elements hands, this setting used to be called Full Color Management.)

- **Allow Me to Choose.** This option assumes that you're using the sRGB space, but lets you assign either an Adobe RGB tag, an sRGB tag, or no tag at all. If you've selected "Allow Me to Choose," each time you open a file, you see the dialog box shown in Figure 7-5. You can use this dialog box to assign a different profile to a photo. Just save it once without a profile (turn off the ICC [International Color Consortium] Profile checkbox in the Save As dialog box), and then reopen it and choose the profile you want from the dialog box. Or there's an easier way to convert a color profile if you need to make a change. See the box on page 183 to learn how.

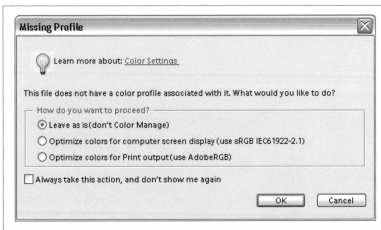

Figure 7-5:
If you select the "Allow Me to Choose" option for color management, you see the Missing Profile dialog box each time you open a previously untagged image. Here's where you can decide whether or not to tag your file and how to tag it. (See page 46 for more about tags.)

POWER USERS' CLINIC

Converting Profiles in Elements

If you're a color-management maven, Elements gives you a feature you'll really appreciate—the ability to convert an image's ICC profile from one color space to another. If you've been working in, say, sRGB, and now you want your photo to have the Adobe RGB profile, you can convert it by going to Image → Convert Color Profile and choosing Apply Adobe RGB profile in the pop-out menu.

You can choose to remove a profile, or convert to sRGB or Adobe RGB; your current color profile choice is grayed out.

This is a true conversion. Your photo's colors don't shift the way they might if you just tag a photo with a different profile. Why would you want to perform such a conversion? Well, for example, if you use Adobe RGB when editing your photos, but you're sending your pictures to an online printing service that wants sRGB instead. Then you may want to think about converting.

NOTE   Elements 5, like its predecessor Elements 4, automatically opens files tagged with a color space other than the one you're working in without letting you know what it's just done. (Except when you open a file in a color space that Elements can't handle at all, like CMYK. In that case, Elements offers to convert it to a mode you can use.) So, if you have an Adobe RGB file and you're working in "Always Optimize for Computer Screens," Elements doesn't warn you about the profile mismatch the way early versions did—it just opens the file.

So what's your best option? Once again, if everything is looking good, leave it alone. Otherwise, for general use, you're probably best off starting with No Color Management. Then try the others if that doesn't work well for you.

If you choose one of the other three options, when you save your file, Elements attempts to embed the file with a *tag*, or information about the file's color space—either Adobe RGB or sRGB. (Incidentally, this tag isn't related to the Organizer tags that you read about in Chapter 2.) If you don't want a color tag—also known as an *ICC Profile*—in your file, just turn off the checkbox before you save your file. Figure 7-6 shows where to find the profile information in the Save As dialog box, and how to turn the whole process off.

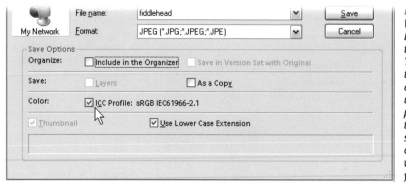

Figure 7-6:
When you save a file, Elements offers to embed the color tag in the file. You can safely turn off the ICC Profile checkbox and leave the file untagged. (Assigning a profile is helpful because then any program that sees your file knows what color standards you're working with. But if you're new to Elements, you'll usually have an easier time if you don't start embedding profiles in files without a good reason.)

Using Levels

People who've used Elements for a while will tell you that the Levels command is one of the program's most essential tools. You can fix an amazing array of problems simply by adjusting the level of each *color channel*. (On your monitor, each color you see is composed of red, green, and blue. In Elements, you can make very precise adjustments to your images by adjusting these color channels separately.)

Just as its name suggests, Levels adjusts the level of each color within your image. There are several different adjustments you can make using Levels, from general brightening of your colors to fixing a color cast (more about color casts later in this chapter). Most digital photo enthusiasts treat almost every picture they take to a dose of Levels, because there's no better way to polish up the color in your photo.

The way Levels works is fairly complex. Start by thinking of the possible range of brightness in any photo on a scale from 0 (black) to 255 (white). Some photos may have pixels in them that fall at both those extremes, but most photos don't. And even the ones that do may not have the full range of brightness in each individual color channel. Most of the time, there's going to be some empty space at one or both ends of the scale.

When you use Levels, you tell Elements to consider the range of colors available in *your* photo as the *total* tonal range it has to work with. Elements redistributes your colors accordingly. Basically, you just get rid of the empty space at the ends of the scale of possibilities. This can dramatically readjust the color distribution in your photo, as you can see in Figure 7-7.

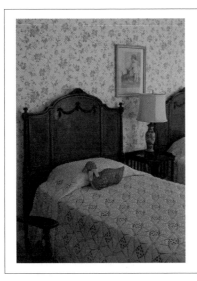 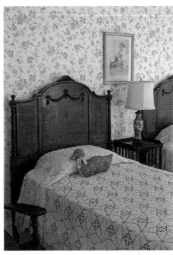

Figure 7-7:
A simple Levels adjustment can make a huge difference in the way your photo looks.

Left: The slight yellow cast to this photo makes everything look dull.

Right: Levels not only got rid of the yellow cast, but the photo also gives the impression of having better contrast and sharpness.

It's much, much easier to use Levels than to understand it, as you know if you've already tried Auto Levels in Quick Fix (page 99). That command is great for, well, quick fixes. But if you really need to massage your image, Levels has a lot more under the hood than you can see there. The next section shows you how to get at these settings.

Understanding the Histogram

Before you can get started adjusting Levels, you first need to understand the heart, soul, and brain of the Levels dialog box: the Histogram (shown in Figure 7-8).

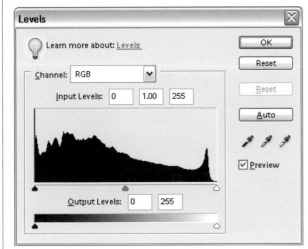

Figure 7-8:
One of the scariest sights in Elements, the Levels dialog box is actually your very good friend. If it frightens you, take comfort in knowing that you've always got the Auto button here, which is the same Auto Levels command as in Quick Fix. But it's worth persevering: the other options here give you much better control over the end results.

The Histogram is the black bumpy mound in the window. It's really nothing more than a bar graph indicating the distribution of the colors in your photo. (It's a bar graph, but there's no space between the bars, which is what causes the mountainous look.)

From left to right, the Histogram shows the brightness range from dark to light (the 0 to 255 mentioned earlier in this section). The height of the "mountain" at any given point shows how many pixels in your photo are that particular brightness. You can tell a lot about your photo by where the mound of color is before you adjust it, as demonstrated in Figure 7-9.

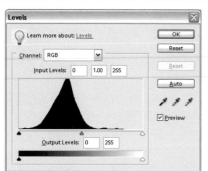

Figure 7-9:
Top: If the bars in your Histogram are all smushed together, your photo doesn't have a lot of tonal range. As long as you like how the photo looks, that's not important. But if you're unhappy with the color in the photo, it's usually going to be harder to get it exactly right compared to a photo with a wider tonal distribution.

Middle: If all your colors are bunched up on the left side, your photo is underexposed.

Bottom: If you just have a big lump that's all on the right side, your photo is overexposed.

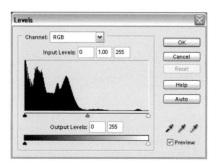

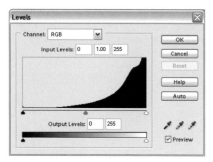

If you look above the Histogram, you can see that there's a little menu that says RGB. If you pull that down, you can also see a separate Histogram for each individual color. You can adjust all three channels at once in the RGB setting, or change each channel separately for maximum control over your colors.

The Histogram contains so much information about your photo that Adobe also makes it available in the Full Editor in its own palette; this way, you can always see it and use it to monitor how you're changing the colors in your image. The Histogram palette is shown in Figure 7-10. Once you get fluent in reading Histogramese, you'll probably want to keep this palette around.

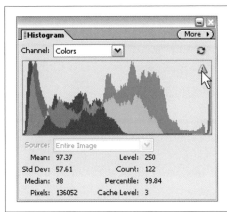

Figure 7-10:
If you keep the Histogram on your desktop, you can always see what effect your changes are having on the color distribution in your photo. To get this nifty Technicolor view, go to Window → Histogram and then choose Colors from the pull-down menu on the palette. To update a Histogram, click the triangle as shown. If you're really into statistical information, there's a bunch of it available from this palette, but if you're not a pro, you can safely ignore these numbers.

The Histogram is just a graph, and you don't do anything to it directly. What you do when you use Levels is use the Histogram as a guide so that you can tell Elements what to consider as the black and white points—that is, the darkest and lightest points, in your photo. (Remember, you're thinking in terms of brightness values, not shades of color, for these settings.)

Once you've set the end points, you can adjust the *gamma*—the tones in between that would appear gray in a black-and-white photo. If that sounds complicated, it's not—not when you're actually doing it. Once you've made a Levels adjustment, the next time you open the Levels dialog box, you'll see that your Histogram now runs the entire length of the scale because you've told Elements to redistribute your colors so that they cover the full dark-to-light range.

The next two sections show you—finally!—how to actually adjust your image's Levels.

NOTE   Once you learn how to interpret the Histograms in Elements, you can try your hand with your camera's histogram (if it has one). It's really hard to judge how well your picture turned out when all you have to go by is your camera's tiny LCD screen, so the histogram can be a big help. By looking at your camera's histogram, you can tell how well exposed your shot was.

Levels Before Curves

The colors in my photo are so far off that everybody looks seasick! Which feature should I use to get that greenish cast out of my family's faces—Levels or Curves?

Elements 5 brings a much requested feature over from Photoshop—*Color Curves.* Despite the name, the Curves tool isn't some kind of arc drawing tool. Instead, it's yet another sophisticated method of adjusting the color in your photos. Curves works something like Levels, but with many more available points of correction.

In Elements, you get a simplified version of the Photoshop Curves dialog box, with a few preset settings. You don't get quite as many points of adjustment, so you get much of the advanced color control of Curves without all the complexity.

Generally speaking, a quick Levels adjustment is usually all you need to achieve good, realistic color. If you still aren't satisfied with the contrast in your image, or you want to create funky artistic effects, check out Color Curves (explained in detail on page 248).

Adjusting Levels: The Eyedropper Method

One way to adjust Levels is to set the black, white, and/or gray points by using the eyedroppers on the right side of the Levels dialog box. It's quite simple—just follow these steps:

1. **Bring up the Levels dialog box by selecting Layer → New Fill or Adjustment Layer → Levels.**

   If for some reason you don't want a separate layer for your Levels adjustment, go to Enhance → Adjust Lighting → Levels or press Ctrl+L instead. But making the Levels changes on an Adjustment layer gives you more flexibility for making changes in the future.

2. **Move the Levels dialog box out of the way so that you get a good view of your photo.**

   The dialog box loves to plunk itself down smack in the middle of the most important part of your image. Just grab it by the top bar and drag it to where it's not covering up a crucial part of your photo.

3. **In the Levels dialog box, click the black eyedropper.**

   From left to right, the eyedroppers are black, gray, and white. You can kind of see the colors if you look closely.

4. **Move your cursor back over your photo and click an area of your photo that should be black.**

   Should be, not *is.* That's a mistake lots of people make the first time they use this tool. They get the gray eyedropper, say, and click a spot that appears gray rather than one that *ought to be* gray.

5. Repeat with the other eyedroppers for their respective colors.

In other words, now find a white point and a gray point. That's the way it's supposed to work, but it's not always possible to use all of them in any one photo. Experiment to see what gives you the best-looking results.

NOTE   You don't always need to set a gray point. If you try to set it and think your photo looked better without it, just skip that step.

6. When you're happy with what you see, click OK.

See, it's not so hard. If you mess up, just click the Reset button, and you can start over again.

Adjusting Levels: The Slider Controls

The eyedropper method works fine if your photo has spots that should be black, white, or gray, but a lot of the time, your picture may not have any of these colors.

Fortunately, the Levels sliders give you yet another way to apply Levels, and it's by far the most popular method. Using the sliders gives you maximum control over your colors, and it works great even for photos that don't have a white, black, or gray point to click.

If you look directly under the Histogram, you'll see three little triangles, called *Input sliders.* The left triangle is the slider for setting the black point in your photo, the right slider sets the white point, and the middle slider adjusts your gamma (gray). You just drag them to make changes to the color levels in your photo, as shown in Figure 7-11.

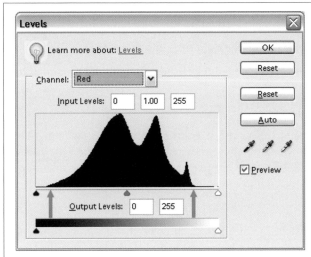

Figure 7-11:
Here's how to use the Levels sliders. You want to move the sliders from the ends of the track until they're under the outer edges of the color data in the graph. If there's empty space on the end, just move the slider until it's under the first mound of data. The red arrows in this figure show where you'd position the left and right sliders for this photo.

When you move the left Input slider, you tell Levels, "Take all the pixels from this point down and consider them black." With the right slider, you're saying, "Make this pixel and all higher values white." The middle slider, the gamma slider, adjusts the brightness value that's considered medium gray. All three adjustments improve the contrast of your image.

> **TIP** If there are small amounts of data, like a flat line at the ends or if all your data is bunched in the middle of the graph, watch the preview in your photo to decide how far toward the mountain you should bring the sliders. Moving it all the way in may be too drastic. Your own taste should always be the deciding factor when you're adjusting a photo.

The easiest way to use the Levels sliders is to:

1. **Bring up the Levels dialog box.**

   Use one of the methods described in step 1 of the Eyedropper method (page 188).

2. **Move the Levels dialog box so you've got a clear view of your photo and then grab the black Input slider.**

   That's the one on the left side of the Histogram box.

3. **Slide it to the right, if necessary.**

   Move it over until it's under the left-most part of the Histogram that has a "mound" of color in it. If you glance back at Figure 7-11, you'd move the left slider to where the left red arrow is. (Incidentally, although you're adjusting the colors in your image, the Levels Histogram stays black and white no matter what you do—you don't get any color in the dialog box itself.)

   You may not need to move the slider at all if there's already a good bit of data at the end of the Histogram. It's not mandatory to adjust everything every time.

4. **Grab the white slider (the one on the right side) and move it left.**

   Bring it under the farthest right area of the Histogram that has a mound of data in it.

5. **Now adjust the gray slider.**

   This is called the *gamma* slider, and it adjusts the midtones of your photo. Move it back and forth while watching your photo until you like what you see. Gamma makes the most impact on the overall result, so take some time to play with this slider.

6. **Click OK.**

You can adjust your entire image or adjust each color channel individually. The most accurate way is to first choose each color channel separately from the Channel drop-down menu in the Levels dialog box. Adjust the end points for each channel by itself, and then go back to RGB and tweak just the gamma slider.

TIP   If you know the numerical value of the pixels you want to designate for any of these settings—you geek!—you can type that information into the boxes. You can set the gamma value from
.10 to 9.99. It's set at 1.00 automatically.

The last control you may want to use in the Levels dialog box is the Output Levels slider. Output Levels work roughly the same way as your brightness and contrast controls on your TV. Moving these sliders makes the darkest pixels darker and the lightest pixels lighter. Among pros, this is known as adjusting the tonal range of a photo.

Adjusting Levels will improve almost every photo you take, but if your photo has a bad *color cast*—if it's too orange or too blue—you may need something else. The next section shows you how to get rid of unwanted color.

Removing Unwanted Color

It's not uncommon for an otherwise good photo to have a *color cast*—that is, to have all the tonal values shifted so that the photo is too blue, like Figure 7-12, or too orange.

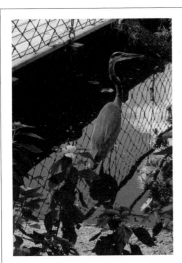 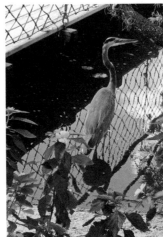

Figure 7-12:
Left: You may wind up with a photo like this every once in a while if you forget to change the white balance— your camera's special setting for the type of lighting conditions you're shooting in (common settings are daylight, fluorescent, and so on). This is an outdoor photo taken with the camera set for tungsten indoor lighting.

Right: Elements fixes that wicked color cast in a jiffy. The photo still needs other adjustments, but the color is back in the ballpark.

Elements gives you several ways to correct color cast problems:

- **Auto Color Correction** doesn't give you any control over how Elements works, but it often does a good job. To use it, go to Enhance → Auto Color Correction or press Ctrl+Shift+B.

- **Levels** gives you the finest control of the methods in this list. You can often eliminate a color cast by adjusting the individual color channels till the extra color is gone (as explained in the previous section). The downside is that Levels can be very fiddly for this sort of work, and one of the other ways may be much faster at getting you the results you want.

- **Remove Color Cast** is the special command for correcting a color cast with one-click ease. The next section explains how to use this tool.

- **The Color Variations** dialog box is helpful in figuring out which colors you need more or less of, but it has some limitations. It's covered on page 193.

- **The Photo Filter command** gives you much more control than the Color Cast tool, and you can apply Photo Filters as Adjustment layers, too. Photo Filters are covered on page 224.

- **The Average Blur Filter,** used along with a blend mode, lets you fix a color cast. As you'll read on page 355, it's something like creating a custom photo filter.

- **Adjust Color for Skin Tone** lets Elements adjust your photos based on the skin colors in the image. In practice, this adjustment may be more likely to introduce a color cast than to correct one, but if your photo has a slight bluish cast that's visible in the skin of the people in the photo (as explained on page 106), it may do the trick. This option works best for slight, annoying casts that are too subtle for the other methods in this list.

All these tools are useful for fixing a color cast, depending on exactly what your problem is. Usually you'd start with Levels and then move on to the Color Cast tool or the Photo Filter. (To practice any of the fixes you're about to learn, download the photo heron.jpg from the "Missing CD" page at *www.missingmanuals. com.*)

Silver Window Borders in Elements

I've set my computer to use the standard blue Windows theme, but all my Elements windows are bordered in silver. What gives?

If you use the standard Windows XP theme with the blue top bars on the windows, you may wonder what happened when you installed Elements, since all your Elements windows are silver. There's nothing wrong with your computer. Bright colors like the Windows shade of

blue tend to confuse your ability to judge colors. So Adobe did you a favor and chose a neutral noninterfering color scheme instead.

You may notice, however, that if you use Windows blue for the rest of your system, your floating palettes will revert to blue when you pull them out of the Palette bin and go back to gray when you put them back in the bin.

Using the Color Cast Tool

The Color Cast tool is another eyedropper sampling tool that adjusts the colors in your photo based on the pixels you click. In this case, you show Elements where a neutral color should be. As you saw with the heron in Figure 7-12, the Color Cast command can make a big difference with just one click. To use it:

1. Go to Enhance → Adjust Color → Remove Color Cast.

   Your cursor should change to an eyedropper when you move it over your photo. If it doesn't change, go to the dialog box and click the Eyedropper icon.

2. **Click an area that should be gray, white, or black.**

   You only have to click once in your photo for this tool to work. As with the Levels eyedropper tool, click an area that *should be* gray, white, or black (as opposed to looking for an area that's currently one of these colors). If several of these colors appear, you can try different spots in your photo, clicking Reset in between each sample, until you find the spot that gives you the most natural-looking color.

3. **Click OK.**

The Color Cast tool works pretty well if your image has areas that should be black, white, or gray, even if they're very tiny. The tricky thing is when you have an image that doesn't have a good area to sample—when there isn't any black, white, or gray anywhere in the picture. If that's the case, consider using the Photo Filter (page 224).

> **TIP** If you generally like what Auto Levels does for your photos, but you feel like it leaves behind a slight color cast, a click with the Color Cast tool may be just the right finishing touch.

Using Color Variations

The Color Variations window (Figure 7-13) is very appealing to many Elements beginners, because it gives you a visual clue about what to do to fix the color in your photo. You just click the little preview thumbnail that shows the color balance you like best, and Elements applies the necessary change to make your photo look like the thumbnail.

However, Color Variations has some pretty severe limitations, most notably the microscopic size of the thumbnails. It's very hard to see what you're doing, and even newcomers can usually get better results in Quick Fix (page 91).

Still, Color Variations is useful for those times when you know something is not quite right in your color but you can't figure out exactly what to do about it. And because it's adjustable, Color Variations is good for when you do know what you want but you want to make only the tiniest sliver of a difference to your photo's color.

To use the Color Variations tool:

1. **Open your photo.**

   You may want to make a duplicate layer (page 147) for the adjustments, so that you'll have the option to discard your changes if you're not happy with them. If you don't work on a duplicate, keep in mind that the changes you make here aren't undoable after you've closed the photo.

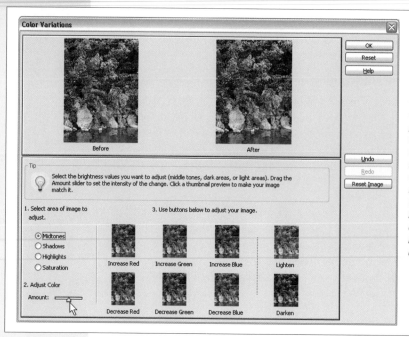

2. Go to Enhance → Adjust Color → Color Variations.

   You see the dialog box pictured in Figure 7-13.

3. **On the lower-left corner of the dialog box (where it says "Select area of image to adjust"), click a radio button to choose whether you want to adjust highlights, shadows, midtones, or saturation.**

   Color Variations begins by selecting midtones, which is usually what you want. But experiment with the other settings to see what they do. The Saturation button works just like Saturation in Quick Fix (page 91).

4. **Use the slider at the bottom of the dialog box to control how drastic the adjustment should be.**

   The farther you push the slider to the right, the more dramatic the change. Usually, just a smidgen is enough to make a noticeable change.

5. **Just below where it says "Use buttons below to adjust your image," click one of the color buttons to make your photo look more like one of the thumbnail photos.**

   You can always Undo or Redo using the buttons on the right side of the window, or use Reset Image to put your photo back to where it was when you started.

6. **When you're happy with the result, click OK.**

Choosing the Color You Want

So far, the color corrections you've been reading about in this chapter have all done most of the color assigning for you. But a lot of the time, you want to be able to *tell* Elements what colors to work with—like when you're selecting the color for a background or Fill layer (page 166), or when you want to paint on an image.

Although you can use any of the millions of colors your screen can display, Elements loads only two colors at a time. You choose these colors using the Foreground and Background color squares at the bottom of the Toolbox (see Figure 7-14).

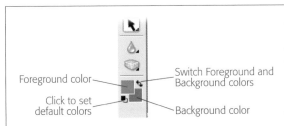

Foreground color

Switch Foreground and Background colors

Click to set default colors

Background color

Figure 7-14:
The top square is your Foreground color, and the bottom is your Background color. You can also use keystrokes to reset the standard black and white colors or switch the colors. Pressing D resets your colors to Elements standard colors of black for the Foreground and white for the Background. Click the curved double-headed arrows or press X to swap the Foreground and Background values.

Foreground and Background mean just what they sound like—use the Background color to fill in backgrounds, and use the Foreground color with the Elements tools, like the Brush or the Paint Bucket. You can use as many colors as you want, of course. The color-picking tools at the bottom of the Toolbox let you control the color you're using in a number of different ways:

- **Reset default colors.** Click the tiny black and white squares to return to the standard settings of black for the Foreground color and white for the Background color.

- **Switch Foreground and Background colors.** Click the little curved arrows above and to the right of the squares, and your Background color becomes the Foreground color, and vice versa. This is very helpful when you've inadvertently made your color selection in the wrong box. (For example, if you've set the Foreground color to yellow, but you actually meant to make the Background color yellow, just click these arrows, and you're all set).

- **Change either the Foreground or Background color to whatever color you want.** You can choose any color you like for either color square. Click either square to call up the Color Picker (explained later) to make your new choice. There's no limit on the colors you can select to use in Elements. Well, technically there is, but it's in the millions, so you should find enough choices for anything you want to do.

You actually have a few different ways to select your Foreground and Background colors. The next few sections show you how to use the Color Picker, the Eyedropper tool (to pick a color from an existing image), or the Color Swatches palette.

When you're working with some of the Elements tools, like the Type tool, you can choose a color in the tool's Options bar settings. Adobe knows that, given a choice, most people tend to prefer working with either the Color Swatches or the Color Picker, so they've come up with a clever way to accommodate both camps, as shown in Figure 7-15.

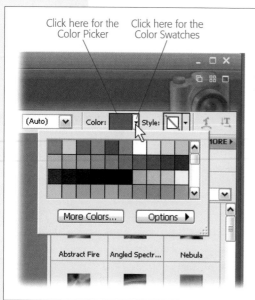

Click here for the Color Picker   Click here for the Color Swatches

Figure 7-15:
Whether you prefer using Color Swatches or the Color Picker, you can choose your favorite (for most tools) in the Options bar. Click the color sample in the box to bring up the Color Picker, or, if you're a Swatcher, click the arrow to the right of the box to reveal the Color Swatches palette.

The Color Picker

Figure 7-16 shows you the Color Picker. It has an intimidating number of options, but, most of the time, you don't need them all. Picking a color is as easy as clicking wherever you see the color you want.

The Color Picker is actually pretty simple to use:

1. **Click the Foreground or Background color square in the Toolbox.**

   The Color Picker launches. Some other tools—like the Paint Bucket (page 318) and the mask color option for the Selection brush (page 125)—also use the Color Picker. It works the same way no matter how you get to it.

2. **Choose the color range you want to select from.**

   Use the vertical Color Slider in the middle of the Color Picker. Slide through the spectrum until you see the color you want in the Color Field.

3. **Click the exact spot in the Color Field where you see the particular shade you want.**

   You can keep clicking around to watch the color in the top box in the window change to reflect the color you've chosen. The bottom box continues to show your original color for comparison.

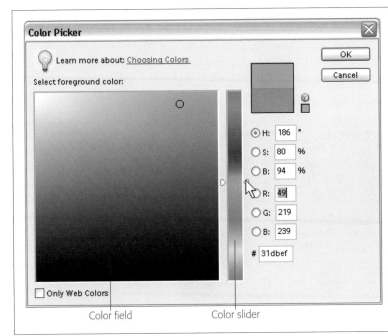

Figure 7-16:
For most beginners, the most important parts of the Elements Color Picker are the slider in the middle (called, appropriately enough, the Color Slider), and the square window, which Adobe calls the Color Field. Use the Slider to get the general color you want, and then click in the Field on the exact shade.

4. **Click OK.**

The color you selected is now your option in the Foreground or Background square in the Toolbox.

That's the basic way to use the Color Picker. See the box on page 199 for ways to enter a numeric value for your color if you know it, or to change the shades the Color Picker is offering you.

> **TIP** You're not limited to Elements' Color Picker. You can also opt to use the Windows Color Picker instead, if you prefer. To change the Color Picker, go to Edit → Preferences → General. The Windows Color Picker opens up looking pretty feeble—just a few colored squares and some plain white ones, but if you click "Define Custom Colors," it expands, giving you access to most of the features in the Adobe picker. (The plain white squares are like little pigeonholes where your color choices are saved.)

The Eyedropper Tool

If you've ever repainted your house, you've probably had the frustrating experience of spotting the *exact* color you want—if only there were a way to capture that color. That's one problem you'll never run into in Elements, thanks to the handy Eyedropper tool that lets you sample any color you see on your monitor and then automatically make it the Foreground color in Elements. If you can get a color into your computer, Elements can grab it.

Sampling a color (that is, snagging it for your own use) couldn't be simpler than it is with the Eyedropper. Just move your cursor over the color you want and click. It even works on colors that aren't already in Elements, as explained in Figure 7-17. Sampling is perfect for projects like scrapbook pages, where you might want to use, say, the color from an event program cover as a theme color for the project. Just scan the program and sample the color with the Eyedropper.

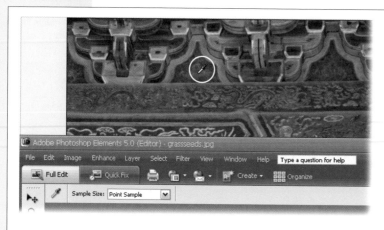

Figure 7-17:
To use the Eyedropper tool to sample colors outside of Elements, start by clicking anywhere inside your Elements file. Then, while still holding your mouse button down, move your cursor over to the non-Elements object (a Web page, for instance), until the eyedropper is over the area you want to sample. Then you can let go, and you'll see the new color in the Elements color squares. If you let go before you get to the non-Elements object, it won't work. Here, the Eyedropper (circled) is sampling the red color from a photo in Windows Picture and Fax Viewer. If you don't have a big monitor, it can take a bit of maneuvering to get the program windows positioned so that you can perform this procedure.

By now, you may be thinking that Elements has more eyedroppers than your medicine cabinet. But this time, the Eyedropper in question is the Official Elements Eyedropper tool that has its own place in the Toolbox. It's one of the easiest tools to use:

1. **Click the Eyedropper in the Toolbox or just press I.**

   Your cursor changes into a tiny eyedropper.

2. **Move the Eyedropper over the color you want to sample.**

   You can watch the color change in the Foreground color box as you move the Eyedropper around.

3. **Click when you see the color you want.**

   Your color choice is loaded up, ready to use, as your Foreground color in the Color Squares. To make it a Background color instead, Alt+click the color in your source.

If you want to keep your color sample around so that you can use it another time without having to get the Eyedropper out again, you can save your color samples in the Swatches palette. Then you can quickly choose those exact colors again any time you want. See the next section for directions on how to do this.

TIP   Since there may be some slight pixel-to-pixel variation in a color, you can set the Eyedropper to sample a little block of pixels and average them. In the Eyedropper Options bar settings, you can choose between the exact pixel you click (point sample), a 3-pixel square average or a 5-pixel one. Oddly enough, this Eyedropper setting also applies to the Magic Wand. Change it here and you change it for the Wand, too.

POWER USERS' CLINIC

Paint by Number

The Elements Color Picker also includes some very sophisticated controls that most folks can live a long and happy life without ever understanding. For the curious or more advanced, here's what the rest of the Color Picker does.

- **HSB buttons.** These numbers control the hue, saturation, and brightness of your color. The settings control pretty much the same values as the Hue/Saturation adjustment. (See page 102 for more about hue and saturation.)

- **RGB buttons.** The RGB buttons let you specify the amount of red, green, and blue you want in the color you're picking. Each button can have a numerical value anywhere from 0 to 255. A lower number means less of the color, a higher number means more. For example, 128, 128, 128 is neutral gray. By changing the numbers, you can change the blend of the color.

- **Hex number.** Below the radio buttons is a box that lets you enter a special six-character hexadecimal code that you use when you're creating Web graphics. These codes tell Web browsers which colors to display. You can also click a color in the window to see the hex number for that shade.

- **Only Web Colors checkbox.** Turning on this box insures that the colors you see in the main color box are drawn only from the 216 colors that antique Web browsers can display. For example, if you're creating a Web site and you're really worried about color compatibility with Netscape 4.0, this box is for you. If you see a tiny cube just to the left of the Help button, the color you're using isn't deemed Web safe.

The Color Swatches Palette

The Color Swatches palette holds several little preloaded libraries of sample colors for you to use in picking a color. Go to Window → Color Swatches to call up the Color Swatches palette. You can park the Color Swatches palette in the Palette bin just like any other palette, if you like, or leave it floating on your desktop. When you're ready to choose a color, just click the swatch you want, and it appears in the Foreground color square or the color box of the tool you're using.

The Color Swatches palette is very handy when you want to keep certain color choices at your fingertips. For instance, you can put your logo colors into it, and then you always have those colors available for any graphics or ads you create in Elements.

Elements starts you off with several different libraries (groups) of Color Swatches. Click the More button on the Swatches palette to see them all. A swatch you create appears at the bottom of the current library, and you can save it there, or you can create your own swatch libraries if you'd rather do that.

Using the Color Swatches to select your Foreground or Background color is as easy as using the Eyedropper tool. Figure 7-18 shows you how.

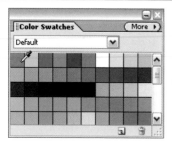

Figure 7-18:
When you move your cursor over the Color Swatches palette, it changes to an eyedropper. Click to select a color. If you're using a preloaded palette you'll see color name labels as you move over each square. If you use the swatches a lot, choose "Place in Palette Bin when closed" from the More menu so the Swatches palette is always there.

To use the Color Swatches palette:

- **To pick a foreground color**: Click the color you want. It appears as the Foreground color choice.

- **To pick a background color**: Ctrl+click a color, and Elements makes it the Background color.

You can also change the way the Color Swatches palette displays swatch information, as shown in Figure 7-19.

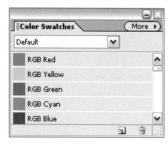

Figure 7-19:
On the Color Swatches palette, click the More button → Small List, and depending on the collection you're using, you can see the names or hex numbers for each color (in addition to a small thumbnail of the color). In some of the tools, like the Type tools, you'll need to click the Options button instead of the More button.

Saving colors in the Swatches palette

Any colors you've picked using the Color Picker or Eyedropper tool, you can save as swatches. If you don't save them, you lose them as soon as you select a different library or close the palette.

To add a swatch, you can do one of two things:

- **Click the New Swatch icon at the bottom of the Color Swatch palette.** It's the same square that stands for "new" in the Layers palette.
- **Click the More button on the palette, and choose New Swatch.**

In either case, you get a chance to name and save the new swatch. The name shows up as tooltips text when you hover your mouse over the swatch in the palette. (Don't change the save location if you want Elements to continue to recognize it as a swatch.) Your swatch gets saved at the bottom of the current swatch library. To delete a swatch that you've saved, drag it to the Trash icon in the Color Swatches palette.

You can also create your own libraries, if you want to keep your own swatches separate from the ones Elements gives you. Go to the More button on the palette and pick Save Color Swatches. Then give your new library a name and save it.

> **NOTE** If you save a new swatch library, it doesn't show up in the list of libraries until the next time you start Elements.

Sharpening Your Images

Digital cameras are wonderful, but often it's hard to tell how well you've focused until you download the photos to your computer. And due to the way a camera's digital sensors process information, most digital image data usually needs to be *sharpened*. Sharpening is an image-editing trick that makes your pictures look more clearly focused.

Elements includes some almost miraculous tools for sharpening your images. (It's pretty darned good at blurring them, too, if you want; see page 353.) And Elements 5 adds yet another—Adjust Sharpness. (It's a cousin to Smart Sharpening, one of Photoshop's most popular features.)

> **NOTE** If you've used previous versions of Elements, you may be searching in vain on the Filter menu for the Sharpen filters. It's true—your old friends Sharpen and Sharpen More are gone. In their place, the nifty new Adjust Sharpness appears at the bottom of the Enhance menu, along with the Unsharp Mask. (Both of these features are explained in the following sections.) If you miss the one-click ease of Sharpen and Sharpen More, just head over to the Quick Fix and use its Auto button to get the same effect.

Unsharp Mask

Although it sounds like the last thing you'd ever want to do to a photo, the Unsharp Mask reigned as the Supreme Sharpener for many generations of image correction, despite the fact that it has the most counterintuitive name in all of Elements.

To be fair, it's not Adobe's fault. *Unsharp Mask* is an old darkroom term, and it actually does make sense if you know how our film ancestors used to improve a picture's focus. (Its name refers to a complicated darkroom technique that involved making a blurred copy of the photo at one point in the process.)

Prior to Elements 5, Unsharp Mask ranked right up there with Levels as a contender for most useful tool in Elements, and some people still think it's the best way to sharpen a photo. Figure 7-20 shows how much a little Unsharp Masking can do for your photos.

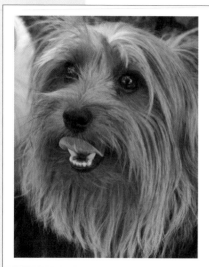
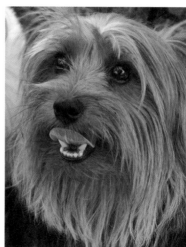

Figure 7-20:
Left: The photo as it came from the camera.

Right: The photo was treated with a dose of Unsharp Mask. Notice how much clearer the individual hairs in the dog's coat are and how much better defined its eyes and mouth are.

To use the Unsharp Mask, first finish all your other corrections and changes. The Unsharp Mask (or any sharpening tool) can undermine other adjustments you make later on, so always sharpen as the very last step. A good rule to remember when sharpening is "last and once." Repeatedly applying sharpening can degrade your image's quality.

> **NOTE** An exception to the rule about sharpening only once occurs when you're converting RAW images (page 211). You can usually sharpen both in the RAW converter and then again as a last step without causing problems.

If you're sharpening an image with layers, be sure the active layer has something in it. Applying sharpening to a Levels Adjustment layer, for example, won't do anything. Also, perform any format conversions (page 58) before applying sharpening. Finally, you may want a duplicate layer for the sharpening if you want the ability to undo your changes later on. Press Ctrl+J to create the duplicate layer.

> **NOTE** It's helpful to understand just exactly what Elements does when it "sharpens" your photo. It doesn't magically correct the focus. As a matter of fact, it doesn't really sharpen anything. What it does is deepen the contrast where colors meet, giving the impression of a crisper focus. So while Elements can dramatically improve a shot that's just faintly out of focus or a little soft, even Elements can't fix that old double exposure or a shot where the subject is just a blur of motion.

When you're ready to apply the Unsharp Mask:

1. **Go to Enhance → Unsharp Mask.**

2. **Adjust the settings in the Unsharp Mask dialog box until you like what you see.**

   Move the sliders until you're happy with the sharpness of your photo. Your adjustment options are explained in the following list. In the Preview window, you can zoom in and out and grab the photo to adjust which part you see.

3. **When you're satisfied, click OK.**

The sliders for the Unsharp Mask work very much like the sliders in several of the other tools:

- **Amount.** This tells Elements how much to sharpen, in percent terms. A higher number means more sharpening.

- **Radius.** This tells Elements how far from an edge Elements should look when increasing the contrast.

- **Threshold.** This is how different a pixel needs to be from the surrounding pixels before Elements should consider it an edge and sharpen it. If the threshold is left at zero—which is the standard setting—Elements sharpens all the pixels in an image.

There are many, many different schools of thought about which values to plug into each box. Whatever works for you is fine. The one thing you want to watch out for is oversharpening. Figure 7-21 tells you how to know if you've gone too far.

You'll probably need to do a bit of experimenting to find out which settings work best for you. Photos you want to print usually need to be sharpened to an extent that makes them look over-sharpened when viewed on your monitor. Therefore, you may want to create separate versions of your photo (one for onscreen viewing and one for printing). Version sets (page 54) in the Organizer are great for keeping track of multiple copies like this.

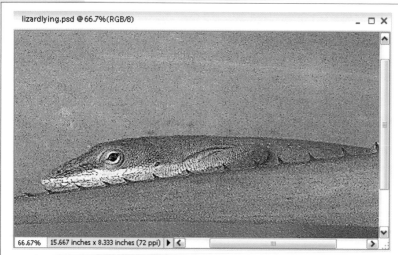

lizardlying.psd @ 66.7%(RGB/8)

66.67% 15.667 inches x 8.333 inches (72 ppi)

Figure 7-21:
The perils of oversharpening. This lizard may have a suspicious attitude, but he didn't have a skin condition. The flaky look comes from overapplying sharpening, and the white flecks are called artifacts. If you look very closely, you can also see how oversharpening causes a halo effect around the lizard. The appearance of halos is often your first clue that you've oversharpened your image.

Adjust Sharpness

Unsharp masking has been around since long before digital imaging. A lot of people (including the folks at Adobe) have been thinking that, in the computer age, there's got to be a better way to sharpen, and now there is. In Elements 5, you get to try out the latest tool in the war on poor focus—Adjust Sharpness.

The Unsharp Mask tool you learned about in the previous section helps boost a photo's sharpness by reducing Gaussian blur (page 353). Problem is, Gaussian blurring is rarely the cause of your picture's poor focus, so there's only so much Unsharp Mask can fix. In real life, blurry photos usually come from one of two causes:

- **Lens blur.** Your camera's prime focal point is not directly over your subject. Or perhaps your lens is not quite as sharp as you'd like it to be.

- **Motion blur.** You moved the camera—or your subject moved—while you pressed the shutter.

Adjust Sharpness is as easy to use as the Unsharp Mask, and it gives you settings to correct all three causes of blur—Gaussian, lens, and motion. When you first open the Adjust Sharpness dialog box, its settings are almost identical to Unsharp Mask. It's the extra things Adjust Sharpness can do that make it a more versatile tool. Here's how to use it:

1. **Make sure the layer you want to sharpen is the active layer in your photo.**

   See Chapter 6 if you need a refresher on layers.

2. **Go to Enhance → Adjust Sharpness.**

You can reach this menu item from either Full Edit or Quick Fix.

3. **Make your adjustments in the Adjust Sharpness dialog box.**

As shown in Figure 7-22, the dialog box gives you a nice big preview. It's usually best to stick to 50 or 100 percent zoom (use the plus and minus buttons below the preview) for the most accurate view. The settings are explained in detail on page below.

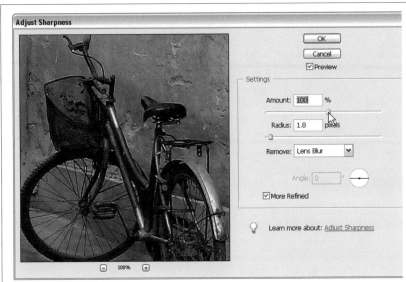

Figure 7-22:
The Adjust Sharpness dialog box shows you a good-sized preview of your image. But position the dialog box so you can see the main image window as well. That way you can keep an eye on any changes happening in areas outside the preview frame.

4. **When you like the way your photo is sharpened, click OK.**

The first two settings in the Adjust Sharpness dialog box, Amount and Radius, work exactly the same way they do in the Unsharp Mask. Adjust Sharpness also has a couple of additional settings of its own:

- **Remove.** Here's where you choose what kind of fuzziness to fix: Gaussian, lens, or motion blur, as explained on page 353. If you aren't sure which you want, try all three and see which best suits your photo.

- **Angle.** In a motion blur, you can improve your results by telling Elements the angle of the motion. For example, if your grip on the camera slipped, the direction of motion would be downward. Move the line in the little circle or type a number in degrees to approximate the angle. (It's awfully tricky to get the angle exactly right, so you may find it easier to sharpen without messing with this setting.)

• **More Refined.** Turn this checkbox on, and Elements takes a tad longer to apply sharpening since it sharpens more details. Generally you'll want to leave this setting off for photos with lots of little details, like leaves or fur (and people's faces, unless you like to look at pores). But you might want it on for bold desert landscapes, for example, or other subjects without lots of fiddly small parts. Noise, artifacts, and dust become much more prominent when you turn on More Refined, since they get sharpened along with the details of your photo. Experiment, and watch the main image window as well as the preview, to see how it's affecting your photo.

Many people who've used Smart Sharpening in Photoshop swear they'll never go back to plain unsharp masking. Try out Adjust Sharpness and see if you agree. To give you an idea of the difference between the two methods, Figure 7-23 shows the dog from Figure 7-20 again, only this time with Adjust Sharpness instead of Unsharp Masking.

> **TIP** Although Amount and Radius mean the same things as they do in Unsharp Masking, don't assume that you can just plug your favorite Unsharp Mask settings into Adjust Sharpness and get the same results. Experiment, and don't be surprised if you prefer very different numbers in these settings for the new tool.

The High-Pass Filter

Unsharp Mask is definitely the traditional favorite, and Adjust Sharpness is the latest thing in sharpening, but there's an alternative method that many people prefer because you do it on a dedicated layer and can back the effect off later by adjusting the layer's opacity, if you like. Moreover, you can use this method to punch up the colors in your photo as you sharpen. It's called *High-Pass* sharpening. All sharpening methods have their virtues, and you may find that you choose your technique according to the content of your photo. Try the following procedure out for yourself by downloading the photo waterlillies.jpg from the "Missing CD" page at *www. missingmanuals.com*.

1. **Open your photo and make sure the layer you want to sharpen is the active layer.**

2. **Duplicate your layer by pressing Ctrl+J.**

   If you have a multi-layered image and you want to sharpen all the layers, first flatten your image or use the Stamp Visible command (see the box on page 162), so everything is all in one layer.

3. **Go to Filter → Other → High-Pass.**

   Your photo now looks like the victim of a mudslide, buried in featureless gray. That's what you want for right now.

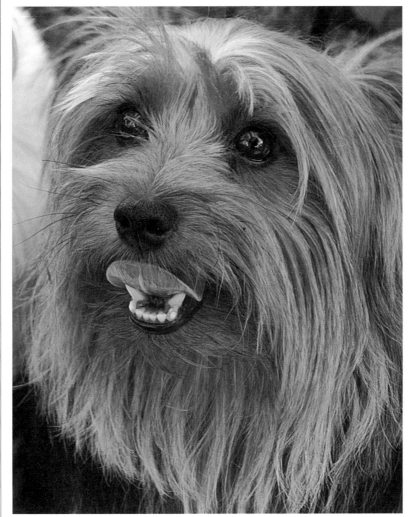

Figure 7-23:
Here's the terrier from Figure 7-20, only this time he's been sharpened using Adjust Sharpness. Notice how much more each hair in his coat stands out, and how much more detail you can see in his nose and mouth.

4. **Move the slider until you can barely see the outlines of your subject.**

   Usually that means picking a setting somewhere roughly between 1.5 and 3.5. If you can see colors, your setting is too high. If you can't quite eliminate every trace of color without totally losing the outline, a tiny bit of color is OK. Keep in mind that the edges you see through the gray are the ones that you'll be sharpening the most. Use that as your guide to how much detail to include.

5. **Click OK.**

6. In the Layers palette, set the blend mode for the new layer to Overlay.

Ta-da! Your subject is back again in glowing, sharper color, as shown in Figure 7-24.

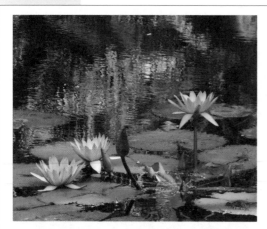

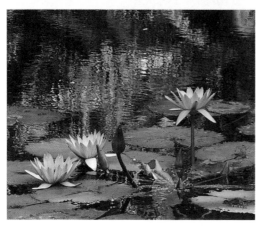

Figure 7-24:
Top: The original photo.

Bottom: High-Pass sharpening using Vivid Light makes the colors more vivid, but the ripples are much harder-edged than they were in the original. For high-pass sharpening, you can use any of the blend modes in the group with Overlay, except Hard Mix and Pin Light. Vivid Light can make your colors pop, but watch out for sharpening artifacts, since they'll be more vivid, too. Overlay gives a softer effect.

The Sharpen Tool

Elements also gives you a dedicated Sharpen tool (Figure 7-25). It's a special brush that sharpens instead of adding color to the areas you drag it over. To get to it, go to the Blur tool and choose the Sharpen tool from the fly-out menu.

The Sharpen tool has a couple of settings in the Options bar, in addition to the brush choices, which work the way they do for the regular Brush tool (see page 306 for more about brush settings). The Strength setting adjusts how much the brush sharpens what it passes over. A higher number means more sharpening.

The Mode setting lets you increase the visibility of an object's edge by choosing
Darken or Lighten, but usually Normal gives the most predictable results.

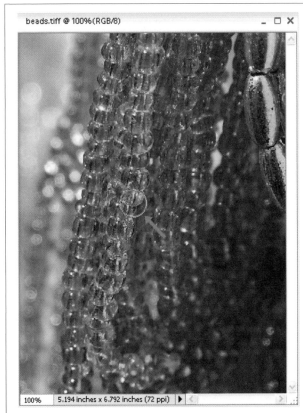

Figure 7-25:
*The Sharpen tool isn't meant to sharpen an entire
photo, but it's great for detail sharpening. Here, it's
being used to bring out the detail in the front strand
of beads. (The red arrow helps you find the cursor.)
Approach this tool with caution; it's very easy to
overdo things with it. One pass too many or a too-
high setting, and you start seeing artifacts right
away.*

beads.tiff @ 100%(RGB/8)

100%   5.194 inches x 6.792 inches (72 ppi)

Elements for Digital Photographers

If you're a fairly serious digital photographer, you'll be delighted to know that Adobe hasn't just loaded Elements with easy-to-use features, aimed at beginners. Elements is also brimming with a collection of pretty advanced tools pulled straight from Photoshop.

Number one on the list is the famous *Adobe Camera RAW Converter*, which takes RAW files—a format some cameras use to give you maximum editing control—and lets you convert and edit them in Elements. In this chapter, you'll learn lots more about what RAW is, and why you may or may not want to use it in your own photography.

You'll also get to know the Photo Filter command, which helps adjust image colors by replicating the old-school effect of placing filters over a camera's lens. And last but not least, Elements includes some truly useful batch-processing tools, including features to help rename files, perform format conversions, and even apply basic retouching to multiple photos.

The RAW Converter

Probably the most useful thing Adobe has done for photography buffs in Elements is including the Adobe Camera RAW Converter. For many people, this feature alone is well worth the price of the program, since you just can't beat the convenience of being able to perform conversions in the same program you use for editing.

If you don't know what RAW is, it's just a file format (a group of formats, really, since every camera maker has its own proprietary RAW format). But it's a very special one. Your digital camera actually contains a little computer that does a certain amount of processing to your photos right inside the camera itself. If you shoot in JPEG format, for instance, your camera has already made some decisions about things like sharpness, color saturation, and contrast before it saves the JPEG files to your memory card.

If your camera lets you shoot RAW files, on the other hand, you get the unprocessed data straight from the camera. Shooting in RAW lets you make your own decisions about how your photo should look, to a much greater degree than you can with any other format. It's something like getting a negative from your digital camera—what you do to it in your digital darkroom is up to you.

That's the big advantage of RAW—total control. The downside is that every camera manufacturer has its own proprietary RAW format, and the format may even vary between models from the same manufacturer. No regular graphics program can edit these files, and very few programs can even view them. Instead, you need special software to convert your RAW files to a format that you can work with. In the past, that usually meant you needed to use software from the manufacturer before you could move your photo into an editing program like Elements.

Enter Adobe Camera RAW, which lets you convert your files right in Elements. Not only that, but the Adobe Camera RAW plug-in that comes with Elements lets you make very sophisticated corrections to your photos—before you even open them. Many times, you can do everything you need right in the converter, so that you're done as soon as you open your converted file. (You can, of course, still use any of Elements' regular tools once you've opened a RAW file.) Using Adobe Camera RAW saves you a ton of time, and it's compatible with most cameras' RAW files.

NOTE   Adobe regularly updates the RAW Converter to include new versions produced by different cameras, so if your camera's RAW files don't open, check for a newer version of the plug-in. You can download the latest version by going to *www.adobe.com/support/downloads* and scrolling down to the section for Photoshop CS2. (Elements and Photoshop use the same plug-in, but you don't see all the features in Elements.) You'll also find a standalone version of the DNG converter (see page 223) there, which you can use without launching Elements.

Using the RAW Converter

For all the options it gives you, the RAW Converter is very easy to use. Adobe has designed it so that it *automatically* calculates and applies what it thinks are the correct settings for exposure, shadows, brightness, and contrast. You can accept the Converter's decisions or override them and do everything yourself—it's your call.

To get started, you first need to open your images. You can keep track of RAW files in the Organizer (page 15), but the Organizer doesn't open them. You have to be in the Editor to actually convert the files. The Organizer displays thumbnails of your RAW files before you open them so that you can choose the photo you want. If you'd like some practice with RAW, there's a sample image (RAW_practice. mrw) available on the "Missing CD" page (*www.missingmanuals.com*), but be warned: it's a very large file (7.2 MB).

FREQUENTLY ASKED QUESTION

To Shoot in the RAW or Not

Should I shoot my pictures in the RAW format?

It depends. There are pros and cons to using the RAW format. It may surprise you to learn that some professional photographers choose *not* to use RAW. For example, not many journalists use it, and it's not common with sports photographers, either. Here's a quick look at the advantages and disadvantages to help you decide if you want to get involved with RAW.

On the plus side, you get:

- **More control.** With RAW you have a lot of extra chances to tweak your photos, and you get to call the shots, instead of the processing choices made by your camera.

- **More fixes.** If you're not a perfect photographer, RAW is more forgiving—you can fix a lot of mistakes in RAW, although even RAW won't make a bad photo into a great photo.

- **No need to fuss with your white balance all the time while shooting.** Although you'll still get better input if your camera's white balance settings are correct.

- **Non-destructive editing.** The changes you make in the RAW converter don't change your original image one jot. It's always there for a fresh start, if need be.

But RAW also has some significant drawbacks. For one thing, you can't just open up a file and start using the photo the way you do with a JPEG file. You always have to convert it first, whether you use the Elements Converter or one supplied by the manufacturer. Other disadvantages include:

- **Larger file size.** RAW files are smaller than TIFFs, but they're usually much bigger than the highest-quality JPEGs. Consequently, you'll need bigger (or more) memory cards if you regularly shoot RAW.

- **Speed.** It generally takes your camera longer to save RAW files than JPEGs—a significant consideration for action shots. Newer cameras have a buffer that holds several shots and lets you keep shooting while the camera is working, but you'll hit the wall pretty quickly if you're using burst (rapid-advance) mode. Then you just have to wait.

- **Worse in-camera preview.** For many cameras, you have some pretty significant limitations for digitally zooming the view in the viewfinder when using RAW.

You may want to try a few shots of the same subject in both RAW and JPEG to see whether you notice a difference in your final results. Generally speaking, RAW offers the most leeway if you want to make significant edits, but you need to understand what you're doing. JPEG is easier if you're a beginner.

It's really your call. There are some excellent photographers who wouldn't think of shooting in anything but RAW, and other excellent photographers who think it's too time consuming.

To start converting your file, in the Organizer, highlight the file and then click Edit → Full Edit (or press Ctrl+I). That brings up the Converter window.

> **NOTE** You may not be able to open your RAW files by double-clicking them outside of Elements (from the Windows desktop, for instance). You'll probably get a message to the effect that your computer has no idea what program to use to open that file. You can make sure that Elements is the program that's always used to open your RAW files by following the steps described on page 37.

One important point about RAW files: Elements never overwrites your original file. As a matter of fact, Elements *can't* in any way modify the original RAW file. This means that your original is always there for you if you want to try converting your photo again later on using different settings. It's something like having a negative that you can always get more prints from.

> **NOTE** The Organizer can store your RAW files with no problems, but the Photo Downloader tends to be very slow about importing them and has been known to choke when working with RAW files. You may well find you prefer to get your RAW photos into your computer using one of the other methods discussed in Chapter 2.

Adjusting the view

When the RAW Converter opens, you'll see something like Figure 8-1. Before you decide whether to accept the auto settings that Elements offers or to perform further tweaking, you need to get a good close look at your image. The Converter makes it easy to do this by giving you a large preview of your image and a handful of tools to help adjust what you're looking at.

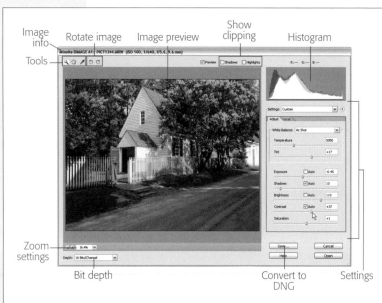

Image info — Rotate image — Image preview — Show clipping — Histogram — Tools — Zoom settings — Bit depth — Convert to DNG — Settings

Figure 8-1:
The Elements RAW Converter packs a number of powerful tools into one window. Besides the large preview window, you get a small tool set (in the upper-left corner) containing some old friends, and a specialized tool for adjusting your white balance (explained on page 217), as well as the panel on the right where you tweak your settings. Below your photo, the Converter gives you a few view-adjusting tools, including a drop-down menu (lower-left) where you can choose zoom settings. If you need to rotate your image, the rotate arrows are above the preview area, on the left side.

- **Hand and Zoom tools.** These tools are in the Toolbox above the upper-left corner of the Converter window. You use them here exactly the same way you would anywhere else in Elements. You'll find more about the Hand tool on page 80; the Zoom tool is described on page 79. The keyboard shortcuts for adjusting the view (page 80) also work in the RAW Converter.

- **Rotation arrows.** If you need to rotate your photo, click one of the arrows above the preview window.

- **View percentage.** You get a pop-up menu with preset sizes below the lower-left corner of the preview window. Just choose the size you want, or click the + or – buttons to zoom in or out.

Once you've gotten a good close look at your photo, you need to decide: did Elements do a good enough job of choosing the settings for you? If so, you're done. Just click Open, and Elements opens your photo in the Editor, ready for any artistic changes or cropping. If you prefer to make adjustments to your photo in the Converter, read on. (If you're happy with Elements' conversion, but you want to sharpen your picture, skip ahead to page 221.)

The RAW Converter's Settings menu

The long strip down the right side of the RAW Converter gives you many ways to tweak and correct the color, exposure, sharpness, brightness, and noise level of your photo. The strip is divided into two tabs. The one you see first, labeled Adjust, contains the basic settings for the major adjustments. (The other tab, Detail, is for fine-tuning your photo. See page 221.) When you first open a file in the Converter, Elements makes its best guess for the settings it thinks your photo needs.

That's a feature you'll either love or hate. The good news is that you don't have to live with the decisions Elements makes for you. If all this auto stuff drives you crazy, you can turn it off completely. You'll learn how in a minute.

If you look at the upper-right corner of the Converter, you see a Histogram at the top of the window. The Histogram helps you keep track of how your changes are affecting the colors in your photo. (Flip back to page 185 for more on the fine art of reading Histograms.)

Just below the Histogram is a pull-down menu that says Camera Raw Defaults. It also offers you a couple of other options. Whatever is chosen in this menu determines how Elements converts your photo. Here's a look at what the choices mean:

- **Image Settings.** This is the "undo all my changes" option. In other words, if you've made some changes in the Converter, and you want to revert to the settings Elements presented you with when you first opened this photo, choose this option.

- **Camera Raw Defaults.** Elements contains a profile of normal RAW settings for your camera model that it uses as its baseline for the adjustments it makes. That's what you get when you pick Camera Raw Defaults.

- **Previous Conversion.** If you've already processed a photo and want to apply the same settings to your currently opened photo, choosing this setting applies the settings from the last RAW image you opened (but only if it's from the same camera).

- **Custom.** Once you start changing settings, you see this instead of one of the other choices.

Since individual cameras, even if they're the exact same model, may vary a bit (as a result of the manufacturing process), the Camera Raw Defaults settings may not be the best ones for *your* camera. You can override the default settings and create a new set of default settings for any camera. You also use pretty much the same procedure if you just want to get Elements out of Auto mode (in which Elements picks the settings it thinks work best). In either case, you need to create your own default settings. This is very easy to do, using the pop-out menu shown in Figure 8-2.

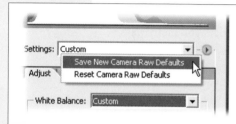

Figure 8-2:
If you don't like the way Elements converts your photos, you can turn off the Auto buttons (in the main settings area, not shown here) or make any other changes to your settings. Then click the triangle inside the blue circle and select Save New Camera Raw Defaults. From now on when you open a photo, you'll see the settings you've chosen.

- **To turn off the Auto settings:** If you just want to put Elements in manual mode, turn off all four Auto checkboxes, and then click the blue triangle (to the right of the Settings drop-down menu) and choose Save New Camera Raw Defaults. You're still using the same basic settings, but Elements won't do the Auto thing anymore when you open new photos in the Converter.

- **To change your camera's settings:** If you know that you always want a different setting for one of the sliders—like maybe your Shadows setting at 13 instead of the factory setting of 9—move all the sliders (not just the ones with Auto boxes) to where you want them and choose Save New Camera Raw Defaults. From now on, Elements opens your photos with these settings as your starting point.

- **To revert to the original Elements settings for your camera:** If you want to go back to the way things were originally, click the arrow and choose Reset Camera Raw Defaults. This also turns the Auto settings back on.

TIP   If you have a lot of RAW files to process, there's a way to quickly apply the same settings to a whole bunch of images. First, in the Organizer, select all the photos you want to convert before you call up the RAW Converter. When you press Ctrl+I or choose Edit → Go to Full Edit, the first photo appears in the RAW Converter. (When you open a group of photos, Elements tends to open the files in the order they appear in the Photo Browser.) Then, in the RAW Converter, Alt+click the Open button to apply the settings from the first photo to the subsequent photos without actually opening those files. When you Alt+click the Open button, it changes to say Update. As you click Update, each new photo from the group you selected appears in the Converter in turn.

White Balance

If you decide to adjust your photos yourself, the first control you'll see listed is for white balance. Adjusting white balance is often the most important change when it comes to making your photos look their best.

The White Balance control adjusts all the colors in your photo by creating a neutral white tone. If that sounds a little strange, stop and think about it for a minute. The color you think of as *white* actually changes depending on the current lighting conditions. In the late afternoon, white is much warmer due to the sun's low rays, while at noon, there's no warmth (no orange/yellow color) to the light at all. In the same way, tungsten lighting is much warmer than fluorescent lighting, which makes whites rather bluish.

Most digital cameras have a white balance setting on them, although you may have to take your camera out of Auto or Program mode to see it. Your camera white balance choices are usually something like Auto, Daylight, Cloudy, Tungsten, Fluorescent, and Custom. When you shoot JPEGs, getting the correct setting here really matters, because it's tough to readjust white balance, even in a program like Elements. With RAW, you can afford to be a little sloppier about setting your white balance, because you can easily tweak it in the RAW Converter.

Getting the white balance right can make a very big difference in how your photo looks, as you can see in Figure 8-3.

Elements gives you several ways to adjust the white balance in your image:

- **Pull-down menu.** The menu just below the Histogram starts out by displaying As Shot, which means Elements is showing you your camera's settings. You can use the menu to change this setting, choosing from Auto, Daylight, Cloudy, and other options. From Daylight down through the other choices on the list, each setting is slightly warmer than the one above it. It's worth giving Auto a try because it picks the correct settings a surprising percent of the time for many cameras.

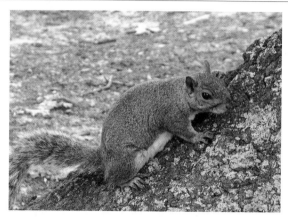

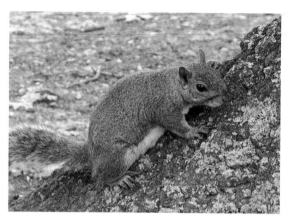

Figure 8-3:
Top: The blue-green color seen in this photo is typical of photos with poor white balance.

Bottom: By using the tools Elements gives you, you can easily correct the white balance, which also makes your photo appear more vivid and improves the contrast.

- **Temperature.** Use this slider to make your photo warmer (more orange) or cooler (more blue). Moving the slider to the left cools your photo, while moving it to the right warms it. You can also type a temperature in the box in degrees Kelvin (the official measurement for color temperature), if you're experienced in doing this by the numbers. Use the Temperature slider and the Tint slider (described next) in conjunction for a perfect white balance.

- **Tint.** Tint adjusts the green/magenta balance of your photo, pretty much the way it does in Quick Fix (see page 103). Move it to the left to increase the green in your photo and to the right for more magenta.

- **Eyedropper tool.** The RAW window has its own special Eyedropper tool. You click a white or light gray spot in your photo with it, and Elements calculates the white balance based on those pixels. This is the most accurate method, but it may be hard to find white pixels to use it on.

If you're a good photographer, much of the time a good white balance and a little sharpening may be all your photo needs before it's ready to go out into the world.

Adjusting Exposure, Shadows, Brightness, Contrast, and Saturation

The final group of settings on the Adjust tab includes the adjustments that Elements makes to your photo automatically: Exposure, Shadows, Brightness, and Contrast. (There's also a slider for Saturation, but it has no Auto setting.) If you like the Auto results, that's great, and Elements is fairly talented at picking the best settings. But you may find that for some photos, the Auto settings just don't work, as in Figure 8-4, or you may just prefer to tweak things yourself.

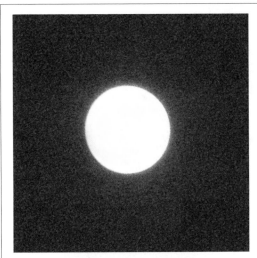

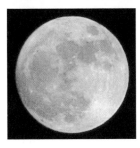

Figure 8-4:
Top: The RAW Converter's suggested settings for this moon shot. (If you've been wondering what noise is, this is an outstanding example of that annoying problem.)

Bottom: With a little bit of manual adjustment, the photo reveals that the camera actually captured plenty of detail.

Here's what each of the four settings does for your photo:

- **Exposure.** A properly exposed photo shows the largest possible range of detail. Shadows aren't so dark that all details are lost, and highlights aren't so bright that all you're seeing is white. Move the slider to the left to decrease exposure and to the right to increase it. (The values on the scale are equivalent to f-stops.) Too high a choice here will *clip* some of your highlights. (That is, they'll be so bright you won't see any detail in them.) See Figure 8-5.

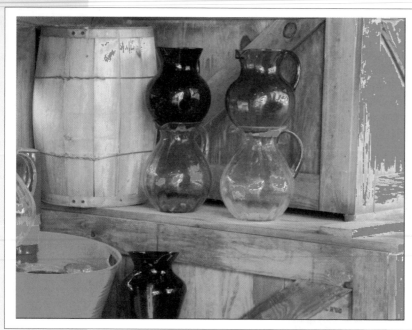

Figure 8-5:
To help you get the Exposure and Shadows settings right, Elements includes checkboxes above the preview window where you can turn on special masks that show you where your highlights (in red) or your shadows (in blue) lose detail at your current settings. In this photo, Elements is warning that the areas where you see what looks like red paint will get clipped when you open the photo unless you change the settings.

- **Shadows.** This slider increases the shadow values and determines which pixels become black in your photo. Increasing the Shadows value may give an effect of increased contrast in your photo. Move the slider to the right to increase shadows or to the left to decrease them. A very little change here goes a long way. Move too far to the right and you'll clip your shadows. (In other words, they'll become plain black, with no details.)

- **Brightness.** This is somewhat similar to exposure in that moving the slider to the right lightens your image and moving it to the left darkens it. But the Brightness slider won't clip your photo the way the other two may. Use this slider to set the overall brightness of your image after you've used the Exposure and Shadows sliders to set the outer range of your photo.

- **Contrast.** Contrast adjusts the midtones in your image. Move this slider to the right for greater contrast in those tones and to the left for less. It's usually the last of the four sliders to use.

Most of the time, you'll want to adjust all four of these sliders to get a perfectly exposed photo. There's one other adjustment on this tab, one that has no Auto setting, because you may or may not want to use it.

- **Saturation.** Saturation controls how vivid your colors are. Most RAW files have lower saturation to start with than you'd see in the same photo shot as a JPEG, so it's common to want to boost their saturation a bit. Move the slider to the right for more intense color, and to the left for more muted color. If you know you always want to change the saturation, you can change the standard setting by moving the slider and creating a new camera default setting, as described on page 216.

Adjusting Sharpness and Reducing Noise

Once you've got your exposure and white balance right, you may be almost done with your photo. But in most cases, you'll still want to click over to the RAW Converter's Detail tab to do a little sharpening.

There are two other important adjustments available here as well: *luminance smoothing* and *noise reduction* (both described in a moment). None of the adjustments on this tab have Auto settings, although you can change the standard settings by moving their sliders where you want them and then creating a new camera default, as described earlier.

- **Sharpness.** Use this slider to increase the edge contrast in your photo, which makes it appear more crisply focused. If you're not planning on making any further edits to your photo when you leave the RAW Converter, go ahead and sharpen it here by dragging the slider to the right to increase sharpness.

    On the other hand, some people prefer to wait to sharpen until they finish all their other adjustments in Full Edit mode, so they skip this slider. But in fact you can usually sharpen here, and then sharpen again later on, outside the Converter without causing yourself any trouble.

The next two settings work together to reduce the *noise* (graininess) of your photo. Noise is a big problem in digital photos, especially with 5-plus megapixel cameras that don't have the large sensors found in true SLR cameras. Elements gives you two adjustments here that may help.

- **Luminance Smoothing.** This setting reduces grayscale noise, which causes an overall grainy appearance to your photo—something like what you'd see in old newspaper photos. The slider is always at zero to start with since you don't want to use it more than you can help. That's because moving to the right reduces noise, but it also softens the detail in your photo.

- **Color Noise Reduction.** If you look at what should be evenly colored areas of your photo, and you see obvious clumps of differently colored pixels, this setting can help smooth things out. Drag the slider to the right to reduce the amount of color noise.

In most cases, it may take a fair amount of fiddling with these sliders to come up with the best compromise between sharpness and smoothness. It helps if you zoom the view up to 100 percent or more when using them.

Choosing bit depth: 8 or 16 bits?

Once you've got your photo looking good, you have one more important choice to make: do you want to open it as an 8-bit or a 16-bit file? *Bit depth* refers to the number of pieces of color data, or *bits*, that each pixel in your image can hold. A

---

single pixel of an 8-bit image can have 24 bits of information in it, 8 for each of the three color channels (red, green, and blue). A 16-bit image holds far more color information than an 8-bit photo. How much more? An 8-bit image can hold up to 16 million colors, while a 16-bit image can hold up to 281 *trillion* colors.

NOTE   You can adjust 16-bit images with microscopic precision, but in the real world, your home printer only provides 8-bit color anyway. If you want to do all your editing (or at least 90 percent of it) in 16-bit color, consider upgrading to Photoshop.

Most digital cameras produce RAW files with 10 or 12 bits per channel, although a few can shoot 16-bit files. You'd think it makes perfect sense to save your digital files at the largest possible bit depth, but the fact is you'll find quite a few restrictions on how much you can do to a 16-bit file in Elements. You can open it, make some corrections, and save it, but that's about all. You can't work with layers or apply the more artistic filters, or use many of the Auto commands on a 16-bit file.

NOTE   Your scanner may say it handles 24-bit color, but this is actually the same as what Elements calls 8-bit. Elements goes by the number of bits per color channel, whereas some scanner manufacturers try to impress you by giving you the total for all three channels (8 x 3 = 24). When you see very high bit numbers—assuming you aren't a commercial printer—you can usually get the Elements equivalent number by dividing by three.

Once you've decided between 8- and 16-bit color, just make your selection in the Depth drop-down menu (in the lower-left corner of the RAW Converter window). The RAW bit-depth setting is "sticky," so if you change it, all your images open in that color depth until you change it again. If you ever forget what bit depth you've chosen, your image's title bar will tell you, as shown in Figure 8-6.

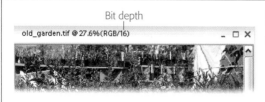

Bit depth

old_garden.tif @ 27.6% (RGB/16)

Figure 8-6:
You can always tell an image's bit depth by looking in the title bar of any image window. This image is 16-bit.

NOTE   If you do decide to create a 16-bit image and you become frustrated by your lack of editing choices, you can convert your image to 8-bit by choosing Image → Mode → 8 Bits/Channel. You can't convert an 8-bit image to 16-bit.

If you want to take advantage of any 16-bit files you might have, you may want to use either Save As or the Organizer's version set option (see page 54) for the copy you plan to convert to 8 bit. That way you'll still have the 16-bit file for future reference. Incidentally, your Save options are different for the two bit depths. JPEG, for instance, is available only for 8-bit files. If you wonder why you only have choices like JPEG 2000 when you save a file, then you've got yourself a 16-bit file.

A popular choice when you're thinking about your order of operations (workflow, in photo-industry speak) is to first convert your RAW file as a 16-bit image to take advantage of the increased color information while making any basic corrections, and then convert to 8-bit for the fancy stuff like the artistic filters or layer creation.

Converting to DNG

There's been a lot of buzz lately about Adobe's new DNG (digital negative) format, and if you shoot RAW, you should know what's going on. As you read at the beginning of this chapter, every manufacturer uses a different format for RAW files. Even the formats for different cameras from the same manufacturer differ. It's a recipe for an industry-wide headache.

Adobe's solution is the DNG format, which the company envisions as a more standardized alternative to RAW files. Here's how it works. If you convert your RAW file to a DNG file, it still behaves like a RAW file—you can still tweak your settings in the Converter when you open it, and you still have to save it in a standard image format like TIFF or JPEG to use it in a project. But the idea behind DNG is that if you keep your RAW files in this format, you don't have to worry about whether or not Elements version 35 can open them. Adobe clearly hopes that all camera manufacturers will adopt this standard, putting an end to the mishmash of different formats that make RAW files such a nuisance to deal with. If every camera used DNG, you'd never have to worry, every time you bought a new camera, if your programs could view the camera's images.

You can create DNG files from your RAW files right in the Converter. Just click the Save button at the bottom of the window, and you see the DNG Converter, shown in Figure 8-8. Choose a destination, and then select how you want to name the DNG file. You get the same naming options as in Process Multiple files (page 227), but since you convert only one file at a time here, you may as well keep the photo's current name and just add the .dng extension.

Of course, the jury is still out on whether DNG is going to become an industry standard. There have been other good ideas over the years, like the JPEG 2000 format (see page 55), that never really took off. It's up to you whether or not to create DNG files from your RAW files, but for now, it's probably prudent to hang onto the original files as well, if you do decide to do so.

> **TIP** If you want to batch convert your RAW files to DNG, the easiest way is to go to Adobe's Web site (*www.adobe.com/products/dng/index.html*) and download the standalone DNG converter, which you can leave on your desktop. Then just drop a folder of RAW images onto its icon, and the DNG Converter lets you process the whole folder at once. (The standalone Converter is part of the RAW Converter update (page 212). If your RAW Converter is up to date already, just remove the DNG Converter and discard the rest of the download.)

Digital Blending

With most digital cameras, you're likely to hit the clipping point (page 219) in an image much sooner than you want to. If you up the exposure so that the shadows are nice and detailed, about half the time you've blown the highlights. On the other hand, if you adjust your exposure settings down to favor the highlights, your shadows are murkier than an Enron annual report.

Photographers try to get around these limitations with a technique called *digital blending*, in which you *bracket* your shots. That is, you take two identical shots of your subject at different settings—one exposed for shadows and one for highlights—and then combine them, choosing the best bits of each one.

That technique is great for landscapes. But if you're shooting hummingbirds, roller-skating chimps, or toddlers, you know it's just about impossible to get two identical shots of a moving subject. And if you're like many amateur photographers, you may not realize you didn't capture what you wanted until you're home and see the shot on your computer.

If you shoot in RAW mode, you can use the Converter to help you fake digital blending, sort of. It's not as good as planning ahead, but you can often salvage another stop or two of detail. Just follow these steps:

1. **Run your photo through the Converter twice, one time exposing for the highlights and once for the shadows.**

2. **Drag one image onto the other—the way you would if you were creating a new layer (page 168).**

   Put the image with the largest area that you want to use on top, so you'll have less to change.

3. **Use the Eraser tool (page 325) to rub out the bad spots on the top photo, revealing those areas in the bottom layer.**

   Figure 8-7 shows this process in action.

When you're done, you can merge the layers (page 162) if you want.

If you'd like to try your hand at the real thing, you'll find an excellent tutorial at The Luminous Landscape: *http://luminous-landscape.com/tutorials/digital-blending.shtml*. Every digital photographer should bookmark this site. You're sure to find a ton of valuable information there, including lots of fine tutorials.

Photo Filter

The Photo Filter command gives you a host of nifty new photo filters that are the digital equivalent of the many-colored lens-mounted filters used in traditional film photography. You can use them to correct problems with your image's white balance, as well as for a bunch of other fixes, from the seriously photographic to the downright silly. For example, you can correct a bad skin tone or dig out an old photo of your fifth-grade nemesis and make him green, literally. Figure 8-9 shows one Photo Filter in action.

Elements comes with 20 Photo Filters, but for most people, the important ones are the top 6: three warming filters and three cooling filters. You use these filters to get rid of the color casts that come from a poor white balance (see page 217).

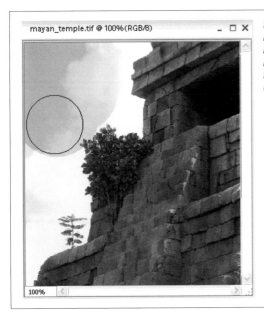

mayan_temple.tif @ 100%(RGB/8)   _ □ X

100%

Figure 8-7:
Digital blending (see the box on page 224) in action. Here, the blown-out sky in the top image is being erased to reveal the blue sky in the bottom layer. This maneuver is similar to the technique you'll use for creating spot or accent color, explained on page 270.

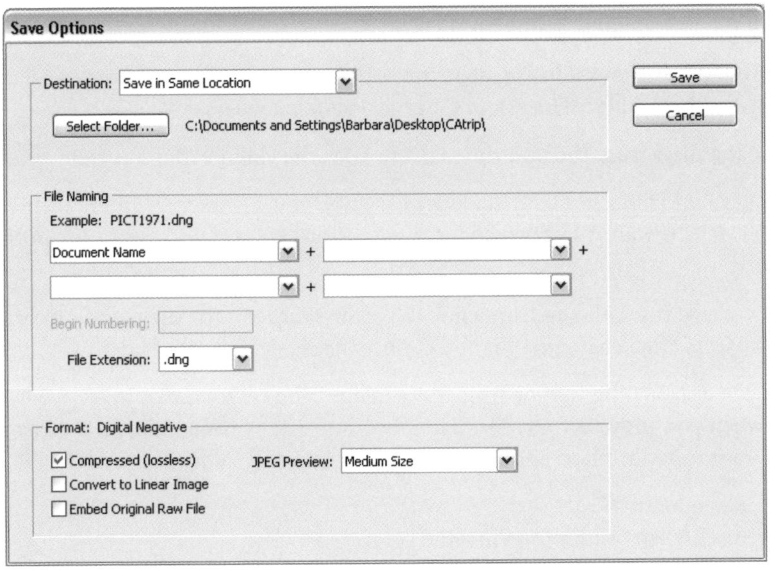

Save Options

Destination: Save in Same Location

Select Folder...   C:\Documents and Settings\Barbara\Desktop\CAtrip\

Save

Cancel

File Naming

Example: PICT1971.dng

Document Name   +

+

Begin Numbering:

File Extension: .dng

Format: Digital Negative

☑ Compressed (lossless)   JPEG Preview: Medium Size
☐ Convert to Linear Image
☐ Embed Original Raw File

Figure 8-8:
The DNG Converter. The bottom section of the Converter window lets you choose whether or not to compress the file, how to handle the image preview, and whether or not to embed your original RAW file in the new one. Generally, you're best off leaving the settings in this section the way you see them in the illustration.

The filters are an improvement over the Color Cast eyedropper (page 192) because you can control the strength with which you apply them (using the Density slider, explained later). And you can also apply them as Adjustment layers (page 166), so you can tweak them later on.

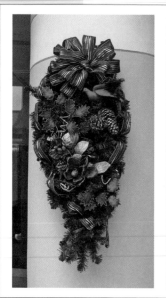 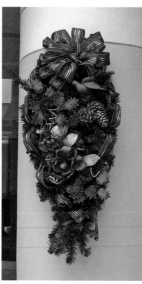

Figure 8-9:
You can use the Photo Filter to correct the color casts you get from artificial lighting.

Left: This photo had a strong bluish tinge from nearby fluorescent lighting.

Right: The Warming Filter (85) took care of it. Use Cooling Filter (80) or Cooling Filter (82) to counteract the orange cast from tungsten lighting. (The numbers stand for the numbers of glass filters you'd use on a film camera.)

To apply a Photo Filter:

1. **Open the Photo Filter dialog box.**

   Go to Layer → New Adjustment Layer → Photo Filter, or go to Filter → Adjustments → Photo Filter. The Photo Filter dialog box appears.

2. **Choose a filter from the pull-down list or click the Color radio button.**

   You get two choices. The pull-down list gives you a choice of filters in preset colors. If you want to choose your own custom color, click the Color button instead.

3. **If you chose the Color button, click the color square in the dialog box to bring up the Color Picker (page 196) and choose the shade you want.**

   You can also sample a color from your image. The cursor turns to an eyedropper when you move it from the dialog box into your photo. Just click the color you want for your filter, and that color appears in the color square in the dialog box.

4. **Move the Density slider to adjust the color.**

   Moving the Density slider to the right increases the filter's effect; moving it to the left decreases it. If you leave Preserve Luminosity turned on, the filter won't darken your image. Turn off Preserve Luminosity and your photo gets darker when you apply the filter.

5. **Click OK.**

Processing Multiple Files

If you're addicted to batch processing your photos, you'll love the Elements equivalent: Process Multiple Files. In addition to renaming your files and changing their formats, you can do a lot of other very useful things with this tool, like adding copyright information or captions to multiple files, or even using some of the Quick Fix auto commands.

To call up the batch-processing window, in the Editor, go to File → Process Multiple Files. You see yet another of the headache-inducing giant Elements dialog boxes, but this one is actually pretty easy to understand. If you look closely, you see that the dialog box is divided into sections, each with a different specialty (see Figure 8-10).

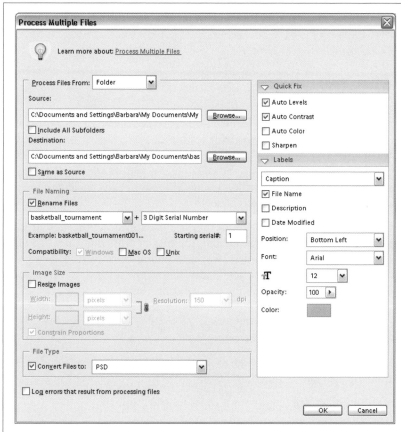

Figure 8-10:
You could also call Process Multiple Files "Computer: Earn Your Keep," because you can make so many changes at once. This dialog box is set up to apply the following changes: rename every file (from PICT8983 to basketball_ tournament001), change them to the .psd format, apply Auto Levels and Auto Contrast, and add the file name as a caption. You make all that happen by clicking the OK button.

NOTE   Process *Multiple* Files is the name of the command, but you can run it on just one photo if you want, although it would usually be easier just to do a regular Save As (see Chapter 2 for more about saving files). Just open your photo, go to File → Process Multiple Files, and choose Opened Files as your source. You can even opt to save the new version to the desktop without overwriting your original.

The following sections cover each main section of the Process Multiple Files dialog box. You have to use the first section (which tells Elements which files you want to process), but you'll probably only want to make use of one or two of the other sections at any one time. (Of course, you can use them all, as shown in Figure 8-10.)

TIP   If you're working in the Organizer, you can do some batch processing without going to the Editor. Select the files you want, and then go to File → Export → To Computer (or press Ctrl+E). You get a dialog box that lets you change the format, choose a new size from a list of presets, set a destination for the new images, and choose a new "common base name" if you want. If you choose this option, your files get the new name plus a sequential number. (By the way, this export feature is a great way to create a folder of JPEGs to send to an online photo service.)

Choose Your Files

In the first section of the dialog box, in the upper-left corner, you identify the files you want to convert and then tell Elements where to put them once it's processed them. You have several options here, which you pick from the Process Files From pull-down menu. You can choose your currently open files, the contents of a folder, or "Import," which brings up the same options you see when you go to File → Import, like your camera or scanner. Using this option, you can choose to convert your files as you bring them into Elements.

If you want to include files scattered around in different locations on your hard drive, you can speed things up by opening the files or gathering them into one folder. If you have a couple of folders' worth of photos to convert, you can save time by putting all the folders into one folder and using the "include all subfolders" option explained later. Then all the files get converted at once.

Here's how to get started:

1. **Choose the files you want to convert.**

   Use the Process Files From pull-down menu to tell Elements which kind of files you want: opened files, a folder, or files imported from your camera or scanner.

2. **If you chose Folder, tell Elements which folder you want.**

   Click the Browse button and, in the dialog box that appears, choose the folder you want. Files for processing must be in a folder if they aren't already open.

   If you have folders within a folder and you want to change all those files, turn on the Include All Subfolders checkbox. Otherwise, Elements changes only the files at the top level of the folder.

3. **Pick a destination.**

This is where the files will end up once they've been processed. Most of the time, you'll want a new folder for this, so click Browse, and then click New Folder in the window that opens. You can also choose an existing folder in the Browse window if you prefer. You need to be careful about choosing "Same as Source," as Figure 8-11 explains.

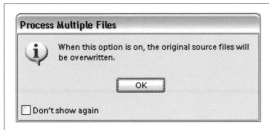

Figure 8-11:
If you turn on the "Same as Source" checkbox, Elements warns that it's going to replace your originals with the new versions. That's a timesaver, but it's dangerous, too. If something goes wrong, your originals can be messed up, so don't choose the Same as Source checkbox unless you have backup copies someplace else.

File Renaming

Being able to rename a group of files all in one fell swoop is a very cool feature, but it has a few limitations. Yes, you can rename your files here, but if you think that means you can give each photo a name like "Keisha and Gram at the Park," followed by "Fred's New Newt" for the next photo, you're going to be disappointed. Instead, what Elements offers when you use its file-renaming feature is a quick way of applying a similar name to a group of files. That means it's easy to transform a folder filled with files named DSCF001.jpg, DSCF0002.jpg, and so on, into the slightly friendlier Keisha and Gram001.jpg, Keisha and Gram002.jpg.

To rename your files, turn on the Rename Files option in the dialog box. You then see two active text boxes with pull-down menus next to them (a + sign separates the menus). You can enter any text you like, and it will replace every file name in the group, or you can choose any of the options in the menus. (Both menus are the same.)

The menus offer you a choice of the document name (in three different capitalization formats), serial numbers, serial letters, dates, extensions, or nothing at all. Figure 8-12 shows the many choices you get.

> **TIP** If you choose to add serial numbers, there's a box ("Starting serial#") where you can designate the starting number. Your first choice is always 1, which actually shows up as 001 because the leading zeros are needed for your computer to recognize the file order. The tenth figure in your batch would be numbered 010, one hundred would be 100, and so on.

So if you type *tongue_piercing_day* in the text box and choose the three-digit serial number, Elements names your photos tongue_piercing_day001.jpg, tongue_piercing_day002.jpg, and so on.

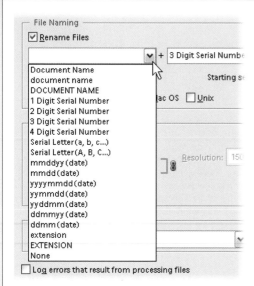

Figure 8-12:
Elements offers lots of naming options to suit whatever you eventually plan to do with your photos. If you select Document Name, for example, your photos retain their original names (plus whatever you choose from the right-side pull-down menu). DOCUMENT NAME gets you the same file names in all capital letters, "1 Digit Serial Number" starts you off with the number 1, and so on.

You also get to designate which operating systems' naming conventions Elements should respect when assigning the new names, as explained in Figure 8-13. If you send files to people or servers using other operating systems, you know how important this is. If you don't, play it safe and leave all three checkboxes turned on. You never know when you may need to send a photo to your nephew who uses Linux.

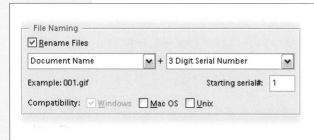

Figure 8-13:
The Compatibility checkboxes tell Elements to watch out for any characters that would violate the naming conventions of the operating systems you check. This is very handy if, say, your Web site is hosted on a Unix server and you want to be sure your file names won't create a problem for it. You can choose to be compatible with either or neither of the other operating systems, but the Windows checkbox is always turned on.

Changing Image Size and File Type

The Image Size and File Type sections let you resize your photos and change your images' file formats. The Image Size settings work best when you're trying to reduce file sizes (for example, with a folder of images that you've converted for Web use but found are still too big).

> **NOTE** Before you make any big changes to a group of files, it's important that you understand the concept of how changes in an image's resolution and file size affect its appearance. See page 82 for a refresher.

To apply image size changes, turn on the Resize Images checkbox and then adjust the Width, Height, and Resolution settings, all of which work the same way as those described on page 86.

In the File Type section, you can convert files from one format to another. This is probably the most popular batching activity. If your camera creates JPEGs and you want TIFFs for editing work, you can change an entire folder at once. From the pull-down menu, just select the file type you want to create.

The final setting in the left half of the window is the checkbox for logging errors in processing your files. It's a good idea to turn this checkbox on, as explained in Figure 8-14.

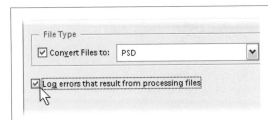

Figure 8-14:
If you turn on "Log Errors that result from processing files," Elements lets you know if it runs into any problems while converting your files. You'll find a little text log file in the folder with your completed images, whether there were problems or not.

Applying Quick Fix Commands

In the upper-right corner of Process Multiple Files, you'll find some of the same Quick Fix commands you have in the regular Quick Fix window. If you consistently get good results with the Auto commands there, you can run them on a whole folder at once here.

You can run Auto Levels, Auto Contrast, Auto Color, Auto Sharpen, or any combination of those commands that you like on all the files in your folder. (Unfortunately, you can't batch run the Auto Smart Fix command.) If you don't see the list, click the flippy triangle next to Quick Fix to expand it. If you need a refresher on what each one does, see Chapter 4, beginning on page 99.

Attaching Labels

The tools in the Labels section let you add captions and copyright notices, which Elements calls *watermarks*, to your images (see Figure 8-15). Watermarks and captions get imprinted right onto the photo itself. The procedure is the same for both, only the content differs. A watermark contains any text you choose, while a caption is limited to your choices from a group of checkboxes.

First, you need to choose whether you want a watermark or a caption (choose from the pull-down menu right below the Label tab). You can't do both at once, so if you want both, add one and then run Process Multiple Files again on the resulting images to add the other. You can download wagonwheels.jpg from the "Missing CD" page at *www.missingmanuals.com* to try adding your own watermarks and captions.

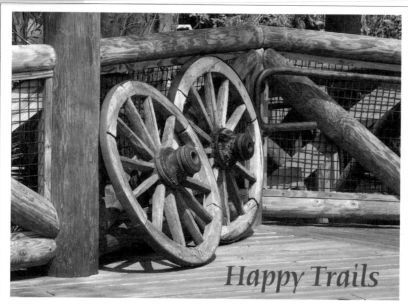

Figure 8-15:
Adobe calls the "Happy Trails" custom text in this image a watermark. Elements is very flexible about the fonts and sizes you can choose for a watermark or caption, but you don't get much say in where it goes on your photo if you use Process Multiple Files. For maximum flexibility, use the Type tool, as explained on page 375. The drawback: you can't batch process using that method.

Happy Trails

Watermarks

If you want to create a watermark, you first need to enter some text in the Custom Text box. You can enter any text you want. Then choose the position and appearance of your text as explained later.

Text you enter here gets applied to every photo in the batch, so this is a great way to add copyright or contact info that you want on every photo. If you want different text on each photo, check out the Description option for captions, as shown in Figure 8-16.

> **TIP**   If you want to include the copyright symbol (©), hold Alt while typing 0169 (on the number pad, not the top row of the keyboard).

Adding captions

For a caption, you can choose any of the following, separately or in combination:

- **File Name.** You can choose to show the file's name as the caption. If you choose to run the rename option at the same time, you get the new name you're assigning.

- **Description.** Turn this checkbox on to use any text you have entered in the Description section of the File Info dialog box (File → File Info) as your caption. This is your most flexible option for entering text, and the only way to batch different caption text for each photo. Just enter the text for each photo in File → File Info → Description.

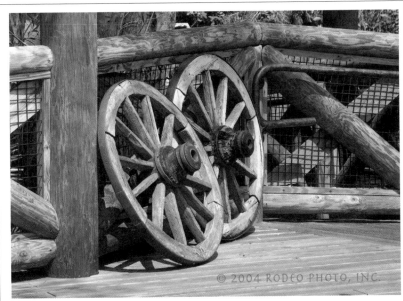

Figure 8-16:
You just can't beat Process Multiple Files for adding quick copyright information to your photo, although there are other methods that give a more sophisticated look, as described in the Note at the end of this chapter (page 234).

- **Date Modified.** This is the date your file was last changed. In practice, that usually means today's date, because you're modifying your file by running Process Multiple Files on it.

Once you've decided what you want your caption to say, you need to make some choices about its position and size. These choices are the same whether you're adding a watermark or a caption, and if you switch from one to the other, your previous choices will appear.

- **Position.** This tells Elements where to put your caption. Your options are Bottom Left, Bottom Right, or Centered. Centered doesn't mean bottom center, incidentally. It puts the text smack in the middle of your image.

- **Font.** From the pull-down menu, choose any font on your system. Chapter 13 has much more information about fonts.

- **Size.** This setting determines the size of your type. Click the menu next to the two little Ts to choose from several preset sizes, up to 72 point.

- **Opacity.** Use this to adjust how solidly your text prints. Choose 100% for maximum readability or move the slider to the left for watermark type that lets you see the image underneath it.

- **Color.** Use this setting to choose your text color. Click the box to bring up the color picker and make your choice.

NOTE If you want to use a logo as a watermark, you can't use the Process Multiple Files tool. But there is a way to apply a logo to a bunch of images. Here's how. First, create your logo on a new layer in one of the images. Adjust the opacity with the slider in the Layers palette until you like the results. Save the file. Now you can drag that layer from the Layers palette onto each photo where you need it. You can also do this with Adjustment layers (page 166) to give yourself a sort of batch-processing capability for applying the same adjustments to multiple files.

Retouching 102: Fine-Tuning Your Images

Basic edits like exposure fixes and sharpening are fine if all you want to make are simple adjustments. But Elements also gives you the tools to make sophisticated changes that aren't hard to apply, and that can make the difference between a ho-hum photo and a fabulous one. This chapter introduces you to some advanced editing maneuvers that will greatly help you either rescue damaged photos or give good ones that little extra zing.

The first part of the chapter shows you how to get rid of blemishes—not only those that affect skin, but also dust, scratches, stains, and other photographic imperfections. You'll also learn some powerful color-improving techniques, including the newly arrived—and much requested—Color Curves tool, which gives you a powerful new way to improve your image's contrast and color.

Fixing Blemishes

It's an imperfect world, but in your photos, it doesn't have to be. Elements gives you some amazing tools for fixing the flaws in your subjects. You can erase crow's feet and blemishes, eliminate power lines in an otherwise perfect view, or even hide objects you wish weren't in your photo. Not only that, but these same tools are great for fixing problems like tears, folds, and stains—the great foes of photo-scanning veterans. With a little effort, you can bring back photos that seem beyond help. Figure 9-1 shows an example of the kind of restoration you can accomplish with a little persistence and Elements.

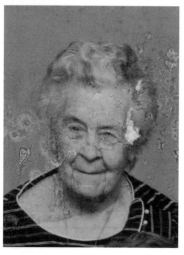

Figure 9-1:
You can do some amazing repair work with Elements if you have the patience.

Top: Here's a section of a water-damaged family portrait. The grandmother's face is almost obliterated.

Bottom: The same image after repairing with Elements. It took a lot of cloning and healing to get even this close, but if you keep at it, you can do the kind of work that would have required professional help before Elements. If you're interested in restoring old photographs, check out Katrin Eismann's books on the subject. They're written for Photoshop, but you can adapt most of the techniques for Elements.

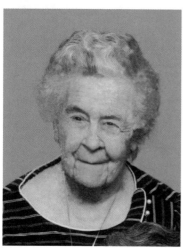

Elements gives you three main tools for this kind of work:

- **The Spot Healing brush** is the easiest way to repair your photo. Just drag over the area you want to fix. Elements searches the surrounding area and blends that information into the troubled spot, making it indistinguishable from the background. It usually works best on small areas, for the reasons explained later.

- **The Healing brush** works similarly to the Spot Healing brush, only you tell the Healing brush the part of your photo to use as a source for the material you want to blend in. This makes the Healing brush more flexible than the Spot Healing brush, and better suited to large areas, because you don't have to worry about inadvertently dragging in unwanted details.

- **The Clone Stamp** offers another way to make repairs. It works like the Healing brush in that you sample a good area and apply it to the area you want to fix. But instead of blending the repair in, the Clone Stamp actually covers the bad area with the replacement. The Clone Stamp is best for situations when you want to completely hide the underlying area, as opposed to letting any of what's already there blend into your repair (which is how things work with the Healing brushes). The Clone Stamp is also your best option when you want to create a realistic copy of detail that's elsewhere in your photo. You can clone over some leaves to fill in a bare branch, or replace a knothole in a fence board with good wood, for instance.

All three tools work similarly: you just drag each tool over the area you want to change. It's as simple as using a brush. In fact, each of these tools requires you to choose a brush, just like the ones you'll learn about in Chapter 12. But brush selection is pretty straightforward; in this chapter you'll learn everything you need to make basic brush choices.

The Spot Healing Brush: Fixing Small Areas

The Spot Healing brush excels at fixing minor blemishes: pimples, lipstick smudges, stray lint, and so on. You simply paint over the area you want to repair, and the Spot Healing brush automatically searches the surrounding areas and blends that into the spot you're brushing. Figure 9-2 shows what a great job the Spot Healing brush can do. (Download the file radish.jpg from the "Missing CD" page at *www.missingmanuals.com*, if you'd like to try this tool out.)

The Spot Healing brush's ability to borrow information from surrounding areas is great, but it's also a drawback. The larger the area you drag the brush over, the wider Elements searches for replacement material. So, if there's contrasting material too close to the area you're trying to fix, it can unintentionally get pulled into the repair. For instance, if you're trying to fix a spot on an eyelid, you may wind up with some of the color from the eye itself mixed in with your repair.

You get best results from this brush when you choose a brush size that just barely covers the spot you're trying to fix. If you need to drag to fix an oblong area, use a brush the minimum width that covers the flaw. The Spot Healing brush also works much better when there's a large surrounding area that looks the way you want your repaired spot to look.

The Spot Healing Brush has only three settings in the Options bar. From left to right, they are:

- **Brush.** You can use the pull-down menu to choose a different brush style if you prefer (see Chapter 12 for lots more about brushes), but generally, you're best off sticking to the standard brush that Elements starts out with and just changing the size, if necessary.

- **Size.** Use this slider to set the brush size.

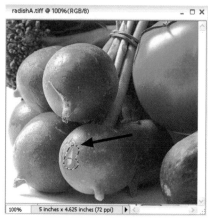

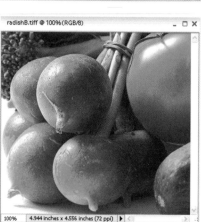

Figure 9-2:
The trick to using the Spot Healing brush is to work in very tiny areas. If you choose too large a brush or drag over too large an area, you're more likely to pick up undesired shades and details from the surrounding area.

Top: The radish in the bottom row has a large gouge in it.

Bottom: By dragging with a brush barely the width of the scar, you can make a truly invisible fix.

- **Proximity.** Use these radio buttons to adjust how the brush works. Proximity tells the Spot Healing brush to search the surrounding area for replacement pixels. Create Texture tells it to blend only from the area you drag it over. Generally speaking, if Proximity doesn't work well, you'll get better results by switching to the regular Healing brush than by choosing Create Texture.

You won't believe how easy it is to fix problem areas with the Spot Healing brush. All you do is:

1. **Activate the Spot Healing brush.**

   Press J and choose the Spot Healing brush in the Options bar (the left icon—the one with the little selection dotted lines extending from it), or click the Healing brush icon (the band-aid) in the Toolbox, and choose the Spot Healing brush from the pop-out menu.

2. **Choose a brush size just barely bigger than the flaw.**

   You can choose your brush size from the Options bar Size slider or by pressing] (the close bracket key) for a larger brush or [(open bracket key) for a smaller brush.

3. **Click the bad spot.**

   If the brush doesn't quite cover the flaw, drag over the area.

4. **When you release the mouse button, Elements repairs the blemish.**

   You won't see any change to your image while you drag, only after you let go.

Sometimes you get great results with the Spot Healing brush on a larger area if it's surrounded by a large field of good material that's similar in tone to the spot you're trying to fix. Most of the time, though, you're better off with the regular Healing brush for large areas, as well as for flaws whose replacement material isn't right next to the bad spot.

GEM IN THE ROUGH

Dust and Scratches

Scratched, dusty prints can create giant headaches when you scan them. Cleaning your scanner's glass helps, but lots of photos come with plenty of dust marks already in the print, or in the file itself if the lens or sensor of your digital camera was dusty.

A similar problem is caused by *artifacts*, blobbish areas of color caused by JPEG compression. If you take a close look at the sky in a JPEG photo, for instance, you may see that instead of a smooth swathe of blue, you see lots of little distinct clumps of each shade of blue.

The Healing brushes are usually your best first line of defense for fixing these problems, but if the specks are very widespread, Elements offers a couple other options you may want to try.

The first is the JPEG artifacts option in the Reduce Noise filter (page 350). Hopefully, that should take care of things.

If it doesn't, other possible solutions include the Despeckle filter (Filter → Noise → Despeckle), which is sometimes effective for JPEG artifacts. If that doesn't get everything, you can undo it and try the Dust and Scratches filter (Filter → Noise → Dust and Scratches), or the Median Filter (Filter → Noise → Median). The Radius setting for these last two filters tells Elements how far to search for dissimilar pixels for its calculations. Keep that number as low as possible. The downside to the filters in this group is that they smooth things out in a way that can make your image look blurred. Generally, Despeckle is the filter that's least destructive to your image's focus.

The Healing Brush: Fixing Larger Areas

The Healing brush lets you fix much larger areas than you can usually manage with the Spot Healing brush. The main difference between the two tools is that with the regular Healing brush, you choose the area that's going to be blended into the repair. The blending makes your repair look very natural. Figure 9-3 shows what great results you can get with this tool.

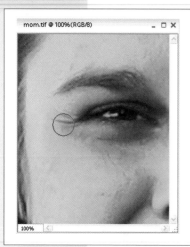 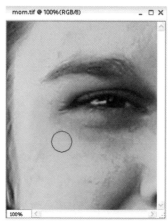

Figure 9-3:
The Healing brush is especially remarkable because it also blends the textures of the areas where you use it.

Left: This photo shows the crow's feet at the corner of the woman's eye.

Right: The Healing brush eliminates them without creating a phony, airbrushed effect.

The repair material doesn't have to be nearby; in fact, you can sample from a totally different photo if you like. To sample material from another photo, just get both photos arranged on the desktop so that you can easily move the cursor from one to the other.

The basic procedure for using the Healing brush is similar to that for the Spot Healing brush: you drag over the flaw you want to fix. The difference is that with the Healing brush, you first Alt+click where you want Elements to look for replacement pixels.

The Healing brush offers you several choices in the Options bar:

- **Brush.** Click the brush thumbnail to bring up the Brush Dynamics palette, explained on page 311. This lets you customize the size, shape, and hardness of your brush. But generally, the standard brush works well, so you don't have to change things other than the size if you don't want to.

- **Mode.** You can choose some blend modes (see page 332) here, but most of the time, you want to choose between the top two options: Normal and Replace. Normal is usually your best choice. Sometimes, though, your replacement pixels may make the area you work on show a visibly different texture than the surrounding area. In that case, choose Replace, which preserves the grain of your photo.

- **Source.** You can choose to sample an area to use as a replacement, or you can blend in a pattern. Using the Healing brush with patterns is explained in the section "Applying Patterns" on page 245.

- **Pattern thumbnails.** If you chose to use a pattern, this box becomes active. Click it to select the pattern you want to use.

- **Aligned.** If you turn on the Aligned checkbox, Elements keeps sampling new material in your source as you use the tool. The sampling follows the direction of your brush. Even if you let go of the mouse button, Elements continues to sample new material as long as you continue brushing. If you leave Aligned turned off, all the material comes from the area where you first defined your source point.

  Generally, for both the Healing brush and the Clone Stamp, it's easier to leave Aligned turned off. You can still change your source point by Alt+clicking another spot, but you often get better results if *you* make the decision about when to move on to another location rather than letting Elements decide.

- **Sample All Layers.** If you turn on this option, Elements samples from all the visible layers (page 150) in the area where you set your source point. Turn it off and Elements samples only the active layer.

It's almost as simple to use the Healing brush as it is to use the Spot Healing brush.

1. **Activate the Healing brush.**

   Press J and choose it from the Options bar, or click the Healing brush icon (the band-aid) in the Toolbox and choose it from the pop-out menu.

2. **Find a good spot you want to sample to use in the repair and Alt+click it.**

   When you click the good spot, your cursor temporarily turns into a circle with crosshairs in it to indicate that this is the point where Elements will retrieve your repair material from. (If you want to use a source point in a different photo, both the source photo and the one you're repairing must be in the same color mode. See page 40 for more about color modes.)

3. **Drag over the area you want to repair.**

   You can see where Elements is sampling the repair material from: you'll see a cross marking the sampling point.

4. **When you release the mouse, Elements blends the sampled area into the problem area.**

   Often you don't know how effective you were until Elements is through working its magic, because it takes a few seconds for Elements to finish its calculations and blend in the repair. If you don't like what Elements did, press Ctrl+Z to undo and try again.

You can choose to heal on a separate layer. The advantage to doing this is that if you find the end result is a little too much—your granny suddenly looks like a Stepford wife—you can back things off a bit by reducing the opacity of the healed layer to let the original show through. This is a good plan when using the Clone tool, too. Just press Ctrl+Shift+N to create a new layer and then turn on Sample All Layers in the Options bar.

The Clone Stamp

The Clone Stamp is like the Healing brush in some ways. You add material from a source point that you select. The main difference with the Clone Stamp is that it doesn't *blend in* when the new material is applied. Instead, the Clone Stamp works by covering up the underlying area completely. This makes the Clone Stamp your tool of choice when you don't want to leave any visible trace of what you're repairing. Figure 9-4 shows an example of when cloning is a better choice than healing.

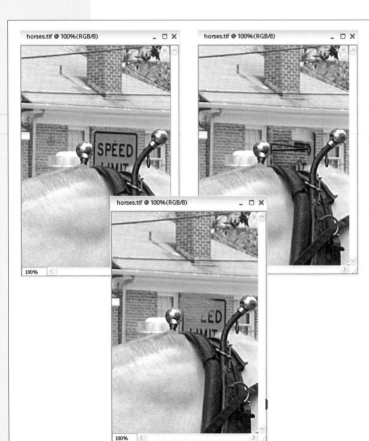

Figure 9-4:
Here's an example of when you'd choose cloning over healing.

Top left: This photo has a very distracting Speed Limit sign just above the horse's collar.

Top right: In this photo, the Healing brush does a lousy job covering up the sign.

Bottom: The Clone Stamp works much better. Only the upper-left corner has been fixed, but you can see how much better the Clone Stamp covers up the sign.

The choices you make in the Options bar for the Clone Stamp are very important in getting the best results possible.

- **Brush.** You can use the pull-down menu to select a different brush style (see Chapter 12 for more about brushes), but the standard brush style usually works pretty well. If the soft edges of your cloned areas bother you, you may be tempted to switch to a harder brush. But that usually makes your photo look like you strewed confetti on it, because hard edges don't blend well with what's already in your photo.

• **Size.** Choose a brush that's just big enough to get your sample without picking up a lot of other details that you don't want in your repair. While it may be tempting to clone huge chunks at once to get it done faster, most of the time, you'll do better using the smallest brush that gets the sample you want.

• **Mode.** You can choose any blend mode (see page 322) for cloning, but Normal is usually your best bet. Other modes can create interesting special effects.

• **Opacity.** Elements automatically uses 100-percent opacity for cloning, but you can reduce opacity to let some details from your original show through.

TIP   You gain more control by placing your clone on another layer (see page 146) than by adjusting the Clone Stamp's opacity.

• **Aligned.** This setting works exactly the way it does for the Healing brush (described earlier in this chapter). Turn it on and Elements keeps sampling at the same distance from your cursor as you clone. Turn it off and you keep putting down the same source material. Figure 9-5 shows an example of when you'd turn on Aligned.

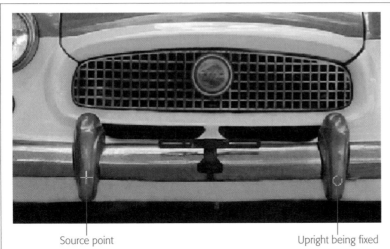

Figure 9-5:
The right-hand upright on this car's bumper was badly damaged. To restore it, the Clone Stamp's align option was used to pull detail from the left bumper, replacing the missing pieces. Leaving the Clone Stamp aligned lets you choose just the details you want for your restoration work, which is especially helpful if the area you're working on is oddly shaped.

Source point   Upright being fixed

• **Sample All Layers.** When you turn on Sample All Layers, Elements takes its samples from all the visible layers in the area where you set your source point. Turn it off and Elements samples only the active layer.

The Clone Stamp shares its space in the Toolbox with the Pattern Stamp, which is explained later. (You can tell which is which because the Pattern Stamp icon has a little checkerboard on it.) Using the Clone Stamp is very much like using the Healing brush. Only the result is different.

Repairing Tears and Stains

With Elements, you can do a great deal to bring damaged old photos back to life. The Healing brush and the Clone Stamp are major players when it comes to restoring pictures. It's fiddly work and takes some persistence, but you can achieve wonders if you have the patience.

That said, if you're lucky enough to have good-sized useable replacement sections elsewhere in your photo, you can use the Move tool to copy the good bits into the problem area. First, select the part you want to copy. Then press M to activate the Move tool and Alt+drag the good piece where you want it. (There's more about the Move tool on page 136.)

You can use the Rotate commands to flip your selection if you need a mirror image. For example, if the left leg of a chair is fine but the right one is missing, try selecting and Alt+dragging the left leg with the Move tool. When it's where you want it, go to Image → Rotate → Flip Selection Horizontal to turn the copied left leg into a new right leg.

If you don't need to rotate an object, sometimes you may be able to just increase the Clone Stamp brush size and clone your object where you need a duplicate. Cloning objects works well only when your background is the same for both areas.

1. **Activate the Clone Stamp.**

   Press S and choose it in the Options bar, or click its icon (the rubber stamp) in the Toolbox and choose it from the pop-out menu.

2. **Find the spot in your photo that you want to repair.**

   You may need to zoom way, way in to get a good enough look at what you're doing. See page 77 for how to adjust the view.

3. **Find a good spot to sample as a replacement for the bad area.**

   You want an area that has the same tone as the area you're fixing. The Clone Stamp doesn't do any blending the way the Healing brush does, so tone differences are pretty obvious.

4. **Alt+click the spot you want to clone from.**

   When you click, your cursor turns to a circle with crosshairs in it, indicating the source point for the repair. Once you're actually working with the Clone Stamp, you see a cross marking the sampling point.

5. **Click the spot you want to cover.**

   Elements puts whatever you just selected down on top of your image, concealing the original. You can drag with the Clone Stamp, but it almost always goes into Aligned mode (described earlier) when you do, so often it's preferable to use multiple clicks instead for areas that are larger than your sample.

6. **Continue until you've covered the area.**

   With the Clone Stamp, unlike the Healing brush, what you see as you click is what you get. Elements doesn't do any further blending or smoothing.

The Clone Stamp is a very powerful tool, but it's crotchety, too. See the box below for some suggestions on how to make it behave.

You can clone on a separate layer, just the way you would with the Healing tool. This lets you adjust the opacity of your repair afterwards. Press Ctrl+Shift+N to create a new layer and then turn on Sample All Layers in the Options bar. It's almost always a good idea to clone on a separate layer when you can do so, since cloning is so much more opaque than healing.

TROUBLESHOOTING MOMENT

Keeping the Clone Stamp Under Control

The clone tool is a great resource, but it definitely has a mind of its own sometimes.

If you suddenly see spots of a different shade appearing as you clone, take a look in the Options bar at the Aligned box. It has a tendency to insist on staying turned on, and even if you turn it off, it can turn itself back on when you aren't paying attention.

Once in a great while, the Clone Stamp just won't reset itself when you try to select a new sampling point. If you think about it, it's surprising that this doesn't happen more often. For such an amazing tool, it works most of the time.

Try clicking the Clone Stamp's icon on the left side of the Options bar and choosing the Reset Tool option, as shown Figure 9-6. If that doesn't do it, restart the Editor and delete Elements' preferences file. Here's how: hold down Ctrl+Alt+Shift immediately after launching the Editor. You get a dialog box asking if you want to delete the Elements settings. Say yes. This returns all your Elements settings to where they were the first time you launched the program. (Resetting the preferences cures about 80 percent of the problems you may run into in Elements.)

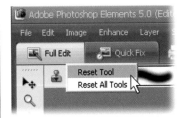

Figure 9-6:
You can reset the Clone Stamp (or, for that matter, any Elements tool) by clicking its icon at the left end of the Options bar, then choosing Reset tool. If you want to reset the whole Toolbox, choose Reset All Tools. This clears up a lot of the little problems you may have when trying to make a tool behave correctly.

Applying Patterns

Besides applying solid colors to your images, Elements lets you add patterns to your pictures. You get quite a few patterns with Elements when you buy it, and you can also download more patterns from online sources (see page 475) or create your own. You can use patterns to add interesting designs to your image, or to give a more realistic texture to certain repairs.

You can use either the Healing brush or the Pattern Stamp to apply patterns. The Healing brush has a pattern option in the Options bar. The Pattern Stamp shares the toolbox slot with the Clone Stamp, and it works very much like the Clone Stamp, but it puts down a preselected pattern instead of a sampled area.

> NOTE   Elements actually gives you lots of ways to use patterns, including creating a Fill layer that's entirely covered with the pattern of your choice. Fill layers are covered on page 166.

The tool you choose to apply your pattern makes a big difference, as you can see from Figure 9-7. The next two sections explain how to use both tools.

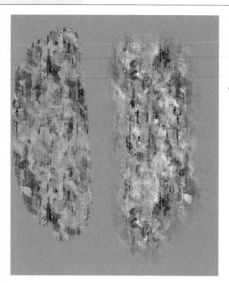

Figure 9-7:
The same pattern applied with the Healing brush (left) and the Pattern Stamp (right). The Healing brush blends the pattern into the underlying color (and texture, when there is any), while the Pattern Stamp just plunks down the pattern as it appears in the pop-out palette.

The Healing Brush

The Healing brush in Pattern mode is great for things like improving the texture of someone's skin by applying just the skin texture from another photo.

Using patterns with the Healing brush is just as easy and works the same way as using the brush in normal healing mode: you just drag across the area you want to fix. The only difference is that you don't have to choose a sampling point, since the pattern is your source point. When you drag, the pattern you selected blends into your photo.

Click the Pattern button in the Options bar and then choose a pattern from the palette by clicking the pattern thumbnail. There are more pattern libraries available if you click the More button on the Pattern palette, or you can create your own patterns. Figure 9-8 explains how to create custom patterns for use with either the Healing brush or the Pattern Stamp.

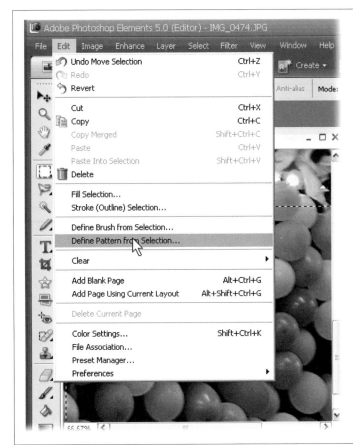

Figure 9-8:
You can create your own patterns very easily. On any image, make a rectangular selection, and then choose Edit → Define Pattern from Selection. Your pattern appears at the bottom of the current pattern palette, and a dialog box pops up and asks you to type a name. To rename or delete a pattern later, right-click it in the Pattern palette and make your choice. You can also download hundreds of different patterns from various online sources (see page 475).

TIP You can create some very interesting effects by changing the blend mode (page 322) when using patterns.

The Pattern Stamp

The Pattern Stamp is just like the Clone Stamp, only instead of copying sampled areas, it puts down a predefined pattern that you select from the Pattern palette. The Pattern Stamp is useful when you want to apply a pattern to your image without mixing it in with what's already there. For instance, if you want to see what your patio would look like if it were a garden instead, you could use the Pattern stamp to paint a lawn and a flower border on a photo of your patio.

To get started, click the pattern thumbnail in the Options bar. The Pattern palette opens, which is where you choose a pattern. Other options for this brush, like the size, hardness, and so on, are the same as for the Clone Stamp. The one difference is the Impressionist option demonstrated in Figure 9-9.

Once you've selected a pattern, just drag in your photo where you want the pattern to appear.

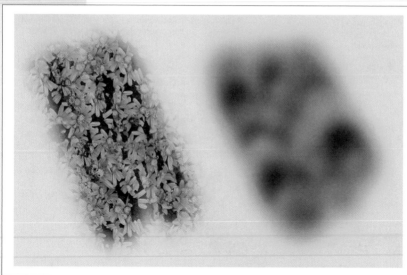

Figure 9-9:
If you turn on Impressionist in the Options bar, your pattern is blurred, giving an effect vaguely like an Impressionist painting. Here, you can see a pattern put down with the regular Pattern Stamp (left) and the Impressionist stamp (right).

Curves: Enhancing Tone and Contrast

The Color Curves tool is probably Elements' most-requested new feature ever. Legions of photo-editing veterans begged for this tool, which works much like Levels (see page 184), but with many more points of correction. Unlike Levels, in which you set your entire photo's white point, black point, and gamma settings, Curves let you target specific tonal regions. For instance, Curves let you make only your shadows lighter or only your highlights darker. Maybe that's why some pros say, "Curves are Levels on steroids." (For advice on when to use Levels and when to use Color Curves, see the box on page 188.)

Elements' Color Curves tool is a slightly restricted version of its counterpart (just called Curves) in the full version of Photoshop. In the more powerful Curves tool, you can work on each color channel separately, as you do in the Levels dialog box. You can also drag any point on the Curves graph (like the one you see in Figure 9-10) to manipulate it directly. For example, you can drag to adjust just the middle range of your greens. Elements doesn't give you that kind of flexibility.

Since Curves, in its original-strength version, is a pretty complicated tool, Adobe makes it easier to use in Elements. To start with, you get a group of preset curves adjustments to choose from (see Figure 9-10). These presets offer the types of basic enhancements you'll use most often. Just click the one that looks good to you. If you like what it does, you're done. But if you aren't quite satisfied with a preset, you have a simple way to make adjustments in the Adjust Color Curves dialog box's Advanced Options.

Here's how to improve a photo's appearance with Color Curves:

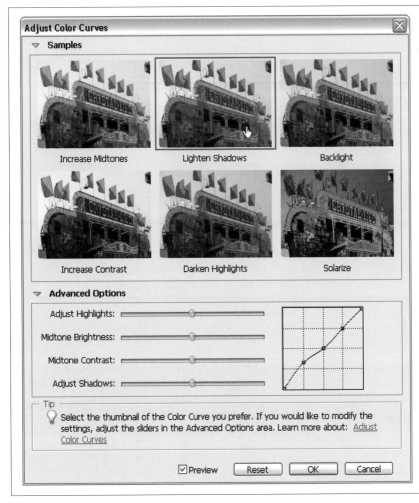

1. **Open your photo and make a duplicate layer.**

   Press Ctrl+J or go to Layer → Duplicate Layer. Elements doesn't let you use Curves as an Adjustment layer (unlike Photoshop), so you're safer applying it to a duplicate layer in case you want to change something later.

   TIP   If you want to restrict your adjustment to a particular area in your photo, select it first so Color Curves changes only the selected area. For instance, if you're happy with everything in your shot of your son's Little League game except the catcher in the foreground, select him, and you can do a Color Curves adjustment that affects him alone—not the rest of the photo.

2. **Go to Enhance → Adjust Color → Adjust Color Curves.**

   The Color Curves dialog box opens. As shown in Figure 9-10, the Increase Midtones preset starts out selected.

3. **Choose a Color Curves preset.**

Look at the thumbnails and click the preset that's closest to what you want your photo to look like. Try clicking different presets. (As long as you're just clicking thumbnails, you don't need to click Reset between each one, since Elements starts from your original each time you click.)

You can see the preview right in your image as well, so drag the dialog box out of the way and check your actual photo to get a better idea of how you're changing things before you make your final choice.

4. **Apply the changes, or tweak them some more.**

If you're satisfied, click OK. If not, go to the next step. (And if you don't want to apply any Color Curves adjustment at all, click Cancel.)

5. **Make any further adjustments.**

If you think your photo still doesn't look quite right, click the flippy triangle next to Advanced Options to see the sliders shown in Figure 9-11. Use the sliders to make any additional changes, as described on page 251. Click Reset if you want to undo any of the changes you make with the sliders.

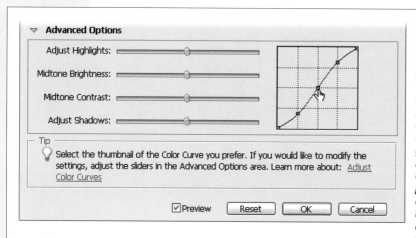

Figure 9-11:
The graph indicated by the hand cursor is where the Color Curves feature gets its name. With no Curves adjustments at all, this graph would look like a straight line. The adjustments you make cause the points on the graph to move, resulting in a curved line. (Because one of the Color Curves presets is always pre-applied when you open the dialog box, you never actually see a straight line.)

NOTE   Clicking Reset doesn't return the sliders to the 0 position in the middle. That's OK: Reset simply returns your photo to the way it was when you first arrived in the Color Curves dialog box (that is, with the Increase Midtones preset selected).

6. **When you're happy with your photo's new look, click OK.**

Don't forget to save your changes. If you used a duplicate layer, you can always change your mind about them later on.

NOTE   If you've used Curves add-ons in an older version of Elements (like those from Richard Lynch or Grant Dixon, for example), the new Color Curves tool may take some getting used to. (You power user, you!) Unfortunately, those add-ons no longer work in Elements 5. If you want to make the more elaborate adjustments you got from your old add-ons, your only option is to hang on to your copy of Elements 2 or 3 and use it to create Curves Adjustment layers.

Once you've got some Color Curves experience under your belt, you probably won't be satisfied with the results you get from the presets. So don't hesitate to use the sliders under Advanced Options to adjust different tonal regions in your photo:

- **Adjust Highlights.** Move the slider to the left to darken the highlights in your photo; move it to the right to lighten them.

- **Midtone Brightness.** If you'd like the middle range of colors to be darker, move this slider to the left. Move it to the right to make the midtones brighter.

- **Midtone Contrast.** This slider works just like the one in the Shadows/Highlights feature (see page 178). Move it to the right to increase the contrast in your photo, and to the left to reduce the contrast.

- **Adjust Shadows.** If you want to lighten shadows, move the slider to the right. To darken the shadow areas of your photo, move it to the left.

As you move the sliders, you can see the point you're adjusting move on the graph and watch the curve change shape. Although it's fun to see what's going on in the graph, you should pay more attention to what's happening in your photo.

Color Curves is such a potent tool, it can change your photo in ways you don't intend. Rather than using Color Curves to make huge adjustments, try another tool first. Then come back and use Color Curves for the final, subtle tweaks. On the other hand, you can also use Color Curves to create some wild special effects, if that's what you're after. See Figure 9-12 for an example.

Making Your Colors More Vibrant

Do you drool over the luscious photos in travel magazines, the ones that make it look like the world's full of destinations so vivid they make your regular life seem pretty drab in comparison? What *is* it about those photos that makes things look so dramatic?

Often the answer is the *saturation*, or intensity, of the colors. Supersaturated color makes for darned appealing landscape and object photos, regardless of how the real thing may rate on the vividness scale.

There are a variety of ways to adjust the saturation of your photos. Some cameras offer you settings to help control it, but Elements lets you go even further. For example, by increasing or decreasing a photo's saturation, you can shift the perceived focal point, change the mood of the picture, or just make your photo more eye-catching in general.

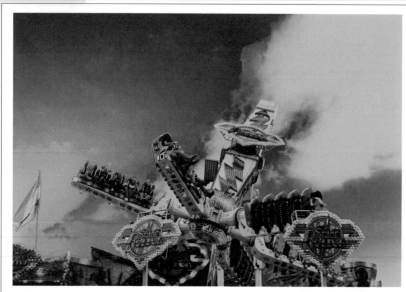

Figure 9-12:
Many people prefer to use Color Curves for artwork and special effects rather than adjusting photos. Jimi Hendrix fans may like the Solarize preset, which Adobe includes to give you a starting point for funky pictures like this one. (Others say this preset should serve as a warning about going overboard with this tool.)

By increasing your subject's saturation and decreasing it in the rest of the photo you can focus your viewer's attention, even in a crowded photo. Figure 9-13 shows a somewhat exaggerated use of this technique; you can download the photo (shelf-sitter.jpg) from the "Missing CD" page at *www.missingmanuals.com* to try it out for yourself.

It's quite easy to change saturation. You can use either the Hue/Saturation dialog box or the Sponge tool, which are explained in the following sections. For big areas, or when you want a lot of control, use Hue/Saturation. If you just want to quickly paint a different saturation level (either more or less saturation) on a small spot in your photo, the Sponge tool is faster.

> **TIP** Many consumer-grade digital cameras are set to crank the saturation of your JPEG photos into the stratosphere. That's great if you love all the color. If you prefer not to live in a Technicolor universe, you may wish to desaturate your photos in Elements to remove some of the excess color.

Using the Hue/Saturation Dialog Box

Hue/Saturation is one of the most popular commands in Elements. If you aren't satisfied with the results of a simple Levels adjustment, you may want to work on the hue or saturation as the next step toward getting really eye-catching color.

Hue simply means the color of your image—whether it's blue or brown or purple or green. Most people use the saturation adjustments more than the hue controls, but both hue and saturation are controlled from the same dialog box. You can adjust both or just one.

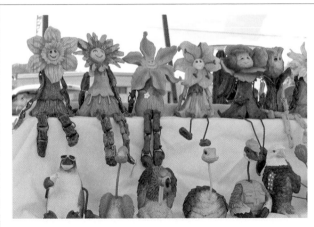

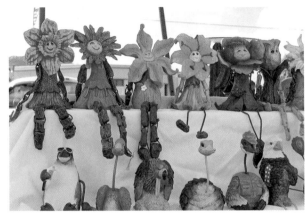

Figure 9-13:
Top: In this photo, all the little shelfsitter figures are about equal in brightness.

Bottom: To make one figure stand out from the crowd, the figure was selected and the saturation was increased. Meanwhile, the rest of the photo was desaturated. The effect is exaggerated here, but a subtler use of this technique can work wonders for spotlighting objects in your photos.

It's possible in Elements to use the Hue slider to actually change the color of objects in your photos, but you probably want to adjust saturation far more often than you want to shift the hue of a photo.

When you use Hue/Saturation, it's a good idea to make most of your other corrections—like Levels or exposure corrections (see page 174)—first. When you're ready to use the Hue/Saturation command, just follow these steps:

1. **If you want to adjust only part of your photo, select the area you want.**

   Use whatever selection tools you prefer. (See Chapter 5 for more about making selections.)

2. **Call up the Hue/Saturation Adjustment dialog box.**

   Go to Enhance → Adjust Color → Adjust Hue/Saturation or to Layer → New Adjustment Layer → Hue/Saturation. As always, if you don't want to make irrevocable changes, use an Adjustment layer instead of working directly on your photo.

3. **Move the sliders until you see what you want.**

If you want to adjust only saturation, you can ignore the Hue slider. Move the Saturation slider to the right to increase the amount of saturation (more color) or to the left to decrease it. If necessary, move the Lightness slider to the left to make the color darker, or move it to the right to make the color lighter. Incidentally, you don't have to change all the colors in your photo equally. See Figure 9-14 for how to focus on individual color channels.

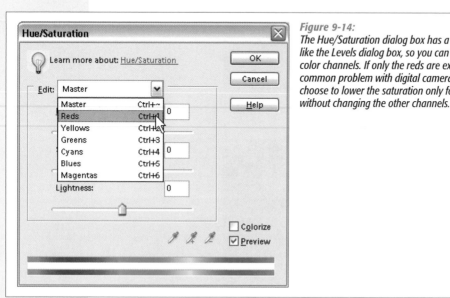

Figure 9-14:
The Hue/Saturation dialog box has a pull-down menu like the Levels dialog box, so you can adjust individual color channels. If only the reds are excessive (a common problem with digital cameras), you can choose to lower the saturation only for the reds without changing the other channels.

TIP Generally speaking, if you want to change a pastel to a more intense color, you'll need to reduce the lightness in addition to increasing the saturation—if you don't want your color to look radioactive.

Adjusting Saturation with the Sponge Tool

You can also adjust saturation with the Sponge tool. The Sponge tool is very handy for working on small areas, but all that dragging gets old pretty fast when you're working on a large chunk of your image. For those situations, use Hue/Saturation instead.

Although it's called a sponge, the Sponge tool works like any other brush tool in Elements. Choosing the size and hardness are just the same as choosing them for any other brush (see page 306). The Sponge has a couple of unique settings of its own as well:

• **Mode.** Choose here whether to saturate (add color) or desaturate (remove color).

• **Flow.** Flow governs how intense the effect is. A higher number means more intensity.

To use the Sponge tool, drag over the area you want to change. Figure 9-15 shows an example of the kind of work the Sponge does.

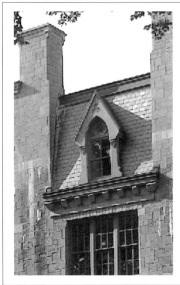

Figure 9-15:
Here, the Sponge tool has been applied to the left side of the window frame and the roof beside it, increasing the color saturation in those areas. Approach the Sponge tool with some caution. It doesn't take much to cause degradation in your image, especially if you've made lots of other adjustments to it. If you start to see noise (graininess), undo your sponging and try it again at a reduced setting.

You may want to press Ctrl+J to create a duplicate layer before you use the Sponge. Then you can always throw out the duplicate layer later on if you change your mind about the changes you made.

1. **Activate the Sponge tool.**

   Click the icon on the toolbar, or press O and choose the Sponge icon. Choose the brush size and the settings you want in the Options bar.

2. **Drag in the area you want to change.**

   If you aren't seeing enough of a difference, up the Flow setting a little. If it's too strong, reduce the number for the Flow.

   TIP   If you have a hard time coloring (or decoloring) inside the lines, you can select the area you want before you start sponging. Then the brush won't do anything outside the selection, allowing you to be as sloppy as you like.

Changing the Color of an Object

In Chapter 4, you saw one way to change the color of an object—select it and use the Hue/Saturation sliders in Quick Fix. Elements also gives you some other ways to do this: you can use an Adjustment layer, the Replace Color command, or the Color Replacement tool.

The method you choose depends to some extent on your photo and to some extent on your own preference. Using an Adjustment layer gives you the most flexibility if you want to make other changes later on. Replace Color is the fastest way to change one color that's widely scattered throughout your whole image, and the Color Replacement tool lets you quickly brush a replacement color over the color you want to change. Whichever method you choose, Figure 9-16 shows the kind of complex color change you can make in a jiffy using any one of these methods.

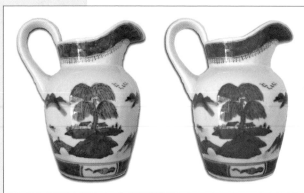

Figure 9-16:
What if you have a blue and white jug, but what you really want is a brown and white one? Just call up the Replace Color tool. Elements actually gives you several ways to make a complicated color substitution like this one, all of which are covered in this section.

Using an Adjustment Layer

You can use a Hue/Saturation Adjustment layer to make the same kind of changes to the color that you saw on page 252. The advantage of the Adjustment layer is that later on, you can change the settings or the area affected by the layer (as opposed to changing your whole image). The procedure is exactly the same as that described in the section "Using the Hue/Saturation Dialog Box," only this time, you start by selecting the object you want to change.

1. **Select the object whose color you want to change.**

   Use any of the Selection tools (Chapter 5). (If you don't make a selection before creating the Adjustment layer, you'll change your entire photo.)

2. **Create a new Hue/Saturation Adjustment layer.**

   Go to Layer → New Adjustment Layer → Hue/Saturation. The new layer affects only the area you selected.

3. **Use the sliders in the dialog box to adjust the color until you see what you want, and then click OK.**

   You need to use the Hue slider to start with. Use it to pick the color you want, and when you've gotten that into the ballpark of what you want, use the Saturation and Lightness sliders to adjust the vividness and darkness of the new color.

This method is fine if you have one area of color that's easily selectable. But what if you have a bunch of different areas or you want to change one shade everywhere it appears in your photo? For that, Elements offers the Replace Color command.

Replacing Specific Colors

Take a look at the blue pitcher in Figure 9-16 again. Do you have to tediously select each blue area one by one if you want to make a brown and white jug?

You can do it that way, of course, but an easier way is to use the Replace Color command. It's one of those Elements dialog boxes that look a bit intimidating, but it's a snap to use once you understand how it works. Replace Color changes every instance of the color that you select, no matter how many times it appears in your image.

You don't need to start by making a selection when you use Replace Color. As usual, if you want to keep your options for future changes open, make a duplicate layer (Ctrl+J). When you start, be sure your active layer isn't an Adjustment layer, or Replace Color won't work.

1. **Open the Replace Color dialog box.**

   Go to Enhance → Adjust Color → Replace Color. The Replace Color dialog box in Figure 9-17 appears.

2. **Move your cursor over your photo.**

   The cursor changes to an eyedropper. Take a moment to confirm that the left eyedropper in the Replace Color dialog box is the active one. That's the one without a plus or minus sign.

   TIP   If you want to protect a particular area of your chosen color from being changed, paint a mask on it by using the Selection brush in Mask mode (page 125) before you use the eyedroppers.

3. **Click an area of the color you want to replace.**

   All the areas matching that particular shade are selected, but you won't see the marching ants in your image the way you do with the Selection tools. If you click more than once, you just change your selection instead of adding to it, just the way you would with any of the regular Selection tools (see page 115). To add to your selection (that is, to select additional shades), hold down the Shift key and click in your photo again.

   Another way to add more shades is to select the middle eyedropper (the one with the + sign next to it) and click in your photo again. To remove a color, select the right eyedropper (with the – sign) and click. Alternatively, Alt+click with the first eyedropper, and the shade you click is removed from the selection. If you want to start your selection all over again, Alt+click the Cancel button to turn it to a Reset button.

4. **When you've selected everything you want to change, move the sliders to replace the color.**

   The Hue, Saturation, and Lightness sliders work exactly the way they do in Hue/Saturation (explained earlier in this chapter). Move them and watch the

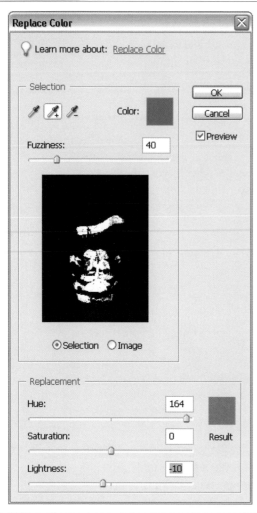

color box in the Replace Color window to see what color you're concocting. You can also click the color box to bring up the Color Picker (see page 196) and choose a color there. If you need to tweak the area of color you're changing, the Fuzziness slider adjusts the range of colors that Color Replacement affects, as shown in Figure 9-18.

Look at your photo after you've chosen your replacement color. If the preview doesn't show the color in all the areas you want, just click the missing spots with the middle eyedropper to fix them.

5. **Click OK.**

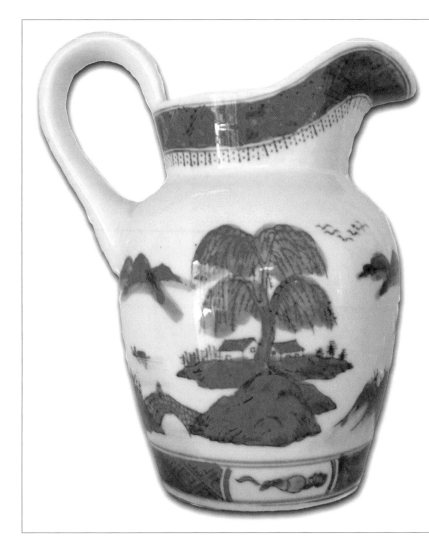

Figure 9-18:
Fuzziness is similar to the Tolerance setting for the Magic Wand (page 116). Take a look at the brown areas of the jug. There's still a lot of blue around them. Set Fuzziness higher to include more shades than you've previously been changing (in this figure, making such a change would cause all the blue to get turned to brown). If you find you're picking up little bits of areas you don't want, set Fuzziness lower. Move the slider to the right for more fuzziness and to the left for less.

Using a Brush to Replace Colors

The Color Replacement tool gives you yet another way to change the colors in your photo. It lets you brush a replacement color onto the area you want to change, without changing any other colors in your photo except the one you target. Figure 9-19 shows how great this tool is for changing hard-to-isolate areas like feathers.

The Color Replacement tool shares a slot with the Brush tool in the Toolbox. To select it, press B or click the Brush tool. Choose the Color Replacement tool from the pop-out list, or click it in the Options bar (it's the third icon from the left).

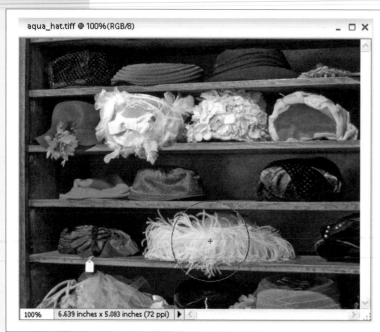

aqua_hat.tiff @ 100%(RGB/8)

100%   6.639 inches x 5.083 inches (72 ppi)

Figure 9-19:
Feathers, hair, and fur are usually completely exasperating to try to select. But the Color Replacement tool saves you from having to fool with selections. Just move the crosshairs in the cursor over the area you want to change and click or drag. It would have taken hours to get a good selection on this marabou hat, but the Color Replacement tool is smart enough to find all those drifting white areas and change them to aqua—without bleeding the color into other light areas, like the price tag on the adjacent hat.

The Options bar settings make a big difference in the way the Color Replacement tool works:

- **Brush Options.** These settings (size, hardness, angle, and so on) work the same way they do for any brush. See Chapter 12 for more information about brushes.

- **Mode.** This is the blend mode (page 322) the tool uses. Generally you want Color or Hue, although you can get some funky special effects with Saturation.

- **Sampling.** These choices appear as icons in the Options bar. Click one to tell the tool how to look for colors in your image. From left to right, they stand for Continuous, Once, and Background Swatch. If you choose Continuous, the brush changes every color that falls under the crosshairs as you move through your photo. Choosing Once means that no matter how far you travel while holding the mouse button, Elements replaces only the color that was under the crosshairs when you first clicked. Background Swatch means that Elements replaces only the color currently featured in the Background color swatch.

- **Limits.** This setting tells the Color Replacement tool which areas of your photo to look at in its search for color. Contiguous means only areas that touch each other get changed. Discontiguous means the tool changes all the places it finds a color—whether they're touching one another or not.

- **Tolerance.** This is just like the Tolerance setting for the Magic Wand: the higher the number, the more shades of color are affected by the tool. Getting this setting right is the key to getting good results with the Color Replacement tool.

- **Anti-alias.** This setting smoothes the edges of the replacement color. It's best to leave it turned on.

Using the Color Replacement tool is very straightforward:

1. **Pick the color you're going to use as a replacement.**

   Elements uses the current Foreground color as the replacement color. To choose a new Foreground color, click the Foreground color square in the Toolbox and choose a new color from the Color Picker (page 196) when it appears.

2. **Activate the Color Replacement tool and pick a brush size.**

   See Chapter 12 for help with using brushes. Generally for this tool, you want a fairly large brush, as shown in Figure 9-19.

3. **Click or drag in your photo to change the color.**

   Elements targets the color that is under the crosshairs in the center of the brush.

The Color Replacement tool is great for changing large areas of color to an equivalent tone, but if you want to replace dark red with pale yellow you probably won't like the results. It's not great for colors where the lightness is very different.

> **TIP** You may want to use the Color Replacement tool on a duplicate layer (Ctrl+J) so that you can adjust the layer opacity to control the effect.

Special Effects

Elements gives you some other useful ways of drastically changing the look of your image. You can apply these effects as Adjustment layers (Layer → New Adjustment Layer) or by going to Filter → Adjustments (there's much more about filters in Chapter 13). Either way gives you the same options for their settings. You can see them in action in Figure 9-20.

In most cases, you use these adjustments as steps along the way in a more complex treatment of your photo, but they're effective by themselves, too. Here's what each does:

- **Gradient Map** is pretty complicated. According to Adobe, it "maps the grayscale range of an image to the colors of a specified gradient fill." If you want to know what the heck *that* means, turn to page 371. Basically, a gradient map lets you apply a gradient based on the light and dark areas of your photo. The gradient colors replace the existing colors in your photo. There's a lot more to it than that, though.

- **Equalize** makes the darkest pixel black and the lightest white, and redistributes the brightness values for all the colors in a photo to give them all equal weight. The dialog box lets you choose between simply equalizing your whole photo and equalizing it based on a selection. It doesn't always work, but sometimes Equalize is great for bringing up the brightness level of a dim photo.

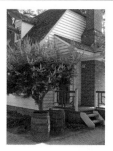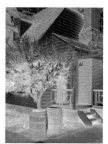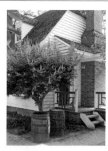

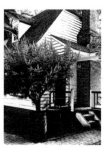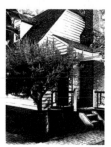

Figure 9-20:
You can get some interesting special effects with the Adjustment commands, whether you apply them as filters or as Adjustment layers. If you want to use them as filters, it's not a bad idea to start with a duplicate layer.

Top row (left to right): The original photo, Invert, Equalize.

Bottom row: Posterize and Threshold.

- **Invert** makes your photo look like a negative. It's so useful in doing artistic effects that you can also invert any time in the Editor just by pressing Ctrl+I.

  NOTE   If you think choosing the Invert option sounds like a great way to get your negatives scanned in with a basic flatbed scanner and turned to positive images, sorry, but you need to think again. Color negatives have an orange mask on them that Elements can't easily undo. You're best off with a dedicated film scanner that's designed to cope with negatives, or at least with a scanner that has software designed to deal with the mask.

- **Posterize** reduces the total number of colors in your photo, giving a less detailed, more poster-like effect. The lower the number you enter in the dialog box, the fewer colors you'll get (thus, the more extreme the result). If you want blocky, poster-like edges in your photo, try Filter → Artistic → Poster Edges instead of or in addition to this.

- **Threshold** turns every pixel in your photo to pure white or pure black. You won't find any shades of gray here. Figure 9-21 explains how to adjust the settings for the Threshold command.

- **Photo Filter** makes color corrections, like removing color casts from your photos. You can read about them in detail on page 224.

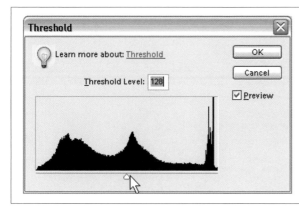

Figure 9-21:
This slider controls the dividing point between black and white pixels in a Threshold adjustment. Slide to the left if you want more white pixels, and to the right for more dark ones.

Removing and Adding Color

If you love classic black-and-white photography, or if you yearn to be the next Ansel Adams, then you'll be over the moon with Elements 5. For the first time, you can easily do a high-quality black-and-white conversion in Elements. (Previous versions of Elements let you remove the color from a photo, but as art photography aficionados can tell you, there's a world of difference between just dumping the color from a photo and creating a true work of black-and-white art.)

If you can't imagine why anyone would willingly abandon color, consider that in a world crammed full of eye-popping colors, black and white really stands out. Also, you may be planning to have something printed where you can't use color illustrations. And of course, for artistic photography, there's still nothing like black and white, where tone and contrast make or break the photo, without any pretty colors to distract you from the picture's underlying structure

In this chapter, you'll learn how to make a color photo black and white, and how to create images that are partly in color and partly in black and white. You'll also learn how to colorize a black-and-white image, and, along the way, how to use and edit *layer masks*, an important technique for advanced Elements work.

Method One: Making Color Photos Black and White

A good black-and-white image is so much more than just a color photo without color. Generally, just removing the color from a photo produces a pretty flat-looking, uninteresting image. A good black-and-white photo usually needs more contrast. You can create very different effects and totally different moods in your photo, depending on what you decide to emphasize in the black-and-white version.

Black-and-white conversion has traditionally been regarded as a pretty complicated process. When you do a Google search, you can find literally dozens of different recipes for making conversions. Fortunately for you, Elements 5 makes it really easy to perform these conversions, and even to do sophisticated tweaking of the different color channels. (Read more about conversion below.)

Just follow these steps:

1. **Open the photo you want to convert.**

   If the photo has multiple layers, flatten it (Layer → Flatten Image), or make sure the layer you want to convert is the active layer (click it in the Layers palette). If you want to convert only a part of your photo, then select the area you want to make black and white. (See Chapter 5 for more on selections.)

2. **Go to Enhance → Convert to Black and White.**

   You see the dialog box shown in Figure 10-1.

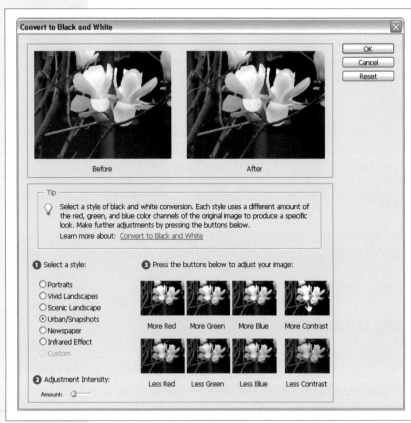

Figure 10-1:
The new "Convert to Black and White" dialog box makes it very easy to create effective transformations, even if you don't have any idea what you're doing. First, choose a conversion style from the radio buttons on the left, and then click the little thumbnails to tweak your conversion, if necessary. It's just like using Color Variations (page 193), only these are colorless variations.

3. **Choose a conversion style.**

Elements gives you a variety of different preset styles for the conversion. Click the button next to a style to try it on your photo. Try different styles to see which suits your photo best.

4. **Tweak the conversion, if necessary.**

Use the buttons below the preview area (More Red, More Green, and so on) to increase or decrease the prominence of each color channel. (These buttons are explained in more detail below.) Each thumbnail photo gives you a minuscule preview of how your image will look if you apply its effect. Use the Adjust Intensity Amount slider to strengthen or weaken the effect you'll get when you click the button.

If you want to start from scratch, click Reset.

TIP   You may find it very difficult to see any differences between all those little thumbnails. If so, move the Amount slider to the right till you can see a difference in the thumbnails, and then put the slider back to where it was, so that you don't make radical changes to your photo. A very small amount makes a big difference in your photo.

5. **When you're satisfied with how your photo looks, click OK.**

Be sure to examine your actual image carefully. Move the "Convert to Black and White" dialog box around so that you can see all the regions of your photo before you accept the conversion. If you decide against creating a black-and-white image, then click Cancel.

TIP   The adjustments you can make in the "Convert to Black and White" window change your entire photo. Very often, you may prefer to further emphasize certain details in your photo without making global changes. To do that, use the Dodge and Burn tools (page 319), once you've completed your conversion.

While the different conversion styles have descriptive names, like Portrait and Urban Landscape, don't put too much stock in the names themselves. Instead, test out the various styles to see which best matches your photo. For instance, you may vastly prefer the way Uncle Julio looks when you choose the Newspaper style instead of the Portraits style. Basically, the names are just a less intimidating way of describing preset collections of settings to the color channels in your photo.

But wait a minute: changes to the color channels? That's right. Back in Chapter 7, you read about how your photo consists of three separate color channels: red, blue, and green. What you may not realize is that, in your original camera file, each of these channels is recorded merely as variations in light and dark tones, in other words, a black-and-white image. Your image file tells the computer or printer to make a particular channel all red, blue, or green, and the blending of the three monotone channels makes all the colors you see.

Now when you convert your photo back to black and white, each of these channels contains varying amounts of details from your photo, depending on the color of your original subject. So, the green channel might have more detail from your subject's eyelashes, while the red channel has more detail from the bark on the tree she's standing under. (Remember, the color channels themselves don't necessarily correspond to the color of the objects you see in your final photo. Or, put another way: your camera needs to use a mixture of red, blue, and green to create what looks like bark to us humans.) Noise (see page 350) often happens much more in one channel than the others, as well.

The buttons in the dialog box (More Red, More Green, and so on) let you increase or decrease the presence of each color channel. So you can adjust how prominent various details in your photo are by changing the importance of that color channel in the complete photo. These adjustments can greatly change the appearance of the final conversion.

That's the theory behind those color channel buttons, but, fortunately, you don't have to understand it to use them effectively. Just be sure you can get a good view of your photo, and click till you're happy with what you see. If you plan to print your converted photo, read the box on page 270 for some tips on how to get a good black-and-white print from a color inkjet printer.

> **TIP** Elements gives you an easier way to convert your photo to black and white, but it's an all or nothing scenario—you don't get any options for adjusting the tones in your image. There's a very nice black-and-white tint effect in the Photo Effects part of the Artwork and Effects palette's Special Effects section. You can apply it by double-clicking it. Also, several of the new Frames in the Artwork section of the Artwork and Effects palette automatically convert your photo to black and white when you place the photo into the frame. The Vintage frames and some of the Professional frames turn your photo black and white, as well as framing it. See page 402 for details on how to use these frames.

Method Two: Removing Color from a Photo

Since one size never fits all, Elements gives you a few other, fundamentally different ways to remove the color from your image. Most times, you should follow the instructions in the preceding section to convert your photo to black and white. But if you want to drain the color from a particular part of your photo, or if you're looking to do something artistic, like changing a color photo into a drawing or a painting, then you'll probably want to try one of these three methods:

• **Convert Mode.** You may remember from page 40 that you need to choose a color mode for your photo, either RGB, Bitmap, or Grayscale. You can remove the color from your photo by changing its mode to Grayscale. To do this, choose Image → Mode → Grayscale. This method is quick, but it's also a bit destructive, since you can't apply it to a layer: your entire photo is either grayscale or not.

• **Remove Color.** You can also keep your photo as an RGB file and drain the color from it, by going to Enhance → Adjust Color → Remove Color (or pressing Ctrl+Shift+U). This removes the color from the active layer only, so if your photo has more than one layer, you need to flatten it first (Layer → Flatten Image), or the other layers keep their color.

Remove Color is really just another way to completely desaturate your photo as you might when using the Hue/Saturation command (described in the next option). It's faster than using the Hue/Saturation dialog box, but you don't get the control that the dialog box gives you. Figure 10-2 shows you the difference between applying the Remove Color command versus converting your entire image to grayscale.

Figure 10-2:
Uncoloring your photo can give you very different results depending on the method you use.

Top: Each star, when first created, has a pure color value of 255. In other words, you're looking at stars that are 100 percent purple, red, and green, with zero as the number for the other two channels.

Middle: The same images with the mode converted to grayscale (Image → Mode → Grayscale).

Bottom: Using the Remove Color command causes a very different change.

• **Hue/Saturation.** You can also call up the Hue/Saturation dialog box (page 252), and move the Saturation slider all the way to the left, or type "–100" into the Saturation box. The advantage to this method is that if you don't care for the shade of gray you get, you can desaturate each color channel separately by using the pull-down menu in the dialog box. With this method, you can tweak your settings a bit to eliminate any color cast you may get from your printer.

NOTE   If you're planning to print the results of your conversion, the paper you use can make a *big* difference in the gray tones you get. If you don't like the results from your usual paper, then try a different weight or brand. You'll need to experiment because the inks for different printer models react differently with different brands of paper.

OUTSIDE ELEMENTS

Digital Black and White

If you love black-and-white photography, there's good news for you in the digital world. The quality of digital black-and-white printing is improving by leaps and bounds, and now you can get decent black-and-white photos from even some of the lowest-priced printers, if you shop carefully and investigate your options before you buy.

For all the wonders of digitizing, though, there's still nothing that can exactly duplicate the effect of a traditional silver oxide print—although digital printing has made great strides in the past couple of years.

If you want to print black-and-white photos, you may still want to look into a photo printer that allows you to substitute several shades of gray for your color cartridges. The special inks available are constantly improving, and you can get much better prints now than you could even a year or two ago. You can now purchase special grayscale ink cartridge sets for even very inexpensive inkjet printers, and more printer drivers have settings for grayscale printing. (Printer driver controls appear when you launch the Elements Print dialog box, as explained on page 418.) You have many more options than you did even a year ago.

Creating Spot Color

Removing almost all the color from a photo but leaving one or two objects in vivid tones, called *spot color*, is a very effective artistic device that's long been popular in the print industry. (The term can also have a different meaning among those in the commercial printing business, where it refers to the use of a special ink for a particular color in a multi-colored image.) Figure 10-3 shows an example of spot color. To practice the maneuvers you're about to learn, download the photo (barn. jpg) from the "Missing CD" page at *www.missingmanuals.com*.

This section walks you through three of the easiest methods. You can erase your way back to color, change only a selected area to black and white, or use an Adjustment layer. In learning to use the last method, you'll also learn how to edit the layer mask of an Adjustment layer so that you can change the area the adjustment affects.

The end result looks the same no matter which of these methods you choose. Just select the one you find easiest for the particular photo you want to change.

TIP   If you have a newish digital camera, check your special effects settings for a spot or accent color setting. Many cameras can now create a black-and-white image with only one shade left in color.

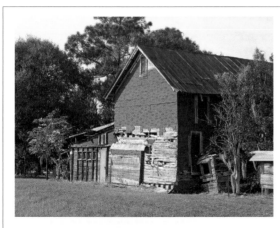

Figure 10-3:
With Elements, you can easily remove the color from only part of an image.

Top: Here, the photo is a regular color image.

Bottom: In Elements, it's easy to remove the color from everything except the barn. You'll learn three easy methods in this section.

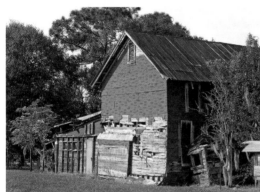

POWER USERS' CLINIC

Faking Photoshop

In Chapter 6, you learned about the basics of layer masks and how to use a blank Adjustment layer as a mask by grouping it with the layer you want to mask.

If you're trying to follow a tutorial written for full Photoshop, sometimes you can get closer to the way a layer mask works in full Photoshop by placing your mask *underneath* the layer you're grouping it with. If you remember, in grouped layers (page 160), the bottom layer calls the shots for things like color and opacity.

If you want to control visibility for parts of the masked layer, if you put the mask layer below it, you can adjust what shows and what's hidden on the real layer, by painting on the layer mask.

Both ways, above and below, have their uses, but they give you control in different ways. If you do a little experimenting, it won't take long to develop a sense for which one you want in a particular situation.

Erasing Colors from a Duplicate Layer

The simplest way to remove colors from your image is to use the Eraser tool. (See page 325 for more about the different Erasers.) When you use this method, you place a color-free layer over your colored original and erase bits of the top layer to let the color below show through.

1. **Make a duplicate layer.**

   Press Ctrl+J or go to Layer → Duplicate layer. This is the layer that's going to be black and white.

2. **Remove the color from the new top layer.**

   Go to Enhance → Convert to Black and White, or to Enhance → Adjust Color → Remove Color. (Be sure the top layer is the active one before you do this.) You should now see only a black-and-white image.

3. **Erase the areas on the top layer where you want to see color.**

   Use the Eraser tool (page 326) to remove parts of the top layer so the colored layer underneath shows through. Usually you'll get best results with a fairly soft brush.

If you want to have an image that's mostly colored with only a few black-and-white areas, reverse the technique—remove the color from the bottom layer and leave the top layer in color. Then erase as described above.

When you're finished, you can flatten the layers if you want, but if you do keep them separate, you can always go back and erase more of the top layer later on. And you'll still have the option of trashing the layer you erased and making a new duplicate of the bottom layer, if you want to start over.

Removing Color from Selections

If you don't want to have multiple layers, you can also use Convert to Black and White or the Remove Color command on a selection. (See Chapter 5 for more about making selections.) Just make sure you save your image as a version (page 54), or perform this method on a copy, if your photo isn't in the Organizer. You don't want to risk wrecking your original photo.

The procedure for changing a selected area to black and white is very simple.

1. **Mask out the area where you want to keep the color in your image.**

   Use the Selection brush in Mask mode (see page 125) to paint a mask over the area where you want to *keep* the color, to protect it from being changed in step 2. In other words, you're going to make everything black and white *except* where you paint with the Selection brush.

   If you want to keep the color in most of your photo and remove the color from only one or two objects, paint over them with the brush in Selection mode instead of Mask mode.

2. **Remove the color from the selected area.**

Go to Enhance → Convert to Black and White, or to Enhance → Adjust Color → Remove Color, or press Ctrl+Shift+U. The color disappears from the areas not protected by the mask, but the area under the mask is untouched. (You can also do this step by going to Enhance → Adjust Color → Adjust Hue/Saturation and moving the Saturation slider all the way to the left.)

You should see a photo with color only in the areas that you didn't select. This method's the least flexible. Once you close your image, the change is permanent and not undoable, which is why you don't want to use this method on your original photo.

SPECIAL EFFECTS

Hints for Coloring Old Photographs

It's easier to put each element of a face that you're going to color–lips, eyes, cheek color, skin–on a separate layer. That way, you can change just one color later without a lot of hassle. You can always merge the layers (Layer → Merge Visible, or Merge Down) later, once you know for sure that you're done.

If you want the effect of a photo that was hand-colored a century ago, paint at less than 100-percent opacity. The tinting on old photos is very transparent.

If you select the area before you paint, you won't have to worry about getting color outside of where you want it, because your paint is confined to your selection.

Skin colors are very hard to create in the color picker. Try sampling skin tones from another photo instead. If it's a family photo, after all, the odds are good that the current generation's basic skin tones are reasonably close to Great-Granddad's.

Using a Layer Mask and the Saturation Slider

If you'd like to keep the option of easily changing your mind about which areas keep the color, it's best to remove the color with a Hue/Saturation Adjustment layer. This is your most flexible choice (though it doesn't offer you the tone adjustments you can make when using "Convert to Black and White"). Using an Adjustment layer lets you both add and subtract areas of color later if you like.

1. **Select the area where you want to remove the color.**

Use any Selection tool you like (see Chapter 5 for more about Selection tools). If you think it would be easier to select the area where you want to keep the color, do that, and then press Shift+Ctrl+I to invert your selection so that the area that's going to lose the color is selected instead.

2. **Create a Hue/Saturation Adjustment layer.**

Go to Layer → New Adjustment Layer → Hue/Saturation, or click the New Adjustment Layer icon on the Layers palette and choose a Hue/Saturation layer.

3. **In the Hue/Saturation dialog box that appears, remove the color.**

Move the Saturation slider all the way to the left to remove the color.

Why is this method better? Well, for one, you can always discard the Adjustment layer if you change your mind. But that's not all. You can actually edit the Adjustment layer's layer mask (see page 167 for more about what a layer mask is) so that you can change which parts of your photo are in color, even days or weeks later.

Don't want that tree as well as the vine on the house? Or maybe you wish you'd left all the window frames in color? All are easily fixed by editing the layer mask. The next section tells you how.

Editing a layer mask

Elements gives you the ability to make changes to the layer mask of an Adjustment layer any time you want to—as long as the layer hasn't been merged into another layer and the image hasn't been flattened. You may want to edit your layer mask when you realize your original selection needs some cleaning up, or when you want to make changes to the area the Adjustment layer affects.

> **NOTE** Remember that masking something means it *won't* be affected by a change. So the area that shows up in black or red on your layer mask is the area that *isn't* going to be changed by your adjustment. If you don't see any black or red when you look at a layer mask, then the Adjustment layer is going to change your whole photo.

You can work on the mask directly in your photo, or you can make the layer mask visible and work on the mask itself. Here's the simplest way to make changes to the area covered by a layer mask:

1. **Set your foreground/background colors to black and white.**

    Just press D. If you want to paint with white, press X to swap the colors so that white (the background) becomes the foreground color.

2. **Paint directly on your image.**

    Use the Brush tool to paint. Paint with black to keep an area from being affected by your adjustment. Paint with white to increase the area affected by the adjustment. In other words, black masks an area, while white increases your selected area.

    You can also use the Selection tools (the same way you would on any other selection) to change the mask's area. Just keep in mind that what's selected gets changed by the adjustment, while what's masked doesn't change. See Chapter 5 if you need help making selections. If you watch the layer mask icon in the layers palette, you'll see that it also changes to show where you've painted.

To make a layer mask visible, click it in the Layers palette. Elements gives you a choice of two different ways to see the masked area, as shown in Figure 10-4. You merely Alt+click the right-side thumbnail for the Adjustment layer in the Layers palette, and then you'll see the black layer mask (instead of your photo) in the image window. Add the Shift key when you click to see a red overlay over the photo instead of the black-and-white view.

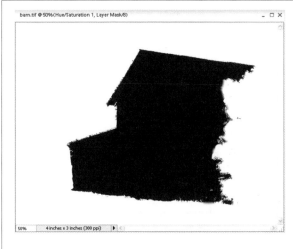

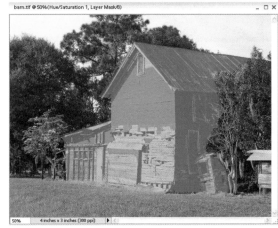

Figure 10-4:
Elements not only lets you edit your layer mask, but gives you two different ways to see it.

Top: To see the masked area in black, Alt+click the right thumbnail for the layer in the Layers palette.

Bottom: To see the masked area in red, Alt+Shift+click the layer's thumbnail.

The black mask view shows only the mask itself, not your photo beneath it. This is a good choice when you're checking to see how clean the edges of your selection are. If you're adding or subtracting areas of your photo, then choose the red overlay view so that you can see the objects in your photo as you paint over them. You can use the method described above to paint in either view.

That's all there is to it, but that's not all you can do to edit a layer mask. You can use shades of gray to adjust the transparency of the mask. When you paint on your mask with gray, you can change the opacity of the changes made by the Adjustment layer. You can let a little color show through the mask, for instance, without letting the full vividness of the color come through. Figure 10-5 shows an example of how you'd use this technique.

The lighter the shade of gray you choose, the more color shows through.

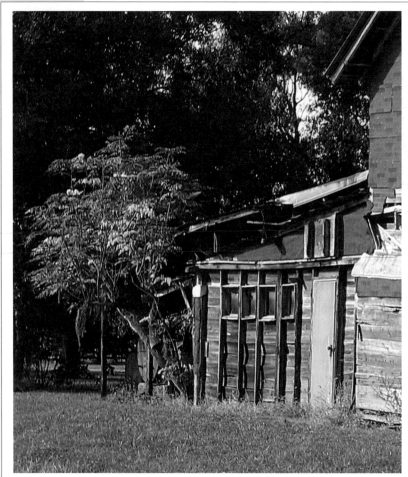

Figure 10-5:
By painting with different
shades of gray on the
layer mask, you can
cause the effect of the
adjustment to be partially
transparent. Here, a
fairly light gray was used
to paint over the tree so
that a little green shows,
but it's not the bright,
saturated green of the
original photo. Only part
of the tree was painted to
make it easy to see the
contrast with what was
there before.

Colorizing a Black-and-White Photo

So far, you've read about ways to keep color in an image while you make part of it black and white. But what about when you've got a black-and-white photo and you want to add color to it? Elements makes things easy (or if not easy, then at least possible). For instance, you can give an old photo the sort of hand-tinted effect you sometimes see in antique prints, as shown in Figure 10-6.

You can easily color things with Elements. Before you start tinting your photo, first make any needed repairs. See page 235 for repair strategies. For fixes to the exposure, see page 174.

1. **Make sure your photo's in RGB mode.**

   Go to Image → Mode → RGB. Your photo must be in RGB mode or you can't color it.

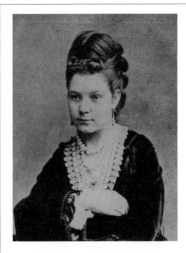

Figure 10-6:

Top: If you decide to color an old black-and-white or sepia photo, put each color on its own layer. That way you can adjust the transparency or change the hue or saturation for one color without changing the other colors, too.

Bottom: A very low opacity is enough for really old photos like this one if you want to give the effect of a print that was hand-colored.

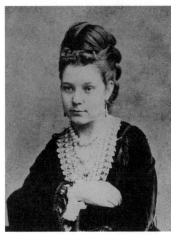

2. **Create a new layer in Color mode.**

   Go to Layer → New → Layer and select Color as the layer mode. By choosing Color as your layer mode, you can paint on the layer and the image details still show through.

3. **Paint on the layer.**

   Use the Brush tool (page 306) and choose a color in the Toolbox's Foreground color square (page 195). Keep changing the foreground color as much as you need to. If the coverage is too heavy, then in the Options bar, reduce the opacity of the brush.

You can also paint directly on the original layer. But the problem with that is that it's far more difficult to fix things if you make a mistake when you're well into your project. Using the original layer also doesn't give you much of an out if you decide later on that the lip color you painted first doesn't look so great with the skin color you just chose.

Tinting an Entire Photo

You can give an entire photo a single color tint all over, even if the original is a grayscale photo. In fact, you can use tinting to create a variety of different moods.

You have two basic ways to tint your photo. Actually, there are lots more than two, but two should give you the idea. The first method (Layer style) described here is faster, but the second (Colorize) lets you tweak your settings more. Figure 10-7 shows the result of using the Layer style method on a color photo. (For a more subtle effect, you can also use the Photo Filters, described on page 224.) There are also some terrific monotone tint effects in the Photo Effects, as explained on page 356.

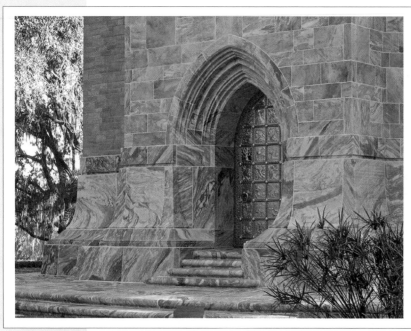

Figure 10-7:
The easiest way to create a monochrome color scheme for your photo is with the Photographic Layer styles, which are explained in Chapter 13. Shown here is the Gray-Green Tone style applied to the original color photo. It removes the existing color and recolors your image in one click. The downside is that you can't edit the color once you're done if you decide you'd rather have, say, orange.

For either method, if you want to keep the original color (or lack thereof) in part of your photo, use the Selection brush in Mask mode (page 125) to mask out the area you don't want to change.

> NOTE   New to Elements 5: Some of the frame effects in the Artwork and Effects palette auto-matically add a tint to your photo when you apply them. There are also some handy mono-chrome tint effects among the Photo Effects.

Using a Layer style

Although many people never dig down far enough to find them, Adobe gives you some Photographic Layer styles that make tinting a photo as easy as double-clicking. You'll learn more about Layer styles on page 358, but this section tells you all you need to know to use the Photographic styles. It's a very simple procedure.

1. **Create a duplicate layer.**

   Go to Layer → Duplicate Layer or press Ctrl+J. (If you don't create a duplicate layer and your original has only a Background layer, you'll get asked to convert it to a layer when you apply the style. Say yes.)

2. **If necessary, change the mode to RGB.**

   Go to Image → Mode → RGB. With this method, it doesn't matter if your original is in color or not. The Layer style gets rid of the original color and tints the photo all at the same time.

3. **Choose a Layer style.**

   Go to the Artwork and Effects palette, click the Effects, Filters, and Layer Styles button, and then choose Layer Styles from the left menu, and Photographic Effects from the right. Double-click the style of your choice, drag it to the photo, or click it once in the palette and then click Apply. You can click around and try different styles to see which you prefer. Undo (Ctrl+Z) after each style that you try.

4. **When you see what you like, click OK.**

   The drawback to this method is that you can't easily go back and edit the color you get from the Layer style. When you call up the Style Settings (see page 361), you won't see any active checkboxes, because these styles don't use those settings. Instead, you'd need to use a Hue/Saturation adjustment (see page 256) or Color Variations (page 193) to go back later and change the Layer style's tint color.

Additional tint effects from the Artwork and Effects palette

The new frames in the Artwork and Effects palette include some frames that automatically apply a tint to your photo, as shown in Figure 10-8. These range from simple all-over colors like Sepia, to fading gradients. (See page 362 for more about gradients.)

You can read more about using the Frames from the Artwork and Effects palette on page 402. To tint your photo, choose (logically enough) the Color Tints section of the Artwork Frames.

There are also some very effective color tints in the Photo Effects, found in the Special Effects section of the palette. Read about how to apply Effects on page 356.

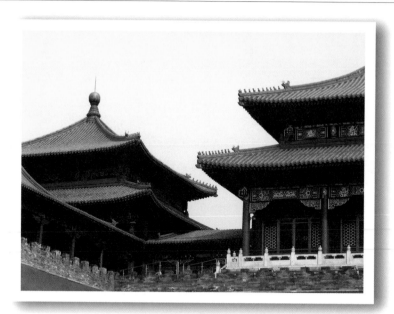

Figure 10-8:
Using the new artwork in Elements 5, you can apply elaborate effects, like this fading gradient, drop shadow, and the frame, with just a double-click. The effect used here is the Blue Fadeout (from Artwork → Frames → Color Tints), plus a little editing of the frame's drop shadow (see page 402).

Using Colorize

You can use the Colorize checkbox in the Hue/Saturation dialog box to add a color tint to a grayscale photo or to change the color of a photo that already has color in it. With this method, you can choose any color you like, as opposed to the limited color choices of the Layer styles in the previous section. You can also adjust the intensity of the color with the Saturation slider once you've selected the shade you want.

Figure 10-9 explains how the Colorize setting changes the way the Hue/Saturation command works.

1. **Remove the color from your photo, if necessary.**

   Press Ctrl+Shift+U to remove the color. Do this if the photo has become yellowed or discolored (because of age, for example).

2. **Make sure your photo is in RGB mode.**

   Go to Image → Mode → RGB.

3. **Colorize your photo on a new layer.**

   Go to Layer → New Adjustment Layer → Hue/Saturation and turn on the Colorize checkbox. When you turn this setting on, your image becomes filled with the foreground color. If you don't like it, that's fine. You're going to change it right now.

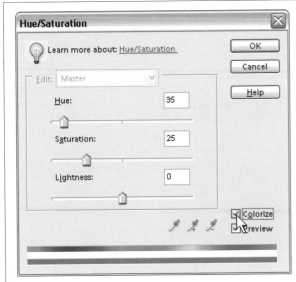

Figure 10-9:
If you want to color something that has no color
information in it, like a white shirt or a grayscale
image, then in the Hue/Saturation dialog box, turn on
Colorize to add color to the image. If you don't turn
on the Colorize checkbox, you can adjust the hue,
saturation, and lightness of white all day long, and all
you'll do is go from white to gray to black because
there's no color info there for Elements to work on.

4. **Adjust the color until it looks the way you want it to.**

Move the sliders for Hue, Saturation, and Lightness until you find the look you
want, and then click OK. Figure 10-10 shows the results.

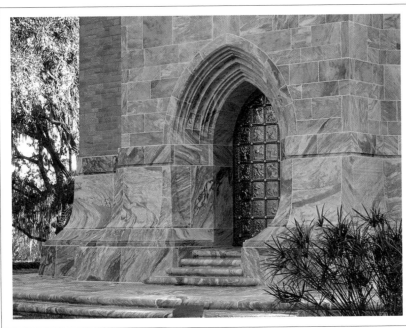

Figure 10-10:
Here's the photo tinted
with a purple tone by
turning on the Colorize
checkbox in the Hue/
Saturation dialog box.
The door was masked
out so that it stays in full
color.

If you selected and masked an area, that part should still show the original color.

You can change your mind about the colorizing by double-clicking the left icon on the layer in the Layers palette. That brings up the controls for the Hue/Saturation adjustment again so you can change your settings. And you can also edit the layer mask, as described on page 274, if you want to change the area that's affected by the Adjustment layer.

When you're done, if you merge layers, or press Ctrl+Alt+Shift+N+E to produce a new merged layer above the old ones, you can use Levels (page 184), Color Variations (page 193), and the other color-editing tools to tweak the tint effect.

Creating Panoramas and Correcting Perspective

Everyone's had the experience of trying to photograph an awesome view—a city skyline or a mountain range, for instance—only to find the whole scene won't fit into one picture, because it's just too wide. Elements, once again, comes to the rescue. With Elements' Photomerge command, you can stitch together a group of photos that you've taken while panning across the horizon. You end up with a panorama that's much larger than any single photo your camera can take. Panoramas can become addicting once you've tried them, and they're a great way to get those wide, wide shots that are beyond the capability of your camera lens.

The general procedure for creating a panorama in Elements is pretty straightforward, but the devil is in the details. In the first part of this chapter, you'll learn how to use the Photomerge command to make panoramas. Because the angle of your image may need a little correcting afterwards, you'll also learn how to use the Transform commands to adjust the images you've created.

If you're into photographing buildings (especially tall ones), you'll know that you often need some kind of perspective correction: a building appears to be leaning backward or sideways as a result of distortion caused by your camera's lens. You'll learn how to use the new Correct Camera Distortion filter to straighten things back up.

> **NOTE** Photomerge is great for making larger images by combining photos at their edges. But if you want to combine elements of different photos into one image, like putting a picture of your new girlfriend's face onto a picture of your old girlfriend, page 168 shows you how to do that by putting each element on its own layer.

Creating Panoramas

It's a lot of fun to combine your photos into panoramas using the Photomerge command. Start with a group of photos you've taken that can fit together side by side to show a more complete view of your subject in one image. Figure 11-1 shows a three-photo panorama and the photos that went into it. You can download these photos (pavilion1.jpg, pavilion2.jpg, and pavilion3.jpg) from the "Missing CD" page at *www.missingmanuals.com*, if you'd like to try panorama-making.

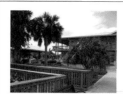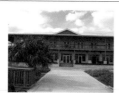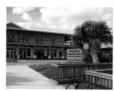

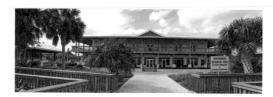

Figure 11-1:
With Elements, you can easily stitch together many different shots to make one large image that shows the entire view. Elements easily blended the three photos you see at the top of the figure into the completed panorama you see below them.

Elements can merge together as many photos as you want to include in a panorama. The only real size limitation comes when you want to print out your merges. If you have only letter-sized paper and you create a five-photo horizontal panorama, it's going to be only a couple of inches high, even if you rotate your panorama to print lengthwise. (You can buy printers with attachments that let you print on rolls of paper, so that there's no limit to the longest dimension of your panorama. These printers are very popular with panorama addicts. You can also use an online printing service, like the Kodak EasyShare Gallery to get larger prints than you can make at home. See page 410 for more about how to order online prints from the Organizer.)

You'll get the best results creating a panorama if you plan ahead when shooting your photos. The pictures should be side by side, of course, and you get much better results if they overlap each other by at least 30 percent. Also, you'll minimize the biggest panorama problem—matching the color of your photos—if you make sure they all have identical exposures. The box on page 290 has some suggestions.

When you use the Photomerge command, you start by telling Elements which photos to combine, or you choose your files in the Photomerge's Browse window. When you've got all the photos you want, the actual Photomerge window appears, shown in Figure 11-2. Elements starts things off by doing the heavy lifting of actually merging the photos into one, but you still have to go in and do the clean-up work (trimming, correcting the blending, and so on) if you want stellar results.

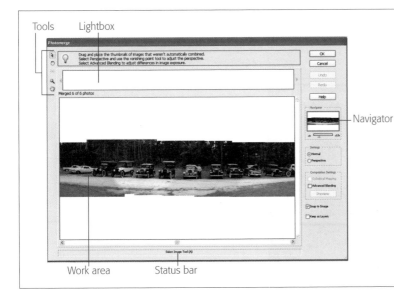

Tools Lightbox

Navigator

Work area   Status bar

Select Image Tool (A)

Figure 11-2:
The Elements Photomerge window is your workshop for joining two or more photos into a panorama. If Elements can't figure out how to place a photo, it gets left in the Lightbox at the top of the window. You can position it manually and then adjust it using the tools from the toolbox on the left side of the window. Although Elements does a lot of the work automatically, you'll get better results if you go in to tweak things, using the settings on the right side of the window, once Elements has created the basic merge for you.

TIP You can also create vertical panoramas—Elements automatically figures out which way your photos fit together.

Selecting Files and Merging Them

The first part of creating a panorama is selecting the photos you want to include. You can save yourself a lot of time and trouble if you go through your photos first, to be sure the color in all the photos matches, *before* you start your panorama. Figure 11-3 shows why you need to take this step.

When you're ready to create a panorama, just follow these steps:

1. **Go through the photos you want to use and make sure the colors match as closely as possible.**

   Use any of the editing tools in Quick Fix (see page 91) or the more advanced options described in Chapter 7 to modify colors and exposure levels. Figure 11-4 demonstrates how to compare the color in your photos as you work.

2. **Start your panorama.**

   To begin a new Photomerge, go to File → New → Photomerge Panorama. This brings up the Photomerge Browse window, which is where you choose the photos you want to combine. You must have at least one photo open in the Editor to start a Photomerge (otherwise the menu item is grayed out).

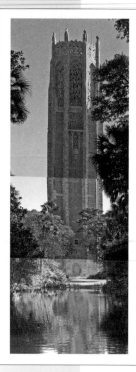 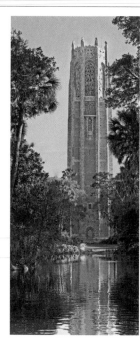

Figure 11-3:

Left: This three-photo panorama shows the biggest problem most people face when merging images— exposure differences from shot to shot.

Right: As you can see in the repaired version, it was necessary to sacrifice some color from the best photo (the top one) to get everything matched up. The Advanced Blending option joined the bottom two images fairly seamlessly, though. The sky was repaired with a combination of the Clone Stamp (page 242), the Healing brush (page 246), and the Paint Bucket (page 318) tools.

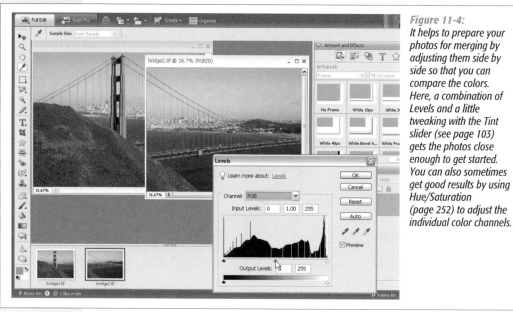

Figure 11-4:

It helps to prepare your photos for merging by adjusting them side by side so that you can compare the colors. Here, a combination of Levels and a little tweaking with the Tint slider (see page 103) gets the photos close enough to get started. You can also sometimes get good results by using Hue/Saturation (page 252) to adjust the individual color channels.

3. **Choose the photos you want to include.**

   Click the Browse button in the window to see a list of the folders and files on your hard drive. Navigate to the one you want and click Choose. If you can't select all the photos at once because they aren't all in the same folder, you can click Browse as many times as you want, and the new files get added to the list in the window.

   If you have photos already open in Elements, they're automatically loaded in the Browse window. So if you want to merge photos from several different folders, opening all of them is one way to get them into the mix faster than by navigating to each folder separately.

   Photomerge copies each file as it adds it to the panorama and doesn't change your originals. You don't need to worry about making copies especially for your panoramas.

4. **Add more photos if necessary.**

   If you need files from several folders and you didn't get them ahead of time, just keep going back until you've rounded them all up. Just click the Browse button again. If you inadvertently have more photos than you want, highlight the unwanted photo(s) in the list and click the Remove button.

5. **When you've got all the images you want, click OK.**

   If your photos weren't already open, you see them open one by one as Elements starts performing its merge magic. You can watch exactly what Elements is doing if you have the Layers palette (page 142) out where you can see it, since Elements places each merged photo on its own layer before combining them.

   If you want your photos to remain on their own layers in the completed panorama, make sure the Keep as Layers checkbox is turned on.

Elements' first pass isn't always perfect, as you can see in Figure 11-5, top. The next section explains how to help Elements out when it can't quite figure out how to put things together, and how to improve the look of the combined image.

Adjusting Your Photos

Once your photos appear in the Photomerge window, you see Elements' best-guess effort at combining them. Now your part of the work begins, since you usually need to do a fair bit of tweaking here to get the best results.

Sometimes, for example, as shown in Figure 11-5, Elements gets confused and combines your photos randomly. In other cases, it just can't figure out where to put a photo at all. When that happens, Elements leaves the photos it can't place up at the top of the window, in the area called the Lightbox.

You can manually drag files from the Lightbox into the merge and also reposition photos already in your panorama. Just grab them with the Select Image tool (explained on page 288) and drag them to the correct location in the merge.

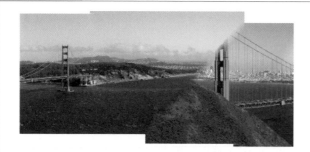

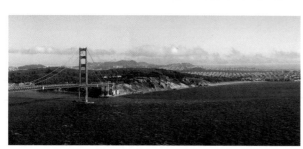

Figure 11-5:
Elements valiantly tries to combine your photos, but sometimes it has trouble lining images up exactly or figuring out how to fit a particular photo into the merge.

Top: Here, Elements guesses more wildly than a 10th grader on a pop quiz.

Bottom: Here's the final result, showing the end result of a five-photo merge. As you can see, with a little help, Elements can usually do a fine job of combining images—even when it doesn't know where to start.

If you try to nudge the position of a photo and it keeps jumping away from where you've placed it, turn off Snap to Image on the right side of the Photomerge window. Then you should be able to put your photo exactly where you want it. However, Elements isn't doing the figuring for you anymore, so use the Zoom tool to get a good look at the alignment afterwards. You may need to micro-adjust the photo's exact position.

At the top left of the Photomerge window is a little Toolbox. Some tools are familiar; others are special tools just for panoramas.

- **Select Image.** Use this tool to move individual photos into or out of your merge or to reposition them within it. When the Select Image tool is active, you can drag photos into or out of the Lightbox. Press A from the keyboard or click the tool to activate it.

- **Rotate Image.** Elements usually rotates images automatically when merging them, but if it doesn't, or guesses wrong, press R to activate this tool and then click the photo you want to rotate. You see handles on the image, just the way you would with the regular Rotate commands (page 65). Then just grab a corner and turn the photo until it fits in properly. Usually, you won't need to drastically change a photo's orientation, but this tool helps make the small changes often needed to line things up better.

- **Set Vanishing Point.** To understand what this tool does, think of standing on a long, straight, country road and looking off into the distance. The point at which the two parallel lines of the road seem to converge and meet the horizon is called the *vanishing point*. The Vanishing Point tool in Elements tells

Photomerge where you want that point to be in your finished panorama. Knowing the vanishing point helps Elements figure out the correct perspective. Press V to activate the Vanishing Point tool. Figure 11-6 shows an example of how it can change your results.

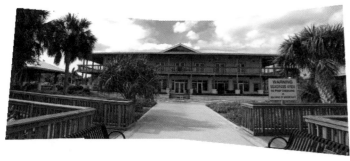

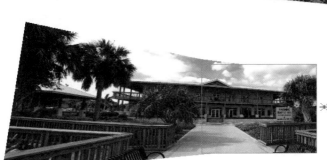

Figure 11-6:
You can radically alter the perspective of your panorama by selecting a vanishing point.

Top: Here you see the result of clicking in the center.

Bottom: Here you see the result of clicking on the right-hand image. Note that the tool selects only the image, not the actual point. You can click any photo to put your vanishing point there, but if you subsequently try to tweak it by clicking a higher or lower point within the same photo, nothing happens.

- **Zoom tool.** This is the same Zoom tool (page 79) you meet everywhere else in Elements. Click the magnifying glass in the Toolbox or press Z to activate it.

- **Hand tool.** Use the Hand tool (page 80) here when you need to scoot your *entire* merged image around to see a different part of it. Click the Hand icon in the Toolbox or press H to activate it. When moving an individual photo within your panorama, use the Select Image tool.

You have a few other aids on the right side of the window. Some, like Advanced Blending, adjust the way your photos blend together. Others, like Cylindrical Mapping adjust the camera's-eye view angle. (More on both in a moment.)

To control your onscreen view of your panorama, Elements gives you the Navigator on the right side of the Photomerge window. It works just like the regular Navigator described on page 81. Move the slider to resize the view of your panorama.

Drag to the right to zoom in on one area, or to the left to shrink the view so that you can see the whole thing at once. If you want to target a particular spot in your merge, drag the red rectangle to control the area that's onscreen.

Shooting Tips for Good Merges

The most important part of creating an impressive and plausible panorama starts before you even launch Elements. You can save yourself a lot of grief by planning ahead when shooting photos for a panorama.

Most of the time, you know *before* you shoot that you'll want to try to merge your photos. You don't often say, "Wow, I can't believe I've got seven photos of the Dr. Dre balloon at the Thanksgiving Day parade that just happen to be exactly in line and have a 30-percent overlap between each one! Guess I'll try a merge."

If you know you want to create a panorama, when you're taking pictures, set your camera to be as much in manual mode as possible. The biggest headache in panorama making is trying to get the exposure, color, brightness, and so on to blend seamlessly. Elements is darned good about blending the outlines of the physical objects in your photos. Lock your camera settings so that the exposure of each image is as identical as possible.

Even on small digital cameras that don't have much in the way of manual controls, you may have some kind of panorama setting, like Canon's Stitch Assist mode, that does the same thing.

(To be honest, your camera may make merges itself that work better than what Elements can do, because the camera's doing the image-blending internally. Check out whether your model has a panorama feature.)

The more your photos overlap, the better. Elements does what it can with what you give it, but it's really happy if you can arrange a 30- or 40-percent overlap between images.

It's helpful to use a tripod if you have one, and *pan heads* (tripod heads that let you swivel your camera in an absolutely straight line) were made for panoramas. Actually, as long as your shots aren't wildly out of line, Elements can usually cope. But you may have to do quite a bit of cropping to get even edges on the finished result if you don't use a tripod.

Whether you use a tripod or not, keep the camera—rather than the horizon—level to avoid distortion. In other words, focus your attention more on leveling the body of the camera than what you see through the viewfinder. Use the same focal length for each image, and try not to use the zoom, unless it's manual, so that you can keep it exactly the same for every image.

Fine-Tuning Your Panorama

Once you get all your photos positioned to suit you, you may want to adjust the result to make things look a bit smoother. Elements has several other commands to help you do so.

On the right side of the Photomerge window, you see several rows of buttons and checkboxes. You'll usually want to try at least a couple of these settings to improve your panorama. At the top, you see the usual OK and Cancel buttons for when you're ready to create your panorama or when you change your mind about the whole process.

Next are the Undo and Redo buttons. If you Undo something and change your mind again, click Redo. Both Undo and Redo are grayed out until you do something they can change. The Help button takes you straight to the Photomerge section of the Elements Help files (see page 24).

Below the Navigator box (page 289) you see two radio buttons—Normal and Perspective—that adjust the viewing angle of your panorama. You can choose one or the other, but not both.

- **Normal.** This radio button gives you your panorama as Elements combined it, with no changes to the perspective. If you don't like the way the angles in your panorama look, try clicking Perspective instead.

- **Perspective.** If you click this button, Elements attempts to apply perspective to your panorama to make it look more realistic. Sometimes Elements does a bang-up job, but usually you'll get better results if you help it out by setting a vanishing point, as explained earlier. Sometimes adding cylindrical mapping, explained later in this chapter, can help. If you still get a totally weird result, go ahead and just create the merge anyway. Then correct the perspective yourself afterward using one of the Transform commands, covered in the next section.

The Composition settings further down the window aren't mutually exclusive. You can add either (or both) of them—Cylindrical Mapping or Advanced Blending—to your panorama if you think it needs their help. Just turn on their checkboxes to use them.

To see what they do to your photo, you need to click the Preview button after turning on their checkboxes. While you're looking at the preview, you can't make any other changes to your panorama. You have to click Exit Preview before you can tweak your panorama any further. You won't see the effect of these settings again until you click OK to tell Elements you're ready for a finished panorama.

> **TIP** If you use the preview, take a good look at the joined seams of your merge when Elements is finished. Once in a while it has trouble getting things put back exactly where they were before previewing. In that case, just close the merge without saving and try again.

- **Cylindrical Mapping.** When you apply perspective to your panorama, you may wind up with an image that looks like a giant bow tie. Cylindrical mapping helps put your images back into a more normal perspective by vertically stretching the middle section to make everything the same height. It's called "cylindrical" because it gives an effect like that of looking at a label on a bottle—the middle seems largest, and the image gets smaller as it fades into the distance (on the sides around the back of the bottle). This setting is available only if you select Perspective in the settings above it. If you choose Normal, it's grayed out.

- **Advanced Blending.** It's very rare to get photos with colors that match exactly. Advanced blending tries to smooth out the differences by averaging the color between the photos, and it does help some, but usually not enough.

The following two settings really should be at the top of the list because they're the ones you'd use first when making a panorama.

• **Snap to Image.** When you drag photos into the merge from the Lightbox, Elements automatically places your photos in the panorama exactly where it thinks they should go. If you want to override Elements and position your photos yourself, turn off "Snap to Image."

• **Keep as Layers.** When you create a panorama, Elements ordinarily combines all your photos into an image that has only one layer in it. If you turn on "Keep as Layers," you get a multi-layered panorama in which each photo is on its own layer (page 139). This makes it a bit easier to go back and apply corrections to one of the photos after the merge, but it also makes for a hugely larger file. Generally, you're better off canceling a merge and working on the photo by itself and then remerging.

NOTE   There are many other panorama creation programs available, like Canon's PhotoStitch software. You may find you prefer these dedicated programs since they automate more of the work than Elements does.

Finishing Up: Creating Your Panorama

Once you're happy with your panorama, click the OK button and wait while Elements puts everything together for you. You may need to wait awhile, especially on a memory-challenged computer, so don't worry if it seems like nothing's happening—Elements is calculating like mad.

Usually you have to crop (see page 71) your panorama to get rid of the ragged edges, but once you do, it's quite remarkable how much it looks like a single photo. At this point, it's a single image, so you can edit it the way you would a normal photo. You need to name and save it (page 52), also.

Correcting Lens Distortion

If you ever photograph buildings, you know that it can be tough getting good shots with a fixed-lens digital camera. When you get too close to the building, your lens starts to cause distortion, as shown in Figure 11-7. There are special perspective-correcting lenses available, but they're expensive (and if you have a pocket camera, they aren't even an option). One of Elements 5's niftiest new features is the Correct Camera Distortion filter. It's another very popular Photoshop tool that Adobe transferred over to Elements, minus a couple of advanced options. Correct Camera Distortion is a terrifically helpful filter, and not just for buildings. You can also use it to correct the slight balloon effect you sometimes see in closeups of people's faces (especially with a wide-angle setting). You can even deploy the filter for creative purposes. For example, you can create the effect of a fish-eye lens by pushing the filter's settings to their extremes. You can also use it to create (or banish) *vignetting* (those shadowy corners caused by a lens or lens hood).

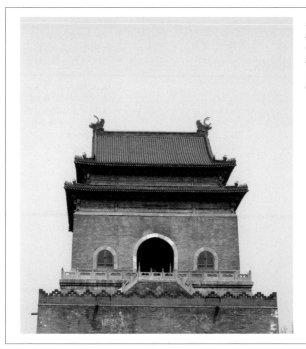

Figure 11-7:
Here's a classic example of a candidate for Elements'
Correct Camera Distortion filter. See how the top of
the building appears to be leaning away from you?
You can fix such problems in a jiffy with the help of
this filter.

Here are some telltale signs that it's time to summon Correct Camera Distortion:

- You've used the Straighten tool (page 67), but things still don't look right.

- Your horizon is straight, but there are no true right angles in your photo. In other words, the objects in your photo lean in misleading ways. For instance, buildings lean in from the edges of the frame, or back away from you.

- Every time you straighten to a new reference line, something else gets out of whack. For example, say you keep choosing different lines in your photo that ought to be level, but no matter which one you choose, something else in the photo goes out of plumb.

- If you have a problem with vignetting—a dark, shadowy effect in your photo's corners—you can also fix that with Correct Camera Distortion.

Adobe's made this filter extremely easy to use. Just follow these steps:

1. **Open a photo, and then go to Filter → Correct Camera Distortion.**

   The large dialog box shown in Figure 11-8 appears.

   NOTE Even though Correct Camera Distortion is in the Filter menu, you can't reapply it using the Ctrl+F shortcut, the way you can with most other filters. You always have to select it from the Filter menu.

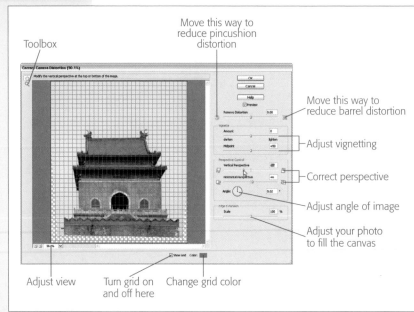

Toolbox

Move this way to
reduce pincushion
distortion

Move this way to
reduce barrel distortion

Adjust vignetting

Correct perspective

Adjust angle of image

Adjust your photo
to fill the canvas

Figure 11-8:
To use Correct Camera
Distortion, look at the
little icons next to each
slider, which show you
what happens when you
move the slider toward
the icon. For instance, if
your photo suffers from
barrel distortion, move
the Distortion slider
towards the pinched-in
pincushion. The icon
illustrates exactly what
you want to do to your
photo—slim it down.

Adjust view

Turn grid on
and off here

Change grid color

2. **Use the Hand tool (page 80) to adjust your photo in the window so that, ideally, a line in the photo is along one of the grid lines.**

   If the distortion is very bad, this mission may be impossible, but get at least one line as closely aligned to the grid as you can, so you have a reference for how you're changing the photo. You can also use the usual view adjustment controls (including zoom in and out buttons) in the lower-left corner of the dialog box.

   The Show Grid checkbox lets you turn the grid on and off, but since you're going to be aligning your image you'll almost always want to keep it on. To change the color of the grid, click the Color box next to the Show Grid checkbox.

3. **Make your adjustments.**

   The filter lets you fix three different kinds of problems: barrel/pincushion distortion, vignetting, and perspective problems. These are the most common distortion errors you're likely to run into, and correcting them is as easy as dragging sliders around. The small icons on each side of most of the sliders show you how your photo will change if you move in that direction. You may only need to make one adjustment, or you may need many (the list on the next page will help you decide which controls to use).

   Watch the grid carefully to see how things are lining up. When you get everything straightened to your satisfaction, you're done. If you want to start over, Alt+click the Cancel button to change it to a Reset button and return your photo to where you began.

4. **Scale your photo, if you wish.**

As you make your adjustments, you'll probably notice some empty space appearing on either side of your canvas (see Figure 11-8 for an example). That's often what happens when Elements pinches and stretches your photo to correct the distortion. To make things right, you've got two options. You can click OK now and crop the photo yourself (using any of the options you learned about back on page 71). Or, you can stay here and use the Edge Extension slider to enlarge your photo so that it fills up the visible window. If you use this method, Elements crops away some of the photo anyway.

> **TIP** Edge Extension is handy, but gives you little control over how the photo is cropped. After all the effort you made using this filter, you may as well do your own cropping to get the best possible results.

5. **Click OK to apply your changes.**

If you don't like the way things are turning out, you can reset your photo by Alt+clicking the Cancel button. Also, you can get a quick look at where you started from by toggling the Preview checkbox on and off.

The Correct Camera Distortion filter gives you a few different ways to adjust your image. Your choices are divided into sections, according to the different kinds of distortion they fix:

- **Remove Distortion.** Use this slider to fix *barrel distortion* (objects in your photo balloon out, like the sides of a barrel, as shown in Figure 11-9), and its opposite, *pincushion distortion* (your photo has a pinched look, with the edges of objects pushing in toward the center). Move the slider to the right to fix barrel distortion and to the left to fix pincushion distortion.

> **TIP** Barrel distortion is usually worst when you use wide-angle lens settings, while pincushion distortion generally appears when telephoto lenses are fully extended. Barreling's more common than the pincushion effect, especially when you use a small point-and-shoot camera at a wide-angle lense setting. You can often reduce barrel distortion in a small camera by simply avoiding your lens's widest setting. For instance, if you go from f2.8 to f5.6, you may see significantly less distortion.

- **Vignette.** If you see dark corners in your photo (usually caused by shadows from the lens or lens hood) you need to spend time with these sliders. This problem typically afflicts owners of digital SLR (single lens reflex) camera, or people who use add-on lenses with fixed-lens cameras. Move the Amount slider to the right to lighten the corners, and to the left to darken them. The Midpoint slider controls how much of your photo is affected by the Amount slider. Move it to the left to increase the area (to bring it towards the center of the photo), or to the right to keep the vignette correction more toward the edges. Also consider turning off the Show Grid checkbox, so that you have an unobstructed

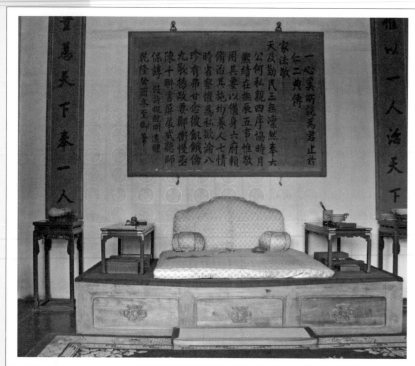

view of how you're changing the lightness values in your photo. Turn it back on again if you have other adjustments to make afterward.

• **Perspective Control.** Use these sliders to correct objects like buildings that appear to be tilted or leaning backwards. It's easiest to understand these sliders by looking at the icons at each end of their sliders. Vertical Perspective spreads the top of your photo wider as you move the slider to the left, and makes the bottom wider as you move it to the right. (If buildings seem like they're leaning backwards, move it to the left first.) Horizontal Perspective is for when your subject doesn't seem to be straight on in relation to the lens (for example, if it appears to be rotated a few degrees to the right or left). Move the slider to the left to bring the left side of the photo towards you, and to the right to bring the right side closer.

• **Angle.** You can rotate your entire photo here, by moving the line in the circle to the angle you want, or by typing a number into the box. A very small change here has a huge effect. The circle tool is easy to work with, but if you prefer, you can type a precise angle, in degrees. Here's how it works: there are 360 degrees in a circle. Your photo's starting point is 0.00 degrees. To rotate your photo to the left (counterclockwise), start from 0.01 and go up in small increments to increase the rotation. To go clockwise, start with 359.99 and then reduce the number. In other words, 350 is further to the right than 355.

NOTE   Each of the adjustment settings is accompanied by a box where you can type a number instead of using the sliders. If you want to make the same adjustments to many photos, take note of the numbers you used to fix your first photo. Then just plug those numbers into the boxes for the other photos.

- **Edge Extension.** As explained above, when you're done fixing your photo, you're likely to end up with some blank areas along the edge of your photo's canvas, as shown in Figure 11-8. Use the Scale slider to enlarge the photo, thereby getting rid of the blank areas. (You can also use this slider to shrink your photo, but you'll rarely need to do that.) Move the slider to the right to enlarge your image, and to the left to shrink it.

    The Scale slider changes your actual photo, not just your view of it (as would be the case when using the Zoom tool). When you click OK, Elements resizes and crops your photo. If you want the objects in your photo to stay the same size they were, don't use this slider. Instead, just click OK and then crop using any of the methods discussed starting on page 71.

The most important thing to remember when using Correct Camera Distortion is that a little goes a long way. For most of the corrections, start small and work in small increments. These distortions can be very subtle, and it often takes subtle adjustments to correct them.

TIP   This filter isn't just for corrections. You can use it to make your sour-tempered boss look truly prune-y, for example, by pincushioning him (just make sure you do it at home!). Or, you can add vignettes to photos for special effects. You can also use the filter on simplified shapes, artwork, or anything else that strikes your fancy.

Transforming Images

In Elements 5, you'll probably end up using the Correct Camera Distortion filter, as explained in the previous section, for all your straightening and dewarping needs. But Elements still includes a series of Transform commands that you can also use, as shown in Figure 11-10. For example, Transforming comes in handy when you want to make a change to just *one* side of a photo, or for final tweaking to a correction you made with Correct Camera Distortion. You can also apply these commands just for fun to create wacky photos or text effects.

Skew, Distort, Perspective

Elements gives you four commands to help straighten up the objects in your photos. While they all move your photo in different directions, the way you use them is the same. The Transform commands have the same box-like handles that you see on the Move tool, for example. You choose the command you want, and then the handles appear around your photo. Just drag a handle in the direction you want your photo to move. Figure 11-11 shows how to use the Transform commands.

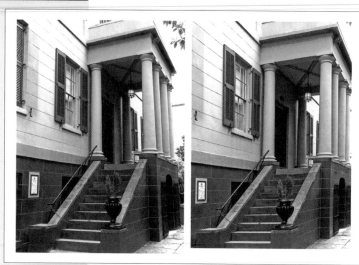

Figure 11-10:
Left: While you'd usually use Correct Camera Distortion (page 292) to straighten a slanting building like this, you can also use the Transform commands. You just have more limited choices with Transform.

Right: Here, it took only a dose of Skew and a bit of Distort to pull the building straight and make it tall enough again.

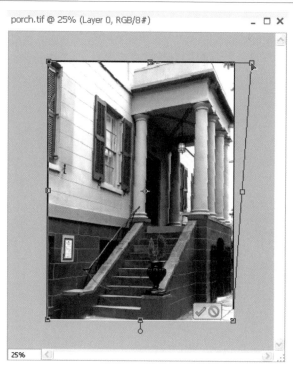

Figure 11-11:
Here's an example of how you'd use the Skew command to pull a building straight upright. The trick to applying the Transform commands is to make sure you can reach the handles on the corners. It helps to enlarge your image window far beyond the size of the actual image to give yourself room to pull. To do that, just drag the window corner, or better yet, click the large square on the far right of the Shortcuts bar to get into Maximize view.

To see the list of Transform commands, go to Image → Transform. The first one, Free Transform, is the most powerful because it includes all the others. There's more about Free Transform in the next section.

The other Transform commands, which are more specialized, are:

- **Skew** slants an image. If you have a building that looks like it's leaning to the right, you can use Skew to pull it to the left and straighten it back up again.

- **Distort** stretches your photo in the direction you want to pull it. Use it to make buildings (or people) taller and skinnier, or shorter and squatter.

- **Perspective** stretches your photo to make it look like parts are nearer or farther away. For example, if a building in your photo looks like it's leaning away from you, you can use Perspective to pull the top back toward the viewer.

Although Free Transform is the most capable, it can also be trickier to use. You may find it easier to use one of the one-way commands from the previous list so you don't have to worry about inadvertently moving a photo in an unwanted direction.

> **NOTE** If you have an active selection in your image, you can apply the Transform commands just to the selection, as long as you're not working on a background layer.

All the Transform commands, including Free Transform, offer the same settings in the Options bar, which are shown in Figure 11-12.

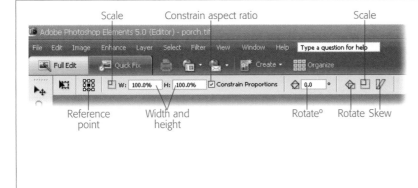

Figure 11-12:
The Options bar for the Transform commands. The width and height boxes let you manually specify dimensions when resizing your image (click the Scale button to their left once you're done entering the numbers). To scale by dragging, click the Scale button on the right side of the Options bar and drag any of the scaling boxes (not shown) that appear in the bounding box surrounding your image.

From left to right, the Option bar settings control:

- **Reference Point Location.** This strange little doodad (shown in Figure 11-13) lets you tell Elements where the fixed point should be when you transform something. It's a miniature cousin of the placement grid you see in the Canvas Size dialog box (page 89). The reference point starts out in the image's center, but you can tell Elements to move everything using the upper-left corner or the bottom-right corner as the reference point instead. To do that, click the square you want to use as the reference.

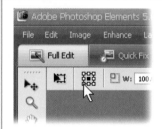

Figure 11-13:
This 9-box icon in the Options bar is where you set the reference point for transformations, which tells Elements the central point for rotations. For example, if you want your photo to spin around the lower-left corner instead of the center, click the lower-left square (where the cursor is). For the Transform commands, this also tells Elements the point to work from.

- **Scale.** You can resize your image by dragging, or enter a percentage in the width or height box here. Turn on the Constrain Proportions checkbox to keep the original proportions of your image.

- **Rotate.** The box next to the little triangle in the Options bar lets you enter the number of degrees to rotate your image or selection.

- **Rotate.** Click this next triangle and you can grab a corner of your image to make a free rotation (see page 69).

  TIP   If you Shift+drag when turning your image, you force it to turn in 15-degree increments.

- **Scale.** Click here if you want to resize your image by dragging—as opposed to entering numbers in the Scale boxes to the left of the Options bar.

- **Skew.** Click here and you can pull a corner of your image to the left or right, the way you do with the Skew command.

In most cases, you can transform your object without paying much attention to these settings. Truly, the easiest way to transform your photo is to grab a handle and drag. Here's how you can proceed:

1. **Position your image to give yourself room to work.**

   You need to position your photo so that you have room to drag the handles far beyond its edges. Figure 11-11 is a good example of an image that's sufficiently expanded to make lots of transformations.

2. **Choose how you want to transform your image.**

   Go to Image → Transform and select the command you want. It's not always apparent which is best for a given photo, so you may want to try all three in turn. You can always change your mind and undo your changes by pressing Escape before you accept a change, or undo using Ctrl+Z once the change has been made.

   You can apply transform commands only to layers, so if your image has only a Background layer, the first thing Elements does when you choose one is to ask you convert it to a regular layer. Just say yes and go on. Once the Transform command is active, you see the handles around your image.

3. **Transform your image.**

Grab a handle and pull in the direction you want the image to move. You can switch to another handle to pull in a different direction, too. If you decide you made a mistake, just press the Escape key (Esc) to return to your original photo.

4. **When you're happy with how your photo looks, accept the change.**

Click the Commit button (the checkmark) in your photo, or press Enter. Click the Cancel button (the "no" symbol) instead if you decide not to apply your transformation to your photo.

TIP   Before you click the Commit button, you can switch to another Transform command and add that transformation to your image, too.

Free Transform

Free Transform combines all the other Transform commands and lets you warp your image in many different ways. If you aren't sure what you need to do, Free Transform is a good choice because it combines all the other Transform commands into one.

You use Free Transform exactly the way you use the other Transform tools, following the steps listed earlier. The difference is that with Free Transform, you can pull in *any* direction, using keystroke combinations to tell Elements which kind of transformation you want to apply. Each particular transformation, listed as follows, does exactly the same thing it would if you selected that transformation from the Image → Transform menu:

- **Distort.** To make your photo taller or shorter, Ctrl+drag any handle. You should see a gray arrowhead for your cursor.

- **Skew.** To make your photo lean to the left or right, Ctrl+Shift+drag a handle in the middle of a side. You should see the gray arrow with a tiny double-arrow attached to it.

- **Perspective.** To correct the way an object appears so that it leans away from or towards you, press Ctrl+Alt+Shift and drag a corner. You see the same gray arrowhead that you see when you're distorting.

The Free Transform command is the most powerful of all the transformational commands, but when you're pulling in several different directions, it's tricky to keep your photo from warping. Consequently, some people prefer to use the simpler Transform commands and apply multiple transformations instead.

Part Four: Artistic Elements

4

Drawing with Brushes, Shapes, and Other Tools

If you're not of the artistic persuasion, you may feel tempted to skip this chapter. After all, you probably just want to fix and enhance your photos. What do you care about brush technique? Surprisingly enough, you should care quite a lot. In Elements, brushes aren't just for painting a moustache and horns on a picture of someone you don't like, or for blackening your sister's teeth in that old school photo.

Many tools in Elements use brushes to apply their effects. So far, you've already run into the Selection brush, the Clone Stamp, and the Color Replacement brush, to name just a few. And even with the Brush tool, you can paint with lots of things besides color—like lights or shadows, for example. In Elements, when you want to apply an effect in a precise manner, you're often going to use some sort of brush to do it.

If you're used to working with real brushes, their digital cousins can take some getting used to, but there are many serious artists now who paint primarily in Photoshop. With Elements, you now have access to most of the same tools as in Photoshop, if not quite all the settings available for each tool. Figure 12-1 shows an example of the detailed work you can do with Elements and some artistic ability.

This chapter explains how to use the Brush tool, some of the other brush-like tools (like the Erasers), and how to draw shapes even if you can't hold a pencil steady. You also get some practical applications for your new skills, like dodging and burning your photos to enhance them, and a super-easy way to create sophisticated artistic crops for your photos—a favorite feature for scrapbooking.

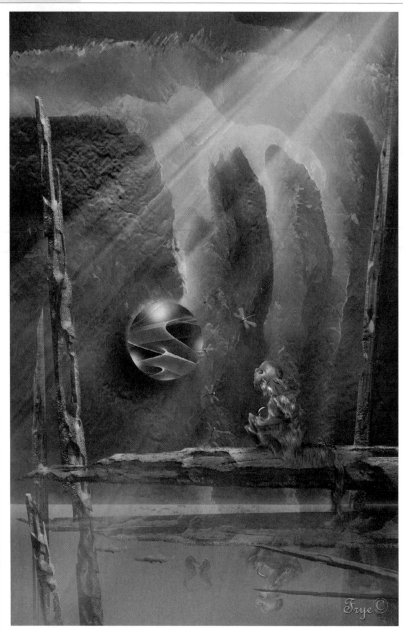

Figure 12-1:
This complex drawing by artist Jodi Frye was done entirely in Elements. If you learn to wield all the drawing power in Elements, you can create amazingly detailed artwork. Jodi has a gallery of many more Elements drawings in a wide variety of styles at www.frontiernet.net/ ~jlfrye.

Picking and Using a Basic Brush

If you look at the Toolbox, you'll see the Brush tool icon just below the Eraser. (Don't confuse it with the Selection brushes, which are up above the Type tool.) Click the Brush tool's icon or press B to activate it.

The Brush is one of the tools that include a hidden pop-out drawer—you can choose between the Brush, the Impressionist brush, the Pencil tool, and the Color Replacement brush. You can read about the Impressionist brush and the Pencil tool later in this chapter, and about the Color Replacement brush on page 259. This section is about the regular Brush tool.

If you look at the Options bar (Figure 12-2), you can see that the Brush offers you lots of ways to customize the tool.

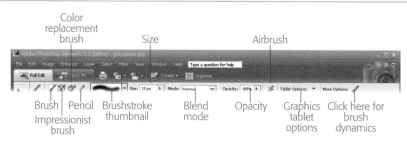

Figure 12-2:
These are the Options bar settings for the Brush tool. By changing the settings shown here, as well as the hidden settings—revealed when you click the More Options button—you can dramatically alter the behavior of any brush.

Here's a quick rundown (from left to right) of the available Brush options:

- **Brush, Impressionist brush, Color Replacement brush, or Pencil.** Click any of these four icons to activate the particular brush tool you want. The Impressionist brush applies a painting style effect. The Color Replacement brush (page 259) lets you brush in a replacement color for any particular color in your image. The Pencil tool is explained on page 317.

- **The Brushstroke thumbnail.** The Options bar displays a thumbnail of the stroke you'd get with the current brush. Click the brushstroke thumbnail to see the Brush palette. Elements gives you a bunch of basic brush collections, which you can view and select here. You can also download many more from various Web sites (see page 475).

    If you click the pull-down menu, you'll see that you get more than just hard or soft brushes of various sizes (see Figure 12-3). You also get special brushes for drop shadows, brushes that are sensitive to pen pressure if you're using a graphics tablet (although they also work if you're using the mouse—you just don't have as many options), and brushes that paint shapes and designs.

    NOTE   One very cool feature of the brushes in Elements is that any changes you make to a brush are shown in the little brushstroke thumbnail in the Brush palette.

- **Size.** This pull-down menu lets you adjust the size of your brush—anywhere from one pixel up to sizes that may be too big to fit on your monitor. Or you can just type in a size. Figure 12-4 shows you an easy way to adjust brush size using your mouse. You can also press the close bracket key (]) to quickly increase brush size or the open bracket key ([) to decrease it as you're working.

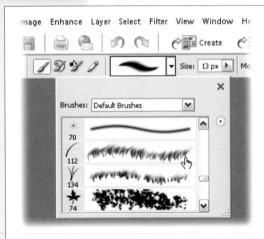

Figure 12-3:
Elements gives you a pretty good list of different brushes to choose from, or you can add your own. You can make brushes, too, as explained on page 315.

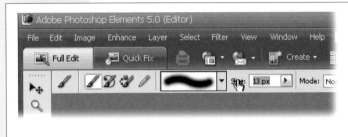

Figure 12-4:
You don't need to open pull-down menus like this one to adjust their contents. Just move your cursor onto the word "size" (the word is covered by the hand here), and your cursor changes into a hand-with-double-headed-arrow. Now you can "scrub" back and forth right on the Options bar to make the changes—left for smaller, right for larger. This trick also works anywhere in Elements you see a numerical pop-out slider (as in the Layers palette's Opacity menu, for example).

- **Mode.** Choices in this pull-down menu determine your blend mode. The modes determine how the brush color interacts with what's in your image. For example, Normal simply paints the current foreground color (more about all the Mode choices later).

- **Opacity.** Opacity controls how thoroughly your brushing covers what's beneath it. You can use the pull-down menu's slider or type in any number you like, from 1 to 100. 100 percent gets you total coverage. (Or you can scrub, as shown in Figure 12-4.)

- **Airbrush.** Clicking the little pen-like brush just to the right of the Opacity control lets you use the brush as an airbrush. Figure 12-5 shows you how this works.

- **Tablet Options.** If you use a graphics tablet, you can use these settings to tell Elements which brush characteristics should respond to the pressure of your stroke. There's more about graphics tablets on page 473.

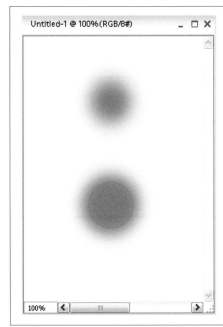

Figure 12-5:
As with real airbrushes, Elements' airbrush option causes Elements to continue to "spray" paint as long as you hold down the mouse cursor, regardless of whether the mouse is moving or not.

Top: Notice the effect of one click with the brush in Regular mode.

Bottom: Here's the effect of one click with the same brush in Airbrush mode. See how far the color has spread out beyond the actual brush cursor when using the airbrush? Not every brush offers the airbrush option.

- **More Options.** Clicking this icon gets you the Brush Dynamics palette, which gives you oodles of ways to customize your brush, which are covered in the next section. If you're using your brush for artistic purposes, you should familiarize yourself with these settings, since this is where you can set a chiseled stroke or a fade, for example.

To actually use the Brush, you enter your settings—make sure you've selected the color you want in the Foreground color square (page 195)—and then just drag across your image wherever you want to paint.

> **TIP** If you ever want to return a brush to its original settings, click the Brush button on the far-left side of the Options bar and then click Reset Tool from the pop-up menu.

One of the biggest differences between drawing with a mouse and drawing with a real brush is that, on a computer, it doesn't matter how hard you press the mouse. But if you've got a *graphics tablet*, an electronic pad that causes your pen movements to appear instantly onscreen, you can replicate real-world brushing, including pressure effects. Page 473 tells you all about using a tablet.

> **TIP** Tip: If you're used to painting with long, sweeping strokes, keep in mind that in Elements, that technique can be frustrating. That's because when you undo a mistake (by pressing Ctrl+Z), Elements undoes *everything* you've done while you've been holding down the mouse button.
>
> In tricky spots, you can save yourself some aggravation by using shorter strokes so you don't have to lose that whole long curve you painstakingly worked on just because you wobbled a bit at the end. (The Eraser tool [page 325] is handy in these situations, too, for tidying up.)

TROUBLESHOOTING MOMENT

What Happened to My Cursor?

One thing that drives newcomers to Elements nuts is having the Brush cursor change from a circle to little crosshairs, seemingly spontaneously. This is one of those "It's not a bug; it's a feature" situations. Many tools in Elements offer you the option of what is called the *precise cursor*, shown in Figure 12-6. There are situations where you may prefer to see those little crosshairs so that you can tell *exactly* where you're working.

You toggle the precise cursor by pressing the Caps Lock key. So, if you hit that key by accident, you may find yourself in precise cursor mode with no idea of how you got there. Just press it again to turn it off.

There's one other way you may wind up with the precise cursor, and this time you have no choice in the matter. It happens when your image is so small in proportion to the cursor that Elements *must* display the crosshairs to show the brush in the right scale for your image. Zooming

the view out usually gets your regular cursor back, unless you're working with a 1-pixel brush, which always uses crosshairs.

There's another wrinkle to the mysterious cursor problem. Your cursor may look like a tiny icon instead of the brush circle. Once again, you can control this by adjusting an Elements preference setting. Go to Edit → Preferences → Display & Cursors → Painting Cursors → Normal Brush Tip to get back the normal brush. This preference window also lets you turn off the specialized cursors for tools like the Lasso tools. To do so, in the Other Cursors box, choose Precise.

You can also choose to always see the crosshairs within the regular cursor circle if you want. In the Preferences dialog box, at the bottom of the list of Brush Size options, turn on the checkbox for "Show Crosshair in Brush Tip," and you'll always have a mark for the exact center of your brush.

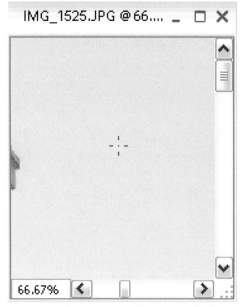

Figure 12-6:
Adobe calls these crosshairs the precise cursor. Elements sometimes makes your tool look like this when you're zoomed way in on an image. To get the normal cursor back, you can zoom out some, and read the box above for further advice.

TIP To draw or paint a straight line, hold down the Shift key while you move your mouse. If you click where you want your line to start, and press and hold Shift, and then click at the end point, Elements draws a straight line between those two points. It's important to click first and then press Shift, or you may draw lines where you don't want them.

Modifying Your Brush

When you click the More Options button in the Options bar, you'll see a palette that lets you customize the brush in a number of ways. Its official name is the *Brush Dynamics palette*. You'll also run into a version of this palette for some of the other brush-like tools, like the Healing brush. The Brush Dynamics palette options let you change the way your brush behaves in a number of sophisticated and fun ways. Mastering these settings goes a long way toward getting artistic results in Elements.

- **Spacing** controls how far apart the brush marks get laid down when you apply the brush. A lower number makes them close together, a higher number farther apart, as shown in Figure 12-7.

Figure 12-7:
The same brush stroke with the spacing set at 5 percent, 75 percent, and 150 percent (respectively, from top to bottom). You may have been wondering why some of the brush thumbnails look like long caterpillars, when the brush should paint an object, like a star or leaf. The reason? Cramped spacing: the thumbnail shows the spacing as Elements originally sets it. Widen the spacing to see separate objects instead of a clump.

- **Fade** controls how fast the brush stroke fades out—just the way a real brush does when you run out of paint. Think of the numbers as sort of "how many steps" it would take to run out of paint. A lower number means it fades out very fast (very few steps) while a higher one means the fade happens later (more steps). You can pick a number up to 9999, so with a little fiddling, you should be able to get just what you want.

  If the brush isn't fading fast enough, decrease the number. If it fades too fast, increase it. A smaller brush usually needs a higher number than a larger brush would. You may find that you need to set the spacing up into the 20s or higher to make fading show any visible effect.

- **Hue Jitter** controls how fast the brush switches between the background and foreground colors. Some brushes, especially the ones that you'd use to paint objects like leaves, automatically vary the color for a more interesting or realistic effect. The higher the number here, the faster the color moves from foreground to background. A lower number means the brush takes a longer distance to get from one color to the other. Brushes that acknowledge hue jitter don't put down only the two colors, but a range of hues in between. Not all brushes respond to this setting, but for the ones that do, it's a pretty cool feature. Figure 12-8 shows you how it works.

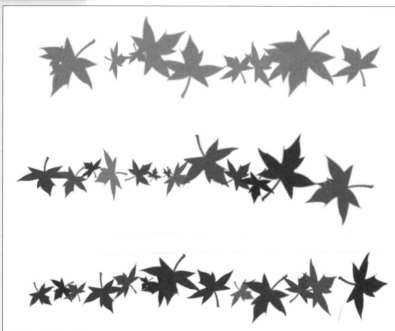

Figure 12-8:
*Top: A brushstroke with no
hue jitter.*

*Middle: The same
brushstroke with a medium
hue jitter value.*

*Bottom: The same
brushstroke with a high hue
jitter value. The foreground/
background colors here are
red and blue. Notice how the
brush automatically does a
little shading, even without
allowing for jitter. It takes a
fairly high number to get all
the way to blue in a stroke of
this length.*

- **Scatter** means just what it says—how far the marks get distributed in your stroke. If scatter is very low, you get a dense, line-like stroke, whereas a higher value gives an effect more like random spots.

- **Hardness** controls whether the brush edge is sharp or fuzzy. This setting isn't available with all brush types, but when it is, you can choose any value between zero and 100 percent.

- **Angle and Roundness**. If you've ever painted with a real brush, you should understand Angle and Roundness right away. They let you create a more chiseled edge to your brush and also rotate it so that it's not always painting with the edge facing the same direction. Painters don't use only round brushes, and you don't have to in Elements, either.

There are some brushes in the libraries that aren't round, like the calligraphy and chalk brushes. But you can adjust the roundness of any brush to make it more suitable for chiseled strokes, as shown in Figure 12-9.

There's also a checkbox (Keep These Settings For All Brushes) you can turn on if you want to make all your brushes behave exactly the same way.

Saving Modified Brush Settings

If you modify a brush and you like the result, you can save it as a custom brush. You can alter any of the existing brushes and save the result—a great feature if you're working on a project that's going to last a while and you don't want to have to keep modifying the settings again and again. (Don't worry: When you modify

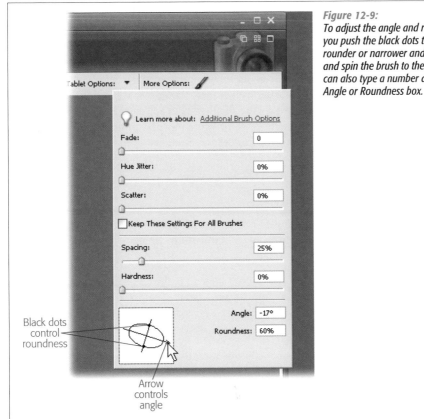

Figure 12-9:
To adjust the angle and roundness of a brush, you push the black dots to make the brush rounder or narrower and then grab the arrow and spin the brush to the angle you want. You can also type a number directly into either the Angle or Roundness box.

an existing brush, Elements preserves a copy of the original.) To create your own brush, just:

1. **Choose a brush to modify.**

   Select a brush in the Brush palette. You can customize any of the brushes.

2. **Make the changes you want.**

   Change the brush settings until you get what you're after. Watch the brush thumbnail in the Options bar as you go. It changes to reflect your new settings.

3. **Tell Elements you want to keep the new brush.**

   Click the arrow in the upper-right corner of the brush thumbnails palette and choose Save Brush. Elements asks you to name it. You don't absolutely have to, but naming brushes makes them easier to keep track of.

4. **Click OK.**

   The brush shows up in the bottom of your list of brushes.

Deleting brushes is pretty straightforward. You can select the brush in the Brush palette and then choose Delete Brush from the pop-out menu. Or, you can Alt+click the brush thumbnail. The cursor will change to a pair of scissors when you hold down the key. Clicking with the scissors deletes the brush.

You can also make a selection from an image and save it as a brush, if you like (the next section shows you how). Just remember, though, that brushes by definition don't have color, so you save only the shape of your selection, not the full coloring of it. The color you get is whichever color you choose to apply. If you want to save a full color sample, try saving your sample as a pattern (page 245) or just use the clone stamp repeatedly instead.

The Specialty Brushes

So far you've been reading about brushes that behave pretty much as brushes do in the real world—they paint a stripe of something, whether color, light, or even transparency.

But in the digital world, a brush doesn't have to be just a brush. With some of the brushes included in Elements, you can paint stars, flowers, disembodied eyeballs, gravel, or even rubber ducks with just one swipe of the brush, as shown in Figure 12-10.

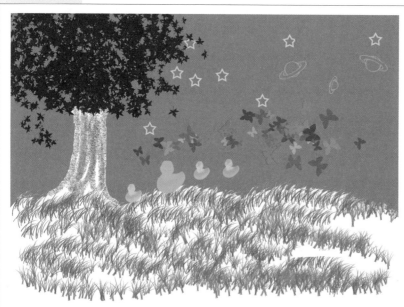

Figure 12-10:
You can digitally doodle using the Elements brushes, even if you can't draw a straight line. Everything in this lovely drawing was done with brushes included with Elements. The leaves were painted with a brush that paints leaves; the yellow ducks come from a brush that paints rubber ducks, and so on.

If you click the arrow next to the brush thumbnail in the Options bar, you'll see the list of brushes in the current category and a pull-down menu that lets you investigate the other brush sets you got with Elements. The brushes used in Figure 12-10, for example, came from several different categories, but you have all of them if you have Elements. Some brushes are sensitive to your pen pressure if you're using a graphics tablet (page 473).

The Specialty brushes respond very readily to changes in the Brush Dynamics settings (covered earlier in this chapter). Your choices there can make a huge difference in the effect you get—whether you're painting swathes of smooth grass, like a lawn, or scattered sprigs of dune grass, for instance. You get the exact same list of choices described in the previous section on the Brush Dynamics palette: spacing, fade, hue jitter, and so on.

> **TIP** If you've tried some of the special effects brushes and found the results rather anemic, you can always go back once you've painted and punch up the color with a Multiply layer, just as you would do for an overexposed photo (see page 175).

Making a Custom Brush

You can turn any picture, or selection within a picture, into a brush that paints the shape you've selected. Figure 12-11 shows what a wreath looks—and behaves like—when it's been turned into a brush.

It's surprisingly easy to create a custom brush from any object you have a picture of.

1. **Open a photo or drawing that includes what you want to use as a brush.**

   You can choose an area as large as 2,500 pixels square. (Remember, you can resize your selection once it's a brush, just the way you can resize any other brush, so don't worry if it's a big area.)

2. **Select the object or region you want.**

   Use any of the Selection tools. It's a good idea to check your selection with the Selection brush in Mask mode as a last step (page 125). That's because any stray areas you included by mistake get painted down with each stroke—just as if you wanted them to be there.

3. **Create your brush.**

   Go to Edit → Define Brush from Selection. You see a dialog box showing the shape and asking you to name your new brush. Check the thumbnail to be sure it's exactly what you had in mind. If not, click Cancel and try again. If you like what you've got, click OK.

The new brush shows up at the bottom of your Default list of brushes. If you want to get rid of it, highlight the thumbnail in the brush thumbnails, click the arrow on the right side of the palette, and go to Delete Brush.

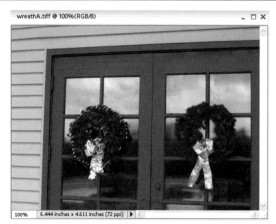

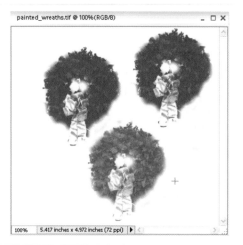

Figure 12-11:
Top: If you want to make a brush to draw holiday wreaths, just select a wreath in a photo and save it as a brush.

Bottom: You can paint better than you thought! Notice, too, that some of the ragged edges of the wreath were left out to improve the shape of the brush.

The Impressionist Brush

When you paint with the Impressionist brush, you blur and blend the edges of the objects in your photo, just like an Impressionist painting. At least that's what's *supposed* to happen. This brush is very tricky to control, but you can get some very interesting effects, especially if you paint with it on a duplicate layer and play with the Opacity control (page 151). Usually you want a very low opacity with this brush, or some of the curlier styles will make your image look like it's made from poodle hair.

The Impressionist brush has most of the same options as the regular Brush, but if you click the More Options button, you'll see three new choices:

- **Style** determines what kind of brushstroke effect you want to create.

- **Area** tells Elements the size and number of brushstrokes.

• **Tolerance** is how similar in color pixels have to be before they're affected by the brush.

If you really want to create a hand-painted look, you may prefer the brushstroke filters (Filter → Brush Strokes). Page 342 explains how to use them. The Impressionist brush is really not the best tool for true Impressionist effects, although its blurring qualities can sometimes be useful, because it covers large areas faster than the Blur tool. The Smudge tool (page 323) is another excellent, though time-consuming, way to create a painted effect.

The Pencil Tool

The Pencil tool is basically just another brush. It shares the Brush tool's slot in the Toolbox. Click its icon in the Options bar or press N to activate the Pencil.

> **NOTE**   If you're already using the Brush tool when you want the Pencil, you can also click the Pencil icon in the Options bar to switch to the Pencil.

The Pencil has many of the same setting options as the Brush—like size, mode, and opacity—but it offers only hard-edged brushes. In other words, you can't draw fuzzy lines with the pencil, not even the kind of lines you'd sketch with a soft pencil. The Pencil's lines are always very well defined. It's especially useful when you want to work on a pixel-by-pixel basis.

You use the Pencil tool the same way you use any other brush. The big difference is the Auto Erase option (the checkbox is located in the Options bar). Auto Erase makes the Pencil paint with the background color over areas that contain the foreground color. But if you start dragging in an area that doesn't contain the foreground color, it paints with the foreground color instead. This is really confusing until you try it, but then it's pretty easy to understand. Take a look at Figure 12-12 for some help in understanding what's going on, or better yet, create a blank document (page 39) and try it yourself.

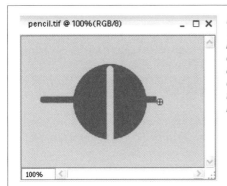

Figure 12-12:
The slightly confusing Auto Erase option, used to create two lines: a horizontal one consisting of the foreground color (blue) and a vertical one consisting of the background color (pink). The horizontal line was drawn by starting with the cursor in the background (thus, the pencil erased the pink, leaving a blue line across the circle). On the other hand, the pink line was drawn by starting inside the blue circle, causing the background color to be exposed.

The Paint Bucket

When you want to fill a large area with color in a hurry, the Paint Bucket's the tool for you. It's right below the Brush tool in the Toolbox. If you click it or press K to activate it and then click in your image, the entire available area (either your whole image or the current selection) gets flooded with color. It works something like the Magic Wand: Just as the Magic Wand selects the color you click, the Paint Bucket fills only the color you click.

Use this tool to change the color of a solid layer with one click. Most of the Options bar settings for the Paint Bucket are probably familiar:

- **Fill.** Choose to fill the area with the foreground color (page 195) or a pattern (page 245). You can choose from any of the existing patterns (listed in the Pattern drop-down menu on the Options bar). Or you can create your own, just as you would with the Pattern Stamp (see page 247).

- **Mode.** Use the Paint Bucket in any blend mode, as explained later in this chapter on page 322.

- **Opacity.** 100-percent opacity gives you total coverage; nothing shows through the paint you put down. Lower the percentage for a more transparent effect.

- **Tolerance.** This setting works the same way it does for the Magic Wand (page 116). The higher the number, the more shades the paint fills.

- **Anti-alias.** This setting smoothes the edges of the fill. Leave it turned on unless you have a specific reason not to.

- **Contiguous.** This is another old familiar from the Magic Wand (page 116). If you leave Contiguous on, you change only areas of the chosen color that touch each other. Turn it off, and all areas of the color you click get changed, whether they're contiguous or not.

- **Use All Layers.** Fills any pixels that meet your criteria, no matter what layer they're on. (The Paint Bucket actually paints on the active layer, but it looks for pixels to change based on all the layers in your image.) To keep out just one layer, click the Eyeball icon on the Layers palette to hide the layer you want to exclude. Turn it back on by clicking the same spot again after using the Paint Bucket. Don't forget that you can lock the transparent and translucent parts of layers in the Layers palette (see page 151).

You can undo a Paint Bucket fill with the usual Ctrl+Z.

> **TIP**   You can sometimes improve blown-out skies by using the Eyedropper to select an appropriate shade of blue from another photo and then filling the blown-out areas of your sky using the Paint Bucket at a very low opacity.

Dodging and Burning

Like the Unsharp Mask, dodging and burning are old darkroom techniques to enhance photos and emphasize particular areas. Dodging *lightens* shadows and brings out the details hidden in them, and burning *darkens* highlights, bringing out their details. Both tools live with the Sponge tool in the Toolbox, so you may have run into them while you were using the Sponge.

You may think that since you have the Shadows/Highlights command, you don't have any need for these tools. But they still serve a useful purpose because they let you make selective changes, rather than affecting the entire image the way Shadows/Highlights does. Figure 12-13 gives an example of when you might need to work on a particular area. Of course, you can also make a selection (see Chapter 5) and then use Shadows/Highlights just on that area, which is another technique that you may want to try as well as dodging and burning.

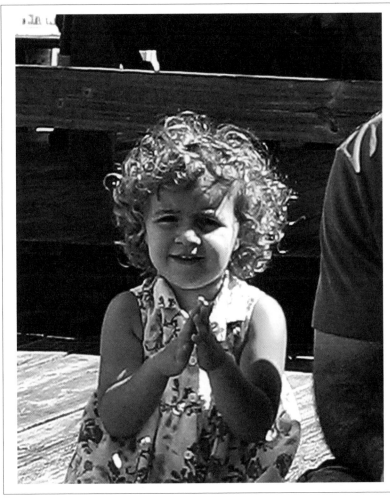

Figure 12-13:
Although the overall shadow/highlight balance of this photo is about right, the detail in the face of this little concert-goer is obscured by backlighting and by her father's shadow. Careful dodging and burning can really improve these problems, as you can see in Figure 12-14.

Skillful use of dodging and burning can greatly improve your photo, although it helps to have an artistic eye to spot what you want to emphasize and what you want to downplay. When you use the new black and white conversion feature (page 265), use the Dodge and Burn tools to emphasize certain areas of your photos. The real masters of black and white photography, like Ansel Adams, relied heavily on dodging and burning (in the darkroom, in those days) to create their greatest images.

Both the Dodge and Burn tools are really just variants of the Brush tool, except that they don't apply color directly—they just affect the colors and tones that are already present in your photo. Adobe refers to these two as the "toning tools."

One caution about these tools, though—unless you use them on a duplicate layer, you can't undo the effect once you close your photo. So you need to be careful how you use them. Actually, many people prefer to dodge and burn using the method described on page 326, rather than with the actual Dodge and Burn tools, unless they're working on a black and white photo.

Dodging

The Dodge tool is used to lighten areas of your image and to bring out details that may be hidden in shadows. You can use dodging to create highlights or to even out areas that have been too deeply shadowed. It's a good idea to create a separate layer (Layer → Duplicate Layer or Ctrl+J) when you use this tool, to preserve your image if you go overboard. Be sure you're applying the Dodge tool to a layer that has something in it, or nothing happens.

1. **Activate the Dodge tool.**

   Click the Sponge tool in the Toolbox and choose the Dodge tool (the lollipop-like paddle) from the pop-out menu, or press O and click the Dodge tool in the Options bar. You'll see the usual brush options, but with two differences: a choice of whether the tool should work on highlights, midtones, or shadows, and a setting called Exposure, which determines the strength of the effect.

2. **Drag over the area you want to change.**

   Choose a very low Exposure setting for these tools and drag more than once to get a more realistic result (see Figure 12-14). After you're done, if you think the Dodge tool's effect is still too strong, you can always reduce the opacity of the layer in the Layers palette.

Burning

The Burn tool does exactly the opposite of what the Dodge tool does: it darkens. You can use the Burn tool to make highlights show more details. Of course, there have to be *some* details there for the tool to work. If your photo's highlights are blown out (see page 179), you won't get any results, no matter how much you apply the tool.

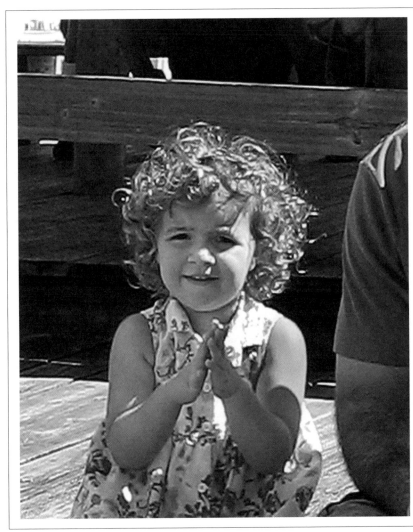

Figure 12-14:
Figure 12-13 after the Dodge and Burn tools. The girl's features are much easier to see, but if you look closely, you can see that the colors in her face are a bit flat. See Figure 12-19 on page 327 to compare a different method for selectively adjusting highlights and shadows. Both solutions have advantages and disadvantages. Things are deliberately a bit too strong in both figures to show you the perils of getting overzealous with either method.

The Burn tool is applied exactly the same way the Dodge tool is, and most of the time, you'll probably want to use these tools in combination. They can help draw attention to specific parts of your photo, but they work best for subtle changes. Applying them too vigorously—especially on color photos—gives an obviously faked look to your photo. Black-and-white photos (or color photos converted to black and white) can generally stand much stronger contrasts.

TIP You can switch between the Dodge and Burn tools by pressing the O key until the tool you want is highlighted in the Options bar.

Blending and Smudging

In Elements, you can control how the color you add to your image blends with the colors that are already there. This section takes a look at blending in two different ways—using the Smudge tool to literally mix elements of your image together, and using *blend modes* to determine how the colors you paint change what's already in your image. Blend modes are almost limitless in how you can use them to manipulate your images.

Blend Modes

Blend modes control how the color you add when you paint reacts with the existing pixels in your image—whether you just add color (Normal mode), make the existing color darker (Multiply mode), or change the saturation (Saturation mode).

Many uses for the blend modes are more advanced and beyond the scope of this book (and would make the book over a thousand pages long). But Figure 12-15 shows a few examples of how simply changing the brush blend mode can radically change your result.

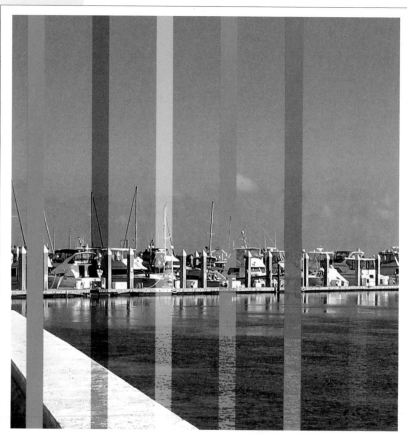

Figure 12-15:
This photo shows the effect of some of the different blend modes when used with the Brush tool. The same color was used for every one of the vertical stripes—you can see how different the result is from just changing the mode.

From left to right, the modes are: Normal, Color Burn, Color Dodge, Vivid Light, Difference, and Saturation.

There are so many ways to combine blend modes that even Elements pros can't always predict the results, so experimenting is the best way to learn about them. Also, many of the more advanced books on Elements include projects that require using the different modes.

Blend modes are grouped according to the effects that they have. The top group includes what you might call painting modes, followed by modes for darkening, lightening, adjusting light, special effects modes, and adjusting color.

It's also important to be aware that the modes work quite differently with layers than with tools. In other words, painting with a brush in Dissolve mode is going to produce an effect quite different than creating a layer in Dissolve mode and painting on it, as shown in Figure 12-16.

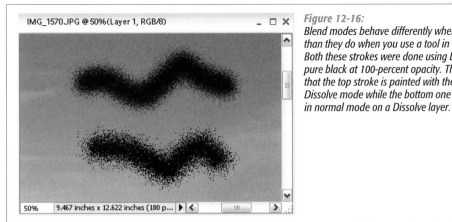

Figure 12-16:
Blend modes behave differently when used in layers than they do when you use a tool in the same mode. Both these strokes were done using Dissolve mode in pure black at 100-percent opacity. The difference is that the top stroke is painted with the Brush tool in Dissolve mode while the bottom one is a brush stroke in normal mode on a Dissolve layer.

Modes are really cool and very useful once you get used to using them, but if you're just starting out in Elements, there's no need to worry about them right away.

> **TIP** If you'd like to learn more about how each mode works, there are a lot of useful tutorials on the Web. A good place to start is *www.photoshopgurus.com/tutorials.html*. Click the Beginner Tutorials section. The document *Photoshop Blend Modes.pdf* (toward the bottom of the scroll-down list) is particularly helpful. (Ignore the section "Additional BLEND MODE information." That's only for Photoshop.)

The Smudge Tool

The Smudge tool does just what its name says. You can use it to smear the colors in your image, just as if you had rubbed them with your finger. You can even "finger paint" with the Smudge tool, if you feel the call of your inner fifth grader. Adobe describes the effect of the Smudge tool as being "like a finger dragged through wet paint." It's sort of like a cousin to the Liquify filter (page 388), but without so many options.

If you're interested in turning your photos into paintings (Figure 12-17), the humble Smudge tool is your most valuable resource. For artistic smudging, you need a graphics tablet so you can vary the stroke pressure. You can use the Smudge tool without a tablet, but you won't get nearly as good an effect. If you'd like to learn more about this kind of smudging, you'll find some excellent tutorials by going to the Retouching forum at *www.dpreview.com* (search for *smudging*). The forums at *www.retouchpro.com* are also a favorite hangout for expert smudgers.

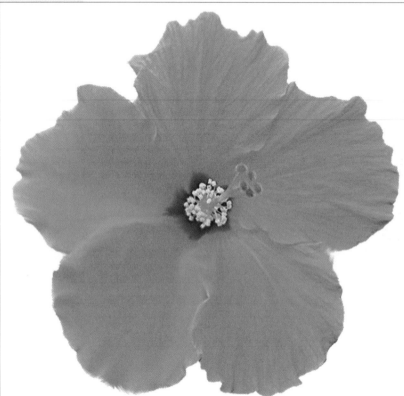

Figure 12-17:
With the help of a graphics tablet, you can join the ranks of the many skilled smudgers who create amazing effects using only this tool. The two petals on the left side of this hibiscus blossom show preliminary smudging results. The brushes you use determine whether the effect is smooth, as you see here, or more heavily stroked. When you want to blend in other colors, use the Finger Painting option. In effect, the Smudge tool lets you turn your photo into a painting.

A warning—if you have a slow computer, there's quite a bit of lag time between when you apply the Smudge tool and when the effect actually shows up. This delay makes the tool tricky to control, because you need to resist the temptation to keep going over the area until you see results.

The Smudge tool hides under the Blur tool in the Toolbox. Click the Blur tool and, from the pop-out menu, choose the Smudge tool (its icon is a finger, painting), or press R and keep pressing it till the Smudge tool's icon is active.

The Smudge tool offers mostly the same settings as a regular brush, but it also includes the Sample All Layers option (page 241), like the Healing brush or Clone Stamp. It also has two additional settings: Strength and Finger Painting.

- **Strength.** This setting means just what it says—it controls how hard the tool smudges the colors together. A higher number results in more blending.

- **Finger Painting.** Turning on this box makes the Smudge tool smear the foreground color at the start of each stroke. Otherwise, the tool uses the color that's under the cursor at the start of each stroke. Figure 12-18 helps you understand the difference. This option is very useful for creating artistic smudges. If you want a bit of a contrasting color to help your strokes stand out more, choose a foreground color (page 195) and turn this on.

TIP   Use the Eyedropper (page 197) to sample other areas of your image to add Finger Painting colors that harmonize well with the area you're smudging.

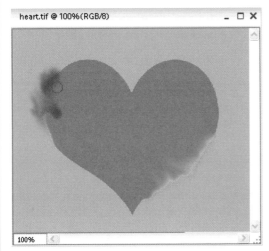

Figure 12-18:
The Smudge tool smears colors together. The stroke on the left was done with the Finger Painting checkbox turned on, which lets you introduce a bit of the foreground color (green, in this case) into the beginning of each stroke. This is very useful for shading or when you need to mix in just a touch of another color. The smudging on the right was done with Finger Painting off, so it uses only the colors that are already in your image.

Once you've chosen your settings, smudge away.

NOTE   When using the Smudge tool, you only see results where two colors come together. It blends together the pixel colors where edges meet. If you use Smudge in the middle of an area of solid color, nothing happens.

The Eraser Tool

Everyone makes mistakes sometimes. Adobe has thoughtfully included three different mistake-fixers. If you click and hold the Eraser icon in the Toolbox, you'll see the Eraser, the Magic Eraser, and the Background Eraser. You'll probably use all three Erasers at one time or another. You can also activate the Eraser by pressing E and then clicking the one you want in the Options bar.

POWER USERS' CLINIC

Blend Modes Instead of Dodge and Burn

You can do a lot in Elements without ever getting down and dirty with blend modes, but there are a lot of things you can do more effectively and easily if you take the time to familiarize yourself with them. For instance, you may prefer the effect you get using a layer in Overlay mode to that of the Dodge and Burn tools.

To adjust a photo using an Overlay blend mode layer instead of the Dodge and Burn tools, you'd first make basic adjustments like Levels or Shadows/Highlights. Then, when you're ready to fine-tune your photo by painting over the details you want to enhance, here are the steps you'd follow:

1. **Create a new layer.**

   Go to Layer → New → Layer or press Ctrl+Shift+N.

2. **Before you dismiss the New Layer dialog box, choose the Overlay blend mode for your new layer.**

   Select Overlay in the Layer mode menu and turn on the box that says "Fill with Overlay-neutral color (50% gray)." You won't see anything happen yet.

3. **Set the foreground and background colors to their original settings.**

   Press D to set the colors in the Foreground/Background squares to black and white.

4. **Activate the Brush tool.**

   Choose a brush (set to Normal mode) and set the opacity very low, maybe 17 percent or even less. You'll need to experiment a bit to see how low a setting is low enough.

5. **Paint on the areas you want to adjust.**

   Paint with white to bring up the detail in dark areas and with black to darken overly light areas. (Remember that you can switch colors by pressing X.) The detail on your photo comes up just like magic.

Figure 12-19 shows the results of using Overlay mode on the image from Figure 12-13 so that you can compare the different results. This method has the added advantage of being adjustable by changing the opacity of the Overlay layer. You can also carry this technique to extremes for very interesting results, when you want an artistic rather than a realistic result.

Using the Eraser

The Eraser is basically just another kind of brush tool, only instead of adding color to your image, it removes color from the pixels. How it works varies a little, depending on where you use it.

If you use the Eraser on a regular layer, it replaces the color with transparency. On a Background layer, or one in which transparency is locked, it replaces whatever color is there with the background color (see Chapter 6 for more about how layers work).

The settings for the Eraser are pretty much the same as for any other brush—including brush style, size, and opacity—but the Eraser has a couple of options of its own:

- **Mode.** For the Eraser, Mode doesn't have anything to do with blend modes (page 322), but rather tells Elements the shape of the eraser you want to work with. Your choices are Brush, Pencil, and Block.

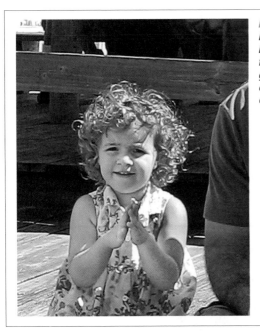

Figure 12-19:
Here's Figure 12-13 again, this time after using Overlay blending, as described in the box on page 326. Unlike the results from the actual Dodge and Burn tools, this time the color isn't grayish—as dodging made it—but the contrast where shadowed areas meet bright ones still needs some work. This figure is just one example of what you can do with modes.

You can see the difference in how the Eraser is going to work by watching the brush style preview in the Options bar as you change Modes. Picking the Brush or Pencil lets you use the Eraser as you would those tools—in other words, by choosing a brush, you can choose any brush you like. The Brush option lets you make soft-edged erasures, while Pencil mode makes only hard-edged erasures. Choosing Block changes the cursor to a square, so that you can use it just the way you would a regular artist's erasing block—sort of.

• **Opacity** determines how much of the color is removed—at 100 percent, it's all gone (or all replaced with the background).

To use the Eraser:

1. **Activate the Eraser.**

   Click the Eraser tool in the Toolbox or press E. The tool looks like an eraser, so it's easy to find.

2. **Choose your settings.**

   Select the kind of Eraser you want, select a mode, and then choose the eraser's size and opacity.

   These choices work the same way they do for regular brushes, except for Mode, as noted earlier. The next two sections tell you all about the Magic Eraser and the Background Eraser.

3. **Drag anywhere in your image to remove what you don't want.**

You may need to change the size of the Eraser a few times. It's usually easiest to use a small eraser (or the Background Eraser as explained later) to accurately clear around the edges of the object you want to keep, as shown in Figure 12-20. Then you can use a larger brush to get rid of the remaining chunks, once you don't have to worry about accidentally going into the area you want to keep.

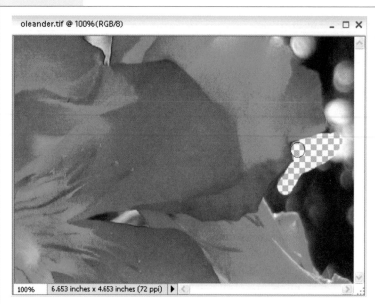

oleander.tif @ 100%(RGB/8)

100%   6.653 inches x 4.653 inches (72 ppi)

Figure 12-20:
Accurate erasing around an object usually means zooming way, way in so that you can control which pixels the Eraser is changing.

> **TIP**   You can use a selection (see Chapter 5) to limit where the Eraser operates.

It's tedious to erase around a long outline or to remove entire backgrounds, so Elements has two other kinds of Erasers for those situations.

The Magic Eraser

Once you try it, you're likely to wonder why the heck Adobe gave this pedestrian tool such an intriguing name. What's so magic about the Magic Eraser?

Well, not much, really. It's a "Magic" Eraser as in the "Magic" Wand, because it works very much like the Magic Wand tool (page 116). Use it to select pixels of a single color or range (depending on the tolerance settings). It even has the same little sparklies as the Magic Wand does in its icon to remind you of the relationship.

The problem, as Figure 12-21 shows you, is that the Magic Eraser isn't as clean in its work as the other erasers. Still, it can be a big help in eliminating large chunks of solid color. Moreover, if you're lucky, you may be able to clean the edges right up with the Defringe command (Enhance → Adjust Color → Defringe Layer). There's more about Defringing on page 132.

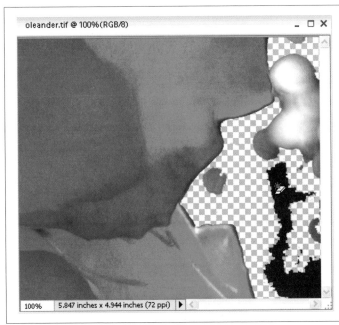

oleander.tif @ 100%(RGB/8)

100%   5.847 inches x 4.944 inches (72 ppi)

Figure 12-21:
This figure shows a close-up look at the Magic Eraser at work on the flower petals from Figure 12-20. One click of the Magic Eraser got rid of a bunch of the background, and setting the Tolerance higher would've gotten even more. But if you look closely, you can see the disadvantage of the Magic Eraser—the edges of the flowers are fringed with dark ragged areas it didn't eliminate. It doesn't always work, but you may be able to clean up the edges by going to Enhance → Adjust Color → Defringe Layer (see page 132).

It's usually best to use the Magic Eraser in combination with at least one of the other erasers if you're looking to achieve really clean results.

The Background Eraser

Lots of people think this eraser deserves the name "Magic" much more than the Magic Eraser does. The Background Eraser is a tremendous help when you want to remove all the background around an object. For example, say you've got a photo of a football and you want to quickly remove the ball from the background.

The Background Eraser erases all the pixels under the brush (but outside the edges of the object) and renders the area it's used on transparent, even if it's a Background layer. (If you click with it on a Background layer, your computer may hesitate initially because it's busy transforming your Background to a regular layer.)

Here's how to use it:

1. **Select the Background Eraser.**

   Either go to the Toolbox, click the Eraser icon, and then select it from the pop-out menu, or press E and click its icon in the Options bar. It's the eraser with a pair of scissors next to it.

2. **In the Options bar, choose a brush size.**

   The cursor turns to a circle with crosshairs in it. These crosshairs are important. They're the Background Eraser's "hotspot." Any color that you drag them over is turned to transparency. The circle size changes depending on how large a brush you've chosen, but the crosshairs stay the same size. As you can see in Figure 12-22, with a large brush, there may be a lot of space around the crosshairs, so it's easy to remove big chunks of the background at once, since everything in the circle is going to get eliminated.

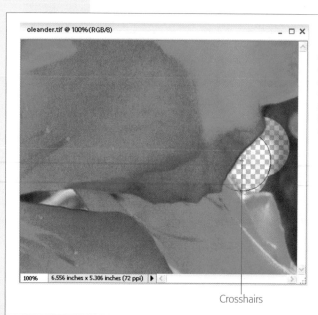

oleander.tif @ 100%(RGB/8)

100%   6.556 inches x 5.306 inches (72 ppi)

Crosshairs

Figure 12-22:
The Background Eraser does a very careful job of separating the flowers from their background. Just be sure to keep the little crosshairs outside the color you want to keep. Here, because the crosshairs are outside the petals, only the background is getting removed. But if you moved the crosshairs into the flower, you'd be biting chunks out of it with the tool.

If you start seeing *all* your brushes (not just the Background Eraser) as circles with crosshairs, take a look at the box on page 310 to see how to get back to your regular cursor.

3. **Drag in your photo.**

    Move around the edge of the object you want to keep, being very careful not to let the crosshairs move into the object, or else you'll start erasing that, too. If you make a mistake, just use Ctrl+Z to undo your actions.

If you want to remove the background from around an object, you may find it most effective to start with the Background Eraser around the edge of your object. Then, use the other Erasers to clean up afterward. The advantage to working this way is that you don't have to clean up junk left over from the Magic Eraser. It's also easier to maneuver the Background Eraser than the regular Eraser, especially if you don't have a graphics tablet.

Drawing with Shapes

Wow, so many brush options and Adobe still isn't done—there's yet another way to draw things in Elements. Elements includes a Shape tool (actually a group of tools that share one slot in the Toolbox), which lets you draw geometrically perfect shapes, regardless of your artistic ability. And not just simple shapes like circles and rectangles. You can draw animals, plants, starbursts, picture frames—all sorts of things, as shown in Figure 12-23. This tool should appeal to anyone whose grade school masterpieces always seemed to get put up on the wall behind the piano somewhere.

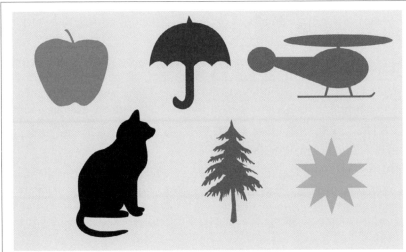

Figure 12-23:
Here are just a few of the shapes that you can draw with Elements, even if you flunked art class in elementary school. These objects look much more impressive once you gussy them up with Layer styles (page 358).

Turning yourself into an artist by using Elements' Shape tool is easy. Just follow these steps:

1. **Open an image or create a new one.**

   You can add shapes to any file that you can open in Elements.

2. **Activate the Shape tool.**

   Click the Shape tool in the Toolbox, or press U. The Shape tool is sometimes a little confusing to newcomers to Elements, because the icon reflects the shape that's currently active—so you may see a rectangle, a polygon, or a line, for instance. The little cartoon speech balloon of the Custom Shape tool is the icon Elements initially presents you with.

3. **Select the kind of shape you want to draw.**

   Click the shape you want in the Options bar. You can choose a rectangle, a rounded rectangle, an ellipse, a polygon, a line, or a custom shape. (If you choose the custom shape, you have many different shapes to choose from.) All the shapes, and their accompanying options, are described in the following sections.

4. **Adjust your settings in the Options bar.**

Choose a color by clicking the color square in the Options bar or use the foreground color (page 195). If you click the Options bar color square, you see the Color Picker (page 196). If you click the arrow to the right of the square, you get the Color Swatches palette instead (page 199).

If you have special requirements, like a rectangle that's exactly 1"×2", click the arrow next to the shape thumbnail for the Shape Options palette and enter the size of your shape.

There's also an Options bar setting that lets you apply a layer style (see page 358) as you draw your shape. Just click the drop-down arrow on the right side of the Style box and choose the style you want from the pop-out palette. To go back to drawing without a style, choose the rectangle with the diagonal red line through it.

5. **Drag in your image to draw the shape.**

Notice that *how* you drag the cursor affects the final appearance of the shape. For example, the way you drag determines the proportions of your figure. If you're drawing a fish, you can drag so that it's long and skinny or short and fat. Even with practice, it may take a couple of tries to get exactly the proportions you want.

> **TIP** If you're trying to create exact copies of a particular shape, use the Shape Selection tool, described later, to create duplicates of the first shape.

The Shape tool automatically puts each shape on its own layer. If you don't want to do that, or you need to control how shapes interact, you can use the squares in the middle of the Options bar. They're the same as the ones for managing selections (page 115). Use them to add more than one shape to a layer, subtract a shape from a shape, keep only the area where shapes intersect, or exclude the areas where they intersect.

> **TIP** If you want to draw multiple shapes on one layer, click the "Add to Shape" rectangle in the Options bar. Then, everything you do is on the same layer. Shapes don't have to touch or overlap to use this option.

You can also turn any shape from a vector image (infinitely resizable) into a raster image (drawn pixel by pixel) by clicking the Simplify button in the Options bar. The box "Rasterizing Vector Shapes" on page 333 tells you everything you need to know about the difference between vector and raster images.

You can also add custom shapes by choosing them in the Artwork and Effects Panel. Just double-click the one you want, or click its palette thumbnail and then click Apply.

The following sections describe all of the main shape categories and their special settings.

Rasterizing Vector Shapes

Back in Chapter 3, you read about how the majority of your images (definitely your photos) are just a bunch of pixels to Elements. These images are known as *raster* images. The shapes you draw with the Shape tools work a little differently. They're called *vector* images.

A vector image is made up of a set of directions, specifying what kind of geometric shapes should be drawn. The advantage of vector images is that you can size them way up or down without producing the kind of pixelation you see when you resize a raster image too much.

Your shape keeps its vector characteristics until you *simplify* the layer that it's on. Simplifying, also called *rasterizing*, just means that Elements turns your shape into regular pixels. Once you simplify, you have the same limitations on resizing as you do for a regular photo. For example, you can make your image smaller, but you can't make it larger than 100 percent without losing quality. Sooner or later, you may want to transform your vector image to a regular raster image so that you can do certain things to it, like adding filters or effects.

If you try to do something that requires simplifying a layer, Elements generally asks you to do so, via a pop-up dialog box. To rasterize your shape, just click OK, or click the Simplify button in the Options bar. Remember that once you've rasterized a shape, if you try to resize, you won't get the nice, clean unpixelated results that you got when it was a vector image. If you need to resize a shape, it's easiest to start over with a new shape—if that's feasible (which is yet another good reason to use layers).

Also, it may puzzle you that, where at one time you were able to change the color of an existing shape by clicking the color box, now, all of a sudden, the shape totally ignores what you do in the Options bar. That's because you simplified the shape layer. Simplifying always affects the entire layer—everything on it is simplified, or nothing is. Once your shape is simplified, you have to make a selection and change the color the way you would on any detail in a photo.

The Artwork and Effects palette in Elements 5 brings a new wrinkle to the raster/vector situation—Smart Shapes. The items on the Artwork and Effects palette (the frames, backgrounds, and other doodads) act as vector objects, except that may seek out a particular place in the layer stack. (See page 402 for more on Smart Shapes.)

Rectangle and Rounded Rectangle

The Rectangle and Rounded Rectangle tools work pretty much the same way and are very popular for creating Web page buttons. They both have Shape options settings in the Options bar for:

- **Unconstrained.** Choose Unconstrained to draw a rectangle of whatever dimensions you want. How you drag determines the proportions of your shape.

- **Square.** To draw a square instead of a rectangle, click this radio button before you start, or just hold down the Shift key as you drag.

- **Fixed Size.** This setting makes Elements draw your shape the size you specify. Just enter the dimensions you want in inches, pixels, or centimeters.

- **Proportional.** Use this setting if you know the proportions you want your rectangle to have, but not the exact size. Just type in the proportions. So if you enter a length of 2 and a height of 1, no matter where you drag, the shape is always twice as long as it is high.

- **From Center.** This setting lets you draw your shape from its center instead of from a corner. It's useful when you know exactly where you want the shape but aren't sure exactly how big it needs to be.

- **Snap to Pixels.** This setting makes sure that the edge of your rectangle falls exactly on the edge of a pixel. You'll get crisper-looking edges with it turned on. It's available only for the Rectangle and Rounded Rectangle tools.

Most of the Shape tools have similar options. The Rounded Rectangle has one option of its own, though: *Radius*. Radius is the amount, in pixels, that the corners are rounded off. A higher number means more rounding.

> **TIP** Looking to add a simple, empty rectangle, square, circle, or ellipse? See the box on page 338.

Ellipse

The Ellipse has the same Shape Options as the Rectangle tool. The only difference is that you can opt for a circle instead of a square. The Shift key constrains the Ellipse to a circle.

Polygon

You can draw any kind of polygon using this tool. You set the number of sides yourself in the Options bar.

The shape options in the Options bar pull-down menu are a bit different for this tool:

- **Radius.** This setting sets the distance from the center to the outermost points.

- **Smooth Corners.** If you don't want sharp edges at the corners, choose Smooth Corners.

- **Star.** This setting inverts the angles to create a star-like shape, as shown in Figure 12-24.

- **Indent Sides by.** If you're drawing a star, this sets how much (in percent) you want the sides to indent.

- **Smooth Indents.** Use Smooth Indents if you don't want sharp angles on your star.

Line Tool

Use this tool for drawing straight lines and arrows. Specify the weight (the width) of the line in pixels in the Options bar. If you want an arrowhead on your line, the Shape options give you some settings for adding one to your line as you draw:

- **Start/End.** Do you want the arrowhead at the start or the end of the line you draw? Tell Elements your preference with this setting.

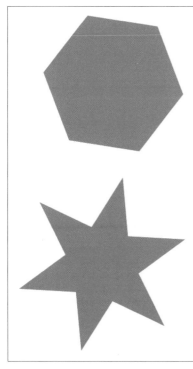

Figure 12-24:
Top: A hexagon drawn with the Shape tool.

Bottom: Turning on the Star option inverts the angles on a polygon, so that instead of drawing a hexagon, you create a star.

- **Width and Length.** This setting determines how wide and how long you want the arrowhead to be. The measurement unit is the percentage of the line width, so if you enter a number lower than 100, your arrowhead is narrower than the line it's attached to. You can pick values between 10 and 5,000 percent.

- **Concavity.** Use this setting if you want the sides of the arrowhead indented. The number determines the amount of curvature on the widest part of the arrowhead. See Figure 12-25. Pick a setting between –50 percent and +50 percent.

TIP   There are also arrows available in the Custom Shape tool if you want something fancier.

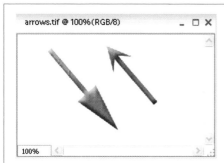

Figure 12-25:
Two arrows drawn with the Line tool.

Left: An arrow with no concavity.

Right: An arrow with concavity set to 50 percent. Both arrows have Layer styles applied to them so they don't look so flat. You can read more about how to do that in the next chapter.

The Custom Shape Tool

The Custom Shape lets you draw a huge variety of different objects, as you can see in Figure 12-26. Its icon is the little cartoon talk bubble shape in the Toolbox. Click it or press U to activate the Custom Shape tool.

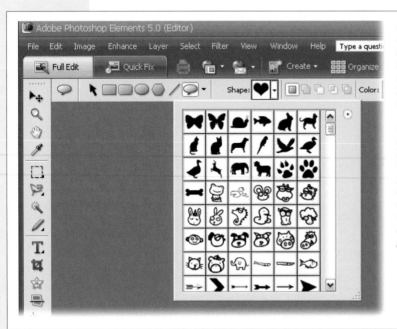

Figure 12-26:
Here's just a small part of the shape library you can choose from in the Shape Picker. To add more custom shapes to your repertoire, you can download and add them to C: \Program files\Adobe Photoshop Elements 5\ Presets\Custom shapes. Look for the file extension .csh when you want shapes that you can add to your library. Downloaded shapes that you add show up as drawing options when you click the More button on the Shapes palette.

Once the Custom Shape tool is active, if you look in the Options bar, you see a little window labeled Shape with the arrow for a pull-down menu next to it. Click this arrow to bring up the Elements Shape Picker.

There are a variety of different shapes in the Default group but if you click the arrow at the upper-right corner of the window, you get a menu giving you lots more choices. To scroll through all of them, just choose All Elements Shapes.

> TIP   There's a copyright symbol available in the custom shapes if you prefer not to use text to create one.

The Custom shape also has a few optional settings, like the other Shape tools. They are:

- **Unconstrained.** Control the proportions of your shape by the way you drag.
- **Defined Proportions.** The shape always has the proportions the designer gave it when it was created.

- **Defined Size.** The shape is always the size it was originally created to be—dragging won't make it bigger or smaller. It just plinks out at a fixed size that you can't control, except by resizing after the fact.

- **Fixed Size.** Enter the dimensions you want in inches, pixels, or centimeters.

- **From Center.** Start drawing in the center of the object.

The Shape Selection Tool

The arrow in the Options bar just to the left of the Rectangle tool is the Shape Selection tool. This is a special kind of Move tool (page 136) that works only on shapes that haven't been simplified yet, as explained in Figure 12-27.

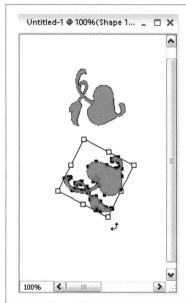

Figure 12-27:
The Shape Selection tool gives you the same kind of bounding box as the Move tool, and it works the same way, but only on shapes that haven't been simplified yet. You can apply transformations like skewing and rotating, too, when the Shape Selection tool is active. Once you've simplified a shape layer, you need the regular Move tool to move it around. You can always use the Move tool, even on shapes where you can use the Shape Selection tool. But the Shape Selection tool works only on shapes that haven't been simplified yet.

It may seem unnecessary, but if you're working with shapes, it saves a lot of time not to have to keep switching tools when you want to move one shape.

Click the Shape Selection tool and then move your shape. Your shape doesn't have to be on the active layer. You can also use the Shape Selection tool to combine multiple shapes into one by clicking the Combine button.

The Shape Selection tool works just like the Move tool. You can drag to move, hold down Alt to copy (instead of moving) the original shape, drag the handles to resize the shape, and so on. Unfortunately, you can't align and distribute shapes with this tool the way you can with the Move tool (see page 136). If you need to line things up, use the regular Move tool instead.

Drawing Outlines and Borders

If you've played around at all with the Shape tool, you may have noticed that you can't draw shapes that are just outlines (that is, that aren't filled with color). No matter what you do, your shape is always a solid shape (except for the frame shapes).

Even if you haven't ever touched the Shape tool, you may be wondering how the heck to get a simple plain colored border around a photo.

The easiest way to create an outline is to make a selection using the Marquee tool or other selection tools and then select Edit → Stroke (Outline) Selection. The Stroke dialog box pops up and lets you enter the width of the line in pixels and choose a color.

You'll also see choices for Location, which tell Elements where you want the line—around the inside edge of the selection, centered on the edge of the selection, or around the outside. If you're bordering an entire photo, don't choose Outside, or the border won't show because it's off the edge of your image.

You can choose a blend mode (page 332) if you like and set the opacity. Using a mode can give you a more subtle edge than a normal stroke does. The Transparency setting just ensures that any transparent areas in your layer stay transparent. When you're finished adjusting the settings in the Stroke dialog box, click OK, turn off your Marquee, and you've got yourself an outlined shape.

Also check out some of the simpler frame designs in the Artwork and Effects palette's All Occasions section (page 344). They let you apply a simple border with just a double-click.

The Cookie Cutter

At first glance, you may think the Cookie Cutter is a pretty silly tool. Actually, it's a very handy tool that you may use all the time, once you understand it. The Cookie Cutter creates the same shapes as the Custom Shape tool, but you use it on a photo to crop it to the shape you chose. Want a heart-shaped portrait of your sweetie? The Cookie Cutter is your tool. If you're a scrapbooker, with a couple of clicks you can get results that would have taken ages and a bunch of special scissors to create with paper.

If you're not into that sort of thing, don't go away, because hidden away in the shapes library are some of the most sophisticated artistic crop shapes you can find. You can use them to get the kinds of effects that people pay commercial artists big bucks to create—like creating abstract crops that give a jagged or worn edge to your photo (an effect that's great for contemporary effects).

You can also combine the result with a stroked edge, as explained in the box above, and maybe even a Layer style (page 358). Even without any additional frills, your photo's shape will appear more interesting, as shown in Figure 12-28.

TIP   Elements gives you a couple of other ways to create cutouts and fancy edge effects, which you might want to check out. If you plan to print out your cropped photo, for use in a scrapbooking project, for example, check out the Picture Package (page 422). The frames there include some shape crops, and you can do everything right in the Organizer Print dialog box, if those shapes work for you. (Despite the name, you can make a Picture Package with only one print of one photo.)

The Frames section of the Art and Effects palette also includes a bunch of crops, ranging from simple shapes like stars to elaborate edges that make your photo look like a half-completed jigsaw puzzle.

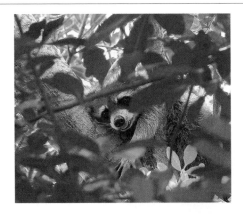

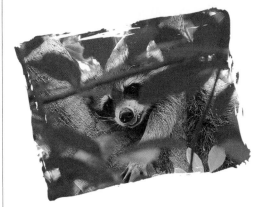

Figure 12-28:
A quick drag with the Cookie Cutter is all it took to create the bottom graphic from the top photo. If you want to create custom album or scrapbook pages, you can rotate or skew your crops before you commit them. See page 65 for how to rotate and skew your images.

You use the Cookie Cutter just the way you use the Custom Shape tool, but you use it on a photo.

1. **Activate the Cookie Cutter tool.**

   Click the Cookie Cutter in the Toolbox (the icon looks like a heart), or press Q.

2. **Select the shape you want your photo to be.**

   Choose a shape from the Shapes palette by clicking the downward arrow next to the shape display in the Options bar. You have access to all the Custom Shapes, but pay special attention to the Crop Shapes category. Click the More button on the Shape Picker to see all the shape categories it contains, or choose All Elements Shapes.

3. **Adjust your settings, if necessary.**

   You have the same Shape Options described earlier for the Custom Shapes (page 336), so you can set a fixed size or constrain proportions if you want. Click the Shape Options button to see your choices.

   You can choose to feather the edge of your shape, too. Just enter the amount in pixels. (See page 117 for more about feathering.) The other option, Crop, crops the edges of your photo so they're just large enough to contain the shape.

4. **Drag in your photo.**

   A mask appears over your photo and you see only the area that will still be there once you crop, surrounded by transparency.

5. **Adjust your crop if necessary.**

   You can reposition the shape mask or drag the corners to resize it. Although the cropped areas disappear, they'll reappear as you reposition the mask if you move it so that they're included again.

   Once you've created the shape, you'll see the Transform options (page 299) in the Options bar (which means that you can skew or distort it if you want) until you commit your shape, as explained in the next step. You can drag the mask around to reposition it if you'd like, or Shift+drag a corner to resize it without altering the proportions. It may take a little maneuvering to get exactly the parts of your photo that you want inside the crop.

6. **When you've gotten everything lined up the way you want, click the Commit button in the image window or just press Enter.**

   If you don't like the results, click the Cancel button in the window, or press Escape (Esc). Once you've made your crop, you can use Ctrl+Z if you want to undo it to try something else.

   NOTE The Cookie Cutter replaces the areas it removes with transparency. If the transparency checkerboard makes it too hard for you to get a clear look at what you've done, temporarily create a new white or colored Fill layer (page 166) beneath the cropped layer. You can delete it once you're sure you're happy with your crop.

Filters, Effects, Layer Styles, and Gradients

There's a popular saying among artistic types who use software in their studios: *tools don't equal talent*. And it's true: no mere program is going to turn a klutz into a Klimt. But Elements has a few special tools—*filters, effects*, and *Layer styles*—that can sure help you fool a lot of people into thinking you're a better artist than you actually are. It's amazing what a difference you can make to the appearance of any image with only a couple of clicks.

Filters are an automated way to change the appearance of your image. You can use filters for enhancing and correcting your image, but Elements also gives you a bunch of other filters that are great for unleashing all your artistic impulses, as shown in Figure 13-1. You'll find the original photos (courthouse.jpg and paulownia.jpg) on the "Missing CD" page at *www.missingmanuals.com*, if you want to play around with these images yourself.

Most filters have settings that you can adjust to control how the filter changes your photo. Because you get more than a hundred different filters with Elements, there isn't room in this chapter to cover each filter individually, but you'll learn the basics of applying filters, and you'll get in-depth coverage of some of the filters you're most likely to use frequently.

Effects are like little macros or scripts, designed to make very elaborate changes to your image, like creating a three-dimensional frame around it or making it look like a pencil sketch or an oil pastel. They're very easy to apply—you just double-click a button—but tweaking their settings isn't as easy to do as it is with filters, since effects are programmed to make very specific changes. (Adobe calls them Photo Effects, but you can apply them to any kind of image, not just a photo.)

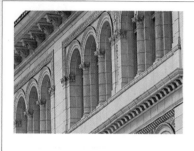
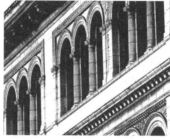
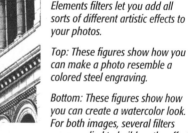
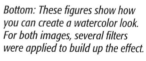
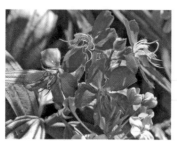
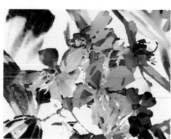

Figure 13-1:
Elements filters let you add all sorts of different artistic effects to your photos.

Top: These figures show how you can make a photo resemble a colored steel engraving.

Bottom: These figures show how you can create a watercolor look. For both images, several filters were applied to build up the effect.

Layer styles change the appearance of just one layer (see page 139) of your photo. They're very popular for creating impressive-looking text, but you also can apply them to objects and shapes. Some Layer styles produce results similar to what you can get from one of the effects, but Layer styles and effects are very different under the hood in what happens to your photo when you apply them. Most Layer styles include settings you can easily modify.

You can combine filters, effects, and Layer styles on one image if you like. And you may spend hours trying different groupings, because it's addicting to watch the often unpredictable results you get when you mix them up.

The last section of this chapter focuses on *gradients*. A gradient is a rainbow-like range of color that you can use to color in an object or a background. But that's not all gradients are good for. You can also use gradients and *Gradient Maps*—gradients that get distributed according to the brightness values in your photo—for very precise retouching effects.

Using Filters

Filters make it possible for you to change the look of your photos in very complex ways; using them is as easy as double-clicking a button. Elements gives you a huge number of filters, which are grouped in categories to help you choose the one that does what you need. This section offers a quick tour through the filter categories as well as some information about using a few of the most popular filters, like the Noise and Blur filters.

To make it easy to apply filters, Elements presents your filters in two different places: the Filter menu, where you choose them from the list that appears, and the Artwork and Effects palette. (The menu is the only place where you can see every filter. Some filters, like the Adjustment filters, don't appear in the palette.) There's also a Filter Gallery, a great feature that makes it very easy to get a good idea of how your photo will look when you apply the artistic filters. The next part of this section explains how to use all three methods.

Applying Filters

In the Filter menu, you choose your filter by name from the list. In the Artwork and Effects palette, thumbnail images give you a preview of what the filters do. The filters do exactly the same thing no matter which way you choose them.

The Filter Gallery gives you a good preview of what a filter looks like when applied to your image. Some filters automatically open the Filter Gallery when you choose them from the menu or the palette. Or you can call up the Gallery itself (without first choosing a filter) by going to Filter → Filter Gallery. Not every filter can be applied from the Gallery—only some of the filters with adjustable settings.

> **TIP** Elements makes it easy to apply the same filter repeatedly. Press the Ctrl+F keyboard shortcut, and Elements applies the last filter you used, with whatever settings you last used. The top listing in the Filter menu also shows the name of this same filter (selecting it works the same way as the keyboard shortcut: you get the same settings you just used).

Filter menu

The Filter menu groups filters into 14 main categories. Correct Camera Distortion (page 292) is all by itself at the top of the list. You'll also see a divider below the bottom category (called Other). When you first install Elements, the Digimarc filter is the only filter below this line, but other filters you download or purchase will appear here, too.

When you choose a filter from the list, one of three things happens:

- **Elements applies the filter automatically.** This happens if the filter's name in the list doesn't have an ellipsis (…) after it. Just look at the result in your photo and undo it (Ctrl+Z) if you don't like its effect. If you do like it, you don't have to do anything else.

- **You see a dialog box.** The Elements filters that have adjustable settings have an ellipsis (…) after their names. Some of them (mostly correctional filters) open a dialog box where you can tweak the settings. Set everything as you want it, watching the small preview in the dialog box to see what you're doing. Then click OK.

- **You see the Filter Gallery.** Some of the more artistic, adjustable filters call up the Filter Gallery so that you can get a nice large preview of what you're doing and also so you can rearrange the order of multiple filters before applying them. Applying filters from the Gallery is explained later.

Regardless of how you've applied the filter, once you're done, you can always undo it (Ctrl+Z) if you're not happy with the effect. If you like it, there's no need to do anything else, except of course to eventually save your image.

> **TIP** Since there's no way to undo filters after you've closed your image, many people apply filters to a duplicate layer. Press Ctrl+J to create a duplicate layer.

Artwork and Effects palette

If you're more comfortable with visual clues when choosing a filter, you can also find most filters in the Artwork and Effects palette (Figure 13-2), which is, logically enough, also where you apply effects.

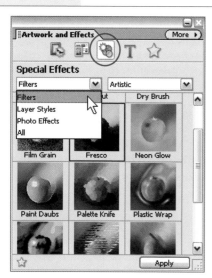

Figure 13-2:
The Artwork and Effects palette gives you a preview of what every filter looks like when applied to the same picture of a green apple. Click the Special Effects button (circled) to get to this section of the palette, and then choose Filters from the pull-down menu. If you know what you want a filter to do but don't know what name to look for, scrolling through these thumbnail images should help you find the one you want. To apply a filter from the palette, double-click the thumbnail, or click the thumbnail once and then click Apply. You can also drag the filter's thumbnail from the palette onto your image.

The Artwork and Effects palette is usually one of the palettes in the Palette bin the first time you launch Elements. If it's not there waiting for you, go to Window → Artwork and Effects, and then click the Special Effects button (see Figure 13-2). Choose Filters from the left pull-down menu, and then you can use the menu on the right to limit your viewing options to filters in any particular category, if you like. The categories are the same ones you see in the Filter menu, except that Adjustments is available only through the menu, and Sharpen appears in the palette but not the Filter menu.

To apply a filter from the palette, double-click its thumbnail, or drag the thumbnail onto your image. If the filter has settings, you get the same dialog box or Filter Gallery you'd see if you'd applied the filter from the Filter menu, as described earlier.

One small drawback to applying filters from the palette is that you can't tell from the thumbnail whether a filter is one that applies automatically. There's no clue like the ellipsis (…) to tell you which group a filter falls into.

> **TIP** If you're experienced with Elements, it may bug you how much farther you've got to dig down in this version to get to the stuff that used to be in the Styles and Effects palette. Try using the Artwork and Effects palette's Favorites section, as described on page 404, for faster access to the filters, styles, and effects you use most often.

Filter Gallery

The Filter Gallery, shown in Figure 13-3, is one of Elements' more popular features. It gives you a large preview window, a look at all the little green apple thumbnails so you have a visual guide to what your filter will do, and most importantly, it lets you apply filters like layers—you can stack them up and change the order in which they're applied to your image. Changing the order of filters can make some big differences in how they affect your image. For example, you get very different results if you apply Ink Outlines *after* the Sprayed Strokes filter than you do if you apply Ink Outlines first. The Gallery lets you play around and experiment to see which order gives you the exact look you want. The layer-like behavior of the filters in the gallery is only for previewing, though. They don't end up as real layers.

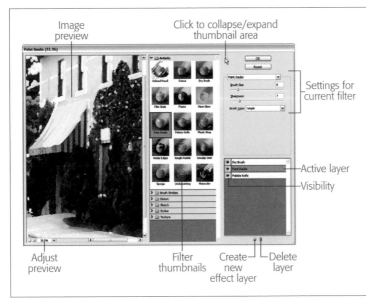

Image preview | Click to collapse/expand thumbnail area

Figure 13-3:
The Filter Gallery. If you want an even larger preview, you can click the arrow that the cursor is over in the figure to collapse the thumbnails and regain that entire section for preview space.

Settings for current filter

Active layer

Visibility

Adjust preview | Filter thumbnails | Create new effect layer | Delete layer

---

The Gallery is more for artistic filters than for corrective filters. You can't apply the Adjustment or Noise filters from the Gallery, for instance. All the Gallery filters are in the artistic, brush stroke, distort, sketch, stylize, and texture categories. (See the next section for an overview of all the filter categories.)

The Filter Gallery is divided into three panes. On the left side is a preview of what your image will look like when you apply the filter. The center holds the thumbnails for the different filters, and the right side contains the settings for the currently chosen filter. At the bottom of the settings pane are your filter layers. You can see what filters you've applied, and add or subtract layers and rearrange their order here.

> **NOTE** Filter layers work something like regular layers (see Chapter 6) with one important difference: your filter layers are what you might call "working" layers. In other words, you only have separate filter layers until you click OK. Then all your chosen filters get applied to your image at once. You can't close your photo and come back later and still expect to see the filters as individual, changeable layers after you've actually applied the filters. And most importantly, your filters become part of the layer you apply them to. You aren't creating a new permanent layer when you use the Filter Gallery.

In addition to letting you adjust the settings for a given filter, the Filter Gallery lets you perform a few other tricks:

- **Adjust the preview magnification of your image.** In the lower-left corner of the Gallery, click directly on the percentage listing or click the arrow next to it for a list of preset sizes to choose from. You can also click the + and–buttons to zoom the view in or out. Easier still, use the Ctrl+= and Ctrl+– (the Ctrl key plus the minus key) shortcuts to zoom in and out from the keyboard.

- **Choose a new filter.** Just click a filter's thumbnail once, and you get the settings for the new filter and the preview image updates right away—usually (see the box on page 349).

- **Add a new filter layer.** You can stack up filters in layers in the Filter Gallery the way you would layers in the Layers palette. Each time you click the New Filter Layer icon (see Figure 13-4), you add another filter layer to the ones you already have.

- **Change the position of filter layers.** Just drag them up and down in the stack like regular layers (page 153) to changer the order in which they'll get applied to your image.

- **Hide filter layers.** Click the eye next to a filter layer in the filter layer palette to turn off visibility, just like in the regular Layers palette (page 150).

- **Delete filter layers.** Highlight any filter layer by clicking it, and then click the Trash icon to delete it.

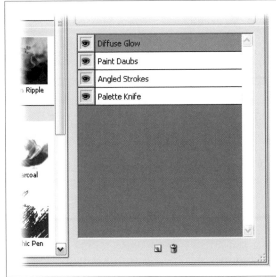

Figure 13-4:
If you've used layers before (see Chapter 6), these little icons should look familiar. In the Filter Gallery, they make new filter layers instead of regular layers. Click the square to add a new filter layer to your image. Click the trash icon to delete a filter layer. The eye icons next to your filter layers turn visibility on and off just as they do in the Layers palette. It's true that the filters preview in layers, but they don't show up as real layers in the Layers palette—only in the Filter Gallery.

- **Change the content of a layer.** You can change what kind of filter is in a particular layer. For instance, if you applied, say, the Smudge Stick, and you like all your other changes, but wish you had used the Glass filter instead, you don't have to delete the Smudge Stick layer. Instead, just highlight the Smudge layer and click the Glass filter button to change the layer's contents.

TIP   Ctrl+F reapplies all the filters that were in your last gallery set if you press it again after using the Filter Gallery.

Filter Categories

Elements divides the filters into categories to help make it easier for you to track down the filter you want. Some of the categories, like Distort, contain filters that vary hugely in what they do to your photo. Other categories, like the Brush Stroke filters, contain filters that are all pretty obviously related to one another. Here's a quick breakdown of the categories:

- **Correct Camera Distortion.** This is a new filter that lets you correct perspective distortion (think: tall buildings) as well as vignetting (shadows) caused by your camera's lens. It's explained in detail on page 292.

- **Adjustments.** These filters apply some photographic, stylistic, and artistic changes to your photo. Most of the adjustments are explained on page 261, but you can find more information on Photo Filters on page 224.

- **Artistic.** This is a huge group of filters that do everything from making your photo look like it was cut from paper (Cutout) to making it look like a quick sketch (Rough Pastels). You generally get the best effects with these filters by using multiple filters or applying the same one multiple times.

- **Blur.** The blur filters let you soften the focus of your photo and add artistic effects. They're explained later in this chapter.

- **Brush Strokes.** These filters apply brush stroke effects to your photo to give it a hand-painted look.

- **Distort.** These filters warp your image in a great variety of ways. The Liquify filter is the most powerful, and you'll find a tutorial for using it on page 388.

- **Noise.** Use these filters to add or remove grain from your image. They're explained later in this chapter.

- **Pixelate.** The Pixelate filters break your image up in different ways, making it show the dot pattern of a magazine halftone, or the fragmented look you see on television where they're concealing someone's identity.

NOTE   The Color Halftone filter makes your photo look like a *halftone*, a one-color image whose pixels simulate the shades of gray you see in a black-and-white photo. It's not the same as true halftone screening, which isn't available in Elements. If the print shop you're working with needs a halftone, you either need to get Photoshop or ask the printer to do the conversion for you.

- **Render.** This group includes a pretty diverse bunch of filters that let you do things like create a lens-flare effect (Lens Flare), transform a flat object so it looks three dimensional (3D Transform), and make fibers (Fibers) or clouds (Clouds). The Lighting Effects filter, a powerful but confusing filter that's like a whole program in itself, helps you change the way lighting appears in your image. For a full rundown on what this filter does, as well as how to use it, check out the "Missing CD" page at *www.missingmanuals.com*.

- **Sharpen.** Unsharp Mask (page 202) appears in the palette but not the Filter menu. (The sharpening commands are in the Enhance menu.)

- **Sketch.** These filters not only make your photo look like it was drawn with different instruments (like charcoal, chalk, and crayon)—you can also make your photo look like it was embossed in wet plaster, photocopied, or stamped with a rubber stamp.

- **Stylize.** These filters create special effects by increasing the contrast in your photo and displacing pixels. You can make your photo look radioactive, reduce it to outlines, or make it look like it's moving fast with the Wind filter.

- **Texture.** These filters change the surface of your photo to look like it was made from another material. Use them to create a crackled finish (the Craquelure filter), stained glass (Stained Glass), or a mosaic effect (Mosaic Tiles).

- **Video.** These filters are for use in creating and editing images for (and from) videos.

- **Other.** This is a group of fairly technical filters that you can highly customize. The High Pass filter is explained on page 206. You can use Offset to shift an image or a layer a little bit.

- **Digimarc.** Use this filter to check for Digimarc watermarks in photos. Digimarc is a company that lets subscribers enter their information in a database so that anyone who gets one of their photos can find out who the copyright holder is.

You can find a number of filter plug-ins online, ranging from free to very expensive. Page 475 gives you some suggestions for places to start looking. Once you've installed new filters, you access them at the bottom of the list in the Filter menu.

> **NOTE** Filters are platform specific, so you can't use plug-ins written for Macs if you're using Windows. Only Windows plug-ins work with the Windows version of Elements.

UNDER THE HOOD

Filter Performance Hints

If Elements could speak, it would say, "Easy for *you*," when it comes to filters and effects. Although you don't have to do much to apply them, Elements has a huge amount of work to do on its end. Elements 5 is pretty fast, but if your computer is slow or memory-challenged, it can take a long time to apply filters and even to update the preview. You can speed things up by applying filters to a selection for previewing. Filters that have their own dialog boxes (as opposed to the Filter Gallery) will show a flashing line under the size percentage below the preview area to indicate the progress they're making. A few other filter-related tips are worth remembering:

- Filters won't do anything if they don't have pixels to work on, so be sure you're targeting a layer with something in it and not an Adjustment layer.

- If you apply a filter to a selection, you'll usually want to feather (page 117) the edges a fair amount to help the filter edges blend into the rest of your photo.

- Alt+click the Cancel button to turn it to a Reset button. Clicking Cancel makes the window go away, while Reset lets you start over without having to call up the filter again.

- If your filters are grayed out in the Filter menu, check to be sure you're not in 16-bit mode (page 221) or in grayscale, bitmapped, or index color (all these color modes are explained on page 40).

Useful Filter Solutions

This section shows you how to use some of Elements' most popular and useful filters to correct your photos and create a few special effects. You'll learn how to modify the graininess of your photos to create an aged effect or smooth out a repair job. And you'll also see how to blur your photos to create a soft-focus effect, or to make your subjects look like they're moving.

Removing noise: getting rid of graininess

Noise, the appearance of undesired graininess in an image, is a big problem with many digital cameras, especially those with small sensors and high megapixel counts. It's rare to find a fixed-lens camera with more than 5 megapixels that doesn't have some trouble with noise, especially in underexposed areas. If you shoot using the RAW format, you can correct a fair amount of noise right in the RAW Converter (page 211). But the RAW Converter won't help if you're shooting JPEGs. And even RAW files may need further noise reduction once you've edited your photo after converting it.

Elements includes the Reduce Noise filter, which is designed specifically to help you get rid of noise in your photos. To get to it, go to Filter → Noise → Reduce Noise. You get a dialog box with a preview window on the left side and settings adjustments on the right. To use the filter, first use the controls below the preview to set the view to at least 100 percent, or preferably even higher. It's important to be able to see the pixels in your photo so that you can see how the filter is changing them as you adjust the settings.

You get three settings, each of which you control by using a slider:

- **Strength.** This controls the overall impact of the filter. This setting controls the same kind of noise as the Luminance Smoothing setting in the RAW converter (page 221). The stronger you set it, the greater the risk of softening your photo.

- **Preserve Details.** Using noise reduction can soften the appearance of your photo. This setting tells Elements how much care to take to preserve the details of your image.

- **Reduce Color Noise.** This setting adjusts uneven distribution of color in your image. You can set this slider pretty high without a negative impact on your photo.

There's also a checkbox for minimizing JPEG artifacts, as explained in Figure 13-5.

For each setting, move the slider to the right if you want more and to the left if you want less, while watching the effect in the preview window. You may notice a little lag time before the preview updates. When you see what you want, click OK to apply the filter.

The Elements Reduce Noise filter does a fine job on areas with a small amount of noise, like the skies in many JPEG photos. But if your camera has major noise problems, you may find you still need third-party noise reduction software. The two most popular programs are probably Noise Ninja (*www.picturecode.com*) and Neat Image (*www.neatimage.com*). Both have demo versions you can download to try out the programs. If you search with Google for "noise reduction software," you'll get a variety of other options as well, including several free programs.

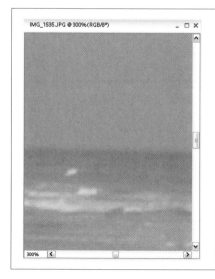 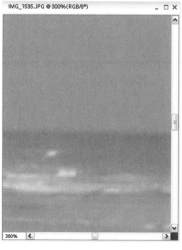

Figure 13-5:
Many JPEG photos have a problem with artifacts, uneven areas of color caused by JPEG compression (see page 57).

Left: Here's an extreme closeup of a JPEG photo. The herringbone pattern you see in the sky is typical of the kind of artifacts you sometimes get in JPEG photos.

Right: Turning on the checkbox in the Reduce Noise filter helps to smooth out the color.

Adding noise: smoothing out repair jobs

Elements also gives you a filter for *creating* noise. Why do that when most of the time you try so hard to get rid of noise? One reason is when you're trying to age the appearance of your photo. If you want to make a photo look like it came from an old newspaper, for instance, you'd add some noise.

The other most common use for noise is to help make repaired spots blend in with the rest of an image. If you've altered part of a photo in Elements, especially by painting on it, odds are that the repaired area is going to look perfectly smooth. That's great if the rest of the photo is noise free. But if the rest of the photo is a little grainy, that smooth patch is going to stand out like a sore thumb. Add a bit of noise to make it blend in better with the rest of the photo, as shown in Figure 13-6.

To add noise to a photo, start by selecting the area where you want to add the noise (if you don't want to change your whole photo). Using a duplicate layer (Ctrl+J) for the noise is a safe step, since you can always undo your changes if you've got them on a layer.

1. **Call up the Add Noise filter.**

   Go to Filter → Noise → Add Noise to bring up the dialog box with the settings for the filter.

2. **Adjust the settings to your liking.**

   The settings are explained in the following list. Use the preview window in the dialog box to check how the changes are affecting your photo.

3. **When you're satisfied, click OK.**

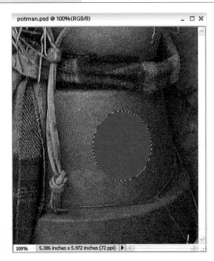

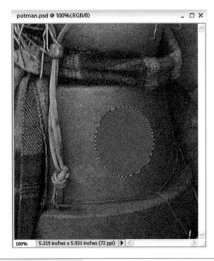

Figure 13-6:

Top: If you use the Average Blur filter in a repair on this noisy photo, the blended area stands out, making your repair very obvious.

Bottom: If you add some noise, the changes you've made become much less noticeable.

You have three options in the Add Noise dialog box:

- **Amount.** This option controls how heavy the noise is going to be. Just drag the slider to the right for more noise or to the left for less. You can also type in a number. A higher percentage means more noise.

- **Uniform or Gaussian.** These buttons let you control how the noise gets distributed through your image. Uniform is just what it says—the same all over. Gaussian distributes the noise to produce a more speckled effect.

  If you're adding noise to duplicate existing noise in a grainy photo, you'll probably want a Gaussian distribution. For an old newspaper photo look, try Uniform. In either case, experiment until you get what you want.

• **Monochromatic.** This setting limits noise to the colors already existing in your photo. Take a look at the middle image in Figure 13-7 and notice how many more colors you can see inside the noise, compared to the solid red of the original. The noise was applied with the Monochromatic setting turned off.

Noise can also help you when you want to apply special effects to blocks of solid color, as shown in Figure 13-7. If you try to apply the Angled Strokes filter to a solid color, you won't see the strokes. Adding noise gives the filter something to work on.

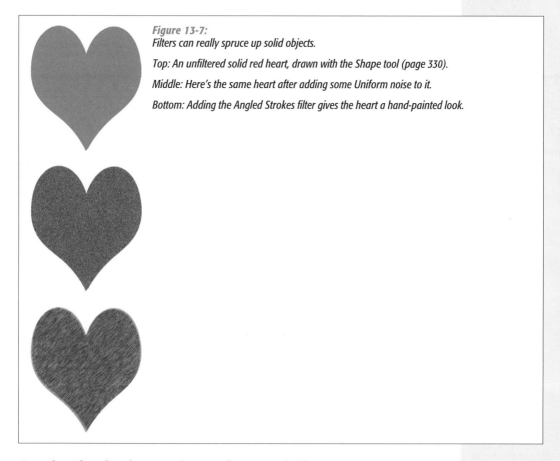

Figure 13-7:
Filters can really spruce up solid objects.

Top: An unfiltered solid red heart, drawn with the Shape tool (page 330).

Middle: Here's the same heart after adding some Uniform noise to it.

Bottom: Adding the Angled Strokes filter gives the heart a hand-painted look.

Gaussian Blur: drawing attention to a foreground object

The Gaussian Blur filter lets you control how much your image is blurred. The Gaussian blur is probably the most frequently used of the Blur filters. Besides blurring large areas of your photo, like the background in the bottom photo in Figure 13-8, you can apply a Gaussian Blur at a very low setting to soften lines—very useful when you're trying to achieve a sketched effect. If you'd like to try out the different blurs, you'll find the hawk photo (hawk.jpg) on the "Missing CD" page at *www.missingmanuals.com*.

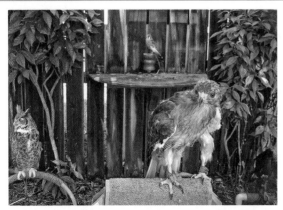

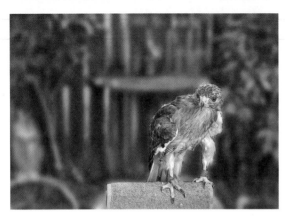

Figure 13-8:
Top: This photo could use some help from the Blur filters. The hawk is hard to distinguish from the rest of the photo; blurring helps center the focus on the hawk.

Bottom: With a Gaussian Blur filter applied to the background, the hawk becomes the clear focal point of the photo.

When you use the Gaussian Blur, you have to set the *radius*, which controls how much you want the filter to blur things. A higher radius produces more blurring; use the filter's preview window to see what you're doing.

Radial Blur: producing a sense of motion

As you can see in Figure 13-9, the Radial Blur really produces a sense of motion. It has two available styles: Zoom, which is designed to give the effect of a camera zooming in, and Spin, which produces a circular effect around your designated center point.

The Radial Blur dialog box may look a bit complicated, but it's really not. Unfortunately, you don't get a preview with this filter, because it drains so much processor power. That's why you have a choice between Draft, Good, and Best Quality. Use Draft for a quick look at roughly what you'll get. Then, most of the time, choose Good for the final version. There's not much difference between Good and Best except on large images, so don't feel that you must choose Best for the final version all the time.

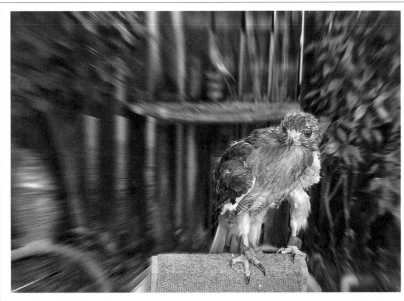

Figure 13-9:
A Radial Blur applied in Zoom mode. As you can see, this filter can produce an almost vertiginous sense of motion. If you don't want to give people motion sickness, go easy on the Amount setting.

Once you've chosen your method (Zoom or Spin), set the amount, which controls the intensity of the blur that's applied. Next, click inside the Blur Center box to identify the point where you want the blur to center, as shown in Figure 13-10. Finally, click OK when you're finished.

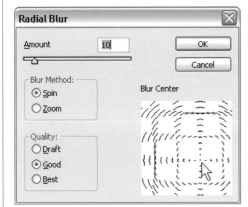

Figure 13-10:
The Blur Center box lets you identify the center point of the Radial Blur's effect (whether you've chosen Zoom or Spin mode). Drag the ripple drawing inside the box in any direction; here, the center point has been moved just to the right and down from its original position in the center of the box.

Color correcting with the Average Blur filter

If you've already given the Average Blur filter a whirl you may be wondering what on earth Adobe was thinking when they created it. Use it on your entire photo, and your image disappears under a hideous soup, something like what you'd get by pureeing together all the colors in your photo. Oddly enough, this effect makes the filter a great tool for getting rid of color casts (see page 191). You can use the Average Blur to create a sort of custom Photo Filter (see page 224), toned specially for the image you use it on. The secret is in using blend modes. Here's how:

1. **Open your image and make a duplicate layer.**

   Just press Ctrl+J, or go to Layer → Duplicate Layer.

2. **Apply the Average Blur filter.**

   Make sure your duplicate layer is the active layer (click it in the Layers palette if it isn't), and then go to Filter → Blur → Average. Your photo disappears under a layer of (probably) very unpleasing solid color, but you'll fix that next.

3. **Change the blend mode of the blur layer.**

   In the Layers palette, choose Color from the Mode pull-down menu. Already things are starting to look better.

4. **Reduce the opacity of the blur layer, and do other tweaking, if necessary.**

   Use the opacity slider in the Layers palette. Try 50 percent. By now, the color should look right—no more color cast. Tweak if necessary, and save your work.

   You may want to add a Hue/Saturation layer (see page 256) if you find that no matter how you adjust the opacity slider, the photo looks a little flat.

The Average Blur filter is a particularly good way to color-correct underwater photos, where it's very hard to get a realistic white balance using your camera's built-in settings.

Adding Effects

Like filters, effects give you loads of ways to really change the appearance of your photo—from adding green slime textures to surrounding your photos with classy picture frames. Although you apply effects with a simple double-click of your mouse, these clicks actually trigger a sequence of changes that Elements applies to your image. Some of the effects involve many complex steps, although Elements 5 works so quickly you might not even notice all the changes taking place.

Adobe puts effects in two places in the Artwork and Effects palette. Along with the usual Photo Effects, there are some effects in the Text section of the palette. Both Photo and Text effects work the same way.

> **NOTE** You usually can't customize or change an effect's settings. Effects are typically an all-or-nothing deal. For example, if you use one of the Pattern Frame effects, you either take the pattern as Elements applies it to your image, or you don't. No need to ask if you can adjust the scale of the pattern—you can't.

You apply effects from the Artwork and Effects palette (choose Window → Artwork and Effects). Then click the Special Effects button and, from the left pull-down menu, choose Photo Effects. Photo Effects are subdivided into Image Effects and frames, as shown in Figure 13-11.

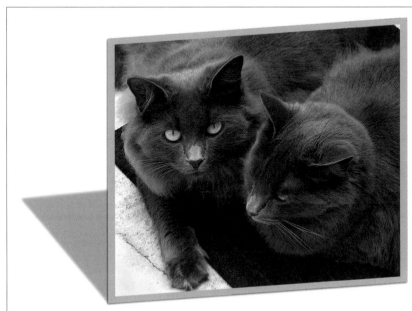

Figure 13-11:
The Artwork and Effects palette's Photo Effects section offers some excellent frame effects, like this standup frame. But there are also many more frame styles in the Artwork section (see page 515).

Just as with filters, use the right menu on the Artwork and Effects palette to see all your choices, or pick from only one category. The thumbnail images give you a preview of what the effect will do to your image.

> **NOTE** Effects don't get their own menu the way filters do. The only way to apply them is from the Artwork and Effects palette.

To apply an effect, double-click its thumbnail in the Artwork and Effects palette, click the thumbnail once and click Apply, or just drag the thumbnail onto your photo. That's all there is to it. If you don't like the result, press Ctrl+Z to undo it, but there's not much you can tweak in the effects.

Here are a few other effects-related tips to help you get the most out of these nifty-but-quirky features:

• A few effects flatten (page 164) or simplify (page 333) your image. Therefore, it's usually best to make a copy of your image, or wait until you're done making all your other edits, before applying an effect.

• Some effects create additional layers; check the Layers palette once you're done applying them. You may want to flatten your image to reduce the file size before printing or storing it. (See Chapter 6 if you need a refresher on using layers.)

Adding Layer Styles

Like filters and effects, Layer styles let you transform objects by giving them new characteristics, like Drop Shadows, for instance. Layer styles are especially useful for modifying individual objects, like text and buttons, because you can edit the text and change the button's shape even *after* you've applied the Layer style.

Layer styles, as their name suggests, work on the contents of one layer—rather than on your whole image. That's important. A Layer style affects the *entire* contents of a layer. If you want to apply a Layer style to just one object in your picture, select the object and put it on a layer of its own (Ctrl+J or Layer → New → Layer via Copy, or Ctrl+Shft+J or New → Layer via Cut). Figure 13-12 shows what you can do with Layer styles.

 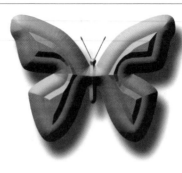

Figure 13-12:
Layer styles are great for making fancy buttons for Web sites. Changing this plain black Custom Shape was as simple as clicking the Sunset Sky Layer style (in Complex Styles), adding a bevel, and then making the bevel bigger. (Keep reading to learn how to edit Layer styles.)

You apply Layer styles from the Artwork and Effects palette (Window → Artwork and Effects). Click the Special Effects button (see Figure 13-2) and, from the palette's left-side pull-down menu, choose Layer Styles. Then, from the menu on the right, choose a Layer style category. Finally, select the layer you want to modify (by highlighting it in the Layers palette), and then click the Layer style you want to use. The box on page 360 shows you how to modify any style's settings.

> **NOTE** Some tools, like the Type tool (see page 375), have an Options bar box that lets you choose a Layer style.

Here's a quick rundown of the choices available in each Layer style category:

- **Bevels.** Bevels give objects a 3-D look by making them appear raised from the page or embossed into it. Figure 13-13 shows an example of how combining a bevel and a drop shadow can add a lot of dimension to even a simple shape.

- **Complex.** Includes a variety of elaborate Layer styles that make an object look like it's made from metal, cactus, and several other materials. These styles are particularly useful for applying to type.

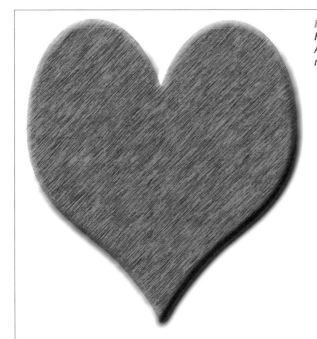

Figure 13-13:
Here's the heart image from earlier in this chapter. Adding a bevel and a drop shadow gives it much more dimension and depth.

- **Drop Shadows.** Adds shadows that make your object look like it's floating above the page.

   NOTE   Adding a drop shadow to an entire photo requires adding canvas (see page 89) to give the shadow someplace to fall. The easiest way to add a drop shadow around an entire photo is to use the Drop Shadow effect from the Frame effects, rather than using a Layer style.

- **Glass Buttons.** These styles are supposed to make objects look like glass buttons, but many people think they look more like plastic. They're useful for creating Web page buttons.

- **Image Effects.** This group gives you a wealth of ways to transform your photo, including fading it and making it look like the pieces of a puzzle or a tile mosaic.

- **Inner Glows.** Adding an Inner Glow adds light around the inside edge of your object.

- **Inner Shadows.** Inner Shadows give your image a hollow or recessed effect by casting a shadow within the object, rather than outside it the way drop shadows do.

- **Outer Glows.** Outer Glows create the same kind of light effects that Inner Glows do, only they go around the outer edge of your image.

- **Patterns.** These styles apply an overall pattern to your image. Want to make something look like it's made from metal or dried mud, or to fill in a dull background with a really vivid pattern? You'll find lots of choices here.

- **Photographic Effects.** This group includes several favorite traditional photographic techniques. You can add a variety of monochrome effects, like good old-fashioned sepia.

- **Visibility.** These styles change the opacity and visibility of your layer. Use them to create a ghosted effect—or when you're applying multiple Layer styles and you want to use the outlined shape of an object without having the object itself visible.

- **Wow Chrome, Neon, Plastic Styles.** Use these styles to make an object look like it's made from shiny chrome, outlined in neon, or made from plastic.

    NOTE   You can apply Layer styles only to regular layers, so if you try to apply one to a Background layer, Elements will ask you to convert it to a regular layer before the style will take effect.

If someone sends you a file made using Layer styles that you don't have, you can snag them for your own use by highlighting the layer with the styles on it, and then going to Layer → Layer Style → Copy Layer Style. Then, in an image where you want to use the styles, click the layer that you want to modify and then choose Layer → Layer Style → Paste Layer Style. This command applies all the styles used in the original image to the layer you targeted.

POWER USERS' CLINIC

Editing Layer Styles

Elements 5 has a powerful new dialog box for editing Layer styles (see Figure 13-14). It gives you many more editing options than you had in previous versions of Elements. Once you've applied a Layer style, you can edit it as much as you like. Just double-click the Layer Styles icon in the Layers Palette (it looks like a little blue-edged white starburst) or select Layer → Layer Style → Style Settings.

Once the Style Settings dialog box appears, you can edit your style in many different ways:

- **Drop Shadow.** You can change the shadow's direction, distance, opacity, or even its color. Once the Style Settings dialog box is open, you can drag the shadow around, right in your image window, until it's positioned where you want it.

- **Glow.** You can set the color, size, and opacity for both inner and outer glows, and turn each one on or off individually.

- **Bevel.** Change the size or direction of the bevel.

- **Stroke.** A stroke is a border around the edge of the style (like a line). You can change the color, size, and opacity of the stroke.

With Elements 5, you can customize styles in so many ways that you can practically make your own style from any existing one. There's only one hitch: There's no way to change the standard settings for each style, so changes you make only affect the style as you're currently applying it.

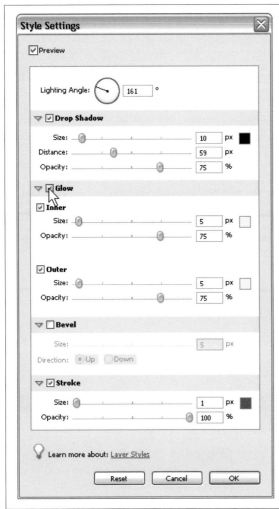

To remove a Layer style, right-click the layer in the Layers palette and choose Clear Layer Style, or go to Layer → Layer Style → Clear Layer Style. These commands are all-or-nothing: if your layer has multiple styles, they all go away at once. To remove one style at a time, use the Undo History palette (page 26).

> **TIP** If you want to see what your image looks like without the styles you've applied to it, go to Layer → Layer Style → Hide All Effects.

You can download hundreds of additional Layer styles from the Web (see page 475 for tips on where to look). It's easy to get addicted to collecting Layer styles because they're so much fun to use.

Applying Gradients

You may have noticed that a few of the Layer styles and Image Effects fade out a color at the edges. In fact, Elements lets you fade colors in many different ways by using *gradients*, in which colors blend and fade in almost any way you can imagine. Use gradients to create anything from a multi-colored rainbow extravaganza to a single color that fades away into transparency. Figure 13-15 shows you a few examples of what you can do with gradients. The only limit is your imagination.

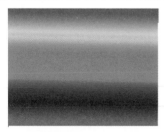
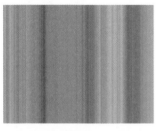
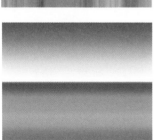

Figure 13-15:
Here are three examples of gradients drawn with the Gradient tool.

Top: This figure shows a gradient that creates a rainbow effect.

Middle: If you play with the Gradient Editor (page 368), you can create all sorts of interesting effects. Here's the gradient from the top figure again, only this time it's applied left to right instead of top to bottom. It looks so different because the noise option is used here (see page 370). Click the Randomize button a couple of times for this effect.

Bottom: This figure shows a gradient you can create if you want a landscape background for artwork.

You can apply gradients directly to your image using the Gradient tool, or you can create *Gradient Fill layers*, which are entire layers filled with—you guessed it—gradients. You can even edit gradients and create new ones using the Gradient Editor. Finally, there's a special kind of gradient called a *Gradient Map* that lets you replace the colors in your image with the colors from a gradient. This section covers the basics of using all these tools and methods.

The Gradient Tool

If you want to apply a gradient to a particular object in your image, the Gradient tool is the fastest way to do it. The Gradient tool may seem complicated when you first see it, but it's actually pretty easy to use. Start by activating the Gradient tool in the Toolbox (the fading purple rectangle) or by pressing G. Figure 13-16 shows the Gradient tool's Options bar.

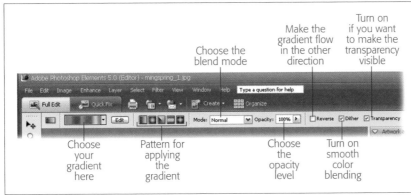

Figure 13-16:
The Gradient tool's Options bar gives you lots of choices for customizing how you apply your gradient.

Using the Gradient tool is as easy as dragging. Click where you want the gradient to begin and then drag to the point where you want it to stop (you'll see a line connecting your beginning and ending points). When you release the mouse, the gradient covers the entire available space.

For example, say you're using a yellow-to-white gradient. If you click to end the gradient one-third of the way into your photo, the yellow stops transitioning at that point, but the remaining two-thirds of your photo is covered with white. Drag the gradient within a selection if you want to confine the area it covers (see Chapter 5 if you need a refresher on making selections).

> **NOTE** The Gradient tool puts the gradient on the same layer as the image you apply it to, which means that it's hard to change anything about your gradient after it's applied. If you think you might want to alter your gradient, use the Gradient Fill layer, described later.

Some gradients use your chosen foreground and background colors as the two colors that generate the gradient. But Elements also offers a number of preset gradients, which are gradients in different color schemes that Adobe has created for you.

Click the arrow to the right of the gradient thumbnail in the Options bar and you'll see a little palette of different gradients, some of which use your selected colors and others that are preset with their own color scheme. The gradients are grouped into categories; you can only work with the gradients in one category at a time.

Click the arrow on the upper-right corner of the gradient thumbnails pop-out menu to see all the available gradient categories. Choose one, and the available gradients change to reflect those in the new category.

You can also download gradients from the Web and add them to your library, or you can create your own gradients from scratch. (See page 475 for some ideas about where to look for new gradients.) Creating and editing gradients is explained later, in the section about the Gradient Editor.

You can customize your gradient in several ways, even without using the Gradient Editor. When the Gradient tool is active, you see several choices in the Options bar:

- **Gradient.** Click the arrow to the right of the thumbnail to choose a different gradient than the one displayed.

- **Edit.** Click this button to bring up the Gradient Editor (explained later).

- **Gradient types.** Use this setting to determine the way the colors flow in your gradient. Click a thumbnail to choose how to apply the gradient. From left to right, your choices are: Linear (in a straight line), Radial (a sunburst effect), Angle (a counterclockwise sweep around the starting point), Reflected (from the center out to each edge in a mirror image), and Diamond. Figure 13-17 shows what each one looks like.

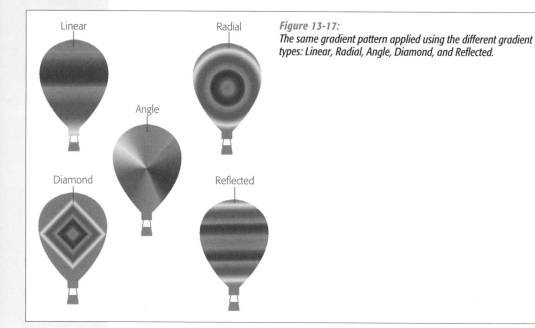

Figure 13-17:
The same gradient pattern applied using the different gradient types: Linear, Radial, Angle, Diamond, and Reflected.

- **Mode.** You can apply a gradient in any blend mode (see page 322).

- **Opacity.** If you want your image to be visible through the gradient, reduce the opacity here.

- **Reverse.** This setting changes the direction in which the colors are applied so that instead of yellow to blue from left to right, you get blue to yellow, for instance.

- **Dither.** Turning on this checkbox makes the edges of the color transitions blend together.

- **Transparency.** If you want to shade to transparency anywhere in your gradient, you need to turn Transparency on. Otherwise, the gradient can't show transparent regions.

Using the Gradient tool

To apply a gradient with the Gradient tool, first make a selection if you don't want to see the gradient in your whole image. Then:

1. **Choose the colors you want to use for your gradient.**

   Click the Foreground/Background color squares (page 195) to choose colors. (Some gradient choices ignore these colors and use their own preset colors instead.)

2. **Activate the Gradient tool.**

   Click it in the Toolbox or press G.

3. **Select a gradient.**

   Go to the Options bar and click the Gradient thumbnail and choose the gradient style you want. Then make any other changes to the Options bar settings, like reversing the gradient, if necessary.

4. **Apply your gradient.**

   Drag in your image from the starting point to the ending point, marking where the gradient should run. If you're using a linear gradient, you can make the gradient run vertically by dragging up or down. Or you can make it go left to right by dragging sideways. For Radial, Reflection, and Diamond gradients, try dragging from the center of your image to one edge. If you don't like your results, Ctrl+Z to undo it. Once you like the way the gradient looks in your image, you don't need to do anything special to accept it, except of course to save your image before you close it.

Gradient Fill Layer

You can also apply your gradient using a special fill layer. Most of the time, this is a better choice than the Gradient tool, especially if you want to be able to make changes to your gradient later on.

To create a Gradient Fill layer, go to Layer → New Fill Layer → Gradient. The New Layer dialog box appears, which lets you set the opacity for the layer and choose a blend mode (page 153), if you like. Once you click OK, the new layer immediately fills with the currently selected gradient, and the dialog box shown in Figure 13-18 pops up. You can change many of the settings for your gradient here or choose a different gradient.

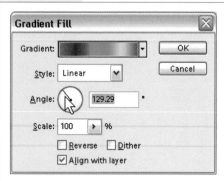

Figure 13-18:
The Gradient Fill dialog box gives you access to most of the same settings you find in the Options bar for the Gradient tool. The major difference is that in the fill layer, you set the direction of your gradient by typing in a number for the angle or by changing the direction of the line as shown here. You don't get a chance to set the direction by dragging, as you do with the Gradient tool.

The settings in the Gradient Fill dialog box are pretty much the same as those in the Options bar for the Gradient tool:

- **Gradient.** To choose a different gradient, click the arrow next to the thumbnail for the Gradient palette. To choose from a different gradient category, click the arrow on the palette and choose the category you want.

- **Style.** You get the same choices you do for the tool (for example, Linear, Diamond, and so on). In this case, you see only the name of the style. Choose a different style and it previews in the layer itself.

- **Angle.** This setting controls the direction the colors will run. Enter a number in degrees or spin the line in the circle by moving it with your mouse to change the direction of the flow.

- **Scale.** This setting determines how large your gradient is relative to the layer. 100 percent means they're the same size. If you choose 150 percent, for example, the gradient exceeds the size of your layer, which means you'll see only a portion of the gradient in the layer. For example, if you had a black-to-white gradient, you'd see only shades of gray in your image. If you turn off "Align with Layer," you can adjust the location of the gradient relative to your image. Just drag the gradient in your image.

- **Reverse.** Turn Reverse on to make colors flow in the opposite direction.

- **Dither.** Use this setting to create smooth color transitions.

- **Align with Layer.** This setting keeps the gradient in line with the layer. Turn it off, and you can pull the gradient around in your image to place it exactly where you want it.

When you've gotten the gradient looking the way you like, click OK to create your layer. You can edit it later by double-clicking the left icon for the layer in the Layers palette.

Editing a Gradient

The Elements Gradient Editor lets you create gradients that include any color combination you like. You can even make gradients in which the color fades to transparency, or you can modify existing gradients. For instance, you can easily make a two-color gradient where the fade is very one-sided, if you want a large plain area where you can put text (the plain area helps keep the text readable).

The Gradient Editor isn't the easiest tool in the world to use. This section will give you the basics you need to get started. Then, like much of Elements, a little bit of playing around with it will help you understand how the Gradient Editor works.

The Gradient tool must be active to launch the Gradient Editor. Click the Edit button in the Options bar to see the Gradient Editor (see Figure 13-19).

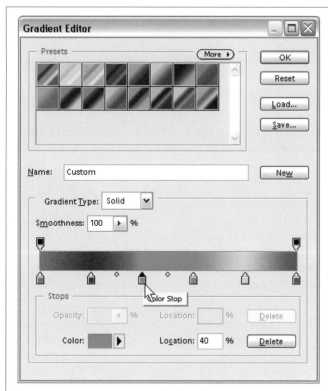

Figure 13-19:
The powerful and complex Gradient Editor. You won't see the little diamonds under the Gradient bar until you click a Color Stop (see the cursor) to edit a color. The black triangle on the Stop is another indication that it's the active Stop.

The Gradient Editor opens showing the currently selected gradient. You can choose a different gradient by picking from the thumbnails at the top of the Gradient Editor window, or by clicking the arrow to the right and choosing a new category from the list. You'll learn how to save your gradients later in the chapter.

Using the Gradient Editor

To get started using the Gradient Editor, first choose your gradient's type and smoothness settings:

- **Gradient Type.** Your choices are Solid or Noise. Solid gradients are the most common types of gradient; they let you create transitions between solid blocks of color. Noise gradients, which are covered later in this section, produce bands of color, as you might see in a spectrometer.

- **Smoothness.** This setting controls how even the transition appears between colors.

Most of the work you'll do in the Gradient Editor takes place in the *Gradient bar*, the long colored bar where your chosen gradient is displayed. The little boxes (also called *stops*) and diamonds surrounding the Gradient bar let you control the color and transparency of your gradient.

For now, you care only about the stops *beneath* the Gradient bar. Each is a Color Stop; it represents where a particular color falls in the gradient. You always need at least two Color Stops in a gradient.

If you click a stop, the pointed end turns black, letting you know that it's the active stop. Anything you do at this point is going to affect the area governed by that stop. You can slide the stops around to change where the colors change in your gradients. The Color Stops let you customize your gradient in lots of different ways. Using them, you can:

- **Change where the color transitions.** Click a Color Stop, and you see a tiny diamond appear under the bar. The diamond is the midpoint of the color change. Diamonds always appear between two Color Stops. You can drag the diamond in either direction to skew the color range between two Color Stops so that it more heavily represents one color over another. Wherever you place the diamond tells Elements the point at which the color change should be half completed.

- **Change one of the colors in the gradient.** Click any Color Stop and then click the color square (at the bottom of the Gradient Editor, in the Stops section) to bring up the Color Picker (page 196). Choose a new color, and the gradient automatically alters to reflect your change. You can also pick a new color by moving your cursor over the Gradient bar. The cursor turns to an eyedropper that lets you sample a color from the bar or from anywhere in your image.

- **Add a color to the gradient.** Click a Color Stop and then click again (not in the bar, but anywhere just beneath it) to indicate where you want the new color to appear. You see a new Color Stop where you clicked. Next, click the color-picking window to choose the color you want to add. The new color appears in the gradient at the new stop. Repeat as many times as you want, adding a new color each time.

- **Remove a color from a gradient.** If there's a gradient that's *almost* what you want but you don't like one of the colors, you don't have to live with it. You can remove a color by clicking its stop to make it the active color. Then click the Delete button to remove that color, or just drag its stop downward off the bar. The Delete button is grayed out if no Color Stop is active.

Transparency in gradients

You can also use the Gradient Editor to adjust the transparency in a gradient. Elements gives you nearly unlimited control over the transparency in your gradients and over the opacity of any color at any point in the gradient. Adjusting opacity in the Gradient Editor works very much like using the Color Stops to edit the colors. Instead of Color Stops, you use Opacity Stops.

> **NOTE** Transparency is particularly nice in images for Web use, but remember that you need to save in a format that supports transparency, like GIF, or you lose the transparency. If you save your file as a JPEG, the transparent areas become opaque white. See page 428 for more about file formats for the Web.

The Opacity Stops are the little boxes *above* the Gradient bar. You can move an Opacity Stop to wherever you want and then adjust the transparency by using the settings in the Stops section of the Gradient Editor. Click the Gradient bar wherever you want to add more Opacity Stops (click above the Gradient bar, rather than in it). The more Opacity Stops your Gradient bar has, the more points at which you can adjust your gradient's opacity.

Here's how to add an Opacity Stop and then adjust its opacity setting:

1. **Click one of the existing Opacity Stops.**

   If the little square on the stop is dark, it means the stop is completely opaque. A white square is totally transparent. The new stop will have the same opacity as the stop you click, but you can adjust the new stop once you've created it.

2. **Add a stop.**

   Click anywhere along the Gradient bar where you want to add a stop. If you want your gradient to be precisely positioned, you can enter numbers (indicating percent) in the Location box below the gradient bar. For example, 50 percent positions a stop at the midpoint of the Gradient bar.

3. **Adjust the new stop's opacity.**

Go to the Opacity box below the Gradient bar and either enter a percentage or click the arrow to the right of the number and move the slider to change the opacity setting. If you want to get rid of a stop, click its tab and press Delete.

By adding stops, you can make your gradient fade in and out, as shown in the background of Figure 13-20, which shows a simple vertical blue to transparent linear gradient that's been edited so that it fades in and out a few times.

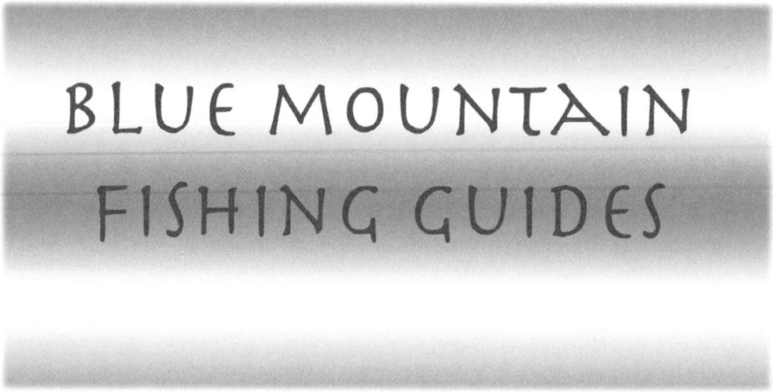

Figure 13-20:
You can make a gradient fade in and out like this background by adding more Opacity stops and reducing the opacity level of each stop.

Creating noise gradients

Elements also lets you create what Adobe calls *noise gradients*. A noise gradient isn't speckled (as you might expect if you're thinking of camera noise). Instead, noise gradients randomly distribute their colors within the range you specify, giving a banded or spectrometer-like effect to the gradient. The effect is interesting, but noise gradients can be a bit unpredictable. The noisier a gradient is, the more banding of the colors you'll see, and the greater the number of random colors.

You can create a noise gradient by clicking the More button on the Options bar gradient pop-out menu and selecting Noise Samples in the pop-out list of categories. Or you can click the Edit button to bring up the Gradient Editor and choose Noise as your Gradient Type.

Noise gradients have some special settings of their own in the Gradient Editor:

• **Roughness** controls the percent of noise in the gradient (see Figure 13-21).

• **Color Model** determines which color mode you work in—RGB or HSB. RGB gives you red, green, and blue color sliders, while HSB lets you set hue, saturation, and brightness (see page 199 for more information about these settings).

• **Restrict Colors** keeps your colors from getting too saturated.

• **Add Transparency** puts random amounts of transparency into your gradient.

- **Randomize.** Click this button to add random colors (and transparency if you turned on that checkbox). Keep clicking the Randomize button until you see an effect you like.

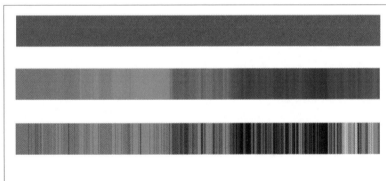

Figure 13-21:
The amount of noise in a gradient can make quite a difference in the effect you get.

Top: Here is a Solid gradient.

Middle: A gradient with the same colors and 50-percent noise.

Bottom: A gradient with the same colors and 90-percent noise.

Saving Gradients

After all that work, you'll probably want to save your gradient so you can use it again. To save a gradient, you have two options:

- **Click the New button in the Editor.** Enter a name for your new gradient in the Name box. Your gradient gets added to the current category. Elements creates a new preset gradient for you that's now available in the Gradient thumbnails.

- **Click Save.** The Save dialog box appears, and Elements asks you to name the gradient. You'll save the new gradients in a special Gradients folder, which Elements automatically takes you to in the Save dialog box. When you want to use the gradient again, click Load, and then select it from the list of gradients that appear.

  NOTE   You can also save and load gradients from the More menu on the Options bar Gradient pop-out menu.

Gradient Maps

Gradient Maps let you use gradients in nonlinear ways. In other words, instead of a rainbow that shades from one direction to another, in a Gradient Map, the gradient colors are substituted for the existing colors in your image. You can use Gradient Maps for funky special effects or for serious photo corrections.

What Elements does when you create a Gradient Map is map the brightness values of your image to a gradient (light to dark), and then replace the existing colors with the gradient you choose, using the lightness values as a guide for which color goes where.

That may sound complicated, but if you try it, you'll quickly see what's going on. Take a look at Figure 13-22, for instance. Applying a Gradient Map dramatically livens up this really dull photo, but that's not all Gradient Maps are good for. Gradients and Gradient Maps can also be valuable tools for straight retouching. See the box on page 373 for how to use gradients to fix the color in your photo.

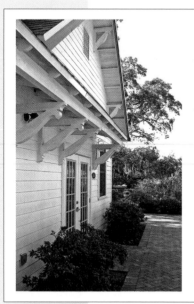 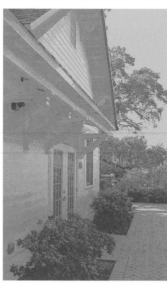

Figure 13-22:
Left: A boring shot with a totally blown-out sky.

Right: The image becomes something altogether different when you apply a Gradient Map adjustment.

You can apply a Gradient Map directly to your image by going to Filter → Adjustments → Gradient Map. But most times, you'll want to use a Gradient Map Adjustment layer, because it's easier to edit after you've created the layer. Here's how:

1. **Create a Gradient Map Adjustment layer.**

   Go to Layer → New Adjustment Layer → Gradient Map. You see the dialog box shown in Figure 13-23.

2. **Choose a gradient.**

   You'll see a gradient in the dialog box. The gradient color is based on your current Foreground/Background colors (see page 195). That's the map of the lightness/ darkness values that Elements has made for your image. If you want your image to show color, you need to choose a color gradient. Click the arrow at the right of the Gradient bar and choose a color gradient.

   The Dither setting adds a little random noise to make smoother transitions. The Reverse setting switches the direction the gradient is applied to the map. For example, if you chose a red-to-green gradient, reversing it would put green where it would have previously put red, and vice versa. It's worth giving this setting a try—you can get some very interesting effects.

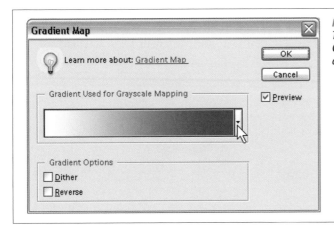

Figure 13-23:
The Gradient Map Adjustment layer dialog box. Clicking the drop-down menu shows you the available gradient patterns.

3. **Click OK when you're satisfied with the result.**

Elements automatically replaces the colors in your image with the equivalent values from the gradient you chose.

Remember, too, that you don't have to use your gradient in Normal mode. You can use any blend mode (page 153). You can spend hours playing around with the different effects you can get with the Gradient Map. Other filters and adjustments can produce unexpected results when used with it.

> **TIP**   Try Equalizing your image (Filter → Adjustments → Equalize) after applying a Gradient Map adjustment. The colors can shift quite dramatically. Equalize is a good thing to try if you find that your Gradient Map makes your image look dull or dingy. You may need to merge the layers (page 162) to get this command to work though, since you can't equalize an Adjustment layer. (See page 261 for more about the Equalize command.)

POWER USERS' CLINIC

Using Gradients for Color Correction

If your only interest in Elements is enhancing and correcting your photos, you may think that all this gradient business is a big waste of time. But keep in mind that gradients and Gradient Maps aren't just for introducing lurid colors into your photos. They're powerful tools to help you correct your photographs.

For instance, say you've got a photo where one side is much darker than the other. You may want to apply an Adjustment layer so it affects only the dark side of the image.

You can do this by bringing up the layer mask of the Adjustment layer (see page 274) and applying your gradient directly to the mask.

You can also use Gradient Map Adjustment layers in different blend modes to help balance out the colors in your photos, although you may need to use the Gradient Editor to play with the distribution of light and dark values to get the best effect.

Gradient maps are also useful for colorizing skin in black and white photos. Set up a gradient based on three or more skintones, and you can get a more realistic distribution of color tones than you could get by painting.

Type in Elements

If you want to add text to your images, Elements makes it easy. You can quickly create all kinds of fancy text to use on greeting cards, as newsletter headlines, or as graphics for Web pages.

Elements gives you lots of ways to jazz up your text: you can apply Layer styles, special effects, and gradients, or you can warp your type into psychedelic shapes. And the Type Mask tools let you fill individual letters with the contents of a photo. Best of all, most type tools let you change your text with just a few button clicks (see Figure 14-1). By the time you finish this chapter, you'll have learned about all the ways that Elements can add pizzazz to your text.

Adding Type to an Image

It's a cinch to add text to an image in Elements. Just select the Type tool, choose your font from the Options bar, and type away. The Type tool has a Toolbox icon that's easy to recognize: a capital T. Elements actually gives you four different type tools, all of which are hidden behind the Toolbox icon's pop-out menu: the Horizontal Type tool, the Vertical Type tool, the Horizontal Type Mask, and the Vertical Type Mask.

You'll learn about the Type Mask tools later in this chapter (see page 391). To get started, you'll focus on the regular Horizontal and Vertical Type tools. As their names imply, the Horizontal Type tool lets you enter type that runs left to right, while the Vertical Type tool is for creating type that runs down the page.

When you use the Type tools, Elements automatically puts your text on its own layer, which makes it easy to throw out your text and start over again later.

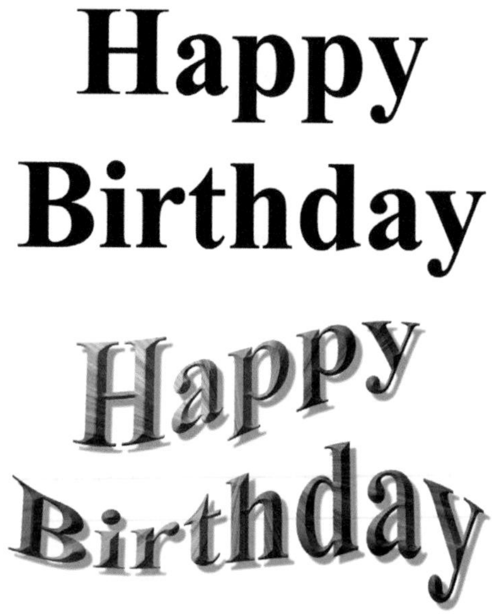

Happy Birthday

Figure 14-1:
With Elements, you can take basic type and turn it into the same kind of snazzy headlines you see on greeting cards and magazine covers. It took only a couple of clicks—a couple of Layer styles and some warping—to turn the plain black type (top) to the extravaganza below.

Happy Birthday

TROUBLESHOOTING MOMENT

Why Does the Type Tool Turn My Photo Red?

If your image gets covered with an ugly orange-red film every time you click it with the Type tool, you've got one of the Type Mask tools turned on. (Type Masks are useful when you want to create text that's cut from an image. They're covered later in this chapter, starting on page 391.)

To switch over to the regular Type tools, click the Type tool icon in the Elements Toolbox. Use the pop-out menu to select either of the regular Type tools (horizontal or vertical). Or you can click the correct icon in the Options bar. (If you're in doubt, hover your mouse over the icons to see labels describing each.)

Type Options

Whether you select the Horizontal or Vertical Type tool, the first thing you're going to want to do is take a look at the many settings available in the Options bar (Figure 14-2). These choices let you control pretty much every aspect of your type, including font selection, font color, and alignment.

Your choices from left to right are:

- **Tool Selection.** These buttons select which Type tool you want to use. From left to right, your choices are Horizontal Type, Vertical Type, Horizontal Type Mask, and Vertical Type Mask. Once you select one tool and click in your image, the other tools disappear. Go to the Toolbox icon's pop-out menu if you want to change your tool selection.

NOTE   If you choose the Vertical Type tool, your columns of type run from right to left (each time you start a new column) instead of left to right. If you want vertical type columns to run left to right, you need to put each column on its own layer and position them manually.

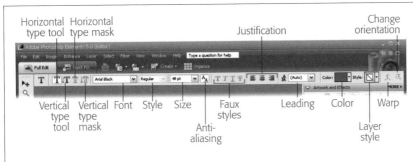

Figure 14-2:
The Type Options bar lets you control lots of different settings, most of which are pretty standard, like the font you want to use and the size of the letters. It's the choices toward the right end–like Warping and Layer style–where the fun begins.

- **Font.** Choose your font, listed here by name. Elements uses the fonts installed on your computer.

TIP   The font menu displays the font names in the actual fonts to make it easier for you to find the one you want. To see all the fonts, in the Options bar, click the down arrow to the right of the font name for a pop-out menu. You can also adjust the size of the preview samples by going to Edit → Preferences → Type.

- **Style.** Here's where you select the styles available for your font, like Bold or Italic.

- **Point Size.** This is where you choose how big your type should be. Text is traditionally measured in *points*. You can choose from the list of preset sizes in the pull-down menu or just type in the size you want. You aren't limited to the sizes shown in the menu—you can type in any number you want. See the box on page 382 for help understanding the relationship between points and actual size in Elements.

  If points make you nervous, you can change the type measurement unit to millimeters, pixels, or picas in Edit → Preferences → Units and Rulers.

- **Anti-aliasing.** This setting smoothes the edges of your type. Turn it on or off by clicking the little square with "AA" on it. Anti-aliasing is explained later, but usually you want it turned on.

- **Faux Styles.** Faux as in "fake." If your chosen font doesn't have a Bold, Italic, Underline, or Strikethrough version, you can tell Elements to simulate it here by clicking the appropriate icon. (This option isn't available for some fonts.)

- **Justification.** These buttons tell Elements how to align your text, just like in a word processor. If you enter multiple lines of type, here's where you tell Elements whether you want it lined up left, right, or centered (for horizontal type).

If you select the Vertical Type tool, you see squares of type that are aligned top, bottom, or middle.

- **Leading** (rhymes with "bedding"). This setting controls the amount of spacing between the lines of type, measured in points. For horizontal type, leading is the difference between the baselines (the bottom of the letters) on each line. For vertical type, leading is the distance from the center of one column to the center of the column next to it. Figure 14-3 demonstrates what a difference leading can make to the appearance of your text. The first setting you'll always see is Auto, which is Elements' guess about what looks best. You can change leading by choosing a number from the list or entering the amount you want (in points).

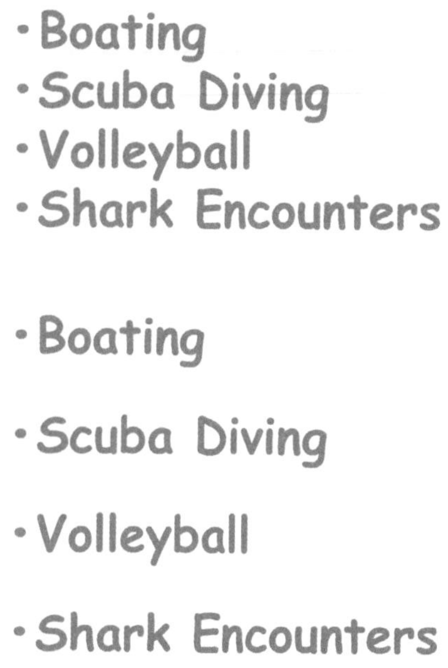

- Boating
- Scuba Diving
- Volleyball
- Shark Encounters

Figure 14-3:
Leading is the space between lines of type.

Top: Here, you can see a list with Auto leading.

Bottom: Here's one with the leading number set much higher. If you change the leading of vertical type, you change the space between the vertical columns of type, rather than the space between letters in an individual column. See the box on page 383 for how to tighten up the space between letters that are stacked vertically.

- Boating

- Scuba Diving

- Volleyball

- Shark Encounters

- **Color.** Click this square to set your text's color. Alternatively, click the arrow to the color square's right to bring up the Color Swatches (page 199). When you've made your selection, the Foreground color square (page 195) changes to show the new color.

NOTE   When the Type tool cursor is active in your image, you can't use the keyboard commands to reset Elements' standard colors (black and white) or to switch them. You'll need to click the relevant buttons in the Toolbox instead. (See page 195 for how to use the Toolbox's color-picking squares.)

- **Layer Style.** Layer styles (page 358) let you add funky visual effects to your type. First, enter some text and then, on the Options bar, click the Commit button (the green checkmark). Next, click the Layer style box and choose a style from the pop-out palette. If you want to remove a style that you've just applied, choose Remove Style from the More button/menu (on the upper-right corner of the Layer styles palette).

The next two choices are grayed out until you create some text for them to work on:

- **Warp.** The little T over a curved line hides a multitude of options for distorting your type in lots of interesting ways. There's more about this option on page 385. (The Warp Text command is also available from Layer → Type → Warp Text.)

- **Orientation.** This button changes your text from horizontal to vertical, or vice versa (you first need to type some text for this option to become active). You can also change type orientation by going to Layer → Type → Horizontal or Vertical.

These two choices don't show up at all until you've typed something:

- **Cancel.** When you add type to your image, the text automatically gets placed on its own layer. Click this button to delete this newly created text layer. This Cancel button works only if you click it before you click the Commit checkmark. To delete text after you've committed it, drag its layer to the Trash in the Layers palette.

- **Commit.** Click this green checkmark after you type on your image to tell Elements that yes, you want the text to remain as it appears. Committing your type gives you access to the other tools again.

If you see either of these buttons, you haven't committed your type, and many menu selections and other tools won't be available until you do. When you see the Cancel and Commit buttons in the Options bar, you're in what Elements calls "Edit mode," where you can make changes to your type, but most of the rest of Elements isn't available to you. Just click Commit or Cancel to get the rest of the program options back.

Creating Text

Now that you're familiar with the choices you've got in the Options bar, you're ready to start adding text to your image. You can add type to an existing image, or start by creating a new file (if you want to create type to use as a graphic by itself). To use either the Horizontal or Vertical Type tools, just follow these steps:

1. **Activate the Type tool.**

   Click the tool in the Toolbox or press T, and then select the Horizontal Type tool or the Vertical Type tool from the pop-out menu.

2. **Modify any settings you want to change on the Options bar.**

   See the list in the previous section for a run-down of your choices. You can make changes after you enter your type, too, so your choices aren't set in stone yet. Elements lets your type remain editable until you simplify the layer. (See page 164 for more about what simplifying a layer means.)

3. **Enter your text.**

   Click in your image where you'd like your text to go and then begin typing. The Type tools automatically create a new layer for your text. If you're using the Horizontal Type tool, the horizontal line you see is the baseline your letters sit on. If you're typing vertically, the vertical part of the cursor is the centerline of your character.

   Type the way you would in a word processor, using the Enter key to create a new line. If you want Elements to *wrap* your type (adjust it to fit a given space), drag a text box with the Type tool before you start typing. Otherwise, you need to make your returns manually. If you create a text box, you can resize it to adjust the type flow by dragging the handles after you finish typing. This won't work anymore after you simplify the layer.

   As noted earlier, if you want to use the Vertical Type tool, you can't make the columns of type run left to right. If you need multiple vertical columns of English language text, enter one column and then click the Commit button. Then start over again for the next column, so that each column is on its own layer.

4. **Use the Move tool if you don't like where the text is positioned.**

   Sometimes the text isn't placed exactly where you want it. The Move tool helps you reposition your text. If you need to move vertical type columns, wait until you've committed the type to rearrange the columns.

5. **If you like what you see, click the checkmark in the Options bar to commit the type.**

   When you commit your type, you tell Elements that you accept what you've created. The Type tool cursor is no longer active in your photo once you commit. If, on the other hand, you don't like what you typed, click the Cancel button in the Options bar, and the whole type layer goes away.

Once you've entered type, you can modify it using most of Elements editing tools—you can add Layer styles (page 358), move it with the Move tool (page 136), rotate it, make color adjustments, and so on.

> **TIP** If you try to paste text into Elements by copying it from your word processor, the results are unpredictable. Sometimes things work fine, but you may find the text comes in as one endlessly long line of words. If that happens, it's easier to type your text in Elements from scratch than to try to reformat the text.

Editing Type

In Elements, you can change your text after you've entered it, just like in a word processor. Elements lets you change not only words, but the font and its size, too, even if you've applied lots of Layer styles (see Figure 14-4). You modify text by highlighting it and making the correction or changing your settings in the Options bar.

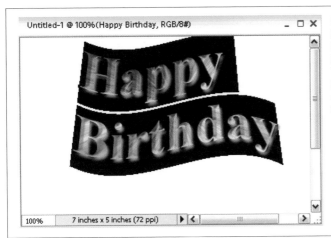

Untitled-1 @ 100%(Happy Birthday, RGB/8#)

100%   7 inches x 5 inches (72 ppi)

Figure 14-4:
*If you change your mind about what you want
to say, no problem. Here, the text is
highlighted so that the words can be changed.
The best part is that you can change the text to
say anything, and all the formatting stays
exactly the same. You can't do this after you
simplify a type layer, though.*

TIP   As mentioned earlier, you can see the font names in the menu displayed in the actual fonts themselves. Even better, Elements also gives you a quick way to preview what your actual text will look like in other fonts. First, select the text, and then click in the Font box in the Options bar. Use your mouse's scroll wheel (or up and down arrow keys) to run down the font list. You'll see your words appear in each font as you go down the list.

You can make all these changes as long as you don't *simplify* your type. Simplifying is the process of changing text from an easily editable vector shape to a rasterized graphic. In this respect, text works just like the shapes you learned about in Chapter 11 (see page 333): Once you simplify text, Elements doesn't see it as text anymore, just as a bunch of regular pixels. (Page 164 has more information about simplifying.)

You can either choose to simplify text yourself (by selecting Layer → Simplify Layer), or you can wait for Elements to prompt you to simplify, which it will do when you try to do things like apply a filter or add an effect to your type.

NOTE   Some text effects automatically simplify your text without asking first. So, make sure you've made all the edits you want to your text before using these effects.

How Resolution Affects Font Size

It's easy enough to pick the font size in the Text tool's Options bar. But you may find that what you thought would be big, bold, headline-size type is almost invisible on your image because it looks tiny. What gives?

In Elements, the actual size of text in your image is tied to the resolution of your image. So, if you thought that choosing 72-point type would give you a headline that's an inch high, it will, but only if the *resolution* of your file is also 72 pixels per inch (ppi). The more you increase the resolution, the smaller that same type is going to be. If you double the resolution to 144 ppi, your 72-point text prints half an inch high. If you triple it to 216 ppi, it's one-third of an inch high.

If you're working with high-resolution images, you have to increase the size of your fonts to allow for the extra pixel packing that comes from increased resolution.

It's not uncommon to have to choose sizes that are much higher than anything listed in the size menu in the Options bar. Don't be afraid of really big sizes if you need them—just keep entering larger numbers in the size box until the text looks right in proportion to your image.

Another thing that sometimes causes confusion is that you have to remember that Elements is creating the type based on the actual size of your image, not the view size. People often try to put very small type on a very big image and wonder why it looks so bad. If you aren't sure about the actual size of your document, try going to View → Print Size before typing. This view offers only an approximation, but it will help you get a better idea of what your text will look like.

Smoothing type: anti-aliasing

Anti-aliasing smoothes the edges of your type. It gets rid of the "jaggies" by blending the edge pixels on letters to make the outline look even, as shown in Figure 14-5. In Chapter 5 (page 117), you read about anti-aliasing for graphics; anti-aliasing has a similar effect on type.

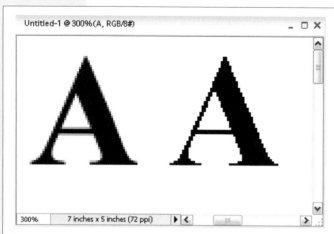

Figure 14-5:
An extremely close look at the same letter with and without anti-aliasing. The left letter A has anti-aliasing turned on, making the edges smooth. If you look at the letter A on the right, you can see how the edges are much more jagged and rough looking.

Elements always starts you off with anti-aliasing turned on, and 99 percent of the time you'll want to keep it on. The main reason to turn it off is to avoid *fringing*—a line of unwanted pixels that make it look like the text was cut out from an image with a colored background.

You turn anti-aliasing on and off by clicking the Anti-aliasing button (the two As) in the Options bar. The button shows a dark outline when anti-aliasing is on. You can also turn anti-aliasing off and on by going to Layer → Type → Anti-Alias Off or Anti-Alias On. Once you simplify type, you can't change the anti-aliasing setting for the type.

> **TIP**   If you're seeing really jagged type even with anti-aliasing turned on, check your resolution. Type often looks poor at low resolution settings—just as photos do. See page 82 for more about resolution.

WORKAROUND WORKSHOP

Using Asian Text Options to Control Text Spacing

Getting letters spaced correctly when using the Vertical Type tool can be tough. Elements lets you set the *leading*, but with vertical type, your leading setting affects the spacing between *columns* of letters, not the spacing of the letters within a column.

Also, sometimes you may want to adjust the spacing between letters written in horizontal text. Elements lets you make either of these fixes, but you need to use the Asian Text Options, even if you're writing in English.

To get started, go to Edit → Preferences → Type and turn on the checkbox for Show Asian Text Options. Then, the next time you click in an image with the Type tool, you'll see an Asian character in the Options bar, just to the left of the Cancel button.

Click the symbol for a pop-out menu with three options: *tate-chuu-yoko, mojikumi,* and a pull-down menu with percentages on it. You want the pull-down menu, which is for *tsume*. Tsume reduces the amount of space around the characters or letters you apply it to.

To apply tsume, just highlight the characters you want to change and select a percentage from the pull-down menu. The higher the percentage, the tighter the spacing becomes.

You can select a single letter or a whole word for tsume. Since it reduces the space all the way around each letter you apply it to, you can use it for either vertical or horizontal text, although for horizontal type, you'd be most likely to use it to tidy up the spacing of just one or two letters. For vertical type, tsume is a great way to tighten up the vertical spacing of your text.

Warping Type

With Elements, you can warp the shape of your type in all sorts of fun ways. You can make it wave like a flag, bulge out, twist like a fish, arc up or down, and lots more. These complex effects are really easy, too, and best of all, you can still edit the type once you've applied the effects. Figure 14-6 shows just a few examples of what you can do. If you add a Layer style (explained on page 358), warps are even more effective.

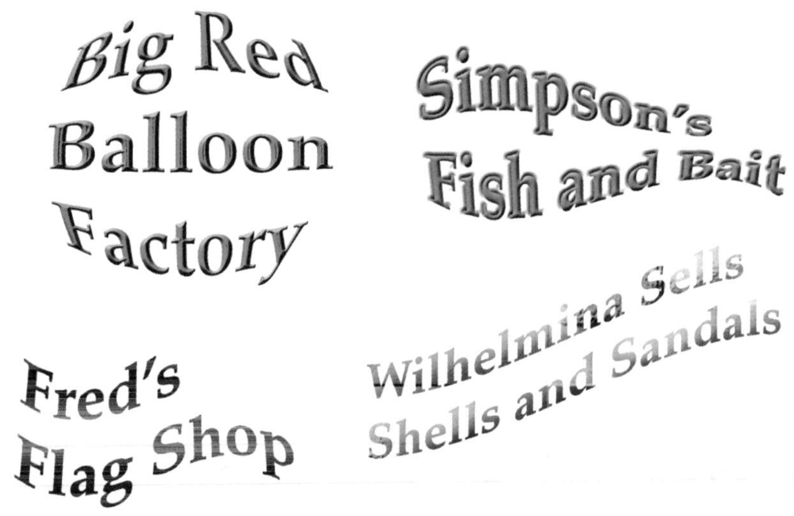

Big Red Balloon Factory

Simpson's Fish and Bait

Fred's Flag Shop

Wilhelmina Sells Shells and Sandals

Figure 14-6:
Elements gives you oodles of ways to warp your type. Here are just a few of the basic warps, applied using their standard settings.

Clockwise from the upper left: Inflate, Fish, Rise, and Flag. You can tweak these effects endlessly using the sliders in the Warp dialog box. (These examples also have Layer styles applied to them.)

To warp your type, follow these steps:

1. **Enter the text you want.**

   Use the Move tool (page 136) to reposition your text if necessary.

2. **Select the text you want to warp.**

   Make sure the Text layer is the active layer, or you won't be able to select what you typed. Click the Text layer in the Layers palette if it's not already highlighted there.

3. **Click the Create Warped Text button in the Options bar.**

   It's the T with a curved line under it. The Warp Text dialog box, shown in Figure 14-7, appears.

4. **Tell Elements how to warp your text.**

   Select a warp style from the pull-down list. Next, make any changes you want to the sliders or the horizontal/vertical orientation of the warp. Tweaking these settings can radically alter the effect. Push the sliders around to experiment. You can preview the results right in your image. Your choices are described in more detail in the next section.

5. **When you come up with something you like, click OK.**

   NOTE   You can't warp type that has the Faux Bold style applied to it. If you forget and try to do so, Elements politely reminds you. The program even offers to remove the style and continue with your warp.

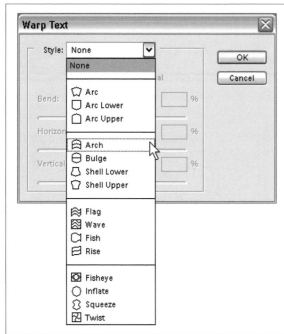

Figure 14-7:
As you see, you have a lot of choices for how to warp your text. Once you choose a warp style, you see sliders in the dialog box that you can use to further customize the effect.

Elements gives you lots of different warp styles to choose from, and you can customize the look of each style by using the settings in the Warp Text dialog box, described in the next section.

The Warp Text Dialog Box

The little dialog box that comes up when you click the Create Warped Text button is pretty straightforward. Your setting choices are:

- **Warp Style.** This is where you choose your warp style: Arc, Flag, and so on. To help you choose a style, Elements gives you thumbnail icons demonstrating the general shape of each warp.

- **Horizontal/Vertical.** These radio buttons control the orientation of the warping. Most of the time, you'll want to leave the button the same as the text's orientation, but you can get interesting effects by warping the opposite way.

  A vertical warp on horizontal text gives more of a perspective effect, like the text is moving towards you or away from you. You can get some very funky effects by putting a horizontal warp on vertical text.

- **Bend.** This is where you tell Elements how much of an arc you want. If you want to change the arc from Element's standard setting, type a percentage in the box or just move the slider until you get what you want. A higher positive percentage makes a bigger warp. A negative number makes your text warp in the opposite direction. For example, if you want an inverted arc, choose the Arc style and move the slider into the negative region.

- **Horizontal/Vertical Distortion.** These settings control how much your text warps in the horizontal or vertical plane. Moving the sliders gives you a very high degree of control over just how and where your text warps. They work pretty much the same way as the Bend setting—type a negative or positive percentage or move the sliders.

The best way to find the look you want is to experiment. It's lots of fun, especially if you apply a Layer style first (page 358) to give your type a 3-D look before warping it.

> **TIP** Many of the Warps look best on two lines of type, so that the lines bend in opposite directions. However, you can also get very interesting effects by putting two lines of type on separate layers and applying a different warp to each.

To edit your warp after it's done, double-click the Warp thumbnail icon in the Layers palette. Doing that automatically makes the text layer active and highlights the text. Then, click the Warp icon in the Options bar again. The Warp dialog box opens and shows your current settings. Make any changes you want or set the style to None to get rid of it.

> **TIP** Elements gives you helpful step-by-step instructions for warping text in the How To palette. Go to Window → How To if the palette isn't already in the Palette bin, and click the flippy triangle next to "Working with Text." Then choose Warping Text.

Adding Special Effects

Besides warping your type, you can apply all kinds of Layer styles, filters, and special Text effects to give your text a more elaborate appearance. You can change your text's color, make it look 3-D, add brushstrokes for a painted effect, and so on. (There's more about Layer styles, filters, and effects in Chapter 13.)

Elements gives you lots of different ways to add special effects to your text. The following sections show you three of the most interesting: applying the Text effects, using a gradient to make rainbow-colored type, and using the Liquify filter to warp your text in truly odd ways.

Text Effects

The Artwork and Effects palette contains an entire category dedicated to special Text effects (Figure 14-8). You apply Text effects just the way you would apply any other effect—make the type layer active and double-click the effect you want.

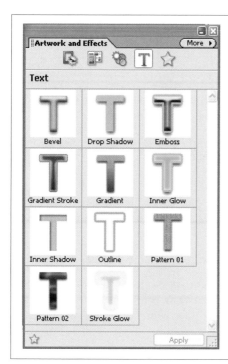

Figure 14-8:
The Artwork and Effects palette includes an entire section for Type effects. Some, like Pattern 02, are unique to this section. Others, like the Bevel and Drop Shadow, are just shortcuts for effects you could also achieve using Layer styles.

If you already have Layer styles on your text, it's hard to predict how much the effects will respect the Layer styles. Some effects build onto the changes you've previously made with Layer styles; most undo anything you've done before. Experimenting is the best way to find out what happens when you combine Layer styles and effects.

Type Gradients

Gradient patterns fill your text with a spectrum of color. The simplest way to get these rainbow effects is to apply one of the Layer styles or Type effects that include a gradient. On the other hand, these features give you no control over the colors or direction of the gradient. If you have a specific look in mind, you may have to start from scratch and do it yourself.

The easiest way is to start with a Type Mask, as explained on page 391. But if you already have some existing text, as long as it's not yet simplified, you can easily fill it with a gradient.

NOTE   A heavier, chunky font shows off your rainbow better than a thin, spidery one. Fonts with names that end in Extended, Black, or Extra Bold are good, like Arial Black or Rockwell Extra Bold.

First, make sure you've got some text in your image, and then follow these steps:

1. **Create a new layer for your gradient. Make sure it's directly above your text layer in the Layers palette.**

    You're going to group the two layers, which is why they need to be next to each other. To create the new layer, press Ctrl+Shift+N or go to Layer → New → Layer. In the New Layer dialog box, turn on "Group with Previous Layer."

    Look at the Layers palette to be sure the new layer is the active layer. If it isn't, give it a click in the Layers palette to highlight it.

2. **Activate the Gradient tool.**

    Click the Gradient tool in the Toolbox and choose a gradient style in the Options bar. (See page 362 for more about how to select, modify, and apply gradients.)

3. **Drag across your new layer in the direction you want the gradient to run.**

    Because the layers are grouped, the gradient appears only in your type. If you don't like the effect, press Ctrl+Z and drag again until you like what you see. That's all you have to do, except of course, save your work if you want to keep it.

Applying the Liquify Filter to Type

The Warp Text button in the Options bar (explained earlier, on page 383) gives you lots of ways to reshape your type. But there's an even more powerful way to warp type: the Liquify filter (see Figure 14-9).

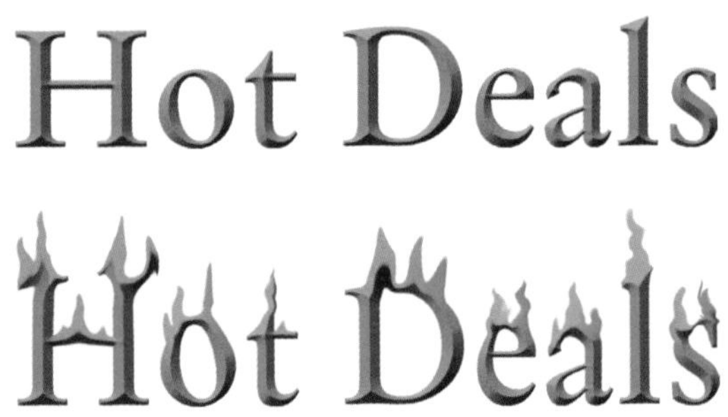

Figure 14-9:
The Liquify filter can reshape text in many different ways, including adding a flame-like effect (shown here), making letters twirl around on themselves, or making text undulate like it's underwater.

Top: Text with a bevel Layer style applied.

Bottom: Use the Liquify filter's Warp tool to pull these little "flames" from the text.

TIP   You can actually use the Liquify filter to warp anything in an image—not just text. Use it to alter objects in photographs and drawings, for example. Fix someone's nose, make your brother look like E.T., give a scene a watery reflection, and so on.

To use the Liquify filter, you first need to simplify the layer your text is on (Layer → Simplify Layer or just click OK when the Liquify filter asks if you want to simplify). (Remember, you can no longer edit your text once you simplify it.) Then, call up the Liquify filter dialog box by going to Filter → Distort → Liquify. You can also get to it by double-clicking the Liquify filter thumbnail in the Distort section of the filters in the Artwork and Effects palette.

You see yet another large Elements dialog box. Like most of them, it's fairly straightforward once you learn your way around it. In the upper-left corner of the Liquify dialog box is a little Toolbox with some very special tools in it (see Figure 14-10).

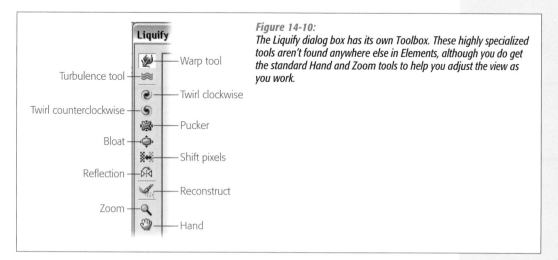

Figure 14-10:
The Liquify dialog box has its own Toolbox. These highly specialized tools aren't found anywhere else in Elements, although you do get the standard Hand and Zoom tools to help you adjust the view as you work.

From top to bottom they are:

- **Warp tool.** This lets you push the pixels of your image in whichever direction you want, although it usually takes a fair amount of coaxing to create much of an effect.

- **Turbulence tool.** You can use the Turbulence tool to create clouds and waves. This tool is very dependent on the Turbulent Jitter setting on the right side of the window (explained later). A higher number creates a smoother effect.

- **Twirl Clockwise.** Hold this tool down on your image, and the pixels under your cursor spin in a clockwise direction. The longer you apply this tool, the more extreme the spin effect.

- **Twirl Counterclockwise.** The opposite of the Twirl Clockwise tool. It makes the pixels under the cursor spin counterclockwise.

- **Pucker.** This tool makes the pixels under the cursor move toward the center of the brush.

- **Bloat.** The opposite of the Pucker tool. It makes pixels move *away* from the center of the brush.

- **Shift Pixels.** The pixels you drag this tool over move perpendicularly in relation to the direction of your stroke. For example, if you drag from the top of an image in a straight line down, the pixels you pass over will move to the right. Alt+drag to change the direction of the shift.

- **Reflection.** Drag to create a reflection of the area the tool passes over. Overlapping strokes create a watery effect.

- **Reconstruct.** Pass this wonderful tool over areas where you've gone too far, and you selectively return them to their original condition without wrecking the rest of your changes.

- **Zoom and Hand tools.** These are the same Zoom (page 79) and Hand (page 80) tools you find elsewhere in Elements.

Your image appears in the preview window in the center of the dialog box. You can adjust the view with the Zoom tool or by using the magnification menu in the lower-left corner of the image area.

> **TIP**   It often helps to zoom in very closely when using the Liquify filter. If you've added text to a large image, select the text with the Marquee tool (page 113) before activating the Liquify filter. Then you'll see only the selected area in the filter preview, which makes it easier to get a high zoom level.

At the right side of the dialog box are the Tool Options settings:

- **Brush Size.** You can enter a number as low as 1 pixel or as large as 600 in the space provided.

- **Brush Pressure.** This is how much the brush affects the pixels you drag over. The range is from one to 100. The higher the pressure, the stronger the effect of the brush. If you're using a graphics tablet, turn on Stylus Pressure so that the harder you press, the more effect you get.

- **Turbulent Jitter.** This controls how smooth your changes look. The higher the number, the smoother the effect you get from your changes.

To use the filter, just pick your tool, modify your Tool Options (if you want), and then drag across your image. This is a very processor-intense filter, so there may be a fair amount of lag time before you see results, especially if your computer's slow. Give the filter time to work.

There's a Revert button, which returns your image to its original condition before you started using the Liquify filter. You can also Alt+click the Cancel button to turn it to a Reset button (which resets the tool settings as well as your photo). When you like what you see in the preview, click OK and wait a few seconds while Elements applies your transformations. Then you're done.

Type Masks: Setting an Image in Type

So far in this chapter, you've been reading about how to create regular type and how to glam it up by applying Layer styles and effects. But in Elements, you can also create type by filling letters with the contents of a photo, as shown in Figure 14-11. (You'll find gourds.jpg, the photo used as the basis for Figures 14-11 and 14-13, on the "Missing CD" page at *www.missingmanuals.com*.)

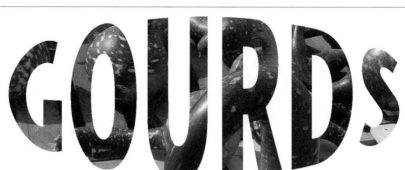

Figure 14-11:
By using the Type Mask tools, you can create type that's made from an image. You can also use the Type Mask tools to emboss type into your photo. See Figure 14-13.

The Type Mask tools work by making a selection in the shape of your letters. Essentially, you're creating a kind of stencil that you'll place on top of your image.

Once you've used the Type Mask to create your text-shaped selections, you can perform all sorts of neat modifications to your text. You can emboss type into your image (which makes it looks like it's been stamped into your image); you can apply a stroke to the outline of your text (useful if your font doesn't have a built-in out-line option); or you can copy and move your text to another document entirely.

Using the Type Mask Tools

The following steps show you how to create a Type Mask and lay it over an image so that the letters you create are filled with whatever's in your image:

1. **Open the image that you want to use as your source for creating the text.**

2. **Activate the Type Mask tool.**

   Click the Type tool in the Toolbox or press T. Select the Type Mask tool you want—horizontal or vertical. (Use the pop-out menu or click the icon in the Options bar.) The Type Mask tools behave just like the regular Type tools—a horizontal mask goes across the page, a vertical mask goes up and down.

3. **Click your image and start typing.**

   When you click, a red film covers your entire image. The red indicates the area that *won't* be part of your letters. By typing, you're going to cut a visible selection through the red area (see Chapter 5 if you need a refresher on selections).

When you type, instead of creating regular type, you're creating a type-shaped selection. You can see the shape of the selection as you go.

It's important to choose a very blocky font for the type mask, since you can't see much of the image if you use thin or small type.

It's hard to reposition your words once you've committed them, so take a good look at what you've got. While the mask is active, you can move the mask by dragging it, as explained in Figure 14-12.

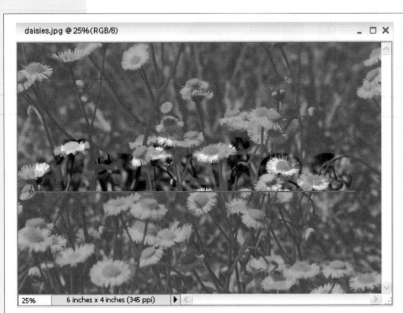

daisies.jpg @ 25%(RGB/8)

25%   6 inches x 4 inches (345 ppi)

Figure 14-12:
Once you've activated the Type Mask tool and clicked on your image, you'll see a red mask appear across your picture. As you start typing, your text appears, as shown here. To move a selection made with the Type Mask tool, hold down Ctrl, and then you can easily drag your selection around in your image as long as you haven't committed it yet.

4. **Don't click the Commit button until you're satisfied with what you have.**

   Once you click the Commit button (the checkmark icon on the right side of the Options bar), you can't alter your type as easily as you can with the regular Type tool. That's because the regular tools create their own layers, while the Type Mask tools just create selections. Once you commit, your type is just like any other selection—Elements doesn't see it as type anymore, so you can no longer change the size by highlighting the text and picking a different size, for example.

5. **When you're happy with your selection, finish by clicking the Commit button.**

   Once you click the Commit button, you see the outline of your type as an active selection. You can move the selection outline by nudging it with the arrow keys.

6. **Remove the non-text portion of your image.**

   Go to Select → Inverse and press Backspace to remove the rest of the image. Alternatively, you could copy and paste the selection into another document.

Figure 14-13 shows the effect of pressing Ctrl+J and placing a Type Mask selection on a duplicate layer of its own, and then adding Layer styles (page 358) to the new layer.

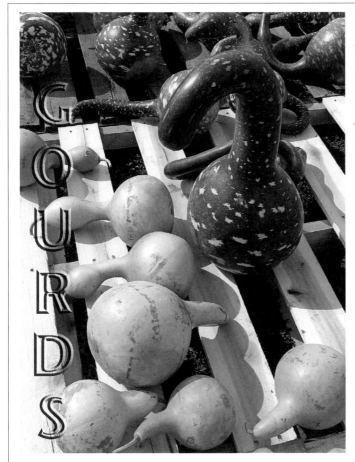

Figure 14-13:
By copying text to another layer, you can bevel or emboss it into your photo. Notice that this photo shows what you need to watch out for–the G is kind of hard to see because it blends right into the image. You may need to place your text a few times before you get it positioned correctly. Or you could also add a colored outline to make it stand out more, as described below.

Creating Outlined Type

If the font you're using doesn't come with a built-in outline style, there's no quick option for creating outlined type in Elements (the way you can in Microsoft Word, for example). By using the Type Mask tools, though, you can create outlined text quite easily.

To make a text outline like the one shown in Figure 14-14:

1. **Open your image or create a new one (if you just want the type by itself). Activate the Type Mask tool of your choice.**

   Click the Type tool or press T. Then select either of the Type Mask tools.

2. **Choose your font and size.**

Use the settings in the Options bar. Outlined type works better with a fairly heavy font rather than a slender one. Bold fonts also work well here, rather than regular fonts.

3. **Enter your type.**

Type in your image where you want the text to go. If you want to warp your type, do it now, before you commit the type.

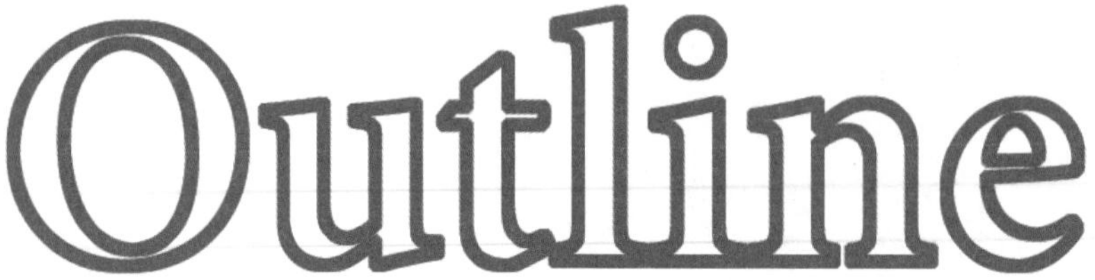

Figure 14-14:
By using the Type Mask tools, you can create outline type almost as quickly as ordinary type.

4. **Click the Commit button (the checkmark).**

Be sure you like what you've got before you do, because once you commit the text, it changes to a selection that's hard to edit. If you'd rather start over, click the Cancel button (the No symbol) instead.

5. **Add a stroke to your outline.**

Be sure the type selection is active, and then go to Edit → Stroke (Outline) Selection. Choose a line width in pixels and the color you want, and then click OK. (There's more about your choices in this dialog box on page 338.) Your selection is now a linear outline of the text you typed.

5

Part Five:
Sharing Your Images

Creating Projects

If you make scrapbooks, photo albums, and other crafty projects, Elements 5 was made for you. You can create the projects of your dreams without using—or buying—any other software. Elements 5 is crammed with all kinds of graphics, frames, and other special effects you can use in your projects. For the first time, too, it's easy to create multiple page documents with Elements.

You put together these projects using the new Photo Creations feature. Once you learn the steps for Photo Layouts in the first section, you can make any Elements project, since the basic method is the same for all Photo Creations. This chapter describes the features unique to each type of project. In addition, you'll learn how to create photo books and calendars using Kodak EasyShare, Adobe's online photo-printing partner.

> **NOTE**   You can also create Photo galleries (photo-filled Web pages) and slideshows in Elements. You can learn about those projects in Chapters 17 and 18.

Photo Layouts

Elements 5 gives you new wizards to help create fancy pages featuring your photos, which you can then share either by printing or as digital files. Although Elements gives you lots of preset layouts to start from, you can customize every aspect of these layouts to create projects that are totally your own.

A Photo Layout is a page displaying one or more of your photos, with or without a themed background. (Flip ahead to Figure 15-3 to get a glimpse of what Elements can help you do.) Elements' wizards all start you off with one or more suggested photo placeholders, but you can add or remove photos at will. You can also change the background, frame styles, and other details.

To create a Photo Layout:

1. **In the Organizer, select the photos you want to include.**

   Actually, you don't have to preselect your photos, since you'll have a chance to add or change photos once your project's begun. You can also start with open photos in the Editor, but that way takes a little more work. Or, you can start without choosing any photos.

   NOTE Photo Layouts, like all the printable projects on the Create menu, start off at a resolution of 220 ppi. That's perfectly fine for most people's taste. But if you want a higher resolution, your best bet is to cook up your own project from scratch, since increasing the resolution of a prebuilt Elements project often throws the layout out of whack.

2. **Go to Create → Photo Layout.**

   The window shown in Figure 15-1 appears.

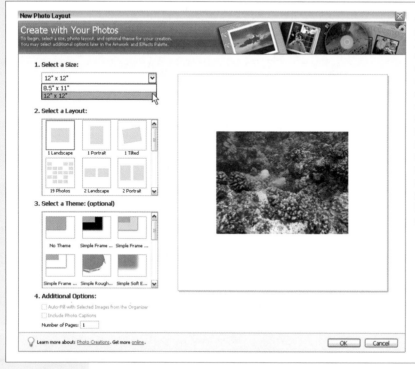

Figure 15-1:
If you like to scrapbook, you'll be pleased to see Elements' 12"×12" Photo Layout page size option. Every change you make in this dialog box (except for the items controlled by the checkboxes at bottom) is reflected in the preview area on the right. (If your computer doesn't have a lot of horsepower, Elements may take a while to update things after you click.)

3. **Choose your page size from the Select a Size pull-down menu.**

   Then, from the Select a Layout box, pick a general layout for the number of photos you want. The preview on the right side of the window changes to show your current choice.

   NOTE If you've already selected photos in the Organizer, you won't see them until the next window.

4. **From the Select a Theme box, if you want, choose a theme.**

   Themes give you coordinated backgrounds and frames for your photos. Investigate the different themes, even if none of them particularly appeal to you at first. The frames in these themes have some wonderful photo effects—fades, black and white, ragged cutouts, old photos, and so on. You can always choose a different background later if you don't like the one that goes with the frames.

5. **Choose from the Additional Options, if desired.**

   If you leave "Auto-Fill with Selected Images from the Organizer" turned on, the pictures you chose in the Organizer automatically appear in your layout when Elements creates it. (The checkboxes are grayed out if you didn't select any photos. If you selected photos and you don't actually want them in your layout, turn it off.)

   There's also a checkbox for having captions you've added to your photos appear in the layout. (You can add or edit the captions later, so you're not tied to what's in the Caption field.)

   If you selected some photos before you started, the Number of Pages box tells you how many pages long your creation will be. This number updates to reflect your current Layout choice. So, for example, if you select three photos in the Organizer and choose a single photo per page, the number of pages is three. If you click a layout that uses three photos per page, the number of pages changes to one. (If you haven't selected any photos yet, you can specify how many pages you want by typing a number.)

6. **When you've made all your choices, click OK.**

   Elements zips over to the Editor and gets to work creating your layout. You may have to wait several seconds. (If you watch the Layers palette, you can see how busy the program is.) If you preselected photos and left Auto-Fill turned on, Elements puts your photos right into the frames for you. If you didn't start from a photo, you see "Click here to add photo or Drag photo here." That's fine, because you can add photos in the next step.

7. **Adjust your photos.**

   If you haven't already picked photos for your project, click a frame and then choose a photo from the dialog box that appears. Or, if you have photos open in the Editor, drag them from the Photo bin right into a frame.

Regardless of how you get your photos into the layout, you can make a number of adjustments to them once they're in. Double-click any photo and you see the controls shown in Figure 15-2, which let you make a number of different changes to your photo. Click the green checkmark to apply your changes, or the red Cancel button to get rid of them. (These controls change only your photo, not the frame itself. For that, use the Move tool, as described in the next step.)

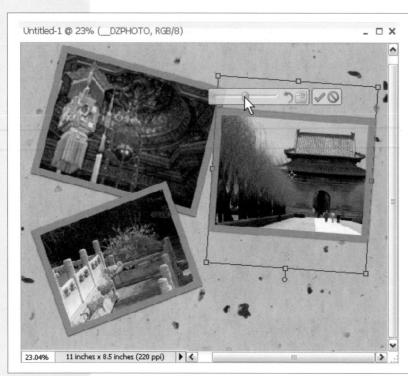

Untitled-1 @ 23% (__DZPHOTO, RGB/8)

23.04%   11 inches x 8.5 inches (220 ppi)

Figure 15-2:
When you double-click a photo, you get controls for adjusting it. To resize your picture, move the slider to the left (smaller) or right (larger). You can rotate your photo by clicking the curved blue arrow, or click the folder icon to choose a different photo. You can also drag a corner to scale your photo or do a manual rotation.

TIP   You can also change the frame style by clicking a photo, then choosing a new style from the Artwork and Effects palette (page 23). Just double-click the new style and drag it to the photo, or click it once and then click Apply. The frames wrap around your photo automatically so you don't have to do any juggling in the layer stack.

8. **Customize your layout.**

Here's the fun part. You can change your layout using any Elements tool you want. Use the Move tool (page 136) to drag your photos into different positions. Apply Effects or Layer Styles (page 358), or drag in art from the Artwork and Effects palette. These graphics are vector images (page 333), which means they'll look great no matter how big or small you resize them. You can also add text to your layout (Chapter 14). You can change the background by selecting a new one in the Artwork and Effects palette (see the box on page 402). You can even flatten your image and use filters on the entire page, as shown in Figure 15-3.

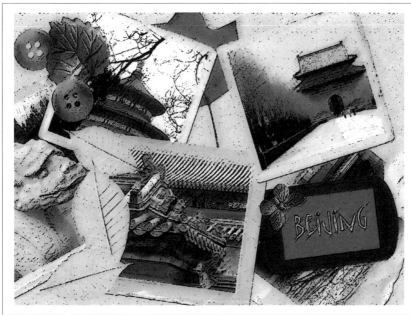

Figure 15-3:
This collage was created in the Photo Layout page. Except for the photos themselves, all the additional artwork came from the Artwork and Effects palette. Some of the frames automatically create a black and white photo, as you see here. To get this hand-painted appearance, the whole layout was flattened, and then the Poster Edges and Watercolor filters (page 515) were applied.

9. **Save your layout.**

   When you're done, press Ctrl+S to name your layout and save it. You can save it in any standard file format, but if you want it to behave like a Photo Layout the next time you open it, leave the format as PSE, which is a special format just for Photo Creations.

There's almost no limit to what you can do in a Photo Layout. Anything you've read in the other chapters of this book works here, too. Plus, here are a few special things you can do with photos in a layout:

- **Remove a photo from your layout.** Right-click and choose Clear Photo. To remove the photo's placeholder and frame as well, choose Clear Frame.

- **Make your photo appear without a frame.** Right-click and choose Clear Frame.

- **Resize a Frame.** You can use the Move tool (page 136) to resize a frame, either before or after you put a photo into it. Resizing after adding a photo is a two-step process, though: First, use the Move tool to resize the frame. Then, click the photo itself to bring back the photo controls (Figure 15-2) so you can adjust it, too, if necessary.

- **Resize the frame to fit the photo.** If you want to make the frame fit the photo, instead of the other way around (as explained in step 4 on page 399), right-click and choose "Fit Frame to Photo."

- **Change your theme.** If you create a Photo Layout and then wish you'd gone with a different theme, click the New Theme button at the top of the Artwork and Effects palette (it's the second from the left). Elements presents all the possible themes for your particular Photo Creation. Double-click a thumbnail and then drag the new theme to your photo, or click the thumbnail once and then click Apply. Presto—you've got your existing layout with new frames and background.

- **Edit the Layer style of a Frame.** In the Layers palette, most of the frames have a Layer style icon. Double-click the icon to edit things like the size of the drop shadow on the frame. (See page 360 for more about editing Layer styles.)

What's more, you can add and delete pages from Photo Layouts, as the next section explains.

POWER USERS' CLINIC

Smart Objects

Smart Objects are one of the ways Adobe made Elements 5 projects so fun and easy. Like their big-shot cousins in the full version of Photoshop, these objects seem to know where they are and what you're trying to do—and behave accordingly. Here are some of the things that make Smart Objects so smart:

- When you apply a new background from the Artwork and Effects palette, it immediately zooms down to the bottom of the layer stack to replace the existing background, without any assistance from you.

- Similarly, the frames in the Artwork section of the palette automatically target your photos. (This behavior can be a little quirky, though, and you may find that your frames aren't so smart if you try to apply them to a layered photo. Instead, they just sit there and wait for you to help them out by placing the photo inside them.)

- You can scale, resize, and transform or distort objects from the Artwork section of the palette as much as you want without affecting the image quality. This behavior is something like how vector art works, but what's going on under the hood is quite a bit different. (The preview may appear pixelated if you hugely resize a graphic, but the actual object should be okay once you click the green checkmark.)

By the way, if you've used Photoshop CS2, you'll find that Smart Objects in Elements don't do nearly as many interesting things as they do in the full version of Photoshop. You can't create linked objects, for instance, where painting on one makes your painting appear on all of them. In fact, if you try to paint on a Smart Object in Elements, you just get the dialog box shown in Figure 15-4.

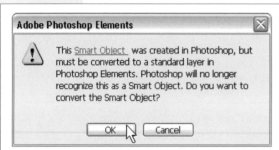

Figure 15-4:
You can enlarge, reduce, transform, and distort Smart Objects, but if you try to paint on them, or to apply filters or effects, you get this message. It's fine to click OK, but once you do, your formerly Smart Object will behave like any other object. (You can't increase its size to more than 100 percent, for instance, or it'll go all pixely on you.)

TIP   You can apply artwork from the Artwork and Effects palette to any image, not just those in Photo Layouts and other Create projects.

Creating Multi-Page Documents

In Elements 5—*finally*—you can create a file that's more than one page long. Photo Layouts automatically start with as many pages as needed to hold all your preselected photos, but you can add and remove pages from a layout anytime. (You can also add pages to any Elements file, not just to the Create projects.)

The size and resolution of your existing page determines the size and resolution of pages you add. In other words, if you have a 3"×5" photo and you add a page to it, you get a 3"×5" page. If you want to add a letter-sized page to a small photo file, you must first add canvas to the photo (page 89) or resize it. (But check page 88 to see why resizing probably won't work.)

To add a new page to your document, go to the Editor's Edit menu and choose one of the following commands:

- **Add Blank Page.** Creates a new, totally empty page with the same dimensions and resolution as your existing page.

- **Add Page Using Current Layout.** When you choose this option, Elements creates a page that's exactly like the current state of your existing page, including any changes you've made. Instead of photos, there are placeholders for you to fill in. So, for example, if you've changed frame styles and dragged a photo to another position, the new frame and positioning (without the photo) appears in your new page. Any graphics you've added from the Graphics section of the Artwork and Effects palette show up as well. This option is a big help when you're making photo books or scrapbooks.

You can navigate through all of the pages in your document using the Photo bin, as shown in Figure 15-5. If you decide you've got too many pages, go to Edit → Delete Current Page, and the currently active page is history.

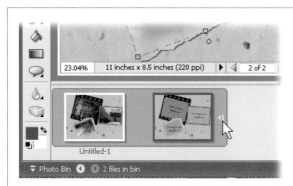

Figure 15-5:
You can expand and collapse the pages of your file so it doesn't hog all the visible space in the Photo bin. Just click the arrow (where the cursor is) to collapse your document into a single item. Collapsed multi-page documents have a special outline in the bin to make them easy to recognize.

No matter what kind of file you start with—whether it's from the Create menu or just a regular JPEG—you must save your file as a PSE format file if you add pages to it. Elements reminds you with the dialog box in Figure 15-6. While it's very, very nice to be able to create multi-page documents in Elements, the PSE format has some drawbacks, too, as explained in the box below.

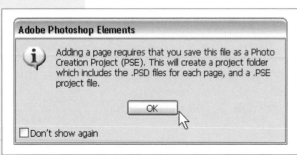

Figure 15-6:
You can't save a document with multiple pages in common file formats like TIFF or PSD. Your only option is PSE, as this dialog box reminds you every time you add a second page to any document. See the box below to learn why PSE is a mixed blessing.

TROUBLESHOOTING MOMENT

About PSE Files

Anytime you create a multipage document in Elements 5, you get one file format choice when it's time to save—PSE. This special new format has both advantages and disadvantages.

A PSE file is really a folder containing all the information Elements needs to reassemble your document the next time you open it. That's very handy when you're working in Elements, but the drawback is that hardly any other program can read these files. PSE files work just fine if you print at home or use Kodak EasyShare for online printing. You can send PSE files to EasyShare as easily as you send JPEGs.

The rub comes if you want to use a different printing service. If you make, say, a book that you want to print at Lulu.com or MyPublisher.com, there's no way they can work with your PSE file—at least not at this writing. Most printing services require PDF format files.

You can save individual pages as PDF files in Elements, but you'll have a bunch of separate files instead of one longer one. A possible workaround is to save individual pages as PDF files and then use another program, like Adobe Acrobat, to combine them into one PDF file for printing. (Be aware, though, that Elements makes very large PDF files.)

Adding Favorites to the Artwork and Effects Palette

If you use the same effects, graphics, and styles over and over, you may find it tedious to keep navigating to them in the Artwork and Effects palette (especially if you've used a previous version of Elements where Styles and Effects were right out in front). You can make your life simpler by saving your Artwork and Effects standbys in the palette's Favorites section. Then you can get to these items with just a click or two.

To add an item to Favorites, right-click its thumbnail and choose Add to Favorites. To view all your favorites, click the star button at the top of the palette. So, for instance, say you're creating a scrapbook where you're using the Old Paper effect on lots of pages. Save the effect as a Favorite, and then you can just go to Favorites

→ Old Paper to summon Ye Old Paper. The Favorites section is a big timesaver, especially since you can save art from the palette, along with filters, frames, and Layer styles, and have them all in one place to choose from.

To delete a favorite, right-click its thumbnail and choose Remove from Favorites.

Photo Book Pages

Elements lets you create 10.25"×9" pages for use in bound photo books—a very popular gift item. If you wish to order your photo book from Kodak EasyShare (see page 410 to learn how to set up an account), you need at least 20 pages. (You can create a PSE file with fewer pages, but you'll end up with blank pages at the back of your book.) Use the wizard for Photo Book Pages exactly the same way you use the Photo Layout wizard (page 397).

> **NOTE**   If you want to print your Photo Book Pages elsewhere, you may have a bit of a dilemma, as explained in the box on page 404.

You can also create a photo book without using the Photo Book Pages at all. You can connect to EasyShare and upload your photos themselves, as explained on page 407. (You don't get any page decorations or layout choices when you use the EasyShare wizard, though.) One thing to keep in mind if you're creating a bound photo book: Whether you order from EasyShare or another publisher, almost all books use only a single photo for the first page because that's what shows through the cover cutout.

Album Pages

You create album pages (to insert into a scrapbook or binder) exactly the same way you create Photo Layouts. As a matter of fact, you may notice that the Album Pages templates look exactly like the ones for Photo Layouts, and both offer a size choice of 11"×8.5". You also get a 10.25"×9" size option for Album Pages.

> **NOTE**   All the choices for both Album Pages and Photo Layouts are landscape-oriented pages. If you want a portrait-oriented page (tall rather than wide) for your Album or Photo Layout, just pick the landscape template that's closest to what you want and then go to Image → Rotate and choose one of the 90 degree options to change the orientation.

Greeting Cards

Adobe calls them "Greeting Cards," but they're more like what *you* call postcards. An Elements Greeting Card is a 4"×6" or 5"×7" single-sided page rather than a folded card. The layout and template choices are a bit different from what's offered for Photo Layouts, but the procedure is exactly the same. Just follow the steps for Photo Layouts (page 397).

TIP   You can also order greeting cards from Kodak EasyShare, as explained on page 407.

CD Jacket

You can create CD jewel box inserts in Elements 5. These inserts appear on the front and backside of the CD case. Just go to Create → CD Jacket, and you get a variety of different templates, all the correct size for use in a CD case.

The steps for creating your CD Jacket are the same as for a Photo Layout, but the layout choices, of course, are different. Pay special attention to the photo placement when choosing your layout: the right side of the layout is the front cover.

Unfortunately, none of the designs mark out the spine area where most CDs display their titles (although the "2 Centered" template has the gap between the photos in the correct place for spine text). If you decide to enter text that you want to appear on the spine, click the Horizontal Type tool (page 375), type away, and then go to Image → Rotate → Layer 90° Left. Then use the Move tool to place the text where you want it.

TIP   If you use a theme (page 399) and you want to add spine text, remember that home inkjet printers don't do a good job printing small white type on a dark background. You're better off going with dark type on a light background.

DVD Jacket

You can also make inserts for DVD cases. Unlike Elements' CD Jacket templates, many DVD Jacket themes give you a designated area to put text along the skinny edge of the DVD case, so you can tell one DVD from another on the shelf. DVD Jackets work just like Photo Layouts, so follow the same steps you'd use to create a Photo Layout.

To add spine text, use the Horizontal Type tool (page 375) to enter it, choose Image → Rotate → Layer 90° Left, and then use the Move tool to put the text where you want it. Remember, though, that if you choose a different background or theme from the Artwork and Effects palette, the new background won't show the different shading in the spine area that helps you place your text correctly.

CD/DVD Label

You can create stick-on labels for CDs and DVDs with Elements and print them on blank label sheets from any office supply store. Elements gives you templates that create a single label layout, and when you're done, you need to place your work into the template that goes with your brand of labels. (Most CD or DVD labels print two to a page.) The major brands, like Avery and Neato, have free downloadable templates on their Web sites to help you position your labels properly on the page.

NOTE   While labels make your discs look great, it's risky to put a stick-on label on any disc you'll use in a computer. If the label gets stuck in the disk drive, you may have to replace the drive. Consider using a marker to label discs for computer use.

Online Creations

Besides what you can do in Elements, you can create a handful of projects online at Kodak EasyShare (page 410). First, select your photos in the Organizer. Then, in the Shortcuts bar, click the Order button and choose Order Kodak Photo book or Order Photo Greeting Card. Elements automatically uploads your photos, and you see them in the EasyShare wizard, which walks you through creating and ordering your book or cards. You need to set up an EasyShare account the first time you use the service. Setting up an account and using EasyShare are explained on page 410.

You can also create calendars with EasyShare. Before you start, you must select twelve photos in the Organizer. Then go to Create → Photo Calendar, and Elements 5 whisks you off to Kodak's EasyShare service. You can access the Photo Calendar menu choice from either the Organizer or the Editor, but it's the photos you've selected in the Organizer that get uploaded. If you select fewer than 12 photos, the EasyShare wizard nags you to add more, and you don't have the option of using the same photo for each month. (Unlike Elements 3 and 4, Elements 5 doesn't include templates for creating calendars to print at home or take to your local print shop.)

Another online ordering option—PhotoStamps. These are real, legitimate postage that features a photo of your choice. If you've always wanted to be immortalized on a stamp, here's your opportunity. Select one or more photos in the Organizer, then go to Create → PhotoStamps. Elements automatically uploads your photos to Stamps.com. Create an account with Stamps.com, and then you can order your stamps.

NOTE   While Photo Stamps are fun, they're definitely for people with lots of disposable income. Check the price list before you spend a lot of time preparing photos to see whether you really think they're going to be worth the cost.

Printing Your Photos

Now that you've gone to so much trouble making your photos look terrific, you'll probably want to share them with other people. The next three chapters look at the many different options Elements gives you for sharing your photos with the world at large.

This chapter covers the traditional method: printing your photos. You can print your photos at home on an inkjet printer, take them to a printing kiosk at a local store, or use an online printing service. Elements makes it especially simple to use Kodak's EasyShare Gallery, Adobe's online printing partner. You also get an easy connection to several other popular online photo services (see page 442). And you're not limited to merely ordinary prints these days. You can create hardcover books, calendars, album pages, and greeting cards, too.

Getting Ready to Print

Whether you're going to print at home or send your photos out, you need to make sure your image file is set up to give you good-looking prints.

The first thing to check is your photo's resolution, which controls the number of pixels in your image. When you don't have enough pixels in your photo, you're not going to get a good print. 300 pixels per inch (ppi) is usually considered optimum, and a quality print needs a resolution of at least 150 ppi to avoid the grainy look you see in low-resolution photos (see page 82 for more on setting your photo's resolution).

TIP   Be sure you set your resolution to a whole number—decimals may cause black lines on your prints with some printers. In other words, 247 ppi is fine, but you may have problems if the ppi is 247.32.

If you're printing on photo paper or sending your photos out for printing, check to be sure that your photos are cropped to a standard paper size. (See page 71 if you need help with cropping.) And when you're printing at home, the paper you print on makes a big difference in the color and quality of your output. You'll get the best results if you use your printer manufacturer's recommended paper and ink.

Ordering Prints

You don't even need to own a printer to print your photos. There's no shortage of companies hoping you'll choose them for the privilege of printing your photos. You can order prints online or use a print kiosk at a local store. Elements makes it very easy to prepare your photos for printing either way. Just save your photos in a compatible file format (see page 428 for more about picking different file formats). The JPEG format is usually your best bet, but always check with the service you plan to use to see if they have any special requirements.

If you plan to physically take your photos in for printing (as opposed to ordering them online), burn the photos to a CD and take that in. You'll have fewer problems than you would if you tried copying your edited photos back onto your camera's memory card. (When you use the Organizer, export your photos to the desktop, as explained in Figure 16-1.)

Ordering Prints Online

Adobe has partnered with Kodak's online photo-printing service, EasyShare Gallery, to make it easy to upload photos directly from the Organizer. You can share photos with other EasyShare account holders (creating an account is free), or order prints or books. (There are many other online printing services that you can also use [see page 442], but the process isn't integrated right into Elements the way it is with EasyShare.)

NOTE   If you've ordered online from an earlier version of Elements but haven't done so in a while, the EasyShare Gallery is the current name for what used to be Ofoto.com. If you have an Ofoto account, you can still use it with EasyShare.

Elements sports an Order Prints palette in the Organize bin, just below where you see your Tags and Collections (see Figure 16-2). This palette makes ordering prints from EasyShare extremely easy—just drag your photos from the Photo Browser right onto the palette, or click the Order Online button and then select Order Prints.

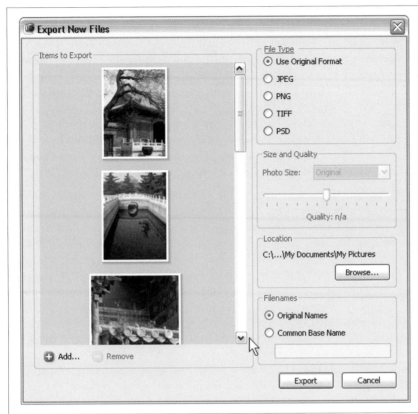

Figure 16-1:
Use the Export New Files dialog box to get your images ready for in-store printing (at a kiosk, for example). First, select your photos in the Photo Browser. Then choose File → Export → As New File(s) to send them to the desktop for easy burning to a CD. Click the Browse button to choose the desktop as your location, and change the format if needed (if you have TIFFs and the store wants JPEGs, for example).

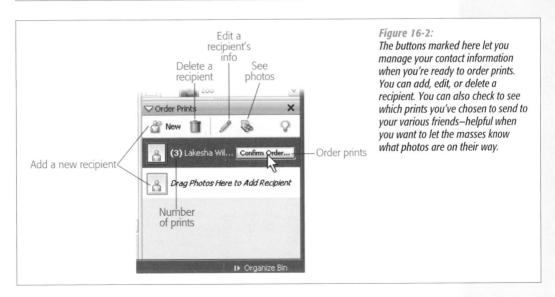

Figure 16-2:
The buttons marked here let you manage your contact information when you're ready to order prints. You can add, edit, or delete a recipient. You can also check to see which prints you've chosen to send to your various friends—helpful when you want to let the masses know what photos are on their way.

The palette lets you enter information about your regular recipients to simplify the process of ordering and sharing. You need to enter the person's name and shipping information, and Elements remembers it for you. Click the Create New Order Prints Recipient button and then enter the information for the person in the window that appears. When you want to send prints to someone, drag the photos to his name in the list. (If you haven't set someone up as a recipient yet, you can also drag the photos to where it says Drag Photos Here to Add Recipient, which brings up the same window.) To use EasyShare, you'll need to create an account for yourself, if you don't already have one, but you can wait to do that until you're ready to order. The first time you connect to EasyShare, you see a window where you can set up a new account or log in to your existing one.

Then you tell EasyShare how many prints you want of each photo you've selected and which sizes they should be. Confirm your order, and then, in a few days—presto—your prints arrive in the mail. The entire process is very easy, and the pricing is competitive with most drugstore photo printing. The only difference between prints ordered online and regular film prints is that the envelope Easy-Share sends you contains a contact sheet (a page of thumbnail-sized photos), instead of negatives. (You still have your "negatives," which are your original files.)

> **NOTE** Elements automatically checks for updates to the EasyShare services (and any additional online services Adobe may choose to offer), and also automatically assumes you want to be notified of special promotions. You can turn off either automatic update in Edit → Preferences → Services. You can also tell Elements how to handle updates when it finds them by going to Organizer → Help → Updates → Preferences, where you can choose whether Elements should check for updates and install them automatically, or ask you before it installs anything.

Once your photos are edited and you're ready to order prints, follow these steps:

1. **In the Organizer, select the photos you want to print.**

   If the photos you want are scattered around, you may find it easier to make a temporary collection (see page 48) so that you can easily see them all once. Alternatively, you can also just Ctrl+click to select the photos you want.

2. **Select a recipient.**

   Drag the photos to the name of the person you want to receive the prints. If the person isn't already in your list, then drag the photos to where it says Drag Photos Here to Order Prints. The New Order Prints Recipient window opens so you can type in their info, and then the photos become associated with that name when you click OK. You can also use your Contact Book (page 438) to create a new recipient, as explained in Figure 16-3.

3. **Confirm your order.**

   If you want to review which photos you've chosen, click the "View Photos in Order" button to see them. It's the button just to the right of the Edit Contact button (the pencil icon) at the top of the Order Prints Pane. Hover your mouse

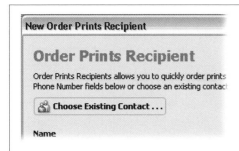

New Order Prints Recipient

Order Prints Recipient

Order Prints Recipients allows you to quickly order prints
Phone Number fields below or choose an existing contac

Choose Existing Contact . . .

Name

Figure 16-3:
*You can set up a recipient by copying information that's already
stored in your Contact Book. To do so, click the Create New Order
Prints Recipient button and then click Choose Existing Contact.
Elements automatically creates a new Print Order recipient for the
name you choose.*

over each button to see the tooltips text if you aren't sure which is which. When
the "View Photos in Order" window opens, you can add or delete photos there
before confirming the order. You can also add more photos by dragging them
to the name in the Order Prints pane, but the "View Photos in Order" window
is the easiest way to remove photos before you start the ordering process. You
can also delete a photo from your order once you're in the EasyShare window
(Figure 16-4) by clicking Remove under the photo's EasyShare thumbnail.

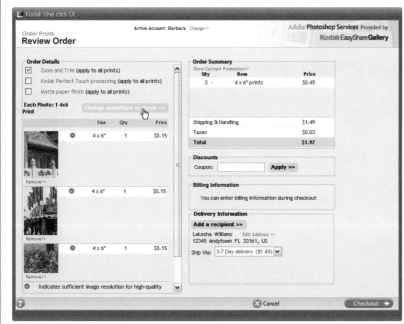

Figure 16-4:
*You can add additional
sizes or order more than
one copy of a particular
photo once you're in the
EasyShare wizard. If your
photo's resolution (see
page 82) is too low for a
good print, you see the
red circle next to it, as
you can see in the top
and bottom photos here.*

The number of photos ordered for each person appears in parentheses to the
left of the person's name in the recipient list. When you're ready to order, click
the Confirm Order button and Elements whisks you off to the EasyShare site
(although you're still actually in an Elements window, bearing the headline
"Welcome to Adobe Photoshop Services").

4. **Order your prints.**

An easy-to-follow wizard appears to help you set up your account. (If you already have an EasyShare account, just log in.) Select the size and number of prints for each photo, as shown in Figure 16-4. You'll receive an envelope of prints in the mail in a few days.

Elements makes ordering prints from EasyShare very convenient. Of course, you can use EasyShare without the Organizer, and you can use other online print services like Shutterfly (*www.shutterfly.com*) or Snapfish (*www.snapfish.com*) if you like. The real advantage of ordering from Elements is the convenience of being able to work right from the Organizer. (You can also order prints from many online photo-sharing sites, like the ones discussed on page 442. To use them, upload your photos, and then use the site's own wizard to order prints, mugs, tote bags, or whatever other merchandise they offer.)

NOTE   You need to create recipients for only those people you regularly share photos with. If you're only going to send photos to someone one time, like guests from a wedding whom you rarely see, then skip the whole New Recipient thing by selecting your photos, and then going to File → Order Prints. Or you can click the Order Prints shortcut button and choose Order Prints from the pop-out menu. Either option takes you to EasyShare, and you can enter the recipients' information there instead.

Printing at Home (The Editor)

If you want to do your own printing, you can print directly from the Elements Editor. You can print only one photo at a time from the Editor, but at least you don't have to switch to the Organizer every time you want to print a photo. (Printing multiple photos, like contact sheets, is handled by the Organizer, which is explained later.)

Before you actually print your photos, for best results, you need to check the settings in two windows: the Page Setup dialog box, and the Elements Print Preview Window.

Page Setup

The Page Setup window is the same for all the programs you have on your computer. It's where you set your page size and orientation and tell the computer which printer you want to use, if you have more than one printer.

You get to Page Setup by going to File → Page Setup. You can also press Ctrl+Shift+P or click the Page Setup button on the Elements Print Preview window (explained later).

In Page Setup, start by choosing the correct printer by clicking the Printer button. Next, in the main Page Setup window, choose the paper size you want and the orientation (portrait or landscape). When you've selected these settings, you're ready to go to the Elements Print Preview dialog box.

Print Preview

Print Preview is your control center for printing from Elements. It offers you lots of ways to tweak your prints, from simply positioning your photo correctly to making very sophisticated color adjustments.

Press Ctrl+P in the Editor to call up the Print Preview window. For simple printing, make sure the photo is properly positioned on the page and click Print. If you're lucky, you'll get a perfect-looking print. If you don't like the color, the next section on color management explains your options.

Don't be intimidated by the Print Preview window, which is shown in Figure 16-5. You probably won't need all the settings every time you print, but each setting comes in handy sooner or later.

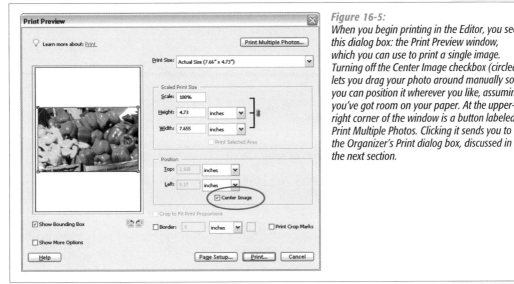

Figure 16-5:
When you begin printing in the Editor, you see this dialog box: the Print Preview window, which you can use to print a single image. Turning off the Center Image checkbox (circled) lets you drag your photo around manually so you can position it wherever you like, assuming you've got room on your paper. At the upper-right corner of the window is a button labeled Print Multiple Photos. Clicking it sends you to the Organizer's Print dialog box, discussed in the next section.

On the left side of the Print Preview window is a thumbnail showing the location where your photo will print. Normally, Elements shows a *bounding box*, the black outline with handles on the corners indicating the edges of your photo. Don't worry, the bounding box itself doesn't print along with your photo. The box gives you a way to move and resize your image by dragging the handles. If seeing the bounding box bothers you, then get rid of it by turning off the Show Bounding Box checkbox.

The familiar Elements Rotate symbols appear below the right corner of the image window. Use these if you need to change the orientation of your photo.

If you want to print only part of a photo, Figure 16-6 shows how. Your selection must be a plain rectangle or a square without any feathering (see page 117), or Elements won't print it.

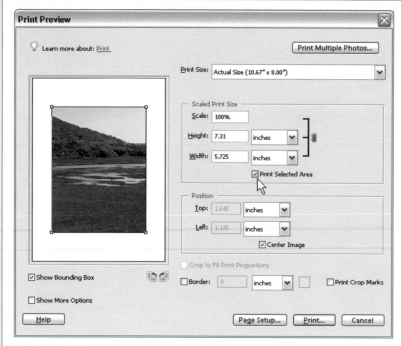

Figure 16-6:
If you don't want to print your entire photo, you don't actually have to crop it before printing it. You can select the area you want to print and then turn on Print Selected Area (where the cursor is here). The rest of your photo vanishes, and you see only the part you selected. You can treat the selection like an entire image—move it, resize it, put a border around it, and so on.

You can resize your photo in Print Preview in several ways:

- **Print Size menu.** Choose any print size from the list or enter a Custom Size. Fit On Page changes the size of your image, if necessary, to fit the size of the paper you're using.

- **Scaled Print Size.** Resize your photo by a certain percent or by entering new dimensions here. (If you want a custom size, enter the size here. You don't have to change the Print Size pull-down menu, too.)

- **Bounding Box.** You can also use the bounding box to change the size of your image. Drag one of the tiny white boxes (on any of the bounding box's corners) to make your image larger or smaller.

- **Crop to Fit Print Proportions.** If your image has a different aspect ratio (length to width proportions) than the paper you're printing on, and you're feeling lazy, then turn this checkbox on, and Elements crops your print for you.

You need to be cautious about resizing in Print Preview, though. Elements resamples your image (see page 88) to make it fit the size you choose. Don't go larger than 100 percent, or the quality of your photo starts to deteriorate and you'll get a warning from Elements (see Figure 16-7).

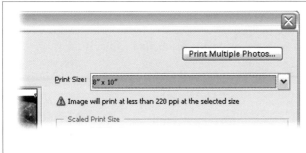

Figure 16-7:
When your resizing activities are going to reduce your photo's resolution below 220 ppi, Elements warns you about the result. Generally, it's better to do most resizing—especially any resizing upward—before you get to Print Preview. Enlarging your photo in Print Preview can make for grainy, poor-quality prints. If you can see pixelation in the preview window, then you know that something's amiss, and you should start by checking your resolution.

The other settings in the main part of the Print Preview window are:

- **Position.** This setting tells Elements where to put your photo on the page. Elements starts you out with the Center Image checkbox turned on. You need to turn it off before you can reposition your image. To change the location of your photo, either drag its thumbnail or type the amount of offset you want in the boxes provided. (Top controls how far your image is from the top of the page; Left controls the distance from the left edge of the page.)

- **Border.** When you want to add a border to your photo, turn on the Border checkbox and enter the size you want for your border (in inches, millimeters, or points). Elements shrinks your photo to accommodate the border. Then click the white square to bring up the Elements Color Picker (see page 196) so that you can choose a color for your border.

- **Print Crop Marks.** This setting, found to the right of the Border settings, lets you print guidelines in the margins of your photo to make it easier to trim it exactly. Crop marks are mainly useful for trimming bordered photos so that the borders are exactly even.

There are two more basic settings that don't appear until you turn on Show More Options, which is just above the Help button. When you do so, the Print Preview window expands and you see:

- **Label.** Directly under the Show More Options box are the label settings. You can print the file name or caption directly on your photo by turning on the relevant checkbox. The thumbnail window shows you where your text gets printed.

- **Invert Image.** This setting horizontally reverses your image. Use it when printing transfers for projects like t-shirts. It's located on the lower-right side of the Print Preview window.

The other settings that appear when you expand the window are advanced color settings. They're explained in the next section.

NOTE   Print Preview isn't *color managed*, which means that what you see in the window isn't meant to show you the exact colors you'll get when you print. Instead, you're looking only at the position of your photo.

More printing options—color management

Elements gives you several advanced color-related settings in the Print Preview window. If you're content with the way your prints look without adjusting these settings, just be happy and ignore them. But if you don't like the color you're getting from Elements, then turn on Show More Options at the bottom of the Print Preview window, which expands to show you these advanced controls.

If you remember from Chapter 7, Elements is a *color-managed* program, which means it tries to coordinate the color settings used by a wide variety of devices and programs: your photo (which may retain color settings applied by your camera), your monitor, your Elements settings, and your printer. Sometimes you need to step in and help Elements decide which settings are best, since different devices can have different interpretations of what individual colors look like.

The most important choice you need to make is whether you want Elements or your printer to manage your photo's color settings. (It's possible to let both Elements *and* your printer have a say in color management, but that almost always mucks things up.) You make your decision in the Color Management section of the Print Preview dialog box, where you'll see three settings:

- **Source Space.** This setting shows you which, if any, color space your file's tagged with (for example, sRGB or Adobe RGB). You don't actually choose a setting here; instead, this line tells you the color space associated with your file. See page 181 for more about color spaces.

- **Printer Profile.** This is where you decide whether Elements or your printer handles color management. If you choose Printer Color Management, you're letting your printer take over the color management duties. You can also leave this setting at "Same as Source," or you can let Elements take over by assigning one of the many profiles shown in the list.

- **Intent.** Intent tells Elements what to do if your photo contains colors that fall outside the range of the print space you're using. Your choices are explained in the box "What's Your Intent?" on page 423. When you choose "Same as Source" for your Printer Profile, this setting isn't available.

The easiest way to set up color management, and a good way to start, is to choose Printer Color Management or "Same as Source" for the Printer Profile setting. This means that Elements hands your photo over to your printer and lets your printer take care of the color management duties. Then all you need to do is select the proper paper profile and settings for your printer.

Selecting a paper profile sounds complicated, but it's usually as simple as choosing, say, Photo Paper Plus Glossy from the list of options in your *printer driver*, the utility program that lets you control your printer's settings. You'll find these options in Page Setup → Printer → Properties. The exact wording differs depending on what kind of printer you've got, but Figure 16-8 shows a popular printer's settings.

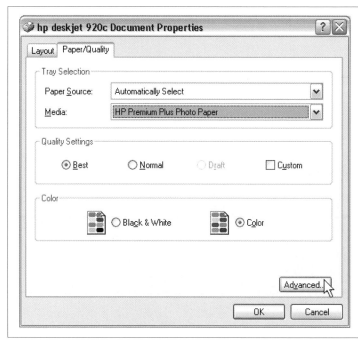

Figure 16-8:
Even a basic model like this older HP inkjet printer includes some options for color management, if you feel you need them. Clicking the Advanced button calls up another window that shows your color management options. Most of the time, selecting the right settings in Elements' Print Preview window and choosing the correct paper type gives you good prints. Most modern printer drivers automatically choose the correct ink setting for the paper you've chosen. Don't override these settings unless you've got a good reason.

NOTE   If your camera takes photos in sRGB and you've been editing them in No Color Management or "Always Optimize Colors for Computer Screens," then don't alter your workflow by choosing Adobe RGB for the printer profile. Your colors may shift drastically. If for some reason you want to change the color space for the printer, first go to Image → Convert Color Profile, and then apply the Adobe RGB profile to your photo. If you aren't absolutely sure that your printer understands Adobe RGB (many inkjets don't), and you don't have a compelling reason for changing, then it's best to leave things alone.

There are limitless variations on how you can use the color settings in Elements, and you may need to experiment a bit to find what works best for you. See the box "Economical Print Experiments for advice on how to cheaply test out a bunch of different print settings. If you go looking around for more information, you'll find that this is a very controversial subject. Everyone has a different approach that's the "right" one. In fact, you have many options that can lead to good results.

Printing at Home (The Organizer)

Elements also lets you print from the Organizer, which gives you many more output options than the Editor, including the ability to print several photos on one page. You can create contact sheets of thumbnails, picture packages (like you'd order from a professional photographer), and labels. You can also easily add all kinds of fancy borders to your photos in the Organizer.

The Print Selected Photos dialog box is the Organizer's print control center. Press Ctrl+P or click the Print shortcut icon and then choose Print to bring it up (see Figure 16-9).

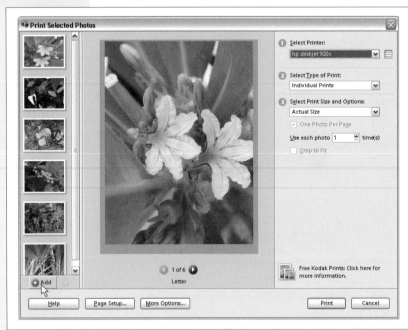

Figure 16-9:
Your control center for printing from the Organizer. The strip on the left side of the window holds thumbnails for all the photos you plan to print. When you're creating a picture package or a contact sheet, you can add or remove images by clicking the + or – buttons at the bottom of the thumbnail strip.

Print Selected Photos has a strip down the left side of the window that displays the thumbnails of the photos you've selected for printing. You can add or remove photos here by using the buttons in the lower-left corner of the window. Click Add to bring up a window where you can search for additional photos, or highlight a photo's thumbnail and click the red minus button to remove it.

There's a preview window in the center of the dialog box, and the right side of the dialog box gives you a few easy-to-understand options to choose from:

- **Select Printer.** Choose the printer you want to use if you have more than one printer. The little icon to the right of the printer name is a shortcut to your printer preferences.

- **Select Type of Print.** You can choose to make individual prints, a contact sheet, a picture package of multiple photos, or pick from a few different label styles. The next sections explain how to use the multiple print options.

- **Select Print Size and Options.** This is where you select the size of your prints and how many times you want to use each photo, if you're printing multiple images. For example, you can choose to print one photo four times or four different photos one time each. If you're printing picture packages and you turn on the One Photo Per Page checkbox, each image prints out on a separate page.

Crop to Fit tells Elements to perform any cropping necessary (if you want to decide where to crop your photos, use the cropping tools you learned about on page 71).

NOTE The size options you see are dependent on the page size you selected in Print Setup. So if you see only letter-sized options and you want, say, A4, then check to be sure you've chosen A4 as your paper size.

Click More Options at the bottom of the Print Selected Photos window, and you'll get the same options for captions, inverting, and color management that you get in the Editor. When you're ready to print, enter your settings and click Print.

WORKAROUND WORKSHOP

Economical Print Experiments

If you've just gone out and bought top-quality photo paper, you may be suffering from a bit of sticker shock and perhaps even thinking, "Oh yeah, great. Now I'm supposed to use this stuff up experimenting? At that price?"

The good news is, while you have to bite the bullet and sacrifice a sheet or two, you don't need to waste the whole box. Instead, try this: Make a small selection somewhere in a photo you want to print, press Ctrl+C, and go to File → New from Clipboard. You get a new file with only a small piece of your photo in it.

This is your test print. In Print Preview, turn off the Center Image checkbox and drag your small photo to the upper-left corner of the page. Run the page through your printer using Elements' standard settings. When your print looks good, you're ready to print the whole photo.

On the other hand, if you don't like the result, then press Ctrl+P to bring up Print Preview again. This time, move your test strip over to the right a little bit. Change your settings (keeping note of the changes you've made) and print again on the same piece of paper. Your new test prints out beside the first strip. Keep moving the test area around on the page, and you can try out quite a few different combinations of settings, all on the same sheet of paper.

Printing Multiple Photos

The Organizer really shines when it comes to printing more than one photo at a time. You can print a contact sheet that shows small thumbnails of many images. You can also choose to create a picture package that features multiple pictures in multiple sizes. Finally, you can choose to print your pictures on a limited selection of label sizes.

Contact Sheets

Contact sheets show thumbnail views of multiple images on a single page. They're great for creating a visual reference guide to the photos you've archived onto a CD, for instance. Or you may want to print a contact sheet of all the photos on a memory card as soon as you download the photos to your computer, even before editing them (see Figure 16-10).

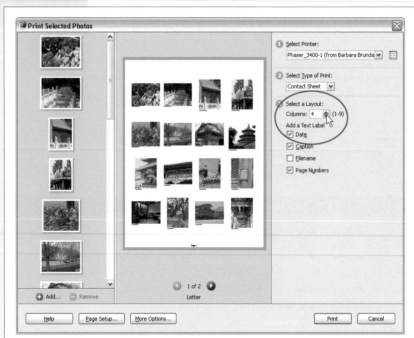

Figure 16-10:
An Elements contact sheet. The Columns menu, in the "Select a Layout" section (circled), lets you decide how many columns appear on your contact sheet.

To print a contact sheet, in the Print Selected Photos dialog box, go to "Select Type of Print" and choose Contact Sheet. Your options immediately change to show "Select a Layout," and you can use the following settings to customize your contact sheet:

- **Columns.** Here's where you decide how many vertical rows of photos to have on a page. Choose up to nine columns per page. The more columns you have, the smaller your thumbnails are. Even if you have only one image currently chosen, increasing the number of columns shrinks the thumbnail size.

- **Add a Text Label.** When you want a caption on each image, choose the Date, Caption (any text in the image's caption field), and/or Filename here.

- **Page Numbers.** You can add page numbers if you're printing multiple pages. When all your photos fit on one page, this choice is grayed out.

You can add and remove images as explained earlier. When you like your layout, click Print.

Picture Package

Elements' Picture Package tool lets you print several images on one sheet. You can print a package that's one photo printed repeatedly, or create a package that includes multiple photos.

What's Your Intent?

The Intent setting in Elements Print Preview window is the most confusing of the color management options for most people. Here are the basics of what you need to know to choose a setting. Sometimes your photo may contain colors that fall outside the boundaries of the print space you're using. Intent just tells Elements what to do if that happens. You have four choices:

- **Perceptual** tells Elements to preserve the relationship between the colors in your image—even if that means Elements has to do some visible color shifting to make all the colors fit.

- **Relative Colorimetric** tries to preserve the colors in both the source and the output space by shifting things to the closest matching color in the printer profile's space. Relative Colorimetric is Elements' standard setting, and it's usually what you want because it keeps your colors as close as possible to what you see on your screen.

- **Saturation** makes colors very vivid but not necessarily very accurate. This setting is more for special effects than for regular photo printing.

- **Absolute Colorimetric** lets you simulate another printer and paper. This setting is for specialized proofing situations.

To get started, press Ctrl+P, and the Print Selected Photos dialog box appears. Go to "Select Type of Print" and choose Picture Package. Next, under "Select a Layout," choose which composition style you want (choices include four 3"×5" photos, one 5"×7" photo, and so on). Then choose a frame, if you'd like one, by picking from the "Select a Frame" drop-down menu. Add photos to your package by clicking on the Add button in the lower-left corner of the dialog box. Figure 16-11 shows you how to change the layout of your photos once they're on the page. If you turn on Fill Page With First Photo, then you get an entire page dedicated to each photo showing multiple sizes of the image, instead of a group of different photos on each page.

Elements crops your photos to fit their slots if you turn on "Crop to Fit," but you're probably better off doing that yourself in the Editor (page 71) before you start. When you've got your package arranged as you want it, click Print.

Labels

You can also use the Organizer to print your photos on sticky labels. Elements gives you choices based on the popular Avery brand label sizes. You can use other brands, too, but you have to figure out which labels correlate to the Avery sizes listed.

You get a choice of four Avery label sizes, as shown in Figure 16-12. If you print labels from the Organizer, print a test copy on regular paper first and check the alignment of the labels and your paper. If necessary, use the Offset boxes to adjust the location of the labels on the sheet.

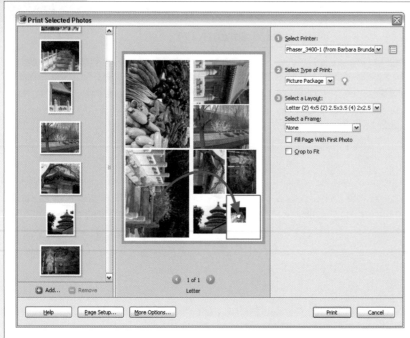

Figure 16-11:
Reorganizing your package is drag-and-drop easy. If you have empty space in your layout and you want to fill it, then drag a thumbnail from a slot in the layout, or from a thumbnail on the left, into the slot where you want to use the photo again. Here you see a photo being dragged from one of the large slots into an empty part of the layout to also create a smaller print of the same photo. Changing the size of a photo is also easy. Just drag it from the box it's currently in to a different-sized box. To remove a photo from the package, highlight it on the left side of the main window and click the red minus button (grayed out in the illustration).

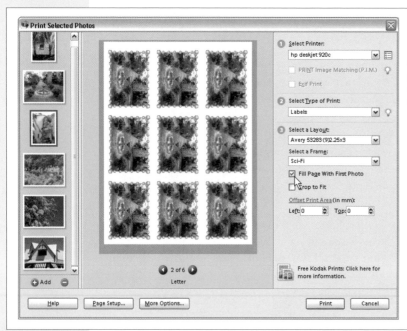

Figure 16-12:
Elements lets you add fancy borders to your Avery labels (or picture package). The labels shown here are the smallest size (2.25" × 3.0").

Creating Your Own Package

You may find that you want a different layout for your picture package than any of the choices that Elements offers. You can make your own picture package from scratch, and it's not hard to do.

1. Save all the photos you want to use at the same resolution.

2. In the Editor, create a new document (Ctrl+N or File → New). Make sure it's the size you want your complete package to be. Also make sure it has the same resolution as your photos. (See page 40 for more about setting a file's resolution.) You can save time by choosing the Letter preset size from the New file menu. That's already set to 300 ppi.

3. Drag each photo into your new document. Drag the photos from the Layers palette (see page 168) and then position them as you wish. You can use the Move tool or scale to resize them (see page 136).

When you have all your photos positioned and sized to suit you, save the combined file and print it. You can create a smaller file size by flattening the layers first (Layer → Flatten Image). Flatten only if you don't think you'll want to tweak your layout later on.

You can also create new layouts for yourself in the Organizer. Go to *C:\Program files\Adobe\Photoshop Elements 5.0\shared_assets\layouts*. Choose the layout that's closest to what you want and duplicate it. Then open it in a text editor and make the changes you want. (The layouts aren't easy to figure out, but fortunately, you have a read-me file that explains what to do. You'll find it in *C:\Program files\Adobe\Photoshop Elements 5.0\shared_assets\ReadMe*.) When you're done, save the altered text file under a new name back into the same folder.

Elements and the Web

Printing your photos is great, but it costs money, takes time, and doesn't do much to instantly impress faraway friends with your newfound photo prowess. Fortunately, Elements comes packed with tools that make it easy to email your photos and post them on the Web.

Elements 5 makes it easy to send photos to several different popular online sharing services, right from the Organizer. You can even send your photos to cellphones and electronic picture frames. If you want, you can place your photos on a Yahoo map and share the map, a very fun feature. In this chapter, you'll learn about all these sharing techniques. You can also create elaborate slideshows and mini Web sites featuring your pictures, which Chapter 18 covers in detail.

Image Formats and the Web

Back in the Web's early days, making your graphic files small was important, because most Internet connections were about as quick as camels. Nowadays, file size isn't as crucial; your main obligation when creating graphics for the Web is ensuring they're compatible with the Web browsers people use to view your Web pages. That means you'll probably want to use either of the two most popular image formats, JPEG or GIF:

- **JPEG** (Joint Photographic Experts' Group). Use this format for images with lots of detail and where you need smooth color transitions. For example, photos are almost always posted on the Web as JPEGs.

NOTE JPEGs can't have transparent areas, although there's a workaround for that: fill the background around your image with the same color as the Web page you want to post it on. The background blends into the Web page, giving the impression that your object is surrounded by transparency. See Figure 17-4 for details about how this trick works.

- **GIFs** (Graphics Interchange Format) are great for images with limited numbers of colors, like corporate logos and headlines. Text looks much sharper in the GIF format than it does as a JPEG. GIFs also allow you to keep transparency as part of your image.

- **PNG** (Portable Network Graphic) is another Web graphics format that was created to overcome some of the disadvantages of JPEGs and GIFs. There's a lot to like about PNG files. They can include transparent areas, and the format reduces the file size of photographs without the loss of data that happens with JPEG files (see page 57 for more about that). The big drawback to PNG files is that only newer Web browsers deal with them very well. Older versions of Internet Explorer are notorious for not supporting the PNG format, so if you've got potential viewers with ancient computers, you probably won't want to use PNG.

Elements makes it easy to save your images in any of these formats. You do so by using the Save For Web dialog box, which is covered in the next section.

Saving Images for the Web or Email

If you plan to email your photos or put them up on your Web site, Save For Web is a terrific tool that takes any open image and saves it in a Web friendly format; it also gives you lots of options to help achieve maximum image quality while keeping file size to a minimum. The goal of Save For Web is to create as small a file as you can without compromising the image's onscreen quality.

Save For Web creates smaller JPEG files than you get by merely using Save As, because it strips out the EXIF data, the information about your camera (see page 51). To get started with Save For Web, go to File → Save for Web or press Ctrl+Alt+Shift+S. The dialog box shown in Figure 17-1 appears.

The most important point to remember when saving images for the Web is that the resolution (measured in pixels per inch, or ppi) is completely irrelevant. All you care about are the image's pixel dimensions, such as 400×600. When you have a photo that you've optimized for print, you'll almost certainly need to drastically downsize it. This is easy to do in Save For Web.

Elements gives you a lot of useful tools in Save For Web. In the top-left corner is a Toolbox, featuring the Hand, Zoom, and Eyedropper tools, with a color square below the Eyedropper. The Hand and Zoom work the same way they do elsewhere in Elements. (See page 80 for more about the Hand tool and page 79 for more about the Zoom tool.)

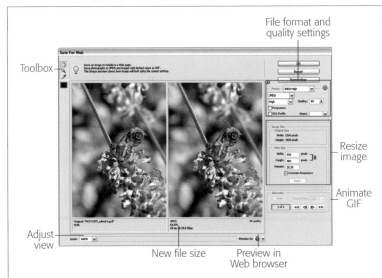

File format and
quality settings

Toolbox

Resize
image

Animate
GIF

Adjust
view

New file size   Preview in
Web browser

Figure 17-1:
The Save For Web dialog box
makes it easy to get the exact
image size and quality you want.
The left-side preview shows your
original image. The right-side
preview shows what your newly
sized image will look like at its
new file size.

Below each image preview, you'll see the file size and the estimated download time, which you can adjust by modifying your assumptions about your recipient's Internet connection speed, as explained in Figure 17-2. You can also adjust the zoom percentage (using the Zoom menu at the bottom of the window), but usually you'll want to stick to 100 percent because that's the size your image will be on the Web.

In the upper-right corner of the window are your file format and quality choices. What you see varies a bit depending on which format you've chosen. Below that are your options for resizing your image. If you want to create animated GIFs (those tiny moving images you see on Web pages), then set up the animation at the bottom of the settings panel. How to create animated GIFs is explained later.

Using Save For Web

When you're ready to use Save For Web, follow these steps:

1. **Open the image you want to modify.**

2. **Launch the Save For Web dialog box.**

   Go to File → Save for Web or press Ctrl+Alt+Shift+S. The Save For Web dialog box appears.

3. **Choose the format and quality settings you want for your Web image.**

   Your choices are explained in the following section.

4. **If necessary, resize your image so it fits onscreen without having to scroll.**

   If you want to make sure that anyone can see the whole image (no matter how small the monitor), enter 650 pixels or less for the longest side of your photo in the New Size area. (650 pixels is about the largest size that can fit on small

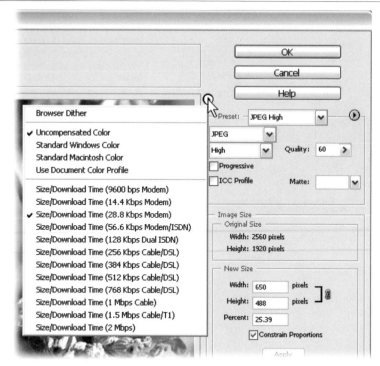

Figure 17-2:
The Save For Web window gives you an estimate of how long it's going to take to download your image. If you want to change the download assumptions (for example, the speed of the Internet connection), then go to the upper-right corner of the preview area and click the arrow button for the pop-out list shown here.

monitors without scrolling, but if you're sending to someone with an older monitor you may want to stay below 500 pixels.) As long as Constrain Proportions is turned on, you don't have to enter the dimension for the other side. You can also resize your image by entering a percent (for example, entering 90 shrinks your image by 10 percent). When you're finished entering the new dimensions, click Apply.

5. **Check your results.**

    Look at the file size again to see if it's small enough and take a close look at the image quality in the preview area. Use Elements file size optimization feature, if necessary, as explained in Figure 17-3. You can also preview your image in your actual Web browser (see the section "Previewing Images and Adjusting Color" on page 433).

6. **When everything looks good, click OK.**

    You're asked to name the new file and choose a location to save it in.

Save for Web file format options

One way to reduce your file size is to reduce the physical size, as explained in step 3. But you can also make your file smaller by adjusting the quality settings. Your quality options vary depending on which format you're using.

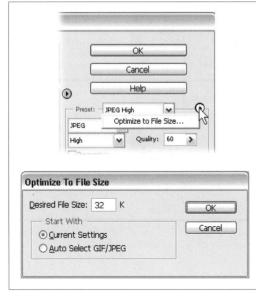

Figure 17-3:
Elements' Save For Web dialog box has a helpful file-size optimization feature for when you need to send a file to someplace that puts limits on your total file size.

Top: When you click the triangle next to the Preset menu and choose Optimize to File Size, Elements gives you a dialog box so you can enter a desired file size.

Bottom: Use K (kilobytes) as your unit of measurement in the Optimize To File Size dialog box. Picking Current Settings tells Elements to use whatever settings you've entered in the main Save For Web window, like the format and quality. Autoselect GIF/JPEG means you want Elements to decide between GIF and JPEG for you. Once you've finished making your selections, click OK. Elements then reduces your image to the size you requested.

- **JPEG.** Elements offers you a variety of basic quality settings for your JPEGs: Low, Medium, High, Very High, and Maximum. You can further adjust the quality by entering a number in the Quality box on the right. A higher number means higher quality. Generally, Medium is usually enough if you're saving for Web use. If you use Save For Web to make JPEG files for printing, then you'll want Maximum.

  If you turn on the Progressive checkbox, your JPEG loads from the top down. This option was popular for large files when everyone had slow dial-up connections, but it makes a slightly larger file, so it's not as popular today. Using the ICC profile checkbox, you can keep any color space profile embedded in your image. (See page 181 for more about color spaces.) With Matte, you can set the color of any area that's transparent in your original (see Figure 17-4). When you don't set a matte color, you get white. By choosing a matte color that matches the background of your Web page, you can make it look like your image is surrounded by transparency. In Elements, you have three ways to select your color: click the arrow on the right side of the box, sample a color from your image with the eyedropper tool, or click the color square in the matte box to call up the Color Picker. (See page 196 for more about using the Color Picker.)

- **GIF.** GIFs get smaller the fewer colors they contain. Elements GIF format names tell you the number of colors that will be in your GIF. For example, when you see GIF-128, GIF-32, and so on, the number is the number of colors in the GIF. You can also use the colors box to set your own number of colors. Use the arrows on the left edge of the box to scroll to the number you want, or just type it into the box.

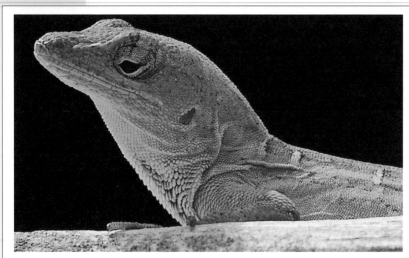

Figure 17-4:
The JPEG format doesn't preserve transparent areas when you save your image. But Elements helps you simulate transparency by letting you choose a matte color, which replaces the transparency. When you choose a matte color that's identical to your Web page's background, you create a transparent effect. The black matte around this lizard will blend into the black background of the page it goes on.

If you turn on Interlacing, your image will download in multiple passes (sort of like an image that's slowly coming into focus). With today's computers, interlacing isn't as useful as it used to be on slower machines. If you want to keep transparent areas transparent, then leave Transparency turned on. If you don't want transparency, then choose a matte color the way you do for a JPEG. When you create a GIF you plan to animate, turn on Animate. (See page 434 for more about animated GIFs.)

Dithering is an important setting. The GIF format works by compressing and flattening large areas of colors. When you choose dithering, Elements blends existing colors to make it look like you have more colors than are actually in your GIF. For instance, Elements may mix red and blue pixels in an area to create purple. You can choose how much dither you want. Sometimes you don't want any dithering—it depends on the image.

- **PNG-8.** PNG-8 is the more basic of your PNG choices in Elements, and you get pretty much the same options as you do for a GIF.

Both PNG-8 and GIF also give you advanced options for how to display colors (generating the color lookup table if you're a Web-design maven). You can totally forget this option even exists, but if you're curious, these are your choices: Selective, the standard setting, favors broad areas of color and keeps to Web-safe colors; Perceptual favors colors that the human eye is more sensitive to; Adaptive samples colors from the spectrum appearing most commonly in the image; and Restrictive keeps everything within the old 216-color Web palette.

- **PNG-24.** This is the more advanced level of PNG, which lets you use transparency. Your save options are the same as those for JPEG files.

NOTE   The Elements Color Picker lets you limit your choices to Web Safe Colors. But do you need to stick to this limited color palette for Web graphics? Not really. You need to be seriously concerned about keeping to Web-safe colors only if you know the majority of people looking at your image will be using very old Web browsers. All modern Web browsers have been able to cope with a normal color range for several years now.

Getting colors to display consistently in all browsers is another kettle of fish entirely. See the next section, "Previewing Images and Adjusting Color."

Previewing Images and Adjusting Color

Elements gives you a few different ways to preview how your image will look in a Web browser. You can start by looking at your image in any Web browser you have on your computer (see Figure 17-5).

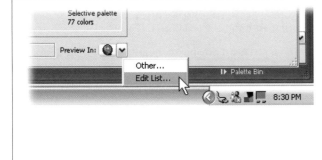

Figure 17-5:
To preview your image in a Web browser, click the Preview In icon to launch your computer's standard Web browser, or click the arrow and choose a browser from the list. The first time you click this icon, you need to go to Edit List, as shown in the illustration, and then click Find All. Elements sniffs out every browser on your computer and automatically adds what it finds to the list of available browsers. The icon you see may vary, because Elements uses your particular browser's icon (or the last browser you used for previewing in Elements).

To add a new browser, in the Save For Web dialog box, click the Preview In drop-down list and choose Edit List. Then, in the dialog box that appears, click Add Browser and navigate to the one you want. If you want to have all your browsers listed, then click Find All. From now on you can pick any browser from the list. When you do, Elements launches the browser with your image in it.

If you want to get a very rough idea of how your image will look on other people's monitors, click the arrow that's just above the upper-right corner of the right pre-view window. Above the modem specifications, you see a list of color options:

- **Uncompensated Color.** This option shows colors the way they normally appear on your monitor. This setting makes no adjustment to the color. It's what you usually see.

- **Standard Windows Color.** The Standard Windows Color option shows colors the way they should look on an average Windows monitor.

- **Standard Macintosh Color.** This option shows colors the way they should look on an average Mac monitor.

• **Use Document Color Profile.** If you kept the ICC profile (page 181), this setting tries to match how your image will look as a result of that.

These are all only rough approximations. You need only take a stroll down the monitor aisle at your local electronics chain to see what a wacky bunch of color variations are possible. You really can't control how other people are going to see your image unless you go to their homes and adjust their monitors for them.

NOTE   Changing any of these color options affects only the way the image displays on your monitor; it doesn't change anything in the image itself.

Creating Animated GIFs

Elements makes it easy to create *animated GIFs*, those little animated illustrations that make Web pages look annoyingly jumbled or delightfully active, depending on your tastes. If you've ever seen a strip of movie film or the cels for a cartoon, Elements does something similar with these specialized GIFs.

Animated GIFs are made in layers. (If you download an animated GIF and open it up in Elements, it appears as a multi-layered image.) When you create an animated GIF, you make a new layer for each frame. Save For Web creates the actual animation, which you can preview in a Web browser.

NOTE   It's a shame that you can't easily animate a JPEG the way you can a GIF. Most elaborate Web animations involving photographs are done with Flash, which is another program altogether. You can learn a little more about Flash on page 447. However, Elements 5 offers another option if you want to make a standalone animation as opposed to an animated graphic for a Web page. Check out flipbooks on page 468. You can build cartoon-like Windows Media format animations using flipbooks.

Probably the best way to learn how to create an animated GIF is to make one. Here's a little tutorial on making twinkling stars.

Before you start, set your background color to black and your foreground color to some shade of yellow. (See page 195 if you need help setting your foreground/background colors.)

1. **Create a new document.**

   Press Ctrl+N. Set the size to 200 pixels by 200 pixels, choose RGB for the Color mode, and then choose Background Color for your Background Contents.

2. **Activate the Custom Shape Tool.**

   From the Shapes palette (in the Options bar), click the triangle inside the blue circle and then select Nature. Choose the Sun 2 shape, which is in the top row, second from the left.

3. **Draw some stars.**

Draw one yellow star, and then click the "add to shape area" square in the Options bar before drawing four or five more stars. (This puts all the stars on the same layer, which is important, since then you won't have a bunch of layers to merge.)

4. **Merge the star layer and the background layer.**

Choose Layer → Merge Down. You now have one layer containing yellow stars on a black background, like the bottom layer shown in Figure 17-6.

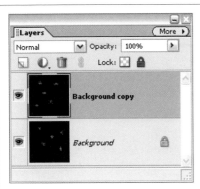

Figure 17-6:
There are only two frames in this animated GIF, which makes for a pretty crude animation. The more frames you have, the smoother the animation. But more frames makes a bigger file. On a tiny image like this one, size doesn't matter, but with a larger image, your file can get huge pretty fast.

5. **Duplicate the layer.**

Choose Layer → Duplicate Layer. You now have two identical layers.

6. **Rotate the top layer 90 degrees.**

Click any other tool in the Toolbox and then go to Image → Rotate → Layer 90° Left (if the Move Custom Shape tool is active, the Rotate command doesn't work). You should now have two layers with stars in different places on each one, which is why you did the rotation.

7. **Animate your GIF.**

Go to File → Save For Web and turn on the Animate checkbox. (Select GIF as your Save format if Elements didn't already do so for you—you won't see the Animate checkbox for other formats.) You can adjust the time between slides if you want. Leave Loop turned on. That makes the animation repeat over and over. When you turn Loop off, your animation plays once and stops.

8. **Preview your animation.**

You can use the arrows in the animation controls to step through your animation one frame at a time, but for a more realistic preview, view the image in a Web browser (explained in the previous section). The stars should twinkle. Well, OK, they flash off and on—think of twinkle lights. Save your animation, if you like, by clicking OK.

Creating Web Buttons

Elements makes it a snap to create buttons to use on Web pages. Here's what you need to do:

1. **Set the Foreground color square to the color you want to use for your button, and use the Shape tool to draw the shape you want.**

   (It helps to choose Actual Pixels for your view size when doing Web work, because that gives you the same size you'll see in a Web browser.)

2. **Apply one or more Layer styles (page 358) to make your button look more three-dimensional.**

   Bevels, some of the Complex Layer styles, or the Wow Layer styles are all popular choices.

3. **Add any necessary text using the Type tool (page 375).**

   You may want to apply a Layer style to the text, too.

4. **Save as a GIF.**

Emailing Your Photos

Elements makes it easy to email your photos. With just a few clicks, Elements preps your image, fires up your email program, and attaches your image to an outgoing email. Of course, you can email your images yourself (without Elements' help), and you may prefer that method since you get more freedom to specify settings like file size. When you email images from within Elements, the program controls the size of the files you can send. The Organizer gives you a lot of fancy templates for creating specially designed email.

Emailing Images

The Organizer gives you an almost bewildering array of formatting choices for emailing your photos. You can send pre-arranged groups of photos, frame your photos, change the background color, and so on. There's one big annoyance when you send from the Organizer, though: You get an ad for Elements in every message you send from Elements.

> **TIP** Don't want to be in the advertising business? To get rid of the Adobe ad at the bottom of your messages, highlight it in the message and press Backspace. Or, if you want to eliminate it from all your Elements emails, go to *C:\Program Files\Adobe\Photoshop Elements 5.0\shared_ assets\locales\en_us\email\signatures*. Open the files you find there using a text editor like Notepad and remove the advertising lines. From now on, your mail is ad-free.

To use the Elements email features, go to File → E-mail (in the Editor or Organizer), or in the Organizer, click the Share button on the shortcuts bar and choose E-mail (or press Ctrl+Shift+E).

Even if you start from the Editor, you get bounced over to the Organizer to set up and send your message. Wherever you start from, you'll see the window shown in Figure 17-7.

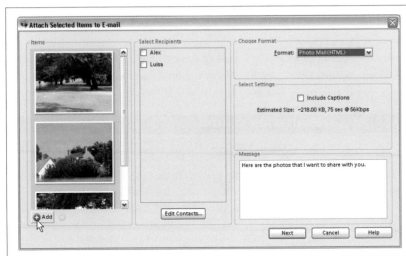

Figure 17-7:
The setup window for emailing from the Organizer is pretty easy to use. You can start with one photo or a selected group. To send more photos, click the Add button at the bottom of the window (where the cursor is in the illustration), navigate to the one(s) you want, and click OK. Remove photos you don't want by highlighting them and clicking Delete (the red – button, which is currently grayed out).

Next, decide whether you want to enter an email address now. You can:

- **Do nothing.** Wait until Elements is through, and then type the address in the completed email before you send it.

- **Choose a Recipient from the list.** Elements keeps a *Contact Book*, a list of people you regularly send emails to. You can just select names from the list. Read more about this in the box "The Contact Book" on page 438. If you haven't used the Elements email feature before, start by clicking Edit Contacts and entering the information for your recipient.

- **Edit Contacts.** If you want to enter a new recipient, or change the information for someone in your list, then click this button and enter the information in the Contact Book.

The next important decision you have to make is what kind of email you'd like to send:

- **Photo Mail (HTML).** Elements lets you send emails formatted in HTML, the language used to create Web pages. This option gives you all kinds of fancy design choices; your photo gets embedded in the body of the email.

  The catch is that the recipient has to be using a mail program that understands HTML mail. Most newer email programs are fine with this type of email, but if you're mailing to someone using ancient software like AOL 4, for instance, your email formatting isn't going to appear correctly. (Even if a mail program allows HTML mail, if your recipient has that option turned off, your email won't appear with all its formatting intact.) The next section gives you more information about Elements' HTML mail options.

- **Simple Slide Show.** This option creates a basic PDF format slideshow of all your images. All you have to do is name your slideshow. Read more about slideshows on page 454.

- **Individual Attachments.** This is your most traditional choice. Selecting this option sends each photo as a standard email attachment. The "Convert Photos to JPEGs" option automatically changes your files to JPEGs if they aren't already in that format. If they are, the option is grayed out.

ORGANIZATION STATION

The Contact Book

The Organizer makes it easy to call up the addresses of people you regularly email by keeping a Contact Book. Any time you send email to a new recipient, you first have to add the address to the Contact Book by clicking Edit Contacts in the E-mail window. You can also get to the Contact Book by choosing Edit → Contact Book in the Photo Browser or Date view.

Once you've got the Contact Book open, click the New Contact button to add an address. Then you can enter a name, email address, phone number, and other contact info. To edit or delete a contact, just highlight it in the list and click the relevant button.

You can also create groups of names in the Contact book, for times when you want to send the same photo to several people at once. To do this, click New Group, enter a name for the group, and then select an entry or entries in the Contact Book and click Add. The name goes into the Members list. To remove a name from the group, highlight it in the Members list and click Remove.

You can easily coordinate the Contact Book with your existing address book. You can choose to import addresses from Microsoft Outlook, Outlook Express, or any addresses you saved as V-cards in other programs. Just click Import and choose your source. You can also export your Contact Book addresses as V-cards for use in other programs. (V-cards are an industry standard for digitally storing business card information.)

HTML mail options

Elements also gives you a ton of options for gussying up your photos if you choose Photo Mail (HTML). When you send HTML mail, your message gets formatted using a *template*, a stationery design in which your photo appears.

Once you select Photo Mail (HTML), you see the estimated download time (for an ordinary dial-up modem) to help you determine if your email is reasonably sized. You can choose whether to display captions, and below that, you can highlight the standard message text that says "Here are the photos that I want to share with you," and change it to whatever you like. If you forget this step, you can still change it later, as shown in Figure 17-8, or you can permanently get rid of it using the same procedure described in the Tip on page 436 for getting rid of the Adobe ad in your signature.

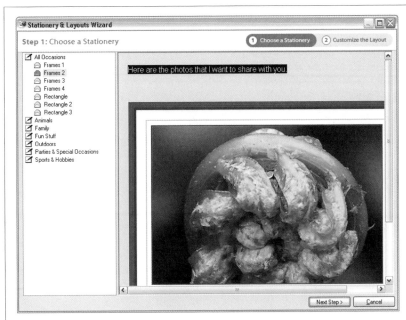

Figure 17-8:
If you forget to enter your own message before clicking Next, and you find yourself in "Choose a Stationery," don't worry. You can still highlight your text in the Stationery window and change it here, along with choosing your theme or frame. You can also type in a caption where it says "Enter caption here."

When you click Next, a wizard presents a long list of stationery theme categories with several choices in each. The preview window updates to show each one as you click it. You can add a caption to any photo in this window by highlighting the text below the photo and typing what you want. When you find a style you like, click Next Step to go to the next window.

In the Customize window, you can change the size of your photo(s) if you wish. When you're mailing more than one photo, you have a choice of several different page layouts. Below the layouts, you can choose a typeface (from a list of five common fonts). Click the box to the right of the font name to choose a color for the text. If you've chosen a frame style that leaves empty space around the photo, you can customize the background color of your email. For some styles, you can adjust the padding (the matte-like space between the photo and the frame) and the frame size. Each time you make a change in the left pane of the window, Elements updates the preview so you can see just what you're getting.

When you've adjusted everything to your liking, click Next. (Click Cancel if you don't want to send the email after all, or Previous Step if you want to go back and choose a different theme.) Elements now creates your ready-to-send email. You can make any changes to the message and address just as you would to any other email. And you send it off like any other email, too.

PDF slideshows

You can also email a group of your photos as a slideshow. Elements uses the popular PDF format, which lets your recipients page through each slide using the ubiquitous Adobe Reader program. They just launch the slideshow and view the photos one by one. You can create a PDF slideshow from the Create menu's Slide Show Editor (see page 454), or you can make a slideshow right in the E-mail window if you don't want to deal with the Slide Show Editor.

To do so, just select your photos as described earlier, and then choose Simple Slide Show (PDF) as your format in the E-mail dialog box. You get offered a choice of sizes, including Use Original Size. Name the slideshow and click OK. Elements generates a standard email message with the slideshow as a PDF attachment.

Sending Photos to Other Gear

Now that practically everyone has a cellphone with a camera and a viewing screen, Adobe has kept pace by making it easy for you to send your photos to cellphones. If you live the high-tech lifestyle, Elements gives you several ways to get your photos to and from your gear:

- **Send to cellphone.** If you and your friends like to look at tiny pictures on tiny screens, you can send photos directly to a cellphone. Go to Share → E-Mail to Mobile Phone, and you see the dialog box shown in Figure 17-9.

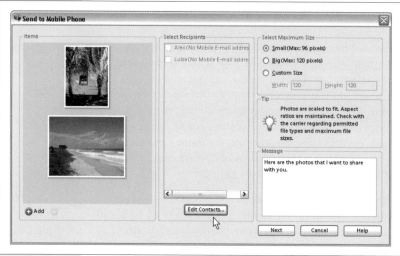

Figure 17-9:
The window for emailing to a cellphone is very similar to the regular email window. The big difference is that your size choices are very limited. The Contact Book displays any numbers you've entered as mobile phone numbers; otherwise, entering addresses is exactly the same as for regular email.

- **Get photos from cellphone.** If you have a camera phone and you'd like to import the photos into Elements, then go to File → Get Photos → from Mobile Phone or press Ctrl+Shift+M. You can specify a download folder and also designate it as a watched folder. (See page 486 for more about watched folders.)

You can also choose or change this folder in Edit → Preferences → Mobile Phone. Finally, you can choose whether or not to have Elements automatically fix red eyes in the phone photos it imports. (See page 95 for more about the Red Eye tool.) You'll find a checkbox in the import window (Automatically Fix Red Eyes) and also in the Mobile Phone preferences window.

- **Send to a Ceiva Frame.** If you have a Ceiva Digital Picture Receiver, Elements 5 makes it very simple to send your photos to it. (The Ceiva Receiver is an electronic gadget which looks like a regular picture frame, but displays photos you send to it digitally over a phone line.) Just choose Share → Send to your Ceiva Frame to connect and upload your photos. A basic Ceiva account that lets you send photos to someone's frame is free, but you have to sign up for it; the frames themselves are pretty expensive. Connect to the service from the Share menu or go to *www.ceiva.com* to learn more.

NOTE   If you used Elements 4, you may have noticed that Elements 5 is missing the feature that lets you send photos to Palm-based computers. Here's Adobe's suggested workaround for sending photos to your Palm handheld with Elements 5. Create a slideshow (see page 454) from photos sized to fit the screen of the device you want to use as a viewer, and then save in the PDF format. Upload the PDF file using whatever software you normally use to send files to your Palm, and then use Adobe Reader for Palm OS to view the show. (You can download Reader for Palm OS at *www.adobe.com/products/acrobat/readerforpalm.html*.)

Sharing Photos with Yahoo Maps

Elements 5 brings a fun new way to share your photos online: placing your photos as virtual pins stuck in a Yahoo map. Your first reaction may be a yawn and, "So what? I know where I've been." But this is actually a very cool feature. What makes it so great is that you can choose to use a satellite view of the map, and in many places, you can zoom in to the level where you can see individual buildings. This means you can place your photos *exactly* where you took them. Want to sell your house? Find it on the map and attach your photos. Click the mountain lodge where you spent your vacation and attach your photos. Trace out the route of your trip to Europe and place the photos of each site you visited.

Once you've created your photo-speckled map, you aren't limited to admiring your work on your own computer. You can create a Photo Gallery to post it online, where your friends can click the pins on the map to view a slideshow of your photos for that spot. Adobe has made this very easy by building the map feature right into the Organizer. There's even a map view in the Organizer, as explained in Figure 17-10.

NOTE   If you have one of the new camera models with GPS (a Global Positioning System that always knows where the camera is), then Elements automatically reads your GPS data and places your photos on the map. The camera writes the GPS coordinates into your EXIF data (see page 51). You don't have to do a thing except enjoy the view.

Sharing Photos Online

With Elements 5, Adobe makes it easy to post your photos to several popular online services, so that your friends can view your photos online. Adobe offers its own online service, and you can quickly send your photos to Kodak EasyShare Gallery, SmugMug, and others. (The list changes depending on Adobe's current partnerships.) Once your photos are posted, you and your friends can order not only prints, but t-shirts, mugs, bags, and other items with your photos on them. (Merchandise options vary, depending on which service you're using.) Here's a quick rundown of what you can do with each service, and what it'll cost you:

- **Adobe Photoshop Services Showcase.** Adobe's own site where you can post Photo galleries (see page 410), photos, or even movies. It's very easy to use, and it's free. You can choose whether to make your photos and galleries public (so everyone can see them) or private (visible only to the people you invite).

- **Kodak EasyShare.** Besides ordering prints from EasyShare, you can upload your photos for your friends to view online. Once your friends set up free accounts, they can order prints directly from Kodak. EasyShare also offers a wide variety of gift items with your photos on them, like mugs, bags, shirts, and more. EasyShare's free, except for the cost of what you order.

- **SmugMug.** SmugMug is another online gallery service with a lot of different gift items you and your friends can order. It has a seven-day free trial, and your friends can order prints and merchandise without a paid account. If you want to maintain a gallery there, however, it's $39.95 a year after the trial period expires.

To upload a photo to any of these services, just select it in the Organizer, and then click the Share button and choose the service you want. (You can also select and upload more than one photo at a time.)

You'll be asked to sign in if you already have an account, or to create one if you don't. Each site has a simple-to-use wizard that walks you through the sign-up process, and they also have tours so that you can take a look around before you decide to join.

If you aren't sure which one(s) to try, ask your friends which one they like. Each service has pros and cons. You may want to try them all out before you decide.

To create a map with your photos, just follow these steps:

1. **Place your photos on the Map.**

   You have several choices for getting your photos onto the Map:

   - Right-click a photo icon, and then choose Place on Map. You get a dialog box where you can enter the general location (London, for example, or North Carolina) or even the specific address where your photos should go.

   - Drag and drop photos where you want them, when the Map pane is open. You may need to use the Map Move tool (more on how to use that in a moment) to reposition the photos exactly where you want them.

   - Assign a Place tag (page 46) to a group of photos, and then place the tag on the map using either of the two previous methods. All photos tagged with this Place tag get positioned on your map.

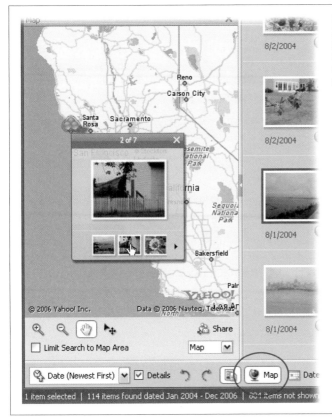

TIP The map is pretty grabby. When you're dragging in a photo to a location *close* to a spot where you already have photos, it may get sucked into the existing group, even though that's not where you want it. Sometimes it's easier to drop a photo some distance from where you want it, and then use the Move tool to bring it to a location close to existing pins.

Use the Map tools to adjust the view to your liking, and then use the Map Move tool (see Figure 17-11) to reposition your photos, if necessary. The more you zoom the view, the more accurate your placement.

2. **View your photos on the map.**

Click any visible pin to display the little pop-up window you can see in Figure 17-10. To see a particular photo, click it in the little thumbnail strip along the bottom of the pop-up window.

NOTE The pin icon is either one pin for a single photo, or three pins for multiple photos. It would be nice if the number of pins corresponded to the number of photos, but whether you have two photos or 20 attached to a particular spot on the map, the icon shows three pins for any group of photos.

3. **When you've got all your photos positioned as you want them, share your map.**

   Click the Share button and choose how you want to share your map. Your choices are explained below. If you aren't ready to share it yet, your pins will stay on the map even if you don't use the Share button—you don't need to do anything special to save them for later.

The map pane gives you three ways to view the map. If you click the Map pull-down menu you can see:

- **Map.** This is a standard street map type view, a drawing with street names and numbers on it.

- **Hybrid.** Hybrid combines the satellite view and the map view, so you see a satellite photo with the street names marked on it.

- **Satellite.** This is an aerial photo of the map area, taken by satellite, but the detail level is pretty amazing if you zoom it all the way in. (Not all areas have the same zoom level available. The map tells you if it can't zoom to the maximum level.)

The Map pane also includes a little tool set below the map to help you get things arranged to your liking. You can see it in Figure 17-11.

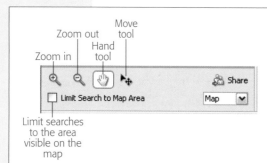

Figure 17-11:
The Map pane has its own little toolbox, used only to adjust your view of the map and to rearrange your photos, if necessary. Click one of the Zoom tools, and then click the map to zoom in or out. The area you click becomes the center of the map. The Hand tool works just like the regular Hand tool (page 80), but only moves the Map around. The Map Move tool lets you reposition your photos on the map when you need to move them.

The Zoom and Hand tools work like the regular Elements Zoom (page 79) and Hand tools (page 80), but they work only on the map. The Map Move tool is very handy. It's tough to position your photos precisely on the first try. Click the Map Move tool, and then grab a pin and drag it where you want it. If you have multiple photos on a pin and you want to move only one photo, the easiest way is to right-click it and choose Remove from Map, and then add it in again.

> **TIP** The map can be a little cranky about scrolling long distances. If you find it's hard to maneuver the map to the spot where you want to put your photos, then try right-clicking a photo and choosing Place on Map, and then entering your area in the search box. You can always remove the photo (right-click → Remove from Map) once the map shows the region you want.

If you've already placed a photo on a map, you can go right to that location by right-clicking the photo in the Photo Browser and choosing Show on Map. The Map pane opens, showing your photo's current location. When you want to get rid of a photo, right-click it and choose Remove from Map. (You can do this in the Photo Browser or from its pin in the map.)

Once you've arranged all your photos to your satisfaction, you can share your map. Click the Share button and you get a window that offers you two choices: to create a Photo Gallery (see page 447), or to share to the Flickr online service (see page 447). The Photo Gallery ultimately gives you the most sharing options. Photo galleries are covered in detail starting on page 447.

NOTE   When you share a map, the Photo page that Elements generates automatically opens with the plain Map view showing, so you'll need to explain to friends how to change to one of the other views (Hybrid or Satellite) for a better look.

The Yahoo Map Gallery (see Figure 17-12) looks a lot like a Photo Web Gallery (a collection of photos on a Web page; covered in Chapter 18), but you don't get as many choices for customizing it. You do get all the same sharing options, though, including sending it to Adobe Photoshop Services Showcase if you don't have any Web space of your own to use for hosting it.

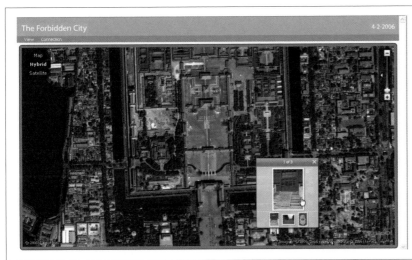

Figure 17-12:
Here's an example of a completed Yahoo Map Photo Gallery. It's a great way to share your photos with friends. All they need to do is click a thumbtack to see the photos "pinned" to a particular location.

Photo Galleries, Slideshows, and Flipbooks

Last chapter, you learned how to email your photos. But what if you've got legions of friends? Do you have to email your pictures to everyone? Not with Elements, which lets you create *Photo Galleries,* collections of ready-made photo Web pages. You can make galleries with all kinds of special effects, like having your photos on a revolving carousel, or on book pages that you can "turn" with a mouse. You can even upload your gallery to the Web and share it with the world (or just a few friends).

Elements can also help you put together elaborate standalone slideshows, complete with fancy between-photo transitions, clip art, and even audio. And for the perfect combination of high-tech wizardry and old-school charm, you can make *flipbooks*, simple slideshows that are easy to share with friends. Like the flipbooks of yore, these little shows can make a series of still photos appear to move, like an animated cartoon. In this chapter, you'll learn the ins and outs of all these ways of sharing your photos.

Photo Galleries

Elements' Web page presentation kit uses Flash, an Adobe program that creates nifty little animations that are small enough to easily share over the Web. When you create a Photo Gallery, Elements whips up a folder containing your images and everything needed to view them on the Internet (like navigation buttons). Once you post the gallery to a Web site, you can give the Web address to your friends so they can see your photos in a Web browser. Folks can see your photos, attractively arranged, without having to download every single photo or wait for you to have extra prints made. Figure 18-1 shows you a completed Photo Gallery.

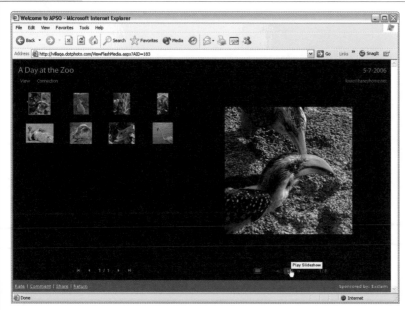

Figure 18-1:
Choose some photos and a gallery style, and Elements creates a professional-looking gallery such as this. You can choose from a wide variety of styles and color schemes. Some Photo Galleries, like this one, feature only thumbnails and a slideshow, while others let you add more text to create a gallery that's more like an online journal.

NOTE   You need to finish any editing, cropping, or enhancing of your photos before you start creating your Photo Gallery. You can't edit pictures once they're in the gallery.

Creating a Photo Gallery is simple. You choose the photos and the gallery style you want, and then Elements does the rest. The program writes the code, prepares the thumbnails, and creates any animations (if you've chosen a style that uses them). When Elements is done, it saves the necessary files in a folder, which you then upload to the Web. (You can use your own Web site, if you have one, or some Adobe-sponsored Web space—more details on that later.) The next section describes the entire process from creation to upload.

NOTE   Elements' Photo galleries are mostly for still photos, but you can add movies, too. The catch is that the video must be in the Flash FLV format, which means you must create your flicks in Premiere Elements, the commercial version of Flash, or a similar program.

Creating a Photo Gallery

It's amazingly simple to set up a Photo Gallery in Elements. The hardest part is choosing from among the delicious variety of options.

1. **In the Organizer, choose the photos you want to include.**

   You don't have to preselect every last photo, but it does speed things up.

2. **Then, in the Shortcuts bar, choose Create → Photo Gallery.**

   The Photoshop Elements Photo Gallery wizard appears.

3. **In the wizard, choose a gallery style and make any changes to the photos you want to include.**

There are three types of Photo galleries: Web Galleries, Animated, and Interactive.

- **Web Galleries.** These traditional designs display a collection of thumbnails on the left side of the screen and a slideshow view of your photos on the right (Figure 18-1). You get a lot of options for color schemes and themes, and different layouts (larger thumbnails, centered slideshow, and so on). Choosing a Web Gallery style is a two-step process. First, in the top part of the Gallery wizard, choose a template layout. Then, in the bottom section, pick a color scheme. Once you click a template layout the choices at the bottom change to reflect the themes available in that layout. Of the three types, Web Galleries give you the most customization options.

- **Animated.** These galleries feature cartoon-like animations that introduce your photos. For instance, if you choose the Baby Gallery, a stork flies in before the slideshow starts (awwww). Click a template thumbnail, and you see a preview of the animation below. Your customization options here are generally limited to Title, Subtitle, and an email address.

- **Interactive.** These galleries are also animated, but require your viewer to do something to see the photos—turn the pages of a book or shuffle a pile of slides around to zoom in on particular photos, for example. Like the animated galleries, you don't get many custom choices. Click a template thumbnail to see a preview of what it does.

NOTE   A particularly fun kind of Photo Gallery is the Yahoo Map Gallery, which displays your photos as "pins" stuck into a map. Clicking the pins starts a slideshow of photos for that location. The Map Gallery's design is similar to a Web Gallery, but with fewer customization options. See page 441 for more on how to create one.

4. **Once you choose a general gallery type, choose the specific design.**

Now's also the time to add, remove, or rearrange your photos, if you'd like. In the panel on the left side of the wizard, click the green button to choose more photos to add to your gallery. If you don't want to include a photo, click it and then click the red button to delete it. You can also drag your photos around to change their order. When you're all set, click Next Step.

5. **Make any changes to your gallery's settings.**

For most Web Gallery styles, you can customize almost everything about your page (Figure 18-2). The Animated and Interactive styles also have some options you can change—like adding an email address so visitors can contact you—but these styles don't have as many custom settings.

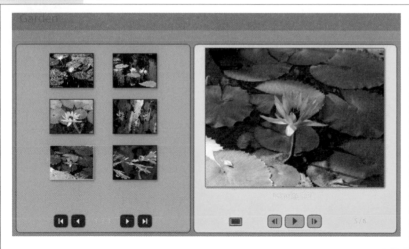

Figure 18-2:
You can truly make your gallery design your own. This kitschy extravaganza began as the Green Leaf Web Gallery template, although the only remaining trace of the original color scheme is the buttons and the border around the thumbnail and slideshow sections. If you want to save your changes as a template, click the Yes button in the wizard (next to "You have made changes to the style's setting. Do you want to save this as a new style?") and then give your template a name. From now on, the template appears at the end of the list of available designs.

Here's a list of what's available in the Photo Gallery wizard's Customize pane. (You don't have to make any changes if you don't want to, except you probably want to at least give your gallery a title.)

- **Gallery Title.** The name you type here appears at the top of most designs.

- **Gallery Caption.** For some designs, you'll see Subtitle instead of Caption. Either way, it's a chance to add some supplementary words along with your title.

- **About This Gallery.** You can enter a longer description of your photos here. This information is only visible when someone clicks View → About These Photos on your gallery page.

- **Your Name.** If you want a visible credit on the page, enter it here.

- **E-mail Address.** If you want a way for visitors to your page to contact you, enter an address here.

TIP   Unless you think you don't get enough spam, don't enter an email address using the regular address format, like *hlector@quietlambs.net*. The Web's teeming with automated robots endlessly searching for readable addresses. Instead, try something like *hlectorATquietlambsDOTnet*, and tell your friends to replace the AT with @ and DOT with a period.

- **Slideshow.** Using this section's pull-down menus, you can set how long each photo appears onscreen (Duration), and the kind of transition you want between each slide.

- **Optimize for.** Use this menu to determine whether your gallery should be sized for visitors with broadband connections or for people using dial-up. (If you want to see the difference, click the Connection link when you preview your gallery in a Web browser, and try both choices.)

- **Background.** You can change the colors of the background areas of your gallery here. You get separate choices for Main (the overall background area), the background for the Thumbnails area, and the background for the Slideshow area. Click the color square next to the one you want to change, and the Color Picker (page 196) appears so you can choose a new color.

  This section also includes sliders that let you reduce the opacity of the navigation buttons and the borders around the thumbnails. Just move them to the left to lower the opacity. You can see your changes in the Preview area.

NOTE   Not every design lets you change the color. If the color squares are blank, that usually means that choosing a different color won't change the color in your gallery. For example, if you're using the Hand Made Paper design, it always uses the original color scheme.

- **Title Bar.** The Web Gallery designs include a title area across the top of the page. Here you can change the background color (Color), the Text Color, and choose which font you prefer. (Your font choices are limited to Myriad or Times.) To choose a new color, click the color square next to your choice for changing, and the Elements Color Picker (page 196) appears. Pick a new color, and it appears in the preview area (although you might need to click the Refresh button under the preview area in the wizard to see it).

- **Menu Bar.** There's a narrow strip below the Title Bar where your visitors can make choices like how they want to view your gallery. The Color and Text Color choices work exactly the way they do for the Title Bar. Hover Color determines the color of the Menu Bar background when you move your mouse over the link area.

- **Thumbnail Effects.** When you move your mouse over a thumbnail, it acquires a highlighted outline. That outline changes color when you click to select a photo. If you want to change the color of either of these highlights, click the color square next to it in the list. The Color Picker (page 196) appears, and you can choose a new color.

- **Caption and File Name.** Here you can choose to show the file names or any captions you've created for your photos. Just turn on the relevant checkboxes. You can also choose between the Myriad and Times fonts for their onscreen display.

That's a lot of choices, but most of the time you can safely ignore most of them. Just type a title and any other text you want your visitors to see, including any contact information, and you're good to go. (You can leave out the contact information if you prefer, but people won't have any way to tell you how great your photos are. Unless, of course, they pick up the phone, or see you in person.)

6. **Preview your gallery in your Web browser.**

   To check your work, click "Preview in Browser". Elements launches your usual Web browser (like Internet Explorer or Firefox) and shows you exactly what your gallery will look like with the current settings (Figure 18-3). Close the browser window to return to the wizard.

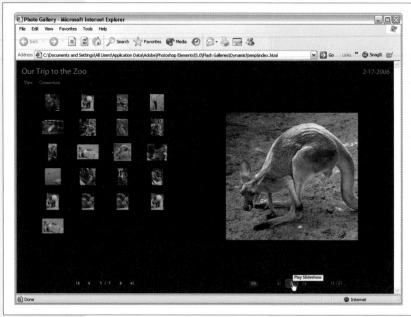

Figure 18-3:
When you click the Photo Gallery wizard's Preview button, you see your gallery in your Web browser, just as it'll appear to anyone who visits your Web site. Click the Play button to see your photos as a slideshow.

NOTE   If you make changes to the settings in the wizard, click the Refresh button in your Web browser before previewing your gallery again. That way, you're sure to see the latest and greatest version of your gallery.

If you want to change the number or order of your photos, click Previous Step to go back one window, and then make your changes there.

7. **Share your gallery.**

   In the Save and Share section of the wizard, name your gallery. Your gallery's name doesn't have to match the title, if any, that you gave it in step 3. If you don't name the gallery, Elements saves and shares it as Untitled.

Once you've got your gallery all arranged to suit you, you have another slew of choices to deal with, this time about what you want to do with your completed gallery. When you're ready to finalize your gallery, the wizard's Share To pull-down menu gives you the following choices:

- **Photoshop Showcase.** Choose this menu item and click Share, and Elements takes you to the Adobe Photoshop Services Showcase Web space. Create an account if you don't already have one, or sign in if you do. Elements then uploads your gallery for you. You can choose to make your gallery public, so that anyone can see it, or restrict it to the people you invite. The site sends invitations for you. This service is free, but it tends to sprinkle lots of ads around your galleries.

- **My FTP Site.** If you have your own Web storage space, choose this option. (FTP, for *File Transfer Protocol*, is the method used to upload files to a Web server.) When you click Share, you see the window shown in Figure 18-4. Enter your information, and Elements sends your gallery to the server.

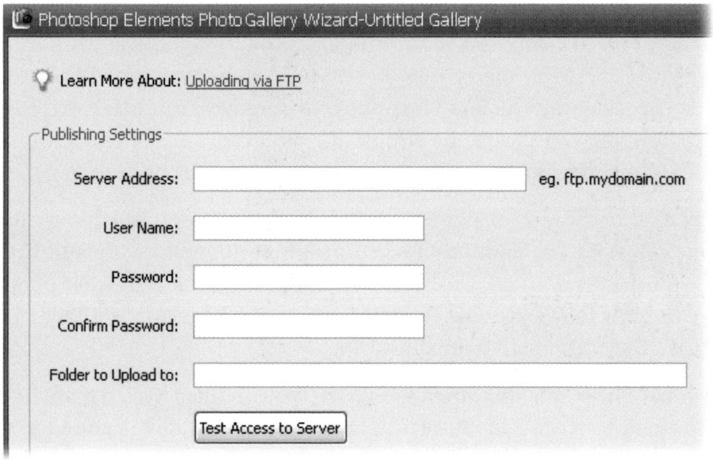

Figure 18-4:
You may already have your own storage space on the Web and not even know it. Most Internet Service Providers (ISPs) offer a certain amount of space as part of your contract with them. Gather the information you need to fill in the blanks in the Upload window of the wizard, shown here. You can usually find FTP information and instructions on your ISP's Web site.

- **CD.** You can burn your gallery to a CD send it to your friends to play on their computers. (They need to have Flash Player installed, but chances are good that they already do.) If the gallery doesn't run automatically, tell them to open the folder and double-click the Index file.

NOTE   Anyone who wants to see your gallery must have Flash Player or a Flash plug-in for their Web browser. Unless your friends still have horse-drawn operating systems, their Web browsers are most likely equipped to play Flash. (If they happen to need a player update to see your show, they'll get a warning notice in their Web browser when they go to your site.) Flash works on all platforms, so your Mac and Linux friends can see your gallery, too. To get the latest player, go to *www.adobe.com*, and click Get Adobe Flash Player.

- **Do Not Share.** This cryptic sentence actually means, "Just save what I've done so far, OK?" Choose this option if you want to store your work in the Organizer for later, and then click Save. To reopen your gallery for more work, right-click its icon in the Photo Browser and choose Edit.

8. **Once you've made your choices, click the Share button (it says Save if you chose the Do Not Share option), and enter any additional information, if necessary.**

   For instance, if you want to send your gallery to your own Web storage space, Elements asks for the information it needs to contact your Web server.

   If you decide not to create a gallery, just click Cancel instead. You can also step backward by clicking Previous Step.

   NOTE   Most Internet service providers (ISPs) give you a reasonable amount of Web server space. If you look on your ISP's Web site, you'll probably find a help page explaining all the details.

Slideshows

Elements makes it easy to create very slick little slideshows—some even with music and fancy transitions between the images—that you can play on your PC or send to your friends. By using the Custom Slide Show feature, you can make extremely elaborate slideshows. If you prefer the simple life, you can quickly create a plain vanilla PDF slideshow in about as much time as it takes to email a photo.

The simple PDF slideshow is really straightforward to create, and looks quite impressive, but you can't add audio to it or control how your slides transition. On the plus side, you can send a PDF slideshow to anyone, regardless of what operating system she uses. As long as your recipients have Adobe Reader or another PDF-viewing program, they can watch your show.

The Custom Slide Show, on the other hand, lets you indulge your creativity to your heart's content. You can add all sorts of fancy transitions, mix in sound in the form of background music or narration, add clip art, pan around your slides, and more. It's a bit more complex to work with the Custom Slide Show window than the PDF one, but the real drawback to the Custom Slide Show comes in your choices for the final output. The Custom Slide Show isn't as universally compatible as the PDF slideshow, as explained below.

   TIP   If you plan to create a simple PDF slideshow, you need to do all your photo editing beforehand, since the Simple Show just sends your photos as is. The Custom Slide Show, on the other hand, lets you edit as much as you like before you finalize your slideshow.

Simple PDF Slideshow

The hardest thing about creating a PDF slideshow in Elements is figuring out where to start. You probably wouldn't expect to create a slideshow in the email window, but that's where Adobe has stuck the Simple Slide Show creator in recent versions of Elements.

On the plus side, creating your slideshow is every bit as easy as emailing a single photo. You just follow the same basic procedure you'd use when emailing a single photo, as explained on page 436. Here's a recap:

1. **Choose at least one photo before you start.**

   You can add and remove photos once you're in the "Attach Selected Items to E-Mail" window, shown in Figure 18-5, but if your photos are widely scattered throughout your catalog, it's usually faster to create a collection first (see page 48) and start from there. A collection is also handy when you want to specify the order in which your photos appear in the slideshow.

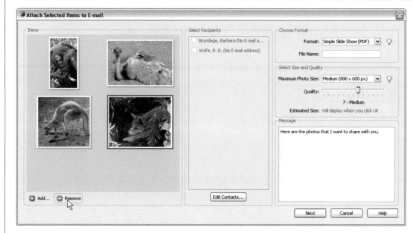

Figure 18-5:
The thumbnail images you see here are just for your convenience while creating your slideshow— the finished version doesn't include thumbnail navigation. To change the order of your photos, just drag the thumbnails into the order in which you want them to appear. Use the green Add button to find additional images, or highlight a photo and then click the red Remove button to get rid of it.

2. **Call up the Attach Selected Items to E-Mail Window, where you'll create your slideshow.**

   In the Organizer's Shortcuts bar, go to Share → E-mail, or press Ctrl+Shift+E; you can also choose File → E-mail.

3. **In the Attach Selected Items to E-Mail window, choose to create a slideshow.**

   From the Format menu, select Simple Slide Show (PDF).

4. **Make any changes to your photos and the slideshow settings.**

   You can add or remove photos from your slideshow by using the buttons below the photo area on the left side of the window. (Due to a little bit of Elements-induced quirkiness, you may not be able to reorder your photos here by dragging them. If you want to change the order, you may need to delete the photos and add them back in the order you want.)

You can select a recipient from the list in the center of the window and replace the Elements "Here are the photos I want to share with you" message text if you wish. (You can also wait until you're in your email program to specify a recipient—you don't have to enter anything now.) See below for info on adjusting your photos' size and image quality.

5. **Find out whether or not your slideshow is a good size for mailing.**

   Click Next. Doing so gives you a pop-up window that tells you the file size of your completed slideshow and the approximate download time for a recipient who's using a dial-up modem. Click OK if the size is acceptable, or Cancel to go back to the "Attach Selected Items to E-Mail" window to make changes.

6. **Finalize your slideshow.**

   When you've got everything the way you want it, click OK. Elements creates your slideshow, launches your email program, and attaches the slideshow to a message. After you've reviewed the email, you're ready to send off your slideshow.

The "Attach Selected Items to E-Mail" window offers you a couple of special settings once you choose to create a slideshow. You'd make your changes to these settings in step 4, above.

- **File Name.** You have to enter a name for your slideshow before Elements can create it.

- **Photo Size.** If you're burning the show to a CD, you can safely leave it at Original and let your friends see your pictures at their actual size. If you want to email the slideshow, you may want to create smaller-sized photos. If you choose a size other than Original, you can also choose an image-quality setting. If you plan to make a CD, you want High. For sending by email, Medium works well.

   TIP   What if you want to burn your slideshow to a CD instead of emailing it? Just use your email program's option to save the attachment and then burn it to a CD the way you would burn any other file, using either the Windows CD-burning utility or any third-party program you may have, like Roxio's Easy CD Creator, for example.

Making a PDF from a Custom Slide Show

There's also another way to create a PDF slideshow, although it's not as obvious as the method just described. When you create a Custom Slide Show, you can choose between making a Windows Media Video (WMV) file or a PDF. You may think this sounds like the best of both worlds—a very compatible format and all the bells and whistles of the Custom Slide Show.

Unfortunately, that's not quite how it works. When you create a PDF this way, you lose the pan and zoom feature, the audio, and the transitions that you set. You do keep any custom slides, text, and clip art that you added, though. On the whole, this feature's best used when you've created a full-scale Custom Slide Show, but one or two of the people you want to send it to won't be able to view it in Windows Media format. The people who get the PDF won't see everything the WMV recipients do, but it's faster than trying to recreate a separate version for the WMV-challenged.

To create a PDF using the Custom Slide Show, just follow the steps outlined in the following section for creating a Custom Slide Show. When you're ready to create your PDF, click Output, and then choose "Save As a File" in the Slide Show Output window that opens. (Or, if you want to make a PDF from an existing slideshow, right-click the slideshow's thumbnail in the Photo Browser and then choose Edit. Once the Slide Show Editor opens, click Output → Save As a File.) Click the PDF File button on the right side of the Slide Show Output window. This brings up a series of settings just for your PDF:

- **Slide Size.** This setting starts out at Small. If you're going to burn a CD, you can choose a larger size. If you want to email the final file, choose Small or Very Small for your images. There's also a Custom choice for when you want to create a size that's different from one of the presets.

- **Loop.** Turn this on, and the slideshow repeats over and over until your viewer stops it by pressing the Escape key.

- **Manual Advance.** If you want recipients to be able to click their way through the slideshow instead of having each slide automatically advance to the next one, turn this on.

- **View Slide Show after Saving.** Turn this on, and as soon as Elements is through creating your slideshow, it launches Adobe Reader so you can watch the results of your work.

When you've got everything set the way you want it, click OK to bring up the Save As dialog box. Name your file and then save it.

> **NOTE** If you'd like to share a slideshow online, the fastest way to create a slideshow for the Web is to create a Photo Gallery (page 447). Your photos play on your Web site in an endlessly looping series, depending on the style you choose.

Custom Slide Show

The Custom Slide Show lets you add audio, clip art, and fancy slide-to-slide transitions. You also get several different ways to share your completed slideshow, including making a Video CD (VCD) or—if you also have Premiere Elements—a DVD that your friends can watch in a regular DVD player. You can also email your slideshow (explained in the previous section) or share it online (see page 442). If your operating system is Windows Media Center Edition, you can even send your slideshow to your TV and watch it there (as long as you have your television hooked up to the computer).

To get started, from the Organizer, select the images you want to include. You may want to set up a temporary collection (see page 48), because you can control the order of your images in a collection. (You can change the order once you're in the Slide Show Editor, but for large shows, you save time if you have things arranged in pretty much the correct order when you start.) You can also start with a single photo and, once you're in the Slide Show Editor, click the Add Media button to add more photos. Then go to Create → Slide Show.

UP TO SPEED

Choosing a Slideshow

A couple of versions ago, people sometimes slammed Elements for not offering much in the way slideshows. In Elements 5, you have so many slideshow options it can be bewildering trying to decide which one to choose. Here are a couple of suggestions to help you out:

- **Slideshows for the Web.** If you want to share your slideshow on the Internet, create a Web Gallery (page 449).

- **Slideshows with Audio.** If you want a soundtrack for your slideshow, use the Slide Show Editor to create your show, and burn it to a disc to share with your friends, who can watch the show on their computers, using Windows Media Player.

- **Slideshows to view on TV.** If you have Windows Media Center Edition, use the Slide Show Editor and choose Send to TV as your output choice. If you want to send a slideshow to someone else to watch on their TV, you can try a VCD. But frankly,

you'd be better off using another program like Adobe's Premiere Elements or any other DVD authoring software to create a true DVD, if your computer has a DVD burner.

- **Slideshows for people uncomfortable with technology.** The simple PDF slideshow (page 454) is probably your best bet. (However, your recipients will still have to have Adobe Reader or another PDF viewer to watch the show. If you know they don't have Reader and won't know how to install it, try a Flipbook [page 468] at the slowest setting.)

Finally, if you still don't think Elements offers enough choices for you, ProShow Gold from Photodex (*www.photodex.com*) is probably the most popular slideshow program for Windows. And if you don't like the Elements Photo Galleries, JAlbum (*http://jalbum.net*) is a popular free alternative, although these days many people just use one of the photo sharing services mentioned on page 442 to create their slideshows online.

Slide Show Preferences

Once you choose to create a slideshow, Elements presents you with the Slide Show Preferences window before you enter the actual Slide Show Editor. You can click right past this window if you like, but it does give you some useful options for telling Elements how you want it to handle certain aspects of all your shows, like the duration of each slide and the color of the background. (You can also change these settings for a particular show in the Slide Show Editor itself.)

In the Slide Show Preferences, you can adjust:

- **Static Duration.** How long each slide displays before it moves on to the next one.

• **Transition.** How Elements should move from one slide to the next. If you choose a different transition from the pop-out menu, you can audition it in the little preview area at the right of the window, as explained in Figure 18-6.

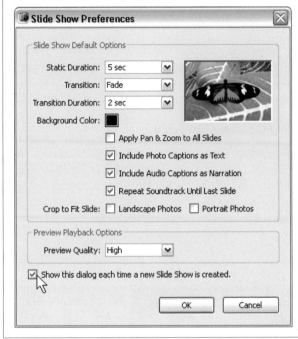

• **Transition Duration.** How fast you want the transition to happen.

• **Background Color.** Click the color square for the Elements Color Picker (see page 196) if you want a different background color.

• **Apply Pan and Zoom to All Slides.** If you set up the Pan and Zoom feature (explained below) for one slide, turn this on and the camera swoops around every slide.

• **Include Photo Captions as Text.** If you want to see whatever is in the Caption field for your photo on the screen with the image, turn on this checkbox. (Elements 3 slideshow veterans will appreciate that this works in reverse, too—you can hide your captions by just turning off this checkbox.)

• **Include Audio Captions as Narration.** If you've recorded audio captions for your slides, leave this checkbox turned on if you want your audience to hear them.

• **Repeat Soundtrack Until Last Slide.** Leave this checkbox turned on, and if you run out of music on your soundtrack, Elements fixes things for you by repeating your song as many times as necessary.

- **Crop to Fit Slide.** Turn either of these checkboxes on, and if your image is too large for the slide, Elements chops off the excess for you. You can choose separately for landscape-and portrait-oriented photos, but it's best if you do any cropping yourself before starting your slideshow (see page 71).

- **Preview Playback Options.** Choose the quality for previewing your show while you're working on it. This doesn't affect the quality of the final slideshow.

Once you're through with these preferences, click OK. If you don't want to see the preferences every time you start a new show, just turn off "Show this dialog each time a new Slide Show is created." You can still get back to the window at any time when you're in the Slide Show Editor by going to Edit → Slide Show Preferences.

Creating your slideshow using the Slide Show Editor

After you click OK in the Slide Show Preferences dialog box, the Elements Slide Show Editor launches (see Figure 18-7). It's crammed with options, but everything is laid out very logically—in fact, it's pretty similar to the Elements Full Edit window. You get a menu bar across the top of the window, but most of the commands here are available elsewhere via a button or a keystroke (like Ctrl+Z to undo your last action).

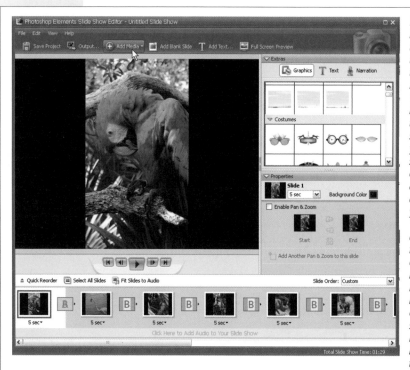

Figure 18-7:
If you want to add photos to your slideshow, click the Add Media button at the top of the Slide Show Editor's preview window. The advantage to bringing your photos in this way (as opposed to selecting them before you start creating your slideshow) is that you can choose to use photos and audio clips that aren't in the Organizer yet, by choosing the "…from folder" option and navigating to the files you want. You can even edit your photos right in the Slide Show Editor. The disadvantage is that you have to choose each photo separately or you'll have no control over the order in which Elements brings them into the show.

On the left side of the window is the preview area. There's a Palette bin on the right side of the screen, and you can collapse it just like the Full Edit Palette bin, by clicking its edge when you want to get it out of your way. Collapsing the bin makes the preview space expand across the window. Click the hidden Palette bin's edge again to bring the bin back onscreen.

At the bottom of the window is the *Storyboard*, where you see your slides and the transitions between them. Click a slide or transition here, and its properties appear in the Palette bin. If you don't want to see the Storyboard anymore, go to the Slide Show Editor's View menu and turn it off by removing the checkmark next to its name. You can turn it back on again there, too.

You can finesse your show in lots of different ways in the Slide Show Editor. For instance, you can:

- **Edit your slide.** You can make any kind of editing changes to your photo right here in the Slide Show Editor. In the preview window, just double-click your image and then, using the choices you see in the Properties palette, you can rotate your slide, change its size, crop it, and apply the Auto Smart Fix (page 97) and the Auto Red Eye Fix (page 95). Figure 18-8 shows you more about all your choices.

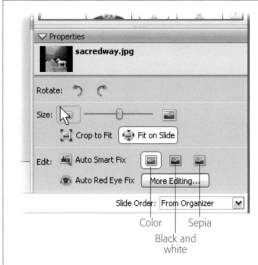

Figure 18-8:
The three little thumbnails to the right of the Slide Show Editor's Auto Smart Fix button let you change your photo to black and white or sepia and back to color again, if you change your mind. Normally, the Color button is active when you start. To change your slide to black and white or sepia, just click the button for the effect you want. (No, you can't bring in a black-and-white slide and colorize it by clicking the Color button. See page 276 if that's what you want to do.) To undo a color change you make here, click the color button. The changes you make with these buttons affect only your slide, not your original photo.

If you want to do more substantial editing, just click the More Editing button, and Elements whisks your slide over to Full Edit.

- **Duration.** You see a duration number listed below each slide, indicating how long a slide appears on the screen before it transitions to the next slide. Click the arrow to the right of the number for a pop-up menu that lets you change how long that particular slide appears onscreen. You don't need to assign the same amount of time to each slide. You can also use the pull-down menu next to the slide's thumbnail in the Properties palette.

- **Transition.** Elements gives you a lot of different ways to get from one slide to the next. These transitions appear in the Storyboard and are represented by tiny thumbnail icons between the two slides they connect. (The transition icon changes to reflect the current transition style when you choose a new transition.)

Click any transition to see a pop-out menu listing all transitions, and choose a different kind of transition, if you like.

Transitions have their own Properties palettes, which appear when you click a transition in the Storyboard. You can choose how long a transition is going to take and, for some transitions, the direction in which you want the transition to move.

If you like to make long slideshows, you'll appreciate the Quick Reorder feature, explained in Figure 18-9. When you switch over to the Quick Reorder window, you see all your slides in a contact sheet-like view, making it easy to reposition slides that would be annoyingly far apart if you had to move them in the Storyboard. In Quick Reorder, you can easily drag them to another spot in the lineup without the hassle of scrolling.

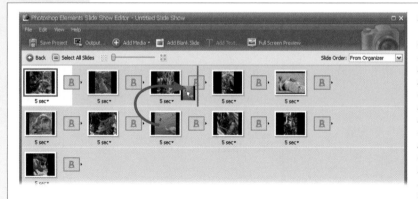

Figure 18-9:
You can reorder slides by dragging them in the Storyboard, but if you have more than a few slides, all that scrolling is a pain. Elements makes it easier with the Quick Reorder window. Just click the Quick Reorder button in the lower-left corner of the Slide Show Editor (just above the Storyboard) to bring up this contact sheet-like view of your slides. Then drag any picture to its new location. You'll see a vertical blue line (here the flamingo is getting moved) when you get the photo to its new location, indicating you can let go. When you're done, click Back in the upper-left corner to return to the main editing window.

You can also change the order of all your slides by using the Slide Order drop-down menu above the right side of the Storyboard, although your choices there are limited. When you start a slideshow from the Organizer, the Slide Order menu reads From Organizer, but you can choose Date (Oldest First), Date (Newest First), Random, Folder Location, Custom (this is what you see if you manually drag slides to new locations), and Reset (which puts your photos back in the order they were in when you first brought them into the Slide Show Editor).

Special effects

Elements gives you all kinds of ways to gussy up your slideshow, including adding clip art, text, and sound. If you want to create a slide that lists credits, for instance, start by creating a blank slide. (Click your last slide, then just click the Add Blank Slide button above the preview area). Elements adds a blank slide, to which you can then add your credits. Here's a rundown of what you can add to your blank slide (or to any of your slides, for that matter, as shown in Figure 18-10). Just click the relevant button (Graphics, Text, or Narration) in the Extras section at the top of the palette to see your options.

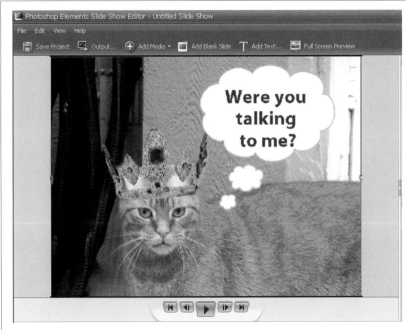

Figure 18-10:
You can add all sorts of clip art to your slides, as well as create slides that include only art or text. If you're wondering how to angle clip art, like the crown here, see the Tip on page 464.

- **Graphics.** Elements gives you a whole library worth of clip art you can add to your slides. The art is divided into these categories: animals, backgrounds, costumes, flowers, food, frames, holidays and special occasions, home items, miscellaneous, ornaments, scrapbooks, sports and hobbies, and thought and speech bubbles.

You'd use the backgrounds on a blank slide, because they cover a whole slide, but the rest of the clip art can be added to slides that already have something on them. To add a piece of clip art to a slide, just double-click the clip art object's thumbnail in the palette. It appears on your slide surrounded by a frame. You can grab the corners of the frame and drag them to resize the clip art object to the size you want. You can also reposition clip art by dragging it.

TIP   If you play around with the costumes (hats, outfits, and glasses that you can paste onto your friends' pictures), you may notice that you can't rotate the clip art on the slide. If you want to adjust the angle for any of the clip art, here's a workaround. All the art lives in *C:\Documents and Set-tings\All Users\Application Data\Adobe\Photoshop Elements\5.0\Slideshow Graphics*. Open your slide in Full Edit and add the clip art there (by importing it from the Graphics folder listed in the previous sentence). Then, use the Move tool (page 136) to place the clip art just so and the trans-form commands (page 297) to adjust the shape, if necessary. When you're done, you can reim-port your image into the Organizer as a version (page 54) and use the new version in your slideshow.

- **Text.** You can add text to your slides, and also apply a number of fancy styles to your text. To add text to a slide, click the Text button at the top of the palette, and then double-click the text style you like. The Edit Text window pops up. Type in the words you want to add to your slide. When you're through typing, click OK. The text appears in your slide, surrounded by a bounding box, which you can use to place the text where you want it.

NOTE   When the Edit Text window is active, you can't click OK by pressing the Enter key. That just creates a line break in your text. You need to click the actual OK button.

At the same time, the Text Properties palette appears at the lower right of the Slide Show Editor. You can change the font, size, color, and style in the palette. You can even choose a different color here for the drop shadow if you're using shadowed text. If you want to edit text later on, just click the letters on the slide to bring back the text bounding box and the Text Properties.

- **Narration.** You can record a narration for your slideshow if you wish. Just click the slide you want to add your voice to, and then click the Narration button in the palette. You'll see the recording window shown in Figure 18-11. (Of course, you need to have some kind of microphone hooked up to your PC to record your voice.)

- **Music.** You can add a full-scale soundtrack to your slideshow. To do that, click at the bottom of the Slide Show Editor where it says "Click Here to add Audio to Your Slide Show." (It looks grayed out, but that's just the way the window is designed. Click it anyway. It works.) In the window that opens, navigate to the audio you want and click Open. You can choose from any MP3, WAV, or WMA files you have on your PC.

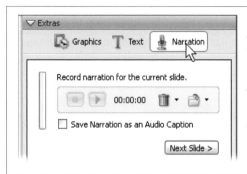

Figure 18-11:
Adding a narration to your slides is as easy as using any home recorder. Just click the Record button and start talking. Click again when you're done. If you don't like how things turned out, click the trash icon and choose Delete This Narration. If you want to permanently save your narration as an audio caption for the original photo, turn on "Save Narration as an Audio Caption." You can also click the folder icon to the right of the recording controls to import an existing audio caption to use with this slide.

NOTE   If you use iTunes, you'll need to convert your iTunes AAC files to one of these formats before Elements will acknowledge their existence. To do so, right-click any song name and choose, from the pop-up menu, "Convert Selection to MP3."

You can make your slideshow fit the duration of the music, if you like. At the top of the Storyboard, click "Fit Slides to Audio," and Elements spins out your slideshow to last the entire length of your song. Or, if you'd rather repeat a short audio clip over and over, go to Edit → Slide Show Preferences and turn on "Repeat Soundtrack until Last Slide." If you don't choose either one, Elements doesn't make any attempt to synchronize the length of the soundtrack and the length of the slideshow.

TIP   If you have problems getting the Organizer to play one of your MP3 files, you may find you have better luck if you use an audio program to re-encode your MP3 as a variable bit-rate MP3 file. Check the audio program's options or help files for instructions on how to do this.

• **Pan and Zoom.** This is the technique made popular by filmmaker Ken Burns, where the camera moves around a still photo, giving the impression of motion. To create this effect in Elements, just click the slide you want to pan over. In the Properties palette, turn on the "Enable Pan and Zoom" checkbox.

When you do so, you see two little thumbnails, Start and End, in the Properties palette. Click the Start thumbnail to choose where to begin panning over your photo. The pan frame appears in your photo, marking the spot where Elements will begin panning over your slide. Drag the frame to another place on the slide to change the starting point for your pan, or drag a corner to resize the frame.

Then, click the End thumbnail in the Properties palette and repeat the process to set the end point for panning and zooming. If you decide you want to edit the effect, you can always click either thumbnail again to bring back the pan frame. You can also click the buttons between the thumbnails to swap where you start and end.

NOTE   Panning and zooming usually looks pretty jerky when you preview your slideshow, but it should be smooth in the final slideshow.

You can pan more than once on a slide, too. To do that, click "Add Another Pan and Zoom to This Slide." If you want all your slides (or selected slides) to show the same pan and zoom you just set up, go to the Edit menu and, from the pop-out menu, choose what you want to do: "Apply Pan and Zoom to Selected Slide(s)," or "Apply Pan and Zoom to All Slides."

TIP   While Elements doesn't give you a way to create scrolling credits, you can fake them by creating a slide with a list of who you want to credit, and then applying the pan and zoom effect to the slide multiple times.

Saving and creating your slideshow

After all your work creating your slideshow, be sure to save it. (If you forget, Elements reminds you to do so when you exit the Slide Show Editor.) As long as you save your slideshow as a Slide Show, you can always go back and edit it whenever you like. To edit an existing slideshow, just right-click its thumbnail in the Organizer and, from the pop-up menu, choose Edit. Elements opens your show up in the Slide Show Editor so that you can make your changes.

NOTE   You can watch a full-screen preview of your slideshow by clicking the Full Screen Preview button above the Palette bin, or by pressing F11.

Once your magnum opus is complete, you're almost ready to save your file. But first you need to decide which format you want to use for finalizing your slideshow. As you can see in Figure 18-12, you have a lot of choices, but it's important to remember that no matter which you choose (except for PDF), you're going to end up with a Windows Media Video (WMV) file.

That doesn't matter as long as everyone you want to share your slideshow with is using a computer or DVD player that uses a recent version of Windows Media Player (it's available as a free download from Microsoft for both Windows and the Mac). But unfortunately, that's not always the case. If you need to send a slideshow to someone who doesn't have Windows Media Player, your only option is to create a PDF file as explained on page 456.

To see your Output options, click the Output button above the Slide Show Editor's preview window. You get a new window (Figure 18-12) where you can choose from several ways to save and share your slideshow.

- **Save As a File.** Choose this option to save your slideshow to your hard drive as a PDF or Windows Media Video (WMV) file. The PDF options are explained on page 456. If you choose WMV, you get several choices for size and quality. There's no need to change the setting that Elements proposes unless you already know how you're going to use the WMV file and which setting you'd want for that use. Otherwise, just leave the menu set to High for now. (If you're curious about the various choices, choose the one you want to know more about, then click the Details button. You get a pop-up window giving more information about that size and its suggested uses.)

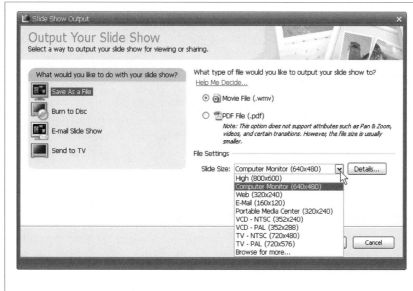

Figure 18-12:
To create your slideshow, in the Slide Show Editor click the Output button above the preview area. This brings up the window you see here. Choose what you want to do from the list on the left. Your options on the right change to reflect your choice. If you're creating a WMV file, you get a number of different slide size choices, shown here. For the items that offer PAL and NTSC variations, PAL is the format you should choose if you plan on viewing the slideshow in Europe or China; choose NTSC for most other areas of the world, including the United States.

- **Burn to Disc.** You can create a Video CD (VCD) using Elements. This is a disc that plays in a DVD player, just like a regular DVD, but you don't need a DVD recorder to create one (because you're just using a plain old CD). The downside is that VCD is a very tricky format—the quality is low and you can expect to have some problems getting the discs to play in some DVD players. If you want to send VCDs, you may want to make a short test slideshow for your friends to be sure they'll be able to watch one before you invest a lot of time in creating a large project.

TIP If you'd like to check which players can handle VCDs, or if you just want to know more about the format, head over to *www.videohelp.com/vcd*, where you'll find links to lists of compatible players and a lot more information.

You can also choose to include other slideshows on the same disc if you turn on the "Include additional slide shows I've made on this disc" checkbox in the Output window. Then click OK to bring up the "Create a VCD with Menu" window where you can choose the slideshows you want to include.

In the "Create a VCD with Menu" window, you must choose between the NTSC or PAL formats for your disc. Choose PAL if you're sending your slideshow to Europe or China, and choose NTSC for most other areas, including the United States. Then click Burn to begin burning your disc.

NOTE   If you also have Adobe's Premiere Elements software (and a drive that can create DVDs), you can send your slideshow to Premiere Elements to make a true DVD. (If you have a DVD recorder, but no Premiere Elements, you can save your slideshow and then use any other DVD authoring software you've got loaded on your PC.)

- **Email Slide Show.** You can send your slideshow via email, either as a WMV file or a PDF document. When choosing a size from the Slide Size pull-down menu in the Output window, just remember that your friends with dial-up Internet connections won't thank you for sending giant files. Even in this day and age of widespread high-speed Internet connections, many mail servers don't let people receive files larger than five megabytes.

- **Send to TV.** If you have Windows Media Center Edition running on your PC, and your television is connected to your computer, you can send your slideshow straight to the TV for large-screen viewing. In the Output window, click "Send to TV," and then type a name for your slideshow in the Name box. Next, choose the option in the Settings pull-down menu that correctly describes your TV, and then click OK. (If you aren't sure what to choose in the Settings menu, click the Details button to learn more about the currently selected choice.)

Flipbooks

Flipbooks are a new feature in Elements 5. In some ways, a flipbook is like a very simple slideshow without any transitions, audio, or fancy panning and zooming. After slogging through the last section, you may be thinking you've had enough slideshow options in Elements, thank you very much. But all that's different about a flipbook is the speed at which the images appear. A flipbook's *frame rate* (how fast one image appears and disappears) is very fast. When you put a stack of photos you took with your camera in burst mode into a flipbook, you can create an animation where the images change so fast it appears that your subject is moving.

> **TIP**   Flipbooks are great for creating a time-lapse effect. For instance, if you take a photo of the building progress of your new house each day from the exact same spot, you can combine all the photos and watch your house go from an empty lot to finished in just a few seconds.

The flipbook effect is similar to an animated GIF, but you can use JPEGs in your flipbook, so the image quality is much higher than with a GIF (see page 55 for more about GIFs). The downside is that you can't easily embed a flipbook as an animated object in a Web page. Your completed flipbook is a Windows Media file, so all you can do is watch it like a movie or regular slideshow. That said, Adobe does give you several different output sizes, so you can pick one that's suitable for watching on a regular television (although you'll need Adobe's Premiere Elements or some other video creation program to create a version your television understands).

You may also want to create a flipbook as a plain old slideshow, since they're quick to create and easy to email. Regardless of how you plan to use your flipbook, here's how to get started:

1. **In the Organizer, select the photos you want to include.**

   You must choose at least two photos, or you'll get a warning (instead of the Flipbook wizard) when you try to continue. You can't add or delete photos once you're in the wizard, so be sure you have all the photos you want before you start. You may want to make a collection (see page 48) to help you keep track.

   NOTE   The flipbook displays your photos in order based on their file names or numbering. For example, files with names like img_0617.jpg, img_0618.jpg, and so on, will appear in numerical order. The only control the Flipbook wizard gives you is that you can reverse the order of the entire group of images.

2. **Go to Create → Flipbook.**

   The Flipbook wizard shows you the window in Figure 18-13. You can preview your flipbook by pressing the Play button below the image area.

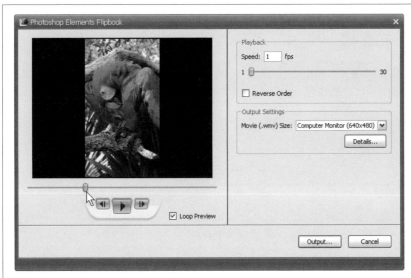

Figure 18-13:
If you wish to step through your photos to make sure you've included the right ones, you can do so by moving this slider. However, you can't add or remove photos once you're in the Flipbook wizard.

3. **Adjust your settings.**

   You only have a limited number of choices in the flipbook window. Because the images move so fast, flipbooks don't allow you to use any kind of transitions between slides. All you can do is to choose:

- **Playback Speed.** The number of frames per second (each photo is one frame). One frame per second is the slowest option, and even that's pretty zippy for a regular slideshow. The more frames per second you choose, the faster and smoother the animation effect will be, and the shorter the total playback time for the flipbook will be.

- **Reverse Order.** If you want to see your slides from last to first, instead of first to last, turn on this checkbox.

- **Output Settings.** These settings determine the final size of your flipbook. You get a variety of file formats to choose from. *Computer Monitor* is a good medium size that gives you a convenient balance between file size and image size. *Web* is a good size for using on a Web page (assuming your viewers have broadband Internet connections). *E-mail* creates a very tiny show that you can send to people with dial-up connections. You can also choose to create your flipbook as *TV-NTSC* or *TV-PAL*. NTSC is for American video players, and PAL is used primarily in Europe and China. (If you choose either of these settings, you'll need a program like Premiere Elements to create your final DVD for television viewing.) Figure 18-14 gives you more advice if you need help choosing a setting.

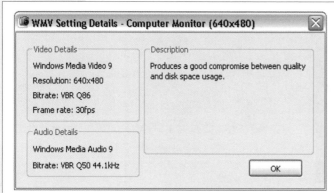

Figure 18-14:
If you're unsure which output format to use for your flipbook, click the Details button in the Photoshop Elements Flipbook window. You get a window with more information, as you see here, about the size you've currently selected.

- **Loop Preview.** Turn this box on, and your preview plays endlessly once you click the Play button, until you stop it by clicking the Pause button.

4. **Create your flipbook.**

   When you're happy with how your flipbook performs, click Output. If you want to make large changes, like adding or removing photos, or if you decide not to make a flipbook at all, click Cancel. (You need to start from the beginning if you wish to change your photo selection.)

   When you click Output, a new window opens where you must name and save your video, which automatically gets added to the Organizer. Then you're all done.

6

Part Six:
Additional Elements

Chapter 19: Beyond the Basics

Beyond the Basics

So far, everything in this book has been about what you can do with Elements right out of the box. But like many things digital, there's a thriving cottage industry devoted to souping up Elements. You can add new brush shapes, Layer styles, and fancy filters. Best of all, a lot of what's out there is free. And many of the tools are especially designed to make Elements behave more like Photoshop. This chapter looks at some of these extras, how to manage the stuff you collect, and how to know when you really do need the full version of Photoshop instead. You'll also learn about the many resources available for expanding your knowledge of Elements beyond this book.

Graphics Tablets

Probably the most popular Elements accessory is a *graphics tablet*, which lets you draw and paint with a pen-like stylus instead of a mouse. If trying to use the Lasso tool with a mouse makes you feel like you're trying to write on a mirror with a bar of soap, then a graphics tablet is for you (Figure 19-1).

> **NOTE** There are deluxe model tablet PCs that act as a monitor and let you work directly on your image. But you need to budget a few thousand dollars for that kind of convenience.

Most tablets work like the one shown in Figure 19-1. You use the special pen on the tablet just as you would a mouse on a mousepad; any changes you make appear right on your monitor.

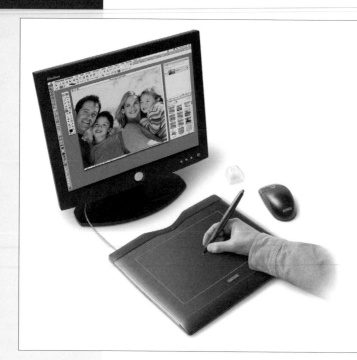

Figure 19-1:
A Wacom Graphire tablet in action. This tablet is 6"×8", a bit larger than the smallest size available (4"×5"). The working area is inside the rectangle on the tablet surface. For basic photo retouching, a small size is usually fine once you get used to it. If you want to do more drawing and you generally use sweeping strokes when you draw, then you may want a larger tablet.

For most people, it's much easier to control fine motions using a tablet's pen compared to a mouse. Moreover, when you use a tablet, many of the brushes and tools in Elements are *pressure sensitive*—the harder you press, the darker and wider the line becomes. The tablet pen lets you create much more realistic paint strokes, as shown in Figure 19-2.

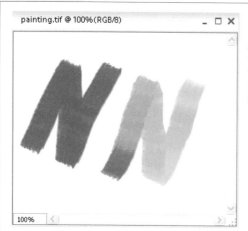

Figure 19-2:
Two almost identical paint strokes, starting with fairly hard pressure and then lightening up. Both were made using the identical brush and color in Elements. The only difference is that the stroke on the left was drawn with a mouse, and the one on the right came from a tablet. You can see what a difference the pressure sensitivity makes.

When using the Brush tool, you'll see Tablet Options next to the Airbrush setting in the Options bar. Many brushes and tools are automatically pressure-sensitive when you hook up a tablet. You can also choose whether to let the pressure control the size, opacity, roundness, hue jitter, and scatter for your brushes. (See page 307 for more about Brush settings.)

With a tablet, you can also create hand-drawn line art—even if you don't have an artistic bone in your body—by placing a picture of what you want to draw on the surface of the tablet and tracing the outline. Also, if you find constant mousing troublesome, you may have fewer hand problems when using a tablet's pen. Most tablets come with a wireless mouse, which you can use on the surface of the tablet, or you can use your regular mouse the way you always do.

Tablet prices start at less than a hundred dollars these days, a big drop from what they used to cost. There are many models available, and the features vary widely. Sophisticated tablets offer more levels of sensitivity and respond when you change the angle at which you hold the stylus.

Wacom, one of the big tablet manufacturers, has some pretty nifty tablet demos on their European Web site (*www.wacom-europe.com/uk/use-it/demos/index.asp*). You can't actually simulate what it's like to use a tablet, but the animations give you a good idea of what your life would be like if you went the tablet route.

Free Stuff from the Internet

You have to spend some money if you want a graphics tablet, but there's a ton of free stuff—tutorials, brushes, textures, and Layer styles, for example—available online that you can add to Elements. Most of these add-ons say they work with Photoshop, but since Elements is based on Photoshop, you can use most of them in Elements, too.

Here are some popular places to go treasure hunting:

- **Adobe Studio Exchange** (*http://share.studio.adobe.com*). On Adobe's own Web site, you can find hundreds and hundreds of downloads, including more Layer styles than you could ever use, brushes, textures, and custom shapes (to use with Shape tool). They're all free, but you have to register. This site is one of the best resources anywhere for extra stuff. About 99 percent of the items listed are made specifically for Photoshop, but Photoshop's brushes, swatches, textures, shapes, and Layer styles work with Elements, too.

- **Creative Mac** (*www.creativemac.com*). Don't let the name put you off. Almost everything on this site works in Windows, too. Here you'll find many great tutorials and a wonderful source for specialty brushes, especially for tricky things like hair and skin.

- **MyJanee** (*www.myjanee.com*). Lots of tutorials and free downloads here.

• **Sue Chastain** (*http://graphicssoft.about.com*). This is another Web site with lots of downloads and many tutorials.

• **Panosfx** (*www.panosfx.com*). Panos Efstathiadis produces some wonderful actions (see the section "When You Really Need Photoshop," below) for Photoshop, and now he's adapted many of them for Elements as well. Most are free; a few are shareware.

• **Optik Verve Labs** (*www.optikvervelabs.com*). This is the home of Virtual Photographer, one of the most amazing plug-ins for Elements. Best of all, it's free.

There are many, many other Web sites. Just enter what you're looking for as your Google search term, and you're bound to see many choices.

> **NOTE** A word of warning: Before setting off on your search, make sure you have a good pop-up window blocker for your Web browser. And be sure you have good anti-virus software installed, as well as detectors for adware and spyware.

If you're willing to pay a little bit, you've got even more choices. You can find everything from more elaborate ways to sharpen your photos to really cool collections of special edges and visual effects. Prices range from donationware (you pay if you like it) to some quite expensive and sophisticated *plug-ins* that cost hundreds of dollars. (A plug-in is a mini program that expands what Elements can do. You get some plug-ins as part of Elements—like the Save For Web dialog box that's described on page 429—and you can add third-party plug-ins, too.) You can also buy books like the *Wow!* series (Peachpit Press), which have very little text and loads of illustrations showing the styles available on the included CD.

> **NOTE** Mac plug-ins don't work in Windows, and vice versa (many plug-ins offer two versions, one for each platform). Elements 5, like Elements 4, is based on Photoshop CS2, so CS2 downloads are compatible. Plug-ins and other goodies designed for older versions of Photoshop or Elements usually work with newer versions, but not the other way around. So a brush made for Photoshop CS2 works in Elements 5 but not Elements 3.

With so many goodies available, it's easy to find yourself overwhelmed trying to keep track of everything you've added to Elements. Your best bet's to make backup copies of anything you download so you'll have it if you ever need to reinstall Elements.

Elements also includes a Preset Manager (Figure 19-3) that can help manage certain kinds of downloads. Go to Edit → Preset Manager to launch it.

> **NOTE** Most Photoshop plug-ins work just fine in Elements, but check with the plug-in's creator before you buy to be sure.

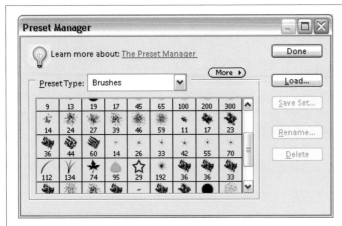

Figure 19-3:
The Elements Preset Manager offers a place to see all your brushes, swatches, gradients, and patterns in one place. You can use it to switch which groups are loaded, to add or remove items, and so on—the same way you do in the main brush window.

When You Really Need Photoshop

You can do an enormous amount with just Elements, but some people do need the full version of Photoshop. For example, if you need the ability to write your own *actions* (actions are little scripts, like macros, that automate certain things you might do in Photoshop) or if you need to work extensively in CMYK mode, then you need Photoshop.

CMYK mode is the color mode used for commercial printing—it stands for Cyan, Magenta, Yellow, and blacK, which are the colors professional printers use. When you send a file to a print shop, they usually tell you it needs to be a CMYK file. You can't convert files to CMYK in Elements. If you need CMYK files on a regular basis, it's worth the extra price of Photoshop to avoid the aggravation. If you only occasionally need CMYK, you might just ask your printer. Most print shops are willing to convert the file for you for an additional charge.

> **NOTE**   Richard Lynch (*www.hiddenelements.com*) created a workaround for CMYK conversion for earlier versions of Elements. You may want to check his Web site to see what he's come up with for Elements 5.

In Photoshop you get more of everything: more choices, more tools, more settings, more types of adjustment layers, and so on.

Beyond This Book

You can do thousands of interesting things with Elements that are beyond the scope of this book. Your bookstore has dozens of titles on Elements and Photoshop, and a lot of things are common to both programs. There are all kinds of specialized books on everything from color management to making selections to scrapbooking.

TIP   If you're looking to learn some photo-shooting and -editing techniques from a pro who's been at it since the birth of digital cameras, then check out *Stephen Johnson on Digital Photography* (O'Reilly).

In addition, you'll find hundreds of tutorial sites on the Web. Besides those mentioned earlier in the chapter, other popular sites include:

- **Adobe** (*www.adobe.com/education/training/photoshop_elements/main.html*). Plenty of free online training for Elements here.

- **Jay Arraich** (*http://arraich.com/elements/psE_intro.htm*). Lots of Elements information, both basic and advanced, from a longtime Photoshop guru.

Two important resources that have all kinds of interesting information are:

- **Elements Challenge pages** (*www.cavesofice.org/~grant/Challenge*). Maintained by Grant Dixon, this site offers you a chance to try your Elements skills with a different Elements challenge every week. Anyone's welcome to participate, no matter what your skill level. If you feel intimidated by some of the entries, don't be. Everyone started off as a beginner. There's also a links page with many tutorial and download sites.

- **Photoshop Elements User** (*www.photoshopelementsuser.com*). This is the Web site for a subscriber-only print newsletter, but it also includes some free online video tutorials, a forum, and a good collection of links. This is the first publication especially for Elements.

If you search Google, you're sure to find a tutorial for any project you might have in mind, although many of them are written for full Photoshop. In most cases, you can adapt them for Elements. If you get stuck or you need help with any other aspect of Elements, there's a very active online community that's sure to have an answer for you. Besides the sites already mentioned, try:

- **Adobe Support forum** (*www.adobe.com/forums*). Scroll down the page to find the Elements User-to-User forum. Lots of helpful and friendly people here. It's your best bet for getting answers without calling Adobe support.

- **Digital Photography Review** (*www.dpreview.com*). You'll find many camera-specific forums on this site. You can also get a lot of Elements answers in the Retouching forum if you specify in your question that you've got Elements rather than Photoshop.

- **Retouch Pro** (*www.retouchpro.cmo/forums*). The forums here cover all kinds of retouching and artistic uses of Elements and Photoshop.

- **Adobe Photoshop Elements Alliance** (*www.elementsusers.com*). Another forum strictly for Photoshop Elements. Not the most active forum, but it offers some helpful information.

As Elements becomes ever more popular with scrapbookers, you're sure to find more sites like:

• Scrapper's Guide (*www.scrappersguide.com*). A commercial site run by Linda Sattgast, for using Elements in scrapbook making.

Adobe's clearly hoping that lots of people will be inspired to create additional graphics and themes for the Artwork and Effects palette, so by the time you're reading this, there may be many more sites like Linda's. Just try a Google search for what you need.

There's no question about it: once you get familiar with Elements, it's addicting! Lots of other folks have found out how much fun this program is, and you shouldn't have any trouble finding the answer to any question you might have.

The only limit to what you can do with Elements is your imagination. Enjoy!

POWER USERS' CLINIC

Making Elements Behave More Like Photoshop

While each version of Elements is more talented than its predecessor, there's one thing about Elements 5 that you may not like if you're a long-time member of the Elements community. Ever since Elements first came out, there's been quite a little cottage industry devoted to figuring out ways to get Elements to behave more like Photoshop.

If you've used Elements 3 or earlier, the odds are pretty good that you're familiar with the extra tools and action players created by Richard Lynch, Paul Shipley, Grant Dixon, and Nero Ling. Unfortunately, Adobe decided to write Elements 4 in a way that disabled the traditional route used by add-on tools to access some of the underlying Photoshop code needed for these additional features to work, so many of the existing add-on tools stopped working in Elements 4.

It's a good news/bad news situation in Elements 5. Adobe has made it easier in some ways to add actions to Elements (just toss them into C: → Documents and Settings → All Users → Application Data → Adobe → Photoshop Elements → 5.0 → Photo Creations → special effects → photo effects). But they didn't restore the "hooks" to the underlying code, so you still have the same problem of not being able to use most actions written for Photoshop. For example, although Elements now has Curves (see page 248), it's not implemented the same way as Photoshop's Curves command. So a Photoshop action that calls up Curves is going to get confused and stop working in Elements when it reaches that step.

For now, it's best to stick to actions that state they're written for Elements 4 or Elements 5, if you want to be sure an action will work.

If you've been using extra tools or actions in Elements 2 or 3, you may want to keep the older version of the program around just for them. (You can have as many different versions of Elements as you like installed on your computer at once, but Adobe recommends that you run only one version at a time.)

Richard Lynch, who has created many tools for earlier versions of Elements, has revised his tools for Elements 5. He's making two of them available for Missing Manual readers (see the "Missing CD" page at *www. missingmanuals.com*). The two tools you'll find there (along with installation instructions and explanations for using them) are Layer Masks, which you can use the way you would in Photoshop (without the hassle of having to create an Adjustment layer first), and a Channel Mixer, which lets you adjust the balance of the different color channels (this is very popular for the kind of black-and-white conversions you can make in Photoshop). Visit *www.hiddenelements.com* for more information about other tools Lynch has created for Elements.

Grant Dixon offers a smaller free tool set for Elements, and it seems likely that others also will soon figure out a way to add more tools to Elements 5.

Part Seven:
Appendixes

7

The Organizer, Menu by Menu

This appendix gives you a quick tour of the main menus in the Organizer. The Organizer has two main windows: Photo Browser and Date View. Both offer the same menu choices—everything listed here is available in either window. There are keyboard shortcuts and buttons in the Organizer windows that give you access to many of these menu items. When there's an alternate method, it's listed in the text.

In addition to the main menus discussed here, the Organizer is chock full of shortcut (also called contextual) menus. You can right-click almost anywhere in the Organizer, and you'll get a menu with several options specific to the object you clicked. Click a tag, for instance, and you get a menu that includes choices for editing the tag or changing it to a category.

> **NOTE**   If you also have Premiere Elements or Photoshop installed, you'll see a few additional menu choices not listed here.

File Menu

This menu is where you import photos, start new projects, manage your catalogs, and export your photos. It's also where you quit the Organizer when you're done.

Get Photos

Here's where you import photos into the Organizer. You can tell Elements to find and import photos from:

- **A camera or card reader** (or press Ctrl+G).

- **A scanner** (or press Ctrl+U).

- **Files and folders** (or press Ctrl+Shift+G).

- **Mobile phones** (or press Ctrl+Shift+M).

- **By Searching** tells Elements to search your computer for photos. You can choose to search all your hard drives (if you have more than one attached to your PC), your C drive only, your My Documents folder, or you can browse to a particular folder or drive to search only its contents.

New

You can choose to create a new blank file that will appear in the Editor. (The Organizer itself doesn't create blank files.) You can also copy a photo in the Organizer (Ctrl+C) and choose to start a new Editor file by copying your photo from the Clipboard (the invisible file that stores what you copy until you paste it somewhere), or start a Photomerge panorama from files you've selected in the Organizer. (Again, this choice takes you to the Editor for the actual merge. See page 284 for more about panoramas.)

Create

From this submenu, you can start many types of projects from the Organizer, although some, like Photo Layouts (page 397), send you to the Editor to put your project together. Here's what you can choose to make:

- **Photo Book Pages** (see page 405)

- **Photo Layout** (page 397)

- **Album Pages** (page 405)

- **Greeting Card** (page 405)

- **CD Jacket** (page 406)

- **DVD Jacket** (page 406)

- **CD/DVD Label** (page 406)

- **Slide Show** (page 457)

- **VCD with Menu** (page 467)

- **Photo Galleries** (page 447)

- **Flipbook** (page 468)

- **Photo Calendar** (page 407)

- **PhotoStamps** (page 407)

Open Recently Edited File in Editor

Choose a file from the list, and the Organizer opens it in the Editor so you can work on it there.

Open Creation

Any Elements project that you've already made (see page 43) appears when you choose this menu item. If you're a scrapbooker, or if you just like to make lots of projects, this is the best way to see a list of all your projects so you can decide which to open for editing or sharing.

Catalog

This is where you manage your catalogs (see page 43). A window opens where you can choose a catalog to open or recover (which repairs and compacts your catalog) from a list of your existing catalogs. You can also create a new catalog. Keyboard shortcut: Ctrl+Shift+C.

Copy/Move Offline

If you want to burn a photo or a group of photos to a CD or DVD, choose this command. Page 58 has more information about backing up your files. Keyboard shortcut: Ctrl+Shift+O.

Backup Catalog

It's wise to keep a good backup of your catalog; this command makes it easy to do so. You can choose to back up your entire catalog or just a few photos. See page 58 for detailed directions on using Backup. Keyboard shortcut: Ctrl+Shift+B.

Restore Catalog

Choose this to replace your catalog with an archived version, if you accidentally delete photos or otherwise run into trouble with the current version. Restore is also a good maintenance tool. If your catalog mysteriously balloons to a huge file size, Restore can usually compress it to bring it back down to a reasonable size. You might want to run Restore every couple of weeks as part of your maintenance routine.

Online Backup

This gives you a link to Iron Mountain, a commercial online backup service (page 61). For a fee, you can store your photos on their servers. Of course, there are many similar services, but the advantage here is the direct connection to the Organizer.

Duplicate

Highlight a photo or a Create project and choose this menu item (or press Ctrl+Shift+D) to make a duplicate.

Reconnect

Sometimes your Organizer catalog (page 43) can't find a file when you ask for it. Usually this happens when you move or rename a file using a method outside of Elements (like Windows Explorer). This command tells the Organizer to find the file again. You can choose to reconnect:

• **Missing File.** Choose this to reconnect one file.

• **All Files.** The Organizer searches for all the files it can't find.

Watch Folders

Use this command if you regularly import photos into certain folders. Elements monitors the folders you choose and checks for new graphics stored inside them. You can tell Elements to automatically place any photos it finds into your catalog, if you want. If you prefer, Elements can just notify you that it found new files and let you decide what to do with them.

Rename

If you want the Organizer to keep track of your photos, you need to move and rename them from within Elements (rather than using, say, Windows Explorer). So if you want to change the name of a photo, choose this menu item or press Ctrl+Shift+N.

Write Tag and Properties Info to Photo(s)

Normally your Organizer tags exist only in your catalog's database. If you want to make the tag information part of the photo file itself (the way keywords are in Photoshop or in the Mac version of Elements), choose this menu item. Elements writes your tags into the file's IPTC metadata (see page 51).

Move

If you want the Organizer to keep track of your photos, you must move them within Elements once they're in your catalog. To move a photo, choose this menu item and then select a destination in the window that appears. You can also move files by dragging them if you go to View → Arrangement → Folder Location. You'll see a new pane on the left of the Photo browser with a schematic view of the folder structure of your hard drive (just like you see elsewhere in Windows). You can drag your photos into the folders you want. Keyboard shortcut: Ctrl+Shift+V.

Export

If you want to export a group of photos for use by another program, this is one way to do it. Choose Export As New File(s) from the menu, and you get a dialog box where you can choose the destination of your files and rename them if you like. You can also choose to convert the exported files to a different format. Your choices are JPG, PSD, TIFF, or PNG. This menu choice is a useful feature if you need to create JPEGs for printing at a store kiosk, for example. The Export menu also lets you export photos to a mobile phone (see page 441).

E-Mail

This brings up the Organizer's email window, which is described in detail on page 436. Keyboard shortcut: Ctrl+Shift+E.

Page Setup

This calls up your system's regular Page Setup window, where you choose the page size and the orientation of your document and the printer you plan to use. Page 419 has more about printing from the Organizer. Keyboard shortcut: Ctrl+Shift+P.

Print

Choose this command, and you get the Organizer's Print Selected Photos window, which is discussed in detail in Chapter 16. Keyboard shortcut: Ctrl+P.

Order Prints

This is one way to connect to the online Kodak EasyShare Gallery to order prints or photo books. See page 410 for details on how to order prints online from the Organizer.

Exit

You can close the Organizer here or by pressing Ctrl+Q. The Editor doesn't quit along with the Organizer. If the Editor is also running, you must exit it separately.

Edit Menu

This menu contains choices that let you make changes to your files. It's also where you can access your Elements preferences to change their settings.

Undo

You can undo your last action in the Organizer by selecting Undo or by pressing Ctrl+Z.

Redo

If you undo something and then change your mind, redo it here or press Ctrl+Y.

Copy

To copy something to the Clipboard, highlight it and select this menu item or press Ctrl+C.

Select All

Choose this to select all the photos in any window in the Organizer, or press Ctrl+A.

Deselect

To clear all selections, choose this or press Ctrl+Shift+A.

Delete from Catalog

This removes a photo from the catalog database. You can also press Delete to do the same thing. If you want to remove the photo from your hard drive as well, the dialog box that appears gives you the option to do so.

Rotate 90° Left

To rotate a photo 90 degrees counterclockwise, select it, and then choose this menu item or just press Ctrl+left arrow key.

Rotate 90° Right

To rotate a photo 90 degrees clockwise, select it, and then choose this menu item or just press Ctrl+right arrow key.

Auto Smart Fix

To instantly apply the Auto Smart Fix command to your photo, choose this item or press Ctrl+Alt+M. See Chapter 4 for more about Auto Smart Fix.

Auto Red Eye Fix

Choose this or press Ctrl+R to automatically find and correct red eye problems in all the selected photos. See page 95 for more about how this feature works.

Edit 3GPP Movie

This is where you can edit movies to send to wireless devices, like cellphones, that also have the ability to play video. Your movie must be in the 3GPP or MPEG-4 format. Select this menu item for a window with your editing controls.

Go to Quick Fix

Choose this item to go to the Editor's Quick Fix window (see Chapter 4).

Go to Full Edit

Choose this item to go to the Editor. Keyboard shortcut: Ctrl+I.

Adjust Date and Time

If you want to adjust a file's date and time settings, select this item or press Ctrl+J. You get three choices:

- **Change to a specified date and time.** This lets you adjust the date and time manually.

- **Change to match the file's date and time.** This changes the time and date to reflect the last time you modified the file.

- **Shift by a set number of hours (time zone adjust).** This lets you change the date and time of a selected group of photos. Any changes you make get made to all the photos you've selected. For example, if you elect to move the time back three hours (via the Time Zone Adjust dialog box), all your selected photos have their times moved back three hours.

Add Caption

To add a caption to an image, choose this menu item or press Ctrl+Shift+T.

Update Thumbnail

If an image thumbnail stops displaying correctly or doesn't show the correct image, choose this menu item or press Ctrl+Shift+U.

Set as Desktop Wallpaper

To use one or more of your photos as wallpaper for your desktop, just click its thumbnail in the Photo Browser, and then choose this menu item or press Ctrl+Shift+W. If you select multiple photos, Elements tiles them so that they all appear as a sort of collage.

Place on Map

Lets you stick photos onto a Yahoo map. Choose this menu item, and you get a dialog box where you can enter the location where they should appear. (There's more about maps on page 441.)

Remove from Map

If your photo already has a place on a Yahoo map and you want to take it off, choose this menu item.

Show on Map

If you've assigned a photo to a spot on a Yahoo map, choose this menu item to see the map showing the photo's location.

Stack

This is where you create and manage *photo stacks*. Stacks are groups of photos that you want to store together. Only the top photo shows in the Photo Browser until you expand the stack. Stacks can be made from unrelated photos, unlike version sets (see later). Your options here are:

- **Automatically Suggest Photo Stacks.** If you've taken photos using your camera's burst or bracket mode, this menu item sorts related photos into their own stacks. (Elements isn't smart enough to look through a folder and find all the photos you took of Yellowstone National Park, though. The photos must be similar in subject and taken very close together in time for this command to work.) Keyboard shortcut: Ctrl+Alt+K.

- **Stack Selected Photos.** Highlight your photos and choose this menu item to put them into a stack. You can also press Ctrl+Alt+S.

- **Unstack Photos.** This modifies a selected photo stack so that the photos it includes are no longer joined together.

- **Expand Photos in Stack.** Choose this or press Ctrl+Alt+R to see all the photos in a stack.

- **Collapse Photos in Stack.** To compress an expanded stack again, choose this command, or press Ctrl+Alt+Shift+R.

- **Flatten Stack.** This reduces your stack to the visible photo, eliminating the hidden photos.

- **Remove Selected Photos from Stack.** Use this to remove one or more photos from a stack.

- **Set as Top Photo.** Highlight a photo and choose this to send that photo to the top of the stack. From now on, it becomes the visible photo.

Version Set

This is where you manage your version sets. When you make changes to a photo in the Editor, you have the option of creating a *version set*, as long as your photo is stored in the Organizer. In a version set, each time you save your photo, Elements saves it as a copy with a new name, that is, a different version. In this way, you can save many files containing your changes and go back to any one at any time. Your options here are:

- **Expand Items in Version Set.** Choose this item, or press Ctrl+Alt+E, to see all your versions at once.

- **Collapse Items in Version Set.** To return an expanded version set to single image view, choose this command, or press Ctrl+Alt+Shift+E.

- **Flatten Version Set.** Use this to reduce a version set to one photo, the top one.

- **Convert Version Set to Individual Items.** If you want to be able to work with the files in a version set as though they were separate photos, choose this item and, instead of a version set, you get multiple individual photos.

- **Revert to Original.** This deletes later versions, leaving only your original photo as it was in when you first brought it into the Organizer.

- **Remove Item(s) from Version Set.** If you find you've saved more versions than you need, highlight the ones you want to get rid of and choose this menu item.

- **Set as Top Item.** Highlight a photo and choose this option to send that photo to the top of the set. From now on, it becomes the visible photo.

Color Settings

This is where you can set your color space. See page 181 for more about color spaces. You can also press Ctrl+Alt+G to bring up Elements color settings.

Contact Book

If you want to see or edit your Contact Book of email addresses (to use when sending your photos from Elements), you can get to it here. See page 438 for more about the Contact Book.

Preferences

This is where you can make changes to your Organizer settings for getting and saving photos; connecting to cameras, scanners, or mobile phones; emailing; editing; and creating tags, collections, and calendars, as well as setting what you want to see in Folder view. You can adjust your settings for using the online Kodak EasyShare Gallery here, and tell Adobe whether or not you want to see ads for special offers. You can also get to the Editor's preferences from this menu.

Find Menu

This menu is really the heart of the Organizer. You can search for your photos in many different ways from this menu.

Set Date Range

Choose this menu item, and a dialog box appears that lets you specify start and end dates. The Organizer shows all the photos that fall in the date range you specify. Keyboard shortcut: Ctrl+Alt+F.

Clear Date Range

After you've searched for a date range, choose this menu item to return to your complete catalog in the Photo Browser, or press Ctrl+Shift+F.

By Caption or Note

When you choose this item, you get a dialog box in which you can search for any text in your captions or notes. It doesn't have to be the entire caption. The Organizer finds all the photos with those words in either field. Keyboard shortcut: Ctrl+Shift+J.

By Filename

Enter part of a file name and the Organizer finds the file for you. Keyboard shortcut: Ctrl+Shift+K.

All Version Sets

Choose this, and Elements shows you all the version sets in your catalog.

All Stacks

This menu item makes Elements show you all the photo stacks you've made.

By History

Choose to find your file based on any of the following factors:

- **Imported On.** This is the date you brought your file into the Organizer.

- **E-mailed to.** You can search by the names of people you've emailed your photos to, but only if you sent the messages from the Organizer.

- **Printed On.** Search for the photos you printed on a certain date.

- **Exported On.** Search for all the photos you exported from the Organizer on a particular date.

- **Ordered Online.** Search for the photos you've ordered from the Kodak Easy-Share Gallery (see page 410).

- **Shared Online.** Search for the photos you've shared on the Kodak EasyShare Gallery (see page 410).

- **Used in Creations.** Search for all the photos you've used in your Create projects.

By Media Type

The Organizer doesn't organize only still photos. You can also use it to keep track of movies and audio files. Here, you can search for all the files of a particular type:

- **Photos.** Find still photos (press Alt+1).

- **Video.** Find video clips (press Alt+2).

- **Audio.** Find your audio files (press Alt+3).

- **Creations.** Find all your Create projects (press Alt+4).

- **Items with Audio Captions.** If you've recorded captions for any of your photos (see Chapter 18), you can search for them by choosing this menu item (or by pressing Alt+5).

- **PDF.** You can import and tag PDF files in the Organizer. If you want to see all your PDFs, choose this or press Alt+6.

- **Photo Creations Format.** To see all the files you've created using the new project types, like Photo Layouts, choose this item or press Alt+7.

By Details (Metadata)

If you want to search your photos according to what's stored in their metadata, like the EXIF information (page 51) from your camera, this is where you start. See page 50 for more about how to perform these searches.

Items with Unknown Date and Time

Choose this menu item if you want to find any photos that haven't been properly tagged with the date and time. Keyboard shortcut: Ctrl+Shift+X.

By Visual Similarity with Selected Photo(s)

This is a very cool feature. If you want to find photos that have colors and tones that are similar to a particular photo (or group of photos), select the photo(s) you want to match, and then choose this item. Elements ranks all your photos by color. The closest matches appear at the top of the list.

Untagged Items

To find photos that you haven't tagged yet, choose this menu item or press Ctrl+Shift+Q.

Items Not in Any Collection

Choose this menu item to find all the photos you haven't used in collections yet.

Find Faces for Tagging

Choose this, and Elements searches your photos for pictures with people's faces in them. You can't choose to search for a particular person, only for all faces. The idea behind this feature is that if you have all your family's and friends' faces in one window, you can quickly tag them with their appropriate tags. Once you've used Find Faces, you can choose to find only untagged photos on future searches, speeding up the process considerably. You can also click the Faces button in the Organize bin to do the same thing.

View Menu

This menu lets you control how your photos are presented in the Organizer. It also includes two very cool ways to look through a group of photos or compare photos.

View Photos in Full Screen

Choose this or press F11, and you get a full-screen slideshow of your photos. Elements presents you with a floating control strip to help you navigate through the photos, but it appears only when you mouse over it. It's a great way to check through a group of newly imported photos, and you can even choose music to listen to while you watch your slideshow.

Compare Photos Side by Side

This is similar to "View Photos in Full Screen in that you get a full-screen view. But in "Compare Photos Side by Side," you get to see any two photos of your choice side by side. It's great for choosing which photos you want to keep or print. You can also get to "Compare Photos Side by Side" by pressing F12. To bring in a new photo for comparison, click the photo that you want to get rid of.

Refresh

If you need to refresh the view, choose this menu item or press F5.

Go To

When you're looking through photos, use this to go:

- **Back** (press Alt+left arrow)
- **Forward** (press Alt+right arrow)

Arrangement

This is an important menu item. It tells the Organizer how you want to see the photos in the Photo Browser. You can choose to arrange your photos by:

- **Date (Newest First)** (Ctrl+Alt+0)
- **Date (Oldest First)** (Ctrl+Alt+1)
- **Import Batch** (Ctrl+Alt+2)
- **Folder Location** (Ctrl+Alt+3)

Media Types

Choose this item to bring up a window where you can choose what kinds of media the Organizer displays. Your choices are photos, videos, audio, creations, PDF files, and the new Photo Creations format. Just turn on the ones you want and turn off the ones you don't.

Details

When Details is turned on, you see the information about your photos in the Photo Browser window, like the date and the tag icons. Turn Details off to see just the thumbnails with no other information. Keyboard shortcut: Ctrl+D.

Timeline

When Timeline is turned on, you see the Timeline above the Image Well (see page 45). To hide the Timeline, turn it off here, or press Ctrl+L.

Collapse All Tags

Choose this item to collapse all the tags in the Organize bin, leaving only their categories showing. You can also press Ctrl+Alt+T.

Expand All Tags

Choose this item to see the list of all your tags expanded in the Organize bin so that every tag is visible. You can also press Ctrl+Alt+X.

Collapse All Collections

Choosing this option collapses, on the Collections tab, all collections, leaving only collection groups visible.

Expand All Collections

Choosing this option expands, on the Collections tab, all collections so that you can see every collection in the list.

Expand All Stacks

To see every photo in every stack, choose this menu item.

Collapse All Stacks

To return all your stacks to single photo view, choose this menu item.

Window Menu

This menu is where you choose which parts of the Organizer are visible. Most of the items are grouped in pairs, because you must choose one or the other. For instance, you have to choose between Photo Browser and Date View for the main Organizer window.

Photo Browser

If you want to see the Photo Browser window, you can choose it here or click the button on the Shortcuts bar, or press Ctrl+Alt+O.

Date View

Date View displays your photos on a calendar. You can switch to Date View here or click the button below the image thumbnails, or press Ctrl+Alt+D.

Organize Bin

The Organize bin at the right of the Photo Browser displays your tag and collections information. You can turn it on and off here, to hide or reveal it.

Tags

To see the Tags tab in the Organize bin, turn it on here, or turn it off to switch to the Collections tab. (You can also just click the tabs themselves in the Organize bin or press Ctrl+T.)

Collections

To see the Collections tab in the Organize bin, turn it on here, or turn it off to switch to the Tags tab. (You can also just click the tabs themselves in the Organize bin, or press Ctrl+Alt+L.)

Order Prints

You can turn the Order Prints pane in the Organize bin on and off here.

Properties

To see the Properties window for a photo, highlight it and then choose this menu item or press Alt+Enter.

Dock Properties in Organize Bin

If you use the Properties window so much that you'd like to keep it around, choose this to send it to live in the Organize bin where you can always see it.

Upload Progress Window

When you send photos to EasyShare for printing or sharing, the Upload Progress Window lets you track how close your upload is to being completed. Turn the window off or on here.

Welcome

Choose this to bring up the Elements Welcome window that you see when the program first launches. If you've chosen to always start in the Organizer and you want to change your startup to the Editor, for instance, call up the Welcome window here and then make your change at the bottom of the window.

Help Menu

This menu is where you find the Elements Help files and tutorials, as well as information about the program itself.

Photoshop Elements Help

You can call up the Elements Help application here, or press F1. Or enter a search term in the box in the menu bar.

About Photoshop Elements

Choose this to see a scrolling window with information about the version of Elements you've got. You'll also see a very long list of patents and credits—an impressive testimony to the complexity of the engineering that went into Elements.

Glossary of Terms

The Elements Help files include a glossary of terms relating to digital imaging. If you're wondering what a term means, this menu item takes you to the glossary index so you can look it up.

Tutorials

The Elements Help files include some excellent tutorials. Choose this item to see a list of them.

System Info

Choose this for a window showing information about Elements itself and also about your Windows operating system. If you can't remember which service pack you have, for instance, you can check here. There's also information about some important plug-ins. If you're not sure whether you have QuickTime, for example, that information is here, too.

Registration

If you didn't register Elements with Adobe the first time you used the program, you can choose this to bring up the registration window again.

Updates

This is where you set your preferences for how you want Elements to handle updates and choose which Elements components you want to update.

Online Support

Choose this option, and Elements launches your Web browser and opens Adobe's support Web site. If it fails because you're not connected to the Internet, Elements launches an Internet connection window.

Photoshop Elements Online

This takes you to the main product page for Photoshop Elements on Adobe's Web site. Like the online support link, Elements launches your browser and offers to connect to the Internet if you're not already online when you chose this menu item.

Online Learning Resources

This also takes you to the main product page for Photoshop Elements on Adobe's Web site.

The Editor, Menu by Menu

The Editor's menus are far more complex than the menus in the Organizer. Both editing modes—Full Edit and Quick Fix—have the same menus, although some choices are grayed out when you're in Quick Fix mode. When you need a menu item that's unavailable in Quick Fix, just switch back to Full Edit to use it.

Several of the menus in Elements are dynamic; they change quite a bit to reflect the choices currently applicable to your image. That means the choices you see in this appendix represent only what you *may* see depending on the situation. The Layer menu, for instance, offers you very different options depending on the current state of your image and which layer's active.

> NOTE   If you have Adobe Premiere Elements installed, then you'll see some extra menu options not included in this basic list.

File Menu

The File menu commands let you create, import, browse, save, and print files.

New

Choose the New menu item if you want to start a new file in Elements. You can choose from:

- **Blank file.** Keyboard shortcut: Ctrl+N.

- **Image from Clipboard.** This automatically pastes anything you've copied into a new file.

• **Photomerge Panorama.** See page 284 for more about how to combine your photos into panoramas.

Create

Create is where you can start many kinds of Elements projects. Most are completed in the Editor, although for some, like Slideshows and Flipbooks, Elements sends you to the Organizer to create your project. You can choose to make:

• **Photo Book Pages** (see page 405)

• **Photo Layout** (page 397)

• **Album Pages** (page 405)

• **Greeting Card** (page 405)

• **CD Jacket** (page 406)

• **DVD Jacket** (page 406)

• **CD/DVD Label** (page 406)

• **Slideshow** (page 457)

• **Photo Galleries** (page 447)

• **Flipbook** (page 468)

• **Photo Calendar** (page 407)

• **PhotoStamps** (page 407)

Open

Choose the Open menu item or press Ctrl+O to open an existing file.

Open As

The Open As menu option (or Alt+Ctrl+O) lets you choose the format for a file as you open it.

Open Recently Edited File

The Open Recently Edited File menu item contains a pop-out list of the most recent files you've had open in Elements.

Duplicate

When you need to make a copy of your photo, choose Duplicate.

Close

To close the active image window, choose Close or press Ctrl+W.

Close All

To close all your open image windows, choose Close All or press Alt+Ctrl+W.

Save

To save your work, choose the Save menu item or press Ctrl+S.

Save As

To save your image under another file name or in a different format, choose Save As or press Shift+Ctrl+S.

Save For Web

To save an image so that it's optimized for posting on a Web page or sending by email, choose the Save for Web menu item or press Alt+Shift+Ctrl+S to bring up the Save For Web window (page 429).

File Info

Choose the File Info menu item to bring up the File Info window, which displays general information (file creation date, file format, and so on) about your image.

Place

Use the Place command to place a PDF, Adobe Illustrator, or EPS file into an image as a new layer. When the artwork's larger than the image you place it in, Elements automatically makes it small enough to fit.

Organize Open Files

Choose the Organize Open Files menu option to add the files you have open in the Editor to the Organizer.

Process Multiple Files

Process Multiple Files is where you batch process your files to rename them, change their format, add copyright information, and so on (see page 237 for everything that Elements lets you do to groups of files).

Import

Import is where you bring certain file formats into Elements. It's also where you can connect to external devices like scanners. (They'll show up in this menu if you install their drivers.) Your basic choices before you connect or install anything are:

- **Frame from Video** (see page 38)
- **WIA Support** (page 38)

Export

The Export command is always grayed out. That's normal. Adobe left it in for the benefit of any third-party plug-ins that may need it to be there. But you don't need it in Elements to use the program's standard tools and commands. (The Organizer contains an active Export command.)

Automation Tools

Like Export, Automation Tools is only here for any old model plug-ins that may need it. Normally, it's grayed out.

Page Setup

Page Setup calls up your system's regular Page Setup window, where you choose the page size and the orientation of your document and select the printer you plan to use. Read more about printing on page 414. Keyboard shortcut: Shift+Ctrl+P.

Print

Choose the Print command, and you get the Print Preview window, which is discussed in detail in Chapter 16. Keyboard shortcut: Ctrl+P.

Print Multiple Photos

Choose the Print Multiple Photos command, and you get the Organizer's Print Selected Photos window, which is discussed in detail on page 419. Keyboard shortcut: Alt+Ctrl+P.

Order Prints

The Order Prints command is your portal to connecting to the Kodak EasyShare Gallery to order prints, calendars, or photo books. See page 410 for how to order prints online from the Organizer.

Exit

You can close the Editor here or by pressing Ctrl+Q. The Organizer doesn't quit along with the Editor. If the Organizer is also running, you must exit it separately.

Edit Menu

The Edit menu contains choices that let you make changes to your files. It's also where you can access your Elements preferences to change their settings.

Undo

You can back out of your last action by selecting Undo or by pressing Ctrl+Z. You can keep applying this command to undo as many steps as you've set in the Undo History palette preferences (Edit → Preferences → General → History States).

Redo

If you undo something and then change your mind again, redo it here or press Ctrl+Y.

Revert

Choose the Revert command to return your image to the state it was in the last time you saved it.

Cut

To remove something from your image and store it on the Clipboard (so that you can paste it into another file), choose Cut or press Ctrl+X.

Copy

To copy something to the Clipboard, highlight it and select the Copy menu item or press Ctrl+C. The Copy command copies only the top layer in a file with layers. To copy all the layers in your selected area, use Copy Merged instead.

Copy Merged

Copy Merged copies all the layers in the selected area to the Clipboard. Keyboard shortcut: Shift+Ctrl+C.

Paste

Use the Paste command or press Ctrl+V to add whatever you have cut or copied into an image.

Paste Into Selection

Paste Into Selection is a special command for pasting something within the confines of an existing selection. See page 115 for more on how this command works. Choose Paste Into Selection here or by pressing Shift+Ctrl+V.

Delete

The Delete command removes what you've selected without copying it to the Clipboard—it's just gone. You can also press Backspace.

Fill, Fill Layer, Fill Selection

Use this to add a Fill layer (see page 166) to your image. When you have no image open, this menu item reads Fill and is grayed out. Open a photo and you see Fill Layer, which lets you create a new Fill layer. When you make a selection in your image, it changes to Fill Selection. Your Fill layer options are a bit different using this item compared to creating a Fill layer from the Layer menu or in the Layers palette. You can't choose to create a Gradient Fill layer here, for instance.

Stroke (Outline) Selection

This command lets you place a colored border around the edges of a selection.

Define Brush, Define Brush from Selection

If you want to create a custom brush from your photo or from an area of your photo, choose this command. The process is explained in detail on page 315.

Define Pattern, Define Pattern from Selection

This command creates a pattern from your image or selection. See page 245 for more about patterns.

Clear

Use these commands to permanently remove information from: the Undo History, Clipboard Contents, or All (both of them). If you have a corrupt image in the Clipboard (or one that's too large), it may cause Elements to slow way down or quit on you. Once in a while, the Clipboard may get stuck too—you try to copy and paste an item but still get whatever you copied previously. Clear fixes all these problems.

Add Blank Page

The Add Blank Page command lets you add a new, blank page to your current project. Find out more about working with multi-page files on page 403.

Add Page Using Current Layout

If you're working with a Photo Layout (page 397) and you want to use that page as a template for new pages, choose Add Page Using Current Layout instead of Add Blank Page.

Delete Current Page

If you're working with a multi-page document and you decide you want to get rid of your current page, choose Delete Current Page.

Color Settings

Color Settings is where you choose your color space for Elements. Keyboard shortcut: Shift+Ctrl+K. See page 181 for more about color spaces.

File Association

The File Association menu item brings up a window where you can choose which file types open automatically in Elements. Or you can set a file to open in a different program instead of Elements.

Preset Manager

The Preset Manager is where you access the Elements Preset Manager, a window that helps you manage your brushes, swatches, gradients, and patterns. See page 476 for more on how the Preset Manager works.

Preferences

The Preferences menu gives you access to the many Elements settings you can customize. The preference screens available from this menu are:

- **General** (Keyboard shortcut: Ctrl+K)
- **Saving Files**
- **Display and Cursors**
- **Transparency**
- **Units and Rulers**
- **Grid**
- **Plug-ins and Scratch Disks**
- **Memory and Image Cache**
- **Type**
- **Organize and Share** (brings up the Organizer's preferences)

Image Menu

The Image menu lets you make changes to your image. Here you can rotate a picture, change its shape, crop or resize it, or change the color mode.

Rotate

These commands let you change the orientation of your image. The first group of choices applies to your whole image. The Rotate commands are explained in detail on page 66. Your options are:

- **90° Left**
- **90° Right**
- **180°**
- **Custom**
- **Flip Horizontal**
- **Flip Vertical**

The next group does the same thing but on a layer or selection. The menu choices change depending on whether you have an active selection in your image. If you have a selection, you'll see Selection instead of Layer.

- Free Rotate Layer
- Layer 90° Left
- Layer 90° Right
- Layer 180°
- Flip Layer Horizontal
- Flip Layer Vertical

Finally you can choose to:

- Straighten and Crop Image
- Straighten Image

These last two commands are mostly for use with scanned images. To straighten the contents of an image, use the Straighten tool (page 67).

Transform

The Transform commands let you change the shape of your image by pulling it in different directions. They're explained in detail on page 297. Your choices are:

- Free Transform incorporates all the other three commands. Keyboard shortcut: Ctrl+T.
- Skew slants an image.
- Distort stretches your photo in the direction you pull it.
- Perspective stretches your photo to make it look like parts are nearer or farther away.

TIP   In Elements 5, you might prefer to use the new Correct Camera Distortion filter for transforming your images to correct perspective. See page 292.

Crop

Choosing the Crop command crops your image to the area you've selected. See page 71.

Divide Scanned Photos

You can create a group scan by placing several photos on your scanner glass at once and then choosing the Divide Scanned Photos command. Elements then cuts your photos apart and straightens and crops each individual photo. See page 63 for more about how this works.

Resize

Here's where you change the actual size of your image (as opposed to changing the size of the view on your screen). Resizing is explained in Chapter 3. Your choices are:

- **Image Size** (page 82).

- **Canvas Size** (page 89).

- **Reveal All.** If you drag a layer from another image into your photo and part of the layer falls outside the perimeter of the target image, then use the Reveal All command to see the entire dragged layer. Also, some versions of Photoshop hide the area outside a selection when you use the Crop tool. When you're dealing with one of these images, use this command to see the area that was hidden by the crop.

- **Scale** (page 300).

Mode

This is where you can change the color mode for your image. See page 40. Your mode choices are:

- **Bitmap**

- **Grayscale**

- **Indexed Color**

- **RGB Color**

You'll find two other commands in this menu:

- **8-bits/Channel** reduces images from 16-bit color to 8-bit (see page 221).

- **Color Table** shows you the color table (the colors of your image shown as swatches) for an Indexed Color image.

Convert Color Profile

If you need to change the ICC profile of an image, you can do it from this menu, which lets you apply an sRGB or Adobe RGB profile, or you can remove the profile from an image. For more on color profiles, go to page 181.

Magic Extractor

Use the Magic Extractor command to call up the Magic Extractor window, which automates the process of selecting an object in your photo and removing it from the background. See page 128 for more.

Enhance Menu

The Enhance menu contains the commands you use to adjust the color and lighting of your images. The top part of the menu contains the commands that apply automatically, and the bottom half includes the changes you can adjust.

Auto Smart Fix

The Auto Smart Fix adjusts lighting and color at the same time. See page 97. Keyboard shortcut: Alt+Ctrl+M.

Auto Levels

Auto Levels adjusts the individual color channels of your image. See page 99. Keyboard shortcut: Shift+Ctrl+L.

Auto Contrast

Auto Contrast adjusts the brightness and darkness of your image without changing the colors. It's explained on page 100. Keyboard shortcut: Alt+Shift+Ctrl+L.

Auto Color Correction

The Auto Color Correction adjusts your color similarly to the way Levels does, but it looks at different information in your photo to make its decisions. See page 102. Keyboard shortcut: Shift+Ctrl+B.

Auto Sharpen

The Auto Sharpen command applies the same one-click sharpening you get when you use the Auto Sharpen button in the Quick Fix. See page 104.

Auto Red Eye Fix

Auto Red Eye Fix applies the same auto red-eye correction found in the Organizer. See page 95. Keyboard shortcut: Ctrl+R.

Adjust Smart Fix

Adjust Smart Fix is the same as the Auto Smart Fix, but you get a slider to adjust the degree of change it makes to your photo. Keyboard shortcut: Shift+Ctrl+M.

Adjust Lighting

The commands under the Adjust Lighting menu item adjust the light and dark values in your photos. Your choices are:

- **Shadows/Highlights** (page 176).

- **Brightness/Contrast** (page 175).

- **Levels.** You can also press Ctrl+L to bring up the Levels dialog box (page 184).

Adjust Color

With these settings you can change a color, replace a color, remove a color cast, remove all the color from your image, or add color to a black-and-white photo. Choose from:

- **Remove Color Cast** (page 192).

- **Adjust Hue/Saturation** (page 252). Keyboard shortcut: Ctrl+U.

- **Remove Color** (page 269). Keyboard shortcut: Shift+Ctrl+U.

- **Replace Color** (page 257).

- **Adjust Color Curves** (page 248). The new Curves tool lets you adjust the brightness and contrast of specific regions (like highlights or midtones) in your photo.

- **Adjust Color for Skin Tone** (page 106). This setting adjusts the colors in your image based on the skin tones of someone whom you select in the photo.

- **Defringe Layer** (page 132). The Defringe Layer setting removes the rim of contrasting pixels you may get when you remove an object from its background.

- **Color Variations** (page 193).

Unsharp Mask

Use the Unsharp Mask filter to apply the most popular traditional method for sharpening your photos. See page 202.

Adjust Sharpness

Choose the Adjust Sharpness menu item to use Adobe's newest sharpening tool. See page 204.

Layer Menu

The Layer menu contains commands for creating and managing Layers. (Chapter 6 is all about Layers.) Layer is the most dynamic menu in Elements—what you see at the bottom of the menu changes very much depending on the layers in your image that's open and the characteristics of the active layer. This is a basic rundown of the main menu options you'll usually see if your open image has only a Background layer. (Sometimes you'll see choices visible but grayed out.) The choices for merging and combining layers change the most as your layers change.

New

This is where you create new, regular (as opposed to Adjustment) layers. You can create a new:

- **Layer.** Keyboard shortcut: Shift+Ctrl+N.

- **Layer from Background.**

- **Layer via Copy.** Keyboard shortcut: Ctrl+J.

- **Layer via Cut.** Keyboard shortcut: Shift+Ctrl+J.

If your image doesn't currently have a Background layer you also see "Background from Layer."

Duplicate Layer

The Duplicate Layer command makes a duplicate of the active layer. As long as you don't have a selection, you can also use Ctrl+J to do the same thing.

Delete Layer

If you want to eliminate a layer, click it in the Layers palette to make it the active layer and choose the Delete Layer command.

Rename Layer

Choose Rename Layer to (you guessed it) rename a layer. You can also double-click the layer's name in the Layers palette.

Layer Style

If a layer has a Layer style applied to it (see page 358), you can adjust it here:

- **Style Settings** brings up the dialog box where you can adjust some of the settings of a Layer style. Double-clicking the Layer style icon in the Layers palette brings up the same dialog box.

- **Copy Layer Style** lets you copy any styles applied to a layer to the Clipboard so you can apply them to another image or layer.

- **Paste Layer Style** applies your copied style to a new layer, even in a new image.

- **Clear Layer Style** removes all the styles applied to a layer.

- **Hide All Effects** hides all the styles applied to a layer so that you can see what your image looks like without them.

- **Scale Effects** lets you adjust the size of certain aspects of Layer styles.

New Fill Layer

New Fill Layer creates a layer that's filled with a color, gradient, or pattern. You can also do this from the Layers palette by clicking the Create Adjustment layer icon. You can choose a layer that's filled with:

- **Solid Color** (page 166)

- **Gradient** (page 362)

- **Pattern** (page 245)

New Adjustment Layer

This command creates a new Adjustment layer. Adjustment layers are explained on page 166. The types of layers you can create are:

- **Levels** (page 184)
- **Brightness/Contrast** (page 175)
- **Hue/Saturation** (page 256)
- **Gradient Map** (page 371)
- **Photo Filter** (page 224)
- **Invert** (page 262)
- **Threshold** (page 262)
- **Posterize** (page 262)

Change Layer Content

For Adjustment and Fill layers, you can change the type of layer you've got, as long as you haven't flattened your layers. For example, you could change a Levels layer into a Hue/Saturation layer. You can also change an Adjustment layer to a Fill layer, and vice versa. The choices include all the layers listed in the two previous sections.

Layer Content Options

Layer Content Options brings up the dialog box for an Adjustment or Fill layer. You can also double click the left icon for the layer in the Layers palette.

Type

The Type command gives you ways to modify a Type layer, as long as it hasn't been simplified. You can choose:

- **Horizontal.** Change vertical type to horizontal type.
- **Vertical.** Change horizontal type to vertical type.
- **Anti-alias Off.** Anti-aliasing is explained on page 382.
- **Anti-alias On.**
- **Warp Text.** See page 383.
- **Update All Text Layers.**
- **Replace All Missing Fonts.** When your image is missing fonts, this command replaces them, but you can't choose the replacement. It's usually just as easy to replace fonts by highlighting the text and selecting a new font in the Options bar.

Simplify Layer

The Simplify Layer command rasterizes your layer, turning the layer content from a vector object to one that's built pixel by pixel. See page 333 for more about the difference between vectors and pixels.

Group with Previous

The Group with Previous command links two layers together in such a way that the bottom layer determines the opacity of the upper layer. See page 160. Keyboard shortcut: Ctrl+G.

Ungroup

The Ungroup command unjoins grouped layers so that they're now two unrelated layers. Keyboard shortcut: Shift+Ctrl+G.

Arrange

Use these commands to change the order of layers in the layers stack, or just drag them in the Layers palette. See page 153. (Front is the top of the stack, and back is directly above the Background layer.)

- **Bring to Front.** Press Shift+Ctrl+].

- **Bring Forward.** Press Ctrl+].

- **Send Backward.** Press Ctrl+[.

- **Send to Back.** Press Shift+Ctrl+[.

- **Reverse.** Select two or more layers, and this command reverses the order in which they appear in the layer stack.

Merge Layers

The Merge Layers command combines multiple layers into one layer. Keyboard shortcut: Ctrl+E. You may also see Merge Down, which merges a layer with the layer immediately beneath it, or Merge Clipping Mask, which merges grouped layers.

Merge Visible

Merge Visible merges all the visible layers into one layer. Keyboard shortcut: Shift+Ctrl+E.

Flatten Image

The Flatten Image command merges all the layers into one Background layer.

Select Menu

The Select menu lets you make, modify, and save selections in your image. See Chapter 5 for more about selections.

All

Choosing All selects your entire image. Keyboard shortcut: Ctrl+A.

Deselect

Use Deselect to remove all selections from your image. Keyboard shortcut: Ctrl+D.

Reselect

If you apply the Deselect command, but then want your selection back again, choose Reselect or press Shift+Ctrl+D.

Inverse

Choosing the Inverse command switches the selected and unselected areas of your image. The area that wasn't previously selected is now selected, and the previously selected area is now unselected. Keyboard shortcut: Shift+Ctrl+I.

All Layers

Choosing All Layers selects all the layers in your image, including hidden layers.

Deselect Layers

The Deselect Layers command unselects all the layers in your image.

Similar Layers

Use the Similar Layers command to select all the layers of your image that are the same type, such as all Adjustment layers or all regular layers.

Feather

Feathering blurs the edges of a selection. See page 117. Keyboard shortcut: Alt+Ctrl+D.

Modify

Modify commands let you change the size or edges of your selection. They're all explained in Chapter 5.

- **Border** selects the edge of your selection (page 135).

- **Smooth** rounds the corners of rectangular selections (page 135).

- **Expand** moves the edge of your selection outward (page 134).

- **Contract** moves the edge of your selection inward (page 134).

Grow

The Grow command expands your selection to include more contiguous areas of similar color. See page 134.

Similar

The Similar command expands your selection to include more areas of similar color, but Similar doesn't restrict the growth areas to only contiguous areas the way Grow does (see page 134).

Load Selection

If you have saved a selection, choose the Load Selection command to use it again.

Save Selection

If you wish to save a selection so that you can use it another time without recreating it, use the Save Selection command. See page 137.

Delete Selection

Use the Delete Selection command to permanently remove a saved selection.

Filter Menu

Filters let you change the appearance of your image in all sorts of ways. Elements comes with some filters that are mostly for correcting and improving your photos, while others create artistic effects. The filters are grouped into categories to make it easier to find one that does exactly what you want. You can also apply filters from the Artwork and Effects palette. Learn more about using filters in Chapter 13. Every image responds to filters differently, so the descriptions here are a very rough guide.

Last Filter

The top item in the Filter menu always features the last filter you've applied. Choose the filter here to use it again with the exact same settings you previously used. You can also press Ctrt+F to reapply the last filter. If you want to change the settings, then you need to choose the filter from its regular place in the list of filters or press Ctrl+Alt+F.

Filter Gallery

The Filter Gallery lets you try the effects of different filters, rearrange them, and preview what they'll look like in your photo. Find out more about the Filter Gallery on page 345.

Correct Camera Distortion

This new filter allows you correct various kinds of lens distortion problems. See page 292.

Adjustments

Adjustments filters are primarily, but not exclusively, for correcting and enhancing photos. These filters are discussed on page 262, unless otherwise noted.

- Equalize
- Gradient Map (page 371)
- Invert (or Ctrl+I)
- Posterize
- Threshold
- Photo Filter (page 224)

Artistic

Artistic filters let you apply a wide variety of artistic effects to your image, ranging from a watercolor effect to making it look like it was sketched with pastels.

- Colored Pencil makes your photo look like it was sketched with a colored pencil on a solid colored background.
- Cutout makes your image look like it was cut from pieces of paper.
- Dry Brush makes your photo look it was painted using dry brush technique.
- Film Grain adds grain to make your photo look like old film.
- Fresco makes your photo look like it was painted quickly in a dabbing style.
- Neon Glow adds vivid color to your image while softening the details.
- Paint Daubs gives your photo a painted look.
- Palette Knife makes your photo look like you painted it using a palette knife. While you may think of using a palette knife as a way to blend heavy paint daubs, Adobe describes the effect of this filter as looking like a thin layer of paint that reveals the canvas beneath it.
- Plastic Wrap makes your image look like it's covered in plastic.
- Poster Edges gives your image accented, dark edges while reducing the number of colors in the rest of the photo.
- Rough Pastels makes your image look like it was quickly sketched with pastels.
- Smudge Stick uses short diagonal strokes that soften the image by smearing the detail.

- **Sponge** paints with highly textured areas of contrasting color like you'd get by sponging on color.

- **Underpainting** makes your image look like it's painted on a textured background.

- **Watercolor** simplifies the details in your image the way they would be if you were creating a watercolor painting.

Blur

Blur filters soften and blur your images. Page 353 tells you all about how to use them.

- **Average**

- **Blur**

- **Blur More**

- **Gaussian Blur**

- **Motion Blur**

- **Radial Blur**

- **Smart Blur**

Brush Strokes

The Brush Strokes filters give your image a hand-painted look.

- **Accented Edges** emphasizes the edges of objects as though they were drawn in black ink or white chalk.

- **Angled Strokes** creates diagonal brush strokes that all run in the same direction.

- **Crosshatch** creates diagonal brush strokes that crisscross.

- **Dark Strokes** paints dark areas of your image with short, tight, dark strokes, and light areas with long, white strokes.

- **Ink Outlines** makes your image look like it was drawn with fine ink lines.

- **Spatter** gives the effect you'd get from a spatter airbrush.

- **Sprayed Strokes** paints your image with diagonal, sprayed strokes in its dominant colors.

- **Sumi-e** gives the effect of drawing with a wet brush full of black ink, in a Japanese-influenced style.

Distort

The Distort filters warp your image in a variety of different ways:

- **Diffuse Glow** makes your image look as though you're viewing it through a soft diffusion filter.

- **Displace** lets you create a map to tell Elements how to distort your image.

- **Glass** makes your image look like you're viewing it through different kinds of glass.

- **Liquify** (page 388).

- **Ocean Ripple** gives an underwater effect by adding ripples to your image.

- **Pinch** pulls the edges of your photo inwards toward the center.

- **Polar Coordinates** lets you create what's called a cylinder anamorphosis. That's the kind of distortion where a distorted image looks normal when you see it in a mirrored cylinder.

- **Ripple** creates a pattern like ripples on the surface of water.

- **Shear** distorts your image along a curve.

- **Spherize** makes your image expand out like a balloon.

- **Twirl** spins your photo, rotating a selection more in the center than at the edge, producing a twirled pattern.

- **Wave** creates a rippled pattern but with more control than the Ripple filter gives you.

- **Zigzag** creates a bent, zigzagging effect that's stronger in the center of the area you apply the filter to.

Noise

You can use Noise filters to add *noise* (grain) to your photos or remove noise from them. They're discussed on page 239.

- **Add Noise**

- **Despeckle**

- **Dust & Scratches**

- **Median**

- **Reduce Noise**

Pixelate

Pixelate filters break up the appearance of your photo into spots or blocks of various kinds.

- **Color Halftone** adds the kind of dotted pattern you see in commercially printed color.

- **Crystallize** breaks your image into polygonal blocks of color.

- **Facet** reduces your image to blocks of solid color.

- **Fragment** makes your image look blurry and offset.

- **Mezzotint** creates an effect something like that of a mezzotint engraving.

- **Mosaic** breaks your image down to square blocks of color.

- **Pointillize** creates a pointillist effect by making your photo look like it's made of many dots of color.

Render

Render is a diverse but powerful group of filters that transform your photo in many ways.

- **3-D Transform** makes your image look like it's on a cube, cylinder, or sphere.

- **Clouds** covers your image with clouds using the foreground/background colors.

- **Difference Clouds** also creates clouds, but the first time you apply it to an image, portions of the image are inverted.

- **Fibers** creates an effect like spun and woven fibers.

- **Lens Flare** creates starry bright spots like you'd get from a camera lens flare.

- **Lighting Effects** is a powerful and complex filter for changing the light in your photo. For an in-depth tutorial on how to use this filter, see the "Missing CD" page at *www.missingmanuals.com*.

- **Texture Fill** lets you use a grayscale image as a texture for your photo.

Sketch

Sketch is another group of artistic filters. Most of them make your image look like it was drawn with a pencil or graphics pen.

- **Bas Relief** gives your photo a slightly raised appearance, as though it's carved in low relief.

- **Chalk & Charcoal** makes your photo look like it was sketched with a combination of chalk and charcoal.

- **Charcoal** gives a smudgy effect to your image, like a charcoal drawing.

- **Chrome** is supposed to make your image look like polished chrome, but you might prefer the Wow chrome Layer styles in the Artwork and Effects palette.

- **Conté Crayon** makes your image look like it was drawn with conté crayons using the foreground/background colors.

- **Graphic Pen** makes the details in your image look like they were drawn with a fine pen using the foreground color, with the background color for the paper color.

- **Halftone Pattern** gives the dotted effect of a halftone screen, like you see in printed illustrations. The effect only *looks* like halftone—this filter doesn't create a true halftone that your printer might request.

- **Note Paper** makes your image look like it's on handmade paper. The background color shows through in spots in dark areas.

- **Photocopy** makes your photo look like a Xerox copy.

- **Plaster** makes your image look like it was molded in wet plaster.

- **Reticulation** creates an effect you might get from film emulsion—dark areas clump and brighter areas appear more lightly grained.

- **Stamp** makes your image look like it was stamped with a rubber stamp.

- **Torn Edges** makes your photo look it's made from torn pieces of paper.

- **Water Paper** makes your photo look like it was painted on wet paper, making the colors run together.

Stylize

Stylize filters create special effects by displacing the pixels in your image or increasing contrast.

- **Diffuse** makes your photo less focused by shuffling the pixels according to the settings you choose.

- **Emboss** makes objects in your image appear stamped or raised.

- **Extrude** gives a 3-D effect by pushing some of the pixels in your image up, something like toothpaste squeezed from a tube.

- **Find Edges** emphasizes the edges of your image against a white background.

- **Glowing Edges** adds a neon-like glow to the edges in your photo.

- **Solarize** produces an effect like what you'd get by briefly exposing a photo print to light while you're developing it. It combines a negative and a positive image.

- **Tiles** breaks your image up into individual tiles. You can choose how much to offset them.

- **Trace Contour** outlines areas where there are major transitions in brightness. The result is supposed to be something like a contour map.

- **Wind** makes your image appear windblown.

Texture

Texture filters change the surface of your photo to look like it was made from another material.

- **Craquelure** produces a surface effect like cracked plaster.

- **Grain** adds different kinds of graininess to your photo.

- **Mosaic Tiles** is supposed to make your photo look like it's made of mosaic tiles with grout in between them.

- **Patchwork** reduces your image to squares filled with the predominant colors.

- **Stained Glass** is supposed to make your photo look like it's made of stained glass. The effect's usually more like a mosaic.

- **Texturizer** makes your photo look like it's on canvas or brick. You can select a file to use as a texture.

Video

Video filters are for use with video images.

- **De-Interlace** smoothes images captured from video by removing the odd or even interlaced lines.

- **NTSC Colors** restricts you colors to those suitable for television reproduction.

Other

This is a group of fairly technical filters.

- **Custom** lets you create your own filter.

- **High Pass** is discussed on page 206.

- **Maximum** replaces pixel brightness values with the highest and lowest values of surrounding pixels. Maximum spreads out white areas and shrinks dark areas.

- **Minimum** is the opposite of the Maximum filter. It spreads out black areas and shrinks white ones.

- **Offset** moves your selection by the number of pixels you specify.

Digimarc

Use the Read Watermark filter to check for Digimarc watermarks in photos. Digimarc is a commercial system that lets subscribers enter their information in a database so that anyone who gets one of their photos can find out who the copyright holder is by searching.

View Menu

The View menu features different ways to adjust how you see your image on your screen. For more details on adjusting your image's view, see page 77.

New Window for...

The New Window for command lets you create a duplicate window for your image so that you can see it at two different magnification levels at once. The new window goes away when you close your image—it doesn't create a copy of your photo.

Zoom In

To increase the view size, you can choose the Zoom In menu item or press Ctrl+=. You can also use the Zoom tool. (See page 79.)

Zoom Out

To reduce the view size, choose the Zoom Out menu item or press Ctrl+−. You can also use the Zoom tool. (See page 79.)

Fit on Screen

Fit on Screen makes your photo as large as it can be without your having to scroll to see part of it. Keyboard shortcut: Ctrl+0.

Actual Pixels

The Actual Pixels view displays your image the exact size it would appear on the Web or in other programs that can't adjust view size (as Elements can). Keyboard shortcut: Alt+Ctrl+0.

Print Size

Elements makes its best guess as to how large your image would print at its current resolution. See page 82.

Selection

When Selection's turned on, the outlines of your selections are visible. You can toggle this setting off and on here, or by pressing Ctrl+H.

Rulers

If you want to see rulers around the edges of your image window, toggle them on and off here. You can adjust the unit of measurement in Edit → Preferences → Units & Rulers.

Grid

If you want to see a measurement and alignment grid on your photos, use the Grid setting to toggle it on and off. You can adjust the grid size in Edit → Preferences → Grid.

Guide Presets

The preset document sizes for new files include a couple of video sizes with guidelines to help you know the workable areas of the document. The Guide Presets menu item becomes active when you're working with a DV (digital video) file. It's grayed out, normally.

Annotations

Annotations is available only for files that contain voice annotations. Toggle the annotation on and off here. You may get a file with a voice annotation from someone working with Photoshop, which lets you record sound annotations that you can add to your files.

Snap to

- **Grid.** When the Grid setting's turned on, Elements automatically jumps to the nearest gridline. If the way your tools and selections keep jumping away from you bothers you, then turn the behavior off here. Then everything stays exactly where you place it.

- **Guides.** When you're working with one of the video document sizes that include guidelines, Guides is where you toggle on and off whether you want objects you add to snap to the guidelines.

Window Menu

The Window menu controls which palettes and bins you see, as well as letting you adjust how your image windows display.

Images

The Images menu item lets you control how your images display. The choices are explained in detail on page 77.

- **Maximize Mode.** Each image takes up the entire available space.

- **Tile.** Your images appear edge to edge so that all windows are equally visible.

- **Cascade.** Image windows tile in overlapping stacks. (Cascade is the usual view in older versions of Elements.)

- **Match Zoom.** Choose Match Zoom to make all open windows zoom to the same extent as the active window.

• **Match Location.** When you have only part of a photo visible in a window, choose Match Location to make all open windows display the same part of their images, too, like the upper-left corner, for example.

Tools

The Tools setting hides and shows the Toolbox.

Artwork and Effects

Artwork and Effects shows and hides the Artwork and Effects palette, from which you apply filters, effects, and Layer styles. It's also where you can add graphics and clip art to your images. See page 23.

Color Swatches

Use Color Swatches to show and hide the Color Swatches palette (see page 199).

Histogram

Use the Histogram to show or hide the Histogram in its own palette (see page 187).

How To

The How To setting shows or hides the How To palette, which contains step-by-step directions for popular Elements tasks and projects (see page 25).

Info

Use the Info setting to bring up a palette with information about your photos, like the file size and dimensions, as well as color value numbers.

Layers

This is where you make the Layers palette visible or hide it. See page 142.

Navigator

Turn the Navigator off and on here. The Navigator lets you adjust which portion of a large image is visible on your screen and also adjust the zoom. See page 81.

Undo History

The Undo History setting makes the Undo History palette visible or hides it. The Undo History palette shows a record of all the changes to your image up to the number of states you set in Edit → Preferences → General → History States. See page 26 for more about the Undo History palette.

Palette Bin

The Palette Bin setting minimizes and maximizes the Palette bin (see page 21). You can also just click the edge of the bin to hide or expand it.

Reset Palette Locations

The Reset Palette Locations command returns all palettes to their original locations.

Welcome

Choose the Welcome menu item to see the Welcome window that appears when Elements starts up. You can then use the menu setting to change the component of Elements that launches when the program starts up.

Photo Bin

The Photo Bin setting minimizes the Photo bin. Select it again to maximize the bin.

Image Windows

At the bottom of the View menu you see a list of all the files you have open in Elements. Choose one to bring it to the front as the active window.

Help Menu

The Help menu is where you find the Elements Help files and tutorials, as well as information about the program itself.

Photoshop Elements Help

You can call up the Elements Help application here, or press F1. Or enter a search term in the box in the menu bar.

About Photoshop Elements

Choose About Photoshop Elements to see a scrolling window with information about the version of Elements you've got. You'll also see a very long list of patents and credits—an impressive testimony to the complexity of the engineering that went into Elements.

About Plug-In

Select the About Plug-In menu item for a long pop-out menu displaying all the plug-ins in your copy of Elements. Choose a plug-in from the list to see its version and date information.

Glossary of Terms

The Elements Help files include a glossary of terms relating to digital imaging. If you're wondering what a term means, this menu item takes you to the glossary index so you can look it up.

Tutorials

The Elements Help files include some excellent tutorials. Choose the Tutorials item to see a list of them.

System Info

Choose System Info for a window showing information about Elements itself and also about your Windows operating system. If you can't remember which service pack you have, for instance, then you can check here. You'll also find information about some important plug-ins. If you're not sure whether you have QuickTime, for example, that information's here, too.

Registration

If you didn't register Elements with Adobe the first time you used the program, you can choose Registration to bring up the registration window again.

Updates

Updates is where you choose which Elements components you want to update, and where you set your preferences for how you want Elements to handle updates.

Online Support

Choose the Online Support option and Elements launches your Web browser and attempts to go to Adobe's support Web site. If you're not connected to the Internet when you select Online Support, then Elements launches an Internet connection window.

Photoshop Elements Online

Photoshop Elements Online takes you to the main product page for Photoshop Elements on Adobe's Web site. Like the online support link, Elements launches your browser and offers to connect to the Internet if you're not already online when you chose this menu item.

Online Learning Resources

Online Learning Resources also takes you to the main product page for Photoshop Elements on Adobe's Web site.

Installation and Troubleshooting

Elements is quite easy to install and is pretty trouble free once you're up and running. This appendix explains a couple of things you can do to ensure that your installation goes smoothly, and also provides cures for most of the little glitches that can crop up once you're using the program.

Installing Elements

Before you install Elements, it helps to make sure your PC is ready to receive its newest arrival.

First of all, if your computer's on a network, then take it off the network temporarily. (You can go back on as soon as you've installed Elements.) Also, it's important to disable any anti-virus software as well as any products from Symantec, including Norton Anti-Virus (which tends to quarrel with Adobe software during installation). You can turn any of these programs back on as soon as you've finished the installation.

Also, you need to install Elements when logged into an administrative account on your computer. (If you've never done anything to change your account and you have only one account on your machine, it's almost certainly an administrative account.)

NOTE   If you already have a previous version of Elements, then there's no need to remove it before installing Elements 5. All versions of Elements run as separate programs, and you can keep the older version, too, if you want. However, if you decide to uninstall an earlier version *after* installing Elements 5, you may lose the Adobe Gamma Utility (see page 180) in the process. If that happens, just reinstall Elements 5.

Make sure you have your Elements serial number handy. You won't be able to install the program without it. If you have a retail version of Elements, the serial number is on the label on the install disc's case. If you got it bundled (when you bought a scanner, for example), you'll usually find the serial number on the paper sleeve the disc's in. (It's not a bad idea to write your serial number right on the disc so that you'll always have it around if you need to reinstall.)

Installing Elements

1. **Put the install disc in your computer's drive.**

   The disc window should open automatically. If for some reason it doesn't, then double-click the disc's icon or right-click it and choose Open.

2. **Choose a language and accept the software agreement.**

3. **Click Install Adobe Photoshop Elements.**

   The installation wizard launches.

4. **Decide whether to remove any older versions of Elements.**

   If you already have a version of Elements on your computer, the installer reminds you about any older versions. It's up to you whether or not to remove them. When you want to remove your older versions, click No to cancel the installation and then remove the older version(s) yourself (Control Panel → Add or Remove Programs) before starting the Elements 5 installer again.

5. **Accept the license agreement.**

   Yes, you already accepted a software agreement. That was for all the stuff on the disc, and this one's specifically for Elements.

6. **Enter your serial number when the installer requests it, and choose where you want Elements to install itself.**

7. **Select which file formats you want Elements to automatically open.**

   If you know which file formats (see page 54) you want Elements to automatically open, you get a chance to tell the installer your preferences. You can also change your file associations later, as explained on page 37.

8. **Click Install to begin the installation.**

   Elements installs. When the installer is done, click Finish to exit the installer, and restart your computer.

The installer creates a desktop shortcut to Elements. To launch Elements, double-click the shortcut or right-click it and choose Open.

Registration

When you first launch Elements, it asks you to register the program. You can run Elements without registering it, but you get a couple of advantages if you register. For one thing, Adobe hangs onto a record of your serial number, so if you ever misplace the number, you can get it from Adobe. Also, when Adobe releases new versions of Elements, there's usually a rebate for registered owners of previous versions.

Scratch Disks

Elements uses a *scratch disk*—reserve space on a hard drive to supplement your PC's memory—when it's busy making your photos gorgeous. The calculations Elements makes behind the scenes are very complex, and Elements needs someplace to write stuff down while it's figuring out how to make changes to your image. It does so by using a scratch disk if the task at hand is too heavy-duty for your system's main memory alone to cope with.

You probably have just one hard drive in your computer, and Elements automatically uses that drive as the scratch disk. That's fine, and Elements can run very happily without a dedicated scratch disk.

> **TIP**   You can make Elements *really* happy by keeping your hard drive defragmented and making sure there's plenty of free space available for Elements to use.

If you're fortunate enough to have a computer with more than one internal drive, you can designate a separate disk as your scratch disk to improve Elements performance. Your scratch disk needs to be as fast as the drive Elements is installed on or there's no point in setting up a special scratch disk. (If you have a USB external drive, for instance, forget it and just leave your main drive as your scratch disk.)

To assign a scratch disk, go to Edit → Preferences → Plug-Ins & Scratch Disks and choose your preferred disk. You can choose up to four disks to use as scratch disks.

Troubleshooting

If Elements behaves badly from the moment you install it, something probably went funky during your installation. That's easy to fix. Uninstall Elements and reinstall it.

To remove Elements, go to Control Panel → Add or Remove Programs and remove Elements. Then reinstall the program. You can't perform a Repair Install for Elements—you just get an error message that keeps asking for the CD. (Repair installs are used for some programs to fix problems without having to do a full reinstall.)

Fortunately, Adobe makes very good software that looks after itself very well. There is, however, one simple procedure you can perform if things start acting funny in Elements: delete your Elements *preferences file*. The preferences file is where Elements keeps track of your preferred settings for the program. Deleting it fixes the overwhelming majority of problems you may develop. In Elements, you're most likely to need to delete the preferences file when dealing with Editor-related problems. The following steps explain what you need to do.

1. **Quit Elements if it's currently running and relaunch the Editor.**

   As soon as you start the program, immediately press Ctrl+Alt+Shift. (You can't press the keys before you start the Editor, and you have to be pretty fast to grab them in time.)

2. **Delete your preferences.**

   A window appears asking if you want to delete the Elements settings. Click Yes. You have to be fairly quick to press the keys in time. If you don't see the window, you were too slow. Quit Elements and try again.

This procedure resets the Editor to the way it was when you launched the program for the very first time. So you'll have to reenter any changes you made to things like your choice of window behavior (page 77) and the Editor's preferences. Your palettes also go back to their original locations; you'll need to rearrange them if you pulled any of them out of the bin. (Deleting the preferences doesn't affect your image files at all.)

It's much less common to need to reset the Organizer's preferences, but if you do want to reset the Organizer, that's easy, too. When you're in the Organizer, go to Edit → Preferences → General and click the Restore Default Settings button at the bottom of the window.

Elements is usually pretty zippy, but if you find that it's really slowing things down on your computer, follow the steps on page 36 for disabling the Photo Downloader, and turn it on only when you need it, or just use the Get Photos command instead. If you still have trouble, then follow step 3 in the box "Avoiding the Organizer" on page 44 to disable the Adobe Active File Monitor in your Windows services. (You'll also lose the ability to use Watched Folders if you do this.)

> **NOTE** Elements stores your catalog (page 43) separately from the actual program files. You can install and uninstall Elements as many times as you like without damaging or losing your existing catalog (if you have one from a previous version of Elements). When you first install Elements 5, if the Organizer doesn't find your existing Elements catalog, go to File → Catalog → Open. Then navigate to your catalog (usually called something like *My Catalog*) and open it. Elements automatically makes a backup copy of your catalog and adds the number -1 to its name (for example, *My Catalog-1*). Elements 5 then uses your existing catalog (the one *without* the -1 in its name). Just remember that any changes you make in Elements 5 won't appear in the old version of the catalog (the one *with* the -1 in its name).

Index

PHOTOSHOP ELEMENTS 5: THE MISSING MANUAL

Colophon

Marlowe Shaeffer was the production editor for *Photoshop Elements 5: The Missing Manual*. Adam Witwer provided quality control. Dawn Mann wrote the index.

The cover of this book is based on a series design by David Freedman. Karen Montgomery produced the cover layout with Adobe InDesign CS using Adobe's Minion and Gill Sans fonts.

David Futato designed the interior layout, based on a series design by Phil Simpson. This book was converted by Abby Fox to FrameMaker 5.5.6. The text font is Adobe Minion; the heading font is Adobe Formata Condensed; and the code font is LucasFont's TheSans Mono Condensed. The illustrations that appear in the book were produced by Robert Romano and Jessamyn Read using Macromedia FreeHand MX and Adobe Photoshop CS.

Better than e-books

Buy *Photoshop Elements 5: The Missing Manual* and access the digital edition FREE on Safari for 45 days.

Go to www.oreilly.com/go/safarienabled
and type in coupon code H5FF-WB2G-BUBE-YIGH-PHVQ

Search
thousands of
top tech books

Download
whole chapters

Cut and Paste
code examples

Find
answers fast

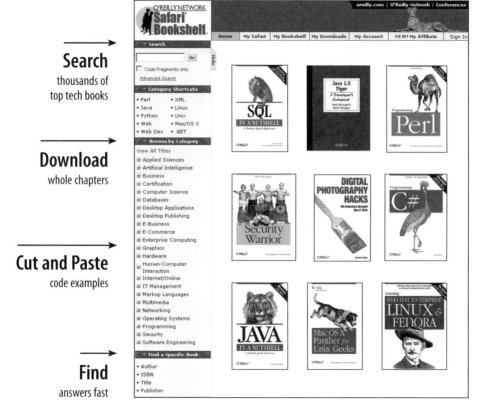

Search Safari! The premier electronic reference
library for programmers and IT professionals.

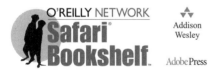